PROGRAMMING IN ADA
plus
LANGUAGE REFERENCE MANUAL
3rd Edition

INTERNATIONAL COMPUTER SCIENCE SERIES

Consulting editors   **A D McGettrick**   University of Strathclyde

J van Leeuwen   University of Utrecht

SELECTED TITLES IN THE SERIES

UNIX℠ is a trademark of AT & T

3rd Edition

PROGRAMMING IN ADA
plus
LANGUAGE REFERENCE MANUAL

J.G.P. Barnes

Alsys Ltd

ADDISON-WESLEY
PUBLISHING
COMPANY

Wokingham, England . Reading, Massachusetts . Menlo Park, California . New York
Don Mills, Ontario . Amsterdam . Bonn . Sydney . Singapore
Tokyo . Madrid . San Juan . Milan . Paris . Mexico City . Seoul . Taipei

Cover designed by Designers & Partners, Oxford.
Printed in the United States of America.

First printed 1991.

British Library Cataloguing in Publication Data
Barnes, J. G. P. (John Gilbert Presslie)
  Programming in ADA plus language
  reference manual.
  005.133

ISBN 0–201–56539–0

Library of Congress Cataloging-in-Publication Data
Barnes, J. G. P. (John Gilbert Presslie)
  Programming in Ada : plus language reference manual / J.G.P. Barnes.
    p.   cm. — (International computer science series)
  Includes bibliographical references and index.
  ISBN 0–201–56539–0
  1. Ada (Computer program language)   I. Title.   II. Series.
QA76.73.A35B38   1991
005.13'3—dc20   91–13685
                                                                      CIP

To BARBARA

Preface to Combined Edition

This new edition brings together the third regular edition of *Programming in Ada* and the Ada *Language Reference Manual*.

The rationale for this edition is simply to provide a single definitive reference for Ada programmers in one convenient volume. *Programming in Ada* is intended for teaching and also as an informal reference. However, it does not cover every fine aspect of Ada and many users find it useful to refer to the *LRM* from time to time.

In combining the two works the opportunity has been taken to remove some of the material in the appendices of the regular edition which essentially reproduced material from the *LRM*. However the full syntax has been kept in both works. This is because it is arranged in a different order and is differently indexed and both versions have their respective merits.

Finally, I am most grateful to the Ada Joint Program Office of the United States Department of Defense for permission to reproduce the *LRM* in its entirety and thereby make this special edition possible.

Reading
March 1991   J. G. P. Barnes

Foreword

In May 1979 came the eagerly awaited announcement by the United States High Order Language Working Group, that 'Green is Ada'.

We were all expecting it in our team and were thus not surprised, but the announcement was certainly an enormous pleasure for all of us. At that time we all considered the preliminary version of Ada to be perfect. It may sound strange, considering the amount of revision that was done in the next fifteen months leading to the July 1980 Ada definition. But there is an easy explanation. In order to design anything you must believe in what you design, you must be continually examining the interweaving of all the features. Certainly, many decisions are the result of compromises between conflicting goals, but after rehearsing time and time again the arguments leading to these compromises you end up by integrating them into the basic assumptions of your design. And so it is not surprising that the result should appear to be the perfect answer.

Clearly, further progress can only come by a reappraisal of implicit assumptions underlying certain compromises. Here is the major contradiction in any design work. On the one hand, one can only reach an harmonious integration of several features by immersing oneself into the logic of the existing parts; it is only in this way that one can achieve a perfect combination. On the other hand, this perception of perfection, and the implied acceptance of certain unconscious assumptions, will prevent further progress.

In the design of Ada, John Barnes has certainly shown a unique ability to switch appropriately between acceptance and reappraisal. In May 1979, John was as proud as anyone else in the design team about our achievement. But, even by the early days of June, John was already reflective, giving a sharp, even severe look to the Ada tasking model as if he had had nothing to do with its design. He authored the first Language study note, of a series of two hundred, called 'Problems with tasking'. The note outlined ten major problems perceived in the preliminary Ada tasking facilities. These problems occupied our team for several months in the Ada revision, and satisfactory solutions could then be given to these ten issues in the final Ada version. In my own case it undoubtedly took me much more time to become objective about preliminary Ada and I certainly was initially upset by John's sacrilege. But with time I have learned to value enormously this kind of interaction with John.

Programming in Ada is thus written by one of the key members of the Ada language design team, by someone who understands all facets of the design of the language, both in a constructive and in a critical manner. I am confident that – with humour as usual – John's enthusiasms and understanding of the spirit of the language will be passed on to readers of this book.

Versailles
May 1981   Jean D. Ichbiah

Preface to the Third Edition

The third edition of this book has not been prompted by any specific event but rather a general feeling that sufficient feedback had been received from the growing use of Ada to make a thorough revision worthwhile.

Before deciding upon the revisions I asked a number of those who had been using the book as a teaching text for their suggestions. Their answers were very helpful although inevitably they were not without conflict. At the end of the day the decisions were mine and I apologize if I have not been able to exactly meet everyone's requirements. Perhaps the most important piece of advice was not to spoil the book by unnecessary change. I hope I have at least succeeded in this.

Users of earlier editions might find it helpful to have a brief list of the major changes.

- Chapter 2 has been considerably enlarged. It now gives an overview of almost all of the language except tasking. In particular it contains enough of generics and input–output to enable the reader to write complete programs right from the beginning. This will be helpful to those who wish to experiment with some of the exercises using a compiler.

- A number of existing sections were rather long and have been subdivided and rearranged so that the reader is spared daunting lumps of material without the relief of some exercises. Section 6.2 on array types and aggregates has thus been split and the material on aggregates (which I always find difficult) has been rewritten with, it is hoped, much greater clarity and rationale. Section 11.1 on discriminated records was also long and has been subdivided with the material on default discriminants rearranged to form a new section. The very long Section 14.4 on the select statement has also been subdivided.

- A number of new sections have been added. Section 6.5 discusses arrays of arrays and slices which were barely covered before. Section 10.3 contains material on the costs of the checks which are required to raise the predefined exceptions. Section 13.4 addresses the use of generics for the mathematical library; much of the discussion is around the draft standard for elementary functions which is being discussed by ISO at the time of writing. Section 16.4 adds further material of a general nature; it discusses the composition of large scale programs from individual components with particular regard to the import and export of entities and the rules for compilation and recompilation.

- Significant additional material has also been added on generic subprogram parameters, fixed point types and the model of the main program which were not fully covered before.

- Since writing the previous edition a number of aspects of the language have been clarified by the publication of Ada Issues as explained in more detail in Chapter 1. This third edition has been revised to conform to the current interpretation of the language and references to relevant approved Issues have been inserted where appropriate.

- Finally, the text has been thoroughly scrutinized for ambiguities, obscurities and errors and polished where necessary. Many additional exercises and examples have also been added where they give additional insight into the use of the language.

It is impossible to remember all those who have helped with this edition in various ways. However, I would particularly like to thank Morteza Anvari, Rodney Bown, Don Greenwell, Charlene Hayden, Stuart Handley, Floyd Holliday, Kit Lester, Fred Long, Peter Martin, Charles Mooney, Ruth Rudolph and Stephen Sangwine for their helpful suggestions on the scope of revision. I would also like to thank Angel Alvarez and Vincent Amiot (who translated the second edition into Spanish and French respectively) for their many comments. Then, I must thank my colleague Alun Tlusty-Sheen with whom I have given many Ada courses for numerous comments and suggestions. Thanks are also due to Vittorio Frigo and Ron Pierce for spotting some nasty bugs, to Graham Hodgson for advice on the mathematical library and to Alison Wearing for many detailed suggestions on improvements to the clarity of the text. Next, I must thank my daughter Janet for suggesting a number of the new exercises and examples and especially for spotting that her ageing father got them wrong on a first writing. Finally, I must thank my wife Barbara for her valued efforts in typing much of the text.

I would also like to continue to record the names of those whose copious comments helped with the second edition. They were Angel Alvarez, Randall Barron, Theodore Chaplin, Donald Clarson, Edward Colbert, Ian Mearns, Mike Tedd and Jo Whitfield.

The original intent of this book was as a comprehensive text to teach the Ada language. It has, however, also found much favour as a friendly reference book. Although these uses conflict I hope that this new edition will be found to be a significant improvement for both purposes.

Reading
December 1988

J. G. P. Barnes

Preface to the First Edition

This book is about Ada, the new and powerful programming language originally developed on behalf of the US Department of Defense for use in embedded systems. Typical of such systems are those for process control, missile guidance or even the sequencing of a dishwasher. Historically these systems have been programmed in languages such as JOVIAL, CORAL 66 and RTL/2.

Based on Pascal, Ada is the first practical language to bring together important features such as data abstraction, multitasking, exception handling, encapsulation and generics. Although originally intended for embedded systems, it is a general purpose language and could, in time, supersede FORTRAN and even COBOL. The political and technical forces behind Ada suggest it will become an important language in the 1980s.

My purpose in writing this book is to present an overall description of Ada. Some knowledge of the principles of programming is assumed and an acquaintance with Pascal would be helpful but is not strictly necessary. The book is written in a tutorial style with numerous examples and exercises. I have also tried to explain the rationale behind many of the features of the language because this not only makes the discussion of more interest but also makes the facts easier to remember. Wherever possible I have tried to use examples which do not assume a particular application background; they are mostly drawn from parallels with normal human life or from mathematics which, after all, is the cornerstone of science and engineering. I hope the reader does not find the occasional attempt at humour misplaced; learning a programming language can be dull and any means of easing the burden seems worthwhile.

I would like to take this opportunity to thank those who directly or indirectly have helped me to write this book. First, I must acknowledge the US Department of Defense for permission to use material from the Ada *Language Reference Manual*. Then, I must acknowledge Jean Ichbiah and Robert Firth with whom I have had the pleasure of giving Ada courses in various parts of the world. These courses not only helped me to gain a useful perspective of the language as a whole but also provided the origins of some of the examples. Next, I must thank Andrew McGettrick for a great number of useful comments on the original draft and for spurring me on to completion with many helpful suggestions. I must also thank my colleagues on the UK Ada Study for their valued comments. Finally, I am deeply grateful to my wife for her untiring efforts in typing the manuscript; without her assistance the labour would have been much prolonged.

Reading
April 1981   J. G. P. Barnes

Contents

Chapter 1
Introduction

Ada is a high level programming language originally sponsored by the US Department of Defense for use in the so-called embedded system application area. (An embedded system is one in which the computer is an integral part of a larger system such as a chemical plant, missile or dishwasher.) In this introductory chapter we briefly trace the development of Ada, its place in the overall language scene and the general structure of the remainder of this book.

1.1 History

The story of Ada goes back to about 1974 when the United States Department of Defense realized that it was spending far too much on software. It carried out a detailed analysis of how its costs were distributed over the various application areas and discovered that over half of them were directly attributed to embedded systems.

Further analysis was directed towards the programming languages in use in the various areas. It was discovered that COBOL was the universal standard for data processing and FORTRAN was a similar standard for scientific and engineering computation. Although these languages were not modern, the fact that they were uniformly applied in their respective areas meant that unnecessary and expensive duplication was avoided.

The situation with regard to embedded systems was, however, quite different. The number of languages in use was enormous. Not only did each of the three Armed Services have their own favourite high level languages, but they also used many assembly languages as well. Moreover, the high level languages had spawned variants. It seemed that successive contracts had encouraged the development of special versions aimed at different applications. The net result was that a lot of money was being spent on an unnecessary number of compilers. There were also all the additional costs of training and maintenance associated with a lack of standardization.

It was therefore realized that standardization had to be established in the embedded system area if the costs were to be contained. The ultimate goal was, of course, a single language. In the short term a list of interim approved languages was introduced. This consisted of CMS-2Y, CMS-2M, SPL/1, TACPOL, JOVIAL J3, JOVIAL J73 and of course COBOL and FORTRAN for the other areas.

The first step in moving towards the development of a single standard was the writing of a document outlining the requirements. The first version was known as Strawman and was published in early 1975. After receiving comments from various sources it was refined and became Woodenman. A further iteration produced Tinman in June 1976. This was quite a specific document and identified the functionality required of the language.

At this stage many existing languages were evaluated against Tinman, partly to see whether one of them could be used as the ultimate standard and partly to invoke detailed evaluation of the requirements themselves. As one might expect, none of the existing languages proved satisfactory; on the other hand the general impression was gained that a single language based on state-of-the-art concepts could be developed to meet the requirements.

The evaluation classified the existing languages into three categories which can be paraphrased as

'not appropriate'	These languages were obsolete or addressed the wrong area and were not to be considered further. This category included FORTRAN and CORAL 66.
'not inappropriate'	These languages were also unsatisfactory as they stood but had some interesting features which could be looked at for inspiration. This category included RTL/2 and LIS.
'recommended bases'	These were the three languages Pascal, PL/I and Algol 68 and were seen as possible starting points for the design of the final language.

At this point the requirements document was revised and reorganized to give Ironman. Proposals were then invited from contractors to design a new language starting from one of the recommended bases. Seventeen proposals were received and four were chosen to go ahead in parallel and in competition. The four contractors with their colour codings were CII Honeywell Bull (Green), Intermetrics (Red), Softech (Blue) and SRI International (Yellow). The colour codings were introduced so that the resulting initial designs could be compared anonymously and hopefully therefore without bias.

The initial designs were delivered in early 1978 and many groups all over the world considered their relative merit. The DoD judged that the Green and Red designs showed more promise than Blue and Yellow and so the latter were eliminated.

The development then entered its second phase and the two remaining contractors were given a further year in which to refine their designs. The requirements were also revised in the light of feedback from the initial designs and became the final document Steelman[1].

The final choice of language was made on 2 May 1979 when the Green language developed at CII Honeywell Bull by an international team led by Jean Ichbiah was declared the winner.

The DoD then announced that the new language would be known as Ada in honour of Augusta Ada Byron, Countess of Lovelace (1815–52). Ada, the daughter of Lord Byron, was the assistant and patron of Charles Babbage and worked on his mechanical analytical engine. In a very real sense she was therefore the world's first programmer.

The development of Ada then entered a third phase. The purpose of this was to expose the language to a significant cross section of eventual users in order to allow them to comment on its suitability for their needs. Various courses were given in the USA and Europe and many teams then settled down to carry out their evaluations. Some 80 general reports were written and presented at a conference in Boston in October 1979. The general conclusion was that Ada was good but a few areas needed further refinement. In addition, nearly a thousand shorter technical language issue reports were received. After all these reports had been considered the preliminary Ada design was revised and this resulted in the publication in July 1980 of the first definitive version of the language. It was then proposed to the American National Standards Institute (ANSI) as a standard.

The ANSI standardization process occupied over two years and resulted in a certain number of changes to Ada. Most of these were small but often of subtle significance especially for the compiler writer. The ANSI standard *Language Reference Manual* (*LRM*) was finally published in January 1983 and it is this edition which forms the subject of this book[2].

ANSI then proposed to the International Standards Organization that Ada become an ISO standard. This resulted in the establishment of an ISO working group which performed the required activities. Ada became ISO standard 8652 in 1987. During this process (and since) a large number of technical queries were and continue to be analysed by the so-called Ada Rapporteur Group (ARG) whose recommendations are passed for approval to both the ISO working group and the USDoD Ada Board, a federal advisory committee established to help the Ada Joint Program Office in its deliberations on how to reap the benefits of Ada. These recommendations are known as Ada Issues (AIs) and come in various categories.

The *LRM* is a complex document and it is not surprising that the ARG identified a number of gaps, ambiguities, inconsistencies, and the occasional plain error. Most of these are subtle and concern fine detail that will rarely impact on the average programmer. However, a few are of note, and they are referred to where appropriate as, for example, AI-6. These references have been inserted so that the reader will not be confused by apparent contradictions between the *LRM* and this book. The AIs are in the public domain, and are available through the various national standards bodies, ISO, the Ada Information Clearinghouse and other Ada related organizations.

The ISO working group is, at the time of writing, considering a number of secondary standards relating to Ada. An important one is that relating to mathematical functions and the current draft is thus treated here very much as if it were part of the language standard.

However, it should not be thought that Ada is just another programming language. Ada is about Software Engineering and by analogy with other branches of engineering it can be seen that there are two main problems with the development of software: the need to reuse software components as much as possible and the need to establish disciplined ways of working.

As a language, Ada largely solves the problem of writing reusable software components (or at least through its excellent ability to prescribe interfaces, provides an enabling technology in which reusable software can be written).

Concerning the establishment of a disciplined way of working, it was realized that the language is just one component, although an important one, of the toolkit that every programmer (and his manager) should have available. It was therefore felt that additional benefit would be achieved if a uniform programming environment could also be established. And so, in parallel with the language design, a series of requirements documents for an Ada Programming Support Environment (APSE) were developed. These were entitled Sandman, Pebbleman and finally Stoneman[3]. These documents are less detailed than the corresponding language documents because the state-of-the-art in this area was (and perhaps still is) in its infancy. A number of grandiose attempts to build an APSE were undertaken in the early 1980s. They failed for a number of reasons – the requirements were not well understood and moreover the hardware technology used for the larger projects, which would benefit most from an APSE, started to undergo a transformation from a central machine with dumb terminals to a distributed intelligent environment requiring a rather different approach. The current situation (1988) is that a number of smaller environment systems are now emerging with longer term efforts being focused on the establishment of Public Tool Interfaces which are intended to allow tools to be moved between the different environments. But that is another story outside the scope of this book.

The failure of the early APSEs coupled with the difficulties in ironing out the problems during ANSI standardization plus the sheer effort required to develop good Ada compilers cast gloom on the development of Ada which is thankfully over. Excellent production quality Ada compilers are now available for all major architectures and millions of lines of real Ada applications have been written. It is now clear that Ada is living up to its promise of providing a language which can reduce the cost of both the initial development of software and its later maintenance. Even if Ada is seen as just another programming language, it reaches parts of the software development process that other languages do not reach.

1.2 Technical background

The evolution of programming languages has apparently occurred in a
rather *ad hoc* fashion, but with hindsight it is now possible to see three
major advances. Each advance seems to be associated with the introduction of a level of abstraction which removes unnecessary and harmful detail
from the program.

The first advance occurred in the early 1950s with high level
languages such as FORTRAN and Autocode which introduced 'expression
abstraction'. It thus became possible to write statements such as

    X=A+B(I)

so that the use of the machine registers to evaluate the expression was
completely hidden from the programmer. In these early languages the
expression abstraction was not perfect since there were somewhat arbitrary
constraints on the complexity of expressions; subscripts had to take a
particularly simple form for instance. Later languages such as Algol 60
removed such constraints and completed the abstraction.

The second advance concerned 'control abstraction'. The prime
example was Algol 60 which took a remarkable step forward; no language
since then has made such an impact on later developments. The point
about control abstraction is that the flow of control is structured and
individual control points do not have to be named or numbered. Thus we
write

    if X=Y **then** P:=Q **else** A:=B

and the compiler generates the gotos and labels which would have to be
explicitly used in languages such as FORTRAN. The imperfection of early
expression abstraction was repeated with control abstraction. In this case
the obvious flaw was the horrid Algol 60 switch which has now been
replaced by the case statement of languages such as Pascal. (The earlier
case clause of Algol 68 had its own problems.)

The third advance which is now occurring is 'data abstraction'. This
means separating the details of the representation of data from the abstract
operations defined upon the data.

Older languages take a very simple view of data types. In all cases
the data is directly described in numerical terms. Thus if the data to be
manipulated is not really numerical (it could be traffic light colours) then
some mapping of the abstract type must be made by the programmer into a
numerical type (usually integer). This mapping is purely in the mind of the
programmer and does not appear in the written program except perhaps as
a comment. It is probably a consequence of this fact that software libraries
have not emerged except in numerical analysis. Numerical algorithms,
such as those for finding eigenvalues of a matrix, are directly concerned
with manipulating numbers and so these languages, whose data values are
numbers, have proved appropriate. The point is that the languages provide
the correct abstract values in this case only. In other cases, libraries are not
successful because there is unlikely to be agreement on the required

mappings. Indeed different situations may best be served by different mappings and these mappings pervade the whole program. A change in mapping usually requires a complete rewrite of the program.

Pascal introduced a certain amount of data abstraction as instanced by the enumeration type. Enumeration types allow us to talk about the traffic light colours in their own terms without our having to know how they are represented in the computer. Moreover, they prevent us from making an important class of programming errors – accidentally mixing traffic lights with other abstract types such as the names of fish. When all such types are described in the program as numerical types, such errors can occur.

Another form of data abstraction concerns visibility. It has long been recognized that the traditional block structure of Algol 60 is not adequate. For example, it is not possible in Algol 60 to write two procedures to operate on some common data and make the procedures accessible without also making the data directly accessible. Many languages have provided control of visibility through separate compilation; this technique is adequate for medium-sized systems but since the separate compilation facility usually depends upon some external system, total control of visibility is not gained. The module of Modula is an example of an appropriate construction.

Another language which made an important contribution to the development of data abstraction is Simula 67 with its concept of class. Many other experimental languages too numerous to mention have also made detailed contributions.

Ada seems to be the first practical language to bring together the various categories of data abstraction. We are probably too close to the current scene to achieve a proper perspective. There are no doubt several imperfections in Ada data abstraction just as FORTRAN expression abstraction and Algol 60 control abstraction were imperfect. However, Ada is an important advance and offers the possibility of writing significant reusable software libraries for areas other than numerical analysis. It should therefore encourage the creation of a software components industry.

1.3   Structure and objectives of this book

Learning a programming language is a bit like learning to drive a car. Certain key things have to be learnt before any real progress is possible. Although we need not know how to use the windscreen washer, nevertheless we must at least be able to start the engine, engage gears, steer and brake. So it is with programming languages. We do not need to know all about Ada before we can write useful programs but quite a lot must be learnt. Moreover many virtues of Ada become apparent only when writing large programs just as many virtues of a Rolls-Royce are not apparent if we only use it to drive to the local shop.

This book is not an introduction to programming but an overall description of programming in Ada. It is assumed that the reader will have a significant knowledge of programming in some high level language. A knowledge of Pascal would be helpful but is certainly not necessary.

It should also be noted that this book strives to remain neutral regarding methods of program design and should therefore prove useful whatever techniques are used. However, certain features of Ada naturally align themselves with different design concepts such as Functional Decomposition (based on control flow) and Object Oriented Design (based on data abstraction) and will be mentioned as appropriate.

Chapter 2 gives a brief overview of some Ada concepts and is designed to give the reader a feel of the style and objectives of Ada. The rest of the book is in a tutorial style and introduces topics in a fairly straightforward sequence. By Chapter 7 we will have covered the traditional facilities of small languages such as Pascal. The remaining chapters cover modern and exciting material associated with data abstraction, programming in the large and parallel processing.

Most sections contain exercises. It is important that the reader does most, if not all, of these since they are an integral part of the discussion and later sections often use the results of earlier exercises. Solutions to all the exercises will be found at the end of the book.

Most chapters conclude with a short checklist of key points to be remembered. Although incomplete, these checklists should help to consolidate understanding. Furthermore the reader is encouraged to refer to the syntax in Appendix 4 which is organized to correspond to the order in which the topics are introduced.

This book covers all aspects of Ada but does not explore every pathological situation. Its purpose is to teach the reader the effect of and intended use of the features of Ada. In two areas the discussion is incomplete; these are machine dependent programming and input–output. Machine dependent programming (as its name implies) is so dependent upon the particular implementation that only a brief overview seems appropriate. Input–output, although important, does not introduce new concepts but is rather a mass (mess?) of detail; again a simple overview is presented. Further details of these areas can be found in the *Language Reference Manual* (*LRM*) which is referred to from time to time and which will be found at the end of this book.

Various appendices are provided. In this edition they mostly refer to corresponding material in the *LRM* but have been formally retained in order to preserve references in the body of the text. Appendix 4 has been retained in full because it is differently arranged to that in the *LRM*.

1.4 References

1   Defense Advanced Research Projects Agency (1978). *Department of Defense Requirements for High Order Computer Programming Languages – 'STEELMAN'*. Arlington, Virginia.
2   United States Department of Defense (1983). *Reference Manual for the Ada Programming Language* (ANSI/MIL-STD-1815A). Washington DC.
3   Defense Advanced Research Projects Agency (1980). *Department of Defense Requirements for Ada Programming Support Environments – 'STONEMAN'*. Arlington, Virginia.

Chapter 2
Ada Concepts

In this chapter we present a brief overview of some of the goals, concepts and features of Ada. Enough material is also given to enable the reader to create a framework in which the exercises and other fragments of program can be executed if desired, before all the required topics (such as input–output) are discussed in depth.

2.1 Key goals

Ada is a large language since it addresses many important issues relevant to the programming of practical systems in the real world. It is, for instance, much larger than Pascal, which, unless extended in some way, is really only suitable for training purposes (for which it was designed) and for small personal programs. Some of the key issues in Ada are

- Readability – it is recognized that professional programs are read much more often than they are written. It is important therefore to avoid an over-terse notation such as in APL which, although allowing a program to be written down quickly, makes it almost impossible to be read except perhaps by the original author soon after it was written.

- Strong typing – this ensures that each object has a clearly defined set of values and prevents confusion between logically distinct concepts. As a consequence many errors are detected by the compiler which in other languages (such as C) would have led to an executable but incorrect program.

- Programming in the large – mechanisms for encapsulation, separate compilation and library management are necessary for the writing of portable and maintainable programs of any size.

- Exception handling – it is a fact of life that programs of consequence are rarely perfect. It is necessary to provide a means whereby a program can be constructed in a layered and partitioned way so that the consequences of unanticipated events in one part can be contained.

- Data abstraction – as mentioned earlier, extra portability and maintainability can be obtained if the details of the representation of data can be kept separate from the specifications of the logical operations on the data.

- Tasking – for many applications it is important that the program be conceived as a series of parallel activities rather than just as a single sequence of actions. Building appropriate facilities into a language rather than adding them via calls to an operating system gives better portability and reliability.

- Generic units – in many cases the logic of part of a program is independent of the types of the values being manipulated. A mechanism is therefore necessary for the creation of related pieces of program from a single template. This is particularly useful for the creation of libraries.

2.2   Overall structure

One of the most important objectives of Software Engineering is to reuse existing pieces of program so that the effort of detailed new coding is kept to a minimum. The concept of a program library naturally emerges and an important aspect of a programming language is therefore its ability to express how to use the items in this library.

Ada recognizes this situation and introduces the concept of library units. A complete Ada program is conceived as a main program (itself a library unit) which calls upon the services of other library units. These library units can be thought of as forming the outermost lexical layer of the total program.

The main program takes the form of a procedure of an appropriate name. The service library units can be subprograms (procedures or functions) but they are more likely to be packages. A package is a group of related items such as subprograms but may be other entities as well.

Suppose we wish to write a program to print out the square root of some number such as 2.5. We can expect various library units to be available to provide us with a means of computing square roots and producing output. Our job is merely to write a main program to use these services as we wish.

For the sake of argument we will suppose that the square root can be obtained by calling a function in our library whose name is SQRT. In addition we will suppose that our library includes a package called

SIMPLE_IO containing various simple input–output facilities. These facilities might include procedures for reading numbers, printing numbers, printing strings of characters and so on.

Our program might look like

```
with SQRT, SIMPLE_IO;
procedure PRINT_ROOT is
    use SIMPLE_IO;
begin
    PUT(SQRT(2.5));
end PRINT_ROOT;
```

The program is written as a procedure called PRINT_ROOT preceded by a with clause giving the names of the library units which it wishes to use. The body of the procedure contains the single statement

```
PUT(SQRT(2.5));
```

which calls the procedure PUT in the package SIMPLE_IO with a parameter which in turn is the result of calling the function SQRT with the parameter 2.5.

Writing

```
use SIMPLE_IO;
```

gives us immediate access to the facilities in the package SIMPLE_IO. If we had omitted this use clause we would have had to write

```
SIMPLE_IO.PUT(SQRT(2.5));
```

in order to indicate where PUT was to be found.

We can make our program more useful by making it read in the number whose square root we require. It might then become

```
with SQRT, SIMPLE_IO;
procedure PRINT_ROOT is
    use SIMPLE_IO;
    X: FLOAT;
begin
    GET(X);
    PUT(SQRT(X));
end PRINT_ROOT;
```

The overall structure of the procedure is now clearer. Between **is** and **begin** we can write declarations and between **begin** and **end** we write statements. Broadly speaking, declarations introduce the entities we wish to manipulate and statements indicate the sequential actions to be performed.

We have now introduced a variable X of type FLOAT which is a predefined language type. Values of this type are a set of certain floating point numbers and the declaration of X indicates that X can have values only from this set. In our example a value is assigned to X by calling the procedure GET which is also in our package SIMPLE_IO.

Some small-scale details should be noted. The various statements and declarations all terminate with a semicolon; this is unlike some other languages such as Algol and Pascal where semicolons are separators rather than terminators. The program contains various identifiers such as **procedure**, PUT and X. These fall into two categories. A few (63 in fact) such as **procedure** and **is** are used to indicate the structure of the program; they are reserved and can be used for no other purpose. All others, such as PUT and X, can be used for whatever purpose we desire. Some of these, notably FLOAT in our example, have a predefined meaning but we can nevertheless reuse them if we so wish although it might be confusing to do so. For clarity in this book we use lower case bold letters for the reserved identifiers and upper case letters for the others. This is purely a notational convenience; the language rules do not distinguish the two cases except when we consider the manipulation of characters themselves. Note also how the underline character is used to break up long identifiers into meaningful parts.

Finally, observe that the name of the procedure, PRINT_ROOT, is repeated between the final **end** and the terminating semicolon. This is optional but is recommended in order to clarify the overall structure although this is obvious in a small example such as this.

Our program is still very simple; it might be more useful to enable it to cater for a whole series of numbers and print out each answer on a separate line. We could stop the program somewhat arbitrarily by giving it a value of zero.

```
with SQRT, SIMPLE_IO;
procedure PRINT_ROOTS is
    use SIMPLE_IO;
    X: FLOAT;
begin
    PUT("Roots of various numbers");
    NEW_LINE(2);
    loop
        GET(X);
        exit when X = 0.0;
        PUT(" Root of ");
        PUT(X);
        PUT(" is ");
        if X < 0.0 then
            PUT("not calculable");
        else
            PUT(SQRT(X));
        end if;
        NEW_LINE;
    end loop;
    NEW_LINE;
    PUT("Program finished");
    NEW_LINE;
end PRINT_ROOTS;
```

The output has been enhanced by the calls of further procedures NEW_LINE and PUT in the package SIMPLE_IO. A call of NEW_LINE will output the number of new lines specified by the parameter (which is of the predefined type INTEGER); the procedure NEW_LINE has been written in such a way that if no parameter is supplied then a default value of one is assumed. There are also calls of PUT with a string as argument. This is in fact a different procedure from the one which prints the number X. The compiler knows which is which because of the different types of parameters. Having more than one procedure with the same name is known as overloading. Note also the form of the string; this is a situation where the case of the letters does matter.

Various new control structures are also introduced. The statements between **loop** and **end loop** are repeated until the condition X = 0.0 in the **exit** statement is found to be true; when this is so the loop is finished and we immediately carry on after **end loop**. We also check that X is not negative; if it is we output the message 'not calculable' rather than attempting to call SQRT. This is done by the if statement; if the condition between **if** and **then** is true, then the statements between **then** and **else** are executed, otherwise those between **else** and **end if** are executed.

The general bracketing structure should be observed; **loop** is matched by **end loop** and **if** by **end if**. All the control structures of Ada have this closed form rather than the open form of Pascal which can lead to poorly structured and incorrect programs.

We will now consider in outline the possible general form of the function SQRT and the package SIMPLE_IO that we have been using.

The function SQRT will have a structure similar to that of our main program; the major difference will be the existence of parameters.

```
function SQRT(F: FLOAT) return FLOAT is
    R: FLOAT;
begin
    -- compute value of SQRT(F) in R
    return R;
end SQRT;
```

We see here the description of the formal parameters (in this case only one) and the type of the result. The details of the calculation are represented by the comment which starts with a double hyphen. The return statement is the means by which the result of the function is indicated. Note the distinction between a function which returns a result and is called as part of an expression and a procedure which does not have a result and is called as a single statement.

The package SIMPLE_IO will be in two parts: the specification which describes its interface to the outside world, and the body which contains the details of how it is implemented. If it just contained the procedures that we have used, its specification might be

```
package SIMPLE_IO is
    procedure GET(F: out FLOAT);
    procedure PUT(F: in FLOAT);
```

```
    procedure PUT(S: in STRING);
    procedure NEW_LINE(N: in INTEGER:= 1);
end SIMPLE_IO;
```

The parameter of GET is an **out** parameter because the effect of calling GET as in

```
GET(X);
```

is to transmit a value out from the procedure to the actual parameter X. The other parameters are all **in** parameters because the value goes in to the procedures.

Only a part of the procedures occurs in the package specification; this part is known as the procedure specification and just gives enough information to enable the procedures to be called.

We see also the two overloaded specifications of PUT, one with a parameter of type FLOAT and the other with a parameter of type STRING. Finally, note how the default value of 1 for the parameter of NEW_LINE is indicated.

The package body for SIMPLE_IO will contain the full procedure bodies plus any other supporting material needed for their implementation and which is naturally hidden from the outside user. In vague outline it might look like

```
with TEXT_IO;
package body SIMPLE_IO is

    ...
    procedure GET(F: out FLOAT) is

        ...
    begin

        ...
    end GET;
    -- other procedures similarly
end SIMPLE_IO;
```

The with clause shows that the implementation of the procedures in SIMPLE_IO uses the more general package TEXT_IO. It should also be noticed how the full body of GET repeats the procedure specification which was given in the corresponding package specification. (The procedure specification is the bit up to but not including **is**.) Note that the package TEXT_IO really exists whereas SIMPLE_IO is a figment of our imagination made up for the purpose of our example. We will say more about TEXT_IO in Section 2.6.

The example in this section has briefly revealed some of the overall structure and control statements of Ada. One purpose of this section has been to stress that the idea of packages is one of the most important concepts in Ada. A program should be conceived as a number of components which provide services to and receive services from each other. In the next few chapters we will of necessity be dealing with the small-scale features of Ada but in doing so we should not lose sight of the overall structure which we will return to in Chapter 8.

Perhaps this is an appropriate point to mention the special package STANDARD. This is a package which exists in every implementation and contains the declarations of all the predefined identifiers such as FLOAT and INTEGER. We can assume access to STANDARD automatically and do not have to give its name in a with clause. It is discussed in detail in Appendix 2.

Exercise 2.2

1   In practice it is likely that the function SQRT will not be in the library on its own but in a package along with other mathematical functions. Suppose this package has the identifier SIMPLE_MATHS and other functions are LOG, LN, EXP, SIN and COS. By analogy with the specification of SIMPLE_IO, write the specification of such a package. How would our program PRINT_ROOTS need to be changed?

2.3   Errors and exceptions

We introduce this topic by considering what would have happened in the example in the previous section if we had not tested for a negative value of X and consequently called SQRT with a negative argument. Assuming that SQRT has itself been written in an appropriate manner then it clearly cannot deliver a value to be used as the parameter of PUT. Instead an exception will be raised. The raising of an exception indicates that something unusual has happened and the normal sequence of execution is broken. In our case the exception might be NUMERIC_ERROR which is a predefined exception declared in the package STANDARD. If we did nothing to cope with this possibility then our program would be terminated and no doubt the Ada Run Time System (that is the non-Ada magic that drives our program from the operating system) will give us a rude message saying that our program has failed and why. We can, however, look out for an exception and take remedial action if it occurs. In fact we could replace the conditional statement

```
if X < 0.0 then
    PUT("not calculable");
else
    PUT(SQRT(X));
end if;
```

by

```
begin
    PUT(SQRT(X));
exception
```

```
        when NUMERIC_ERROR =>
            PUT("not calculable");
    end;
```

This fragment of program is an example of a block. If an exception is raised by the sequence of statements between **begin** and **exception**, then control immediately passes to the one or more statements following the handler for that exception and these are obeyed instead. If there were no handler for the exception (it might be another exception such as STORAGE_ERROR) then control passes up the flow hierarchy until we come to an appropriate handler or fall out of the main program which then becomes terminated as we mentioned with a rude message from the Run Time System.

The above example is not a good illustration of the use of exceptions since the event we are guarding against can easily be tested for directly. Nevertheless it does show the general idea of how we can look out for unexpected events and leads us into a brief consideration of errors in general.

There are two underlying causes of errors in software as perceived externally: an incorrect software specification in which a possible sequence of external events has not been taken into consideration and an incorrect implementation of the software specification itself. The first type of error can be allowed for to some extent by exception handlers. The second type leads to an incorrect Ada program.

From the linguistic viewpoint, an Ada program may be incorrect for various reasons. Four categories are recognized according to how they are detected.

- Some errors will be detected by the compiler – these will include simple punctuation mistakes such as leaving out a semicolon or attempting to violate the type rules such as mixing up colours and fish. In these cases the program will not be executed.

- Other errors are detected when the program is executed. An attempt to find the square root of a negative number or divide by zero are examples of such errors. In these cases an exception is raised as we have just seen and we have an opportunity to recover from the situation.

- There are also certain situations where the program breaks the language rules but there is no simple way in which this violation can be detected. For example, a program should not use a variable before a value is assigned to it. If it does then the behaviour is quite unpredictable and the program is said to be erroneous.

- Finally there are situations where, for implementation reasons, the language does not prescribe the order in which things are to be done. For example, the order in which the parameters of a procedure call are evaluated is not defined. If the behaviour of a program does depend on such an order then it is illegal and said to have an incorrect order dependency.

Care must be taken to avoid writing erroneous programs and those
with incorrect order dependencies. In practice, if we avoid clever tricks
then all will usually be well.

2.4 The type model

We have said that one of the key benefits of Ada is its strong typing. This is
well illustrated by the enumeration type. Consider

```
declare
    type COLOUR is (RED, AMBER, GREEN);
    type FISH is (COD, HAKE, PLAICE);
    X, Y: COLOUR;
    A, B: FISH;
begin
    X:= RED;      -- ok
    A:= HAKE;     -- ok
    B:= X;        -- illegal
    ...
end;
```

Here we have a block which declares two enumeration types
COLOUR and FISH and two variables of each type and then performs
various assignments. The declarations of the types gives the allowed values
of the types. Thus the variable X can only take one of the three values RED,
AMBER or GREEN. The fundamental rule of strong typing is that we cannot
assign a value of one type to a variable of a different type. So we cannot
mix up colours and fish and thus our (presumably accidental) attempt to
assign the value of X to B is illegal and will be detected during compilation.

There are two enumeration types predefined in the package
STANDARD. One is

```
type BOOLEAN is (FALSE, TRUE);
```

which plays a fundamental role in control flow. Thus the predefined
relational operators such as < produce a result of this type and such a value
follows **if** as we saw in the construction

```
if X < 0.0 then
```

in the example of Section 2.2. The other predefined enumeration type is
CHARACTER whose values are the ASCII characters; this type naturally
plays an important role in input–output. The literal values of this type
include the printable characters and these are represented by placing them
in single quotes thus 'X' or 'a' or indeed ' ' '.

The other fundamental types are the numeric types. One way or
another all other data types are built out of enumeration types and numeric
types. The two major classes of numeric types are the integer types and
floating point types (there are also fixed point types which are rather

obscure and deserve no further mention in this brief overview). All implementations will have the types INTEGER and FLOAT used in Section 2.2. In addition, if the architecture is appropriate, an implementation may have other predefined numeric types, LONG_INTEGER, LONG_FLOAT, SHORT_FLOAT and so on.

One of the problems of numeric types is how to obtain both portability and efficiency in the face of variation in machine architecture. In order to explain how this is done in Ada we have to introduce the perhaps surprising concept of a derived type.

A derived type introduces a new type which is almost identical to an existing type except that it is logically distinct. If we write

```
type LIGHT is new COLOUR;
```

then LIGHT will, like COLOUR, be an enumeration type with literals RED, AMBER and GREEN. However, values of the two types cannot be arbitrarily mixed since they are logically distinct. Nevertheless, in recognition of the close relationship, a value of one type can be converted to the other by explicitly using the destination type name. So we can write

```
declare
    type LIGHT is new COLOUR;
    C: COLOUR;
    L: LIGHT;
begin
    L:= AMBER;          -- the light amber, not the colour
    C:= COLOUR(L);      -- explicit conversion
    ...
end;
```

whereas a direct assignment

```
C:= L;              -- illegal
```

would violate the strong typing rule and this violation would be detected during compilation.

Returning now to our numeric types, if we write

```
type REAL is new FLOAT;
```

then REAL will have all the operations ($+$, $-$ etc.) of FLOAT and in general can be considered as equivalent. Now suppose we transfer our program to a different computer on which the predefined type FLOAT is not so accurate and that LONG_FLOAT is necessary. Assuming that our program has been written using REAL rather than FLOAT then replacing our declaration of REAL by

```
type REAL is new LONG_FLOAT;
```

is the only change necessary. We can actually do better than this by directly stating the precision that we require, thus

  type REAL **is digits** 7;

will cause REAL to be derived from the smallest predefined type with at least 7 decimal digits of accuracy.

  The point of all this is that it is not good practice to use the type FLOAT directly and accordingly we will use our type REAL in examples in future.

  A similar approach is possible with integer types but for a number of reasons the predefined type INTEGER has a fundamental place in the language and so we will continue to use it directly. We will say no more about numeric types for the moment except that all the expected operations apply to all integer and floating types.

  Ada naturally enables the creation of composite array and record types and these are discussed in Chapters 6 and 11. There are also access types (the Ada name for pointer types) which allow list processing and these are also discussed in Chapter 11. In conclusion we note that the type STRING which we encountered in Section 2.2 is in fact an array type whose components are of the enumeration type CHARACTER.

2.5 Generics

At the beginning of Section 2.2 we said that an important objective of Software Engineering is to reuse existing software components. However, the strong typing model of Ada rather gets in the way unless we have some method of writing software components which can be used for various different types. For example, the program to do a sort is largely independent of what it is sorting – all it needs is a rule for comparing the values. Record input–output is another example – the actions are quite independent of the contents of the records.

  So we need a means of writing pieces of software which can be parameterized as required for different types. In Ada this is done by the generic mechanism. We can make a package or subprogram generic with respect to one or more parameters which can include types. Such a generic unit provides a template out of which we can create genuine packages and subprograms by so-called instantiation. The full details are quite extensive and will be dealt with in Chapter 13. However, we want to give the reader the immediate ability to do some input–output and the standard packages for this involve the generic mechanism.

  The standard package for the input and output of floating point values in text form is generic with respect to the actual floating type. This is because we want a single package to cope with all the possible floating types such as the underlying machine types FLOAT and LONG_FLOAT as well as our own portable type REAL. Its specification is

  generic
   type NUM **is digits** <>;
  package FLOAT_IO **is**

```
        ...
        procedure GET(ITEM: out NUM; ... );
        procedure PUT(ITEM: in NUM; ... );
        ...
    end FLOAT_IO;
```

where we have omitted various details relating to the format. The one generic parameter is NUM and the notation **digits** <> indicates that it must be a floating point type and echoes the declaration of REAL using **digits** 10 that we briefly mentioned in the last section.

In order to create an actual package to manipulate values of our type REAL, we write

```
    package REAL_IO is new FLOAT_IO(REAL);
```

which creates a package with the name REAL_IO where the formal type NUM has been replaced throughout with our actual type REAL. As a consequence, procedures GET and PUT taking parameters of the type REAL are created and we can then call these as required. But we are straying into the next section.

Another simple area where the Ada generic mechanism is used is for the mathematical library. This library, discussed in detail in Section 13.4, includes a generic package which contains among other things the various familiar elementary functions such as SQRT. Its specification is

```
    with MATHEMATICAL_EXCEPTIONS;
    generic
        type FLOAT_TYPE is digits <>;
    package GENERIC_ELEMENTARY_FUNCTIONS is
        function SQRT(X: FLOAT_TYPE) return FLOAT_TYPE;
        ...    -- and so on
    end;
```

Again there is a single generic parameter giving the floating type. In order to call the function SQRT we must first instantiate the generic package much as we did for FLOAT_IO, thus

```
    package REAL_MATHS is
                    new GENERIC_ELEMENTARY_FUNCTIONS(REAL);
    use REAL_MATHS;
```

and we can then write a call of SQRT directly. Note that the use clause for REAL_MATHS avoids us having to write REAL_MATHS.SQRT everywhere.

The reader will have noticed that the generic package commences with a with clause for MATHEMATICAL_EXCEPTIONS. This is another package which contains just the declaration of a single exception, ARGUMENT_ERROR, thus

```
    package MATHEMATICAL_EXCEPTIONS is
        ARGUMENT_ERROR: exception;
    end MATHEMATICAL_EXCEPTIONS;
```

This exception is raised if the parameter of a function such as SQRT is unacceptable. This contrasts with our hypothetical function SQRT introduced earlier which we assumed raised the predefined exception NUMERIC_ERROR when given a negative parameter. We will see later when we deal with exceptions in detail in Chapter 10 that it is generally better to declare and raise our own exceptions rather than use the predefined ones.

2.6 Input–output

The Ada language is defined in such a way that all input and output is performed in terms of other language features. There are no special intrinsic features just for input and output. In fact input–output is just a service required by a program and so is provided by one or more Ada packages. This approach runs the attendant risk that different implementations will provide different packages and program portability will be compromised. In order to avoid this, the *Language Reference Manual* describes certain standard packages that can be expected to be available. Other, more elaborate, packages may be appropriate to special circumstances and the language does not prevent this. Indeed very simple packages such as our purely illustrative SIMPLE_IO may also be appropriate. Full consideration of input and output is deferred until Chapter 15 when we discuss interfaces between our program and the outside world in general. However, we will now briefly describe how to use some of the features so that the reader will be able to run some simple exercises. We will restrict ourselves to the input and output of simple text.

Text input–output is performed through the use of a standard package called TEXT_IO. Unless we specify otherwise all communication will be through two standard files, one for input and one for output and we will assume that (as is likely for most implementations), these are such that input is from the keyboard and output is to the screen. The full details of TEXT_IO cannot be described here but if we restrict ourselves to just a few useful facilities it looks a bit like

```
with IO_EXCEPTIONS;
package TEXT_IO is
    type COUNT is ...    -- an integer type
    ...
    procedure NEW_LINE(SPACING: in COUNT:= 1);
    procedure SET_COL(TO: in COUNT);
    function COL return COUNT;
    ...
    procedure GET(ITEM: out CHARACTER);
    procedure PUT(ITEM: in CHARACTER);
    procedure PUT(ITEM: in STRING);
    ...
    -- the package FLOAT_IO outlined in the previous section
    -- plus a similar package INTEGER_IO
    ...
end TEXT_IO;
```

Note first that this package commences with a with clause for IO_EXCEPTIONS. This is a further package which contains the declaration of a number of different exceptions relating to a variety of things which can go wrong with input–output. For toy programs the most likely to arise is probably DATA_ERROR which would occur for example if we tried to read in a number from the keyboard but then accidentally typed in something which was not a number at all or was in the wrong format.

The next thing to note is the outline declaration of the type COUNT. This is an integer type having similar properties to the type INTEGER and almost inevitably derived from it (just as our type REAL is likely to be derived from FLOAT). The parameter of NEW_LINE is of the type COUNT rather than plain INTEGER although since the parameter will typically be a literal such as 2 (or be omitted so that the default of 1 applies) this will not be particularly evident.

The procedure SET_COL and function COL are useful for tabulation. The character positions along a line of output are numbered starting at 1. So if we write (and assuming **use** TEXT_IO;)

SET_COL(10);

then the next character output will go at position 10. A call of NEW_LINE naturally sets the current position to 1 so that output commences at the beginning of the line. The function COL returns the current position and so

SET_COL(COL + 10);

will move the position on by 10 and thereby leave 10 spaces. Note that COL is an example of a function that has no parameters.

A single character can be output by for example

PUT('A');

and a string of characters by

PUT("This is a string of characters");

A value of the type REAL can be output in various formats. But first we have to instantiate the package FLOAT_IO mentioned in the previous section and which is declared inside TEXT_IO. Having done that we can call PUT with a single parameter, the value of type REAL to be output, in which case a standard default format is used, or we can add further parameters controlling the format. This is best illustrated by a few examples and we will suppose that our type REAL was declared to have 7 decimal digits as in the example in Section 2.4.

If we do not supply any format parameters then an exponent notation is used with 7 significant digits, 1 before the point and 6 after (the 7 matches the precision given in the declaration of REAL). There is also a leading space or minus sign. The exponent consists of the letter E followed by the exponent sign (+ or −) and then a two-digit decimal exponent. The effect is shown by the following statements with the output given as a comment. For clarity the output is surrounded by quotes and s designates a space; in reality there are no quotes and spaces are spaces.

```
PUT(12.34);          --   "s1.234000E+01"
PUT(-987.65);        --   "-9.876500E+02"
PUT(0.00289);        --   "s2.890000E-03"
```

We can override the default by providing three further parameters which give respectively the number of characters before the point, the number of characters after the point, and the number of characters after E. However, there is still always only one digit before the point. So

```
PUT(12.34, 3, 4, 2);    -- "ss1.2340E+1"
```

If we do not want exponent notation then we simply specify the last parameter as zero and we then get normal decimal notation. So

```
PUT(12.34, 3, 4, 0);    -- "s12.3400"
```

The output of values of type INTEGER follows a similar pattern. First we have to instantiate the generic package inside TEXT_IO which applies to all integer types with the particular type INTEGER thus

```
package INT_IO is new INTEGER_IO(INTEGER);
use INT_IO;
```

and (much as for the type REAL), we can then call PUT with a single parameter, the value of type INTEGER, in which case a standard default field is used, or we can add a further parameter specifying the field. The default field is the smallest which will accommodate all values of the type INTEGER allowing for a leading minus sign. Thus for a 16 bit implementation of INTEGER, the default field is 6. It should be noticed that if we specify a field which is too small then it is expanded as necessary. So

```
PUT(123);        --   "sss123"
PUT(-123);       --   "ss-123"
PUT(123, 4);     --    "s123"
PUT(123, 0);     --    "123"
```

That covers enough output for simple toy programs. The only input likely to be needed is of integer and real values and perhaps single characters. This is easily done by a call of GET with a parameter which must be a variable of the appropriate type just as we wrote GET(X); in the simple program in Section 2.2.

A call of GET with a real or integer parameter will expect us to type in an appropriate number at the keyboard; this must have a decimal point if the parameter is real. It should also be noted that leading blanks (spaces)

and newlines are skipped. A call of GET with a parameter of type CHARACTER will read the very next character and this can be neatly used for controlling the flow of an interactive program, thus

```
C: CHARACTER;
...
PUT("Do you want to stop? Answer Y if so. ");
GET(C);
if C = 'Y' then
...
```

That concludes our brief introduction to input–output which has inevitably been of a rather cookbook nature. Hopefully it has provided enough to enable the reader to drive such trial examples as desired as well as giving some further flavour to the nature of Ada.

2.7 Running a program

We are now in a position to put together a complete program using the proper input–output facilities and avoiding the non-portable type FLOAT. As an example we will rewrite the simple example of Section 2.2 and also use the standard mathematical library. It becomes

```
with TEXT_IO, GENERIC_ELEMENTARY_FUNCTIONS;
procedure PRINT_ROOTS is
    type REAL is digits 7;
    X: REAL;

    use TEXT_IO;
    package REAL_IO is new FLOAT_IO(REAL);
    use REAL_IO;

    package REAL_MATHS is
                new GENERIC_ELEMENTARY_FUNCTIONS(REAL);
    use REAL_MATHS;

begin
    PUT("Roots of various numbers");
    ...
    ...      -- and so on as before
    ...
end PRINT_ROOTS;
```

To have to write all that introductory stuff just to run a toy program each time is rather a burden so we will put it in a standard package of our own and then compile it once so that it is permanently in our program library and can then be accessed without more ado. We can write

```
with TEXT_IO, GENERIC_ELEMENTARY_FUNCTIONS;
package ETC is
```

```
        type REAL is digits 7;

        package REAL_IO is new TEXT_IO.FLOAT_IO(REAL);
        package INT_IO is new TEXT_IO.INTEGER_IO(INTEGER);

        package REAL_MATHS is
                    new GENERIC_ELEMENTARY_FUNCTIONS(REAL);
    end ETC;
```

and having compiled ETC our typical program can look like

```
    with TEXT_IO, ETC;
    use TEXT_IO, ETC;
    procedure PROGRAM is
        use REAL_IO, INT_IO, REAL_MATHS;     -- as required
        ...
        ...
    end PROGRAM;
```

Note that we can put the use clause for the packages mentioned in the with clause immediately after the with clause. The reader will realize that the author had great difficulty in identifying an appropriate and short name for our package ETC and hopes that he is forgiven for the pun on etcetera.

The reader should now be in a position to write complete simple programs. The exercises in this book have been written as fragments rather than complete programs for two reasons: one is that complete programs would take up a lot of space (and actually be rather repetitive) and the other is that Ada is really all about software components anyway.

Unfortunately it is not possible to explain how to call the Ada compiler and manipulate the program library because this depends upon the implementation and so we must leave the reader to find out how to do this last and vital step from the documentation for the implementation concerned.

Exercise 2.7

1   Write a program to output the ten times table. Make each column
     of the table 5 characters wide.

2   Write a program to output a table of square roots of numbers
     from 1 up to some limit specified by the user in response to a
     suitable question. Print the numbers as integers and the square
     roots to 5 decimal places in two columns. Use SET_COL to set the
     second column position so that the program can be easily
     modified. Note that a value N of type INTEGER can be converted
     to the corresponding REAL value by writing REAL(N).

2.8 Terminology

We conclude this introductory chapter with a few remarks on terminology. Every subject has its own terminology or jargon and Ada is no exception. (Indeed in Ada an exception is a kind of error as we have seen!) A full glossary of terms will be found in Appendix 3.

Terminology will generally be introduced as required but before starting off with the detailed description of Ada it is convenient to mention a couple of concepts which will occur from time to time.

The term static refers to things that can be determined at compilation, whereas dynamic refers to things determined during execution. Thus a static expression is one whose value can be determined by the compiler such as

2 + 3

and a static array is one whose bounds are known at compilation time.

Sometimes it is necessary to make a parenthetic remark to the compiler where the remark is often not a part of the program as such but more a useful hint. This can be done by means of a construction known as a pragma. As an example we can indicate that only parts of our program are to be listed by writing

pragma LIST(ON);

and

pragma LIST(OFF);

at appropriate places. Another similar example is

pragma PAGE;

which indicates that a new page should occur in the listing at this point.

Generally a pragma can appear anywhere that a declaration or statement can appear, after any semicolon and in some other contexts also. Sometimes there may be restrictions on the position of a particular pragma. For fuller details on pragmas see Appendix 1.

Chapter 3
Lexical Style

In the previous chapter, we introduced some concepts of Ada and illustrated the general appearance of Ada programs with some simple examples. However, we have so far only talked around the subject. In this chapter we get down to serious detail.

Regrettably it seems best to start with some rather unexciting but essential material – the detailed construction of things such as identifiers and numbers which make up the text of a program. However, it is no good learning a human language without getting the spelling sorted out. And as far as programming languages are concerned, compilers are usually very unforgiving regarding such corresponding and apparently trivial matters.

We also take the opportunity to introduce the notation used to describe the syntax of Ada language constructs. In general we will not use this syntax notation to introduce concepts but, in some cases, it is the easiest way to be precise. Moreover, if the reader wishes to consult the *LRM* then knowledge of the syntax notation is necessary. For completeness and easy reference the full syntax is given in Appendix 4.

3.1   Syntax notation

The syntax of Ada is described using a modified version of Backus-Naur Form or BNF. In this, syntactic categories are represented by lower case names; some of these contain embedded underlines to increase readability. A category is defined in terms of other categories by a sort of equation known as a production. Some categories are atomic and cannot be decomposed further – these are known as terminal symbols. A production consists of the name being defined followed by the special symbol ::= and its defining sequence.

Other symbols used are

[ ]   square brackets enclose optional items,

{ }   braces enclose items which may be omitted, appear once or be repeated many times,

| a vertical bar separates alternatives.

In some cases the name of a category is prefixed by a word in italics. In such cases the prefix is intended to convey some semantic information and can be treated as a form of comment as far as the context free syntax is concerned. Sometimes a production is presented in a form that shows the recommended layout.

3.2 Lexical elements

An Ada program is written as a sequence of lines of text containing the following characters

- the alphabet A–Z
- the digits 0–9
- various other characters " # & ' ( ) * + , – . / : ; < = > _ |
- the space character

The lower case alphabet may be used instead of or in addition to the upper case alphabet, but the two are generally considered the same. (The only exception is where the letters stand for themselves in character strings and character literals.)

Some other special characters such as ! may also be used in strings and literals. Certain of them may be used as alternatives to |, # and " if these are not available. We will not bother with the alternatives and the extra rules associated with them but will stick to the normal characters in this book.

The *LRM* does not prescribe how one proceeds from one line of text to the next. This need not concern us. We can just imagine that we type our Ada program as a series of lines using whatever mechanism the keyboard provides for starting a new line.

A line of Ada text can be thought of as a sequence of groups of characters known as lexical elements. We have already met several forms of lexical elements in Chapter 2. Consider for example

```
AGE:= 43;    -- John's age
```

This consists of five such elements

- the identifier AGE
- the compound symbol :=
- the number 43

- the single symbol ;
- the comment -- John's age

Other classes of lexical element are strings and character literals; they are dealt with in Chapter 6.

Individual lexical elements may not be split by spaces but otherwise spaces may be inserted freely in order to improve the appearance of the program. A most important example of this is the use of indentation to reveal the overall structure. Naturally enough a lexical element must fit on one line.

Particular care should be taken that the following compound delimiters do not contain spaces

=>	used in aggregates, cases, etc.
..	for ranges
**	exponentiation
:=	assignment
/=	not equals
>=	greater than or equals
<=	less than or equals
<<	label bracket
>>	the other label bracket
<>	the 'box' for arrays and generics

However, spaces may occur in strings and character literals where they stand for themselves and also in comments.

Note that adjacent identifiers and numbers must be separated from each other by spaces otherwise they would be confused. Thus we must write **end loop** rather than **endloop**.

3.3 Identifiers

We met identifiers in the simple examples in Chapter 2. As an example of the use of the syntax notation we now consider the following definition of an identifier.

identifier ::= letter {[underline] letter_or_digit}

letter_or_digit ::= letter | digit

letter ::= upper_case_letter | lower_case_letter

This states that an identifier consists of a letter followed by zero, one or more instances of letter_or_digit optionally preceded by a single underline. A letter_or_digit is, as its name implies, either a letter or a digit. Finally a letter is either an upper_case_letter or a lower_case_letter. As far as this example is concerned the categories underline, digit, upper_case_letter and lower_case_letter are not decomposed further and so are considered to be terminal symbols.

In plain English this merely says that an identifier consists of a letter possibly followed by one or more letters or digits with embedded isolated underlines. Either case of letter can be used. What the syntax does not convey is that the meaning attributed to an identifier does not depend upon the case of the letters. In fact identifiers which differ only in the case of corresponding letters are considered to be the same. But, on the other hand, the underline characters are considered to be significant.

Ada does not impose any limit on the number of characters in an identifier. Moreover all are significant. There may however be a practical limit since an identifier must fit onto a single line and an implementation is likely to impose some maximum line length. Programmers are encouraged to use meaningful names such as TIME_OF_DAY rather than cryptic or meaningless names such as T. Long names may seem tedious when first writing a program but in the course of its lifetime a program is read much more often than it is written and clarity aids subsequent understanding both by the original author and by others who may be called upon to maintain the program. Of course, in short mathematical or abstract subprograms, identifiers such as X and Y may be appropriate.

Identifiers are used to name all the various entities in a program. However, some identifiers are reserved for special syntactic significance and may not be reused. We encountered several of these in Chapter 2 such as **if**, **procedure** and **end**. There are 63 reserved words; they are listed in Appendix 1. For readability they are printed in boldface in this book but that is not important. In program text they could, like all identifiers, be in either case or indeed in a mixture of cases – procedure, PROCEDURE and Procedure are all acceptable. Nevertheless some discipline aids understanding and a useful convention is to use lower case for the reserved words and upper case for all others. But this is a matter of taste.

There are minor exceptions regarding the reserved words **delta**, **digits** and **range**. As will be seen later they are also used as attributes DELTA, DIGITS and RANGE. However, when so used they are always preceded by a prime or single quote character and so there is no confusion.

Some identifiers such as INTEGER and TRUE have a predefined meaning from the package STANDARD. These are not reserved and can be reused although to do so is usually unwise since the program could become very confusing.

Exercise 3.3

1   Which of the following are not legal identifiers and why?

(a)	Ada	(d)	UMO164G	(g)	X_
(b)	fish&chips	(e)	TIME__LAG	(h)	tax rate
(c)	RATE–OF–FLOW	(f)	77E2	(i)	goto

3.4 Numbers

Numbers (or numeric literals to use the proper jargon) take two forms
according to whether they denote an integer (an exact whole number) or a
real (an approximate and not usually whole number). The important
distinguishing feature is that real literals always contain a decimal point
whereas integer literals never do. Ada is strict on mixing up types. It is
illegal to use an integer literal where the context demands a real literal and
vice versa. Thus

        AGE: INTEGER:= 43.0;

and

        WEIGHT: REAL:= 150;

are both illegal. (We are using a type REAL rather than FLOAT for reasons
which were outlined in Section 2.4 and will be fully explained later.)
      The simplest form of integer literal is simply a sequence of decimal
digits. If the literal is very long it may be convenient to split it up into
groups of digits by inserting isolated underlines thus

        123_456_789

In contrast to identifiers such underlines are, of course, of no significance
other than to make the literal easier to read.
      The simplest form of real literal is a sequence of decimal digits
containing a decimal point. Note that there must be at least one digit on
either side of the decimal point. Again, isolated underlines may be inserted
to improve legibility provided they are not adjacent to the decimal point;
thus

        3.14159_26536

      Unlike most languages both integer and real literals can have an
exponent. This takes the form of the letter E (either case) followed by a
signed or unsigned decimal integer. This exponent indicates the power of
ten by which the preceding simple literal is to be multiplied. The exponent
cannot be negative in the case of an integer literal – otherwise it might not
be a whole number. (As a trivial point an exponent of −0 is not allowed for
an integer literal but it is for a real literal.)
      Thus the real literal 98.4 could be written with an exponent in any of
the following ways

        9.84E1   98.4e0   984.0e−1   0.984E+2

Note that 984e−1 would not be allowed.
      Similarly, the integer literal 1900 could also be written as

        19E2   190e+1   1900E+0

but not as 19000e−1 nor as 1900E−0.

The exponent may itself contain underlines if it consists of two or more digits but it is unlikely that the exponent would be so large as to make this necessary. However, the exponent may not itself contain an exponent!

A final facility is the ability to express a literal in a base other than 10. This is done by enclosing the digits between # characters and preceding the result by the base. Thus

    2#111#

is an integer literal of value $4 + 2 + 1 = 7$.

Any base from 2 to 16 inclusive can be used and, of course, base 10 can always be expressed explicitly. For bases above 10 the letters A to F are used to represent the superdigits 10 to 15. Thus

    14#ABC#

equals $10 \times 14^2 + 11 \times 14 + 12 = 2126$.

A based literal can also have an exponent. But note carefully that the exponent gives the power of the base by which the simple literal is to be multiplied and not a power of ten – unless, of course, the base happens to be ten. The exponent itself, like the base, is always expressed in normal decimal notation. Thus

    16#A#E2

equals $10 \times 16^2 = 2560$ and

    2#11#E11

equals $3 \times 2^{11} = 6144$.

A based literal can be real. The distinguishing mark is again the point. (We can hardly say 'decimal point' if we are not using a decimal base! A better term is radix point.) So

    2#101.11#

equals $4 + 1 + \frac{1}{2} + \frac{1}{4} = 5.75$ and

    7#3.0#e−1

equals $3\dot{7} = 0.42857\dot{1}$.

The reader may have felt that the possible forms of based literal are unduly elaborate. This is not really so. Based literals are useful – especially for fixed point types since they enable the programmer to represent values in the form in which he or she thinks about them. Obviously bases 2, 8 and 16 will be the most useful. But the notation is applicable to any base and the compiler can compute to any base so why not?

Finally note that a numeric literal cannot be negative. A form such as −3 consists of a literal preceded by the unary minus operator.

Exercise 3.4

1   Which of the following are not legal literals and why? For those that are legal, state whether they are integer or real literals.

(a)	38.6	(e)	2#1011	(i)	16#FfF#
(b)	.5	(f)	2.71828_18285	(j)	1_0#1_0#E1_0
(c)	32e2	(g)	12#ABC#	(k)	27.4e_2
(d)	32e−2	(h)	E+6	(l)	2#11#e−1

2   What is the value of the following?

(a)	16#E#E1	(c)	16#F.FF#E+2
(b)	2#11#E11	(d)	2#1.1111_1111_111#E11

3   How many different ways can you express the following as a numeric literal?

(a)   the integer 41   (b)   the integer 150

(Forget underlines, distinction between E and e, nonsignificant leading zeros and optional + in an exponent.)

3.5 Comments

It is important to add appropriate comments to a program to aid its understanding by someone else or yourself at a later date. We met some comments in Chapter 2.

A comment in Ada is written as an arbitrary piece of text following two hyphens (or minus signs – the same thing). Thus

```
-- this is a comment
```

The comment extends to the end of the line. There is no facility in Ada to insert a comment into the middle of a line. Of course, the comment may be the only thing on the line or it may follow some other Ada text. A long comment that needs several lines is merely written as successive comments.

```
-- this comment is spread
-- over
-- several
-- lines.
```

It is important that the leading hyphens are adjacent and are not separated by spaces.

Exercise 3.5

1   How many lexical elements are there in each of the following lines of text?

    (a)   X:= X+2; –– add two to X
    (b)   –– that was a silly comment
    (c)   –––––––––––––––––––––
    (d)   – – – – – – – – – – – – –

2   Distinguish

    (a)   **delay** 2.0;
    (b)   **delay**2.0;

Checklist 3

The case of a letter is immaterial in all contexts except strings and character literals.

Underlines are significant in identifiers but not in numeric literals.

Spaces are not allowed in lexical elements, except in strings, character literals and comments.

The presence or absence of a point distinguishes real and integer literals.

An integer may not have a negative exponent.

Numeric literals cannot be signed.

Nonsignificant leading zeros are allowed in all parts of a numeric literal.

Chapter 4
Scalar Types

This chapter lays the foundations for the small-scale aspects of Ada. We start by considering the declaration of objects, the assignment of values to them and the ideas of scope and visibility. We then introduce the important concepts of type, subtype and constraints. As examples of types, the remainder of the chapter discusses the numeric types INTEGER and REAL, enumeration types in general, the type BOOLEAN in particular and the operations on them.

4.1 Object declarations and assignments

Values can be stored in objects which are declared to be of a specific type. Objects are either variables, in which case their value may change (or vary) as the program executes, or they may be constants, in which case they keep their same initial value throughout their life.

A variable is introduced into the program by a declaration which consists of the name (that is, the identifier) of the variable followed by a colon and then the name of the type. This can then optionally be followed by the := symbol and an initial value. The declaration terminates with a semicolon. Thus we might write

```
I: INTEGER;
P: INTEGER:= 38;
```

This introduces the variable I of type INTEGER but gives it no particular initial value and then the variable P and gives it the specific initial value of 38.

We can introduce several variables at the same time in one declaration by separating them by commas thus

```
I, J, K: INTEGER;
P, Q, R: INTEGER:= 38;
```

In the second case all of P, Q and R are given the initial value of 38.

If a variable is declared and not given an initial value then great care must be taken not to use the undefined value of the variable until one has been properly given to it. If a program does use the undefined value in an uninitialized variable, its behaviour will be unpredictable; the program is said to be erroneous. As mentioned in Chapter 2, this means that the program is strictly illegal but the compiler and run time system may not be able to tell us.

A common way to give a value to a variable is by using an assignment statement. In this, the identifier of the variable is followed by := and then some expression giving the new value. The statement terminates with a semicolon. Thus

```
I:= 36;
```

and

```
P:= Q+R;
```

are both valid assignment statements and place new values in I and P thereby overwriting their previous values.

Note that := can be followed by any expression provided that it produces a value of the type of the variable being assigned to. We will discuss all the rules about expressions later but it suffices to say at this point that they can consist of variables and constants with operations such as + and round brackets (parentheses) and so on just like an ordinary mathematical expression.

There is a lot of similarity between a declaration containing an initial value and an assignment statement. Both use := before the expression and the expression can be of arbitrary complexity.

An important difference, however, is that although several variables can be declared and given the same initial value together, it is not possible for an assignment statement to give the same value to several variables. This may seem odd but in practice the need to give the same value to several variables usually only arises with initial values anyway.

Perhaps we should remark at this stage that strictly speaking a multiple declaration such as

```
A, B: INTEGER:= E;
```

is really a shorthand for

```
A: INTEGER:= E;
B: INTEGER:= E;
```

This means that in principle the expression E is evaluated for each variable. This is a subtle point and does not usually matter but we will encounter some examples later where the effect is important.

A constant is declared in a similar way to a variable by inserting the reserved word **constant** after the colon. Of course, a constant must be initialized in its declaration otherwise it would be useless. Why? An example might be

      PI: **constant** REAL:= 3.14159_26536;

In the case of numeric types, and only numeric types, it is possible to omit the type from the declaration of a constant thus

      PI: **constant**:= 3.14159_26536;

It is then technically known as a number declaration and merely provides a name for the number. The distinction between integer and real named numbers is made by the form of the initial value. In this case it is real because of the presence of the decimal point. It is usually good practice to omit the type when declaring numeric constants for reasons which will appear later. We will therefore do so in future examples. But note that the type cannot be omitted in numeric variable declarations even when an initial value is provided.

There is an important distinction between the allowed forms of initial values in constant declarations (with a type) and number declarations (without a type). In the former case the initial value may be any expression and is evaluated when the declaration is encountered at run time, whereas in the latter case it must be a static expression and so is evaluated at compilation time. Full details are deferred until Chapter 12.

Exercise 4.1

1   Write a declaration of a real variable R giving it an initial value of one.

2   Write appropriate declarations of real constants ZERO and ONE.

3   What is wrong with the following declarations and statements?

    (a)   **var** I: INTEGER;
    (b)   G: **constant**:= 981
    (c)   P, Q: **constant** INTEGER;
    (d)   P:= Q:= 7;
    (e)   MN: **constant** INTEGER:= M*N;
    (f)   2PI: **constant**:= 2.0*PI;

4.2   Blocks and scopes

Ada carefully distinguishes between declarations which introduce new identifiers and statements which do not. It is clearly only sensible that the declarations which introduce new identifiers should precede the statements which manipulate them. Accordingly, declarations and statements occur in separate places in the program text. The simplest fragment of text which includes declarations and statements is a block.

A block commences with the reserved word **declare**, some declarations, **begin**, some statements and concludes with the reserved word **end** and the terminating semicolon. A trivial example is

```
declare
    I: INTEGER:= 0;    -- declarations here
begin
    I:= I+1;           -- statements here
end;
```

A block is itself an example of a statement and so one of the statements in its body could be another block. This textual nesting of blocks can continue indefinitely.

Since a block is a statement it can be executed like any other statement. When this happens the declarations in its declarative part (the bit between **declare** and **begin**) are elaborated in order and then the statements in the body (between **begin** and **end**) are executed in the usual way. Note the terminology: we elaborate declarations and execute statements. All that the elaboration of a declaration does is make the thing being declared come into existence and then evaluate and assign any initial value to it. When we come to the **end** of the block all the things which were declared in the block automatically cease to exist.

We can now see that the above simple example of a block is rather foolish; it introduces I, adds 1 to it but then loses it before use is made of the resulting value.

Another point to note is that the objects used in an initial value must, of course, exist. They could be declared in the same declarative part but the declarations must precede their use. For example

```
declare
    I: INTEGER:= 0;
    K: INTEGER:= I;
begin
```

is allowed, but

```
declare
    K: INTEGER:= I;
    I: INTEGER:= 0;
begin
```

is generally not. (We will see in a moment that this could have a valid but different meaning.)

This idea of elaborating declarations in order is important; the jargon is 'linear elaboration of declarations'.

Like other block structured languages, Ada also has the idea of hiding. Consider

```
declare
    I, J: INTEGER;
begin
    ...                     -- here I is the outer one
    declare
        I: INTEGER;
    begin
        ...                 -- here I is the inner one
    end;
    ...                     -- here I is the outer one
end;
```

In this, a variable I is declared in an outer block and then redeclared in an inner block. This redeclaration does not cause the outer I to cease to exist but merely makes it temporarily invisible. In the inner block I refers to the new I, but as soon as we leave the inner block, this new I ceases to exist and the outer one again becomes visible.

We distinguish the terms 'scope' and 'visibility'. The scope is the region of text where the entity is potentially visible and it is visible at a given point if its identifier can be used to refer to it at that point. We will now illustrate these terms but a fuller discussion has to be left until Chapter 8.

In the case of a block the scope of a variable (or constant) extends from the start of its declaration until the end of the block. However, it is not visible in its own declaration nor in any inner block after the redeclaration of the same identifier. The regions of scope and visibility are illustrated by the following:

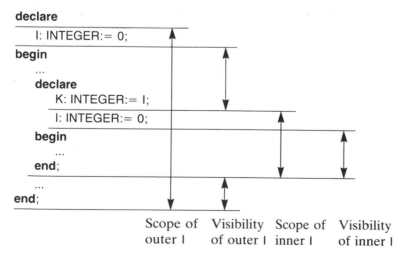

```
declare
    I: INTEGER:= 0;
begin
    ...
    declare
        K: INTEGER:= I;
        I: INTEGER:= 0;
    begin
        ...
    end;
    ...
end;
```

| | Scope of outer I | Visibility of outer I | Scope of inner I | Visibility of inner I |

The initial value of K refers to the outer I because it precedes the introduction of the inner I.

Thus

```
K: INTEGER:= I;
I: INTEGER:= 0;
```

may or may not be legal – it depends upon its environment.

Exercise 4.2

1   How many errors can you see in the following?

```
declare
    I: INTEGER:= 7;
    J, K: INTEGER
begin
    J:= I+K;
    declare
        P: INTEGER=I;
        I, J: INTEGER;
    begin
        I:= P+Q;
        J:= P−Q;
        K:= I*J;
    end;
    PUT(K);          −− output value of K
end;
```

4.3 Types

'A type is characterized by a set of values and a set of operations' (*LRM* 3.3).

In the case of the built-in type INTEGER, the set of values is represented by

$$..., -3, -2, -1, 0, 1, 2, 3, ...$$

and the operations include

$$+, -, \star \text{ and so on.}$$

With two minor exceptions to be discussed later (arrays and tasks) every type has a name which is introduced in a type declaration. (The built-in types such as INTEGER are considered to be declared in the package STANDARD.) Moreover, every type declaration introduces a new type quite distinct from any other type.

The set of values belonging to two distinct types are themselves quite distinct although in some cases the actual lexical form of the values may be identical – which one is meant at any point is determined by the context. The idea of one lexical form representing two or more different things is known as overloading.

Values of one type cannot be assigned to variables of another type. This is the fundamental rule of strong typing. Strong typing, correctly used, is an enormous aid to the rapid development of correct programs since it ensures that many errors are detected at compilation time. (Overused, it can tie one in knots; we will discuss this thought in Chapter 16.)

A type declaration uses a somewhat different syntax to an object declaration in order to emphasize the conceptual difference. It consists of the reserved word **type**, the identifier to be associated with the type, the reserved word **is** and then the definition of the type followed by the terminating semicolon. We can imagine that the package STANDARD contains type declarations such as

type INTEGER **is** ... ;

The type definition between **is** and ; gives in some way the set of values belonging to the type. As a concrete example consider the following

type COLOUR **is** (RED, AMBER, GREEN);

(This is an example of an enumeration type and will be dealt with in more detail in a later section in this chapter.)

This introduces a new type called COLOUR. Moreover, it states that there are only 3 values of this type and they are denoted by the identifiers RED, AMBER and GREEN.

Objects of this type can then be declared in the usual way

C: COLOUR;

An initial value can be supplied

C: COLOUR:= RED;

or a constant can be declared

DEFAULT: **constant** COLOUR:= RED;

We have stated that values of one type cannot be assigned to variables of another type. Therefore one cannot mix colours and integers and so

I: INTEGER;
C: COLOUR;
...
I:= C;

is illegal. In older languages it is often necessary to implement concepts such as enumeration types by more primitive types such as integers and give values such as 0, 1 and 2 to variables named RED, AMBER and GREEN. Thus in Algol 60 one could write

integer RED, AMBER, GREEN;
RED:= 0; AMBER:= 1; GREEN:= 2;

and then use RED, AMBER and GREEN as if they were literal values. Obviously the program would be easier to understand than if the code values 0, 1 and 2 had been used directly. But, on the other hand, the compiler could not detect the accidental assignment of a notional colour to a variable which was, in the mind of the programmer, just an ordinary integer. In Ada, as we have seen, this is detected during compilation, thus making a potentially tricky error quite trivial to discover.

4.4 Subtypes

We now introduce subtypes and constraints. A subtype, as its name suggests, characterizes a set of values which is just a subset of the values of some other type known as the base type. The subset is defined by means of a constraint. Constraints take various forms according to the category of the base type. As is usual with subsets, the subset may be the complete set. There is, however, no way of restricting the set of operations of the base type. The subtype takes all the operations; subsetting applies only to the values.

As an example, suppose we wish to manipulate dates; we know that the day of the month must lie in the range 1 .. 31 so we declare a subtype thus

subtype DAY_NUMBER **is** INTEGER **range** 1 .. 31;

We can then declare variables and constants using the subtype identifier in exactly the same way as a type identifier.

D: DAY_NUMBER;

We are then assured that the variable D can take only integer values from 1 to 31 inclusive. The compiler will insert run-time checks if necessary to ensure that this is so; if a check fails then the CONSTRAINT_ERROR exception is raised.

It is important to realize that a subtype declaration does not introduce a new distinct type. An object such as D is of type INTEGER and so the following is perfectly legal from the syntactic point of view.

D: DAY_NUMBER;
I: INTEGER;
...
D:= I;

Of course, on execution, the value of I may or may not lie in the range 1 .. 31. If it does, then all is well; if not then CONSTRAINT_ERROR will be raised. Assignment in the other direction

I:= D;

will, of course, always work.

It is not always necessary to introduce a subtype explicitly in order to impose a constraint. We could equally have written

D: INTEGER **range** 1 .. 31;

Furthermore a subtype need not impose a constraint. It is perfectly legal to write

subtype DAY_NUMBER **is** INTEGER;

although in this instance it is not of much value.

A subtype (explicit or not) may be defined in terms of a previous subtype

subtype FEB_DAY **is** DAY_NUMBER **range** 1 .. 29;

Any additional constraint must of course satisfy existing constraints

DAY_NUMBER **range** 0 .. 10

would be incorrect and cause CONSTRAINT_ERROR to be raised.

The above examples have shown constraints with static bounds. This is not necessarily the case; in general the bounds can be given by arbitrary expressions and so the set of values of a subtype need not be static, that is known at compilation time. However, it is an important fact that a type is always static.

In conclusion then, a subtype does not introduce a new type but is merely a shorthand for an existing type with an optional constraint. However, in later chapters we will encounter several contexts in which an explicit constraint is not allowed; a subtype has to be introduced for these cases. We refer to a type or subtype name as a type mark and to the form consisting of a type mark followed by an optional constraint as a subtype indication as shown by the syntax

type_mark ::= *type_*name | *subtype_*name
subtype_indication ::= type_mark [constraint]

Thus we can restate the previous remark as saying that there are situations where a type mark has to be used whereas, as we have seen here, the more general subtype indication (which includes a type mark on its own) is allowed in object declarations.

The sensible use of subtypes has two advantages. It can ensure that programming errors are detected earlier by preventing variables from being assigned inappropriate values. It can also increase the execution efficiency of a program. This particularly applies to array subscripts as we shall see later.

We conclude this section by summarizing the assignment statement and the rules of strong typing. Assignment has the form

    VARIABLE := expression;

and the two rules are ,

- both sides must have the same base type,
- the expression must satisfy any constraints on the variable; if it does not, the assignment does not take place, and CONSTRAINT_ERROR is raised instead.

Note carefully the general principle that type errors (violations of the first rule) are detected during compilation whereas subtype errors (violations of the second rule) are detected during execution by the raising of CONSTRAINT_ERROR. (A clever compiler might give a warning during compilation.)

We have now introduced the basic concepts of types and subtypes. The remaining sections of this chapter illustrate these concepts further by considering in more detail the properties of the simple types of Ada.

Exercise 4.4

1   Given the following declarations

        I, J: INTEGER **range** 1 .. 10;
        K : INTEGER **range** 1 .. 20;

which of the following assignment statements could raise CONSTRAINT_ERROR?

    (a)   I:= J;
    (b)   K:= J;
    (c)   J:= K;

4.5 Simple numeric types

Perhaps surprisingly a full description of the numeric types of Ada is deferred until much later in this book. The problems of numerical analysis (error estimates and so on) are complex and Ada is correspondingly complex in this area so that it can cope in a reasonably complete way with the needs of the numerical specialist. For our immediate purposes such complexity can be ignored. Accordingly, in this section, we merely

consolidate a simple understanding of the two numeric types INTEGER and
REAL which we have been using as background for elementary examples.
For the everyday programmer these two numeric types will probably suffice.

First a reminder. The type INTEGER is a genuine built-in Ada type.
But as mentioned in Section 2.4, the type REAL is not. It has to be declared
somewhere in terms of one of the built-in floating point types. The reason for
supposing that this has been done concerns portability and will be discussed
when the truth about numeric types is revealed in more detail. For the
moment, however, we will suppose that REAL is the floating point type. (The
author is not deceiving you but in fact encouraging good Ada programming
practice.)

As we have seen, a constraint may be imposed on the type INTEGER
by using the reserved word **range**. This is then followed by two expressions
separated by two dots which, of course, must produce values of integer type.
These expressions need not be literal constants. One could have

    P: INTEGER **range** 1 .. I+J;

A range can be null as would happen in the above case if I+J turned
out to be zero. Null ranges may seem pretty useless but they often
automatically occur in limiting cases, and to exclude them would mean
taking special action in such cases.

The minimum value of the type INTEGER is given by INTEGER'FIRST
and the maximum value by INTEGER'LAST. These are our first examples of
attributes. Ada contains various attributes denoted by a single quote
followed by an identifier.

The value of INTEGER'FIRST will depend on the implementation but
will always be negative. On a two's complement machine it will be
−INTEGER'LAST−1 whereas on a one's complement machine it will be
−INTEGER'LAST. So on a typical 16 bit two's complement implementation
we will have

    INTEGER'FIRST = −32768
    INTEGER'LAST = +32767

Of course, we should always write INTEG
+32767 if that is what we logically want. Otherwis
could suffer.

Two useful subtypes are

    subtype NATURAL **is** INTEGER **range** 0 .. INTEGER'LAST;
    subtype POSITIVE **is** INTEGER **range** 1 .. INTEGER'LAST;

These are so useful that they are declared for us in the package STANDARD.
The attributes FIRST and LAST also apply to subtypes so

    POSITIVE'FIRST = 1
    NATURAL'LAST = INTEGER'LAST

We turn now to a brief consideration of the type REAL. It is possible to
apply constraints to the type REAL in order to reduce the range and precision

but this takes us into the detail which has been deferred until later. There are also attributes REAL'FIRST and REAL'LAST. It is not really necessary to say any more at this point.

The other predefined operations that can be performed on the types INTEGER and REAL are much as one would expect in a modern programming language. They are summarized below.

+, − These are either unary operators (that is, taking a single operand) or binary operators taking two operands.

In the case of a unary operator, the operand can be either integer or real; the result will be of the same type. Unary + effectively does nothing. Unary − changes the sign.

In the case of a binary operator, both operands must be integer or both operands must be real; the result will be of the type of the operands. Normal addition or subtraction is performed.

* Multiplication; both operands must be integer or both operands must be real; again the result is of the same type.

/ Division; both operands must be integer or both operands must be real; again the result is of the same type. Integer division truncates towards zero.

rem Remainder; in this case both operands must be integer and the result is an integer. It is the remainder on division.

mod Modulo; again both operands must be integer and the result is an integer. This is the mathematical modulo operation.

abs Absolute value; this is a unary operator and the single operand may be integer or real. The result is again of the same type and is the absolute value. That is, if the operand is positive, the result is the same but if it is negative, the result is the corresponding positive value.

** Exponentiation; this raises the first operand to the power of the second. If the first operand is of integer type, the second must be a positive integer or zero. If the first operand is of real type, the second can be any integer. The result is of the same type as the first operand.

In addition, we can perform the operations =, /=, <, <=, > and >= in order to return a Boolean result TRUE or FALSE. Again both operands must be of the same type. Note the form of the not equals operator /=.

Although the above operations are mostly straightforward a few points are worth noting.

It is a general rule that mixed mode arithmetic is not allowed. One cannot, for example, add an integer value to a real value; both must be of the same type. A change of type from INTEGER to REAL or vice versa can be done by using the desired type name (or indeed subtype name) followed by the expression to be converted in brackets.

So given

I: INTEGER:= 3;
R: REAL:= 5.6;

we cannot write

I+R

but we must write

REAL(I)+R

which uses real addition to give the real value 8.6, or

I+INTEGER(R)

which uses integer addition to give the integer value 9.
Conversion from real to integer always rounds rather than truncates,
thus

1.4 becomes 1
1.6 becomes 2

but a value midway between two integers, such as 1.5, may be rounded up
or down according to the implementation.

There is a subtle distinction between **rem** and **mod**. The **rem**
operation produces the remainder corresponding to the integer division
operation /. Integer division truncates towards zero; this means that the
absolute value of the result is always the same as that obtained by dividing
the absolute values of the operands. So

$$
\begin{aligned}
7\ /\ \ \ 3 &=\ \ \ 2 \\
(-7)\ /\ \ \ 3 &= -2 \\
7\ /\ (-3) &= -2 \\
(-7)\ /\ (-3) &=\ \ \ 2
\end{aligned}
$$

and the corresponding remainders are

$$
\begin{aligned}
7\ \mathbf{rem}\ \ \ 3 &=\ \ \ 1 \\
(-7)\ \mathbf{rem}\ \ \ 3 &= -1 \\
7\ \mathbf{rem}\ (-3) &=\ \ \ 1 \\
(-7)\ \mathbf{rem}\ (-3) &= -1
\end{aligned}
$$

The remainder and quotient are always related by

(I/J) ∗ J + I **rem** J = I

and it will also be noted that the sign of the remainder is always equal to
the sign of the first operand I (the dividend).

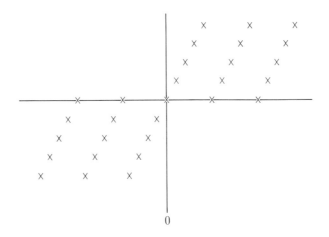

Figure 4.1   Behaviour of I **rem** 5 around zero.

However, **rem** is not always satisfactory. If we plot the values of I **rem** J for a fixed value of J (say 5) for both positive and negative values of I we get the pattern shown in Figure 4.1.

As we can see, the pattern is symmetric about zero and consequently changes its incremental behaviour as we pass through zero.

The **mod** operation, on the other hand, does have uniform incremental behaviour as shown in Figure 4.2.

The **mod** operation enables us to do normal modulo arithmetic. For example

(A+B) **mod** n = (A **mod** n + B **mod** n) **mod** n

for all values of A and B both positive and negative. For positive n, A **mod** n is always in the range 0 .. n−1; for negative n, A **mod** n is always in the range n+1 .. 0. Of course, modulo arithmetic is only usually performed with a positive value for n. But the **mod** operator gives consistent and sensible behaviour for negative values of n also.

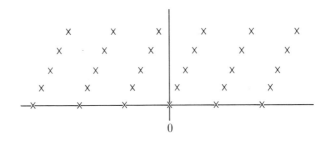

Figure 4.2   Behaviour of I **mod** 5 around zero.

We can look upon r[...]der corresponding to
division with truncation to[...]

$$\frac{7}{3} = 2.33 \Rightarrow 2 \qquad 7-(3\cdot2)=1$$

$$7 \text{ mod } 3 = 1$$
$$(-7) \text{ mod } 3 = 2$$
$$7 \text{ mod } (-3) = -2$$
$$(-7) \text{ mod } (-3) = -1$$

$$-\frac{7}{3} = -2.33 \Rightarrow -3 \qquad -7-(3\cdot-3)=2$$

$$\frac{7}{-3} = -2.33 \Rightarrow -3 \qquad 7-(-3\cdot-3)=-2$$

In the case of **mod** the sign [...] qual to the sign of the
second operand whereas w[...] he first operand.

$$\frac{-7}{-3} = 2.33 \Rightarrow 2 \qquad -7-(-3\cdot2)= -1$$

The reader may hav[...] n has been somewhat
protracted. In summary, i[...] that integer division
with negative operands is [...] and **mod** only differ
when one or both operands is negative. It will be found that in such cases it
is almost always **mod** that is wanted.

Finally some notes on the exponentiation operator **. For a positive
second operand, the operation corresponds to repeated multiplication. So

```
3**4 = 3*3*3*3 = 81
3.0**4 = 3.0*3.0*3.0*3.0 = 81.0
```

The second operand can be 0 and, of course, the result is then always the
value one

```
3**0 = 1
3.0**0 = 1.0
0**0 = 1
0.0**0 = 1.0
```

The second operand cannot be negative if the first operand is an integer,
as the result might not be a whole number. In fact, the exception
CONSTRAINT_ERROR would be raised in such case. But it is allowed for a
real first operand and produces the corresponding reciprocal

```
3.0**(-4) = 1.0/81.0 = 0.0123456780123 ...
```

We conclude this section with a brief discussion on combining
operators in an expression. As is usual the operators have different
precedence levels and the natural precedence can be overruled by the use
of brackets. Operators of the same precedence are applied in order from
left to right. A subexpression in brackets obviously has to be evaluated
before it can be used. But note that the order of evaluation of the two
operands of a binary operator is not specified. The precedence levels of the
operators we have met so far are shown below in increasing order of
precedence

```
= /= < <= > >=
+ -          (binary)
+ -          (unary)
* / mod  rem
** abs
```

Thus

A/B*C	means	(A/B)*C
A+B*C+D	means	A+(B*C)+D
A*B+C*D	means	(A*B)+(C*D)
A*B**C	means	A*(B**C)

In general, as stated above, several operations of the same precedence can be applied from left to right and brackets are not necessary. However, the syntax rules forbid multiple instances of the exponentiating operator without brackets. Thus we cannot write

A**B**C

but must explicitly write either

(A**B)**C   or   A**(B**C)

This restriction avoids the risk of accidentally writing the wrong thing. Note however that the well established forms

A−B−C   and   A/B/C

are allowed. The syntax rules similarly prevent the mixed use of **abs** and ** without brackets.

The precedence of unary minus needs care

−A**B   means   −(A**B)   rather than   (−A)**B

as in Algol 68. Also

A**−B and A*−B

are illegal. Brackets are necessary.

Note finally that the precedence of **abs** is, confusingly, not the same as that of unary minus. As a consequence we can write

− **abs** X   but not   **abs** − X

Exercise 4.5

1   Evaluate the expressions below given the following
        I: INTEGER:= 7;
        J: INTEGER:= −5;
        K: INTEGER:= 3;

(a)	I*J*K	(e)	J + 2 **rem** I
(b)	I/J*K	(f)	K**K**K
(c)	I/J/K	(g)	−J **mod** 3
(d)	J + 2 **mod** I	(h)	−J **rem** 3

2   Rewrite the following mathematical expressions in Ada. Use suitable identifiers of appropriate type.

(a) Mr^2 – moment of inertia of black hole
(b) $b^2 - 4ac$ – discriminant of quadratic
(c) $\tfrac{4}{3}\pi r^3$ – volume of sphere
(d) $\dfrac{p\pi a^4}{8l\eta}$ – viscous flowrate through tube

---

4.6 Enumeration types

Here are some examples of declarations of enumeration types starting with COLOUR which we introduced when discussing types in general.

```
type COLOUR is (RED, AMBER, GREEN);
type DAY is (MON, TUE, WED, THU, FRI, SAT, SUN);
type STONE is (AMBER, BERYL, QUARTZ);
type GROOM is (TINKER, TAILOR, SOLDIER, SAILOR,
               RICH_MAN, POOR_MAN, BEGGAR_MAN, THIEF);
type SOLO is (ALONE);
```

This introduces an example of overloading. The literal AMBER can represent a COLOUR or a STONE. Both meanings of the same name are visible together and the second declaration does not hide the first whether they are declared in the same declarative part or one is in an inner declarative part. We can usually tell which is meant from the context but in those odd cases when we cannot we can always qualify the literal by placing it in brackets and preceding it by an appropriate type mark (that is its type name or a relevant subtype name) and a single quote. Thus

```
COLOUR'(AMBER)
STONE'(AMBER)
```

Examples where this is necessary will occur later.

    Although we can use AMBER as an enumeration literal in two distinct enumeration types, we cannot use it as an enumeration literal and the identifier of a variable at the same time. The declaration of one would hide the other and they could not both be declared in the same declarative part. Later we will see that an enumeration literal can be overloaded with a subprogram.

    There is no upper limit on the number of values in an enumeration type but there must be at least one. An empty enumeration type is not allowed.

    Constraints on enumeration types and subtypes are much as for integers. The constraint has the form

```
range lower_bound_expression .. upper_bound_expression
```

and this indicates the set of values from the lower bound to the upper bound inclusive. So we can write

>**subtype** WEEKDAY **is** DAY **range** MON .. FRI;
>D: WEEKDAY;

or

>D: DAY **range** MON .. FRI;

and then we know that D cannot be SAT or SUN.

If the lower bound is above the upper bound then we get a null range, thus

>**subtype** COLOURLESS **is** COLOUR **range** AMBER .. RED;

Note the curious anomaly that we cannot have a null subtype of a type such as SOLO (since it only has one value).

The attributes FIRST and LAST also apply to enumeration types and subtypes, so

>COLOUR'FIRST = RED
>WEEKDAY'LAST = FRI

There are built-in functional attributes to give the successor or predecessor of an enumeration value. These consist of SUCC or PRED following the type name and a single quote. Thus

>COLOUR'SUCC(AMBER) = GREEN
>STONE'SUCC(AMBER) = BERYL
>DAY'PRED(FRI) = THU

Of course, the thing in brackets can be an arbitrary expression of the appropriate type. If we try to take the predecessor of the first value or the successor of the last then the exception CONSTRAINT_ERROR is raised. In the absence of this exception we have, for any type T and any value X,

>T'SUCC(T'PRED(X)) = X

and vice versa.

Another functional attribute is POS. This gives the position number of the enumeration value, that is the position in the declaration with the first one having a position number of zero. So

>COLOUR'POS(RED) = 0
>COLOUR'POS(AMBER) = 1
>COLOUR'POS(GREEN) = 2

The opposite to POS is VAL. This takes the position number and returns the corresponding enumeration value. So

    COLOUR'VAL(0) = RED
    DAY'VAL(6) = SUN

If we give a position value outside the range, as for example

    SOLO'VAL(1)

then CONSTRAINT_ERROR is raised.
    Clearly we always have

    T'VAL(T'POS(X)) = X

and vice versa.
    We also note that

    T'SUCC(X) = T'VAL(T'POS(X) + 1)

they either both give the same value or both raise an exception.
    It should be noted that these four attributes SUCC, PRED, POS and
VAL may also be applied to subtypes but are then identical to the same
attributes of the corresponding base type.
    It is probably rather bad practice to mess about with POS and VAL
when it can be avoided. To do so encourages the programmer to think in
terms of numbers rather than the enumeration values and hence destroys
the abstraction.
    Finally the operators =, /=, <, <=, > and >= also apply to
enumeration types. The result is defined by the order of the values in the
type declaration. So

    RED < GREEN   is   TRUE
    WED >= THU   is   FALSE

The same result would be obtained by comparing the position values. So

    T'POS(X) < T'POS(Y)   and   X < Y

are always equivalent (except that X < Y might be ambiguous).

Exercise 4.6

1   Evaluate

     (a)   DAY'SUCC(WEEKDAY'LAST)
     (b)   WEEKDAY'SUCC(WEEKDAY'LAST)
     (c)   STONE'POS(QUARTZ)

2   Write suitable declarations of enumeration types for

     (a)   the colours of the rainbow,
     (b)   typical fruits.

3   Write an expression that delivers one's predicted bridegroom after eating a portion of pie containing N stones. Use the type GROOM declared at the beginning of this section.

4   If the first of the month is in D where D is of type DAY, then write an assignment replacing D by the day of the week of the Nth day of the month.

5   Why might X < Y be ambiguous?

4.7 The Boolean type

The Boolean type is a predefined enumeration type whose declaration can be considered to be

> **type** BOOLEAN **is** (FALSE, TRUE);

Boolean values are used in constructions such as the if statement which we briefly met in Chapter 2. Boolean values are produced by the operators =, /=, <, <=, > and >= which have their expected meaning and apply to many types. So we can write constructions such as

> **if** TODAY = SUN **then**
>   TOMORROW:= MON;
> **else**
>   TOMORROW:= DAY'SUCC(TODAY);
> **end if**;

The Boolean type (we capitalize the name in memory of the mathematician Boole) has all the normal properties of an enumeration type, so, for instance

> FALSE < TRUE = TRUE !!
> BOOLEAN'POS(TRUE) = 1

We could even write

> **subtype** ALWAYS **is** BOOLEAN **range** TRUE .. TRUE;

although it would not seem very useful.
    The Boolean type also has other operators which are as follows

not   This is a unary operator and changes TRUE to FALSE and vice versa. It has the same precedence as **abs**.

and   This is a binary operator. The result is TRUE if both operands are TRUE, and FALSE otherwise.

or   This is a binary operator. The result is TRUE if one or other or both operands are TRUE, and FALSE only if they are both FALSE.

    xor   This is also a binary operator. The result is TRUE if one or other operand but not both are TRUE. (Hence the name – eXclusive OR.) Another way of looking at it is to note that the result is TRUE if and only if the operands are different. (The operator is known as 'not equivalent' in some languages.)

The effects of **and**, **or** and **xor** are summarized in the usual truth tables shown in Figure 4.3.

The precedences of **and**, **or** and **xor** are equal to each other but lower than that of any other operator. In particular they are of lower precedence than the relational operators $=$, $/=$, $<$, $<=$, $>$ and $>=$. This is unlike Pascal and as a consequence brackets are not needed in expressions such as

    P $<$ Q **and** I $=$ J

However, although the precedences are equal, **and**, **or** and **xor** cannot be mixed up in an expression without using brackets (unlike $+$ and $-$ for instance). So

    B **and** C **or** D   is illegal

whereas

    I $+$ J $-$ K   is legal

We have to write

    B **and** (C **or** D)   or   (B **and** C) **or** D

in order to emphasize which meaning is required.

The reader familiar with other programming languages will remember that **and** and **or** usually have a different precedence. The problem with this is that the programmer often gets confused and writes the wrong thing. It is to prevent this that Ada makes them the same precedence and insists on brackets. Of course, successive applications of the same operator are permitted so

    B **and** C **and** D   is legal

and as usual evaluation goes from left to right although, of course, it does not matter in this case since the operator **and** is associative.

and	F	T
F	F	F
T	F	T

or	F	T
F	F	T
T	T	T

xor	F	T
F	F	T
T	T	F

Figure 4.3   Truth tables for **and**, **or** and **xor**.

Take care with **not**. Its precedence is higher than **and**, **or** and **xor** as in other languages and so

not A **or** B

means

(**not** A) **or** B

rather than

not (A **or** B)

which those familiar with logic will remember is the same as

(**not** A) **and** (**not** B)

Boolean variables and constants can be declared and manipulated in the usual way.

```
DANGER: BOOLEAN;
SIGNAL: COLOUR;
...
DANGER:= SIGNAL = RED;
```

The variable DANGER is then TRUE if the signal is RED. We can then write

```
if DANGER then
    STOP_TRAIN;
end if;
```

Note that we do not have to write

```
if DANGER = TRUE then
```

although this is perfectly acceptable; it just misses the point that DANGER is already a Boolean and so can be used directly as the condition.
A worse sin is to write

```
if SIGNAL = RED then
    DANGER:= TRUE;
else
    DANGER:= FALSE;
end if;
```

rather than

```
DANGER:= SIGNAL = RED;
```

The literals TRUE and FALSE could be overloaded by declaring for example

type ANSWER **is** (FALSE, DONT_KNOW, TRUE);

but to do so might make the program rather confusing.

Finally, it should be noted that it is often clearer to introduce our own two-valued enumeration type rather than use the type BOOLEAN. Thus instead of

WHEELS_OK: BOOLEAN;
...
if WHEELS_OK **then**

it is much better (and safer!) to write

type WHEEL_STATE **is** (UP, DOWN);
WHEEL_POSITION: WHEEL_STATE;
...
if WHEEL_POSITION = UP **then**

since whether the wheels are OK or not depends upon the situation. Being OK for landing is different to being OK for cruising. The enumeration type removes any doubt as to which is meant.

Exercise 4.7

1   Write declarations of constants T and F having the values TRUE and FALSE.

2   Using T and F from the previous exercise, evaluate

    (a)   T **and** F **and** T   (d)   (F = F) = (F = F)
    (b)   **not** T **or** T   (e)   T < T < T < T
    (c)   F = F = F = F

3   Evaluate

       (A /= B) = (A **xor** B)

for all combinations of values of Boolean variables A and B.

4.8 Type classification

At this point we pause to consolidate the material presented in this chapter so far.

The types in Ada can be classified as shown in Figure 4.4.

This chapter has discussed scalar types. In Chapter 6 we will deal with the composite types but access, private and task types will be dealt with much later.

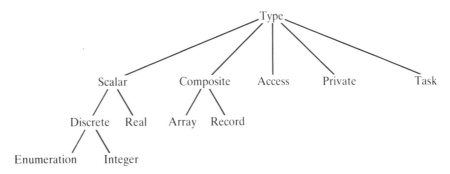

Figure 4.4   Classification of types.

The scalar types themselves can be subdivided into real types and discrete types. Our sole example of a real type has been the type REAL – the other real types are discussed in Chapter 12. The other types, INTEGER, BOOLEAN and enumeration types in general are discrete types – the only other kinds of discrete types to be introduced are other integer types, again dealt with in Chapter 12, and character types which are in fact a form of enumeration type and are dealt with in Chapter 6.

The key abstract distinction between the discrete types and the real types is that the former have a clear-cut set of distinct separate (that is, discrete) values. The type REAL, on the other hand, should be thought of as having a continuous set of values – we know in practice that a finite digital computer must implement a real type as actually a set of distinct values but this is an implementation detail, the abstract concept is of a continuous set of values.

The attributes POS, VAL, SUCC and PRED apply to all discrete types (and subtypes) because the operations reflect the discrete nature of the values. We explained their meaning with enumeration types in Section 4.6. In the case of type INTEGER the position number is simply the number itself so

```
INTEGER'POS(N) = N
INTEGER'VAL(N) = N
INTEGER'SUCC(N) = N+1
INTEGER'PRED(N) = N-1
```

The application of these attributes to integers does at first sight seem pretty futile but when we come to the concept of generic units in Chapter 13 we will see that it is convenient to allow them to apply to all discrete types.

The attributes FIRST and LAST however apply to all scalar types and subtypes including real types.

Again we emphasize that POS, VAL, SUCC and PRED for a subtype are identical to the corresponding operations on the base type, whereas in the case of FIRST and LAST this is not so.

Finally we note the difference between a type conversion and a type qualification.

```
REAL(I)           -- conversion
INTEGER'(I)       -- qualification
```

In the case of a conversion we are changing the type, in the second, we are just stating it (usually to overcome an ambiguity). As a mnemonic aid *qualification* uses a *quote*.

In both cases we can use a subtype name and CONSTRAINT_ERROR could consequently arise. Thus

```
POSITIVE(R)
```

would convert the value of the real variable R to integer and then check that it was positive, whereas

```
POSITIVE'(I)
```

would just check that the value of I was positive. In both cases, of course, the result is the checked value and is then used in an overall expression; these checks cannot just stand alone.

4.9 Expression summary

All the operators introduced so far are shown in Table 4.1 grouped by precedence level.

In all the cases of binary operators except for **, the two operands must be of the same type.

We have actually now introduced all the operators of Ada except for one (&) although as we shall see in Chapter 6 there are further possible meanings to be added.

There are also two membership tests which apply to all scalar types (among others). These are **in** and **not in**. They are technically not operators although their precedence is the same as that of the relational operators =, /= and so on. They enable us to test whether a value lies within a specified range (including the end values) or satisfies a constraint implied by a subtype. The first operand is therefore a scalar expression, the second is a range or type mark and the result is, of course, of type Boolean. Examples are

```
I not in 1 .. 10
I in POSITIVE
TODAY in WEEKDAY
```

Note that this is one of the situations where we have to use a type mark rather than a subtype indication. We could not replace the last example by

```
TODAY in DAY range MON .. FRI
```

Table 4.1 Scalar operators.

Operator	Operation	Operand(s)	Result
and	conjunction	BOOLEAN	BOOLEAN
or	inclusive or	BOOLEAN	BOOLEAN
xor	exclusive or	BOOLEAN	BOOLEAN
=	equality	any	BOOLEAN
/=	inequality	any	BOOLEAN
<	less than	scalar	BOOLEAN
<=	less than or equals	scalar	BOOLEAN
>	greater than	scalar	BOOLEAN
>=	greater than or equals	scalar	BOOLEAN
+	addition	numeric	same
−	subtraction	numeric	same
+	identity	numeric	same
−	negation	numeric	same
*	multiplication	INTEGER	INTEGER
		REAL	REAL
/	division	INTEGER	INTEGER
		REAL	REAL
mod	modulo	INTEGER	INTEGER
rem	remainder	INTEGER	INTEGER
**	exponentiation	INTEGER: NATURAL	INTEGER
		REAL: INTEGER	REAL
not	negation	BOOLEAN	BOOLEAN
abs	absolute value	numeric	same

although we could write

TODAY **in** MON .. FRI

Ada seems a bit curious here!

The test **not in** is equivalent to using **in** and then applying **not** to the result, but **not in** is usually more readable. So the first expression above could be written as

not (I **in** 1 .. 10)

where the brackets are necessary.

The reason that **in** and **not in** are not technically operators is explained in Chapter 7 when we deal with subprograms.

There are also two short circuit control forms **and then** and **or else** which like **in** and **not in** are also not technically classed as operators.

The form **and then** is closely related to the operator **and** whereas

or else is closely related to the operator **or**. They may occur in expressions and have the same precedence as **and**, **or** and **xor**. The difference lies in the rules regarding the evaluation of their operands.

In the case of **and** and **or**, both operands are always evaluated but the order is not specified. In the case of **and then** and **or else** the left hand operand is always evaluated first and the right hand operand is only evaluated if it is necessary in order to determine the result.

So in

X **and then** Y

X is evaluated first. If X is false, the answer is false whatever the value of Y so Y is not evaluated. If X is true, Y has to be evaluated and the value of Y is the answer.

Similarly in

X **or else** Y

X is evaluated first. If X is true, the answer is true whatever the value of Y so Y is not evaluated. If X is false, Y has to be evaluated and the value of Y is the answer.

The forms **and then** and **or else** should be used in cases where the order of evaluation matters. A common circumstance is where the first condition protects against the evaluation of the second condition in circumstances that could raise an exception.

Suppose we need to test

I/J > K

and we wish to avoid the risk that J is zero. In such a case we could write

J /= 0 **and then** I/J > K

and we would then know that if J is zero there is no risk of an attempt to divide by zero. The observant reader will realize that this is not a very good example because one could usually write I>K∗J (assuming J positive) – but even here we could get overflow. Better examples occur with arrays and access types and will be mentioned in due course.

Like **and** and **or**, the forms **and then** and **or else** cannot be mixed without using brackets.

We now summarize the primary components of an expression (that is the things upon which the operators operate) that we have met so far. They are

- identifiers   used for variables, constants, numbers
                                 and enumeration literals
- literals   such as 4.6, 2#101#
- type conversions   such as INTEGER(R)

- qualified expressions   such as COLOUR'(AMBER)
- attributes   such as INTEGER'LAST
- function calls   such as DAY'SUCC(TODAY)

A full consideration of functions and how they are declared and called has to be deferred until later. However, it is worth noting at this point that a function with one parameter is called by following its name by the parameter in brackets. The parameter can be any expression of the appropriate type and could include further function calls. We will assume for the moment that we have available a simple mathematical library containing familiar functions such as

SQRT   square root
LOG   logarithm to base 10
LN   natural logarithm
EXP   exponential function
SIN   sine
COS   cosine

In each case they take a REAL argument and deliver a REAL result.

We are now in a position to write statements such as

```
ROOT:= (−B+SQRT(B**2−4.0*A*C)) / (2.0*A);
SIN2X:= 2.0*SIN(X)*COS(X);
```

Finally a note on errors although this is not the place to deal with them in depth. The reader will have noticed that whenever anything could go wrong we have usually stated that the exception CONSTRAINT_ERROR will be raised. This is a general exception which applies to all sorts of violations of ranges. The only other exception which needs to be mentioned at this point is NUMERIC_ERROR. This will usually be raised if something goes wrong with the evaluation of an arithmetic expression itself before an attempt is made to store the result. An obvious example is an attempt to divide by zero. It might be thought that the distinction between these two exceptions was quite clear. However, consider on the one hand

```
INTEGER'SUCC(INTEGER'LAST)
```

which might be expected to raise CONSTRAINT_ERROR, and on the other hand

```
INTEGER'LAST+1
```

which might be expected to raise NUMERIC_ERROR. In practice, the object code for these two expressions is likely to be the same. As a consequence, AI-387 concludes that CONSTRAINT_ERROR and NUMERIC_ERROR cannot be crisply distinguished and therefore must be considered to be the same exception. (This is our first example of an AI where the language has been concluded not to be quite as it appears from the *LRM*. See Section 1.1.)

As well as exceptions there are erroneous constructs and incorrect order dependencies as mentioned in Chapter 2. The use of a variable before a value has been assigned to it is an important example of an erroneous situation. Two cases which we have encountered so far where the order is not defined are

- The destination variable in an assignment statement may be evaluated before or after the expression to be assigned.
- The order of evaluation of the two operands of a binary operator is not defined.

(In the first case it should be realized that the destination variable could be an array component such as A(I+J) and so the expression I+J has to be evaluated as part of evaluating the destination variable; we will deal with arrays in Chapter 6.) Examples where these orders matter cannot be given until we deal with functions in Chapter 7.

Exercise 4.9

1   Rewrite the following mathematical expressions in Ada.
   (a) $2\pi\sqrt{l/g}$ – period of a pendulum
   (b) $\dfrac{m_0}{\sqrt{1-v^2/c^2}}$ – mass of relativistic particle
   (c) $\sqrt{2\pi n}\,.n^n\,.e^{-n}$ – Stirling's approximation for $n!$ (integral n)

2   Rewrite 1(c) replacing n by the real value x.

Checklist 4

Declarations and statements are terminated by a semicolon.

Initialization, like assignment uses :=.

Any initial value is evaluated for each object in a declaration.

Elaboration of declarations is linear.

An identifier may not be used in its own declaration.

Each type definition introduces a quite distinct type.

A subtype is not a new type but merely a shorthand for a type with a possible constraint.

A type is always static, a subtype need not be.

No mixed mode arithmetic.

Distinguish **rem** and **mod** for negative operands.

Exponentiation with a negative exponent only applies to real types.

Take care with the precedence of the unary operators.

A scalar type cannot be empty, a subtype can.

POS, VAL, SUCC and PRED on subtypes are the same as on the base type.

FIRST and LAST are different for subtypes.

Qualification uses a quote.

Order of evaluation of binary operands is not defined.

Distinguish **and, or** and **and then, or else**.

Chapter 5
Control Structures

This chapter describes the three bracketed sequential control structures of Ada. These are the if statement which we have briefly met before, the case statement and the loop statement. It is now recognized that these three control structures are not only necessary but also sufficient to be able to write programs with a clearly discernible flow of control without recourse to goto statements and labels. However, for pragmatic reasons, Ada does actually contain a goto statement and this is also described in this chapter.

The three control structures exhibit a similar bracketing style. There is an opening reserved word **if**, **case** or **loop** and this is matched at the end of the structure by the same reserved word preceded by **end**. The whole is, as usual, terminated by a semicolon. So we have

if	**case**	**loop**
...	...	...
end if;	**end case**;	**end loop**;

In the case of the loop statement the word loop can be preceded by an iteration clause commencing with **for** or **while**.

5.1   If statements

The simplest form of if statement starts with the reserved word **if** followed by a Boolean expression and the reserved word **then**. This is then followed by a sequence of statements which will be executed if the Boolean expression turns out to be TRUE. The end of the sequence is indicated by the closing **end if**. The Boolean expression can, of course, be of arbitrary complexity and the sequence of statements can be of arbitrary length.

A simple example is

```
if HUNGRY then
    EAT;
end if;
```

In this, HUNGRY is a Boolean variable and EAT is a subprogram describing the details of the eating activity. The statement EAT; merely calls the subprogram (subprograms are dealt with in detail in Chapter 7).

The effect of this if statement is that if variable HUNGRY is TRUE then we call the subprogram EAT and otherwise we do nothing. In either case we then obey the statement following the if statement.

As we have said there could be a long sequence between **then** and **end if**. Thus we might break down the process into more detail

```
if HUNGRY then
    COOK;
    EAT;
    WASH_UP;
end if;
```

Note how we indent the statements to show the flow structure of the program. This is most important since it enables the program to be understood so much more easily. The **end if** should be underneath the corresponding **if** and **then** is best placed on the same line as the **if**.

Sometimes, if the whole statement is very short it can all go on one line.

```
if X < 0.0 then X:= −X; end if;
```

Note that **end if** will always be preceded by a semicolon. This is because the semicolons terminate statements rather than separate them as in Algol and Pascal. Readers familiar with those languages will probably feel initially that the Ada style is irksome. However, it is consistent and makes line by line program editing so much easier.

Often we will want to do alternative actions according to the value of the condition. In this case we add **else** followed by the alternative sequence to be obeyed if the condition is FALSE. We saw an example of this in the last chapter

```
if TODAY = SUN then
    TOMORROW:= MON;
else
    TOMORROW:= DAY'SUCC(TODAY);
end if;
```

Algol 60 and Algol 68 users should note that Ada is not an expression language and so conditional expressions are not allowed. We cannot write something like

```
TOMORROW:=
        if TODAY = SUN then MON else DAY'SUCC(TODAY) end if;
```

The statements in the sequences after **then** and **else** can be quite arbitrary and so could be further nested if statements. Suppose we have to solve the quadratic equation

$$ax^2 + bx + c = 0$$

The first thing to check is a. If $a = 0$ then the equation degenerates into a linear equation with a single root $-c/b$. (Mathematicians will understand that the other root has slipped off to infinity.) If a is not zero then we test the discriminant $b^2 - 4ac$ to see whether the roots are real or complex. We could program this as

```
if A = 0.0 then
            -- linear case
else
    if B**2 − 4.0*A*C >= 0.0 then
            -- real roots
    else
            -- complex roots
    end if;
end if;
```

Observe the repetition of **end if**. This is rather ugly and occurs sufficiently frequently to justify an additional construction. This uses the reserved word **elsif** as follows

```
if A = 0.0 then
            -- linear case
elsif B**2 − 4.0*A*C >= 0.0 then
            -- real roots
else
            -- complex roots
end if;
```

This construction emphasizes the essentially equal status of the three cases and also the sequential nature of the tests.

The **elsif** part can be repeated an arbitrary number of times and the final **else** part is optional. The behaviour is simply that each condition is evaluated in turn until one that is TRUE is encountered; the corresponding sequence is then obeyed. If none of the conditions turns out to be TRUE then the else part, if any, is taken; if there is no else part then none of the sequences is obeyed.

Note the spelling of **elsif**. It is the only reserved word of Ada that is not an English word (apart from operators such as **xor**). Note also the layout – we align **elsif** and **else** with the **if** and **end if** and all the sequences are indented equally.

As a further example, suppose we are drilling soldiers and they can obey four different orders described by

```
type MOVE is (LEFT, RIGHT, BACK, ON);
```

and that their response to these orders is described by calling subprograms TURN_LEFT, TURN_RIGHT and TURN_BACK or by doing nothing at all respectively. Suppose that the variable ORDER of type MOVE contains the order to be obeyed. We could then write the following

```
if ORDER = LEFT then
    TURN_LEFT;
else
    if ORDER = RIGHT then
        TURN_RIGHT;
    else
        if ORDER = BACK then
            TURN_BACK;
        end if;
    end if;
end if;
```

But it is far clearer and neater to write

```
if ORDER = LEFT then
    TURN_LEFT;
elsif ORDER = RIGHT then
    TURN_RIGHT;
elsif ORDER = BACK then
    TURN_BACK;
end if;
```

This illustrates a situation where there is no **else** part. However, although better than using nested if statements, this is still a bad solution because it obscures the symmetry and mutual exclusion of the four cases ('mutual exclusion' means that by their very nature only one can apply). We have been forced to impose an ordering on the tests which is quite arbitrary and not the essence of the problem. The proper solution is to use the case statement as we shall see in the next section.

Contrast this with the quadratic equation. In that example, the cases were not mutually exclusive and the tests had to be performed in order. If we had tested $b^2 - 4ac$ first then we would have been forced to test a against zero in each alternative.

There is no directly corresponding contraction for **then if** as in Algol 68. Instead the short circuit control form **and then** can often be used.

So, rather than

```
if J > 0 then
    if I/J > K then
        ACTION;
    end if;
end if;
```

we can, as we have seen, write

```
if J > 0 and then I/J > K then
    ACTION;
end if;
```

Exercise 5.1

1   The variables DAY, MONTH and YEAR contain today's date. They are declared as

```
DAY: INTEGER range 1 .. 31;
MONTH: MONTH_NAME;
YEAR: INTEGER range 1901 .. 2099;
```

where

```
type MONTH_NAME is (JAN, FEB, MAR, APR, MAY, JUN, JUL,
                    AUG, SEP, OCT, NOV, DEC);
```

Write statements to update the variables to contain tomorrow's date. What happens if today is 31 DEC 2099?

2   X and Y are two real variables. Write statements to swap their values, if necessary, to ensure that the larger value is in X. Use a block to declare a temporary variable T.

5.2 Case statements

A case statement allows us to choose one of several sequences of statements according to the value of an expression. For instance, the example of the drilling soldiers should be written as

```
case ORDER is
    when LEFT => TURN_LEFT;
    when RIGHT => TURN_RIGHT;
    when BACK => TURN_BACK;
    when ON => null;
end case;
```

All possible values of the expression must be provided for in order to guard against accidental omissions. If, as in this example, no action is required for one or more values then the null statement has to be used.
    The null statement, written

```
null;
```

does absolutely nothing but its presence indicates that we truly want to do nothing. The sequence of statements here, as in the if statement, must contain at least one statement. (There is no empty statement as in Algol 60.)

It often happens that the same action is desired for several values of the expression. Consider the following

```
case TODAY is
   when MON | TUES | WED | THU  => WORK;
   when FRI                     => WORK; PARTY;
   when SAT | SUN               => null;
end case;
```

This expresses the idea that on Monday to Thursday we go to work. On Friday we also go to work and then go to a party. At the weekend we do nothing. The alternative values are separated by the vertical bar character. Note again the use of a null statement.

If several successive values have the same action then it is more convenient to use a range

```
when MON .. THU => WORK;
```

Sometimes we wish to express the idea of a default action to be taken by all values not explicitly stated; this is provided for by the reserved word **others**. The above example could be rewritten

```
case TODAY is
   when MON .. THU  => WORK;
   when FRI         => WORK; PARTY;
   when others      => null;
end case;
```

It is possible to have ranges as alternatives. In fact this is probably a situation where the clearest explanation of what is allowed is given by the formal syntax*.

```
case_statement ::=
   case expression is
       case_statement_alternative
       {case_statement_alternative}
   end case;
case_statement_alternative ::=
   when choice { | choice} => sequence_of_statements
choice ::= simple_expression | discrete_range | others |
   component_simple_name
discrete_range ::= discrete_subtype_indication | range
subtype_indication ::= type_mark [constraint]
type_mark ::= type_name | subtype_name
range ::= range_attribute | simple_expression .. simple_expression
```

(*In the production for case_statement_alternative, the vertical bar stands for itself and is not a metasymbol.)

We see that **when** is followed by one or more choices separated by vertical bars and that a choice may be a simple expression, a discrete range or **others**. (The syntax shows that a choice may be a component simple name; however this only applies to choices used in a different situation which we have not yet met and so can be ignored for the moment.) A simple expression, of course, just gives a single value – FRI being a trivial example. A discrete range offers several possibilities. It can be the syntactic form range which the syntax tells us can be two simple expressions separated by two dots – MON .. THU is a simple example; a range can also be given by a range attribute which we will meet in the next chapter. A discrete range can also be a subtype indication which as we know is a type mark (a type name or subtype name) followed optionally by an appropriate constraint. In this case the constraint has to be a range constraint which is merely the reserved word **range** followed by the syntactic form range. Examples of discrete ranges are

```
MON .. THU
DAY range MON .. THU
WEEKDAY
WEEKDAY range MON .. THU
```

All these possibilities may seem unnecessary but as we shall see later the form, discrete range, is used in other contexts as well as the case statement. In the case statement there is not usually much point in using the type name since this is known from the context anyway. Similarly, there is not much point in using the subtype name followed by a constraint since the constraint alone will do. However, it might be useful to use a subtype name alone when that exactly corresponds to the range required. So we could rewrite the example as

```
case TODAY is
   when WEEKDAY  => WORK;
                      if TODAY = FRI then
                         PARTY;
                      end if;
   when others    => null;
end case;
```

although this solution feels untidy.

There are various other restrictions that the syntax does not tell us. One is that if we use **others** then it must appear alone and as the last alternative. As stated earlier it covers all values not explicitly covered by the previous alternatives (one is still allowed to write **others** even if there are no other cases to be considered!).

Another very important restriction is that all the choices must be static so that they can be evaluated at compilation time. Thus all expressions in choices must be static – in practice they will usually be literals as in our examples. Similarly, if a choice is simply a subtype such as WEEKDAY then it too must be static.

Finally we return to the point made at the beginning of this section that all possible values of the expression after **case** must be provided for. This usually means all values of the type of the expression. This is certainly the case of a variable declared as of a type without any constraints (as in the case of TODAY). However, if the expression is of a simple form and belongs to a static subtype (that is one whose constraints are static expressions and so can be determined at compilation time) then only values of that subtype need be provided for. In other words if the compiler can tell that only a subset of values is possible then only that subset need and must be covered. The simple forms allowed for the expression are the name of an object of the static subtype or a qualified or converted expression whose type mark is that of the static subtype.

In the case of our example, if TODAY had been of subtype WEEKDAY then we would know that only the values MON .. FRI are possible and so only these can and need be covered. Even if TODAY is not constrained we can still write our expression as a qualified expression WEEKDAY'(TODAY) and then again only MON .. FRI is possible. So we could write

```
case WEEKDAY'(TODAY) is
   when MON .. THU => WORK;
   when FRI         => WORK; PARTY;
end case;
```

but, of course, if TODAY happens to take a value not in the subtype WEEKDAY (that is, SAT or SUN) then CONSTRAINT_ERROR will be raised. Mere qualification cannot prevent TODAY from being SAT or SUN. So this is not really a solution to our original problem.

As further examples, suppose we had variables

```
I: INTEGER range 1 .. 10;
J: INTEGER range 1 .. N;
```

where N is not static. Then we know that I belongs to a static subtype (albeit anonymous) whereas we cannot say the same about J. If I is used as an expression in a case statement then only the values 1 .. 10 have to be catered for, whereas if J is so used then the full range of values of type INTEGER (INTEGER'FIRST .. INTEGER'LAST) have to be catered for.

The above discussion on the case statement has no doubt given the reader the impression of considerable complexity. It therefore seems wise to summarize the key points which will in practice need to be remembered.

- Every possible value of the expression after **case** must be covered once and once only.

- All values and ranges after **when** must be static.

- If **others** is used it must be last and on its own.

Exercise 5.2

1   Rewrite Exercise 5.1(**1**) to use a case statement to set the correct value in END_OF_MONTH.

2   A vegetable gardener digs in winter, sows seed in spring, tends the growing plants in summer and harvests the crop in the autumn or fall. Write a case statement to call the appropriate subprogram DIG, SOW, TEND or HARVEST according to the month M. Declare appropriate subtypes if desired.

3   An improvident man is paid on the first of each month. For the first ten days he gorges himself, for the next ten he subsists and for the remainder he starves. Call subprograms GORGE, SUBSIST and STARVE according to the day D. Assume END_OF_MONTH has been set and that D is declared as

        D: INTEGER **range** 1 .. END_OF_MONTH;

5.3 Loop statements

The simplest form of loop statement is

```
loop
    sequence_of_statements
end loop;
```

The statements of the sequence are then repeated indefinitely unless one of them terminates the loop by some means. So immortality could be represented by

```
loop
    WORK;
    EAT;
    SLEEP;
end loop;
```

As a more concrete example consider the problem of computing the base e of natural logarithms from the infinite series

$$e = 1 + 1/1! + 1/2! + 1/3! + 1/4! + \ldots$$

where

$$n! = n \times (n - 1) \times (n - 2) \ldots 3 \times 2 \times 1$$

A possible solution is

```
declare
    E: REAL:= 1.0;
    I: INTEGER:= 0;
    TERM: REAL:= 1.0;
begin
    loop
        I:= I + 1;
        TERM:= TERM / REAL(I);
        E:= E + TERM;
    end loop;
    ...
```

Each time around the loop a new term is computed by dividing the previous term by I. The new term is then added to the sum so far which is accumulated in E. The term number I is an integer because it is logically a counter and so we have to write REAL(I) as the divisor. The series is started by setting values in E, I and TERM which correspond to the first term (that for which $I = 0$).

The computation then goes on for ever with E becoming a closer and closer approximation to e. In practice, because of the finite accuracy of the computer, TERM will become zero and continued computation will be pointless. But in any event we presumably want to stop at some point so that we can do something with our computed result. We can do this with the statement

```
exit;
```

If this is obeyed inside a loop then the loop terminates at once and control passes to the point immediately after **end loop**.

Suppose we decide to stop after N terms of the series – that is when $I = N$. We can do this by writing the loop as

```
loop
    if I = N then exit; end if;
    I:= I + 1;
    TERM:= TERM / REAL(I);
    E:= E + TERM;
end loop;
```

The construction

```
if condition then exit; end if;
```

is so common that a special shorthand is provided

```
exit when condition;
```

So we now have

```
loop
    exit when I = N;
    I:= I + 1;
    TERM:= TERM / REAL(I);
    E:= E + TERM;
end loop;
```

Although an exit statement can appear anywhere inside a loop – it could be in the middle or near the end – a special form is provided for the frequent case where we want to test a condition at the start of each iteration. This uses the reserved word **while** and gives the condition for the loop to be continued. So we could write

```
while I /= N loop
    I:= I + 1;
    TERM:= TERM / REAL(I);
    E:= E + TERM;
end loop;
```

The condition is naturally evaluated each time around the loop.

The final form of loop allows for a specific number of iterations with a loop parameter taking in turn all the values of a discrete range. Our example could be recast as

```
for I in 1 .. N loop
    TERM:= TERM / REAL(I);
    E:= E + TERM;
end loop;
```

where I takes the values 1, 2, 3, ... N.

The parameter I is implicitly declared by its appearance in the iteration scheme and does not have to be declared outside. It takes its type from the discrete range and within the loop behaves as a constant so that it cannot be changed except by the loop mechanism itself. When we leave the loop (by whatever means) I ceases to exist (because it was implicitly declared by the loop) and so we cannot read its final value from outside.

We could leave the loop by an exit statement – if we wanted to know the final value we could copy the value of I into a variable declared outside the loop thus

```
if condition_to_exit then
    LAST_I:= I;
    exit;
end if;
```

The values of the discrete range are normally taken in ascending order. Descending order can be specified by writing

```
for I in reverse 1 .. N loop
```

but the range itself is always written in ascending order.

It is not possible to specify a numeric step size of other than 1. This should not be a problem since the vast majority of loops go up by steps of 1 and almost all the rest go down by steps of 1. The very few which do behave otherwise can be explicitly programmed using the while form of loop.

The range can be null (as for instance if N happened to be zero or negative in our example) in which case the sequence of statements will not be obeyed at all. Of course, the range itself is evaluated only once and cannot be changed inside the loop.

Thus

```
N:= 4;
for I in 1 .. N loop
    ...
    N:= 10;
end loop;
```

results in the loop being executed just four times despite the fact that N is changed to ten.

Our examples have all shown the lower bound of the range being 1. This, of course, need not be the case. Both bounds can be arbitrary dynamically evaluated expressions. Furthermore the loop parameter need not be of integer type. It can be of any discrete type, as determined by the discrete range.

We could, for instance, simulate a week's activity by

```
for TODAY in MON .. SUN loop
    case TODAY is
        ...
    end case;
end loop;
```

This implicitly declares TODAY to be of type DAY and obeys the loop with the values MON, TUE, ... SUN in turn.

The other forms of discrete range (using a type or subtype name) are of advantage here. The essence of MON .. SUN is that it embraces all the values of the type DAY. It is therefore better to write the loop using a form of discrete range that conveys the idea of completeness

```
for TODAY in DAY loop
    ...
end loop;
```

And again since we know that we do nothing at weekends anyway we could write

```
for TODAY in DAY range MON .. FRI loop
```

or better

> **for** TODAY **in** WEEKDAY **loop**

It is interesting to note a difference regarding the determination of types in the case statement and for statement. In the case statement, the type of a discrete range after **when** is determined from the type of the expression after **case**. In the for statement, the type of the loop parameter is determined from the type of the discrete range after **in**. The dependency is the other way round.

It is therefore necessary for the type of the discrete range to be unambiguous in the for statement. This is usually the case but if we had two enumeration types with two overloaded literals such as

> **type** PLANET **is** (MERCURY, VENUS, EARTH, MARS, JUPITER,
>   SATURN, URANUS, NEPTUNE, PLUTO);
> **type** ROMAN_GOD **is** (JANUS, MARS, JUPITER, JUNO, VESTA,
>   VULCAN, SATURN, MERCURY, MINERVA);

then

> **for** X **in** MARS .. SATURN **loop**

would be ambiguous and the compiler would not compile our program. We could resolve the problem by qualifying one of the expressions

> **for** X **in** PLANET'(MARS) .. SATURN **loop**

or (probably better) by using a form of discrete range giving the type explicitly

> **for** X **in** PLANET **range** MARS .. SATURN **loop**

When we have dealt with numerics in more detail we will realize that the range 1 .. 10 is not necessarily of type INTEGER. A general application of our rule that the type must not be ambiguous in a for statement would lead us to have to write

> **for** I **in** INTEGER **range** 1 .. 10 **loop**

However, this would be so tedious in such a common case that there is a special rule which applies to discrete ranges in for statements which says that if both bounds are integer literals then type INTEGER is implied. We can therefore conveniently write

> **for** I **in** 1 .. 10 **loop**

But note carefully that we cannot write

> **for** I **in** −1 .. 10 **loop**

because −1 is not a literal as explained in Section 3.4. This perhaps surprising conclusion is confirmed by AI-148. We will return to this topic in Section 12.1.

Finally we reconsider the exit statement. The simple form encountered earlier always transfers control to immediately after the innermost embracing loop. But of course loops may be nested and sometimes we may wish to exit from a nested construction. As an example suppose we are searching in two dimensions

```
for I in 1 .. N loop
    for J in 1 .. M loop
        -- if values of I and J satisfy
        -- some condition then leave nested loop
    end loop;
end loop;
```

A simple exit statement in the inner loop would merely take us to the end of that loop and we would have to recheck the condition and exit again. This can be avoided by naming the outer loop and using the name in the exit statement thus

```
SEARCH:
for I in 1 .. N loop
    for J in 1 .. M loop
        if condition_OK then
            I_VALUE:= I;
            J_VALUE:= J;
            exit SEARCH;
        end if;
    end loop;
end loop SEARCH;
-- control passes here
```

A loop is named by preceding it with an identifier and colon. (It looks remarkably like a label in other languages but it is not and cannot be 'gone to'.) The identifier must be repeated between the corresponding **end loop** and the semicolon.

The conditional form of exit can also refer to a loop by name

```
exit SEARCH when condition;
```

Exercise 5.3

1   The statement GET(I); reads the next value from the input file into the integer variable I. Write statements to read and add together a series of numbers. The end of the series is indicated by a dummy negative value.

2   Write statements to determine the power of 2 in the factorization of N. Compute the result in COUNT but do not alter N.

3   Compute

$$g = \sum_{p=1}^{n} \frac{1}{p} - \log n$$

(As $n \to \infty$, $g \to \gamma = 0.577215665...$)

5.4 Goto statements and labels

Many will be surprised that a modern programming language should contain a goto statement at all. It is now considered to be extremely bad practice to use goto statements because of the resulting difficulty in proving correctness of the program, maintenance and so on. And indeed Ada contains adequate control structures so that it should not normally be necessary to use a goto at all.

So why provide a goto statement? The main reason concerns automatically generated programs. If we try to transliterate (by hand or machine) a program from some other language into Ada then the goto will probably be useful. Another example might be where the program is generated automatically from some high-level specification. Finally there may be cases where the goto is the neatest way – perhaps as a way out of some deeply nested structure – but the alternative of raising an exception (see Chapter 10) could also be considered.

In order to put us off using gotos and labels (and perhaps so that our manager can spot them if we do) the notation for a label is unusual and stands out like a sore thumb. A label is an identifier enclosed in double angled brackets thus

    <<THE_DEVIL>>

and a goto statement takes the expected form of the reserved word **goto** followed by the label identifier and semicolon

    goto THE_DEVIL;

A goto statement cannot be used to transfer control into an if, case or loop statement nor between the arms of an if or case statement.

Exercise 5.4

1   Rewrite the nested loop of Section 5.3 using a label <<SEARCH>> rather than naming the outer loop. Why is this not such a good solution?

5.5   Statement classification

The statements in Ada can be classified as shown in Figure 5.1.

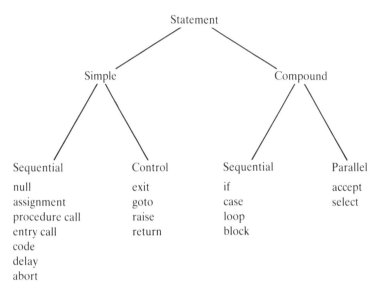

Figure 5.1   Classification of statements.

Further detail on the assignment statement is in the next chapter when we discuss composite types. Procedure calls and return statements are discussed in Chapter 7 and the raise statement which is concerned with exceptions is discussed in Chapter 10. The code statement is mentioned in Chapter 15. The remaining statements (entry call, delay, abort, accept and select) concern tasking and are dealt with in Chapter 14.

All statements can have one or more labels. The simple statements cannot be decomposed lexically into other statements whereas the compound statements can be so decomposed and can therefore be nested. Statements are obeyed sequentially unless one of them is a control statement (or an exception is implicitly raised).

Checklist 5

Statement brackets must match correctly.

Use **elsif** where appropriate.

The choices in a case statement must be static.

All possibilities in a case statement must be catered for.

If **others** is used it must be last and on its own.

The expression after **case** can be qualified in order to reduce the alternatives.

A loop parameter behaves as a constant.

A named loop must have the name at both ends.

Avoid gotos.

Use the recommended layout.

Chapter 6
Composite Types

In this chapter we describe the composite types which are arrays and records. We also complete our discussion of enumeration types by introducing characters and strings. At this stage we discuss arrays fairly completely but consider only simple forms of records. The more elaborate discriminated records which include variant records are deferred until Chapter 11.

6.1   Arrays

An array is a composite object consisting of a number of components all of the same type (strictly, subtype). An array can be of one, two or more dimensions. A typical array declaration might be

```
A: array (INTEGER range 1 .. 6) of REAL;
```

This declares A to be a variable object which has six components, each of which is of type REAL. The individual components are referred to by following the array name with an expression in brackets giving an integer value in the discrete range 1 .. 6. If this expression, known as the index value, has a value outside the range, then the exception CONSTRAINT_ERROR will be raised. We could set zero in each component of A by writing

```
for I in 1 .. 6 loop
    A(I):= 0.0;
end loop;
```

An array can be of several dimensions, in which case a separate range is given for each dimension. So

AA: **array** (INTEGER **range** 0 .. 2, INTEGER **range** 0 .. 3) **of** REAL;

is an array of 12 components in total, each of which is referred to by two integer index values, the first in the range 0 .. 2 and the second in the range 0 .. 3. Each component of this two-dimensional array could be set to zero by a nested loop thus

```
for I in 0 .. 2 loop
    for J in 0 .. 3 loop
        AA(I, J):= 0.0;
    end loop;
end loop;
```

The discrete ranges do not have to be static: one could have

```
N: INTEGER:= ... ;
B: array (INTEGER range 1 .. N) of BOOLEAN;
```

and the value of N at the point when the declaration of B is elaborated would determine the number of components in B. Of course, the declaration of B might be elaborated many times during the course of a program – it might be inside a loop for example – and each elaboration will give rise to a new life of a new array and the value of N could be different each time. Like other declared objects, the array B ceases to exist once we pass the end of the block containing its declaration. Because of 'linear elaboration of declarations' both N and B could be declared in the same declarative part but the declaration of N would have to precede that of B.

The discrete range in an array index follows similar rules to that in a for statement. An important one is that a range such as 1 .. 6 implies type INTEGER so we could have written

A: **array** (1 .. 6) **of** REAL;

However, an array index could be of any discrete type. We could for example have

HOURS_WORKED: **array** (DAY) **of** REAL;

This array has seven components denoted by HOURS_WORKED (MON), ... HOURS_WORKED(SUN). We could set suitable values in these variables by

```
for D in WEEKDAY loop
    HOURS_WORKED(D):= 8.0;
end loop;
HOURS_WORKED(SAT):= 0.0;
HOURS_WORKED(SUN):= 0.0;
```

If we only wanted to declare the array HOURS_WORKED to have components corresponding to MON .. FRI then we could write

HOURS_WORKED: **array** (DAY **range** MON .. FRI) **of** REAL;

or (better)

HOURS_WORKED: **array** (WEEKDAY) **of** REAL;

Arrays have various attributes relating to their indexes. A'FIRST and A'LAST give the lower and upper bound of the first (or only) index of A. So using our last declaration of HOURS_WORKED

HOURS_WORKED'FIRST = MON
HOURS_WORKED'LAST = FRI

A'LENGTH gives the number of values of the first (or only) index.

HOURS_WORKED'LENGTH = 5

A'RANGE is short for A'FIRST .. A'LAST. So

HOURS_WORKED'RANGE   is   MON .. FRI

The same attributes can be applied to the various dimensions of a multidimensional array by adding the dimension number in brackets. It has to be a static expression. So, in the case of our two-dimensional array AA we have

AA'FIRST(1)   = 0
AA'FIRST(2)   = 0
AA'LAST(1)   = 2
AA'LAST(2)   = 3
AA'LENGTH(1) = 3
AA'LENGTH(2) = 4

and

AA'RANGE(1)   is 0 .. 2
AA'RANGE(2)   is 0 .. 3

The first dimension is assumed if (1) is omitted. It is perhaps better practice to specifically state (1) for multidimensional arrays and omit it for one-dimensional arrays.

It is always best to use the attributes where possible in order to reflect relationships among entities in a program because it generally means that if the program is modified, the modifications are localized.

The RANGE attribute is particularly useful with loops. Our earlier examples are better written as

```
for I in A'RANGE loop
    A(I):= 0.0;
end loop;

for I in AA'RANGE(1) loop
    for J in AA'RANGE(2) loop
        AA(I, J):= 0.0;
    end loop;
end loop;
```

The RANGE attribute can also be used in a declaration. Thus

```
J: INTEGER range A'RANGE;
```

is equivalent to

```
J: INTEGER range 1 .. 6;
```

If a variable is to be used to index an array as in A(J) it is usually best if the variable has the same constraints as the discrete range in the array declaration. This will usually minimize the run-time checks necessary. It has been found that in such circumstances it is usually the case that the index variable J is assigned less frequently than the array component A(J) is accessed. We will return to this topic in Section 10.3.

The array components we have seen are just variables in the ordinary way. They can therefore be assigned to and used in expressions.

Like other variable objects, arrays can be given an initial value. This will often be denoted by an aggregate which is the literal form for an array value. The simplest form of aggregate consists of a list of expressions giving the values of the components in order, separated by commas and enclosed in brackets. So we could initialize the array A by

```
A: array (1 .. 6) of REAL:= (0.0, 0.0, 0.0, 0.0, 0.0, 0.0);
```

In the case of a multidimensional array the aggregate is written in a nested form

```
AA: array (0 .. 2, 0 .. 3) of REAL:= ((0.0, 0.0, 0.0, 0.0),
                                       (0.0, 0.0, 0.0, 0.0),
                                       (0.0, 0.0, 0.0, 0.0));
```

and this illustrates that the first index is the 'outer' one. Or thinking in terms of rows and columns, the first index is the row number.

An aggregate must be complete. If we initialize any component of an array, we must initialize them all.

The initial values for the individual components need not be literals, they can be any expressions. These expressions are evaluated when the declaration is elaborated but the order of evaluation of the expressions in the aggregate is not specified.

An array can be declared as constant in which case an initial value is mandatory as explained in Section 4.1. Constant arrays are of frequent value as look-up tables. The following array can be used to determine whether a particular day is a working day or not

> WORK_DAY: **constant array** (DAY) **of** BOOLEAN
>   := (TRUE, TRUE, TRUE, TRUE, TRUE, FALSE, FALSE);

An interesting example would be an array enabling tomorrow to be determined without worrying about the end of the week.

> TOMORROW: **constant array** (DAY) **of** DAY
>   := (TUE, WED, THU, FRI, SAT, SUN, MON);

For any day D, TOMORROW (D) is the following day.

Finally, it should be noted that the array components can be of any type or subtype. Also the dimensions of a multidimensional array can be of different discrete types. An extreme example would be

> STRANGE: **array** (COLOUR, 2 .. 7, WEEKDAY **range** TUE .. THU)
>   **of** PLANET **range** MARS .. SATURN;

Exercise 6.1

1   Declare an array F of integers with index running from 0 to N. Write statements to set the components of F equal to the Fibonacci numbers given by

$$F_0 = 0, F_1 = 1, F_i = F_{i-1} + F_{i-2} \qquad i > 1$$

2   Write statements to find the index values I, J of the maximum component of

> A: **array** (1 .. N, 1 .. M) **of** REAL;

3   Declare an array DAYS_IN_MONTH giving the number of days in each month. See Exercise 5.1(**1**). Use it to rewrite that example. See also Exercise 5.2(**1**).

4   Declare an array YESTERDAY analogous to the example TOMORROW above.

5   Declare a constant array BOR such that

> BOR(P, Q) = P **or** Q

6   Declare a constant unit matrix UNIT of order 3. A unit matrix is one for which all components are zero except those whose indexes are equal which have value one.

6.2 Array types

The arrays we introduced in the last section did not have an explicit type name. They were in fact of anonymous type. This is one of the few cases in Ada where an object can be declared without naming the type – another case is with tasks.

Reconsidering the first example in the previous section, we could write

type VECTOR_6 **is array** (1 .. 6) **of** REAL;

and then declare A using the type name in the usual way

A: VECTOR_6;

An advantage of using a type name is that it enables us to assign whole arrays that have been declared separately. If we also have

B: VECTOR_6;

then we can write

B:= A;

which has the effect of

B(1):= A(1); B(2):= A(2); ... B(6):= A(6);

although the order of assigning the components is not relevant.
On the other hand if we had written

C: **array** (1 .. 6) **of** REAL;
D: **array** (1 .. 6) **of** REAL;

then D:= C; is illegal because C and D are not of the same type. They are of different types both of which are anonymous. The underlying rule is that every type definition introduces a new type and in this case the syntax tells us that an array type definition is the piece of text from **array** up to (but not including) the semicolon.
Moreover, even if we had written

C, D: **array** (1 .. 6) **of** REAL;

then D:= C; would still have been illegal. This is because of the rule mentioned in Section 4.1 that such a multiple declaration is only a shorthand for the two declarations above. There are therefore still two distinct type definitions even though they are not explicit.

Whether or not we introduce a type name for particular arrays depends very much on the abstract view of each situation. If we are thinking of the array as a complete object in its own right then we should use a type name. If, on the other hand, we are thinking of the array as merely an indexable conglomerate not related as a whole to other arrays then it should probably be of an anonymous type.

Arrays like TOMORROW and WORK_DAY of the last section are good examples of arrays which are of the anonymous category. To be forced to introduce a type name for such arrays would introduce unnecessary clutter and a possibly false sense of abstraction.

On the other hand if we are manipulating lots of arrays of reals of length 6 then there is a common underlying abstract type and so it should be named.

The model for array types introduced so far is still not satisfactory. It does not allow us to represent an abstract view that embraces the commonality between arrays which have different bounds but are otherwise of the same type. In particular, it would not allow the writing of subprograms which could take an array of arbitrary bounds as an actual parameter. This is generally recognized as a major difficulty with the original design of Pascal. So the concept of an unconstrained array type is introduced in which the constraints for the indexes are not given. Consider

```
type VECTOR is array (INTEGER range <>) of REAL;
```

(The compound symbol <> is read as 'box'.)

This says that VECTOR is the name of a type which is a one-dimensional array of REAL components with an INTEGER index. But the lower and upper bounds are not given; range <> is meant to convey the notion of information to be added later.

When we declare objects of type VECTOR we must supply the bounds. We can do this in various ways. We can introduce an intermediate subtype and then declare the objects.

```
subtype VECTOR_5 is VECTOR(1 .. 5);
V: VECTOR_5;
```

Or we can declare the objects directly

```
V: VECTOR(1 .. 5);
```

In either case the bounds are given by an index constraint which takes the form of a discrete range in brackets. All the usual forms of discrete range can be used.

The index can also be given by a subtype name, thus

```
type P is array (POSITIVE range <>) of REAL;
```

in which case the actual bounds of any declared object must lie within the range implied by the index subtype POSITIVE. Note that the index subtype must be given by a type mark and not by a subtype indication; this avoids the horrid double use of **range** which could otherwise occur as in

> **type** NASTY **is array** (INTEGER **range** 1 .. 100 **range** <>) **of** ... ;

We can now see that when we wrote

> **type** VECTOR_6 **is array** (1 .. 6) **of** REAL;

this was really a shorthand for

> **subtype** index **is** INTEGER **range** 1 .. 6;
> **type** anon **is array** (index **range** <>) **of** REAL;
> **subtype** VECTOR_6 **is** anon(1 .. 6);

Another useful array type declaration is

> **type** MATRIX **is array** (INTEGER **range** <>, INTEGER **range** <>)
> > **of** REAL;

And again we could introduce subtypes thus

> **subtype** MATRIX_3 **is** MATRIX(1 .. 3, 1 .. 3);
> M: MATRIX_3;

or the objects directly

> M: MATRIX(1 .. 3, 1 .. 3);

An important point to notice is that an array type or subtype must give all the bounds or none at all. It would be perfectly legal to introduce an alternative name for MATRIX by

> **subtype** MAT **is** MATRIX;

in which no bounds are given, but we could not have a type or subtype that just gave the bounds for one dimension but not the other.

In all of the cases we have been discussing, the ranges need not have static bounds. The bounds could be any expressions and are evaluated when the index constraint is encountered. We could have

> M: MATRIX(1 .. N, 1 .. N);

and then the upper bounds of M would be the value of N when M is declared. A range could even be null as would happen in the above case if N turned out to be zero. In this case the matrix M would have no components at all.

There is a further way in which the bounds of an array can be supplied but this only applies to constant arrays which like other constants have to be given an initial value. The bounds can then be taken from the initial value if they are not supplied directly. The initial value can be any expression of the appropriate type but will often be an aggregate as shown in the previous section. The form of aggregate shown there consisted of a list of expressions in brackets. Such an aggregate is known as a positional aggregate since the values are given in position order. In the case of a positional aggregate used as an initial value and supplying the bounds, the lower bound is S'FIRST where S is the subtype of the index. The upper bound is deduced from the number of components. (The bounds of positional aggregates in other contexts will be discussed in the next section.)

Suppose we had

```
type W is array (WEEKDAY range <>) of DAY;
NEXT_WORK_DAY: constant W:= (TUE, WED, THU, FRI, MON);
```

then the lower bound of the array is WEEKDAY'FIRST = MON and the upper bound is FRI. It would not have mattered whether we had written DAY or WEEKDAY in the declaration of W because DAY'FIRST and WEEKDAY'FIRST are the same.

Using initial values to supply the bounds needs care. Consider

```
UNIT_2: constant MATRIX:= ((1.0, 0.0), (0.0, 1.0));
```

intended to declare a 2 × 2 unit matrix with UNIT_2(1, 1) = UNIT_2(2, 2) = 1.0 and UNIT_2(1, 2) = UNIT_2(2, 1) = 0.0.

But disaster! We have actually declared an array whose lower bounds are INTEGER'FIRST which is probably −32768 or some such number but is certainly not 1.

If we declared the type MATRIX as

```
type MATRIX is array (POSITIVE range <>, POSITIVE range <>)
                                                          of REAL;
```

then all would have been well since POSITIVE'FIRST = 1.

So array bounds deduced from an initial value may lead to surprises.

We continue by returning to the topic of whole array assignment. In order to perform such assignment it is necessary that the array value and the array being assigned to have the same type and that the components can be matched. This does not mean that the bounds have to be equal but merely that the number of components in corresponding dimensions is the same. In other words so that one array can be slid onto the other, giving rise to the term 'sliding semantics'. So we can write

```
V: VECTOR(1 .. 5);
W: VECTOR(0 .. 4);
...
V:= W;
```

Both V and W are of type VECTOR and both have five components.
It is also valid to have

```
P: MATRIX(0 .. 1, 0 .. 1);
Q: MATRIX(6 .. 7, N .. N+1);
...
P:= Q;
```

Equality and inequality of arrays follow similar sliding rules to assignment. Two arrays may only be compared if they are of the same type. They are equal if corresponding dimensions have the same number of components and the matching components are themselves equal. Note however that if the dimensions of the two arrays are not of the same length then equality will return FALSE whereas an attempt to assign one array to the other will naturally cause CONSTRAINT_ERROR.

Although assignment and equality can only occur if the arrays are of the same type, nevertheless an array value of one type can be converted to another type if the component types and index types are the same. The usual notation for type conversion is used. So if we have

```
type VECTOR is array (INTEGER range <>) of REAL;
type ROW    is array (INTEGER range <>) of REAL;

V: VECTOR(1 .. 5);
R: ROW(0 .. 4);
```

then

```
R:= ROW(V);
```

is valid. In fact, since ROW is an unconstrained type, the bounds of ROW(V) are those of V. The normal assignment rules then apply. However, if the conversion uses a constrained type or subtype then the bounds are those of the type or subtype and the number of components in corresponding dimensions must be the same. Array type conversion is of particular value when subprograms from different libraries are used together as we shall see later.

We conclude this section by observing that the attributes FIRST, LAST, LENGTH and RANGE, as well as applying to array objects, may also be applied to array types and subtypes provided they are constrained (that is, have their bounds given). So

```
VECTOR_6'LENGTH = 6
```

but

```
VECTOR'LENGTH     is illegal
```

Exercise 6.2

1   Declare an array type BBB corresponding to the array BOR of
         Exercise 6.1(**5**).

2   Declare a two-dimensional array type suitable for declaring
         operator tables on values of

              subtype RING5 **is** INTEGER **range** 0 .. 4;

         Then declare addition and multiplication tables for modulo 5
         arithmetic. Use the tables to formulate the expression (A + B) ⋆ C
         using modulo 5 arithmetic and assign the result to D where A, B, C
         and D have been appropriately declared. See Section 4.5.

6.3 Named array aggregates

There is another form of aggregate known as a named aggregate in which
the component values are preceded by the corresponding index value and
=>. (The symbol => is akin to the ☞ sign encountered in old railway
timetables and used for indicating directions especially on the Paris
Metro.) A simple example would be

      (1 => 0.0, 2 => 0.0, 3 => 0.0, 4 => 0.0, 5 => 0.0, 6 => 0.0)

with the expected extension to several dimensions. The bounds of such an
aggregate are self-evident and so our problem with the unit 2 × 2 matrix of
the previous section could be overcome by writing

      UNIT_2: **constant** MATRIX:= (1 => (1 => 1.0, 2 => 0.0),
                                 2 => (1 => 0.0, 2 => 1.0));

      The rules for named aggregates are very similar to the rules for the
alternatives in a case statement.
      Each choice can be given as a series of alternatives each of which can
be a single value or a discrete range. We could therefore rewrite some
previous examples as follows

      A: **array** (1 .. 6) **of** REAL:= (1 .. 6 => 0.0);

      WORK_DAY: **constant array** (DAY) **of** BOOLEAN
                   := (MON .. FRI => TRUE, SAT | SUN => FALSE);

      In contrast to a positional aggregate, the index values need not
appear in order. We could equally have written

      (SAT | SUN => FALSE, MON .. FRI => TRUE)

We can also use **others** but then as for the case statement it must be last and on its own.

The use of **others** raises some problems since it must be clear what the totality of values is. It should also be realized that although we have been showing aggregates as initial values, they can be used quite generally in any place where an expression of an array type is required. It is therefore necessary that the context supplies the bounds if **others** is used. One way of supplying the context is by qualifying the aggregate as we did to distinguish between overloaded enumeration literals. In order to do this we must have an appropriate (constrained) type or subtype name. So we introduce

type SCHEDULE **is array** (DAY) **of** BOOLEAN;

and can then write an expression such as

SCHEDULE'(MON .. FRI => TRUE, **others** => FALSE)

which could be part of a larger expression or maybe an initial value as we shall see in a moment. (Note that when qualifying an aggregate we do not, as for an expression, need to put it in brackets because it already has brackets.)

Other contexts which supply the bounds will be met in due course when we discuss subprogram parameters and results in Chapter 7 and generic parameters in Chapter 13. These same contexts will also supply the bounds of a positional aggregate; like a named aggregate with **others**, a positional aggregate does not have self-evident bounds.

However, in other contexts such as assignment and as an initial value the bounds are not provided by the context because of the concept of 'sliding semantics' introduced in the previous section. In the case of a positional aggregate in such a context, all is not lost since we recall that the lower bound is taken to be S'FIRST where S is the index subtype and the upper bound is then deduced from the number of components. Of course a named aggregate with **others** cannot use such a rule since the number of components represented by **others** is not known and so such an aggregate is illegal in such a context.

Array aggregates may not mix positional and named notation except that **others** may be used at the end of a positional aggregate. Such a positional aggregate then follows the general rules for a named aggregate with **others**.

Although the context of an assignment or an initial value cannot give the bounds (because of sliding), nevertheless provided the array type is constrained (which it will be unless we are declaring a constant and are going to deduce its bounds from the initial value), the context will tell us the length of the aggregate. So, in the case of a positional aggregate with **others**, taking the lower bound as S'FIRST, we can deduce the upper bound from the length (or in other words the values represented by **others** are taken to follow on from those explicitly given as far as necessary in order to provide the correct length) and so such an aggregate is allowed in a sliding context. However, we cannot do this in the case of a named aggregate with **others** because the whole essence of a named aggregate is that the components are not in order and so such an aggregate is not allowed in a sliding context. There is one exception – a named aggregate with **others** as the only choice is allowed because there can be no ambiguity in that case. So we cannot write

> WORK_DAY: **constant array** (DAY) **of** BOOLEAN
>   := (MON .. FRI => TRUE, **others** => FALSE);   –– illegal

but we must instead write

> WORK_DAY: **constant array** (DAY) **of** BOOLEAN
>   := (TRUE, TRUE, TRUE, TRUE, TRUE, **others** => FALSE);

or change the context by using qualification and write

> WORK_DAY: **constant** SCHEDULE
>   := SCHEDULE'(MON .. FRI => TRUE, **others** => FALSE);

The rules regarding the bounds of array aggregates seem very difficult and to be one of the most curious aspects of Ada. However, if you are very confused, do not be too worried at this point; we will return to this topic when we summarize a number of aspects of expressions in Section 16.1. Meanwhile, remember than an aggregate can always be qualified if in doubt.

Array aggregates really are rather complicated and we still have a few points to make. The first is that in a named aggregate all the ranges and values before => must be static (as in a case statement) except for one special situation. This is where there is only one alternative consisting of a single choice – it could then be a dynamic range or (unlikely) a single dynamic value. An example might be

> A: **array** (1 .. N) **of** INTEGER:= (1 .. N => 0);

This is valid even if N is zero (or negative) and then gives a null array and a null aggregate. The following example illustrates a general rule that the expression after => is evaluated once for each corresponding index value; of course it usually makes no difference but consider

> A: **array** (1 .. N) **of** INTEGER:= (1 .. N => 1/N);

If N is zero then there are no values and so 1/N is not evaluated and NUMERIC_ERROR cannot occur. The reader will recall from Section 4.1 that a similar multiple evaluation also occurs when several objects are declared and initialized together.

In order to avoid awkward problems with null aggregates, a null choice is only allowed if it is the only choice. Foolish aggregates such as

> (7 .. 6 | 1 .. 0 => 0)

are thus forbidden and there is no question of the lower bound of such an aggregate.

Another point is that although we cannot mix named and positional notation within an aggregate, we can, however, use different forms for the different components and levels of a multidimensional aggregate. So the initial value of our matrix UNIT_2 could also be written as

```
(1 => (1.0, 0.0),      or      ((1 => 1.0, 2 => 0.0),
 2 => (0.0, 1.0))               (1 => 0.0, 2 => 1.0))
```

or even as

```
(1 => (1 => 1.0, 2 => 0.0),
 2 => (   0.0,        1.0))
```

and so on.

Note also that the RANGE attribute stands for a range and therefore can be used as one of the choices in a named aggregate. However, we cannot use the range attribute of an object in its own initial value. Thus

```
A: array (1 .. N) of INTEGER:= (A'RANGE => 0);    -- illegal
```

is not allowed. This is because an object is not visible until the end of its declaration. However, we could write

```
A: array (1 .. N) of INTEGER:= (others => 0);
```

and this is probably better than repeating 1 .. N because it localizes the dependency on N.

A final point is that a positional aggregate cannot contain just one component because otherwise it would be ambiguous. We could not distinguish an aggregate of one component from a scalar value which happened to be in brackets. An aggregate of one component must therefore use the named notation. So instead of

```
A: array (1 .. 1) of INTEGER:= (99);    -- illegal
```

we must write

```
A: array (1 .. 1) of INTEGER:= (1 => 99);
```

or even

```
A: array (N .. N) of INTEGER:= (N => 99);
```

which illustrates the obscure case of an aggregate with a single choice and a single dynamic value being that choice.

The reader will by now have concluded that arrays in Ada are somewhat complicated. That is a fair judgement, but in practice there should be few difficulties. There is always the safeguard that if we do something wrong, the compiler will inevitably tell us. In cases of ambiguity, qualification solves the problems provided we have an appropriate type or subtype name to use. Much of the complexity with aggregates is similar to that in the case statement.

We conclude this section by pointing out that the named aggregate notation can greatly increase program legibility. It is especially valuable in initializing large constant arrays and guards against the accidental misplacement of individual values. Consider

```
type EVENT is (BIRTH, ACCESSION, DEATH);
type MONARCH is (WILLIAM_I, WILLIAM_II, HENRY_I, ... ,
                 VICTORIA, EDWARD_VII, GEORGE_V, ... );
...
ROYAL_EVENTS: constant array (MONARCH, EVENT) of INTEGER

   := (WILLIAM_I    => (1027, 1066, 1087),
       WILLIAM_II   => (1056, 1087, 1100),
       HENRY_I      => (1068, 1100, 1135),
       ...
       VICTORIA     => (1819, 1837, 1901),
       EDWARD_VII   => (1841, 1901, 1910),
       GEORGE_V     => (1865, 1910, 1936),
       ...                                 );
```

The accidental interchange of two lines of the aggregate causes no problems, whereas if we had just used the positional notation then an error would have been introduced and this might have been tricky to detect.

Exercise 6.3

1 Rewrite the declaration of the array DAYS_IN_MONTH in Exercise 6.1(**3**) using a named aggregate for an initial value.

2 Declare a constant MATRIX whose bounds are both 1 .. N where N is dynamic and whose components are all zero.

3 Declare a constant MATRIX as in **2** but make it a unit matrix.

4 Declare a constant two-dimensional array which gives the numbers of each atom in a molecule of the various aliphatic alcohols. Declare appropriate enumeration types for both the atoms and the molecules. Consider methanol CH_3OH, ethanol C_2H_5OH, propanol C_3H_7OH and butanol C_4H_9OH.

6.4 Characters and strings

We now complete our discussion of enumeration types by introducing character types. In the enumeration types seen so far such as

```
type COLOUR is (RED, AMBER, GREEN);
```

the values have been represented by identifiers. It is also possible to have an enumeration type in which some or all of the values are represented by character literals.

A character literal is a further form of lexical element. It consists of a single character within a pair of single quotes. The character must be one of the printable characters or it could be a single space. It must not be a control character such as horizontal tabulate or new line.

This is a situation where there is a distinction between upper and lower case letters. The character literals

'A', 'a'

are different.

So we could declare an enumeration type

type ROMAN_DIGIT **is** ('I', 'V', 'X', 'L', 'C', 'D', 'M');

and then

DIG: ROMAN_DIGIT:= 'D';

All the usual properties of enumeration types apply.

ROMAN_DIGIT'FIRST = 'I'
ROMAN_DIGIT'SUCC('X') = 'L'
ROMAN_DIGIT'POS'('M') = 6

DIG < 'L' = FALSE

There is a predefined enumeration type CHARACTER which is (naturally) a character type. We can think of its declaration as being of the form

type CHARACTER **is** (*nul*, ... , '0', '1', '2', ... , 'A', 'B', 'C', ... ,
'a', 'b', 'c', ... , *del*);

but for technical reasons which cannot be explained here the literals which are not actual character literals (such as *nul*) are not really identifiers either (which is why they are represented here in italics). It is however possible to refer to them as ASCII.NUL and so on (or under suitable circumstances to be discussed later as simply NUL). This predefined type CHARACTER represents the standard ASCII character set and describes the set of characters normally used for input and output; for its full declaration see Appendix 2. It is unfortunate that the type CHARACTER is hedged around with subtleties but in practice these do not matter.

It should be noted that the introduction of both the type ROMAN_DIGIT and the predefined type CHARACTER results in overloading of some of the literals. An expression such as

'X' < 'L'

is ambiguous. We do not know whether we are comparing characters of the type ROMAN_DIGIT or CHARACTER. In order to resolve the ambiguity we must qualify one or both literals.

```
CHARACTER'('X') < 'L' = FALSE
ROMAN_DIGIT'('X') < 'L' = TRUE
```

As well as the predefined type CHARACTER there is also the predefined type STRING

type STRING **is array** (POSITIVE **range** <>) **of** CHARACTER;

This is a perfectly normal array type and obeys all the rules of the previous section. So we can write

S: STRING (1 .. 7);

to declare an array of range 1 .. 7. In the case of a constant array the bounds can be deduced from the initial value thus

G: **constant** STRING:= ('P', 'I', 'G');

where the initial value takes the form of a normal positional aggregate. The lower bound of G (that is, G'FIRST) is 1 since the index subtype of STRING is POSITIVE and POSITIVE'FIRST is 1.

An alternative notation is provided for a positional aggregate each of whose components is a character literal. This is the string. So we could more conveniently write

G: **constant** STRING:= "PIG";

The string is the last lexical element to be introduced. It consists of a sequence of printable characters and spaces enclosed in double quotes. A double quote may be represented in a string by two double quotes so that

('A', '"', 'B') = "A""B"

The string may also have just one character or may be null. The equivalent aggregates using character literals have to be written in named notation.

```
(1 => 'A') = "A"
(1 .. 0 => 'A') = ""
```

Note how we have to introduce an arbitrary character in the null named form. Ada has some strange quirks!

Another rule about a lexical string is that it must fit onto a single line. Moreover it cannot contain control characters such as SOH. And, of course, as with character literals, the two cases of alphabet are distinct in strings

"PIG" /= "pig"

In Section 6.6 we will see how to overcome the limitations that a string must fit onto a single line and yet cannot contain control characters.

A major use for strings is, of course, for creating text to be output. A simple sequence of characters can be output by a call of the (overloaded) subprogram PUT. Thus

```
PUT ("The Countess of Lovelace");
```

will output the text

```
The Countess of Lovelace
```

onto some appropriate file.

However, the lexical string is not reserved just for use with the built-in type STRING. It can be used to represent an array of any character type. We can write

```
type ROMAN_NUMBER is array (POSITIVE range <>) of
                                          ROMAN_DIGIT;
```

and then

```
NINETEEN_EIGHTY_FOUR: constant ROMAN_NUMBER :=
                                          "MCMLXXXIV";
```

or indeed

```
FOUR: array (1 .. 2) of ROMAN_DIGIT:= "IV";
```

Exercise 6.4

1   Declare a constant array ROMAN_TO_INTEGER which can be used for table look-up to convert a ROMAN_DIGIT to its normal integer equivalent (for example, converts 'C' to 100).

2   Given an object R of type ROMAN_NUMBER write statements to compute the equivalent integer value V. It may be assumed that R obeys the normal rules of construction of Roman numbers.

6.5   Arrays of arrays and slices

The components of an array can be of any type (or subtype) for which we can declare objects. Thus we can declare arrays of any scalar type; we can also declare arrays of arrays. So we can have

```
type MATRIX_3_6 is array (1 .. 3) of VECTOR_6;
```

where, as in Section 6.2

    type VECTOR_6 **is array** (1 .. 6) **of** REAL;

However, we cannot declare an array of unconstrained arrays (just as we cannot declare an object which is an unconstrained array). So we cannot write

    type MATRIX_3_N **is array** (1 .. 3) **of** VECTOR;   −− illegal

On the other hand there is nothing to prevent us declaring an unconstrained array of constrained arrays thus

    type MATRIX_N_6 **is array** (INTEGER **range** <>) **of** VECTOR_6;

It is instructive to compare the practical differences between declaring an array of arrays

    AOA: MATRIX_3_6;   or   AOA: MATRIX_N_6(1 .. 3);

and the similar multidimensional array

    MDA: MATRIX(1 .. 3, 1 .. 6);

Aggregates for both are completely identical, for example

    ((1.0, 2.0, 3.0, 4.0, 5.0, 6.0),
     (4.0, 4.0, 4.0, 4.0, 4.0, 4.0),
     (6.0, 5.0, 4.0, 3.0, 2.0, 1.0))

but component access is quite different, thus

    AOA(I)(J)
    MDA(I, J)

where in the case of AOA the internal structure is naturally revealed. The individual rows of AOA can be manipulated as arrays in their own right but the structure of MDA cannot be decomposed. So we could change the middle row of AOA to zero by

    AOA(2):= (1 .. 6 => 0.0);

but a similar technique cannot be applied to MDA.

Arrays of arrays are not restricted to one dimension, we can have a multidimensional array of arrays or an array of multidimensional arrays; the notation extends in an obvious way.

Arrays of strings are revealing. Consider

    type STRING_ARRAY **is array** (POSITIVE **range** <>,
                                 POSITIVE **range** <>) **of** CHARACTER;

which is an unconstrained two-dimensional array type. We can then declare

> FARMYARD: **constant** STRING_ARRAY:= ("pig", "cat", "dog",
> "cow", "rat", "ass");

where the bounds are conveniently deduced from the aggregate. But note that we cannot have a ragged array where the individual strings are of different lengths such as

> ZOO: **constant** STRING_ARRAY:= ("aardvark", "baboon", "camel",
> "dolphin", "elephant", ..., "zebra");   −− illegal

This is a real nuisance and means we have to pad the strings to be the same length

> ZOO: **constant** STRING_ARRAY:= ("aardvark",
> "baboon ",
> "camel   ",
> "dolphin ",
> "elephant",
> ...
> "zebra   ");

The next problem is that we cannot select an individual one of the strings. We might want to output one and so attempt

> PUT(FARMYARD(5));

hoping to print the text

> rat

but this is not allowed since we can only select an individual component of an array which in this case is just one character.

An alternative approach is to use an array of arrays. A problem here is that the component in the array type declaration has to be constrained and so we have to decide on the length of our strings right from the beginning thus

> **type** STRING_3_ARRAY **is array** (POSITIVE **range** <>) **of**
> STRING(1 .. 3);

and then

> FARMYARD: **constant** STRING_3_ARRAY:= ("pig", "cat", "dog",
> "cow", "rat", "ass");

With this formulation we can indeed select an individual string as a whole and so the statement PUT(FARMYARD(5)); now works. However, we still cannot declare our ZOO as a ragged array; we will return to this topic in Section 11.2 when another approach will be discussed.

We thus see that arrays of arrays and multidimensional arrays each have their own advantages and disadvantages. Neither is ideal; Ada arrays are rather restrictive and do not offer the flexibility of Algol 68.

A special feature of one-dimensional arrays is the ability to denote a slice of an array object. A slice is written as the name of the object (variable or constant) followed by a discrete range in brackets.

So given

```
S: STRING(1 .. 10);
```

then we can write S(3 .. 8) to denote the middle six characters of S. The bounds of the slice are the bounds of the range and not those of the index subtype. We could write

```
T: constant STRING:= S(3 .. 8);
```

and then T'FIRST = 3, T'LAST = 8.

The bounds of the slice need not be static but can be any expressions. A slice would be null if the range turned out to be null.

The use of slices emphasizes the nature of array assignment. The value of the expression to be assigned is completely evaluated before any components are assigned. No problems arise with overlapping slices. So

```
S(1 .. 4):= "BARA";
S(4 .. 7):= S(1 .. 4);
```

results in S(1 .. 7) = "BARBARA". S(4) is only updated after the expression S(1 .. 4) is safely evaluated. There is no risk of setting S(4) to 'B' and then consequently making the expression "BARB" with the final result of

```
"BARBARB"
```

The ability to use slices is another consideration in deciding between arrays of arrays and multidimensional arrays. With our second FARMYARD we can write

```
PETS: STRING_3_ARRAY(1 .. 2):= FARMYARD(2 .. 3);
```

which uses sliding assignment so that the two components of PETS are "cat" and "dog". Moreover, if we had declared the FARMYARD as a variable rather than a constant then we could also write

```
FARMYARD(1)(1 .. 2):= "ho";
```

which turns the "pig" into a "hog"! We can do none of these things with the old FARMYARD.

Exercise 6.5

1   Write a single assignment statement to swap the first and second rows of AOA.

2   Declare the second FARMYARD as a variable. Then change the cow into a sow.

3   Assume that R contains a Roman number. Write statements to see if the last digit of the corresponding decimal arabic value is a 4 and change it to a 6 if it is.

6.6 One-dimensional array operations

Many of the operators that we met in Chapter 4 may also be applied to one-dimensional arrays.

The Boolean operators **and**, **or**, **xor** and **not** may be applied to one-dimensional Boolean arrays. In the case of the binary operators, the two operands must have the same number of components and be of the same type. The underlying scalar operation is applied component by component and the resulting array is again of the same type. The lower bound of the index of the result is equal to the lower bound of the subtype of the left or only operand.

Consider

```
type BIT_ROW is array (POSITIVE range <>) of BOOLEAN;
A, B: BIT_ROW(1 .. 4);
C, D: array (1 .. 4) of BOOLEAN;
T: constant BOOLEAN:= TRUE;
F: constant BOOLEAN:= FALSE;
```

then we can write

```
A:= (T, T, F, F);
B:= (T, F, T, F);

A:= A and B;
B:= not B;
```

and A now equals (T, F, F, F), and B equals (F, T, F, T). Similarly for **or** and **xor**. But note that C **and** D would not be allowed because they are of different (and anonymous) types because of the rule regarding multiple declarations (Section 4.1). This is clearly a case where it is appropriate to give a name to the array type because we are manipulating the arrays as complete objects.

Note that these operators also use sliding semantics, like assignment as explained in Section 6.2, and so only demand that the types and the number of components are the same. The bounds themselves do not have to be equal. However, if the number of components are not the same then, naturally, CONSTRAINT_ERROR will be raised.

Boolean arrays can be used to represent sets. Consider

```
type PRIMARY is (R, Y, B);
type COLOUR is array (PRIMARY) of BOOLEAN;
C: COLOUR;
```

then there are $8 = 2 \times 2 \times 2$ values that C can take. C is, of course, an array with three components and each of these has value TRUE or FALSE; the three components are

C(R),   C(Y)   and   C(B)

The 8 possible values of the type COLOUR can be represented by suitably named constants as follows

```
WHITE        : constant COLOUR:= (F, F, F);
RED          : constant COLOUR:= (T, F, F);
YELLOW       : constant COLOUR:= (F, T, F);
BLUE         : constant COLOUR:= (F, F, T);
GREEN        : constant COLOUR:= (F, T, T);
PURPLE       : constant COLOUR:= (T, F, T);
ORANGE       : constant COLOUR:= (T, T, F);
BLACK        : constant COLOUR:= (T, T, T);
```

and then we can write expressions such as

RED or YELLOW

which is equal to ORANGE and

not BLACK

which is WHITE.

So the values of our type COLOUR are effectively the set of colours obtained by taking all combinations of the primary colours represented by R, Y, B. The empty set is the value of WHITE and the full set is the value of BLACK. We are using the paint pot mixing colour model rather than light mixing. A value of TRUE for a component means that the primary colour concerned is mixed in our pot. The murky mess we got at school from mixing too many colours together is our black!

The operations or, and and xor may be interpreted as set union, set intersection and symmetric difference. A test for set membership can be made by inspecting the value of the appropriate component of the set. Thus

C(R)

is TRUE if R is in the set represented by C. We cannot use the predefined operation **in** for this. A literal value can be represented using the named aggregate notation, so

(R | Y => T, **others** => F)

has the same value as ORANGE. A more elegant way of doing this will appear in the next chapter.

We now consider the equality and relational operators. The operators = and /= apply to all types anyway and we gave the rules for arrays when we discussed assignment in Section 6.2.

The relational operators <, <=, > and >= may be applied to one-dimensional arrays of a discrete type. (Note discrete.) The result of the comparison is based upon the lexicographic (that is, dictionary) order using the defined order relation for the components. This is best illustrated with strings which we assume for the moment are unambiguously values of the type STRING. The following are all TRUE

```
"CAT" < "DOG"
"CAT" < "CATERPILLAR"
"AZZ" < "B"
""    < "A"
```

The strings are compared component by component until they differ in some position. The string with the lower component is then lower. If one string runs out of components as in CAT versus CATERPILLAR then the shorter one is lower. The null string is lowest of all.

If we assume that we have declared our type ROMAN_NUMBER then

```
"CCL" < "CCXC"
```

is ambiguous since we do not know whether we are comparing type STRING or type ROMAN_NUMBER. We must qualify one or both of the strings. This is done in the usual way but a string, unlike the bracketed form of aggregates, has to be placed in brackets otherwise we would get an ugly juxtaposition of a single and double quote. So

```
STRING'("CCL") < "CCXC"          is TRUE
ROMAN_NUMBER'("CCL") < "CCXC"    is FALSE
```

Note that our compiler is too stupid to know about the interpretation of Roman numbers in our minds and has said that 250 < 290 is false. The only thing that matters is the order relation of the characters 'L' and 'X' in the type definition. In the next chapter we will show how we can redefine < so that it works 'properly' for Roman numbers.

Of course, the relational operators also apply to general expressions and not just to literal strings.

```
NINETEEN_EIGHTY_FOUR < "MM"          is TRUE
```

The relational operators can be applied to arrays of any discrete types. So

```
(1, 2, 3) < (2, 3)
(JAN, JAN) < (1 => FEB)
```

The predefined operators <=, > and >= are defined by analogy with <.

We finally introduce a new binary operator & which denotes catenation (or concatenation) of one-dimensional arrays. It has the same precedence as binary plus and minus. The two operands must be of the same type and the result is an array of the same type whose value is obtained by juxtaposing the two operands. The lower bound of the result is, as usual, the lower bound of the left operand.

So

```
"CAT" & "ERPILLAR" = "CATERPILLAR"
```

String catenation can be used to construct a string which is too long to fit on one line

```
"This string goes" &
"on and on"
```

One or both operands of & can also be a single value of the component type. If the left operand is such a single value then the lower bound of the result is the lower bound of the subtype of the array index.

```
"CAT" & 'S' = "CATS"
'S' & "CAT" = "SCAT"
'S' & 'S' = "SS"
```

This is useful for representing the control characters such as CR and LF in strings.

```
"First line" & ASCII.CR & ASCII.LF & "Next line"
```

Of course, it might be neater to declare

```
CRLF: constant STRING:= (ASCII.CR, ASCII.LF);
```

and then write

```
"First line" & CRLF & "Next line"
```

The operation & can be applied to any one-dimensional array type and so we can apply it to our Roman numbers. Consider

```
R: ROMAN_NUMBER(1 .. 5);
S: STRING(1 .. 5);

R:= "CCL" & "IV";
S:= "CCL" & "IV";
```

This is valid. The context tells us that in the first case we apply & to two Roman numbers whereas in the second we apply it to two values of type STRING. There is no ambiguity as in

B: BOOLEAN:= "CCL" < "IV";

Exercise 6.6

1   Write the eight possible constants WHITE ... BLACK of the type COLOUR in ascending order as determined by the operator < applied to one-dimensional arrays.

2   Evaluate

(a)   RED **or** GREEN

(b)   BLACK **xor** RED

(c)   **not** GREEN

3   Show that **not** (BLACK **xor** C) = C is true for all values of C.

4   Why did we not write

(JAN, JAN) < (FEB)

5   Put in ascending order the following values of type STRING: "ABC", "123", "abc", "Abc", "abC", "aBc".

6   Given

C: CHARACTER;
S: STRING(5 .. 10);

What is the lower bound of

(a)   C & S

(b)   S & C

6.7 Records

As stated at the beginning of this chapter we are only going to consider the simplest form of record at this point. A fuller treatment covering variant records and so on is left until Chapter 11.

A record is a composite object consisting of named components which may be of different types. In contrast to arrays, we cannot have anonymous record types – they all have to be named. Consider

```
type MONTH_NAME is (JAN, FEB, MAR, APR, MAY, JUN, JUL,
                    AUG, SEP, OCT, NOV, DEC);

type DATE is
    record
        DAY: INTEGER range 1 .. 31;
        MONTH: MONTH_NAME;
        YEAR: INTEGER;
    end record;
```

This declares the type DATE to be a record containing three named components: DAY, MONTH and YEAR.

We can declare variables and constants of record types in the usual way.

```
D: DATE;
```

declares an object D which is a date. The individual components of D can be denoted by following D with a dot and the component name. Thus we could write

```
D.DAY:= 4;
D.MONTH:= JUL;
D.YEAR:= 1776;
```

in order to assign new values to the individual components.

Records can be manipulated as whole objects. Literal values can be written as aggregates much like arrays; both positional and named forms can be used. So we could write

```
D: DATE:= (4, JUL, 1776);
E: DATE;
```

and then

```
E:= D;
```

or

```
E:= (MONTH => JUL, DAY => 4, YEAR => 1776);
```

The reader will be relieved to know that much of the complexity of array aggregates does not apply to records. This is because the number of components is always known.

In a positional aggregate the components come in order. In a named aggregate they may be in any order. In the particular example shown the use of a named aggregate avoids the necessity to know on which side of the Atlantic the record type was declared.

A named aggregate cannot use a range because the components are not considered to be closely related and the vertical bar can only be used with components which have the same (base) type. The choice **others** can be used but again only when the remaining components are of the same type.

There is one extra possibility for records and that is that the positional and named notations can be mixed in one aggregate. But if this is done then the positional components must come first and in order (without holes) as usual. So in other words we can change to the named notation at any point in the aggregate but must then stick to it. The above date could therefore also be expressed as

```
(4, JUL, YEAR => 1776)
(4, YEAR => 1776, MONTH => JUL)
```

and so on

It is possible to give default expressions for some or all of the components in the type declaration. Thus

```
type COMPLEX is
    record
        RL: REAL:= 0.0;
        IM: REAL:= 0.0;
    end record;
```

or more succinctly

```
type COMPLEX is
    record
        RL, IM: REAL:= 0.0;
    end record;
```

declares a record type containing two components of type REAL and gives a default expression of 0.0 for each. This record type represents a complex number $x + iy$ where RL and IM are the values of x and y. The default value is thus $(0, 0)$, the origin of the Argand plane. We can now declare

```
C1: COMPLEX;
C2: COMPLEX:= (1.0, 0.0);
```

The object C1 will now have the values 0.0 for its components by default. In the case of C2 we have overridden the default values. Note that, irritatingly, even if there are default expressions, an aggregate must be complete even if it supplies the same values as the default expressions for some of the components.

In this case both components are the same type and so the following named forms are possible

```
(RL | IM => 1.0)
(others => 1.0)
```

The only operations predefined on record types are = and /= as well as assignment of course. Other operations must be performed at the component level or be explicitly defined by a subprogram as we shall see in the next chapter.

A record type may have any number of components. It may pathologically have none in which case its declaration takes the form

```
type HOLE is
    record
        null;
    end record;
```

The reserved word **null** confirms that we meant to declare a null record type. Null records have their uses but they will not be apparent yet.

The components of a record type can be of any type; they can be other records or arrays. However, if a component is an array then it must be fully constrained (that is, its index must not contain <>) and it must be of a named type and not an anonymous type. And obviously a record cannot contain an instance of itself.

The components cannot be constants but the record as a whole can be. Thus

```
I: constant COMPLEX:= (0.0, 1.0);
```

is allowed and represents the square root of −1.

A more elaborate example of a record is

```
type PERSON is
    record
        BIRTH: DATE;
        NAME: STRING(1 .. 20):= (1 .. 20 => ' ');
    end record;
```

The record PERSON has two components, the first is another record, a DATE, the second an array. The array which is a string of length 20 has a default value of all spaces.

We can now write

```
JOHN: PERSON;
JOHN.BIRTH:= (19, AUG, 1937);
JOHN.NAME(1 .. 4):= "JOHN";
```

and we would then have

```
JOHN = ((19, AUG, 1937), "JOHN                ")
```

The notation is as expected. The aggregates nest and for objects we proceed from left to right using the dot notation to select components of a record and indexes in brackets to select components of an array and ranges in brackets to slice arrays. There is no limit. We could have an array of persons

```
PEOPLE: array (1 .. N) of PERSON;
```

and then have

```
PEOPLE(6).BIRTH.DAY:= 19;
PEOPLE(8).NAME(3):= 'H';
```

and so on.

A final point concerns the evaluation of expressions in a record declaration. An expression in a constraint applied to a component is evaluated when the record type is elaborated. So our type PERSON could have

```
NAME: STRING(1 .. N):= (others => ' ');
```

and the length of the component NAME will be the value of N when the type PERSON is elaborated. Of course, N need not be static and so if the type declaration is in a loop, for example, then each execution of the loop might give rise to a type with a different size component. However, for each elaboration of the record type declaration all objects of the type will have the same component size.

On the other hand, a default expression in a record type is only evaluated when an object of the type is declared and only then if no explicit initial value is provided. Of course, in simple cases, like our type COMPLEX, it makes no difference but it could bring surprises. For example, suppose we write the component NAME as

```
NAME: STRING(1 .. N):= (1 .. N => ' ');
```

then the length of the component NAME is the value of N when the record type is declared whereas when a PERSON is subsequently declared without an initial value, the aggregate will be evaluated using the value of N which then applies. Of course, N may by then be different and so CONSTRAINT_ERROR will be raised. This is rather surprising; we do seem to have strayed into an odd backwater of Ada!

Exercise 6.7

1   Rewrite the solution to Exercise 6.1(**3**) using a variable D of type DATE rather than three individual variables.

2   Declare three variables C1, C2 and C3 of type COMPLEX. Write one or more statements to assign (a) the sum, (b) the product, of C1 and C2 to C3.

3   Write statements to find the index of the first person of the array PEOPLE born on or after 1 January 1950.

Checklist 6

Array types can be anonymous, but records cannot.

Aggregates must always be complete.

Distinguish constrained array types from unconstrained array types (those with <>).

Named and positional notations cannot be mixed for array aggregates – they can for records.

An aggregate with **others** must have a context giving its bounds.

A choice in an array aggregate can only be dynamic or null if it is the only choice.

The attributes FIRST, LAST, LENGTH and RANGE apply to array objects and constrained array types and subtypes but not to unconstrained types and subtypes.

For array assignment to be valid, the number of components must be equal for each dimension – not the bounds.

The cases of alphabet are distinct in character literals and strings.

An aggregate with one component must use the named notation. This applies to records as well as to arrays.

A record component cannot be an anonymous array.

A default component expression is only evaluated when an uninitialized object is declared.

Chapter 7
Subprograms

Subprograms are the conventional parameterized unit of programming. In Ada, subprograms fall into two categories: functions and procedures. Functions are called as components of expressions and return a value as part of the expression, whereas procedures are called as statements standing alone.

As we shall see, the actions to be performed when a subprogram is called are described by a subprogram body. Subprogram bodies are declared in the usual way in a declarative part which may for instance be in a block or indeed in another subprogram.

7.1   Functions

A function is a form of subprogram that can be called as part of an expression. In Chapter 4 we met examples of calls of functions such as DAY'SUCC, SQRT and so on.

We now consider the form of a function body which describes the statements to be executed when the function is called. For example the body of the function SQRT might have the form

```
function SQRT(X: REAL) return REAL is
    R: REAL;
begin
    -- compute value of SQRT(X) in R
    return R;
end SQRT;
```

All function bodies start with the reserved word **function** and the designator of the function being defined. If the function has parameters the designator is followed by a list of parameter specifications in brackets. If there are several specifications then they are separated by semicolons. Each specification gives the identifiers of one or more parameters followed by a colon and its type or subtype. The parameter list, if any, is then followed by the reserved word **return** and the type or subtype of the result of the function. In the case of both parameters and result, the type or subtype must be given by a type mark and not by a subtype indication. This is an important example of a situation where an explicit constraint is not allowed; the reason will be mentioned later in this chapter.

The part of the body we have described so far is called the function specification. It specifies the function to the outside world in the sense of providing all the information needed to call the function.

After the specification comes **is** and then the body proper which is just like a block – it has a declarative part, **begin**, a sequence of statements, and then **end**. As for a block the declarative part can be empty but there must be at least one statement in the sequence of statements. Between **end** and the terminating semicolon we may repeat the designator of the function. This is optional but, if present, must correctly match the designator after **function**.

It is often necessary or just convenient to give the specification on its own but without the rest of the body. In such a case it is immediately followed by a semicolon thus

    function SQRT(X: REAL) **return** REAL;

and is then correctly known as a function declaration – although often still carelessly referred to as a specification. The uses of such declarations will be discussed later.

The formal parameters of a function act as local constants whose values are provided by the corresponding actual parameters. When the function is called the declarative part is elaborated in the usual way and then the statements are executed. A return statement is used to indicate the value of the function call and to return control back to the calling expression.

Thus considering our example suppose we had

    S:= SQRT(T + 0.5);

then first T + 0.5 is evaluated and then SQRT is called. Within the body the parameter X behaves as a constant with the initial value given by T + 0.5. It is rather as if we had

    X: **constant** REAL:= T + 0.5;

The declaration of R is then elaborated. We then obey the sequence of statements and assume they compute the square root of X and assign it to R. The last statement is **return** R; this passes control back to the calling expression with the result of the function being the value of R. This value is then assigned to S.

The expression in a return statement can be of arbitrary complexity and must be of the same type as and satisfy any constraints implied by the type mark given in the function specification. If the constraints are violated then, of course, the exception CONSTRAINT_ERROR is raised.

A function body may have several return statements. The execution of any of them will terminate the function. Thus the function SIGN which takes an integer value and returns +1, 0 or −1 according to whether the parameter is positive, zero or negative could be written as

```
function SIGN(X: INTEGER) return INTEGER is
begin
    if X > 0 then
        return +1;
    elsif X < 0 then
        return −1;
    else
        return 0;
    end if;
end SIGN;
```

So we see that the last lexical statement of the body need not be a return statement since there is one in each branch of the statement. Any attempt to 'run' into the final end will raise the exception PROGRAM_ERROR. This is our first example of a situation giving rise to PROGRAM_ERROR; this exception is generally used for situations which would violate the run time control structure.

It should be noted that each call of a function produces a new instance of any objects declared within it (including parameters of course) and these disappear when we leave the function. It is therefore possible for a function to be called recursively without any problems. So the factorial function could be declared as

```
function FACTORIAL(N: POSITIVE) return POSITIVE is
begin
    if N = 1 then
        return 1;
    else
        return N * FACTORIAL(N−1);
    end if;
end FACTORIAL;
```

If we write

```
F:= FACTORIAL(4);
```

then the function calls itself until, on the fourth call (with the other three calls all partly executed and waiting for the result of the call they did before doing the multiply) we find that N is 1 and the calls then all unwind and all the multiplications are performed.

Note that there is no need to check that the parameter N is positive since the parameter is of subtype POSITIVE. So calling FACTORIAL(−2) will result in CONSTRAINT_ERROR. Of course, FACTORIAL(10_000) could result in the computer running out of space in which case STORAGE_ERROR would be raised. The more moderate call FACTORIAL(20) would undoubtedly cause overflow and thus raise NUMERIC_ERROR (or the equivalent CONSTRAINT_ERROR – see Section 4.9).

A formal parameter may be of any type but the type must have a name. It cannot be an anonymous type such as

```
array (1 .. 6) of REAL
```

In any event no actual parameter (other than an aggregate) could match such a formal parameter even if it were allowed since the actual and formal parameters must have the same type.

A formal parameter can, however, be an unconstrained array type such as

```
type VECTOR is array (INTEGER range <>) of REAL;
```

In such a case the bounds of the formal parameter are taken from those of the actual parameter.

Consider

```
function SUM(A: VECTOR) return REAL is
   RESULT: REAL:= 0.0;
begin
   for I in A'RANGE loop
      RESULT:= RESULT + A(I);
   end loop;
   return RESULT;
end SUM;
```

then we can write

```
V: VECTOR(1 .. 4):= (1.0, 2.0, 3.0, 4.0);
S: REAL;
...
S:= SUM(V);
```

The formal parameter A then takes the bounds of the actual parameter V. So for this call we have

```
A'RANGE    is    1 .. 4
```

and the effect of the loop is to compute the sum of A(1), A(2), A(3) and A(4). The final value of RESULT which is returned and assigned to S is therefore 10.0.

The function SUM can be used to sum the components of a vector with any bounds. Ada thus overcomes one of the problems of original

Pascal which insists that array parameters have static bounds. Of course, an Ada function could have a constrained array type as a formal parameter. However, remember that we cannot apply the constraint in the parameter list using a subtype indication as in

function SUM_6(A: VECTOR(1 .. 6)) **return** REAL   -- illegal

but must use the name of a constrained array type such as

type VECTOR_6 **is array** (1 .. 6) **of** REAL;

as a type mark as in

function SUM_6(A: VECTOR_6) **return** REAL

As another example consider

```
function INNER(A, B: VECTOR) return REAL is
    RESULT: REAL:= 0.0;
begin
    for I in A'RANGE loop
        RESULT:= RESULT + A(I)*B(I);
    end loop;
    return RESULT;
end INNER;
```

This computes the inner product of the two vectors A and B by adding together the sum of the products of corresponding components. This is our first example of a function with more than one parameter. Such a function is called by following the function name by a list of the expressions giving the values of the actual parameters separated by commas and in brackets. The order of evaluation of the actual parameters is not defined.
So

```
V: VECTOR(1 .. 3):= (1.0, 2.0, 3.0);
W: VECTOR(1 .. 3):= (2.0, 3.0, 4.0);
R: REAL;
...
R:= INNER(V, W);
```

results in R being assigned the value

$1.0 * 2.0 + 2.0 * 3.0 + 3.0 * 4.0 = 20.0$

Note that the function INNER is not written well since it does not check that the bounds of A and B are the same. It is not symmetric with respect to A and B since I takes (or tries to take) the values of the range A'RANGE irrespective of B'RANGE. So if the array W had bounds of 0 and 2,

CONSTRAINT_ERROR would be raised on the third time round the loop. If the array W had bounds of 1 and 4 then no exception would be raised but the result might not be what we expected.

It would be nice to ensure the equality of the bounds by placing a constraint on B at the time of call but this cannot be done. The best we can do is simply check the bounds for equality inside the function body and perhaps explicitly raise CONSTRAINT_ERROR if they are not equal.

```
if A'FIRST /= B'FIRST or A'LAST /= B'LAST then
    raise CONSTRAINT_ERROR;
end if;
```

(The use of the raise statement is described in detail in Chapter 10.)

We saw above that a formal parameter can be of an unconstrained array type. In a similar way the result of a function can be an array whose bounds are not known until the function is called. The result type can be an unconstrained array and the bounds are then obtained from the expression in the appropriate return statement.

As an example the following function returns a vector which has the same bounds as the parameter but whose component values are in the reverse order

```
function REV(X: VECTOR) return VECTOR is
    R: VECTOR(X'RANGE);
begin
    for I in X'RANGE loop
        R(I):= X(X'FIRST+X'LAST−I);
    end loop;
    return R;
end REV;
```

The variable R is declared to be of type VECTOR with the same bounds as X. Note how the loop reverses the value. The result takes the bounds of the expression R. Note that we have called the function REV rather than REVERSE; this is because **reverse** is a reserved word.

If a function returns a record or array value then a component can be immediately selected, indexed or sliced as appropriate without assigning the value to a variable. So we could write

```
REV(Y)(I)
```

which denotes the component indexed by I of the array returned by the call of REV.

It should be noted that a parameterless function call, like a parameterless procedure call, has no brackets. There is therefore a possible ambiguity between calling a function with one parameter and indexing the result of a parameterless call; such an ambiguity could be resolved by, for example, renaming the functions as will be described in Chapter 8.

Exercise 7.1

1   Write a function EVEN which returns TRUE or FALSE according to
        whether its INTEGER parameter is even or odd.

2   Rewrite the factorial function so that the parameter may be
        positive or zero but not negative. Remember that the value of
        FACTORIAL(0) is to be 1. Use the subtype NATURAL introduced in
        Section 4.5.

3   Write a function OUTER that forms the outer product of two
        vectors. The outer product C of two vectors A and B is a matrix
        such that $C_{ij} = A_i \cdot B_j$.

4   Write a function MAKE_COLOUR which takes an array of values of
        type PRIMARY and returns the corresponding value of type
        COLOUR. See Section 6.6. Check that MAKE_COLOUR((R, Y)) =
        ORANGE.

5   Write a function VALUE which takes a parameter of type
        ROMAN_NUMBER and returns the equivalent integer value. See
        Exercise 6.4(**2**).

6   Write a function MAKE_UNIT that takes a single parameter N and
        returns a unit $N \times N$ real matrix. Use the function to declare a
        constant unit $N \times N$ matrix. See Exercise 6.3(**3**).

7   Write a function GCD to return the greatest common divisor of
        two nonnegative integers. Use Euclid's algorithm that

$$\gcd (x, y) = \gcd (y, x \bmod y) \quad y \neq 0$$
$$\gcd (x, 0) = x$$

        Write the function using recursion and then rewrite it using a loop
        statement.

8   Rewrite the function INNER to use sliding semantics so that it
        works providing the arrays have the same length. Raise
        CONSTRAINT_ERROR (as outlined above) if the arrays do not
        match.

7.2 Operators

In the last section we carefully stated that a function body commenced with
the reserved word **function** followed by the designator of the function. In
all the examples of the last section the designator was in fact an identifier.

However, it can also be a character string provided that the string is one of the following language operators in double quotes

and	or	xor		
=	<	<=	>	>=
+	–	&	abs	not
*	/	mod	rem	**

In such a case the function defines a new meaning of the operator concerned. As an example we can rewrite the function INNER of the last section as an operator.

```
function "*" (A, B: VECTOR) return REAL is
    RESULT: REAL:= 0.0;
begin
    for I in A'RANGE loop
        RESULT:= RESULT + A(I)*B(I);
    end loop;
    return RESULT;
end "*";
```

We call this new function by the normal syntax of uses of the operator "*". Thus instead of

```
R:= INNER(V, W);
```

we now write

```
R:= V*W;
```

This meaning of "*" is distinguished from the existing meanings of integer and real multiplication by the context provided by the types of the actual parameters V and W and the type required by R.

The giving of several meanings to an operator is another instance of overloading which we have already met with enumeration literals. The rules for the overloading of subprograms in general are discussed later in this chapter. It suffices to say at this point that any ambiguity can usually be resolved by qualification. Overloading of predefined operators is not new. It has existed in most programming languages for the past thirty years. What is new is the ability to define additional overloadings and indeed the use of the term 'overloading' is itself relatively new.

We can now see that the predefined meanings of all operators are as if there were a series of functions with declarations such as

```
function "+" (LEFT, RIGHT: INTEGER) return INTEGER;
function "<" (LEFT, RIGHT: INTEGER) return BOOLEAN;
function "<" (LEFT, RIGHT: BOOLEAN) return BOOLEAN;
```

Moreover, every time we declare a new type, new overloadings of some operators such as "=" and "<" may be created.

Although we can add new meanings to operators we cannot change the syntax of the call. Thus the number of parameters of "*" must always be two and the precedence cannot be changed and so on. The operators "+" and "−" are unusual in that a new definition can have either one parameter or two parameters according to whether it is to be called as a unary or binary operator. Thus the function SUM could be rewritten as

```
function "+" (A: VECTOR) return REAL is
    RESULT: REAL:= 0.0;
begin
    for I in A'RANGE loop
        RESULT:= RESULT + A(I);
    end loop;
    return RESULT;
end "+";
```

and we would then write

```
S:= +V;
```

rather than

```
S:= SUM(V);
```

Function bodies whose designators are operators often contain interesting examples of uses of the operator being overloaded. Thus the body of "*" contains a use of "*" in A(I)*B(I). There is, of course, no ambiguity since the expressions A(I) and B(I) are of type REAL whereas our new overloading is for type VECTOR. Sometimes there is the risk of accidental recursion. This particularly applies if we try to replace an existing meaning rather than add a new one.

Apart from the operator "=" there are no special rules regarding the types of the operands and results of new overloadings. Thus a new overloading of "<" need not return a BOOLEAN result. On the other hand, the operator "=" can only be given new overloadings which return a value of type BOOLEAN and then only under special circumstances which will be described in Chapter 9. Note that "/=" may never be explicitly redeclared – it always takes its meaning from "=".

The membership tests **in** and **not in** and the short circuit forms **and then** and **or else** cannot be given new meanings. That is why we said in Section 4.9 that they were not technically classed as operators.

Finally note that in the case of operators represented by reserved words, the characters in the string can be in either case. Thus a new overloading of **or** can be declared as "or" or "OR" or even "Or".

Exercise 7.2

1   Write a function "<" that operates on two Roman numbers and compares them according to their corresponding numeric values. That is, so that "CCL" <"CCXC". Use the function VALUE of Exercise 7.1(**5**).

2   Write functions "+" and "∗" to add and multiply two values of type COMPLEX. See Exercise 6.7(**2**).

3   Write a function "<" to test whether a value of type PRIMARY is in a set represented by a value of type COLOUR. See Section 6.6.

4   Write a function "<=" to test whether one value of type COLOUR is a subset of another.

5   Write a function "<" to compare two values of the type DATE of Section 6.7.

7.3 Procedures

The other form of subprogram is a procedure; a procedure is called as a statement. We have seen many examples of procedure calls where there are no parameters such as WORK; PARTY; ACTION; and so on.

The body of a procedure is very similar to that of a function. The differences are

- a procedure starts with **procedure**,

- its name must be an identifier,

- it does not return a result,

- the parameters may be of three different modes **in**, **out** or **in out**.

The mode of a parameter is indicated by following the colon in the parameter specification by **in** or by **out** or by **in out**. If the mode is omitted then it is taken to be **in**. In the case of functions the only allowed mode is **in**; the examples earlier in this chapter omitted **in** but could have been written for instance, as

```
function SQRT(X: in REAL) return REAL;
function "∗" (A, B: in VECTOR) return REAL;
```

The effect of the three modes is best summarized by quoting the *LRM* (Section 6.2).

in   The formal parameter is a constant and permits only reading of the value of the associated actual parameter.

in out   The formal parameter is a variable and permits both reading and updating of the value of the associated actual parameter.

out   The formal parameter is a variable and permits updating of the value of the associated actual parameter.

As a simple example of the modes **in** and **out** consider

```
procedure ADD(A, B: in INTEGER; C: out INTEGER) is
begin
    C:= A+B;
end ADD;
```

with

```
P, Q: INTEGER;
...
ADD(2+P, 37, Q);
```

On calling ADD, the expressions 2+P and 37 are evaluated (in any order) and assigned to the formals A and B which behave as constants. The value of A+B is then assigned to the formal variable C. On return the value of C is assigned to the variable Q. Thus it is (more or less) as if we had written

```
declare
    A: constant INTEGER:= 2+P;      −− in
    B: constant INTEGER:= 37;       −− in
    C: INTEGER;                     −− out
begin
    C:= A+B;                        −− body
    Q:= C;                          −− out
end;
```

As an example of the mode **in out** consider

```
procedure INCREMENT(X: in out INTEGER) is
begin
    X:= X+1;
end;
```

with

```
I: INTEGER;
...
INCREMENT(I);
```

On calling INCREMENT, the value of I is assigned to the formal variable X. The value of X is then incremented. On return, the final value of X is assigned to the actual parameter I. So it is rather as if we had written

```
declare
    X: INTEGER:= I;
begin
    X:= X+1;
    I:= X;
end;
```

For any scalar type (such as INTEGER) the modes correspond simply to copying the value **in** at the call or **out** upon return or both in the case of **in out**.

If the mode is **in** then the actual parameter may be any expression of the appropriate type or subtype. If the mode is **out** or **in out** then the actual parameter must be a variable. The identity of such a variable is determined when the procedure is called and cannot change during the call.

Suppose we had

```
I: INTEGER;
A: array (1 .. 10) of INTEGER;
procedure SILLY(X: in out INTEGER) is
begin
    I:= I+1;
    X:= X+1;
end;
```

then the statements

```
A(5):= 1;
I:= 5;
SILLY(A(I));
```

result in A(5) becoming 2, I becoming 6, but A(6) is not affected.

If a parameter is a composite type (such as an array or record) then the mechanism of copying, described above, may be used but alternatively an implementation may use a reference mechanism in which the formal parameter provides direct access to the actual parameter. A program which depends on the particular mechanism is erroneous. An example of such a program is given in the exercises at the end of this section. Note that because a formal array parameter takes its bounds from the actual parameter, the bounds are always copied in at the start even in the case of an **out** parameter. Of course, for simplicity, an implementation could always copy in the whole array anyway.

We now discuss the question of constraints on parameters.

In the case of scalar parameters the situation is as expected from the copying model. For an **in** or **in out** parameter any constraint on the formal must be satisfied by the actual at the beginning of the call. Conversely for an **in out** or **out** parameter any constraint on the variable which is the actual parameter must be satisfied by the value of the formal parameter upon return from the subprogram.

In the case of arrays the situation is somewhat different. If the formal parameter is a constrained array type, the bounds of the actual must be identical; it is not enough for the number of components in each dimension to be the same; the parameter mechanism is more rigorous than assignment. If, on the other hand, the formal parameter is an unconstrained array type, then, as we have seen, it takes its bounds from those of the actual. The foregoing applies irrespective of the mode of the array parameter. Similar rules apply to function results; if the result is a constrained array type then the expression in a return statement must have the same bounds. As an aside, one consequence of the parameter and result mechanism being more rigorous than assignment is that array aggregates with **others** are allowed as actual parameters and in return statements. On the other hand, as we saw in Section 6.3, they are not generally allowed in an assignment statement unless qualified.

In the case of the simple records we have discussed so far there are no constraints and so there is nothing to say. The parameter mechanism for other types will be discussed when they are introduced.

We stated above that an actual parameter corresponding to a formal **out** or **in out** parameter must be a variable. This includes the possibility of the actual parameter in turn being a formal parameter of some outer subprogram; but naturally an **out** parameter cannot be an actual parameter to a formal **in out** (or **in**) parameter because otherwise there might (will) be an attempt to read the **out** parameter.

A further possibility is that an actual parameter can also be a type conversion of a variable provided, of course, that the conversion is allowed. As an example, since conversion is allowed between any numeric types, we can write

```
R: REAL;
...
INCREMENT(INTEGER(R));
```

If R initially had the value 2.3, it would be converted to the integer value 2 incremented to give 3 and then on return converted back to 3.0 and assigned to R.

This conversion of **in out** or **out** parameters is particularly useful with arrays. Suppose we write a library of subprograms applying to our type VECTOR and then acquire from someone else some subprograms written to apply to the type ROW of Section 6.2. The types ROW and VECTOR are essentially the same; it just so happened that the authors used different names. Array type conversion allows us to use both sets of subprograms without having to change the type names systematically.

As a final example consider the following

```
procedure QUADRATIC(A, B, C: in REAL; ROOT_1, ROOT_2:
                        out REAL; OK: out BOOLEAN) is
    D: constant REAL:= B**2−4.0*A*C;
begin
    if D<0.0 or A=0.0 then
        OK:= FALSE;
        return;
    end if;
    ROOT_1:= (−B+SQRT(D)) / (2.0*A);
    ROOT_2:= (−B−SQRT(D)) / (2.0*A);
    OK:= TRUE;
end QUADRATIC;
```

The procedure QUADRATIC attempts to solve the equation

$$ax^2 + bx + c = 0$$

If the roots are real they are returned via the parameters ROOT_1 and ROOT_2 and OK is set to TRUE. If the roots are complex (D<0.0) or the equation degenerates (A=0.0) then OK is set to FALSE.

Note the use of the return statement. Since this is a procedure there is no result to be returned and so the word **return** is not followed by an expression. It just updates the **out** or **in out** parameters as necessary and returns control back to where the procedure was called. Note also that unlike a function we can 'run' into the **end**; this is equivalent to obeying **return**.

The reader will note that if OK is set to FALSE then no value is assigned to the **out** parameters ROOT_1 and ROOT_2. The copy rule for scalars then implies that the corresponding actual parameters become undefined. In practice, junk values are presumably assigned to the actual parameters and this could possibly raise CONSTRAINT_ERROR if an actual parameter were constrained. This is probably bad practice and so it might be better to assign safe values such as 0.0 to the roots just in case. (In examples like this, the **out** mechanism does not seem so satisfactory as the simple reference mechanism of Algol 68 or Pascal.)

The procedure could be used in a sequence such as

```
declare
    L, M, N: REAL;
    P, Q: REAL;
    STATUS: BOOLEAN;
begin
    -- sets values into L, M and N
    QUADRATIC(L, M, N, P, Q, STATUS);
    if STATUS then
        -- roots are in P and Q
    else
        -- fails
    end if;
end;
```

This is a good moment to emphasize the point made in Section 4.7 that it is often better to introduce our own two-valued enumeration type rather than use the predefined type BOOLEAN. The above example would be clearer if we had declared

```
type ROOTS is (REAL_ROOTS, COMPLEX_ROOTS);
```

with other appropriate alterations.

We conclude this section by emphasizing that an **out** parameter cannot be treated as a proper variable since it cannot be read. Thus the statements of the above example could not be recast in the form

```
begin
    OK:= D>=0.0 and A/=0.0;
    if not OK then
        return;
```

```
        end if;
        ROOT_1:= ... ;
        ROOT_2:= ... ;
    end QUADRATIC;
```

because the Boolean expression **not** OK attempts to read the **out** parameter OK.

An exception to this rule is that the bounds of an **out** array can be read even though the components cannot. Remember that a formal array always takes its bounds from the actual array. A similar situation applies to discriminants of records which we will meet in Chapter 11.

Exercise 7.3

1   Write a procedure SWAP to interchange the values of the two real parameters.

2   Rewrite the function REV of Section 7.1 as a procedure with a single parameter. Use it to reverse an array R of type ROW.

3   Why is the following erroneous?

```
        A: VECTOR(1 .. 1);

        procedure P(V: VECTOR) is
        begin
            A(1):= V(1)+V(1);
            A(1):= V(1)+V(1);
        end;
        ...
        A(1):= 1.0;
        P(A);
```

4   Draw up a table showing what modes of formal parameter of an outer procedure are possible as actual parameters of various modes of a call of another procedure.

7.4 Named and default parameters

The forms of subprogram call we have been using so far have given the actual parameters in positional order. As with aggregates we can also use the named notation in which the formal parameter name is also supplied; the parameters do not then have to be in order.

So we could write

```
QUADRATIC(A => L, B => M, C => N,
                    ROOT_1 => P, ROOT_2 => Q, OK => STATUS);
INCREMENT(X => I);
ADD(C => Q, A => 2+P, B => 37);
```

We could even write

```
INCREMENT(X => X);
```

the scopes do not interfere.

This notation can also be used with functions

```
F:= FACTORIAL(N => 4);
S:= SQRT(X => T+0.5);
R:= INNER(B => W, A => V);
```

The named notation cannot, however, be used with operators called with the usual infixed syntax (such as V*W) because there is clearly no convenient place to put the names of the formal parameters.

As with record aggregates, the named and positional notations can be mixed and any positional parameters must come first and in their correct order. However, unlike record aggregates, each parameter must be given individually and **others** may not be used. So we could write

```
QUADRATIC(L, M, N,
              ROOT_1 => P, ROOT_2 => Q, OK => STATUS);
```

The named notation leads into the topic of default parameters. It sometimes happens that one or more **in** parameters usually take the same value on each call; we can given a default expression in the subprogram specification and then omit it from the call.

Consider the problem of ordering a dry martini in the USA. One is faced with choices described by the following enumeration types

```
type SPIRIT is (GIN, VODKA);
type STYLE is (ON_THE_ROCKS, STRAIGHT_UP);
type TRIMMING is (OLIVE, TWIST);
```

The standard default expressions can then be given in a procedure specification thus

```
procedure DRY_MARTINI(BASE: SPIRIT:= GIN;
                      HOW: STYLE:= ON_THE_ROCKS;
                      PLUS: TRIMMING:= OLIVE);
```

Typical calls might be

```
DRY_MARTINI(HOW => STRAIGHT_UP);
DRY_MARTINI(VODKA, PLUS => TWIST);
DRY_MARTINI;
DRY_MARTINI(GIN, STRAIGHT_UP);
```

The first call uses the named notation; we get gin, straight up plus olive. The second call mixes the positional and named notations; as soon as a parameter is omitted the named notation must be used. The third call illustrates that all parameters can be omitted. The final call shows that a parameter can, of course, be supplied even if it happens to take the same value as the default expression; in this case it avoids using the named form for the second parameter.

Note that default expressions can only be given for **in** parameters. They cannot be given for operators but they can be given for functions designated by identifiers. Such a default expression (like a default expression for an initial value in a record type declaration) is only evaluated when required; that is, it is evaluated each time the subprogram is called and no corresponding actual parameter is supplied. Hence the default value need not be the same on each call although it usually will be. Default expressions are widely used in the standard input–output package to provide default formats.

Default expressions illustrate the subtle rule that a parameter specification of the form

        P, Q: **in** INTEGER:= E

is strictly equivalent to

        P: **in** INTEGER:= E;
        Q: **In** INTEGER:= E

(The reader will recall a similar rule for object declarations; it also applies to record components.) As a consequence, the default expression is evaluated for each omitted parameter in a call. This does not usually matter but would be significant if the expression E included a function call with side effects.

Exercise 7.4

1   Write a function ADD which returns the sum of the two integer parameters and takes a default value of 1 for the second parameter. How many different ways can it be called to return N+1 where N is the first actual parameter?

2   Rewrite the specification of DRY_MARTINI to reflect that you prefer VODKA at weekends. Hint: declare a function to return your favourite spirit according to the global variable TODAY.

7.5 Overloading

We saw in Section 7.2 how new meanings could be given to existing language operators. This overloading applies to subprograms in general.

A subprogram will overload an existing meaning rather than hide it, provided that its specification is sufficiently different. Hiding will occur if the order and base types of the parameters and result (if any) are the same.

A procedure cannot hide a function and vice versa. Note that the names of the parameters, their mode and the presence or absence of default expressions do not matter. Two or more overloaded subprograms may be declared in the same declarative part.

Subprograms and enumeration literals can overload each other. In fact an enumeration literal is formally thought of as a parameterless function with a result of the enumeration type. There are two classes of uses of identifers – the overloadable ones and the non-overloadable ones. At any point an identifier either refers to a single entity of the non-overloadable class or to one or many of the overloadable class. A declaration of one class hides the other class and cannot occur in the same declaration list.

As we have seen, ambiguities arising from overloading can be resolved by qualification. This was necessary when the operator "<" was used with the strings in Section 6.4. As a further example consider the British Channel Islands; the larger three are Guernsey, Jersey and Alderney. There are woollen garments named after each island.

```
type GARMENT is (GUERNSEY, JERSEY, ALDERNEY);
```

and breeds of cattle named after two of them (the Alderney breed became extinct as a consequence of the Second World War).

```
type COW is (GUERNSEY, JERSEY);
```

and we can imagine (just) shops that sell both garments and cows according to

```
procedure SELL(G: GARMENT);
procedure SELL(C: COW);
```

Although

```
SELL(ALDERNEY);
```

is not ambiguous

```
SELL(JERSEY);
```

is, since we cannot tell which subprogram is being called. We must write for example

```
SELL(COW'(JERSEY));
```

We conclude by noting that ambiguities typically arise only when there are several overloadings. In the case here both SELL and JERSEY are overloaded; in the example in Section 6.4 both the operator "<" and the literals 'X' and 'L' were overloaded.

Exercise 7.5

1   How else could SELL(JERSEY); be made unambiguous?

7.6 Declarations, scopes and visibility

We said earlier that it is sometimes necessary or just convenient to give a subprogram specification on its own without the body. The specification is then followed by a semicolon and is known as a subprogram declaration. A complete subprogram, which always includes the full specification, is known as a subprogram body.

Subprogram declarations and bodies must, like other declarations, occur in a declarative part and a subprogram declaration must be followed by the corresponding body in the same declarative part.

An example of where it is necessary to use a subprogram declaration occurs with mutually recursive procedures. Suppose we wish to declare two procedures F and G which call each other. Because of the rule regarding linear elaboration of declarations we cannot write the call of F in the body of G until after F has been declared and vice versa. Clearly this is impossible if we just write the bodies because one must come second. However, we can write

```
procedure F( ... );      -- declaration of F

procedure G( ... ) is    -- body of G
begin
     F( ... );
end G;

procedure F( ... ) is    -- body of F repeats
begin                    -- its specification
     G( ... );
end F;
```

and then all is well.

If the specification is repeated then it must be given in full and the two must be the same. Technically we say that the two specifications must conform. Some slight variation is allowed. A numeric literal can be replaced by another numeric literal with the same value; an identifier can be replaced by a dotted name as described later in this section; the lexical spacing can be different. It is worth noting that the key reason for not allowing subtype indications in parameter specifications is to remove any problem regarding conformance since there is then no question of evaluating constraint expressions twice and possibly having different results because of side effects. No corresponding question arises with default expressions (which are of course written out twice) since they are only evaluated when the subprogram is called.

Another important case, where we have to write a subprogram declaration as well as a body, occurs in the next chapter when we discuss packages. Even if not always necessary, it is sometimes clearer to write subprogram declarations as well as bodies. An example might be in the case where many subprogram bodies occur together. The subprogram declarations could then be placed together at the head of the declarative part in order to act as a summary of the bodies to come.

Subprogram bodies and other declarations must not be mixed up in an arbitrary way. A body cannot, for example, be followed by object, type and number declarations. This ensures that small declarations are not 'lost' in between large bodies. The rules will be given in more detail when we discuss packages in the next chapter.

Since subprograms occur in declarative parts and themselves contain declarative parts they may be textually nested without limit. The normal hiding rules applicable to blocks described in Section 4.2 also apply to declarations in subprograms. (The only complication concerns overloading as discussed in the previous section.) Consider

```
procedure P is
    I: INTEGER:= 0;

    procedure Q is
        K: INTEGER:= I;
        I: INTEGER;
        J: INTEGER;
    begin
        ...
    end Q;
    ...
end P;
```

Just as for the example in Section 4.2, the inner I hides the outer one and so the outer I is not visible inside the procedure Q after the declaration of the inner I.

However, we can always refer to the outer I by the so-called dotted notation, in which it is prefixed by the name of the unit immediately containing its declaration followed by a dot. So within Q we can refer to the outer I as P.I and so, for example, we could initialize J by writing

```
J: INTEGER:= P.I;
```

If the prefix is itself hidden then it can always be written the same way. Thus the inner I could be referred to as P.Q.I.

An object declared in a block cannot usually be referred to in this way since a block does not normally have a name. However, a block can be named in a similar way to a loop as shown in the following

```
OUTER:
declare
    I: INTEGER:= 0;
```

```
      begin
          ...
          declare
              K: INTEGER:= I;
              I: INTEGER;
              J: INTEGER:= OUTER.I;
          begin
              ...
          end;
      end OUTER;
```

Here the outer block has the identifier OUTER. Unlike subprograms, but like loops, the identifier has to be repeated after the matching **end**. Naming the block enables us to initialize the inner declaration of J with the value of the outer I.

Within a loop it is possible to refer to a hidden loop parameter in the same way. We could even rewrite the example in Section 6.1 of assigning zero to the elements of AA as

```
      L:
      for I in AA'RANGE(1) loop
          for I in AA'RANGE(2) loop
              AA(L.I, I):= 0.0;
          end loop;
      end loop L;
```

although one would be a little crazy to do so!

It should be noted that the dotted form can always be used even if it is not necessary.

This notation can also be applied to operators and character literals. Thus the variable RESULT declared inside "*" can be referred to as "*".RESULT. And equally if "*" were declared inside a block B then it could be referred to as B."*". If it is called with this form of name then the normal function call must be used

```
      R:= B."*"(V, W);
```

Indeed, the functional form can always be used as in

```
      R:= "*"(V, W);
```

and we could then also use the named notation

```
      R:= "*"(A => V, B => W);
```

As we have seen, subprograms can alter global variables and therefore have side effects. (A side effect is one brought about other than via the parameter mechanism.) It is generally considered rather undesirable to write subprograms, especially functions, which have side effects. However, some side effects are beneficial. Any subprogram which performs input–output has a side effect on the file; a function delivering successive members of a sequence of random numbers only works because of its side effects; if we need to count how many times a function is called then we use a side effect; and so on. However, care must be taken when using functions with side effects that the program is correct since there are various circumstances in which the order of evaluation is not defined.

We conclude this section with a brief discussion of the hierarchy of **exit**, **return** and **goto** and the scopes of block and loop identifiers and labels.

A **return** statement terminates the execution of the immediately embracing subprogram. It can occur inside an inner block or inside a loop in the subprogram and therefore also terminate the loop. On the other hand an **exit** statement terminates the named or immediately embracing loop. It can also occur inside an inner block but cannot occur inside a subprogram declared in the loop and thereby also terminate the subprogram. A **goto** statement can transfer control out of a loop or block but not out of a subprogram.

As far as scope is concerned, identifiers of labels, blocks and loops behave as if they are declared at the end of the declarative part of the immediately embracing subprogram or block (or package or task body). Moreover distinct identifiers must be used for all blocks, loops and labels inside the same subprogram (or package or task body) even if some are in inner blocks. Thus two labels in the same subprogram cannot have the same identifier even if they are inside different inner blocks. This rule reduces the risk of goto statements going to the wrong label particularly when a program is amended.

Checklist 7

Parameter and result subtypes must be given by a type mark and not a subtype indication.

A function must return a result and should not run into its final **end** although a procedure can.

The order of evaluation of parameters is not defined.

A default parameter expression is only evaluated when the subprogram is called and the corresponding parameter is omitted.

The actual and formal parameters of a constrained array type must have equal bounds.

Scalar parameters are copied. The mechanism for arrays and records is not defined.

Formal parameter specifications are separated by semicolons not commas.

Chapter 8
Overall Structure

The previous chapters have described the small-scale features of Ada in considerable detail. The language presented so far corresponds to the areas addressed by languages of the 1960s and early 1970s, although Ada provides more functionality in those areas. However, we now come to the new areas which broadly speaking correspond to the concepts of data abstraction and programming in the large which were discussed in Chapter 1.

In this chapter we discuss packages (which is what Ada is all about) and the mechanisms for separate compilation. We also say a little more about scope and visibility.

8.1 Packages

One of the major problems with the traditional block structured languages, such as Algol and Pascal, is that they do not offer enough control of visibility. For example, suppose we have a stack represented by an array and a variable which indexes the current top element, a procedure PUSH to add an item and a function POP to remove an item. We might write

```
MAX: constant:= 100;
S: array (1 .. MAX) of INTEGER;
TOP: INTEGER range 0 .. MAX;
```

to represent the stack and then declare

```
procedure PUSH(X: INTEGER) is
begin
    TOP:= TOP+1;
```

```
        S(TOP):= X;
end PUSH;

function POP return INTEGER is
begin
    TOP:= TOP-1;
    return S(TOP+1);
end POP;
```

In a simple block structured language there is no way in which we can be given access to the subprograms PUSH and POP without also being given direct access to the variables S and TOP. As a consequence we cannot be forced to use the correct protocol and so be prevented from making use of knowledge of how the stack is implemented.

The Ada package overcomes this by allowing us to place a wall around a group of declarations and only permit access to those which we intend to be visible. A package actually comes in two parts: the specification which gives the interface to the outside world, and the body which gives the hidden details.

The above example should be written as

```
package STACK is                    -- specification
    procedure PUSH(X: INTEGER);
    function POP return INTEGER;
end STACK;

package body STACK is               -- body
    MAX: constant:= 100;
    S: array (1 .. MAX) of INTEGER;
    TOP: INTEGER range 0 .. MAX;

    procedure PUSH(X: INTEGER) is
    begin
        TOP:= TOP+1;
        S(TOP):= X;
    end PUSH;

    function POP return INTEGER is
    begin
        TOP:= TOP-1;
        return S(TOP+1);
    end POP;

begin                               -- initialization
    TOP:= 0;
end STACK;
```

The package specification (strictly declaration) starts with the reserved word **package**, the identifier of the package and **is**. This is then followed by declarations of the entities which are to be visible. It finishes with **end**, the identifier (optionally) and the terminating semicolon. In the example we just have the declarations of the two subprograms PUSH and POP.

The package body also starts with **package** but this is then followed by **body**, the identifier and **is**. We then have a normal declarative part, **begin**, sequence of statements, **end**, optional identifier and terminating semicolon just as in a block or subprogram body.

In the example the declarative part contains the variables which represent the stack and the bodies of PUSH and POP. The sequence of statements between **begin** and **end** is executed when the package is declared and can be used for initialization. If there is no need for an initialization sequence, the **begin** can be omitted. Indeed in this example we could equally and perhaps more naturally have performed the initialization by writing

```
TOP: INTEGER range 0 .. MAX:= 0;
```

Note that a package is itself declared and so is just one of the items in an outer declarative part (unless it is a library unit which is the outermost layer anyway).

The package illustrates another case where we need distinct subprogram declarations and bodies. Indeed we cannot put a body into a package specification. And moreover, if a package specification contains the specification of a subprogram, then the package body must contain the corresponding subprogram body. We can think of the package specification and body as being just one large declarative part with only some items visible. But, of course, a subprogram body can be declared in a package body without its specification having to be given in the package specification. Such a subprogram would be internal to the package and could only be called from within, either from other subprograms, some of which would presumably be visible, or perhaps from the initialization sequence.

The elaboration of a package body consists simply of the elaboration of the declarations inside it followed by the execution of the initialization sequence if there is one. The package continues to exist until the end of the scope in which it is declared. Entities declared inside the package have the same lifetime as the package itself. Thus the variables S and TOP can be thought of as 'own' variables in the Algol 60 sense; their values are retained between successive calls of PUSH and POP.

Packages may be declared in any declarative part such as that in a block, subprogram or indeed another package. If a package specification is declared inside another package specification then, as for subprograms, the body of one must be declared in the body of the other. But again both specification and body could be in a package body.

Apart from the rule that a package specification cannot contain bodies, it can contain any of the other kinds of declarations we have met.

Now to return to the use of our package. The package itself has a name and the entities in its visible part (the specification) can be thought of as components of the package in some sense. It is entirely natural therefore that, in order to call PUSH, we must also mention STACK. In fact the dotted notation is used. So we could write

```
declare
   package STACK is        -- specification
      ...                  -- and
      ...                  -- body
   end STACK;
begin
   ...
   STACK.PUSH(M);
   ...
   N:= STACK.POP;
   ...
end;
```

Inside the package we would call PUSH as just PUSH, but we could still write STACK.PUSH just as in the last chapter we saw how we could refer to a local variable X of procedure P as P.X. Inside the package we can refer to S or STACK.S, but outside the package MAX, S and TOP are not accessible in any way.

It would in general be painful always to have to write STACK.PUSH to call PUSH from outside. Instead we can write

```
use STACK;
```

as a sort of declaration and we may then refer to PUSH and POP directly. The use clause could follow the declaration of the specification of STACK in the same declarative part or could be in another declarative part where the package is visible. So we could write

```
declare
   use STACK;
begin
   ...
   PUSH(M);
   ...
   N:= POP;
   ...
end;
```

The use clause is like a declaration and similarly has a scope to the end of the block. Outside we would have to revert to the dotted notation. We could have an inner use clause referring to the same package – it would do no harm.

Two or more packages could be declared in the same declarative part. Generally, we could arrange all the specifications together and then all the bodies, or alternatively the corresponding specifications and bodies, could be together. Thus we could have spec A, spec B, body A, body B, or spec A, body A, spec B, body B.

The rules governing the order are simply

- linear elaboration of declarations,

- specification must precede body for same package (or subprogram),

- small items must generally precede big ones.

More precisely, the last rule is that a body can only be followed by other bodies, subprogram and package (and task) specifications (strictly declarations) or indeed use clauses. The general intent of this rule is to prevent small items from being lost among big ones; the use clause is allowed as a 'big' item (as well as a small item) because it is very convenient to follow the declaration of a package by a corresponding use clause in the same declarative part.

Of course, the specification of a package may contain things other than subprograms. Indeed, an important case is where it does not contain subprograms at all but merely a group of related variables, constants and types. In such a case the package needs no body. It does not provide any hiding properties but merely gives commonality of naming. (A body could be provided; its only purpose would be for initialization.)

As an example we could provide a package containing our type DAY and some useful related constants.

```
package DIURNAL is
    type DAY is (MON, TUE, WED, THU, FRI, SAT, SUN);
    subtype WEEKDAY is DAY range MON .. FRI;
    TOMORROW: constant array (DAY) of DAY
            := (TUE, WED, THU, FRI, SAT, SUN, MON);
    NEXT_WORK_DAY: constant array (WEEKDAY) of WEEKDAY
            := (TUE, WED, THU, FRI, MON);
end DIURNAL;
```

A final point. A subprogram cannot be called successfully during the elaboration of a declarative part if its body appears later. This did not prevent the mutual recursion of the procedures F and G in Section 7.6 because in that case the call of F actually only occurred when we executed the sequence of statements of the body of G. But it does prevent the use of a function in an initial value. So

```
function A return INTEGER;
I: INTEGER:= A;
```

is illegal, and would result in PROGRAM_ERROR being raised.

A similar rule applies to subprograms in packages. If we call a subprogram from outside a package but before the package body has been elaborated, then PROGRAM_ERROR will be raised.

Exercise 8.1

1   The sequence defined by

$$X_{n+1} = X_n.5^5 \bmod 2^{13}$$

provides a crude source of pseudo random numbers. The initial value X_0 should be an odd integer in the range 0 to 2^{13}.
Write a package RANDOM containing a procedure INIT to initialize the sequence and a function NEXT to deliver the next value in the sequence.

2   Write a package COMPLEX_NUMBERS which makes visible

- the type COMPLEX,
- a constant I = $\sqrt{-1}$,
- functions +, −, *, / acting on values of type COMPLEX.

See Exercise 7.2(**2**).

8.2 Library units

Many languages in the past have ignored the simple fact that programs are written in pieces, compiled separately and then joined together. Ada recognizes the need for separate compilation and provides two mechanisms – one top down and one bottom up.

The top down mechanism is appropriate for the development of a large coherent program which nevertheless, for various reasons, is broken down into subunits which can be compiled separately. The subunits are compiled after the unit from which they are taken. This mechanism is described in the next section.

The bottom up mechanism is appropriate for the creation of a program library where units are written for general use and consequently are written before the programs that use them. This mechanism will now be discussed in detail.

A library unit may be a subprogram specification or a package specification; the corresponding bodies are called secondary units. These units may be compiled individually or for convenience several could be submitted to the compiler together. Thus we could compile the specification and body of a package together but as we shall see it may be more convenient to compile them individually. As usual a subprogram body alone is sufficient to define the subprogram fully; it is then classed as a library unit rather than a secondary unit.

When a unit is compiled it goes into a program library. There will obviously be several such libraries according to user and project, etc. The creation and manipulation of libraries is outside the scope of this book. Once in the library, a unit can be used by any subsequently compiled unit but the using unit must indicate the dependency by a with clause.

As a simple example suppose we compile the package STACK. This package depends on no other unit and so it needs no with clause. We will compile both specification and body together so the text submitted will be

```
package STACK is
   ...
end STACK;

package body STACK is
   ...
end STACK;
```

As well as producing the object code corresponding to the package, the compiler also places in the program library the information describing the interface that the package presents to the outside world; this is of course the information in the specification.

We now suppose that we write a procedure MAIN which will use the package STACK. Our procedure MAIN is going to be the main program in the usual sense. It will have no parameters and we can imagine that it is called by some magic outside the language itself. The Ada definition does not prescribe that the main program should have the identifier MAIN; it is merely a convention which we are adopting here because it has to be called something.

The text we submit to the compiler could be

```
with STACK;
procedure MAIN is
    use STACK;
    M, N: INTEGER;
begin
    ...
    PUSH(M);
    ...
    N:= POP;
    ...
end MAIN;
```

The with clause goes before the unit so that the dependency of the unit on other units is clear at a glance. A with clause may not be embedded in an inner scope.

On encountering a with clause the compiler retrieves from the program library the information describing the interface presented by the withed unit so that it can check that the unit being compiled uses the interface correctly. Thus if procedure MAIN tried to call PUSH with the wrong number or type of parameters then this will be detected during compilation. This thorough checking between separately compiled units is a major factor in the increased productivity obtained through using Ada.

If a unit is dependent on several other units then they can go in the one with clause, or it might be a convenience to use distinct with clauses.

Thus we could write

```
with STACK, DIURNAL;
procedure MAIN is
      ...
```

or equally

```
with STACK;
with DIURNAL;
procedure MAIN is
      ...
```

For convenience we can place a use clause after a with clause. Thus

```
with STACK; use STACK;
procedure MAIN is
      ...
```

and then PUSH and POP are directly visible without more ado. A use clause in such a position can only refer to packages mentioned in the with clause.

Only direct dependencies need be given in a with clause. Thus if package P uses the facilities of package Q which in turn uses the facilities of package R, then, unless P also directly uses R, the with clause for P should mention only Q. The user of Q does not care about R and must not need to know since otherwise the hierarchy of development would be made more complicated.

Another point is that the with clause in front of a package or subprogram declaration will also apply to the body. It can, but need not, be repeated. Of course, the body may have additional dependencies which will need indicating with a with clause anyway. Dependencies which apply only to the body should not be given with the specification since otherwise the independence of the body and the specification would be reduced.

If a package specification and body are compiled separately then the body must be compiled after the specification. We say that the body is dependent on the specification. However, any unit using the package is dependent only on the specification and not the body. If the body is changed in a manner consistent with not changing the specification, any unit using the package will not need recompiling. The ability to compile specification and body separately should simplify program maintenance.

The dependencies between the specification and body of the package STACK and the procedure MAIN are illustrated by the graph in Figure 8.1.

The general rule regarding the order of compilation is simply that a unit must be compiled after all units on which it depends. Consequently, if a unit is changed and recompiled then all dependent units must also be recompiled. Any order of compilation consistent with the dependency rule is acceptable.

There is one package that need not be mentioned in a with clause. This is the package STANDARD which effectively contains the declarations

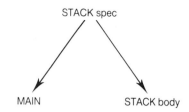

Figure 8.1   Dependencies between units.

of all the predefined types such as INTEGER and BOOLEAN and their
predefined operations. It also contains an internal package ASCII containing constants defining the control characters such as CR and LF. We now
see why the control characters were represented as ASCII.CR etc. in
Chapter 6. By writing **use** ASCII; they can, of course, just be referred
to as CR. The package STANDARD is described in more detail in
Appendix 2.

Finally there are two important rules regarding library units. They
must have distinct identifiers; they cannot be overloaded. Moreover they
cannot be operators. These rules enable an Ada program library to be
implemented quite easily on top of a basic filing system with simple
identifiers.

Exercise 8.2

1   The package D and subprograms P and Q and MAIN have correct
       with clauses as follows

specification of D	no with clause
body of D	**with** P, Q;
subprogram P	no with clause
subprogram Q	no with clause
subprogram MAIN	**with** D;

       Draw a graph showing the dependencies between the units. How
       many different orders of compilation are possible?

8.3   Subunits

In this section we introduce a further form of secondary unit known as a
subunit. The body of a package, subprogram (or task, see Chapter 14) can
be 'taken out' of an immediately embracing library unit or secondary unit
and itself compiled separately. The body in the embracing unit is then
replaced by a body stub. As an example suppose we remove the bodies of

the subprograms PUSH and POP from the package STACK. The body of STACK would then become

```
package body STACK is
    MAX: constant:= 100;
    S: array (1 .. MAX) of INTEGER;
    TOP: INTEGER range 0 .. MAX;
    procedure PUSH(X: INTEGER) is separate;      -- stub
    function POP return INTEGER is separate;     -- stub
begin
    TOP:= 0;
end STACK;
```

The removed units are termed subunits; they may then be compiled separately. They have to be preceded by **separate** followed by the name of the parent unit in brackets. Thus the subunit PUSH becomes

```
separate (STACK)
procedure PUSH(X: INTEGER) is
begin
    TOP:= TOP+1;
    S(TOP):= X;
end PUSH;
```

and similarly for POP.

In the above example the parent unit is (the body of) a library unit. The parent unit could itself be a subunit; in such a case its name must be given in full using the dotted notation starting with the ancestor library unit. Thus if R is a subunit of Q which is a subunit of P which is a library unit, then the text of R must start

```
separate (P.Q)
```

As with library units and for similar reasons, the subunits of a unit must have distinct identifiers. But, of course, this does not prevent subunits of different units having the same identifier. And again subunits cannot be operators.

A subunit is dependent on its parent (and any library units explicitly mentioned) and so must be compiled after them.

Visibility within a subunit is as at the corresponding body stub – it is exactly as if the subunit were plucked out with its environment intact (and indeed the compiler will store the relevant information on compiling the stub and retrieve it on compiling the subunit so that full type checking is maintained). As a consequence any with clause applying to the parent need not be repeated just because the subunit is compiled separately. However, it is possible to give the subunit access to additional library units by preceding it with its own with clauses (and possibly use clauses). Such clauses precede **separate**. So the text of R might commence

```
with X; use X;
separate (P.Q)
...
```

A possible reason for doing this might be if we can then remove any reference to library unit X from the parent P.Q and so reduce the dependencies. This would give us greater freedom with the order of compilation; if X were recompiled for some reason then only R would need recompiling as a consequence and not also Q.

Note that a with clause only refers to library units and never to subunits. Finally observe that several subunits or a mixture of library units, library unit bodies and subunits can be compiled together.

Exercise 8.3

1   Suppose that the package STACK is written with separate subunits PUSH and POP. Draw a graph showing the dependencies between the five units: procedure MAIN, procedure PUSH, function POP, package specification STACK, package body STACK. How many different orders of compilation are possible?

8.4   Scope and visibility

We return once more to the topic of scope and visibility. In this section we summarize the major points which will be relevant to the everyday use of Ada. For some of the fine detail, the reader is referred to the *LRM*. It is perhaps worth mentioning that the *LRM* uses the term declarative region in order to explain the visibility and scope rules. Blocks and subprograms are examples of declarative regions and the scope rules associated with them were described in Sections 4.2 and 7.6. We now have to consider the effect of the introduction of packages.

A package specification and body together constitute a single declarative region. Thus if we declare a variable X in the specification then we cannot redeclare X in the body (except of course in an inner region such as a local subprogram).

In the case of a declaration in the visible part of a package, its scope extends from the declaration to the end of the scope of the package itself. Note that if the package is inside the visible part of another package then this means that, applying the rule again, the scope extends to the end of that of the outer package and so on.

In the case of a declaration in a package body (or in the private part of a package – to be described in the next chapter), its scope extends to the end of the package body.

In the case of the simple nesting of blocks and subprograms an entity is visible throughout its scope unless hidden by another declaration. We saw in Section 7.6 how even if it was hidden it could nevertheless in general be referred to by using the dotted notation where the prefixed name is that of the unit embracing the declaration. In essence, writing the name of the embracing unit makes the entity visible.

In the case of an entity declared in a package the same rules apply inside the package. But outside the package it is not visible unless we write the package name or alternatively write a use clause.

The identifiers visible at a given point are those visible before considering any use clauses plus those made visible by use clauses.

The basic rule is that an identifier in a package is made visible by a use clause provided the same identifier is not also in another package with a use clause and also provided that the identifier is not already visible anyway. If these conditions are not met then the identifier is not made visible and we have to continue to use the dotted notation.

A slightly different rule applies if all the identifiers are subprograms or enumeration literals. In this case they all overload each other unless of course their specifications clash (could hide each other) in which case they are not made visible. Thus an identifier made visible by a use clause can never hide another identifier although it may overload it.

The general purpose of these rules is to ensure that adding a use clause cannot invalidate an existing piece of text. We have only given a brief sketch here and the reader is probably confused. In practice there should be no problems since the Ada compiler will, we hope, indicate any ambiguities or other difficulties and things can always be put right by adding a qualifier or using a dotted name.

There are other rules regarding record component names, subprogram parameters and so on which are as expected. For example there is no conflict between an identifier of a record component and another use of the identifier outside the type definition itself. The reason is that although the scopes may overlap, the regions of visibility do not. Consider

```
declare
    type R is
        record
            I: INTEGER;
        end record;
    type S is
        record
            I: INTEGER;
        end record;
    AR: R;
    AS: S;
    I: INTEGER;
begin
    ...
    I:= AR.I+AS.I;    -- legal
    ...
end;
```

The scope of the I in the type R extends from the component declaration until the end of the block. However, its visibility is confined to within the declaration of R except that it is made visible by the use of AR in the selected component. Hence no conflict.

Similar considerations prevent conflict in named aggregates and in named parameters in subprogram calls.

Observe that a use clause can mention several packages and that it may be necessary for a package name to be given as a selected component itself. A use clause does not take effect until the semicolon. Suppose we have nested packages

```
package P1 is
    package P2 is
        ...
    end P2;
    ...
end P1;
```

then outside P1 we could write

```
use P1; use P2;
```

or

```
use P1, P1.P2;
```

but not

```
use P1, P2;
```

We could even write **use** P1.P2; to gain visibility of the entities in P2 but not those in P1 – however, this seems an odd thing to do. Remember, moreover, that a use clause following a with clause can only refer to packages directly mentioned in the with clause.

Earlier we mentioned the existence of the package STANDARD. This contains all the predefined entities but moreover every library unit should be thought of as being declared inside and at the end of STANDARD. This explains why an explicit use clause for STANDARD is not required. Another important consequence is that, provided we do not hide the name STANDARD by redefining it, a library unit P can always be referred to as STANDARD.P. Hence, in the absence of anonymous blocks, loops and overloading, every identifier in the program has a unique name commencing with STANDARD. Thus we could even pedantically refer to the predefined operators in this way

```
FOUR: INTEGER:= STANDARD."+" (2, 2);
```

It is probably good advice not to redefine STANDARD!

8.5   Renaming

Certain entities can be renamed. As an example we can write

```
declare
    procedure SPUSH(X: INTEGER) renames STACK.PUSH;
    function SPOP return INTEGER renames STACK.POP;
```

```
begin
    ...
    SPUSH(M);
    ...
    N:= SPOP;
    ...
end;
```

A possible reason for doing this is to resolve ambiguities and yet avoid the use of the full dotted notation. Thus if we had two packages with a procedure PUSH (with an INTEGER parameter) then the use clause would be of no benefit since the full name would still be needed to resolve the ambiguity.

There is also a strong school of thought that use clauses are bad for you. Consider the case of a large program with many library units and suppose that the unit we are in has withed several packages. If we have use clauses for all these packages then it is not clear from which package an arbitrary identifier has been imported. In the absence of use clauses we have to use the full dotted notation and the origin of everything is then obvious. However, it is also commonly accepted that long meaningful identifiers should be generally used. A long meaningful package name followed by the long meaningful name of an entity in the package is often too much. However, we can introduce an abbreviation by renaming such as

V: REAL **renames** AEROPLANE_DATA.CURRENT_VELOCITY;

and then compactly use V in local computation and yet still have the full identification available in the text of the current unit.

As another example suppose we wish to use both the function INNER and the equivalent operator "∗" of Chapter 7 without declaring two distinct subprograms. We can write

function "∗" (X, Y: VECTOR) **return** REAL **renames** INNER;

or

function INNER(X, Y: VECTOR) **return** REAL **renames** "∗";

according to which we declare first.

Renaming is also useful in the case of library units. Thus we might wish to have two or more overloaded subprograms and yet compile them separately. This cannot be done directly since library units must have distinct names. However, differently named library units could be renamed so that the user sees the required effect. The restriction that a library unit cannot be an operator can similarly be overcome. The same tricks can be done with subunits.

If a subprogram is renamed, the number, base types and modes of the parameters (and result if a function) must be the same. This informa-tion can be used to resolve overloadings (as in the example of "∗") and, of course, this matching occurs during compilation. Rather strangely, any constraints on the parameters or result in the new subprogram are ignored; those on the original still apply.

On the other hand, the presence, absence or value of default parameters do not have to match. Renaming can be used to introduce, change or delete default expressions; the default parameters associated with the new name are those shown in the renaming declaration. Hence renaming cannot be used as a trick to give an operator default values. Similarly, parameter names do not have to match but naturally the new names must be used for named parameters of calls of the new subprogram.

The unification of subprograms and enumeration literals is further illustrated by the fact that an enumeration literal can be renamed as a parameterless function with the appropriate result. For example

```
function TEN return ROMAN_DIGIT renames 'X';
```

Renaming can also be used to partially evaluate the name of an object. Suppose we have an array of records such as the array PEOPLE in Section 6.7 and that we wish to scan the array and print out the dates of birth in numerical form. We could write

```
for I in PEOPLE'RANGE loop
    PUT(PEOPLE(I).BIRTH.DAY); PUT(":");
    PUT(MONTH_NAME'POS(PEOPLE(I).BIRTH.MONTH)+1);
    PUT(":");
    PUT(PEOPLE(I).BIRTH.YEAR);
end loop;
```

It is clearly painful to repeat PEOPLE(I).BIRTH each time. We could declare a variable D of type DATE and copy PEOPLE(I).BIRTH into it, but this would be very wasteful if the record were at all large. A better technique is to use renaming thus

```
for I in PEOPLE'RANGE loop
    declare
        D: DATE renames PEOPLE(I).BIRTH;
    begin
        PUT(D.DAY); PUT(":");
        PUT(MONTH_NAME'POS(D.MONTH)+1);
        PUT(":");
        PUT(D.YEAR);
    end;
end loop;
```

Beware that renaming does not correspond to text substitution – the identity of the object is determined when the renaming occurs. If any variable in the name subsequently changes then the identity of the object does not change. Any constraints implied by the type mark in the renaming declaration are ignored; those of the original object still apply.

Renaming can be applied to objects (variables and constants), components of composite objects (including slices of arrays), exceptions (see Chapter 10), subprograms and packages. In the case of a package it takes the simple form

package P **renames** STACK;

Although renaming does not directly apply to types an almost identical effect can be achieved by the use of a subtype

subtype S **is** T;

or in order to overcome a lack of standardization even

subtype COLOR **is** COLOUR;

Finally note that renaming does not hide the old name nor does it ever introduce a new entity; it just provides another way of referring to an existing entity (that is why new constraints in a renaming declaration are ignored). Renaming can be very useful at times but the indiscriminate use of renaming should be avoided since the aliases introduced make program proving much more difficult.

Exercise 8.5

1   Declare a renaming of the literal MON of type DAY from the package DIURNAL of Section 8.1.

2   Declare a renaming of DIURNAL.NEXT_WORK_DAY.

3   Declare PETS as a renaming of the relevant part of the second FARMYARD of Section 6.5.

Checklist 8

Variables inside a package exist between calls of subprograms of the package.

A library unit must be compiled after other library units mentioned in its with clause.

A subunit must be compiled after its parent.

A body must be compiled after the corresponding specification.

A package specification and body form a single declarative region.

Do not redefine STANDARD.

Renaming is not text substitution.

Chapter 9
Private Types

We have seen how packages enable us to hide internal objects from the user of a package. Private types enable us to hide the details of the construction of a type from a user.

9.1   Normal private types

In Exercise 8.1(**2**) we wrote a package COMPLEX_NUMBERS providing a type COMPLEX, a constant I and some operations on the type. The specification of the package was

```
package COMPLEX_NUMBERS is
    type COMPLEX is
        record
            RL, IM: REAL;
        end record;

    I: constant COMPLEX:= (0.0, 1.0);

    function "+" (X: COMPLEX) return COMPLEX;        -- unary +
    function "−" (X: COMPLEX) return COMPLEX;        -- unary −

    function "+" (X, Y: COMPLEX) return COMPLEX;
    function "−" (X, Y: COMPLEX) return COMPLEX;
    function "*" (X, Y: COMPLEX) return COMPLEX;
    function "/" (X, Y: COMPLEX) return COMPLEX;
end;
```

The trouble with this formulation is that the user can make use of the fact that the complex numbers are held in cartesian representation.

Rather than always using the complex operator "+", the user could also write things like

    C.IM:= C.IM + 1.0;

rather than the more abstract

    C:= C + I;

In fact, with the above package, the user has to make use of the representation in order to construct values of the type.

We might wish to prevent use of knowledge of the representation so that we could change the representation to perhaps polar form at a later date and know that the user's program would still be correct. We can do this with a private type. Consider

```
package COMPLEX_NUMBERS is
    type COMPLEX is private;
    I: constant COMPLEX;
    function "+" (X: COMPLEX) return COMPLEX;
    function "−" (X: COMPLEX) return COMPLEX;
    function "+" (X, Y: COMPLEX) return COMPLEX;
    function "−" (X, Y: COMPLEX) return COMPLEX;
    function "*" (X, Y: COMPLEX) return COMPLEX;
    function "/" (X, Y: COMPLEX) return COMPLEX;
    function CONS(R, I: REAL) return COMPLEX;
    function RL_PART(X: COMPLEX) return REAL;
    function IM_PART(X: COMPLEX) return REAL;

private
    type COMPLEX is
        record
            RL, IM: REAL;
        end record;
    I: constant COMPLEX:= (0.0, 1.0);
end;
```

The part of the package specification before the reserved word **private** is the visible part and gives the information available externally to the package. The type COMPLEX is declared to be private. This means that outside the package nothing is known of the details of the type. The only operations available are assignment, = and /= plus those added by the writer of the package as subprograms specified in the visible part.

We may also declare constants of a private type such as I, in the visible part. The initial value cannot be given in the visible part because the details of the type are not yet known. Hence we just state that I is a constant; we call it a deferred constant.

After **private** we have to give the details of types declared as private and give the initial values of corresponding deferred constants.

A private type can be implemented in any way consistent with the operations visible to the user. It can be a record as we have shown; equally it could be an array, an enumeration type and so on; it could even be declared in terms of another private type. In our case it is fairly obvious that the type COMPLEX is naturally implemented as a record; but we could equally have used an array of two components such as

type COMPLEX **is array** (1 .. 2) **of** REAL;

Having declared the details of the private type we can use them and so declare the constants properly and give their initial values.

It should be noted that as well as the functions +, −, * and / we have also provided CONS to create a complex number from its real and imaginary components and RL_PART and IM_PART to return the components. Some such functions are necessary because the user no longer has direct access to the internal structure of the type. Of course, the fact that CONS, RL_PART and IM_PART correspond to our thinking externally of the complex numbers in cartesian form does not prevent us from implementing them internally in some other form as we shall see in a moment.

The body of the package is as shown in the answer to Exercise 8.1(**2**) plus the additional functions which are trivial. It is therefore

```
package body COMPLEX_NUMBERS is

    -- unary + -

    function "+" (X, Y: COMPLEX) return COMPLEX is
    begin
        return (X.RL + Y.RL, X.IM + Y.IM);
    end "+";

    -- - * / similarly

    function CONS(R, I: REAL) return COMPLEX is
    begin
        return (R, I);
    end CONS;

    function RL_PART(X: COMPLEX) return REAL is
    begin
        return X.RL;
    end RL_PART;

    -- IM_PART similarly

end COMPLEX_NUMBERS;
```

The package COMPLEX_NUMBERS could be used in a fragment such as

```
declare
    use COMPLEX_NUMBERS;
    C, D: COMPLEX;
    R, S: REAL;
begin
    C:= CONS(1.5, −6.0);
    D:= C + I;                          −− COMPLEX +
    R:= RL_PART(D) + 6.0;               −− REAL +
    ...
end;
```

Outside the package we can declare variables and constants of type COMPLEX in the usual way. Note the use of CONS to create a complex literal. We cannot, of course, do mixed operations between our complex and real numbers. Thus we cannot write

```
C:= 2.0 ⋆ C;
```

but instead must write

```
C:= CONS(2.0, 0.0) ⋆ C;
```

If this is felt to be tedious we could add further overloadings of the operators to allow mixed operations.

Let us suppose that for some reason we now decide to represent the complex numbers in polar form. The visible part of the package will be unchanged but the private part could now become

```
private
    PI: constant:= 3.14159_26536;
    type COMPLEX is
        record
            R: REAL;
            THETA: REAL range 0.0 .. 2.0⋆PI;
        end record;
    I: constant COMPLEX:= (1.0, 0.5⋆PI);
end;
```

Note how the constant PI is for convenience declared in the private part; anything other than a body can be declared in a private part if it suits us − we are not restricted to just declaring the types and constants in full. Things declared in the private part are also available in the body.

The body of our package COMPLEX_NUMBERS will now need completely rewriting. Some functions will become simpler and others will be more intricate. In particular it will be convenient to provide a function to normalize the angle θ so that it lies in the range 0 to 2π. The details are left for the reader.

However, since the visible part has not been changed the user's program will not need changing; we are assured of this since there is no way in which the user could have written anything depending on the details of the private type. Nevertheless, the user's program will need recompiling because of the general dependency rules explained in Section 8.2. This may seem slightly contradictory but remember that the compiler needs the information in the private part in order to be able to allocate storage for objects of the private type declared in the user's program. If we change the private part the size of the objects could change and then the object code of the user's program would change even though the source was the same.

An interesting point is that rather than declare a deferred constant we could provide a parameterless function

function I **return** COMPLEX;

This has the slight advantage that we can change the value returned without changing the package specification and so having to recompile the user's program. Of course in the case of I we are unlikely to need to change the value anyway!

Finally note that between a private type declaration and the later full type declaration, the type is in a curiously half-defined state. Because of this there are severe restrictions on its use; it can only be used to declare deferred constants, other types and subtypes and subprogram specifications (also entries of tasks which we will meet in Chapter 14). It cannot be used to declare variables.

Thus we could write

type COMPLEX_ARRAY **is array** (INTEGER **range** <>) **of** COMPLEX;

and then

C: **constant** COMPLEX_ARRAY;

But until the full declaration is given we cannot declare variables of the type COMPLEX or COMPLEX_ARRAY.

However, we can declare the specifications of subprograms with parameters of the types COMPLEX and COMPLEX_ARRAY and can even supply default expressions. Such default expressions can use deferred constants and functions; this is allowed because of course a default expression is only evaluated when a subprogram is called and this cannot occur until the body of the package has been declared and this is bound to be after the full type declaration.

An interesting point with regard to deferred constants is that the syntax

deferred_constant_declaration ::=
                                        identifier_list : **constant** type_mark;

shows that we cannot use an explicit constraint in their type declaration. This avoids the possibility of a constraint producing a different value when it is repeated in the subsequent full constant declaration. Thus the type marks have to conform just as in repeated subprogram specifications (see Section 7.6). In the case of the array C above the full declaration might be

C: **constant** COMPLEX_ARRAY(1 .. 10):= ... ;

or even

C: **constant** COMPLEX_ARRAY:= ... ;

where in the latter case the bounds are taken from the initial value. If we wish to impose a constraint on the visible deferred constant declaration of C then we would have to introduce a subtype. Similar rules apply to discriminated records which we will discuss in Section 11.1.

There are various other subtle points which need not concern the normal user but which are described in the *LRM*. However, the general rule is that you can only use what you know. Outside the package we know only that the type is private; inside the package and after the full type declaration we know all the properties implied by the declaration.

As an example consider the type COMPLEX_ARRAY and the operator "<". (Remember that "<" only applies to arrays if the component type is discrete.) Outside the package we cannot use "<" since we do not know whether or not type COMPLEX is discrete. Inside the package we find that it is not discrete and so still cannot use "<". If it had been discrete we could have used "<" after the full type declaration but of course we still could not use it outside. On the other hand slicing is applicable to all one-dimensional arrays and so can be used both inside and outside the package.

Exercise 9.1

1   Write additional functions "*" to enable mixed multiplication of real and complex numbers.

2   Rewrite the fragment of user program for complex numbers omitting the use clause.

3   Complete the package RATIONAL_NUMBERS whose visible part is

```
package RATIONAL_NUMBERS is

    type RATIONAL is private;
    function "+" (X: RATIONAL) return RATIONAL; -- unary +
    function "-" (X: RATIONAL) return RATIONAL; -- unary -
    function "+" (X, Y: RATIONAL) return RATIONAL;
    function "-" (X, Y: RATIONAL) return RATIONAL;
    function "*" (X, Y: RATIONAL) return RATIONAL;
    function "/" (X, Y: RATIONAL) return RATIONAL;

    function "/" (X: INTEGER; Y: POSITIVE) return RATIONAL;
```

function NUMERATOR(R: RATIONAL) **return** INTEGER;
function DENOMINATOR(R: RATIONAL) **return** POSITIVE;

private

...

end;

A rational number is a number of the form N/D where N is an integer and D is a positive integer. For predefined equality to work it is essential that rational numbers are always reduced by cancelling out common factors. This may be done using the function GCD of Exercise 7.1(**7**). Ensure that an object of type RATIONAL has an appropriate default value of zero.

4   Why does

function "/" (X: INTEGER; Y: POSITIVE) **return** RATIONAL;

not hide the predefined integer division?

9.2   Limited private types

The operations available on a private type can be completely restricted to those specified in the visible part of the package. This is done by declaring the type as limited as well as private thus

type T **is limited private**;

In such a case assignment and predefined = and /= are not available outside the package. However, the package may define a function "=" if the two parameters are of the same limited type; it must return a value of type BOOLEAN. The operator /= always takes its meaning from = and so cannot be explicitly defined.

An important consequence of the absence of assignment for limited types is that the declaration of an object cannot include an initial value; this in turn implies that a constant cannot be declared outside the defining package. Similarly, a record component of a limited type cannot have a default initial expression. However, remember that the procedure parameter mechanism is not formally assignment and in fact we can declare our own subprograms with limited types as parameters of mode **in** or **in out** outside the defining package and we can even supply default expressions for **in** parameters; parameters of mode **out** are however not allowed for a reason which will become apparent in the next section.

The advantage of making a private type limited is that the package writer has complete control over the objects of the type – the copying of resources can be monitored and so on.

As a simple example consider the following

```
package STACKS is
    type STACK is limited private;
    procedure PUSH(S: in out STACK; X: in INTEGER);
    procedure POP(S: in out STACK; X: out INTEGER);
    function "=" (S, T: STACK) return BOOLEAN;
private
    MAX: constant:= 100;
    type INTEGER_VECTOR is
                            array (INTEGER range <>) of INTEGER;
    type STACK is
        record
            S: INTEGER_VECTOR(1 .. MAX);
            TOP: INTEGER range 0 .. MAX:= 0;
        end record;
end;
```

Each object of type STACK is a record containing an array S and integer TOP. Note that TOP has a default initial value of zero. This ensures that when we declare a stack object, it is correctly initialized to be empty. Note also the introduction of the type INTEGER_VECTOR because a record component may not be an anonymous array.

The body of the package could be

```
package body STACKS is

    procedure PUSH(S: in out STACK; X: in INTEGER) is
    begin
        S.TOP:= S.TOP+1;
        S.S(S.TOP):= X;
    end PUSH;

    procedure POP(S: in out STACK; X: out INTEGER) is
    begin
        X:= S.S(S.TOP);
        S.TOP:= S.TOP-1;
    end POP;

    function "=" (S, T: STACK) return BOOLEAN is
    begin
        if S.TOP /= T.TOP then
            return FALSE;
        end if;
        for I in 1 .. S.TOP loop
            if S.S(I) /= T.S(I) then
                return FALSE;
            end if;
        end loop;
```

```
            return TRUE;
         end "=";

      end STACKS;
```

This example illustrates many points. The parameter S of PUSH has mode
in out because we need both to read from and to write to the stack. Further
note that POP cannot be a function since S has to be **in out** and functions
can only have **in** parameters. However, "=" can be a function because we
only need to read the values of the two stacks and not to update them.

The function "=" has the interpretation that two stacks are equal
only if they have the same number of items and the corresponding items
have the same value. It would obviously be quite wrong to compare the
whole records because the unused components of the arrays would also be
compared. It is because of this that the type STACK has been made limited
private rather than just private. If it were just private then we could not
redefine "=" to give the correct meaning.

This is a typical example of a data structure where the value of the
whole is more than just the sum of the parts; the interpretation of the array
S depends on the value of TOP. Cases where there is such a relationship
usually need a limited private type.

A minor point is that we are using the identifier S in two ways: as the
name of the formal parameter denoting the stack and as the array inside
the record. There is no conflict because, although the scopes overlap, the
regions of visibility do not as was explained in Section 8.4. Of course, it is
rather confusing to the reader and not good practice but it illustrates the
freedom of choice of record component names.

The package could be used in a fragment such as

```
declare
   use STACKS;
   ST: STACK;
   EMPTY: STACK;
   ...
begin
   PUSH(ST, N);
   ...
   POP(ST, M);
   ...
   if ST = EMPTY then
      ...
   end if;
   ...
end;
```

Here we have declared two stacks ST and EMPTY. Both are
originally empty because their internal component TOP has an initial value
of zero. Assuming that we do not manipulate EMPTY then it can be used to
see whether the stack ST is empty or not by calling the function "=". This
seems a rather dubious way of testing for an empty stack since there is no

guarantee that EMPTY has not been manipulated. It would be better if EMPTY were a constant but as mentioned earlier we cannot declare a constant of a limited private type outside the package. We could however declare a constant EMPTY in the visible part of the package. A much better technique for testing the state of a stack would, of course, be to provide a function EMPTY and a corresponding function FULL in the package.

We can write subprograms with limited private types as parameters outside the defining package despite the absence of assignment. As a simple example, the following procedure enables us to determine the top value on the stack without removing it.

```
procedure TOP_OF(S: in out STACK; X: in out INTEGER) is
begin
    POP(S, X);
    PUSH(S, X);
end;
```

The declaration of a function "=" does not have to be confined to the package containing the declaration of the limited type. The only point is that outside the package, we cannot see the structure of the type. Furthermore, a composite type containing one or more components of a limited type is itself considered to be limited and so we could define "=" for such a type. Thus outside the package STACKS we could declare

```
type STACK_ARRAY is array (INTEGER range <>) of STACK;
function "=" (A, B: STACK_ARRAY) return BOOLEAN;
```

where the definition of an appropriate body is left to the reader.

Remember that within the private part (after the full type declaration) and within the body, any private type (limited or not) is treated in terms of how it is represented. Thus within the body of STACKS the type STACK is just a record type and so assignment and things consequential upon assignment (initialization and constants) are allowed. So we could declare a procedure ASSIGN (intended to be used outside the package) as

```
procedure ASSIGN(S: in STACK; T: out STACK) is
begin
    T:= S;
end;
```

The parameter mechanism for a private type is simply that corresponding to how the type is represented. This applies both inside and outside the package. Of course, outside the package, we know nothing of how the type is represented and therefore should make no assumption about the mechanism used.

It is unfortunate that Ada does not separate the ability to permit assignment and redefinition of equality. For instance, it would be reasonable to allow assignment of stacks, but, of course, predefined equality is of no value. Equally in the case of a type such as RATIONAL of Exercise 9.1(2), it would be quite reasonable to allow manipulation – including assignment – of values which were not reduced provided that equality was suitably redefined. We are therefore forced to use a procedural form such as ASSIGN or reduce all values to a canonical form in which component by component equality is satisfactory. In the case of type STACK a suitable form would be one in which all unused elements of the stack had a standard dummy value such as zero.

Exercise 9.2

1   Rewrite the specification of STACKS to include a constant EMPTY in the visible part.

2   Write functions EMPTY and FULL for STACKS.

3   Rewrite the **function** "=" (S, T: STACK) using slices.

4   Write a suitable body for the function "=" applying to the type STACK_ARRAY. Make it conform to the normal rules for array equality which we mentioned towards the end of Section 6.2.

5   Rewrite ASSIGN for STACKS so that only the meaningful part of the record is copied.

6   Rewrite STACKS so that STACK is a normal private type. Ensure that predefined equality is satisfactory.

9.3 Resource management

An important example of the use of a limited private type is in providing controlled resource management. Consider the simple human model where each resource has a corresponding unique key. This key is then issued to the user when the resource is allocated and then has to be shown whenever the resource is accessed. So long as there is only one key and copying and stealing are prevented we know that the system is foolproof. A mechanism for handing in keys and reissuing them is usually necessary if resources are not to be permanently locked up. Typical human examples are the use of metal keys with safe deposit boxes, credit cards and so on.

Now consider the following

```
package KEY_MANAGER is
    type KEY is limited private;
    procedure GET_KEY(K: in out KEY);
    procedure RETURN_KEY(K: in out KEY);
    function VALID(K: KEY) return BOOLEAN;
    ...
    procedure ACTION(K: in KEY; ... );
```

```
                ...
            private
                MAX: constant:= 100;                          -- number of keys
                subtype KEY_CODE is INTEGER range 0 .. MAX;
                type KEY is
                    record
                        CODE: KEY_CODE:= 0;
                    end record;
            end;

            package body KEY_MANAGER is
                FREE: array (KEY_CODE range 1 .. KEY_CODE'LAST) of
                                            BOOLEAN:= (others => TRUE);

                function VALID(K: KEY) return BOOLEAN is
                begin
                    return K.CODE /= 0;
                end VALID;

                procedure GET_KEY(K: in out KEY) is
                begin
                    if K.CODE = 0 then
                        for I in FREE'RANGE loop
                            if FREE(I) then
                                FREE(I):= FALSE;
                                K.CODE:= I;
                                return;
                            end if;
                        end loop;
                                                -- all keys in use
                    end if;
                end GET_KEY;

                procedure RETURN_KEY(K: in out KEY) is
                begin
                    if K.CODE /= 0 then
                        FREE(K.CODE):= TRUE;
                        K.CODE:= 0;
                    end if;
                end RETURN_KEY;
                ...

                procedure ACTION(K: in KEY; ... ) is
                begin
                    if VALID(K) then
                    ...
                end ACTION;

            end KEY_MANAGER;
```

The type KEY is represented by a record with a single component CODE. This has a default value of 0 which represents an unused key. Values from 1 .. MAX represent the allocation of the corresponding resource. When we declare a variable of type KEY it automatically takes an internal code value of zero. In order to use the key we must first call the procedure GET_KEY; this allocates the first free key number to the variable. The key may then be used with various procedures such as ACTION which represents a typical request for some access to the resource guarded by the key.

Finally, the key may be relinquished by calling RETURN_KEY. So a typical fragment of user program might be

```
declare
   use KEY_MANAGER;
   MY_KEY: KEY;
begin
   ...
   GET_KEY(MY_KEY);
   ...
   ACTION(MY_KEY, ... );
   ...
   RETURN_KEY(MY_KEY);
   ...
end;
```

A variable of type KEY can be thought of as a container for a key. When initially declared the default value can be thought of as representing that the container is empty; the type KEY has to be a record because only record components can take default initial values. Note how the various possible misuses of keys are overcome.

- If we call GET_KEY with a variable already containing a valid key then no new key is allocated. It is important not to overwrite an old valid key otherwise that key would be lost.

- A call of RETURN_KEY resets the variable to the default state so that the variable cannot be used as a key until a new one is issued by a call of GET_KEY. Note that the user is unable to retain a copy of the key because assignment is not valid since the type KEY is limited.

The function VALID is provided so that the user can see whether a key variable contains the default value or an allocated value. It is obviously useful to call VALID after GET_KEY to ensure that the key manager was able to provide a new key value; note that once all keys are issued, a call of GET_KEY does nothing.

One apparent flaw is that there is no compulsion to call RETURN_KEY before the scope containing the declaration of MY_KEY is left. The key would then be lost. This corresponds to the real life situation of losing a key (although in our model no one else can find it again – it is as if it were thrown into a black hole). To guard against this the key manager might assume (as in life) that a key not used for a certain period of time is no longer in use. Of course, the same key would not be reissued but the resource guarded might be considered reusable; this would involve keeping separate records of keys in use and resources in use and a cross-reference from keys to resources.

Exercise 9.3

1   Complete the package whose visible part is

```
package BANK is
    subtype MONEY is NATURAL;
    type KEY is limited private;
    procedure OPEN_ACCOUNT(K: in out KEY; M: in MONEY);
        -- open account with initial deposit M
    procedure CLOSE_ACCOUNT(K: in out KEY;
                                         M: out MONEY);
        -- close account and return balance
    procedure DEPOSIT(K: in KEY; M: in MONEY);
        -- deposit amount M
    procedure WITHDRAW(K: in out KEY; M in out MONEY);
        -- withdraw amount M; if account does not contain M
        -- then return what is there and close account
    function STATEMENT(K: KEY) return MONEY;
        -- returns a statement of current balance
    function VALID(K: KEY) return BOOLEAN;
        -- checks the key is valid

private
    ...
```

2   Assuming that your solution to the previous question allowed the bank the use of the deposited money, reformulate the private type to represent a home savings box or safe deposit box where the money is in a box kept by the user.

3   A thief writes the following

```
declare
    use KEY_MANAGER;
    MY_KEY: KEY;
    procedure CHEAT(COPY: in out KEY) is
    begin
        RETURN_KEY(MY_KEY);
        ACTION(COPY, ... );
        ...
    end;
begin
    GET_KEY(MY_KEY);
    CHEAT(MY_KEY);
    ...
end;
```

He attempts to return his key and then use the copy. Why is he thwarted?

4   A vandal writes the following

```
declare
    use KEY_MANAGER;
    MY_KEY: KEY;
    procedure DESTROY(K: out KEY) is
    begin
        null;
    end;
begin
    GET_KEY(MY_KEY);
    DESTROY(MY_KEY);
    ...
end;
```

He attempts to destroy the value in his key by calling a procedure which does not update the **out** parameter; he anticipates that the copy back rule will result in a junk value being assigned to the key. Why is he thwarted?

Checklist 9

For predefined equality to be sensible, the values should be in a canonical form.

An unlimited private type can be implemented in terms of another private type provided it is also unlimited.

A limited private type can be implemented in terms of any private type limited or not.

"/=" can never be defined – it always follows from "=".

"=" can be defined outside the package defining the limited private type concerned.

The rules apply transitively to composite types.

Chapter 10
Exceptions

At various times in the preceding chapters we have said that if something goes wrong when the program is executed, then an exception, often CONSTRAINT_ERROR, will be raised. In this chapter we describe the exception mechanism and show how remedial action can be taken when an exception occurs. We also show how we may define and use our own exceptions. Exceptions concerned with interacting tasks are dealt with when we come to Chapter 14.

10.1   Handling exceptions

We have seen that if we break various language rules then an exception may be raised when we execute the program.

There are five predefined exceptions (declared in the package STANDARD) of which we have met four so far

CONSTRAINT_ERROR	This generally corresponds to something going out of range.
NUMERIC_ERROR	This can occur when something goes wrong with arithmetic such as an attempt to divide by zero. However, as explained in Section 4.9, AI-387 concludes that it is not always possible to distinguish this exception from CONSTRAINT_ERROR and recommends that CONSTRAINT_ERROR should always be raised in such circumstances.
PROGRAM_ERROR	This will occur if we attempt to violate the control structure in some way such as

running into the **end** of a function or calling a subprogram whose body has not yet been elaborated – see Sections 7.1 and 8.1.

STORAGE_ERROR   This will occur if we run out of storage space as, for example, if we called our recursive function FACTORIAL with a large parameter – see Section 7.1.

The other predefined exception is TASKING_ERROR. This is concerned with tasking and so is dealt with in Chapter 14.

If we anticipate that an exception may occur in a part of our program then we can write an exception handler to deal with it. For example, suppose we write

```
begin
    -- sequence of statements
exception
    when CONSTRAINT_ERROR =>
        -- do something
end;
```

If CONSTRAINT_ERROR is raised while we are executing the sequence of statements between **begin** and **exception** then the flow of control is interrupted and immediately transferred to the sequence of statements following the =>. The clause starting **when** is known as an exception handler.

As a trivial example we could compute TOMORROW from TODAY by writing

```
begin
    TOMORROW:= DAY'SUCC(TODAY);
exception
    when CONSTRAINT_ERROR =>
        TOMORROW:= DAY'FIRST;
end;
```

If TODAY is DAY'LAST (that is, SUN) then when we attempt to evaluate DAY'SUCC(TODAY), the exception CONSTRAINT_ERROR is raised. Control is then transferred to the handler for CONSTRAINT_ERROR and the statement TOMORROW:= DAY'FIRST; is executed. Control then passes to the end of the block.

This is really a bad example. Exceptions should be used for rarely occurring cases or those which are inconvenient to test for at their point of occurrence. By no stretch of the imagination is Sunday a rare day. Over 14% of all days are Sundays. Nor is it difficult to test for the condition at the point of occurrence. So we should really have written

```
   if TODAY = DAY'LAST then
      TOMORROW:= DAY'FIRST;
   else
      TOMORROW:= DAY'SUCC(TODAY);
   end if;
```

However, it is a simple example with which to illustrate the mechanism involved.

Several handlers can be written between **exception** and **end**. Consider

```
begin
   -- sequence of statements
exception
   when NUMERIC_ERROR | CONSTRAINT_ERROR =>
      PUT("Numeric or Constraint error occurred");
      ...
   when STORAGE_ERROR =>
      PUT("Ran out of space");
      ...
   when others =>
      PUT("Something else went wrong");
      ...
end;
```

In this example a message is output according to the exception. Note the similarity to the case statement. Each **when** is followed by one or more exception names separated by vertical bars. As usual we can write **others** but it must be last and on its own; it handles any exception not listed in the previous handlers. Note also that we have a common handler for NUMERIC_ERROR and CONSTRAINT_ERROR in accordance with AI-387.

Exception handlers can appear at the end of a block, subprogram body, package body (or task body) and have access to all entities declared in the unit (called a frame in the *LRM* although we will continue to use the more informal term unit). The examples have shown a degenerate block in which there is no **declare** and declarative part; the block was introduced just for the purpose of providing somewhere to hang the handlers. We could rewrite our bad example to determine tomorrow as a function thus

```
function TOMORROW(TODAY: DAY) return DAY is
begin
   return DAY'SUCC(TODAY);
exception
   when CONSTRAINT_ERROR =>
      return DAY'FIRST;
end TOMORROW;
```

It is important to realize that control can never be returned directly to the unit where the exception was raised. The sequence of statements following => replaces the remainder of the unit containing the handler and thereby completes execution of the unit. Hence a handler for a function must generally contain a return statement in order to provide the 'emergency' result.

In particular, a goto statement cannot transfer control from a unit into one of its handlers or vice versa, or from one handler to another. However, the statements of a handler can otherwise be of arbitrary complexity. They can include blocks, calls of subprograms and so on. A handler of a block could contain a goto statement which transferred control to a label outside the block and it could contain an exit statement if the block were inside a loop.

A handler at the end of a package body applies only to the initialization sequence of the package and not to subprograms in the package. Such subprograms must have individual handlers if they are to deal with exceptions.

We now consider the question of what happens if a unit does not provide a handler for a particular exception. The answer is that the exception is propagated dynamically. This simply means that the unit is terminated and the exception is raised at the point where the unit was invoked. In the case of a block we therefore look for a handler in the unit containing the block.

In the case of a subprogram, the call is terminated and we look for a handler in the unit which called the subprogram. This unwinding process is repeated until either we reach a unit containing a handler for the particular exception or come to the top level. If we find a unit containing a relevant handler then the exception is handled at that point. Alternatively we have reached the main program and have still found no handler – the main program is then abandoned and we can expect the run time environment to provide us with a suitable diagnostic message. (Unhandled exceptions in tasks are dealt with in Chapter 14.)

It is most important to understand that exceptions are propagated dynamically and not statically. That is, an exception not handled by a subprogram is propagated to the unit calling the subprogram and not to the unit containing the declaration of the subprogram – these may or may not be the same.

If the statements in a handler themselves raise an exception then the unit is terminated and the exception propagated to the calling unit; the handler does not loop.

Exercise 10.1

Note: these are exercises to check your understanding of exceptions. They do not necessarily reflect good Ada programming techniques.

1   Assuming that calling SQRT with a negative parameter and attempting to divide by zero both raise NUMERIC_ERROR, rewrite the procedure QUADRATIC of Section 7.3 without explicitly testing D and A.

2   Rewrite the function FACTORIAL of Section 7.1 so that if it is called with a negative parameter (which would normally raise CONSTRAINT_ERROR) or a large parameter (which would normally raise STORAGE_ERROR or NUMERIC_ERROR alias

CONSTRAINT_ERROR) then a standard result of say −1 is
returned. Hint: declare an inner function SLAVE which actually
does the work.

10.2   Declaring and raising exceptions

Relying on the predefined exceptions to detect unusual but anticipated
situations is usually bad practice because they do not provide a guarantee
that the exception has in fact been raised because of the anticipated
situation. Something else may have gone wrong instead.

As an illustration consider the package STACK of Section 8.1. If we
call PUSH when the stack is full then the statement TOP:= TOP+1; will raise
CONSTRAINT_ERROR and similarly if we call POP when the stack is empty
then TOP:= TOP−1; will also raise CONSTRAINT_ERROR. Since PUSH and
POP do not themselves have exception handlers, the exception will be
propagated to the unit calling them. So we could write

```
declare
    use STACK;
begin
    ...
    PUSH(M);
    ...
    N:= POP;
    ...
exception
    when CONSTRAINT_ERROR =>
        -- stack manipulation incorrect?
end;
```

and misuse of the stack would then result in control being transferred to
the handler for CONSTRAINT_ERROR. However, there would be no
guarantee that the exception had arisen because of misuse of the stack;
something else in the block could have gone wrong.

A better solution is to raise an exception specifically declared to
indicate misuse of the stack. Thus the package could be rewritten

```
package STACK is
    ERROR: exception;
    procedure PUSH(X: INTEGER);
    function POP return INTEGER;
end STACK;

package body STACK is
    MAX: constant:= 100;
    S: array (1 .. MAX) of INTEGER;
    TOP: INTEGER range 0 .. MAX;
```

```
            procedure PUSH(X: INTEGER) is
            begin
                if TOP = MAX then
                    raise ERROR;
                end if;
                TOP:= TOP+1;
                S(TOP):= X;
            end PUSH;

            function POP return INTEGER is
            begin
                if TOP = 0 then
                    raise ERROR;
                end if;
                TOP:= TOP-1;
                return S(TOP+1);
            end POP;

        begin
            TOP:= 0;
        end STACK;
```

An exception is declared in a similar way to a variable and is raised by an explicit raise statement naming the exception. The handling and propagation rules are just as for the predefined exceptions. We can now write

```
        declare
            use STACK;
        begin
            ...
            PUSH(M);
            ...
            N:= POP;
            ...
        exception
            when ERROR =>
                -- stack manipulation incorrect
            when others =>
                -- something else went wrong
        end;
```

We have now successfully separated the handler for misusing the stack from the handler for other exceptions.

Note that if we had not provided a use clause then we would have had to refer to the exception in the handler as STACK.ERROR; the usual dotted notation applies.

What could we expect to do in the handler in the above case? Apart from reporting that the stack manipulation has gone wrong, we might also

expect to reset the stack to an acceptable state although we have not
provided a convenient means of doing so. A procedure RESET in the
package STACK would be useful. A further thing we might do is relinquish
any resources that were acquired in the block and might otherwise be
inadvertently retained. Suppose for instance that we had also been using
the package KEY_MANAGER of Section 9.3. We might then call
RETURN_KEY to ensure that a key declared and acquired in the block had
been returned. Remember that RETURN_KEY does no harm if called
unnecessarily.

     We would probably also want to reset the stack and return the key in
the case of any other exception as well; so it would be as well to declare a
procedure CLEAN_UP to do all the actions required. So our block might
look like

```
declare
    use STACK, KEY_MANAGER;
    MY_KEY: KEY;

    procedure CLEAN_UP is
    begin
        RESET;
        RETURN_KEY(MY_KEY);
    end;

begin
    GET_KEY(MY_KEY);
    ...
    PUSH(M);
    ...
    ACTION(MY_KEY, ... );
    ...
    N:= POP;
    ...
    RETURN_KEY(MY_KEY);
exception
    when ERROR =>
        PUT("Stack used incorrectly");
        CLEAN_UP;
    when others =>
        PUT("Something else went wrong");
        CLEAN_UP;
end;
```

We have rather assumed that RESET is a further procedure declared in the
package STACK but note that we could write our own procedure externally
as follows

```
procedure RESET is
    JUNK: INTEGER;
    use STACK;
```

```
    begin
        loop
            JUNK:= POP;
        end loop;
    exception
        when ERROR =>
            null;
    end RESET;
```

This works by repeatedly calling POP until ERROR is raised. We then know that the stack is empty. The handler needs to do nothing other than prevent the exception from being propagated; so we merely write **null**. This procedure seems a bit like trickery; it would be far better to have a reset procedure in the package.

Sometimes the actions that require to be taken as a consequence of an exception need to be performed on a layered basis. In the above example we returned the key and then reset the stack but it is probably the case that the block as a whole cannot be assumed to have done its job correctly. We can indicate this by raising an exception as the last action of the handler.

```
    exception
        when ERROR =>
            PUT("Stack used incorrectly");
            CLEAN_UP;
            raise ANOTHER_ERROR;
        when others =>
            ...
    end;
```

The exception ANOTHER_ERROR will then be propagated to the unit containing the block. We could put the statement

```
    raise ANOTHER_ERROR;
```

in the procedure CLEAN_UP.

Sometimes it is convenient to handle an exception and then propagate the same exception. This can be done by just writing

```
    raise;
```

This is particularly useful when we handle several exceptions with the one handler since there is no way in which we can explicitly name the exception which occurred.

So we might have

```
        when others =>
            PUT("Something else went wrong");
            CLEAN_UP;
            raise;
    end;
```

The current exception will be remembered even if the action of the handler raises and handles its own exceptions such as occurred in our trick procedure RESET. However, note that there is a rule that we can only write **raise**; directly in a handler and not for instance in a procedure called by the handler such as CLEAN_UP.

The stack example illustrates a legitimate use of exceptions. The exception ERROR should rarely, if ever, occur and it would also be inconvenient to test for the condition at each possible point of occurrence. To do that we would presumably have to provide an additional parameter to PUSH of type BOOLEAN and mode **out** to indicate that all was not well, and then test it after each call. In the case of POP we would also have to recast it as a procedure since a function cannot take a parameter of mode **out**.

The package specification would then become

```
package STACK is
    procedure PUSH(X: in INTEGER; B: out BOOLEAN);
    procedure POP(X: out INTEGER; B: out BOOLEAN);
end;
```

and we would have to write

```
declare
    use STACK;
    OK: BOOLEAN;
begin
    ...
    PUSH(M, OK);
    if not OK then ...      end if;
    ...
    POP(N, OK);
    if not OK then ...      end if;
end;
```

It is clear that the use of an exception provides a better structured program.

Note finally that nothing prevents us from explicitly raising one of the predefined exceptions. We recall that in Section 7.1 when discussing the function INNER we stated that probably the best way of coping with parameters whose bounds were unequal was to explicitly raise CONSTRAINT_ERROR.

Exercise 10.2

1   Rewrite the package RANDOM of Exercise 8.1(**1**) so that it declares and raises an exception BAD if the initial value is not odd.

2   Rewrite your answer to Exercise 10.1(**2**) so that the function FACTORIAL always raises CONSTRAINT_ERROR if the parameter is negative or too large.

3   Declare a function "+" which takes two parameters of type
VECTOR and returns their sum using sliding semantics by analogy
with the predefined one-dimensional array operations described in
Section 6.6. Use type VECTOR from Section 6.2. Raise
CONSTRAINT_ERROR if the arrays do not match.

4   Are we completely justified in asserting that STACK.ERROR could
only be raised by the stack going wrong?

10.3   Checking and exceptions

In the previous section we came to the conclusion that it was logically
better to check for the stack overflow condition ourselves rather than rely
upon the built-in check associated with the violation of the subtype of TOP.
At first sight the reader may well feel that this would reduce the execution
efficiency of the program. However, this is not necessarily so, assuming a
reasonably intelligent compiler, and this example can be used to illustrate
the advantages of the use of appropriate subtypes.
    We will concentrate on the procedure PUSH, similar arguments
apply to the function POP.
    First consider the original package STACK of Section 8.1. In that we had

```
...
S: array (1 .. MAX) of INTEGER;
TOP: INTEGER range 0 .. MAX;

procedure PUSH(X: INTEGER) is
begin
    TOP:= TOP+1;
    S(TOP):= X;
end PUSH;
```

If the stack is full (that is TOP = MAX) and we call PUSH then it is the
assignment to TOP that raises CONSTRAINT_ERROR. This is because TOP
has a range constraint. However, the only run-time check that needs to be
compiled is that associated with checking the upper bound of TOP. There is
no need to check for violation of the lower bound since the expression
TOP+1 could not be less than 1 (assuming that the value in TOP is always in
range). Note, moreover, that no checks need be compiled with respect to the
assignment to S(TOP). This is because the value of TOP at this stage must lie
in the range 1 .. MAX (which is the index range of S) – it cannot exceed MAX
because this has just been checked by the previous assignment and it cannot
be less than 1 since 1 has just been added to its previous value which could
not have been less than 0. So just one check needs to be compiled in the
procedure PUSH.
    On the other hand, if the variable TOP had not been given a range
constraint but just declared as

```
TOP: INTEGER;
```

then although no checks would have been applied to the assignment to TOP, nevertheless checks would have had to be compiled for the assignment to S(TOP) instead in order to ensure that TOP lay within the index range of S. Two checks would be necessary – one for each end of the index range.

So applying the range constraint to TOP actually reduces the number of checks required. This is typical behaviour given a compiler with a moderate degree of flow analysis. The more you tell the compiler about the properties of the variables (and assuming the constraints on the variables match their usage), the better the object code.

Now consider what happens when we add our own test as in the previous section (and we assume that TOP now has its range constraint)

```
procedure PUSH(X: INTEGER) is
begin
    if TOP = MAX then
        raise ERROR;
    end if;
    TOP:= TOP+1;
    S(TOP):= X;
end PUSH;
```

Clearly we have added a check of our own. However, there is now no need for the compiler to insert the check on the upper bound of TOP in the assignment

```
TOP:= TOP+1;
```

because our own check will have caused control to be transferred away via the raising of the ERROR exception for the one original value of TOP that would have caused trouble. So the net effect of adding our own check is simply to replace a compiler check by our own; the object code is not less efficient.

There are two morals to this tale. The first is that we should tell the compiler the whole truth about our program; the more it knows about the properties of our variables, the more likely it is to be able to keep checks to the appropriate minimum. In fact this is just an extension of the advantage of strong typing discussed in Section 4.3 where we saw how arbitrary run-time errors can be replaced by easily understood compile-time errors.

The second moral is that introducing our own exceptions rather than relying upon the predefined ones need not reduce the efficiency of our program. In fact it is generally considered bad practice to rely upon the predefined exceptions for steering our program and especially bad to raise the predefined exceptions explicitly ourselves. It is all too easy to mask an unexpected genuine error that needs fixing.

It should also be noted that we can always ask the compiler to omit the run-time checks by using the pragma SUPPRESS. This is described in Section 15.5.

Finally, an important warning. Our analysis of when checks can be omitted depends upon all variables satisfying their constraints at all times. Provided checks are not suppressed we can be reasonably assured of this apart from one nasty loophole. This is that we are not obliged to supply initial values in the declarations of variables in the first place. So they can start with a junk value which does not satisfy any constraints and may not even be a value of the base type. If such a variable is read before being updated then our program is erroneous and all our analysis is worthless. It is thus a good idea to initialize all variables unless it is perfectly obvious that updating will occur first.

Exercise 10.3

1   Consider the case of the procedure PUSH with explicit raising of ERROR but suppose that there is no range constraint on TOP.

10.4   Scope of exceptions

To a large extent exceptions follow the same scope rules as other entities. An exception can hide and be hidden by another declaration; it can be made visible by the dotted notation and so on. An exception can be renamed

HELP: **exception renames** BANK.ALARM;

Exceptions are, however, different in many ways. We cannot declare arrays of exceptions, and they cannot be components of records, parameters of subprograms and so on. In short, exceptions are not objects and so cannot be manipulated. They are merely tags.

A very important characteristic of exceptions is that they are not created dynamically as a program executes but should be thought of as existing throughout the life of the program. This relates to the way in which exceptions are propagated dynamically up the chain of execution rather than statically up the chain of scope. An exception can be propagated outside its scope although of course it can then only be handled anonymously by **others**. This is illustrated by the following

```
declare
    procedure P is
        X: exception;
    begin
        raise X;
    end P;
begin
    P;
exception
    when others =>
            -- X handled here
end;
```

The procedure P declares and raises the exception X but does not handle it. When we call P, the exception X is propagated to the block calling P where it is handled anonymously.

It is even possible to propagate an exception out of its scope, where it becomes anonymous, and then back in again where it can once more be handled by its proper name. Consider (and this is really a crazy example)

```
declare
    package P is
        procedure F;
        procedure H;
    end P;

    procedure G is
    begin
        P.H;
    exception
        when others =>
            raise;
    end G;

    package body P is
        X: exception;

        procedure F is
        begin
            G;
        exception
            when X =>
                PUT("Got it!");
        end F;

        procedure H is
        begin
            raise X;
        end H;

    end P;

begin
    P.F;
end;
```

The block declares a package P containing procedures F and H and also a procedure G. The block calls F in P which calls G outside P which in turn calls H back in P. The procedure H raises the exception X whose scope is the body of P. The procedure H does not handle X, so it is propagated to G which called H. The procedure G is outside the package P, so the exception X is now outside its scope; nevertheless G handles the exception anonymously and propagates it further by reraising it. G was called by F so

X is now propagated back into the package and so can be handled by F by its proper name.

A further illustration of the nature of exceptions is afforded by a recursive procedure containing an exception declaration. Unlike variables declared in a procedure we do not get a new exception for each recursive call. Each recursive activation refers to the same exception. Consider the following artificial example

```
procedure F(N: INTEGER) is
    X: exception;
begin
    if N = 0 then
        raise X;
    else
        F(N-1);
    end if;
exception
    when X =>
        PUT("Got it");
        raise;
    when others =>
        null;
end F;
```

Suppose we execute F(4); we get recursive calls F(3), F(2), F(1) and finally F(0). When F is called with parameter zero, it raises the exception X, handles it, prints out a confirmatory message and then reraises it. The calling instance of F (which itself had N = 1) receives the exception and again handles it as X and so on. The message is therefore printed out five times in all and the exception is finally propagated anonymously. Observe that if each recursive activation had created a different exception then the message would only be printed out once.

In all the examples we have seen so far exceptions have been raised in statements. An exception can however also be raised in a declaration. Thus

```
N: POSITIVE:= 0;
```

would raise CONSTRAINT_ERROR because the initial value of N does not satisfy the range constraint 1 .. INTEGER'LAST of the subtype POSITIVE. An exception raised in a declaration is not handled by a handler (if any) of the unit containing the declaration but is immediately propagated up a level. This means that in any handler we are assured that all declarations of the unit were successfully elaborated and so there is no risk of referring to something that does not exist.

Finally, a warning regarding parameters of mode **out** or **in out**. If a subprogram is terminated by an exception then any actual parameter of a scalar type will not have been updated since such updating occurs on a normal return. For an array or record type the parameter mechanism is not so closely specified and the actual parameter may or may not have its original value. A program assuming a particular mechanism is of course erroneous. As an example consider the procedure WITHDRAW of the package BANK in Exercise 9.3(**1**). It would be incorrect to attempt to take the key away and raise an alarm as in

```
procedure WITHDRAW (K: in out KEY; M: in out MONEY) is
begin
    if VALID (K) then
        if M > amount remaining then
            M:= amount remaining;
            FREE(K.CODE):= TRUE;
            K.CODE:= 0;
            raise ALARM;
        else
            ...
        end if;
    end if;
end WITHDRAW;
```

If the parameter mechanism were implemented by copy then the bank would think that the key were now free but would have left the greedy customer with a copy.

Exercise 10.4

1   Rewrite the package BANK of Exercise 9.3(**1**) to declare an exception ALARM and raise it when any illegal banking activity is attempted. Avoid problems with the parameters.

2   Consider the following pathological procedure

```
procedure P is
begin
    P;
exception
    when STORAGE_ERROR =>
        P;
end P;
```

What happens when P is called? To be explicit suppose that there is enough stack space for only *N* simultaneous recursive calls of P but that on the *N* + 1th call the exception STORAGE_ERROR is raised. How many times will P be called in all and what eventually happens?

Checklist 10

Do not use exceptions unnecessarily.

Use specific user declared exceptions rather than predefined exceptions where relevant.

Ensure that handlers return resources correctly.

Match the constraints on index variables to the arrays concerned.

Beware of uninitialized variables.

Out and in out parameters may not be updated correctly if a procedure is terminated by an exception.

Chapter 11
Advanced Types

In this chapter we describe most of the remaining classes of types. These are discriminated record types, access types and derived types. Numeric types, which are explained in terms of derived types, are described in the next chapter and task types are described in Chapter 14.

11.1 Discriminated record types

In the record types we have seen so far there was no formal language dependency between the components. Any dependency was purely in the mind of the programmer as for example in the case of the limited private type STACK in Section 9.2 where the interpretation of the array S depended on the value of the integer TOP.

In the case of a discriminated record type, some of the components are known as discriminants and the remaining components can depend upon these. The discriminants, which have to be of a discrete type, can be thought of as parameterizing the type and the syntax reveals this analogy.

As a simple example, suppose we wish to write a package providing various operations on square matrices and that in particular we wish to write a function TRACE which sums the diagonal elements of a square matrix. We could contemplate using the type MATRIX of Section 6.2.

```
type MATRIX is array (INTEGER range <>, INTEGER range <>)
                                              of REAL;
```

but our function would then have to check that the matrix passed as an actual parameter was indeed square. We would have to write something like

```
function TRACE(M: MATRIX) return REAL is
    SUM: REAL:= 0.0;
begin
    if M'FIRST(1) /= M'FIRST(2) or M'LAST(1) /= M'LAST(2) then
        raise NON_SQUARE;
    end if;
    for I in M'RANGE loop
        SUM:= SUM + M(I, I);
    end loop;
    return SUM;
end TRACE;
```

This is somewhat unsatisfactory; we would prefer to use a formulation which ensured that the matrix was always square and had a lower bound of 1. We can do this using a discriminated type. Consider

```
type SQUARE(ORDER: POSITIVE) is
    record
        MAT: MATRIX(1 .. ORDER, 1 .. ORDER);
    end record;
```

This is a record type having two components: the first, ORDER, is a discriminant of the discrete subtype POSITIVE and the second, MAT, is an array whose bounds depend upon the value of ORDER.

Variables of type SQUARE can be declared in the usual way but a value of the discriminant must be given as a constraint thus

```
M: SQUARE(3);
```

The named form can also be used

```
M: SQUARE(ORDER => 3);
```

The value provided as the constraint could be any dynamic expression but once the variable is declared its constraint cannot be changed. An initial value for M could be provided by an aggregate, but, perhaps surprisingly, this must be complete and repeat the constraint which must match, thus

```
M: SQUARE(3):= (3, (1 .. 3 => (1 .. 3 => 0.0)));
```

However, we could not write

```
M: SQUARE(N):= (M.ORDER, (M.MAT'RANGE(1) =>
                                (M.MAT'RANGE(2) => 0.0)));
```

in order to avoid repeating N because of the rule that we cannot refer to an object in its own declaration. However

```
declare
    M: SQUARE(N);
begin
    M:= (M.ORDER, (M.MAT ' RANGE(1) =>
                        (M.MAT ' RANGE(2) => 0.0)));
```

is perfectly valid. If we attempt to assign a value to M which does not have the correct discriminant value then CONSTRAINT_ERROR will be raised.

Constants can be declared as usual and, like array bounds, the discriminant constraint can be deduced from the initial value.

We can, of course, introduce subtypes

```
subtype SQUARE_3 is SQUARE(3);
M: SQUARE_3;
```

We can now rewrite our function TRACE as follows

```
function TRACE(M: SQUARE) return REAL is
    SUM: REAL:= 0.0;
begin
    for I in M.MAT ' RANGE loop
        SUM:= SUM + M.MAT(I, I);
    end loop;
    return SUM;
end TRACE;
```

There is now no way in which a call of TRACE can be supplied with a non-square matrix. Note that the discriminant of the formal parameter is taken from that of the actual parameter in a similar way to the bounds of an array. Discriminants of parameters have much in common with array bounds. For example a discriminant can be read even in the case of an **out** parameter. Again like arrays, the formal parameter could be constrained as in

```
function TRACE_3(M: SQUARE_3) return REAL;
```

but then the actual parameter would have to have a discriminant value of 3; otherwise CONSTRAINT_ERROR would be raised.

The result of a function could be of a discriminated type and, like arrays, the result could be a value whose discriminant is not known until the function is called. Thus we could write a function to return the transpose of a square matrix

```
function TRANSPOSE(M: SQUARE) return SQUARE is
    R: SQUARE(M.ORDER);
begin
    for I in 1 .. M.ORDER loop
        for J in 1 .. M.ORDER loop
```

```
                    R.MAT(I, J):= M.MAT(J, I);
            end loop;
        end loop;
        return R;
    end TRANSPOSE;
```

A private type can also have discriminants and it must then be implemented in terms of a record type with corresponding discriminants. A good example is provided by considering the type STACK in Section 9.2. We can overcome the problem that all the stacks had the same maximum length of 100 by making MAX a discriminant. Thus we can write

```
    package STACKS is
        type STACK(MAX: NATURAL) is limited private;
        procedure PUSH(S: in out STACK; X: in INTEGER);
        procedure POP(S: in out STACK; X out INTEGER);
        function "=" (S, T: STACK) return BOOLEAN;
    private
        type INTEGER_VECTOR is
                                array (INTEGER range <>) of INTEGER;
        type STACK(MAX: NATURAL) is
            record
                S: INTEGER_VECTOR(1 .. MAX);
                TOP: INTEGER:= 0;
            end record;
    end;
```

Each variable of type STACK now includes a discriminant component giving the maximum stack size. When we declare a stack we must supply the value thus

```
    ST: STACK(100);
```

and as for the type SQUARE the value of the discriminant cannot later be changed. Of course, the discriminant is visible and can be referred to as ST.MAX although the remaining components are private.

The body of the package STACKS remains as before (see Section 9.2). Observe in particular that the function "=" can be used to compare stacks with different values of MAX since it only compares those components of the internal array which are in use.

Although constants of the type STACK cannot be declared outside the defining package (because the type is limited private), we can declare a deferred constant in the visible part. Such a declaration need not supply a value for the discriminant since it will be given in the private part.

This is a good point to mention that discriminants bear a resemblance to subprogram parameters in several respects. The type or subtype of a discriminant must be given by a type mark and not by a subtype indication. This is so that the same simple conformance rules can be used when a discriminant specification has to be repeated in the case of a private type with discriminants, as illustrated by the type STACK above.

A conformance problem also arises in the case of deferred constants with discriminants which are analogous to the deferred array constants discussed in Section 9.1. Suppose we wish to declare a constant STACK with a discriminant of 3. We can omit the discriminant in the visible part and merely write

```
C: constant STACK;
```

and then give the discriminant in the private part either as a constraint or through the mandatory initial value (or both)

```
C: constant STACK(3):= (3, (1, 2, 3), 3);
```

However, if we wish to give the discriminant in the visible part then we must introduce a subtype to do so; we cannot use an explicit constraint in a subtype indication. Having introduced the subtype then the full constant declaration must also use it since the type marks must conform. Thus we can write

```
subtype STACK_3 is STACK(3);
C: constant STACK_3;
```

and then

```
C: constant STACK_3:= (3, (1, 2, 3), 3);
```

in the private part.

It is possible to declare a type with several discriminants. We may for instance wish to manipulate matrices which although not constrained to be square nevertheless have both lower bounds of 1. This could be done by

```
type RECTANGLE(ROWS, COLUMNS: POSITIVE) is
    record
        MAT: MATRIX(1 .. ROWS, 1 .. COLUMNS);
    end record;
```

and we could then declare

```
R: RECTANGLE(2, 3);
```

or

```
R: RECTANGLE(ROWS => 2, COLUMNS => 3);
```

The usual rules apply: positional values must be given in order, named ones may be in any order, mixed notation can be used but the positional ones must come first.

Similarly to multidimensional arrays, a subtype must supply all the constraints or none at all. We could not declare

subtype ROW_3 **is** RECTANGLE(ROWS => 3);

in order to get the equivalent of

type ROW_3(COLUMNS: POSITIVE) **is**
   record
      MAT: MATRIX(1 .. 3, 1 .. COLUMNS);
   end record;

In the examples we have shown, discriminants have been used in index constraints as the upper bounds of arrays; they can also be used as the lower bounds of arrays. In Section 11.3 we will describe how a discriminant can also be used to introduce a variant part. In these cases a discriminant must be used directly and not as part of a larger expression. So we could not declare

type SYMMETRIC_ARRAY(N: POSITIVE) **is**
   record
      A: VECTOR(−N .. N);   −− illegal
   end record;

or

type TWO_BY_ONE(N: POSITIVE) **is**
   record
      A: MATRIX(1 .. N, 1 .. 2*N);   −− illegal
   end record;

Exercise 11.1

1   Suppose that M is an object of the type MATRIX. Write a call of the function TRACE whose parameter is an aggregate of type SQUARE in order to determine the trace of M. What would happen if the two dimensions of M were not equal?

2   Rewrite the specification of STACKS to include a constant EMPTY in the visible part. See also Exercise 9.2(**1**).

3   Write a function FULL for STACKS. See also Exercise 9.2(**2**).

4   Declare a constant SQUARE of order N and initialize it to a unit matrix. Use the function MAKE_UNIT of Exercise 7.1(**6**).

11.2   Default discriminants

The discriminant types we have encountered so far have been such that once a variable is declared, its discriminant cannot be changed. It is possible, however, to provide a default expression for a discriminant and the situation is then different. A variable can then be declared with or without a discriminant constraint. If one is supplied then that value overrides the default and as before the discriminant cannot be changed. If, on the other hand, a variable is declared without a value for the discriminant, then the value of the default expression is taken but it can then be changed by a complete record assignment.

Suppose we wish to manipulate polynomials of the form

$$P(x) = a_0 + a_1 x + a_2 x^2 + \ldots a_n x^n$$

where $a_n \neq 0$ if $n \neq 0$.

Such a polynomial could be represented by

```
type POLY(N: INDEX) is
    record
        A: INTEGER_VECTOR(0 .. N);
    end record;
```

where

```
subtype INDEX is INTEGER range 0 .. MAX;
```

but then a variable of type POLY would have to be declared with a constraint and would thereafter be a polynomial of that fixed size. This would be most inconvenient because the sizes of the polynomials may be determined as the consequences of elaborate calculations. For example, if we subtract two polynomials which have $n = 3$, then the result will only have $n = 3$ if the coefficients of x^3 are different.

However, if we declare

```
type POLYNOMIAL(N: INDEX:= 0) is
    record
        A: INTEGER_VECTOR(0 .. N);
    end record;
```

then we can declare variables

```
P, Q: POLYNOMIAL;
```

which do not have constraints. The initial value of their discriminants would be zero because the default value of N is zero but the discriminants could later be changed by assignment. Note, however, that a discriminant can only be changed by a complete record assignment. So

```
P.N:= 6;
```

would be illegal. This is quite natural since we cannot expect the array P.A to adjust its bounds by magic.

Variables of the type POLYNOMIAL could be declared with constraints

R: POLYNOMIAL(5);

but R would thereafter be constrained forever to be a polynomial with $n = 5$.

Initial values can be given in declarations in the usual way.

P: POLYNOMIAL:= (3, (5, 0, 4, 2));

which represents $5 + 4x^2 + 2x^3$. Note that despite the initial value, P is not constrained.

In practice we would make the type POLYNOMIAL a private type so that we could enforce the rule that $a_n \neq 0$. Observe that predefined equality is satisfactory and so we do not have to make it a limited private type. Both the private type declaration and the full type declaration must give the default expression for N.

Note once more the similarity to subprogram parameters; the default expression is only evaluated when required and so need not produce the same value each time. Moreover, the same conformance rules apply when it has to be written out again in the case of a private type.

If we declare functions such as

function " − " (P, Q: POLYNOMIAL) **return** POLYNOMIAL;

then it will be necessary to ensure that the result is normalized so that a_n is not zero. This could be done by the following function

```
function NORMAL(P: POLYNOMIAL) return POLYNOMIAL is
    SIZE: INTEGER:= P.N;
begin
    while SIZE > 0 and P.A(SIZE) = 0 loop
        SIZE:= SIZE−1;
    end loop;
    return (SIZE, P.A(0 .. SIZE));
end NORMAL;
```

This is a further illustration of a function returning a value whose discriminant is not known until it is called. Note the use of the array slice.

If default expressions are supplied then they must be supplied for all discriminants of the type. Moreover, an object must be fully constrained or not at all; we cannot supply constraints for some discriminants and use the defaults for others.

The attribute CONSTRAINED can be applied to an object of a discriminated type and gives a Boolean value indicating whether the object is constrained or not. For any object of types such as SQUARE and STACK which do not have default values for the discriminants this attribute will, of course, be TRUE. But in the case of objects of a type such as POLYNOMIAL which does have a default value, the attribute may be TRUE or FALSE.

```
P'CONSTRAINED = FALSE
R'CONSTRAINED = TRUE
```

We mentioned above that an unconstrained formal parameter will take the value of the discriminant of the actual parameter. In the case of an **out** or **in out** parameter, the formal parameter will be constrained if the actual parameter is constrained (an **in** parameter is constant anyway). Suppose we declare a procedure to truncate a polynomial by removing its highest order term.

```
procedure TRUNCATE (P: in out POLYNOMIAL) is
begin
    P:= (P.N−1, P.A(0 .. P.N−1));
end;
```

Then given

```
Q: POLYNOMIAL;
R: POLYNOMIAL(5);
```

the statement

```
TRUNCATE(Q);
```

will be successful, but

```
TRUNCATE(R);
```

will result in CONSTRAINT_ERROR being raised.

We conclude this section by considering the problem of variable length strings. In Section 6.5 we noted, when declaring the ZOO, that the animals (or rather their names) all had to be the same length. The strong type model of Ada means that the type STRING does not have the flexibility found in cruder languages such as BASIC. However, with a bit of ingenuity, we can build our own flexibility by using discriminated records. There are a number of possibilities such as

```
subtype STRING_SIZE is INTEGER range 0 .. 80;

type V_STRING(N: STRING_SIZE:= 0) is
    record
        S: STRING(1 .. N);
    end record;
```

The type V_STRING is very similar to the type POLYNOMIAL (the lower bound is different). We have chosen a maximum string size corresponding to a typical page width (or historic punched card).

We can now declare fixed or varying v-strings and make appropriate assignments

V: V_STRING:= (5, "Hello");

We see that although we no longer have to pad the strings to a fixed length, we now have the burden of specifying the length explicitly. However, we can craftily write

```
function "+" (S: STRING) return V_STRING is
begin
    return (S'LENGTH, S);
end "+";
```

and then

```
type V_STRING_ARRAY is array (POSITIVE range <>) of V_STRING;

ZOO: constant V_STRING_ARRAY
        := (+"aardvark", +"baboon", +"camel", +"dolphin",
            +"elephant", ..., +"zebra");
```

Remember from Section 6.5 that we can declare an array of any type or subtype for which we can declare objects. Since v-strings have default discriminants we can declare unconstrained v-strings and hence arrays of them.

We thus see that we have more or less created a ragged array. However, there is a limit of 80 on our strings and, moreover, the storage space for the maximum size string is likely to be allocated irrespective of the actual string. We will return to the topic of ragged arrays when we discuss access types in Section 11.6.

Exercise 11.2

1   Declare a POLYNOMIAL representing zero (that is, $0x^0$).

2   Write a function "*" to multiply two polynomials.

3   Write a function "−" to subtract two polynomials. Use the function NORMAL.

4   Rewrite the procedure TRUNCATE to raise TRUNCATE_ERROR if we attempt to truncate a constrained polynomial.

5   What would be the effect of replacing the discriminant of the type POLYNOMIAL by (N: INTEGER:= 0)?

6   Write a function "&" to concatenate two v-strings.

7   Write the converse unary function "+" which takes a V_STRING as parameter and returns the corresponding STRING. Use this function to output the camel.

11.3 Variant parts

It is sometimes convenient to have a record type in which part of the structure is fixed for all objects of the type but the remainder can take one of several different forms. This can be done using a variant part and the choice between the alternatives is governed by the value of a discriminant.

Consider the following

type GENDER **is** (MALE, FEMALE);

```
type PERSON(SEX: GENDER) Is
    record
        BIRTH: DATE;
        case SEX is
            when MALE =>
                BEARDED: BOOLEAN;
            when FEMALE =>
                CHILDREN: INTEGER;
        end case;
    end record;
```

This declares a record type PERSON with a discriminant SEX. The component BIRTH of type DATE (see Section 6.7) is common to all objects of the type. However, the remaining components depend upon SEX and are declared as a variant part. If the value of SEX is MALE then there is a further component BEARDED whereas if SEX is FEMALE then there is a component CHILDREN. Only men can have beards and only women (directly) have children.

Since no default expression is given for the discriminant all objects of the type must be constrained. We can therefore declare

```
JOHN: PERSON(MALE);
BARBARA: PERSON(FEMALE);
```

or we can introduce subtypes and so write

```
subtype MAN is PERSON(SEX => MALE);
subtype WOMAN is PERSON(SEX => FEMALE);
JOHN: MAN;
BARBARA: WOMAN;
```

Aggregates take the usual form but, of course, give only the components for the corresponding alternative in the variant. The value for a discriminant governing a variant must be static so that the compiler can check the consistency of the aggregate. We can therefore write

```
JOHN:= (MALE, (19, AUG, 1937), FALSE);
BARBARA:= (FEMALE, (13, MAY, 1943), 2);
```

but not

```
S: GENDER:= FEMALE;
BARBARA:= (S, (13, MAY, 1943), 2);
```

because S is not static but a variable.

The components of a variant can be accessed and changed in the usual way. We could write

```
JOHN.BEARDED:= TRUE;
BARBARA.CHILDREN:= BARBARA.CHILDREN+1;
```

but an attempt to access a component of the wrong alternative such as JOHN.CHILDREN would raise CONSTRAINT_ERROR.

Note that although the sex of objects of type PERSON cannot be changed, it need not be known at compilation time. We could have

```
S: GENDER:= ...
CHRIS: PERSON(S);
```

where the sex of CHRIS is not determined until he or she is declared. The rule that a discriminant must be static applies only to aggregates.

The variables of type PERSON are necessarily constrained because the type had no default expression for the discriminant. It is therefore not possible to assign a value which would change the sex; an attempt to do so would raise CONSTRAINT_ERROR. However, as with the type POLYNOMIAL, we could declare a default initial expression for the discriminant and consequently declare unconstrained variables. Such unconstrained variables could then be assigned values with different discriminants but only by a complete record assignment.

We could therefore have

```
type GENDER is (MALE, FEMALE, NEUTER);

type MUTANT(SEX: GENDER:= NEUTER) is
    record
        BIRTH: DATE;
        case SEX is
            when MALE =>
                BEARDED: BOOLEAN;
            when FEMALE =>
                CHILDREN: INTEGER;
            when NEUTER =>
                null;
        end case;
    end record;
```

Note that we have to write **null** as the alternative in the case of NEUTER where we did not want any components. In a similar way to the use of a null statement in a case statement this indicates that we really meant to have no components and did not omit them by accident.

We can now declare

M: MUTANT;

The sex of this unconstrained mutant is neuter by default but can be changed by a whole record assignment.

Note the difference between

M: MUTANT:= (NEUTER, (1, JAN, 1984));

and

N: MUTANT(NEUTER):= (NEUTER, (1, JAN, 1984));

In the first case the mutant is not constrained but just happens to be initially neuter. In the second case the mutant is permanently neuter. This example also illustrates the form of the aggregate when there are no components in the alternative; there are none so we write none – we do not write **null**.

The rules regarding the alternatives closely follow those regarding the case statement described in Section 5.2. Each **when** is followed by one or more choices separated by vertical bars and each choice is either a simple expression or a discrete range. The choice **others** can also be used but must be last and on its own. All values and ranges must be static and all possible values of the discriminant must be covered once and once only. The possible values of the discriminant are those of its static subtype (if there is one) or type. Each alternative can contain several component declarations and as we have seen could also be null.

A record can only contain one variant part and it must follow other components. However, variants can be nested; the component lists in a variant part could themselves contain one variant part but again it must follow other components.

Also observe that it is unfortunately not possible to use the same identifier for components in different alternatives of a variant – all components of a record must have distinct identifiers.

It is perhaps worth emphasizing the rules regarding the changing of discriminants. If an object is declared with a discriminant constraint then it cannot be changed – after all it is a constraint just like a range constraint and so the discriminant must always satisfy the constraint. Because the constraint allows only a single value this naturally means that the discriminant can only take that single value and so cannot be changed.

The other basic consideration is that, for implementation reasons, all objects must have values for discriminant components. Hence, if the type does not provide a default initial expression, the object declaration must and since it is expressed as a constraint the object is then consequently constrained.

There is a restriction on renaming components of a variable of a discriminated type. If the existence of the component depends upon the value of a discriminant then it cannot be renamed if the variable is unconstrained. So we cannot write

C: INTEGER **renames** M.CHILDREN;

because there is no guarantee that the component M.CHILDREN of the mutant M will continue to exist after the renaming even if it does exist at the moment of renaming. However

C: INTEGER **renames** BARBARA.CHILDREN;

is valid because BARBARA is a person and cannot change sex.

Note, amazingly, that we can write

BOBBY: MAN **renames** BARBARA;

because the constraint in the renaming declaration is ignored (see Section 8.5). Barbara has not had a sex change – she is merely in disguise!

We have seen that a discriminant can be used as the bound of an array and also as the expression governing a variant. In a similar way it can also be used as the discriminant constraint of an inner component. We could declare a type representing rational polynomials (that is one polynomial divided by another) by

```
type RATIONAL_POLYNOMIAL(N, D: INDEX:= 0) is
    record
        NUM: POLYNOMIAL(N);
        DEN: POLYNOMIAL(D);
    end record;
```

The relationship between constraints on the rational polynomial as a whole and its component polynomials is interesting. If we declare

R: RATIONAL_POLYNOMIAL(2, 3);

then R is constrained for ever and the components R.NUM and R.DEN are also permanently constrained with constraints 2 and 3 respectively. However

```
P: RATIONAL_POLYNOMIAL:= (2, 3, NUM  => (2, (−1, 0, 1)),
                                DEN  => (3, (−1, 0, 0, 1)));
```

is not constrained. This means that we can assign complete new values to P with different values of N and D. The fact that the components NUM and DEN are declared as constrained does not mean that P.NUM and P.DEN must always have a fixed length but simply that for given N and D they are constrained to have the appropriate length. So we could not write

P.NUM => (1, (1, 1));

because this would violate the constraint on P.NUM. However, we can write

P:= (1, 2, NUM => (1, (1, 1)), DEN => (2, (1, 1, 1)));

because this changes everything together. Of course we can always make a direct assignment to P.NUM that does not change the current value of its own discriminant.

The original value of P represented $(x^2 - 1)/(x^3 - 1)$ and the final value represents $(x + 1)/(x^2 + x + 1)$ which is, in fact, the same with the common factor $(x - 1)$ cancelled. The reader will note the strong analogy between the type RATIONAL_POLYNOMIAL and the type RATIONAL of Exercise 9.1(**3**). We could write an equivalent function NORMAL to cancel common factors of our rational polynomials and the whole package of operations would then follow.

The remaining possible use of a discriminant is as part of the expression giving a default initial value for one of the other record components (but not another discriminant). Although the discriminant value may not be known until an object is declared, this is not a problem since the default initial expression is, of course, only evaluated when the object is declared and no other initial value is supplied.

However, we cannot use a discriminant for any other purpose. This unfortunately meant that when we declared the type STACK in the previous section we could not continue to apply the constraint to TOP by writing

```
type STACK(MAX: NATURAL) is
    record
        S: INTEGER_VECTOR(1 .. MAX);
        TOP: INTEGER range 0 .. MAX:= 0;     -- illegal
    end record;
```

since the use of MAX in the range constraint is not allowed.

Finally, a discriminant need not be used at all. It could just be treated as one component of a record. This might be particularly relevant when we wish to have a type where some components are private and others are visible. As an interesting and extreme example we can reconsider the type KEY of Section 9.3. We could change this to

```
type KEY(CODE: NATURAL:= 0) is limited private;
```

with

```
type KEY(CODE: NATURAL:= 0) is
    record
        null;
    end record;
```

With this formulation the user can read the code number of his key, but cannot change it. There is, however, a small flaw whose detection and cure is left as an exercise. Note also that we have declared CODE as subtype NATURAL rather than subtype KEY_CODE; this is because KEY_CODE is not visible to the user. Of course we could make KEY_CODE visible but this would make MAX visible as well and we might not want the user to know how many keys there are.

We conclude our discussion of discriminated records by recalling the rule in Section 6.5 that the components of an array can be of any type or subtype for which we can declare objects. So we can declare arrays of type MUTANT and subtypes MAN and WOMAN, but not of type PERSON.

Exercise 11.3

1 Write a procedure SHAVE which takes an object of type PERSON and removes any beard if the object is male and raises the exception SHAVING_ERROR if the object is female.

2 Write a procedure STERILIZE which takes an object of type MUTANT and ensures that its sex is NEUTER by changing it if necessary and possible and otherwise raises an appropriate exception.

3 Declare a type OBJECT which describes geometrical objects which are either a circle, a square or a rectangle. A circle is characterized by its radius, a square by its side and a rectangle by its length and breadth.

4 Write a function AREA which returns the area of an OBJECT.

5 Rewrite the declaration of the type POLYNOMIAL of Section 11.2 so that the default initial value of a polynomial of degree n represents x^n. Hint: declare an auxiliary function returning an appropriate array value.

6 What is the flaw in the suggested new formulation for the type KEY? Hint: remember that the user declares keys explicitly. Show how it can be overcome.

7 Write the specification of a package RATIONAL_POLYNOMIALS. Make the type RATIONAL_POLYNOMIAL private with visible discriminants. The functions should correspond to those of the package RATIONAL_NUMBERS of Exercise 9.1(**3**).

11.4 Access types

In the case of the types we have met so far, the name of an object has been bound irretrievably to the object itself, and the lifetime of an object has been from its declaration until control leaves the unit containing the declaration. This is too restrictive for many applications where a more fluid control of the allocation of objects is desired. In Ada this can be done by access types. Objects of an access type, as the name implies, provide access to other objects and these other objects can be allocated in a manner independent of the block structure.

For those familiar with other languages, an access object can be thought of as a reference or pointer. The term reference has been brought into disrepute because of dangling references in Algol 68 and pointer has been brought into disrepute because of anonymous pointers in PL/I. Thus the new term access can be thought of as a polite term for reference or pointer. However, Ada access objects are strongly typed and, as we shall see, there are no dangling reference problems.

One of the simplest uses of an access type is for list processing. Consider

```
type CELL;

type LINK is access CELL;

type CELL is
    record
        VALUE: INTEGER;
        NEXT: LINK;
    end record;

L: LINK;
```

These declarations introduce type LINK which accesses CELL. The variable L can be thought of as a reference variable which can only point at objects of type CELL; these are records with two components, VALUE of type INTEGER and NEXT which is also a LINK and can therefore access (point to or reference) other objects of type CELL. The records can therefore be formed into a linked list. Initially there are no record objects, only the single pointer L which by default takes the value **null** which points nowhere. We could have explicitly given L this default value thus

```
L: LINK:= null;
```

Note the circularity in the definitions of LINK and CELL. Because of this circularity and the rule of linear elaboration it is necessary first to give an incomplete declaration of CELL. Having done this we can declare LINK and then complete the declaration of CELL. Between the incomplete and complete declarations, the type name CELL can only be used in the definition of an access type. Moreover, the incomplete and complete declarations must be in the same list of declarations except for one case which we will mention in the next section.

The accessed objects are created by the execution of an allocator which can (but need not) provide an initial value. An allocator consists of the reserved word **new** followed by either just the type of the new object or a qualified expression providing also the initial value of the object. The result of an allocator is an access value which can then be assigned to a variable of the access type.

So

```
L:= new CELL;
```

Figure 11.1   An access object.

creates a record of type CELL and then assigns to L a designation of
(reference to or pointer to) the object. We can picture the result as in
Figure 11.1. Note that the NEXT component of the record takes the default
value **null** whereas the VALUE component is undefined.

The components of the object referred to by L can be accessed using the
normal dotted notation. So we could assign 37 to the VALUE component by

        L.VALUE:= 37;

Alternatively we could have provided an initial value with the allocator

        L:= **new** CELL'(37, **null**);

The initial value here takes the form of a qualified aggregate and as usual
has to provide values for all the components irrespective of whether some
have default initial expressions.

Of course, the allocator could have been used to initialize L when it
was declared

        L: LINK:= **new** CELL'(37, **null**);

Distinguish carefully the types LINK and CELL. L is of type LINK which
accesses CELL and it is the accessed type which follows **new**.

Suppose we now want to create a further record and link it to our
existing record. We can do this by declaring a further variable

        N: LINK;

and then executing

        N:= **new** CELL'(10, L);
        L:= N;

The effect of these three steps is illustrated in Figure 11.2. Note how
the assignment statement

        L:= N;

copies the access values (that is, the pointers) and not the objects. If we
wanted to copy the objects we could do it component by component.

        L.VALUE:= N.VALUE;
        L.NEXT:= N.NEXT;

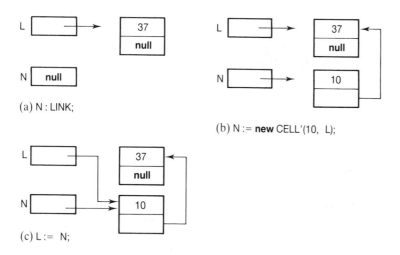

Figure 11.2   Extending a list.

or by using **all**

   L.**all**:= N.**all**;

L.**all** refers to the whole object accessed by L. In fact we can think of
L.VALUE as short for L.**all**.VALUE. Unlike Pascal, dereferencing is
automatic.
  Similarly

   L = N

will be true if L and N refer to the same object, whereas

   L.**all** = N.**all**

will be true if the objects referred to happen to have the same value.
  We could declare a constant of an access type but, of course, since it
is a constant we must supply an initial value.

   C: **constant** LINK:= **new** CELL'(0, **null**);

The fact that C is constant means that it must always refer to the same
object. However, the value of the object could itself be changed. So

   C.**all**:= L.**all**;

is allowed but

   C:= L;

is not.

We did not really need the variable N in order to extend the list since we could simply have written

```
L:= new CELL'(10, L);
```

This statement can be made into a general procedure for creating a new record and adding it to the beginning of a list.

```
procedure ADD_TO_LIST(LIST: in out LINK; V: in INTEGER) is
begin
    LIST:= new CELL'(V, LIST);
end;
```

The new record containing the value 10 can now be added to the list accessed by L by

```
ADD_TO_LIST (L, 10);
```

The parameter passing mechanism for access types is defined to be by copy like that for scalar types. However, in order to prevent an access value from becoming undefined an **out** parameter is always copied in at the start. Remember also that an uninitialized access object takes the specific default value **null**. These two facts prevent undefined access values which could cause a program to go berserk.

The value **null** is useful for determining when a list is empty. The following function returns the sum of the VALUE components of the records in a list.

```
function SUM(LIST: LINK) return INTEGER is
    L: LINK:= LIST;
    S: INTEGER:= 0;
begin
    while L /= null loop
        S:= S+L.VALUE;
        L:= L.NEXT;
    end loop;
    return S;
end SUM;
```

Observe that we have to make a copy of LIST because formal parameters of mode **in** are constants. The variable L is then used to work down the list until we reach the end. The function works even if the list is empty.

A more elaborate data structure is the binary tree. This consists of nodes each of which has a value plus two subtrees one or both of which could be null. Appropriate declarations are

```
type NODE;
type TREE is access NODE;
```

```
type NODE is
   record
      VALUE: REAL;
      LEFT, RIGHT: TREE;
   end record;
```

As an interesting example of the use of trees consider the following procedure SORT which sorts the values in an array into ascending order.

```
procedure SORT(A: in out VECTOR) is
   I: INTEGER;
   BASE: TREE:= null;

   procedure INSERT(T: in out TREE; V: REAL) is
   begin
      if T = null then
         T:= new NODE'(V, null, null);
      else
         if V < T.VALUE then
            INSERT(T.LEFT, V);
         else
            INSERT(T.RIGHT, V);
         end if;
      end if;
   end INSERT;

   procedure OUTPUT(T: TREE) is
   begin
      if T /= null then
         OUTPUT(T.LEFT);
         A(I):= T.VALUE;
         I:= I+1;
         OUTPUT(T.RIGHT);
      end if;
   end OUTPUT;

begin                           -- body of SORT
   for J in A'RANGE loop
      INSERT(BASE, A(J));
   end loop;
   I:= A'FIRST;
   OUTPUT(BASE);
end SORT;
```

The recursive procedure INSERT adds a new node containing the value V to the tree T in such a way that the values in the left subtree of a node are always less than the value at the node and the values in the right subtree are always greater than (or equal to) the value at the node.

The recursive procedure OUTPUT copies the values at all the nodes of the tree into the array A by first outputting the left subtree (which has the smaller values) and then copying the value at the node and finally outputting the right subtree.

The procedure SORT simply builds up the tree by calling INSERT with each of the components of the array in turn and then calls OUTPUT to copy the ordered values back into the array.

The access types we have met so far have referred to records. This will often be the case but an access type can refer to any type, even another access type. So we could have

```
type REF_INT is access INTEGER;
R: REF_INT:= new INTEGER'(46);
```

Note that the value of the integer referred to by R is, perhaps inappropriately, denoted by R.**all**. So we can write

```
R.all:= 13;
```

to change the value from 46 to 13.

It is most important to understand that all objects referred to by access types must be acquired through an allocator. We cannot write

```
C: CELL;
...
L: LINK:= C;    -- illegal
```

This is to avoid the dangling reference problem of Algol 68 where it was possible to leave the scope of the referenced object while still within that of the referring object thus leaving the latter pointing nowhere.

In Ada, the accessed objects form a collection whose scope is that of the access type. The collection will cease to exist only when the scope is finally left but, of course, by then all the access variables will also have ceased to exist; so no dangling reference problems can arise.

If an object becomes inaccessible because no variables refer to it directly or indirectly then the storage it occupies may be reclaimed so that it can be reused by other objects. An implementation may (but need not) provide a garbage collector to do this.

Alternatively, there is a mechanism whereby a program can indicate that an object is no longer required; if, mistakenly, there are still references to such objects then the program is erroneous. For fuller details the reader is referred to Section 15.6. In this chapter we will assume that a garbage collector tidies up for us when necessary.

A few final points of detail. Allocators illustrate the importance of the rules regarding the number of times and when an expression is evaluated in certain contexts. For example, an expression in an aggregate is evaluated for each index value concerned and so

```
A: array (1 .. 10) of LINK:= (1 .. 10 => new CELL);
```

creates an array of ten components and initializes each of them to access a different new cell. As a further example

```
A, B: LINK:= new CELL;
```

creates two new cells (see Section 4.1), whereas

```
A: LINK:= new CELL;
B: LINK:= A;
```

naturally creates only one. Remember also that default expressions for record components, discriminants and subprogram parameters are re-evaluated each time they are required; if such an expression contains an allocator then a new object will be created each time.

If an allocator provides an initial value then this can take the form of any qualified expression. So we could have

```
L: LINK:= new CELL'(N.all);
```

in which case the object is given the same value as the object referred to by N. We could have

```
I: INTEGER:= 46;
R: REF_INT:= new INTEGER'(I);
```

in which case the new object takes the value of I; it does not matter that I is not an access object since only its value concerns us.

The type accessed could be constrained, so we could have

```
type REF_POS is access POSITIVE;
```

or equivalently

```
type REF_POS is access INTEGER range 1 .. INTEGER'LAST;
```

The values of the objects referred to are all constrained to be positive. We can write

```
RN: REF_POS:= new POSITIVE'(10);
```

or even

```
RN: REF_POS:= new INTEGER'(10);
```

Note that if we wrote **new** POSITIVE'(0) then CONSTRAINT_ERROR would be raised because 0 is not of subtype POSITIVE. However, if we wrote **new** INTEGER'(0) then CONSTRAINT_ERROR is only raised because of the context of the allocator.

It is important to realize that each declaration of an access type introduces a new collection. Two collections can be of objects of the same type but the access objects must not refer to objects in the wrong collection. So we could have

```
type REF_INT_A is access INTEGER;
type REF_INT_B is access INTEGER;
RA: REF_INT_A:= new INTEGER'(10);
RB: REF_INT_B:= new INTEGER'(20);
```

The objects created by the two allocators are both of the same type but the access values are of different types determined by the context of the allocator and the objects are in different collections.

So, although we can write

RA.**all**:= RB.**all**;

we cannot write

RA:= RB;   –– illegal

Exercise 11.4

1   Write a

        procedure APPEND(FIRST: **in out** LINK; SECOND: **in** LINK);

which appends the list SECOND (without copying) to the end of the list FIRST. Take care of any special cases.

2   Write a function SIZE which returns the number of nodes in a tree.

3   Write a function COPY which makes a complete copy of a tree.

11.5   Access types and private types

A private type can be implemented as an access type. Consider once more the type STACK and suppose that we wish to impose no maximum stack size other than that imposed by the overall size of the computer. This can be done by representing the stack as a list.

```
package STACKS is
    type STACK is limited private;
    procedure PUSH(S: in out STACK; X: in INTEGER);
    procedure POP(S: in out STACK; X: out INTEGER);
private
    type CELL;
    type STACK is access CELL;
    type CELL is
        record
            VALUE: INTEGER;
            NEXT: STACK;
        end record;
end;
```

```
package body STACKS is

    procedure PUSH(S: in out STACK; X: in INTEGER) is
    begin
        S:= new CELL'(X, S);
    end;

    procedure POP(S: in out STACK; X: out INTEGER) is
    begin
        X:= S.VALUE;
        S:= S.NEXT;
    end;

end STACKS;
```

When the user declares a stack

```
S: STACK;
```

it automatically takes the default initial value **null** which denotes that the stack is empty. If we call POP when the stack is empty then this will result in attempting to evaluate

```
null.VALUE
```

and this will raise CONSTRAINT_ERROR. The only way in which PUSH can fail is by running out of storage; an attempt to evaluate

```
new CELL'(X, S)
```

could raise STORAGE_ERROR.

This formulation of stacks is one in which we have made the type limited private. Predefined equality would merely have tested two stacks to see if they were the same stack rather than if they had the same values, and assignment would, of course, copy only the pointer to the stack rather than the stack itself. The writing of an appropriate function "=" needs some care. We could attempt

```
function "=" (S, T: STACK) return BOOLEAN is
    SS: STACK:= S;
    TT: STACK:= T;
begin
    while SS /= null and TT /= null loop
        SS:= SS.NEXT;
        TT:= TT.NEXT;
        if SS.VALUE /= TT.VALUE then
            return FALSE;
        end if;
```

```
      end loop;
      return SS = TT;          -- TRUE if both null
   end;
```

but this does not work because we have hidden the predefined equality (and hence inequality) which we wish to use inside the body of "=" by the new definition itself. So this function will recurse indefinitely. The solution is to distinguish between the type STACK and its representation in some way. One possibility would be to make the type STACK a record of one component thus

```
   type CELL;
   type LINK is access CELL;
   type CELL is
      record
         VALUE: INTEGER;
         NEXT: LINK;
      end record;
   type STACK is
      record
         LIST: LINK;
      end record;
```

so that we can distinguish between S, the STACK, and S.LIST, its internal representation.

In the previous section we stated that if we had to write an incomplete declaration first because of circularity (as in the type CELL) then there was an exception to the general rule that the complete declaration had to occur in the same list of declarations. The exception is that a private part and the corresponding package body are treated as a single list of declarations as far as this rule is concerned.

Thus, in either of the above formulations the complete declaration of the type CELL could be moved from the private part to the body of the package STACKS. This might be an advantage since it then follows from the dependency rules that a user program would not need recompiling just because the details of the type CELL are changed. In implementation terms it is possible to do this because it is assumed that values of all access types occupy the same space – typically a single word.

Finally, an access type could conversely refer to a private type. So we could have

```
   type REF_STACK is access STACK;
```

The only special point of interest is that if the accessed type is limited private then an allocator cannot provide an initial value since this would be equivalent to assignment and assignment is not allowed for limited types.

Exercise 11.5

1   Assuming that the exception ERROR is declared in the
specification of STACKS, rewrite procedures PUSH and POP so
that they raise ERROR rather than STORAGE_ERROR and
CONSTRAINT_ERROR.

2   Rewrite PUSH, POP and "=" to use the formulation

```
type STACK is
    record
        LIST: LINK;
    end record;
```

Ignore the possibility of exceptions.

3   Complete the package whose visible part is

```
package QUEUES is
    EMPTY: exception;
    type QUEUE is limited private;
    procedure JOIN(Q: in out QUEUE; X: in ITEM);
    procedure REMOVE(Q: in out QUEUE; X: out ITEM);
    function LENGTH(Q: QUEUE) return INTEGER;
private
```

Items join a queue at one end and are removed from the other so
that a normal first-come-first-served protocol is enforced. An
attempt to remove an item from an empty queue raises the
exception EMPTY. Implement the queue as a singly-linked list but
maintain pointers to both ends of the list so that scanning of the
list is avoided. The function LENGTH returns the number of items
in the queue; again, avoid scanning the list.

11.6   Access types and constraints

Access types can also refer to arrays and discriminated record types. In
both cases they can be constrained or not.

     Consider the problem of representing a family tree. We could
declare

```
type PERSON;
type PERSON_NAME is access PERSON;
```

```
type PERSON is
    record
        SEX: GENDER;
        BIRTH: DATE;
        SPOUSE: PERSON_NAME;
        FATHER: PERSON_NAME;
        FIRST_CHILD: PERSON_NAME;
        NEXT_SIBLING: PERSON_NAME;
    end record;
```

This model assumes a monogamous and legitimate system. The children are linked together through the component NEXT_SIBLING and a person's mother is identified as the spouse of the father.

It might however be more useful to use a discriminated type for a person so that different components could exist for the different sexes and more particularly so that appropriate constraints could be applied. Consider

```
type PERSON(SEX: GENDER);
type PERSON_NAME is access PERSON;

type PERSON(SEX: GENDER) is
    record
        BIRTH: DATE;
        FATHER: PERSON_NAME(MALE);
        NEXT_SIBLING: PERSON_NAME;

        case SEX is
            when MALE =>
                WIFE: PERSON_NAME(FEMALE);
            when FEMALE =>
                HUSBAND: PERSON_NAME(MALE);
                FIRST_CHILD: PERSON_NAME;
        end case;

    end record;
```

The incomplete declaration of PERSON also gives the discriminants (and any default initial expressions); these must, of course, conform to those in the subsequent complete declaration. The component FATHER is now constrained always to access a person whose sex is male (or **null** of course). Similarly the components WIFE and HUSBAND are constrained; note that these had to have distinct identifiers and so could not both be SPOUSE. However, the components FIRST_CHILD and NEXT_SIBLING are not constrained and so could access a person of either sex. We have also taken the opportunity to save on storage by making the children belong to the mother only.

When the object of type PERSON is created by an allocator a value must be provided for the discriminant either through an explicit initial value as in

```
    JANET: PERSON_NAME;
    ...
    JANET:= new PERSON'(FEMALE, (22, FEB, 1967), JOHN, others =>
                                                            null);
```

or by supplying a discriminant constraint thus

```
    JANET:= new PERSON(FEMALE);
```

Note the subtle distinction whereby a quote is needed in the case of the full initial value but not when we just give the constraint. This is because the first takes the form of a qualified expression whereas the second is just a subtype indication. Note also the use of **others** in the aggregate; this is allowed because the last three components all have the same base type.

We could not write

```
    JANET:= new PERSON;
```

because the type PERSON does not have a default discriminant. However, we could declare

```
    subtype WOMAN is PERSON(FEMALE);
```

and then

```
    JANET:= new WOMAN;
```

Such an object cannot later have its discriminant changed. This rule applies even if the discriminant has a default initial expression; objects created by an allocator are in this respect different to objects created by a normal declaration where, the reader will recall, a default initial expression allows unconstrained objects to be declared and later to have their discriminant changed.

On the other hand, we see that despite the absence of a default initial expression for the discriminant, we can nevertheless declare unconstrained objects of type PERSON_NAME; such objects, of course, take the default initial value **null** and so no problem arises. Thus although an allocated object cannot have its discriminant changed, nevertheless an unconstrained access object could refer from time to time to objects with different discriminants.

The reason for not allowing an allocated object to have its discriminant changed is that it could be accessed from several constrained objects such as the components FATHER and it would be difficult to ensure that such constraints were not violated.

For convenience we can define subtypes

```
    subtype MANS_NAME is PERSON_NAME(MALE);
    subtype WOMANS_NAME is PERSON_NAME(FEMALE);
```

We can now write a procedure to marry two people.

```
    procedure MARRY(BRIDE: WOMANS_NAME;
                    GROOM: MANS_NAME) is
begin
    if BRIDE.HUSBAND /= null or GROOM.WIFE /= null then
        raise BIGAMY;
    end if;
    BRIDE.HUSBAND:= GROOM;
    GROOM.WIFE:= BRIDE;
end MARRY;
```

The constraints on the parameters are checked when the parameters are passed (remember that access parameters are always implemented by copy). An attempt to marry people of the wrong sex will raise CONSTRAINT_ERROR at the point of call. On the other hand an attempt to marry a nonexistent person will result in CONSTRAINT_ERROR being raised inside the body of the procedure. Remember that although **in** parameters are constants we can change the components of the accessed objects – we are not changing the values of BRIDE and GROOM to access different objects.

A function could return an access value as for example

```
function SPOUSE(P: PERSON_NAME) return PERSON_NAME is
begin
    case P.SEX is
        when MALE =>
            return P.WIFE;
        when FEMALE =>
            return P.HUSBAND;
    end case;
end SPOUSE;
```

The result of such a function call can be directly used as part of a name so we can write

```
SPOUSE(P).BIRTH
```

to give the birthday of the spouse of P. (See the end of Section 7.1.) We could even write

```
SPOUSE(P).BIRTH:= NEWDATE;
```

but this is only possible because the function delivers an access value. It could not be done if the function actually delivered a value of type PERSON rather than PERSON_NAME. However, we cannot write

```
SPOUSE(P):= Q;
```

in an attempt to replace our spouse by someone else, whereas

```
SPOUSE(P).all:= Q.all;
```

is valid and would change all the components of our spouse to be the same as those of Q.

The following function gives birth to a new child. We need the mother, the sex of the child and the date as parameters.

```
function NEW_CHILD(MOTHER: WOMANS_NAME;
                    BOY_OR_GIRL: GENDER; BIRTHDAY: DATE)
                return PERSON_NAME is
    CHILD: PERSON_NAME;
begin
    if MOTHER.HUSBAND = null then
        raise ILLEGITIMATE;
    end if;
    CHILD:= new PERSON(BOY_OR_GIRL);
    CHILD.BIRTH:= BIRTHDAY;
    CHILD.FATHER:= MOTHER.HUSBAND;
    declare
        LAST: PERSON_NAME:= MOTHER.FIRST_CHILD;
    begin
        if LAST = null then
            MOTHER.FIRST_CHILD:= CHILD;
        else
            while LAST.NEXT_SIBLING /= null loop
                LAST:= LAST.NEXT_SIBLING;
            end loop;
            LAST.NEXT_SIBLING:= CHILD;
        end if;
    end;
    return CHILD;
end NEW_CHILD;
```

Observe that a discriminant constraint need not be static – the value of BOY_OR_GIRL is not known until the function is called. As a consequence we cannot give the complete initial value with the allocator because we do not know which components to provide. Hence, we allocate the child with just the value of the discriminant and then separately assign the date of birth and the father. The remaining components take the default value **null**. We can now write

```
HELEN: PERSON_NAME:=
            NEW_CHILD(BARBARA, FEMALE, (28, SEP, 1969));
```

Access types can also refer to constrained and unconstrained arrays. We could have

```
type REF_MATRIX is access MATRIX;
R: REF_MATRIX;
```

and then obtain new matrices with an allocator thus

```
R:= new MATRIX(1 .. 10, 1 .. 10);
```

Alternatively, the matrix could be initialized

R:= **new** MATRIX'(1 .. 10 => (1 .. 10 => 0.0));

but as for discriminated records we could not write just

R:= **new** MATRIX;

because all array objects must have bounds. Moreover the bounds cannot be changed. However, R can refer to matrices of different bounds from time to time.

As expected we can create subtypes

subtype REF_MATRIX_3 **is** REF_MATRIX(1 .. 3, 1 .. 3);
R_3: REF_MATRIX_3;

and R_3 can then only reference matrices with corresponding bounds. Alternatively we could have written

R_3: REF_MATRIX(1 .. 3, 1 .. 3);

Using

subtype MATRIX_3 **is** MATRIX(1 .. 3, 1 .. 3);

we can then write

R_3:= **new** MATRIX_3;

This is allowed because the subtype supplies the array bounds just as we were allowed to write

JANET:= **new** WOMAN;

because the subtype WOMAN supplied the discriminant SEX.

This introduces another example of an array aggregate with **others**. Because the subtype MATRIX_3 supplies the array bounds and qualifies the aggregate, we could initialize the new object as follows

R_3:= **new** MATRIX_3'(**others** => (**others** => 0.0));

The components of an accessed array can be referred to by the usual mechanism, so

R(1, 1):= 0.0;

would set component (1, 1) of the matrix accessed by R to zero. The whole matrix can be referred to by **all**. So

R_3.**all**:= (1 .. 3 => (1 .. 3 => 0.0));

would set all the components of the matrix accessed by R_3 to zero. We can therefore think of R(1, 1) as an abbreviation for R.**all**(1, 1). As with records, dereferencing is automatic. We can also write attributes R'FIRST(1) or alternatively R.**all**'FIRST(1). In the case of a one-dimensional array slicing is also allowed.

We conclude this section by returning to the topic of ragged arrays. By analogy with the type V_STRING of Section 11.2, we can introduce a type A_STRING which uses an access type

```
type A_STRING is access STRING;
```

and then

```
function "+" (S: STRING) return A_STRING is
begin
    return new STRING'(S);
end "+";
```

and

```
type A_STRING_ARRAY is array (POSITIVE range <>) of A_STRING;

ZOO: constant A_STRING_ARRAY
        := (+"aardvark", +"baboon", ..., +"very long animal... ", ...,
            +"zebra");
```

With this formulation there is no limit on the length of the strings. But of course there is the overhead of the access value which is significant if the strings are short.

Exercise 11.6

1   Write a function to return a person's heir. Follow the normal rules of primogeniture – the heir is the eldest son if there is one and otherwise is the eldest daughter. Return **null** if there is no heir.

2   Write a procedure to divorce a woman. Divorce is only permitted if there are no children.

3   Modify the procedure MARRY in order to prevent incest. A person may not marry their sibling, parent or child.

4   Write functions to return the number of children, the number of siblings, the number of grandchildren and the number of cousins of a person.

11.7 Derived types

Sometimes it is useful to introduce a new type which is similar in most respects to an existing type but which is nevertheless a distinct type. If T is a type we can write

type S **is new** T;

and then S is said to be a derived type and T is the parent type of S.

A derived type belongs to the same class of type as its parent. If T is a record type then S will be a record type and its components will have the same names and so on.

It will be remembered that the key things that distinguish a type are its set of values and its set of operations; we now consider these.

The set of values of a derived type is a copy of the set of values of the parent. An important instance of this is that if the parent type is an access type then the derived type is also an access type and they share the same collection. Note that we say that the set of values is a copy; this reflects that they are truly different types and values of one type cannot be assigned to objects of the other type; however, as we shall see in a moment, conversion between the two types is possible. The notation for literals and aggregates (if any) is the same and any default initial expressions for the type or its components are the same.

The operations applicable to a derived type are as follows. First, it has the same attributes as the parent. Second, unless the parent type, and consequently the derived type, are limited, assignment and predefined equality and inequality are also applicable. Third, a derived type will derive or inherit certain subprograms applicable to the parent type. (We say that a subprogram applies to a type if it has one or more parameters or a result of that type or one of its subtypes.) Such derived subprograms are implicitly declared at the place of the derived type definition but may be later redefined in the same declarative region.

If the parent type is a predefined type then the inherited subprograms are just the predefined subprograms. If the parent type is a user defined type then again there will be some predefined subprograms such as "<" and these will be inherited. If the parent type is itself a derived type then its inherited subprograms will be passed on again.

In addition, if the parent type is declared in the visible part of a package then any applicable subprograms declared in that visible part will also be inherited provided that the derived type is declared after the visible part. Thus the new subprograms only really 'belong' to the type in the sense that they can be derived with it when we reach the end of the visible part; this is quite reasonable since it is at this point that the definition of the type and its operations can be considered to be complete in an abstract sense.

We will now illustrate these rules with some examples. If we have

type INTEGER_A **is new** INTEGER;

then INTEGER_A will inherit all the predefined subprograms such as "+", "−" and "abs" as well as attributes such as FIRST and LAST.

If we derive a further type from INTEGER_A then these inherited subprograms are passed on again. However, suppose that INTEGER_A is declared in a package specification and that the specification includes further subprograms, thus

```
package P is
    type INTEGER_A is new INTEGER;
    procedure INCREMENT(I: in out INTEGER_A);
    function "&" (I, J: INTEGER_A) return INTEGER_A;
end;
```

If we now have

```
type INTEGER_B is new INTEGER_A;
```

declared after the end of the specification (either outside the package or in its body) then INTEGER_B will inherit the new subprograms INCREMENT and "&" as well as the predefined ones.

If we do not like one of the inherited subprograms then it can be redefined in the same declarative region. So we could write

```
package Q is
    type INTEGER_X is new INTEGER;
    function "abs" (X: INTEGER_X) return INTEGER_X;
end;
```

in which for some reason we have chosen to replace the predefined operator "abs" by a new version.

If we now write

```
type INTEGER_Y is new INTEGER_X;
```

after the end of the package specification, the new version of "abs" will be inherited rather than the original one.

There are a couple of other minor rules. We cannot derive from a private type until after its full type declaration. Also, if the parent type is itself a derived type declared in the visible part of a package (such as INTEGER_A) then a type derived from it (such as INTEGER_B) cannot be declared inside that visible part. This restriction does not apply if the parent type is not a derived type; but remember that a type so derived from such a parent will inherit just the predefined subprograms and not any new or replaced ones.

Finally, it should be realized that the predefined types are not really a special case since they and the predefined subprograms are considered to be declared in the visible part of the package STANDARD.

Although derived types are distinct, the values can be converted from one to another using the same notation as was used for converting between numeric types. So given

```
type S is new T;
TX: T;
SX: S;
```

we can write

```
TX:= T(SX);
```

or

```
SX:= S(TX);
```

but not

```
TX:= SX;    -- illegal
```

or

```
SX:= TX;    -- illegal
```

If multiple derivations are involved then only the overall conversion is required; the individual steps need not be given. So if we have

```
type SS is new S;
type TT is new T;
SSX: SS;
TTX: TT;
```

then we can laboriously write

```
SSX:= SS(S(TX));
```

and

```
TTX:= TT(T(SX));
```

or merely

```
SSX:= SS(TX);
```

and

```
TTX:= TT(SX);
```

The introduction of derived types extends the possibility of conversion between array types discussed in Section 6.2. In fact, a value of one array type can be converted to another array type if the component types are the same and the index types are the same or convertible to each other.

Having introduced conversion we can now describe the effective specification of a derived subprogram in more detail. It is obtained from that of the parent by simply replacing all instances of the parent base type in the original specification by the new derived type. Subtypes are replaced by equivalent subtypes with corresponding constraints and default initial expressions are converted by adding a type conversion. Any parameters or result of a different type are left unchanged. As an abstract example consider

```
type T is ... ;
subtype S is T range L .. R;

function F(X: T; Y: T:= E; Z: Q) return S;
```

where E is an expression of type T and the type Q is quite unrelated. If we write

```
type TT is new T;
```

then it is as if we had also written

```
subtype SS is TT range TT(L) .. TT(R);
```

and the specification of the derived function F will then be

```
function F(X: TT; Y: TT:= TT(E); Z: Q) return SS;
```

in which we have replaced T by TT, S by SS, added the conversion to the expression E but left the unrelated type Q unchanged. Note that the parameter names are naturally the same.

We can now rewrite the type STACK of Section 11.5 using a derived type as follows

```
type CELL;
type LINK is access CELL;

type CELL is
    record
        VALUE: INTEGER;
        NEXT: LINK;
    end record;

type STACK is new LINK;
```

It is now possible to write the function "=" thus

```
function "=" (S, T: STACK) return BOOLEAN is
    SL: LINK:= LINK(S);
    TL: LINK:= LINK(T);
begin
    -- as the answer to Exercise 11.5(2)
end "=";
```

An advantage of using a derived type rather than making the type STACK into a record of one component is that the procedures PUSH and

POP of Section 11.5 still work and do not have to be modified. This is because the type STACK is still an access type and shares its collection with the type LINK.

Derived types are often used for private types and in fact we have to use a derived type if we want to express the private type as an existing type such as INTEGER.

Another use for derived types is when we want to use the operations of existing types, but wish to avoid the accidental mixing of objects of conceptually different types. Suppose we wish to count apples and oranges. Then we could declare

```
type APPLES is new INTEGER;
type ORANGES is new INTEGER;
NO_OF_APPLES: APPLES;
NO_OF_ORANGES: ORANGES;
```

Since APPLES and ORANGES are derived from the type INTEGER they both inherit "+". So we can write

```
NO_OF_APPLES:= NO_OF_APPLES+1;
```

and

```
NO_OF_ORANGES:= NO_OF_ORANGES+1;
```

but we cannot write

```
NO_OF_APPLES:= NO_OF_ORANGES;
```

If we did want to convert the oranges to apples we would have to write

```
NO_OF_APPLES:= APPLES(NO_OF_ORANGES);
```

In the next chapter we will consider the numeric types in more detail but it is worth mentioning here that strictly speaking a type such as INTEGER has no literals. Literals such as 1 and integer named numbers are of a type known as universal integer and implicit conversion to any integer type occurs if the context so demands. Thus we can use 1 with APPLES and ORANGES because of this implicit conversion and not because the literal is inherited. Enumeration literals on the other hand do properly belong to their type and are inherited; in fact, as mentioned in Section 7.5, enumeration literals behave as parameterless functions and so can be considered to be inherited in the same way as any other applicable subprogram.

Returning to our apples and oranges suppose that we have overloaded procedures to sell them

```
procedure SELL(N: APPLES);
procedure SELL(N: ORANGES);
```

Then we can write

        SELL(NO_OF_APPLES);

but

        SELL(6);

is ambiguous because we do not know which fruit we are selling. We can resolve the ambiguity by qualification thus

        SELL(APPLES'(6));

When a subprogram is derived a new subprogram is not actually created. A call of the derived subprogram is really a call of the parent subprogram; **in** and **in out** parameters are implicitly converted just before the call; **in out** and **out** parameters or a function result are implicitly converted just after the call.
        So

        MY_APPLES + YOUR_APPLES

is effectively

        APPLES(INTEGER(MY_APPLES) + INTEGER(YOUR_APPLES))

Derived types are in some ways an alternative to private types. Derived types have the advantage of inheriting literals but they often have the disadvantage of inheriting too much. For instance, we could derive types LENGTH and AREA from REAL.

        type LENGTH **is new** REAL;
        type AREA **is new** REAL;

We would then be prevented from mixing lengths and areas but we would also have inherited the ability to multiply two lengths to give a length and to multiply two areas to give an area as well as hosts of irrelevant operations such as exponentiation. Of course, it is possible to redefine these operations to be useful or to raise exceptions but it is often simpler to use private types and just define the operations we need.
        As a further example of the use of derived types, reconsider the package BANK of Exercise 9.3(**1**). In that package we declared

        subtype MONEY **is** NATURAL;

in order to introduce the meaningful identifier MONEY and also to ensure that monies were never negative. However, being only a subtype, we could still mix up monies and integers by mistake. It would be far better to write

        type MONEY **is new** NATURAL;

so that the proper distinction is made.

In the private part shown in the solution we should perhaps similarly have written

type KEY_CODE **is new** INTEGER **range** 0 .. MAX;

The above cases illustrate that we can derive from a subtype using either a type mark or the more general subtype indication. The derived type is then actually anonymous and is derived from the underlying base type. In the case of KEY_CODE it is as if we had written

type anon **is new** INTEGER;
subtype KEY_CODE **is** anon **range** 0 .. MAX;

(where there was no need to write anon(0) .. anon(MAX) because the literal 0 and the named number MAX are of type universal integer and conversion is implicit). So KEY_CODE is not really a type at all but a subtype. The set of values of the new derived type is actually the full set of values of the type INTEGER. The derived operations "+", ">" and so on also work on the full set of values. So given

K: KEY_CODE;

we can legally write

K > −2

even though −2 could never be assigned to K. The Boolean expression is, of course, always true.

The reader may have felt that derived types are not very useful because in the examples we have seen there is usually an alternative mechanism open to us – usually involving record types or private types. However, one importance of derived types is that they are crucial to the mechanism for numeric types as we shall see in the next chapter. In truth, derived types are of fundamental importance to the capability to create types; this will become clearer as we proceed.

We finish this chapter by mentioning a curious anomaly concerning the type BOOLEAN which really does not matter so far as the normal user is concerned. If we derive a type from BOOLEAN then the predefined relational operators =, < and so on continue to deliver a result of the predefined type BOOLEAN whereas the logical operators **and**, **or**, **xor** and **not** are inherited normally and deliver a result of the derived type. We cannot go into the reason here other than to say that it is because of the fundamental nature of the type BOOLEAN. However, it does mean that the theorem of Exercise 4.7(**3**) that **xor** and /= are equivalent only applies to the type BOOLEAN and not to a type derived from it.

Exercise 11.7

1   Declare a package containing types LENGTH and AREA with appropriate redeclarations of the incorrect operations "*".

Checklist 11

If a discriminant does not have a default expression then all objects must be constrained.

The discriminant of an unconstrained object can only be changed by a complete record assignment.

Discriminants can only be used as array bounds or to govern variants or as nested discriminants or in default initial expressions for components.

A discriminant in an aggregate and governing a variant must be static.

Any variant must appear last in a component list.

An incomplete declaration can only be used in an access type.

The scope of an accessed object is that of the access type.

If an accessed object has a discriminant then it is always constrained.

Functions returning access values can be used in names.

Access objects have a default initial value of **null**.

An allocator in an aggregate is evaluated for each index value.

An allocator with a complete initial value uses a quote.

Chapter 12
Numeric Types

We now come at last to a more detailed discussion of numeric types. There are two classes of numeric types in Ada: integer types and real types. The real types are further subdivided into floating point types and fixed point types.

There are two problems concerning the representation of numeric types in a computer. First, the range may be restricted and indeed many machines have hardware operations for various ranges so that we can chose our own compromise between range of values and space occupied by values. Second, it may not be possible to represent accurately all the possible values of a type. These difficulties cause problems with program portability because the constraints vary from machine to machine. Ada recognizes these difficulties and provides numeric types in such a way that a recognized minimum set of properties is provided; this enables the programmer to keep portability problems to a minimum.

This chapter starts by discussing integer types because these suffer only from range problems but not from accuracy problems.

12.1   Integer types

All implementations of Ada have the predefined type INTEGER. In addition there may be other predefined types such as LONG_INTEGER, SHORT_INTEGER and so on. The range of values of these predefined types will be symmetric about zero except for an extra negative value in two's complement machines (which now seem to dominate over one's complement machines). All predefined integer types have the same predefined operations that were described in Chapter 4 as applicable to the type INTEGER (except that the second operand of "**" is always just type INTEGER).

Thus we might find that on machine A we have types INTEGER and LONG_INTEGER with

range of INTEGER:
   −32768 .. +32767   (i.e. 16 bits)

range of LONG_INTEGER:
   −21474_83648 .. +21474_83647   (i.e. 32 bits)

whereas on machine B we might have types SHORT_INTEGER, INTEGER and LONG_INTEGER with

range of SHORT_INTEGER:
   −2048 .. +2047   (i.e. 12 bits)

range of INTEGER:
   −83_88608 .. +83_88607   (i.e. 24 bits)

range of LONG_INTEGER:
   −14073_74883_55328 .. +14073_74883_55327   (i.e. 48 bits)

For most purposes the type INTEGER will suffice on either machine and that is why we have simply used INTEGER in examples in this book so far. However, suppose we have an application where we need to manipulate signed values up to a million. The type INTEGER is inadequate on machine A and to use LONG_INTEGER on machine B would be extravagant. We can overcome our problem by using derived types and writing (for machine A)

type MY_INTEGER **is new** LONG_INTEGER;

and then using MY_INTEGER throughout the program. To move the program to machine B we just replace this one declaration by

type MY_INTEGER **is new** INTEGER;

However, Ada enables this choice to be made automatically; if we write

type MY_INTEGER **is range** −1E6 .. 1E6;

then the implementation will implicitly chose the smallest appropriate type and it will be as if we had written either

type MY_INTEGER **is new** LONG_INTEGER **range** −1E6 .. 1E6;

or

type MY_INTEGER **is new** INTEGER **range** −1E6 .. 1E6;

So in fact MY_INTEGER will be a subtype of an anonymous type derived from one of the predefined types and so objects of type MY_INTEGER will be constrained to take only the values in the range $-1E6 .. 1E6$ and not the full range of the anonymous type. Note that the range must have static bounds since the choice of base type is made at compilation time.

If, out of curiosity, we wanted to know the full range we could use MY_INTEGER'BASE'FIRST and MY_INTEGER'BASE'LAST.

The attribute BASE applies to any type or subtype and gives the corresponding base type. It can only be used to form other attributes as in this example. We could even go so far as to ensure that we could use the full range of the predefined type by writing

```
type X is range −1E6 .. 1E6;
type MY_INTEGER is range X'BASE'FIRST .. X'BASE'LAST;
```

This would have the dubious merit of avoiding the constraint checks when values are assigned to objects of type MY_INTEGER and would destroy the very portability we were seeking.

We can convert between one integer type and another by using the normal notation for type conversion. Given

```
type MY_INTEGER is range −1E6 .. 1E6;
type INDEX is range 0 .. 10000;
M: MY_INTEGER;
I: INDEX;
```

then we can write

```
M:= MY_INTEGER(I);
I:= INDEX(M);
```

On machine A a genuine hardware conversion is necessary but on machine B both types will be derived from INTEGER and the conversion will be null.

Note that, as mentioned in the last chapter, we can convert directly between related derived types and do not have to give each individual step. If this were not so we would have to write

```
M:= MY_INTEGER(LONG_INTEGER(INTEGER(I)));
```

on machine A and

```
M:= MY_INTEGER(INTEGER(I));
```

on machine B and our portability would be lost.

The integer literals are considered to belong to a type known as universal integer. The range of this type is at least as large as any of the predefined integer types and it has all the usual operations of an integer type such as $+$, $-$, $<$ and $=$. Integer numbers declared in a number declaration (see Section 4.1) such as

```
TEN: constant:= 10;
```

are also of type universal integer. However, there are no universal integer variables and as a consequence most universal integer expressions are static. The initial value in a number declaration has to be a static universal expression. So

> M: **constant**:= 10;   EVAL AT COMPILE TIME
> MM: **constant**:= M*M;

is allowed since M*M is a static universal expression. However

> N: **constant** INTEGER:= 10;   EVAL AT RUN TIME
> NN: **constant**:= N*N;

is not allowed since N*N is not a static expression of type universal integer but merely a static expression of type INTEGER.

It should be noted that certain attributes such as POS in fact deliver a universal integer value, and since POS can take a dynamic argument it follows that certain universal integer expressions may actually be dynamic.

Conversion of integer literals, integer numbers and universal integer attributes to other integer types is automatic and does not require an explicit type conversion. Problems of ambiguity, however, demand that conversion of more general expressions has to be explicit.

The reader may recall that a range such as 1 .. 10 occurring in a for statement or in an array type definition is considered to be of type INTEGER. The full rule is that the bounds must again be integer literals, integer numbers or universal integer attributes but not a more general expression. Note incidentally that specifying that the range is type INTEGER rather than any other integer type means that the predefined type INTEGER does have rather special properties.

We now see why we could not write

> **for** I **in** −1 .. 10 **loop**

in Section 5.3. But we could introduce an integer number for −1 and then use that as the lower bound

> MINUS_ONE: **constant**:= −1;
> ...
> **for** I **in** MINUS_ONE .. 10 **loop**

The use of integer type declarations which reflect the need of the program rather than the arbitrary use of INTEGER and LONG_INTEGER is good practice because it not only encourages portability but also enables us to distinguish between different classes of objects as, for example, when we were counting apples and oranges in the last chapter.

Consideration of separation of classes is the key to deciding whether or not to use numeric constants (of a specific type) or named numbers (of type universal integer). If a literal value is a pure mathematical number then it should be declared as a named number. If, however, it is a value related naturally to just one of the program types then it should be declared as a constant of that type. Thus if we are counting oranges and are checking against a limit of 100 it is better to write

        MAX_ORANGES: **constant** ORANGES:= 100;

rather than

        MAX_ORANGES: **constant**:= 100;

so that the accidental mixing of types as in

        if NO_OF_APPLES = MAX_ORANGES **then**

will be detected by the compiler.

Returning to the question of portability it should be realized that complete portability is not easily obtained. For example, assume

        type MY_INTEGER **is range** −1E6 .. +1E6;
        I, J: MY_INTEGER;

and consider

        I:= 100000;
        J:= I*I;

In order to understand the behaviour it is most important to remember that MY_INTEGER is really only a subtype of an anonymous type derived from LONG_INTEGER on machine A or INTEGER on machine B. The derived operations +, −, *, / and so on have the anonymous type as operands and results and the subtype constraint is only relevant when we attempt to assign to J. So J:= I*I; is effectively (on machine A)

        J:= anon(LONG_INTEGER(I)*LONG_INTEGER(I));

and the multiplication is performed with the operation of the type LONG_INTEGER. The result is 1E10 and this is well within the range of LONG_INTEGER. However, when we attempt to assign the result to J we get CONSTRAINT_ERROR.

On machine B on the other hand the type is derived from INTEGER and this time the result of the multiplication is outside the range of INTEGER. So NUMERIC_ERROR is raised by the multiplication itself.

Thus, although the program fails in both cases, the actual exception raised could be different. However, we recall from Section 11.1 that NUMERIC_ERROR and CONSTRAINT_ERROR should be treated as the same and so this example is somewhat irrelevant although it does perhaps illustrate another reason for not distinguishing the two exceptions.

A more interesting case is

        I:= 100000;
        J:= (I*I)/100000;

On machine A the intermediate product and final result are computed with no problem and, moreover, the final result lies within the range of J and so no exception is raised. But on machine B we again get NUMERIC_ERROR (alias CONSTRAINT_ERROR).

(The above analysis has ignored the possibility of optimization. The language allows the implementation to use a wider type in order to avoid NUMERIC_ERROR provided that the correct result is obtained. However, the example is certainly valid if machine B did not have a type LONG_INTEGER.)

Finally, we note that the most negative and most positive values supported by the predefined integer types are given by SYSTEM.MIN_INT and SYSTEM.MAX_INT. These are, of course, implementation dependent and are numbers declared in the package SYSTEM which is a predefined library package containing various such implementation dependent constants.

Exercise 12.1

1   What types on machines A and B are used to represent

```
type P is range 1 .. 1000;
type Q is range 0 .. +32768;
type R is range −1E14 .. +1E14;
```

2   Would it make any difference if A and B were one's complement machines with the same number of bits in the representations?

3   Given

```
N: INTEGER:= 6;
P: constant:= 3;
R: MY_INTEGER:= 4;
```

what is the type of

(a)   N+P

(b)   N+R

(c)   P+R

(d)   N∗N

(e)   P∗P

(f)   R∗R

4   Declare a type LONGEST_INTEGER which is the maximum supported by the implementation.

12.2 Real types

Integer types are exact types. Real types, however, are approximate and introduce problems of accuracy which have subtle effects. This book is not a specialized treatise on errors in numerical analysis and so we do not intend to give all the details of how the features of Ada can be used to minimize errors and maximize portability but will concentrate instead on outlining the basic principles.

Real types are subdivided into floating point types and fixed point types. Apart from the details of representation, the key abstract difference is that floating point values have a relative error whereas fixed point values have an absolute error. Concepts common to both floating and fixed point types are dealt with in this section and further details of the individual types are in subsequent sections.

There is a type universal real having similar properties to the type universal integer. Static operations on this type are notionally carried out with infinite accuracy during compilation. The real literals (see Section 3.4) are of type universal real. Real numbers declared in a number declaration such as

PI: **constant**:= 3.14159_26536;

are also of type universal real. (The reader will recall that the difference between an integer literal and a real literal is that a real literal always has a point in it.)

As well as the usual operations on a real type, some mixing of universal real and universal integer operands is also allowed. Specifically, a universal real can be multiplied by a universal integer and vice versa and division is allowed with the first operand being universal real and the second operand being universal integer; in all cases the result is universal real.

So we can write either

TWO_PI: **constant**:= 2*PI;

or

TWO_PI: **constant**:= 2.0*PI;

but not

PI_PLUS_TWO: **constant**:= PI+2;

because mixed addition is not defined. Note that we cannot do an explicit type conversion between universal integer and universal real although we can always convert the former into the latter by multiplying by 1.0.

An important concept is the idea of a model number. When we declare a real type T we demand a certain accuracy. The implementation will, typically, use a greater accuracy just as an implementation of an integer type uses a base type which has a larger range than that requested.

Corresponding to the accuracy requested will be a set of model numbers which are guaranteed to be exactly represented. Because the implemented accuracy will usually be higher, other values will also be represented. Associated with each value will be a model interval. If a value is a model number then the model interval is simply the model number. Otherwise the model interval is the interval consisting of the two model numbers surrounding the value. Special cases arise if a value is greater than the largest model number T'LARGE.

When an operation is performed the bounds of the result are given by the smallest model interval that can arise as a consequence of operating upon any values in the model intervals of the operands.

The relational operators =, > and so on are also defined in terms of model intervals. If the result is the same, whatever values are chosen in the intervals, then its value is clearly not in dispute. If, however, the result depends upon which values in the intervals are chosen then the result is undefined.

Some care is needed in the interpretation of these principles. A key point is that although we may not know where a value lies in a model interval, nevertheless it does have a specific value and should not be treated in a stochastic manner. There is perhaps some philosophical analogy here with Quantum Mechanics – the knowing of the specific value is the collapse of the wave packet! The behaviour of model numbers will be illustrated with examples in the next section and hopefully these remarks will then make more sense.

Exercise 12.2

1   Given

```
TWO: INTEGER:= 2;
E: constant:= 2.71828_18285;
MAX: constant:= 100;
```

what is the type of

(a)   TWO*E
(b)   TWO*MAX
(c)   E*MAX
(d)   TWO*TWO
(e)   E*E
(f)   MAX*MAX

2   Given

```
N: constant:= 100;
```

declare a real number R having the same value as N.

12.3 Floating point types

Our discussion so far has been in terms of a type REAL introduced in Section 2.4. This is not a predefined type but has been used to emphasize that the direct use of the predefined floating point types is not good practice.

In fact, in a similar way to integers, all implementations have a predefined type FLOAT and may also have further predefined types SHORT_FLOAT, LONG_FLOAT and so on with respectively less and more precision. These types all have the predefined operations that were described in Chapter 4 as applicable to the type REAL.

So, as outlined earlier, we can derive our own type directly by

type REAL **is new** FLOAT;

or perhaps

type REAL **is new** LONG_FLOAT;

according to the implemented precision but just as with the integer types it is better to state the precision required and allow the implementation to choose appropriately.

If we write

type REAL **is digits** 7;

then we are asking the implementation to derive REAL from a predefined type with at least 7 decimal digits of precision.

The precise behaviour is defined in terms of our model numbers. Suppose we consider the more general case

type REAL **is digits** D;

where D is a positive static integer expression. D is the number of decimal digits required and we first convert this to B, the corresponding number of binary digits giving at least the same relative precision. B has to be one more than the least integer greater than $D.\log_2 10$ or in other words

$$B-1 < 1 + (3.3219... \times D) < B$$

The binary precision B determines the model numbers; these are defined to be zero plus all numbers of the form

$$sign.mantissa.2^{exponent}$$

where

$sign$ is $+1$ or -1,

$\frac{1}{2} \leqslant mantissa < 1$,

$-4B \leqslant exponent \leqslant +4B$

and the mantissa has exactly B digits after the binary point when expressed in base 2. The range of the exponent, which is an integer, has been chosen to be $\pm 4B$ somewhat arbitrarily after a survey of ranges provided by contemporary architectures.

When we say

```
type REAL is digits 7;
```

we are guaranteed that the model numbers of the predefined floating point type chosen will include the model numbers for decimal precision 7.

As an extreme example suppose we consider

```
type ROUGH is digits 1;
```

Then D is 1 and so B is 5. The model numbers are values where the mantissa can be one of

$$^{16}/_{32},\ ^{17}/_{32},\ \ldots,\ ^{31}/_{32}$$

and the binary exponent lies in -20 .. 20.

The model numbers around one are

$$\ldots,\ ^{30}/_{32},\ ^{31}/_{32},\ 1,\ 1^{1}/_{16},\ 1^{2}/_{16},\ 1^{3}/_{16},\ \ldots$$

and the model numbers around zero are

$$\ldots,\ -^{17}/_{32}\cdot 2^{-20},\ -^{16}/_{32}\cdot 2^{-20},\ 0,\ +^{16}/_{32}\cdot 2^{-20},\ +^{17}/_{32}\cdot 2^{-20},\ \ldots$$

Note the change of absolute accuracy at one and the hole around zero. By the latter we mean the gaps between zero and the smallest model numbers which in this case are 16 times the difference between them and the next model numbers. There is therefore a gross loss of accuracy at zero. These model numbers are illustrated in Figure 12.1.

The largest model numbers are

$$\ldots,\ ^{29}/_{32}\cdot 2^{20},\ ^{30}/_{32}\cdot 2^{20},\ ^{31}/_{32}\cdot 2^{20}$$

or

$$\ldots,\ 950272,\ 983040,\ 1015808$$

```
(a) around 1        ... X X X X   X   X   X ...
                            1

(b) around 0    ... X X X X    X    X X X X ...
                               0
```

Figure 12.1 Model numbers of type ROUGH.

Suppose we write

    R: ROUGH:= 1.05;

then without considering the actual predefined floating point type chosen
for R the literal 1.05 will be converted to a number between 1 and $1\frac{1}{16}$
inclusive which are the model numbers surrounding 1.05 but we do not
know which. So all we know is that the value of R lies in the model interval
$[1, 1\frac{1}{16}]$.

If we compute

    R:= R*R;

then the computed mathematical result must lie between $1^2 = 1$ and
$(1\frac{1}{16})^2 = {}^{289}\!/_{256} = 1\frac{33}{256}$. However, $1\frac{33}{256}$ is not a model number and so we
take the next model number above as the upper bound of the result; this is
$1\frac{3}{16}$. Hence all we can conclude is that R must now lie in the model interval
$[1, 1\frac{3}{16}]$. And this is all we know! Type ROUGH indeed.

The result of

    R > 1.0

is not defined since $1 > 1$ is false but $1\frac{3}{16} > 1$ is true.

Similarly

    R = 1.0

is not defined since $1 = 1$ is true but $1\frac{3}{16} = 1$ is false.

However

    R >= 1.0

is well defined and is true. So, perhaps surprisingly, the operations =, >
and >= do not always have their expected relationship when applied to
floating point types.

The analysis we have just done should be understood to be in terms
of predicting the values before executing the program. Of course, when the
program actually runs, R has a genuine value and is not undefined in any
way. Thus R > 1.0 will have the value true or the value false but will not be
undefined; what is undefined is that we cannot beforehand, just given the
pure Ada and without knowing any extraneous information about the
implementation, predict which of true and false will be the value. In
particular R = R is always true no matter what operations are performed.
Hopefully the remark in the last section about Quantum Mechanics can
now be appreciated. It is as if when we run the program we perform an
observation on R and it then takes on an eigenvalue; but we cannot push
the analogy too far.

The crudity of the type ROUGH in the above example is extreme but
illustrates the dangers of errors. The hole around zero is a particular danger
– if a result falls in that hole then we say that underflow has occurred and all
accuracy will be lost. Our value has gone down a black hole!

In practice we will do rather better because the type ROUGH will undoubtedly be derived from a predefined type with more precision. Suppose that on a particular machine we just have a predefined type FLOAT with D = 7. Then writing

type ROUGH **is digits** 1;

is equivalent to

type anon **is new** FLOAT;
subtype ROUGH **is** anon **digits** 1;

The type ROUGH is therefore really a subtype of the derived type anon and operations on values will be performed with the numbers of the type FLOAT. In order to describe the mechanism more precisely we introduce the concept of safe numbers.

The safe numbers of a type are a superset of the model numbers and have similar computational properties. The safe numbers have the same number of digits B but the exponent range is $\pm E$ where E is at least equal to $4B$. Thus the safe numbers extend the reliable range and allow an implementation to take better advantage of the hardware. Another important difference between model numbers and safe numbers is that the safe numbers of a subtype are those of the base type whereas the model numbers of a subtype are those implied by the accuracy requested in its definition.

As an example, the safe numbers of the type ROUGH are the safe numbers of FLOAT whereas the model numbers of ROUGH are those defined by $D = 1$. The operations apply to the safe numbers and it is these numbers that can be stored in objects of the type ROUGH.

The point of all this is that if we wish to write a portable program then we must stick to the properties of the model numbers, whereas if we wish to get the most out of an implementation then we can exploit the properties of the safe numbers. Note also that an implementation may provide additional numbers to the safe numbers; they cannot be relied upon in the sense that the language does not define their properties other than those implied by the model intervals or safe intervals.

As a minor point we could also impose a range constraint on a floating point subtype or object by for example

R: ROUGH **range** 0.0 .. 100.0;

or

subtype POSITIVE_REAL **is** REAL **range** 0.0 .. REAL'LAST;

and so on. If a range is violated then CONSTRAINT_ERROR is raised.

As well as a type REAL, we might declare a more accurate type LONG_REAL perhaps for the more sensitive parts of our calculation

type LONG_REAL **is digits** 12;

and then declare variables of the two types

```
R: REAL;
LR: LONG_REAL;
```

as required. Conversion between these follows similar rules to integer types

```
R:= REAL(LR);
LR:= LONG_REAL(R);
```

and we need not concern ourselves with whether REAL and LONG_REAL are derived from the same or different predefined types.

Again in a similar manner to integer types, conversion of real literals, real numbers and universal real attributes to floating types is automatic but more general universal real expressions require explicit conversion.

Various attributes are available and they can be used to help in writing more portable programs. For any type (or subtype) F (predefined or not) they are

F'DIGITS	the number of decimal digits, D,
F'MANTISSA	the corresponding number of binary digits, B,
F'EMAX	the maximum exponent, 4*F'MANTISSA,
F'SMALL	the smallest possible model number, 2.0**(−F'EMAX−1),
F'LARGE	the largest positive model number, 2.0**F'EMAX*(1.0−2.0**(−F'MANTISSA)),
F'EPSILON	the difference between 1.0 and the next model number above, 2.0**(1−F'MANTISSA).

In addition there are attributes F'SAFE_EMAX, F'SAFE_SMALL and F'SAFE_LARGE which give the corresponding properties of the safe numbers of the type or subtype.

There are also the usual attributes F'FIRST and F'LAST which need not be model numbers or safe numbers but are the actual extreme values of the type or subtype.

DIGITS, MANTISSA, EMAX and SAFE_EMAX are of type universal integer; SMALL, SAFE_SMALL, LARGE, SAFE_LARGE and EPSILON are of type universal real; FIRST and LAST are of type F.

The attribute BASE can again be used to enable us to find out about the implemented type. So ROUGH'DIGITS=1 and ROUGH'BASE'DIGITS=7.

No more will be said about floating point but it is hoped that the reader will have understood the principles involved. In general one can simply specify the precision required and all will work. But care is sometimes needed and the advice of a professional numerical analyst should be sought when in doubt. For further details the reader should consult the *LRM*.

Exercise 12.3

1   What is the value of ROUGH'EPSILON?

2   Compute the model interval in which the value of R must lie after

```
type REAL is digits 5;

P: REAL:= 2.0;
Q: REAL:= 3.0;
R: REAL:= (P/Q)*Q;
```

3   What would be the effect of writing

```
P: constant:= 2.0;
Q: constant:= 3.0;
R: REAL:= (P/Q)*Q;
S: REAL:= REAL((P/Q)*Q);
```

4   How many model numbers are there of type ROUGH?

5   The function

```
function HYPOTENUSE(X, Y: REAL) return REAL is
begin
    return SQRT(X**2+Y**2);
end;
```

suffers from underflow if X and Y are small. Rewrite it to avoid this by testing X and Y against a suitable value and then rescaling if necessary.

6   Explain why B is not just the least integer greater than $D.\log_2 10$ but one more. Use the type ROUGH to illustrate your answer.

7   What is the ratio between the size of the hole around zero and the gap between the next model numbers for a general value of B?

8   Rewrite the function INNER of Section 7.1 using a local type LONG_REAL with 14 digits accuracy to perform the calculation in the loop.

12.4   Fixed point types

Fixed point is normally used only in specialized applications or for doing approximate arithmetic on machines without floating point hardware.

The general principle of derivation from predefined types applies also to fixed point. However, unlike the integer and floating point types, the predefined fixed point types are anonymous and so cannot be used directly but have to be used via a fixed point declaration. Such a declaration specifies an absolute error and also a mandatory range. It takes the form

type F **is delta** D **range** L .. R;

In effect this is asking for values in the range L to R with an accuracy of D which must be positive. D, L and R must be real and static. The above declaration is essentially equivalent to

type anon **is new** fixed;
subtype F **is** anon **range** anon(L) .. anon(R);

where fixed is an appropriate predefined and anonymous fixed point type.

A fixed point type (or subtype) is characterized by two attributes, a positive integer B and a positive real number *small*. B indicates the number of bits required for the number (apart from the sign) and *small* is the absolute precision. The model numbers are therefore zero plus all numbers of the form

sign.mantissa.small

where

sign is $+1$ or -1
$0 < mantissa < 2^B$

The definition

delta D **range** L .. R

implies a value of *small* which is the largest power of 2 less than or equal to D and a value of B which is the smallest integer such that L and R are no more than *small* from a model number.

As an example, if we have

type T **is delta** 0.1 **range** -1.0 .. $+1.0$;

then *small* will be $\frac{1}{16}$ and B will be 4. The model numbers of T are therefore

$$-{}^{15}\!/_{16}, \ -{}^{14}\!/_{16}, \ ..., \ -{}^{1}\!/_{16}, \ 0, \ +{}^{1}\!/_{16}, \ ..., \ +{}^{14}\!/_{16}, \ +{}^{15}\!/_{16}$$

Note carefully that L and R are actually outside the range of model numbers and are both exactly *small* from a model number; the definition just allows this.

If we have a typical 16 bit implementation then there will be a wide choice of predefined types from which T can be derived. The only requirement is that the model numbers of the predefined type include those of T. Assuming therefore that the predefined type will have $B = 15$, then at one extreme *small* could be 2^{-15} which would give us a much greater accuracy but the same range whereas at the other extreme *small* could be $\frac{1}{16}$ in which case we would have a much greater range but the same accuracy.

If we assume for the sake of argument that the implementation chooses the predefined type with the greatest accuracy then its model numbers will be

$$- \frac{2^{15} - 1}{2^{15}} , \quad \ldots, \quad - \frac{1}{2^{15}} , \quad 0, \quad + \frac{1}{2^{15}} , \quad \ldots, \quad + \frac{2^{15} - 1}{2^{15}}$$

The concept of safe numbers is also defined for fixed point types. The safe numbers of a type are the model numbers of its base type and the safe numbers of a predefined type are just its model numbers. So the safe numbers of T are the model numbers of the chosen predefined type. Similar remarks apply regarding portability as with floating point types. If we just assume the properties of the model numbers then portability is assured but we can also rely upon the safe numbers if we wish to get the best out of a particular implementation.

Returning to the type T, a different implementation might use just eight bits. Moreover, using representation clauses (which will be discussed in more detail in Chapter 15) it is possible to give the compiler more precise instructions. We can say

for T'SIZE **use** 5;

which will force the implementation to use the minimum five bits. Of course, it might be ridiculous for a particular architecture and in fact the compiler is allowed to refuse unreasonable representation clauses.

We can also override the rule that *small* is a power of 2 by using a representation clause. Writing

for T'SIZE **use** 5;
for T'SMALL **use** 0.1;

will result in the model numbers being

$$-1.5, -1.4, \ldots, -0.1, 0, +0.1, \ldots, +1.4, +1.5$$

In this case the predefined type has to have the same model numbers. This is because we have pinned down the possible implementation so tightly that there is only one *a priori* possible value for the predefined *small* anyway. However, and perhaps surprisingly, AI-341 states that specifying *small* via a representation clause always ensures that the selected predefined type will also have this value of *small*. In other words, any spare bits give extra range and not extra accuracy. This is yet another win for the accountants at the expense of the engineers!

The advantage of using the default standard whereby *small* is a power of 2 is that conversion between fixed point and other numeric types can be based on shifting. The use of other values of *small* will in general mean that conversion requires implicit multiplication and division.

It should be realized that the predefined fixed point types are somewhat ephemeral; they are not so much predefined as made up anonymously on the spot as required. However, an implementation is only formally required to have one anonymous predefined type. In such a case the *small* for the one type would inevitably be a power of 2 and so any attempt to specify a value of *small* which was not a multiple of this value would fail. Hence the sophisticated use of fixed point types is very dependent upon the implementation.

A standard simple example is given by

```
DEL: constant:= 2.0**(−15);
type FRAC is delta DEL range −1.0 .. 1.0;
```

which will be represented as a pure fraction on a 16 bit two's complement machine. Note that it does not really matter whether the upper bound is written as 1.0 or 1.0−DEL; the largest model number will be 1.0−DEL in either case. Moreover, −1.0 is not a model number either; the model numbers are symmetric about zero (AI-147).

A good example of the use of a specified value for *small* is given by a type representing an angle and which uses the whole of a 16 bit word

```
type ANGLE is delta 0.1 range −PI .. PI;
for ANGLE'SMALL use PI*2**(−15);
```

Note that the value given for the representation clause for ANGLE'SMALL must not exceed the value for delta which it overrides.

The arithmetic operations +, −, *, / and **abs** can be applied to fixed point values. Addition and subtraction can only be applied to values of the same type and, of course, return that type. Multiplication and division are allowed between different fixed types but always return values of an infinitely accurate type known as universal fixed. Such a value must be explicitly converted by a type conversion to a particular type before any further operation can be performed. Multiplication and division by type INTEGER are also allowed and these return a value of the fixed point type.

The behaviour of fixed point arithmetic is, like floating point arithmetic, defined in terms of the model numbers. Conversion of real literals and other universal real expressions to fixed point types follows similar rules to the floating types.

So given

```
F, G: FRAC;
```

we can write

```
F:= F+G;
```

but not

```
F:= F*G;              -- illegal
```

but must explicitly state

```
F:= FRAC(F*G);
```

It should be noted that multiplication and division between a fixed point type and a universal real operand is not allowed. Moreover, because multiplication and division are defined between any pair of fixed point types it follows that automatic conversion of a simple universal real operand to match a fixed point operand is not possible because there is not a unique fixed point type to which it can be converted. The net result is that we cannot write

```
F:= FRAC(0.5*F);      -- illegal
```

but must explicitly write

```
F:= FRAC(FRAC(0.5)*F);
```

On the other hand we can write

```
F:= F+0.5;
```

because addition is only allowed between the same fixed point types and so the universal real 0.5 is uniquely converted to type FRAC. Note, moreover, that we can write

```
F:= 2*F;
```

because multiplication is defined between fixed point types and INTEGER (and not other integer types) and so the universal integer 2 is uniquely converted to type INTEGER.

As a more detailed example we return to the package COMPLEX_NUMBERS of Section 9.1 and consider how we might implement the package body using a polar representation. Any reader who gave thought to the problem will have realized that writing a function to normalize an angle expressed in radians to lie in the range 0 to 2π using floating point raises problems of accuracy since 2π is not a model number.

An alternative approach is to use a fixed point type. We can then arrange for π to be a model number. Another natural advantage is that fixed point types have uniform absolute error which matches the physical behaviour. The type ANGLE declared above is not quite appropriate because, as we shall see, it will be convenient to allow for angles of up to 2π.

The private part of the package could be

```
private
   PI: constant:= 3.14159_26536;
   type ANGLE is delta 0.1 range −4*PI .. 4*PI;
   for ANGLE'SMALL use PI*2**(−13);
   type COMPLEX is
      record
         R: REAL;
         THETA: ANGLE range −PI .. PI;
      end record;
   I: constant COMPLEX:= (1.0, 0.5*PI);
end;
```

The function for normalizing an angle to lie in the range of the component THETA (which is neater if symmetric about zero) could now be

```
function NORMAL(A: ANGLE) return ANGLE is
begin
   if A >= PI then
      return A − ANGLE(2*PI);
   elsif A < −PI then
      return A + ANGLE(2*PI);
   else
      return A;
   end if;
end NORMAL;
```

Note how we had to use the explicit type conversion in order to convert the universal real expression 2*PI to type ANGLE; remember that automatic conversion of universal real values only applies to single items and not to general expressions. We could alternatively have written

```
      return A − TWO_PI;
```

where TWO_PI is a real number as declared in Section 12.2.

Another interesting point is that the values for THETA that we are using do not include the upper bound of the range +PI; the function NORMAL converts this into the equivalent −PI. Unfortunately, we cannot express the idea of an open bound in Ada although it would be perfectly straightforward to implement the corresponding checks.

The range for the type ANGLE has been chosen so that it will accommodate the sum of any two values of THETA. This includes −2*PI; however, making the lower bound of the range for ANGLE equal to −2*PI is not adequate since there is no guarantee that the lower bound will be a model number − not even on a two's complement implementation. So to be on the safe side we squander a bit on doubling the range.

The various functions in the package body can now be written; we assume that we have access to appropriate trigonometric functions applying to the fixed point type ANGLE and returning results of type REAL. So we might have

```
package body COMPLEX_NUMBERS is
    function NORMAL ...      -- as above
    ...
    function "*" (X, Y: COMPLEX) return COMPLEX is
    begin
        return (X.R * Y.R, NORMAL(X.THETA + Y.THETA));
     end "*";
    ...
    function RL_PART(X: COMPLEX) return REAL is
    begin
        return X.R * COS(X.THETA);
    end RL_PART;
    ...
end COMPLEX_NUMBERS;
```

where we have left the more complicated functions for the enthusiastic reader.

We conclude by noting that the various attributes of a fixed point type or subtype F are as follows

F'DELTA	the requested delta, D,
F'MANTISSA	the number of bits, B,
F'SMALL	the smallest positive model number, *small*,
F'LARGE	the largest positive model number, $(2**F'MANTISSA-1)*F'SMALL$.

In addition there are attributes F'SAFE_SMALL and F'SAFE_LARGE which give the corresponding properties of the safe numbers. Note that F'SAFE_SMALL = F'BASE'SMALL for fixed point types.

There are also the usual attributes F'FIRST and F'LAST which give the actual upper and lower bounds of the type or subtype and of course need not be model numbers.

DELTA, SMALL, SAFE_SMALL, LARGE and SAFE_LARGE are of type universal real; MANTISSA is of type universal integer; FIRST and LAST are of type F.

Exercise 12.4

1   Given F of type FRAC compute the model interval of F after

       F:= 0.1;

2   Why could we not have written

       return A − 2.0*PI;

in the function NORMAL in order to avoid the explicit type conversion?

3   Write the following further function for the package COMPLEX_ NUMBERS implemented as in this section

> **function** "******" (X: COMPLEX; N: INTEGER) **return** COMPLEX;

Remember that if a complex number z is represented in polar form (r, θ), then

$$z^n \equiv (r, \theta)^n = (r^n, n\theta)$$

4   An alternative approach to the representation of angles in fixed point would be to hold the values in degrees. Rewrite the private part and the function NORMAL using a canonical range of 0.0 .. 360.0 for THETA. Make the most of a 16 bit word but use a power of 2 for *small*.

Checklist 12

Use implicitly derived types for increased portability.

Beware of overflow in intermediate expressions.

Use named numbers or typed constants as appropriate.

Beware of underflow into the hole around floating point zero.

Beware of the relational operations with real types.

If in doubt consult a numerical analyst.

Chapter 13
Generics

There are two major concepts in Ada which are static. These are types and subprograms. By this statement we mean that all types and subprograms are identified before program execution. The static nature of these concepts increases the possibility of proving the correctness of programs as well as simplifying implementation considerations. The idea that types are static will be familiar from other languages. However, many languages (such as Algol, FORTRAN and Pascal) have dynamic procedures (at least as parameters to other procedures) and their absence in Ada comes as a bit of a surprise.

In this chapter we describe the generic mechanism which allows us to overcome the static nature of types and subprograms by a special form of parameterization which can be applied to subprograms and packages. The generic parameters can be types and subprograms as well as values and objects.

13.1 Declarations and instantiations

One of the problems with a typed language such as Ada is that all types have to be determined at compilation time. This means naturally that we cannot pass types as run-time parameters. However, we often get the situation that the logic of a piece of program is independent of the types involved and it therefore seems unnecessary to repeat it for all the different types to which we might wish it to apply. A simple example is provided by the procedure SWAP of Exercise 7.3(**1**)

```
procedure SWAP(X, Y: in out REAL) is
    T: REAL;
begin
    T:= X;  X:= Y;  Y:= T;
end;
```

It is clear that the logic is independent of the type of the values being swapped. If we also wanted to swap integers or Booleans we could of course write other procedures but this would be tedious. The generic mechanism allows us to overcome this. We can declare

```
generic
    type ITEM is private;
procedure EXCHANGE(X, Y: in out ITEM);

procedure EXCHANGE(X, Y: in out ITEM) is
    T: ITEM;
begin
    T:= X;  X:= Y;  Y:= T;
end;
```

The subprogram EXCHANGE is a generic subprogram and acts as a kind of template. The subprogram specification is preceded by the generic formal part consisting of the reserved word **generic** followed by a (possibly empty) list of generic formal parameters. The subprogram body is written exactly as normal but note that, in the case of a generic subprogram, we have to give both the body and the specification separately.

The generic procedure cannot be called directly but from it we can create an actual procedure by a mechanism known as generic instantiation. For example, we may write

```
procedure SWAP is new EXCHANGE(REAL);
```

This is a declaration and states that SWAP is to be obtained from the template described by EXCHANGE. Actual generic parameters are provided in a parameter list in the usual way. The actual parameter in this case is the type REAL which corresponds to the formal parameter ITEM. We could also use the named notation

```
procedure SWAP is new EXCHANGE(ITEM => REAL);
```

So we have now created the procedure SWAP acting on type REAL and can henceforth call it in the usual way. We can make further instantiations

```
procedure SWAP is new EXCHANGE(INTEGER);
procedure SWAP is new EXCHANGE(DATE);
```

and so on. We are here creating further overloadings of SWAP which can be distinguished by their parameter types just as if we had laboriously written them out in detail.

Superficially, it may look as if the generic mechanism is merely one of text substitution and indeed in this simple case the behaviour would be the same. However, the important difference relates to the meaning of identifiers in the generic body but which are neither parameters nor local to the body. Such non-local identifiers have meanings appropriate to where the generic body is declared and not to where it is instantiated. If text substitution were used then non-local identifiers would of course take their meaning at the point of instantiation and this could give very surprising results.

As well as generic subprograms we may also have generic packages. A simple example is provided by the package STACK in Section 8.1. The trouble with that package is that it only works on type INTEGER although of course the same logic applies irrespective of the type of the values manipulated. We can also take the opportunity to make MAX a parameter as well so that we are not tied to an arbitrary limit of 100. We write

```
generic
    MAX: POSITIVE;
    type ITEM is private;
package STACK is
    procedure PUSH(X: ITEM);
    function POP return ITEM;
end STACK;

package body STACK is
    S: array (1 .. MAX) of ITEM;
    TOP: INTEGER range 0 .. MAX;
    -- etc. as before but with INTEGER
    -- replaced by ITEM
end STACK;
```

We can now create and use a stack of a particular size and type by instantiating the generic package as in the following

```
declare
    package MY_STACK is new STACK(100, REAL);
    use MY_STACK;
begin
    ...
    PUSH(X);
    ...
    Y:= POP;
    ...
end;
```

The package MY_STACK which results from the instantiation behaves just as a normal directly written out package. The use clause allows us to refer to PUSH and POP directly. If we did a further instantiation

```
package ANOTHER_STACK is new STACK(50, INTEGER);
use ANOTHER_STACK;
```

then PUSH and POP are further overloadings and can be distinguished by the type provided by the context. Of course, if ANOTHER_STACK was also declared with the actual generic parameter being REAL, then we would have to use the dotted notation to distinguish the instances of PUSH and POP despite the use clauses.

Both generic units and generic instantiations may be library units. Thus having put the generic package STACK in the program library an instantiation could itself be separately compiled just on its own thus

```
with STACK;
package BOOLEAN_STACK is new STACK(200, BOOLEAN);
```

If we added an exception ERROR to the package as in Section 10.2 so that the generic package declaration was

```
generic
    MAX: POSITIVE;
    type ITEM is private;
package STACK is
    ERROR: exception;
    procedure PUSH(X: ITEM);
    function POP return ITEM;
end STACK;
```

then each instantiation would give rise to a distinct exception and because exceptions cannot be overloaded we would naturally have to use the dotted notation to distinguish them.

We could, of course, make the exception ERROR common to all instantiations by making it global to the generic package. It and the generic package could perhaps be declared inside a further package

```
package ALL_STACKS is
    ERROR: exception;
    generic
        MAX: POSITIVE;
        type ITEM is private;
    package STACK is
        procedure PUSH(X: ITEM);
        function POP return ITEM;
    end STACK;
end ALL_STACKS;

package body ALL_STACKS is
    package body STACK is
        ...
    end STACK;
end ALL_STACKS;
```

This illustrates the binding of identifiers global to generic units. The meaning of ERROR is determined at the point of the generic declaration irrespective of the meaning at the point of instantiation.

The above examples have illustrated formal parameters which were types and also integers. In fact generic formal parameters can be values and objects much as the parameters applicable to subprograms; they can also be types and subprograms. As we shall see in the following sections, we can express the formal types and subprograms so that we can assume in the generic body that the actual parameters have the properties we require.

In the case of the familiar parameters which also apply to subprograms they can be of mode **in** or **in out** but not **out**. As with subprograms, **in** is taken by default as illustrated by MAX in the example above.

An **in** generic parameter acts as a constant the value of which is provided by the corresponding actual parameter. A default expression is allowed as in the case of parameters of subprograms; such a default expression is evaluated at instantiation if no actual parameter is supplied in the same way that a default expression for a subprogram parameter is evaluated when the subprogram is called if no actual parameter is supplied. Observe that an **in** generic parameter cannot be of a limited type; this is because assignment is not allowed for limited types and the mechanism of giving the value to the parameter is treated as assignment. Note that this is a different mechanism to that used for **in** subprogram parameters where limited types are allowed.

An **in out** parameter, however, acts as a variable renaming the corresponding actual parameter. The actual parameter must therefore be the name of a variable and its identification occurs at the point of instantiation using the same rules as for renaming described in Section 8.5. One such rule is that any constraints on the actual parameter apply to the formal parameter and any constraints implied by the formal type mark are, perhaps surprisingly, completely ignored. Another rule is that if any identifier in the name subsequently changes then the identity of the object referred to by the generic formal parameter does not change. Because of this there is a restriction that the actual parameter cannot be a component of an unconstrained discriminated record if the very existence of the component depends on the value of the discriminant. Thus if M is a MUTANT as in Section 11.3, M.CHILDREN could not be an actual generic parameter because M could have its SEX changed. However, M.BIRTH would be valid. This restriction also applies to renaming itself.

It will now be realized that although the notation **in** and **in out** is identical to subprogram parameters the meaning is somewhat different. Thus there is no question of copying in and out and indeed no such thing as **out** parameters.

Inside the generic body, the formal generic parameters can be used quite freely except for one restriction. This arises because generic parameters (and their attributes) are not considered to be static. There are various places where an expression has to be static such as in the alternatives in a case statement or variant, and in the range in an integer type definition, or the number of digits in a floating point type definition and so on. In all these situations a generic formal parameter cannot be used because the expression would not then be static. A further consequence is that the type of the expression in a case statement and similarly the type of the discriminant in a variant may not be a generic formal type.

Our final example in this section illustrates the nesting of generics. The following generic procedure performs a cyclic interchange of three values and for amusement is written in terms of the generic procedure EXCHANGE.

```
generic
    type THING is private;
procedure CAB(A, B, C: in out THING);

procedure CAB(A, B, C: in out THING) is
    procedure SWAP is new EXCHANGE(ITEM => THING);
begin
    SWAP(A, B);
    SWAP(A, C);
end CAB;
```

Although nesting is allowed, it must not be recursive.

Exercise 13.1

1   Write a generic package declaration based on the package STACKS in Section 11.1 so that stacks of arbitrary type may be declared. Declare a stack S of length 30 and type BOOLEAN. Use named notation.

2   Write a generic package containing both SWAP and CAB.

13.2   Type parameters

In the previous section we introduced types as generic parameters. The examples showed the formal parameter taking the form

    type T **is private**;

In this case, inside the generic subprogram or package, we may assume that assignment and equality are defined for T. We can assume nothing else unless we specifically provide other parameters, as we shall see in a moment. Hence, T behaves in the generic unit much as a private type outside the package defining it; this analogy explains the notation for the formal parameter. The corresponding actual parameter must, of course, provide assignment and equality and so it can be any type except one that is limited.

A formal generic type parameter can take other forms. It can be

    type T **is limited private**;

and in this case assignment and equality are not available automatically. The corresponding actual parameter can be any type.

Either of the above forms could have discriminants

type T(...) **is private**;

and the actual type must then have discriminants with the same types. The formal type must not have default expressions for the discriminants but the actual type can as we shall see later.

The formal parameter could also be one of

type T **is** (<>);
type T **is range** <>;
type T **is digits** <>;
type T **is delta** <>;

In the first case the actual parameter must be a discrete type – an enumeration type or integer type. In the other cases the actual parameter must be an integer type, floating point type or fixed point type respectively. Within the generic unit the appropriate predefined operations and attributes are available.

As a simple example consider

```
generic
    type T Is (<>);
function NEXT(X: T) return T;

function NEXT(X: T) return T is
begin
    if X=T'LAST then
        return T'FIRST;
    else
        return T'SUCC(X);
    end if;
end NEXT;
```

The formal parameter T requires that the actual parameter must be a discrete type. Since all discrete types have attributes FIRST, LAST and SUCC we can use these attributes in the body in the knowledge that the actual parameter will supply them.

We could now write

function TOMORROW **is new** NEXT(DAY);

so that TOMORROW(SUN) = MON.

An actual generic parameter can also be a subtype but an explicit constraint is not allowed; in other words the actual parameter must be just a type mark and not a subtype indication. The formal generic parameter then denotes the subtype. Thus we can have

function NEXT_WORK_DAY **is new** NEXT(WEEKDAY);

so that NEXT_WORK_DAY(FRI) = MON. Note how the behaviour depends on the fact that the LAST attribute applies to the subtype and not to the base type so that DAY'LAST is SUN and WEEKDAY'LAST is FRI.

The actual parameter could also be an integer type so we could have

```
subtype DIGIT is INTEGER range 0 .. 9;
function NEXT_DIGIT is new NEXT(DIGIT);
```

and then NEXT_DIGIT(9) = 0.

Now consider the package COMPLEX_NUMBERS of Section 9.1; this could be made generic so that the particular floating point type upon which the type COMPLEX is based can be a parameter. It would then take the form

```
generic
    type REAL is digits <>;
package GENERIC_COMPLEX_NUMBERS is
    type COMPLEX is private;
    -- as before
    I: constant COMPLEX:= (0.0, 1.0);
end;
```

Note that we can use the literals 0.0 and 1.0 because they are of the universal real type which can be converted to whichever type is passed as actual parameter. The package could then be instantiated by for instance

```
package MY_COMPLEX_NUMBERS is
        new GENERIC_COMPLEX_NUMBERS(MY_REAL);
```

A formal generic parameter can also be an array type. The actual parameter must then also be an array type with the same component type and constraints, if any, the same number of dimensions and the same index subtypes. Either both must be unconstrained arrays or both must be constrained arrays. If they are constrained then the index ranges must be the same for corresponding indexes.

It is possible for one generic formal parameter to depend upon a previous formal parameter which is a type. This will often be the case with arrays. As an example consider the simple function SUM in Section 7.1. This added together the elements of a real array with integer index. We can generalize this to add together the elements of any floating point array with any index type.

```
generic
    type INDEX is (<>);
    type FLOATING is digits <>;
    type VEC is array (INDEX range <>) of FLOATING;
function SUM(A: VEC) return FLOATING;

function SUM(A: VEC) return FLOATING is
    RESULT: FLOATING:= 0.0;
```

```
begin
   for I in A'RANGE loop
      RESULT:= RESULT+A(I);
   end loop;
   return RESULT;
end SUM;
```

Note that although INDEX is a formal parameter it does not explicitly appear in the generic body; nevertheless it is implicitly used since the loop parameter I is of type INDEX.

We could instantiate this by

```
function SUM_VECTOR is new SUM(INTEGER, REAL, VECTOR);
```

and this will give the function SUM of Section 7.1.

The matching of actual and formal arrays takes place after any formal types have been replaced in the formal array by the corresponding actual types. As an example of matching index subtypes note that if we had

```
type VECTOR is array (POSITIVE range <>) of REAL;
```

then we would have to use POSITIVE (or an equivalent subtype) as the actual parameter for the INDEX.

The final possibility for formal type parameters is the case of an access type. The formal can be

```
type A is access T;
```

where T may but need not be a previous formal parameter. The actual parameter corresponding to A must then access T. Constraints on the accessed type must also be the same.

Observe that there is no concept of a formal record type. This is because the internal structure of records is somewhat arbitrary and the possibilities for matching would therefore be rare.

As a final example in this section we return to the question of sets. We saw in Section 6.6 how a Boolean array could be used to represent a set. Exercises 7.1(4), 7.2(3) and 7.2(4) also showed how we could write suitable functions to operate upon sets of the type COLOUR. The generic mechanism allows us to write a package to enable the manipulation of sets of an arbitrary type.

Consider

```
generic
   type BASE is (<>);
package SET_OF is
   type SET is private;
   type LIST is array (POSITIVE range <>) of BASE;

   EMPTY, FULL: constant SET;

   function MAKE_SET(X: LIST) return SET;
```

```
function MAKE_SET(X: BASE) return SET;
function DECOMPOSE(X: SET) return LIST;

function "+" (X, Y: SET) return SET;        -- union
function "*" (X, Y: SET) return SET;        -- intersection
function "-" (X, Y: SET) return SET;        -- symmetric difference
function "<" (X: BASE; Y: SET) return BOOLEAN;    -- inclusion
function "<=" (X, Y: SET) return BOOLEAN;   -- contains
function SIZE(X: SET) return NATURAL;       -- no of elements

private
    type SET is array (BASE) of BOOLEAN;

    EMPTY: constant SET:= (SET'RANGE => FALSE);
    FULL: constant SET:= (SET'RANGE => TRUE);
end;
```

The single generic parameter is the base type which must be discrete. The type SET is made private so that the Boolean operations cannot be directly applied (inadvertently or malevolently). Aggregates of the type LIST are used to represent literal sets. The constants EMPTY and FULL denote the empty and full set respectively. The functions MAKE_SET enable the creation of a set from a list of the base values or a single base value. DECOMPOSE turns a set back into a list.

The operators +, * and − represent union, intersection and symmetric difference; they are chosen as more natural than the underlying **or**, **and** and **xor**. The operator < tests to see whether a base value is in a set. The operator <= tests to see whether one set is a subset of another. Finally, the function SIZE returns the number of base values present in a particular set.

In the private part the type SET is declared as a Boolean array indexed by the base type (which is why the base type had to be discrete). The constants EMPTY and FULL are declared as arrays whose elements are all FALSE and all TRUE respectively. The body of the package is left as an exercise.

Turning back to Section 6.6, we can instantiate the package to work on our type PRIMARY by

```
package PRIMARY_SETS is new SET_OF(PRIMARY);
use PRIMARY_SETS;
```

For comparison we could then write

```
subtype COLOUR is SET;
WHITE: COLOUR renames EMPTY;
BLACK: COLOUR renames FULL;
```

and so on.

We can use this example to explore the creation and composition of types. Our attempt to give the type SET the name COLOUR through a subtype is poor. We would really like to pass the name COLOUR in some way to the generic package as the type to be used. We cannot do this and retain the private nature of the type. But we can use the derived type mechanism to create a proper type COLOUR from the type SET

> **type** COLOUR **is new** SET;

Recalling the rules for inheriting applicable subprograms from Section 11.7, we note that the new type COLOUR automatically inherits all the functions in the specification of SET_OF (strictly the instantiation PRIMARY_SETS) because they all have the type SET as a parameter or result type.

However, this is a bit untidy; the constants EMPTY and FULL will not have been derived and the type LIST will still be as before.

One improvement therefore is to replace the constants EMPTY and FULL by equivalent parameterless functions so that they will also be derived. A better approach to the type LIST is to make it and its index type into further generic parameters. The visible part of the package will then just consist of the type SET and its applicable subprograms

```
generic
    type BASE is (<>);
    type INDEX is (<>);
    type LIST is array (INDEX range <>) of BASE;
package NICE_SET_OF is
    type SET is private;
    function EMPTY return SET;
    function FULL return SET;
    ...
private
```

We can now write

> **type** PRIMARY_LIST **is array** (POSITIVE **range** <>) **of** PRIMARY;

> **package** PRIMARY_SETS **is new** NICE_SET_OF(BASE => PRIMARY,
>   INDEX => POSITIVE,
>   LIST => PRIMARY_LIST);

> **type** COLOUR **is new** PRIMARY_SETS.SET;

The type COLOUR now has all the functions we want and the array type has a name of our choosing. We might still want to rename EMPTY and FULL thus

> **function** WHITE **return** COLOUR **renames** EMPTY;

or we can still declare WHITE as a constant by

> WHITE: **constant** COLOUR:= EMPTY;

As a general rule it is better to use derived types rather than subtypes because of the greater type checking provided during compilation; sometimes, however, derived types introduce a need for lots of explicit type conversions which clutter the program, in which case the formal distinction is probably a mistake and one might as well use subtypes.

We conclude by summarizing the general principle regarding the matching of actual to formal generic types which should now be clear. The formal type represents a class of types which have certain common properties and these properties can be assumed in the generic unit. The corresponding actual type must then supply these properties. The matching rules are designed so that this is assured by reference to the parameters only and without considering the details of the generic body. As a consequence the user of the generic unit need not see the body for debugging purposes. This notion of matching guaranteed by the parameters is termed the contract model.

Unfortunately there is an important violation of the contract model in the case of unconstrained types. If we have the basic formal type

type T **is private**;

then this can be matched by an unconstrained array type such as VECTOR provided that we do not use T in the generic unit in a way that would require the array to be constrained. The most obvious example is that we must not declare an object of type T.

In a similar way the actual type could be an unconstrained discriminated type provided that T is not used in a way that would require constraints. Thus again we could not declare an unconstrained object of type T; but note that if the actual type has default discriminants then the defaults will be used in the generic body and then we will be able to declare an object. This interpretation is given in AI-37 and contrasts with the apparent statement in the *LRM*.

The attribute CONSTRAINED can be applied to the formal type T and gives a Boolean value indicating whether the actual type is a constrained type or not. Thus considering the types of Section 11.3, T'CONSTRAINED would be TRUE if the actual parameter were MAN but FALSE if the actual parameter were PERSON or MUTANT; in the last case the default constraint NEUTER is irrelevant. Remember that the actual parameter must be a type mark and not a subtype indication.

Finally we recall that our use of generic formal parameters within the body is restricted by the rule that they are not static.

Exercise 13.2

1   Instantiate NEXT to give a function behaving like **not**.

2   Rewrite the specification of the package RATIONAL_NUMBERS so that it is a generic package taking the integer type as a parameter. See Exercise 9.1(**3**).

3   Rewrite the function OUTER of Exercise 7.1(**3**) so that it is a generic function with appropriate parameters. Instantiate it to give the original function.

4   Write the body of the package SET_OF.

5   Rewrite the private part of SET_OF so that an object of the type
          SET is by default given the initial value EMPTY when declared.

13.3 Subprogram parameters

As mentioned earlier a generic parameter can also be a subprogram. There
are a number of distinct characteristic applications of this facility and we
introduce the topic by considering the classical problem of sorting.

Suppose we wish to sort an array into ascending order. There are a
number of general algorithms that can be used but they do not depend on
the type of the values being sorted. All we need is some comparison
operation such as "<" which is defined for the type.

We might start by considering the specification

```
generic
    type INDEX is (<>);
    type ITEM is (<>);
    type COLLECTION is array (INDEX range <>) of ITEM;
procedure SORT(C: in out COLLECTION);
```

Although the body is largely irrelevant it might help to illustrate the
problem to consider the following crude possibility

```
procedure SORT(C: in out COLLECTION) is
    MIN: INDEX;
    TEMP: ITEM;
begin
    for I in C'FIRST .. INDEX'PRED(C'LAST) loop
        MIN:= I;
        for J in INDEX'SUCC(I) .. C'LAST loop
            if C(J) < C(MIN) then MIN:= J; end if;     -- use of <
        end loop;
        TEMP:= C(I); C(I):= C(MIN); C(MIN):= TEMP;
    end loop;
end SORT;
```

This trivial algorithm repeatedly scans the part of the array not
sorted, finds the least component (which because of the previous scans will
be not less than any component of the already sorted part) and then swaps
it so that it is then the last element of the now sorted part. Note that
because of the generality we have imposed upon ourselves, we cannot
write

```
for I in C'FIRST .. C'LAST−1 loop
```

because we cannot rely upon the array index being an integer type. We
only know that it is a discrete type and therefore have to use the attributes

INDEX'PRED and INDEX'SUCC which we know to be available since they are common to all discrete types.

However, the main point to note is the call of "<" in the body of SORT. This calls the predefined function corresponding to the type ITEM. We know that there is such a function because we have specified ITEM to be discrete and all discrete types have such a function. Unfortunately the net result is that our generic sort can only sort arrays of discrete types. It cannot sort arrays of floating types. Of course we could write a version for floating types by replacing the generic parameter for ITEM by

```
type ITEM is digits <>;
```

but then it would not work for discrete types. What we really need to do is specify the comparison function to be used in a general manner. We can do this by adding a fourth parameter which is a formal subprogram so that the specification becomes

```
generic
    type INDEX is (<>);
    type ITEM is private;
    type COLLECTION is array (INDEX range <>) of ITEM;
    with function "<" (X, Y: ITEM) return BOOLEAN;
procedure SORT(C: in out COLLECTION);
```

The formal subprogram parameter is like a subprogram declaration preceded by **with**. (The leading **with** is necessary to avoid a syntactic ambiguity and has no other subtle purpose.)

We have also made the type ITEM private since the only common property now required (other than supplied through the parameters) is that the type ITEM can be assigned. The body remains as before.

We can now sort an array of any (unlimited) type provided that we have an appropriate comparison to supply as parameter. So in order to sort an array of our type VECTOR, we first instantiate thus

```
procedure SORT_VECTOR is
    new SORT(INTEGER, REAL, VECTOR, "<");
```

and we can then apply the procedure to the array concerned

```
AN_ARRAY: VECTOR( ... );
...
SORT_VECTOR(AN_ARRAY);
```

Note carefully that our call of "<" inside SORT is actually a call of the function passed as actual parameter; in this case it is indeed the predefined function "<" anyway.

Passing the comparison rule gives our generic sort procedure amazing flexibility. We can, for example, sort in the reverse direction by

```
procedure REVERSE_SORT_VECTOR is
    new SORT(INTEGER, REAL, VECTOR, ">");
...
REVERSE_SORT_VECTOR(AN_ARRAY);
```

This may come as a slight surprise but it is a natural consequence of the call of the formal "<" in

```
if C(J) < C(MIN) then ...
```

being, after instantiation, a call of the actual ">". No confusion should arise because the internal call is hidden but the use of the named notation for instantiation would look curious

```
procedure REVERSE_SORT_VECTOR is
            new SORT(INDEX =>  INTEGER,
                     ITEM =>  REAL,
               COLLECTION =>  VECTOR,
                      "<" =>  ">");
```

We could also sort our second FARMYARD of Section 6.5 assuming it to be a variable

```
subtype STRING_3 is STRING(1 .. 3);

procedure SORT_STRING_3_ARRAY is
        new SORT(POSITIVE, STRING_3, STRING_3_ARRAY, "<");
...
SORT_STRING_3_ARRAY(FARMYARD);
```

The "<" operator passed as parameter is the predefined operation applicable to one-dimensional arrays described in Section 6.6.

The correspondence between formal and actual subprograms is such that the formal subprogram just renames the actual subprogram. Thus the matching rules regarding parameters, results and so on are as described in Section 8.5. In particular the constraints on the parameters are those of the actual subprogram and any implied by the formal subprogram are ignored. A parameterless formal function can also be matched by an enumeration literal of the result type just as for renaming.

Generic subprogram parameters (like generic object parameters) can have default values. These are given in the generic formal part and take two forms. In the above example we could write

```
with function "<" (X, Y: ITEM) return BOOLEAN is <>;
```

This means that we can omit the corresponding actual parameter if there is visible at the point of *instantiation* a unique subprogram with the same designator and matching specification. With this alteration to SORT we could have omitted the last parameter in the instantiation giving SORT_VECTOR.

The other form of default value is where we give an explicit name for the default parameter. The usual rules for defaults apply; the default name is only evaluated if required by the instantiation but the binding of identifiers in the expression which is the name occurs at the point of *declaration* of the generic unit. In our example

with function "<" (X, Y: ITEM) **return** BOOLEAN **is** LESS_THAN;

could never be valid because the specification of LESS_THAN must match that of "<" and yet the parameter ITEM is not known until instantiation. The only valid possibilities are where the formal subprogram has no parameters depending on formal types or the default subprogram is itself another formal parameter or an attribute. Thus we might have

with function NEXT(X: T) **return** T **is** T'SUCC;

The same rules for mixing named and positional notation apply to generic instantiation as to subprogram calls. Hence if a parameter is omitted, subsequent parameters must be given using named notation. Of course, a generic unit need have no parameters in which case the instantiation takes the same form as for a subprogram call – the brackets are omitted.

As a final example of the use of our generic SORT (which we will assume now has a default parameter <> for "<"), we show how any type can be sorted provided we supply an appropriate rule.

Thus consider sorting an array of the type DATE from Section 6.7. We write

```
type DATE_ARRAY is array (POSITIVE range <>) of DATE;
```

```
function "<" (X, Y: DATE) return BOOLEAN is
begin
   if X.YEAR /= Y.YEAR then
      return X.YEAR < Y.YEAR;
   elsif X.MONTH /= Y.MONTH then
      return X.MONTH < Y.MONTH;
   else
      return X.DAY < Y.DAY;
   end if;
end "<";
```

```
procedure SORT_DATE_ARRAY is
   new SORT(POSITIVE, DATE, DATE_ARRAY);
```

where the function "<" is passed through the default mechanism.

It might have been nicer to give our comparison rule a more appropriate name such as

function EARLIER(X, Y: DATE) **return** BOOLEAN;

but we would then have to pass it as an explicit parameter; this might be considered better style anyway.

Formal subprograms can be used to supply further properties of type parameters in a quite general way. Consider the generic function SUM of the last section. We can generalize this even further by passing the adding operator itself as a generic parameter.

```
generic
    type INDEX is (<>);
    type ITEM is private;
    type VEC is array (INDEX range <>) of ITEM;
    with function "+" (X, Y: ITEM) return ITEM;
function APPLY(A: VEC) return ITEM;

function APPLY(A: VEC) return ITEM is
    RESULT: ITEM:= A(A'FIRST);
begin
    for I in INDEX'SUCC(A'FIRST) .. A'LAST loop
        RESULT:= RESULT+A(I);
    end loop;
    return RESULT;
end APPLY;
```

The operator "+" has been added as a parameter and ITEM is now just private and no longer floating. This means that we can apply the generic function to any binary operation on any type. However, we no longer have a zero value and so have to initialize RESULT with the first component of the array A and then iterate through the remainder. In doing this, remember that we cannot write

```
for I in A'FIRST+1 .. A'LAST loop
```

because the type INDEX may not be an integer type.

Our original function SUM of Section 7.1 is now given by

```
function SUM is new APPLY(INTEGER, REAL, VECTOR, "+");
```

We could equally have

```
function PROD is new APPLY(INTEGER, REAL, VECTOR, "*");
```

A very important use of formal subprograms is in mathematical applications such as integration. In traditional languages such as Algol and Pascal, this is done by passing subprograms as parameters to other subprograms. In Ada, subprograms can only be parameters of generic units and so we use the generic mechanism.

We could have a generic function

```
generic
    with function F(X: REAL) return REAL;
function INTEGRATE(A, B: REAL) return REAL;
```

which evaluates

$$\int_a^b f(x)\ dx$$

In order to integrate a particular function we must instantiate INTEGRATE with our function as actual generic parameter. Thus suppose we needed

$$\int_0^P e^t \sin t\ dt$$

We would write

```
function G(T: REAL) return REAL is
begin
    return EXP(T)*SIN(T);
end;

function INTEGRATE_G is new INTEGRATE(G);
```

and then our result is given by the expression

```
INTEGRATE_G(0.0, P)
```

As we have seen, the specification of the formal function could depend on preceding formal types. Thus we could extend our integration function to apply to any floating point type by writing

```
generic
    type FLOATING is digits <>;
    with function F(X: FLOATING) return FLOATING;
function INTEGRATE(A, B: FLOATING) return FLOATING;
```

and then

```
function INTEGRATE_G is new INTEGRATE(REAL, G);
```

In practice the function INTEGRATE would have other parameters indicating the accuracy required and so on.

Examples such as this are often found confusing at first sight. The key point to remember is that there are two distinct levels of parameterization. First, we fix the function to be integrated at instantiation, and then we fix the bounds when we call the integration function thus declared. The sorting examples were similar; first, we fixed the parameters defining the type of array to be sorted and the rule to be used at instantiation, and then we fixed the actual array to be sorted when we called the procedure.

We conclude this section with an important philosophical remark. Generics provide an extremely powerful mechanism for parameterization.

Moreover, this mechanism does not increase run-time costs because all type and subprogram identification is static. Thus Ada enables us to write reusable software of greater applicability without a penalty on run-time performance.

Exercise 13.3

1   Instantiate SORT to apply to

> **type** POLY_ARRAY **is**
> > **array** (INTEGER **range** <>) **of** POLYNOMIAL;

See Section 11.1. Define a sensible ordering for polynomials.

2   Instantiate SORT to apply to an array of the type MUTANT of Section 11.3. Put neuter things first, then females, then males and within each class the younger first. Could we sort an array of the type PERSON from the same section?

3   Sort the array PEOPLE of Section 6.7.

4   What happens if we attempt to sort an array of less than two components?

5   Describe how to make a generic sort procedure based on the procedure SORT of Section 11.4. It should have an identical specification to the procedure SORT of this section.

6   Instantiate APPLY to give a function to "and" together all the components of a Boolean array.

7   Rewrite APPLY so that a null array can be a parameter without raising an exception. Use this new version to redo the previous exercise.

8   Write a generic function EQUALS to define the equality of one-dimensional arrays of a limited private type. See Exercise 9.2(**4**). Instantiate it to give the function "=" applying to the type STACK_ARRAY.

9   Given a function

> **generic**
> > **with function** F(X: REAL) **return** REAL;
> **function** SOLVE **return** REAL;

that finds a root of the equation $f(x) = 0$, show how you would find the root of

> $e^x + x = 7$

13.4 The mathematical library

The reader will be surprised to learn that the *LRM* says nothing about everyday mathematical functions such as SQRT. This is in strong contrast to most languages such as Algol, Pascal and FORTRAN where the provision of standard mathematical functions is taken for granted.

However, the flexibility and generality of Ada is such that the specification of a suitable package is not immediately obvious. There are a number of conflicting requirements

- ease of casual use for simple calculations,

- ability to provide the ultimate in accuracy for serious numerical work,

- portability across different implementations.

Although numerical applications are in a minority, we will nevertheless consider the topic in some detail because it provides a good illustration of the use of generics and other key features of Ada.

The packages to be described are (at the time of writing) proposed ISO standards and therefore subject to change. They were developed by the Ada-Europe and SigAda working groups on Ada Numerics.

First there is a package containing useful numbers of type universal real and given to immense precision. It has no body.

```
package MATHEMATICAL_CONSTANTS is

    PI              : constant:= 3.14159_26535_89793_23846_26433...;
    TWO_PI          : constant:= 2*PI;
    HALF_PI         : constant:= PI/2;
    ONE_OVER_PI     : constant:= 1.0/PI;
    SQRT_PI         : constant:= 1.77245_38509_05516_02729_81674...;

    NATURAL_E       : constant:= 2.71828_18284_59045_23536_02874...;
    ONE_OVER_E      : constant:= 1.0/NATURAL_E;

    GAMMA           : constant:= 0.57721_56649_01532_86060_65120...;

end MATHEMATICAL_CONSTANTS;
```

Then there is a package containing a single exception which is raised under appropriate circumstances. It also has no body.

```
package MATHEMATICAL_EXCEPTIONS is
    ARGUMENT_ERROR: exception;
end MATHEMATICAL_EXCEPTIONS;
```

Finally there is a generic package containing the mathematical functions themselves. Its specification is as follows

```
with MATHEMATICAL_EXCEPTIONS;
generic
    type FLOAT_TYPE is digits <>;
package GENERIC_ELEMENTARY_FUNCTIONS is

    function SQRT (X:        FLOAT_TYPE) return FLOAT_TYPE;
    function LOG (X:         FLOAT_TYPE) return FLOAT_TYPE;
    function LOG (X, BASE:   FLOAT_TYPE) return FLOAT_TYPE;
    function EXP (X:         FLOAT_TYPE) return FLOAT_TYPE;
    function "**" (X, Y:     FLOAT_TYPE) return FLOAT_TYPE;

    function SIN (X:          FLOAT_TYPE) return FLOAT_TYPE;
    function SIN (X, CYCLE:   FLOAT_TYPE) return FLOAT_TYPE;
    function COS (X:          FLOAT_TYPE) return FLOAT_TYPE;
    function COS (X, CYCLE:   FLOAT_TYPE) return FLOAT_TYPE;
    function TAN (X:          FLOAT_TYPE) return FLOAT_TYPE;
    function TAN (X, CYCLE:   FLOAT_TYPE) return FLOAT_TYPE;
    function COT (X:          FLOAT_TYPE) return FLOAT_TYPE;
    function COT (X, CYCLE:   FLOAT_TYPE) return FLOAT_TYPE;
    function ARCSIN (X:       FLOAT_TYPE) return FLOAT_TYPE;
    function ARCSIN (X, CYCLE:  FLOAT_TYPE) return FLOAT_TYPE;
    function ARCCOS (X:       FLOAT_TYPE) return FLOAT_TYPE;
    function ARCCOS (X, CYCLE:FLOAT_TYPE) return FLOAT_TYPE;
    function ARCTAN (Y: FLOAT_TYPE; X: FLOAT_TYPE:= 1.0)
                                            return FLOAT_TYPE;
    function ARCTAN (Y; FLOAT_TYPE; X: FLOAT_TYPE:= 1.0;
                    CYCLE: FLOAT_TYPE) return FLOAT_TYPE;
    function ARCCOT (X: FLOAT_TYPE; Y: FLOAT_TYPE:= 1.0)
                                            return FLOAT_TYPE;
    function ARCCOT (X: FLOAT_TYPE; Y: FLOAT_TYPE:= 1.0;
                    CYCLE: FLOAT_TYPE) return FLOAT_TYPE;

    function SINH (X: FLOAT_TYPE) return FLOAT_TYPE;
    function COSH (X: FLOAT_TYPE) return FLOAT_TYPE;
    function TANH (X: FLOAT_TYPE) return FLOAT_TYPE;
    function COTH (X: FLOAT_TYPE) return FLOAT_TYPE;
    function ARCSINH (X: FLOAT_TYPE) return FLOAT_TYPE;
    function ARCCOSH (X: FLOAT_TYPE) return FLOAT_TYPE;
    function ARCTANH (X: FLOAT_TYPE) return FLOAT_TYPE;
    function ARCCOTH (X: FLOAT_TYPE) return FLOAT_TYPE;

    ARGUMENT_ERROR: exception
        renames MATHEMATICAL_ EXCEPTIONS.ARGUMENT_ERROR;

end GENERIC_ELEMENTARY_FUNCTIONS;
```

The single generic parameter is the floating type. The package might be instantiated with a predefined type such as FLOAT or LONG_FLOAT but hopefully more likely with a user's own type such as REAL.

```
package REAL_ELEMENTARY_FUNCTIONS is
  new GENERIC_ELEMENTARY_FUNCTIONS(REAL);
```

The body could then choose an implementation appropriate to the accuracy of the user's type through the attribute FLOAT_TYPE'DIGITS rather than necessarily using the accuracy of the predefined type from which the user's type has been derived. This could have significant timing advantages.

The functions SQRT and EXP need little comment except perhaps concerning exceptions. Calling SQRT with a negative parameter will raise ARGUMENT_ERROR whereas calling EXP with a large parameter will raise NUMERIC_ERROR (CONSTRAINT_ERROR).

The general principle is that intrinsic mathematical restrictions raise ARGUMENT_ERROR whereas implementation range restrictions raise NUMERIC_ERROR.

Observe that the exception ARGUMENT_ERROR is declared in a separate non-generic package. This means that there is only one such exception which applies to all instantiations of the main package. The renaming declaration enables us to refer to the exception without reference to the package MATHEMATICAL_EXCEPTIONS. We will meet this technique again when we discuss input–output in Chapter 15.

There are two overloadings of LOG. That with a single parameter gives the natural logarithm to base e, whereas that with two parameters allows us to choose any base at all. Thus to find $\log_{10}2$, we write

```
LOG(2.0, 10.0)              -- 0.3010...
```

The reader may wonder why there is not just a single function with a default parameter thus

```
function LOG(X: FLOAT_TYPE; BASE: FLOAT_TYPE:=
  MATHEMATICAL_CONSTANTS.NATURAL_E) return FLOAT_TYPE;
```

which would seem to give the desired result with less fuss. The reason concerns obtaining the ultimate in precision. Passing a default parameter means that the accuracy of the value of e used can only be that of the FLOAT_TYPE. Using a separate function enables the function body to obtain the benefit of the full accuracy of the universal real named number.

The restrictions on the parameters of LOG are X > 0.0, BASE > 0.0 and also BASE /= 1.0. So BASE could be 0.5 which is an amusing thought.

As an aside, we note that we cannot formally rename a named number because renaming requires a type name and the universal types cannot be explicitly named. Consequently we are unable to rename MATHEMATICAL_CONSTANTS.NATURAL_E with a more convenient name such as E. However, there is no need, we can just declare another named number

E: **constant**:= MATHEMATICAL_CONSTANTS.NATURAL_E;

which is no disadvantage because the named numbers are not run-time objects anyway and so there is no duplication.

The function "**" effectively extends the predefined operator to allow non-integral exponents. X must not be negative.

The trigonometric functions SIN, COS, TAN and COT also come in pairs like LOG and for a similar reason. The single parameter versions assume the parameter is in radians whereas the second parameter allows the use of any unit by giving the number of units in a whole cycle. Thus to find the sine of 30 degrees, we write

SIN(30.0, 360.0)   -- 0.5

because there are 360 degrees in a cycle.

In these functions the single parameter versions enable the highly accurate number TWO_PI to be used directly rather than being passed with less accuracy as a parameter.

Of the inverse functions, ARCSIN and ARCCOS need no comment. However, ARCTAN has a default value of 1.0 for a second parameter (the CYCLE then being third). This enables us to call ARCTAN with two parameters giving the classical x- and y-coordinates (thus fully identifying the quadrant). So

ARCTAN(Y => -1.0, X => +1.0)   -- -PI/4
ARCTAN(Y => +1.0, X => -1.0)   -- +3*PI/4

Note carefully that the first parameter of ARCTAN is Y since it is the x-coordinate that is taken to be 1.0 by default. ARCCOT is very similar except that the parameters are naturally in the other order.

There are no obvious comments to make on the hyperbolic functions.

We now turn to an interesting illustration of the use of default subprogram parameters for conveniently passing properties of generic types. Although the example is of a rather mathematical nature it is hoped that the general principles will be appreciated. It follows on from the above elementary functions package and concerns the provision of similar functions but working on complex arguments. Suppose we want to provide the ability to compute SQRT, LOG, EXP, SIN and COS with functions such as

function SQRT(X: COMPLEX_TYPE) **return** COMPLEX_TYPE;

Many readers will have forgotten that this can be done or perhaps never knew. It is not necessary to dwell on the details of how such calculations are performed or their use; the main point is to concentrate on the principles involved. These computations use various operations on the real numbers out of which the complex numbers are formed. Our goal is to write a generic package which works however the complex numbers are implemented (cartesian or polar) and also allows any floating point type as the basis for the underlying real numbers.

Here are the formulae which we will need to compute

Taking, $z \equiv x + iy \equiv r(\cos \theta + i \sin \theta)$, as the argument:

$$\text{sqrt } z = \sqrt{r}(\cos \theta/2 + i \sin \theta/2)$$
$$\log z = \log r + i\,\theta$$
$$\exp z = e^x(\cos y + i \sin y)$$
$$\sin z = \sin x \cosh y + i \cos x \sinh y$$
$$\cos z = \cos x \cosh y - i \sin x \sinh y$$

We thus see that we will need functions to decompose the complex number into both cartesian and polar forms plus SQRT, COS, SIN, LOG, EXP, COSH and SINH applying to the underlying floating type. We also need to be able to put the result together from both cartesian and polar forms.

Our generic package COMPLEX_NUMBERS (see Sections 9.1 and 13.2) is a good starting point. However, it only gives a cartesian view of a complex number and so needs augmenting with additional functions to provide a polar view. We will assume that this has been done and that the extra visible functions are

```
function CONS_POLAR (R, THETA: REAL) return COMPLEX;
function "abs" (X: COMPLEX) return REAL;
function ARG (X: COMPLEX) return REAL;
```

The package GENERIC_ELEMENTARY_FUNCTIONS described above provides all the operations we need on the underlying floating type. Now consider

```
generic
    type REAL_TYPE is digits <>;
    type COMPLEX_TYPE is private;

    with function CONS(R, I: REAL_TYPE) return
                                    COMPLEX_TYPE is <>;
    with function CONS_POLAR(R, THETA: REAL_TYPE) return
                                    COMPLEX_TYPE is <>;
    with function RL_PART(X: COMPLEX_TYPE) return
                                    REAL_TYPE is <>;
    with function IM_PART(X: COMPLEX_TYPE) return
                                    REAL_TYPE is <>;
    with function "abs" (X: COMPLEX_TYPE) return REAL_TYPE
                                    is <>;
    with function ARG (X: COMPLEX_TYPE) return
                                    REAL_TYPE is <>;

    with function SQRT (X: REAL_TYPE) return REAL_TYPE is <>;
    with function LOG   (X: REAL_TYPE) return REAL_TYPE is <>;
```

```
      with function EXP   (X: REAL_TYPE) return REAL_TYPE is <>;
      with function SIN   (X: REAL_TYPE) return REAL_TYPE is <>;
      with function COS   (X: REAL_TYPE) return REAL_TYPE is <>;
      with function SINH  (X: REAL_TYPE) return REAL_TYPE is <>;
      with function COSH (X: REAL_TYPE) return REAL_TYPE is <>;

   package GENERIC_COMPLEX_FUNCTIONS is

      function SQRT (X: COMPLEX_TYPE) return COMPLEX_TYPE;
      function LOG  (X: COMPLEX_TYPE) return COMPLEX_TYPE;
      function EXP  (X: COMPLEX_TYPE) return COMPLEX_TYPE;
      function SIN  (X: COMPLEX_TYPE) return COMPLEX_TYPE;
      function COS  (X: COMPLEX_TYPE) return COMPLEX_TYPE;

   end GENERIC_COMPLEX_FUNCTIONS;
```

This generic package looks extremely tedious to use. Apart from the obviously necessary parameters REAL_TYPE and COMPLEX_TYPE, it has 13 other functions as parameters. However, we note that they all have the default form <>. So, if at the point of instantiation, by good luck or careful planning, we happen to have all the functions visible with the correct names and matching types then we need not mention them in the instantiation. In other words we can pass all the properties of the types on the sly.

So we could write

```
type MY_REAL is digits 9;

package MY_ELEMENTARY_FUNCTIONS is
   new GENERIC_ELEMENTARY_FUNCTIONS(FLOAT_TYPE =>
                                              MY_REAL);

package MY_COMPLEX_NUMBERS is
   new GENERIC_COMPLEX_NUMBERS(REAL => MY_REAL);

use MY_ELEMENTARY_FUNCTIONS, MY_COMPLEX_NUMBERS;

package MY_COMPLEX_FUNCTIONS is
   new GENERIC_COMPLEX_FUNCTIONS(MY_REAL, COMPLEX);

use MY_COMPLEX_FUNCTIONS;
```

and *Hey presto!* it all works. Note that irritatingly the complex type is just COMPLEX and not MY_COMPLEX. We could remedy this using a subtype or derived type as we did for the type COLOUR and the package SET_OF in Section 13.2. Another point to note is that we have to write the use clause for MY_ELEMENTARY_FUNCTIONS and MY_COMPLEX_NUMBERS before the instantiation of GENERIC_COMPLEX_FUNCTIONS otherwise the various exported functions would not be directly visible.

Of course it was not entirely an accident that the parameters matched. But if one of them had not then it could have been explicitly provided. For example the formal parameter for constructing a complex number from its cartesian form might have had the better name CONS_CARTESIAN rather than the rather abbreviated CONS. If that had been the case then the instantiation could be

```
package MY_COMPLEX_FUNCTIONS is
    new GENERIC_COMPLEX_FUNCTIONS(MY_REAL, COMPLEX,
                        CONS_CARTESIAN => CONS);
```

where we have used named notation for the extra parameter although by coincidence it comes next anyway.

Another way to overcome the mismatch is to use renaming. This works because, as mentioned earlier, the matching of actual to formal generic subprogram parameters is defined in terms of renaming anyway. This is a bit tedious because the parameters and result type have to be written out in full and so we leave this as an exercise.

It should also be noted that matching would not have been possible at all if only a single (two parameter) function with default parameter had been provided for LOG, SIN and so on in the package GENERIC_ELEMENTARY_FUNCTIONS. Matching requires that the number of parameters be the same irrespective of any defaults.

As a final point, the astute reader may have realized that adding the polar functions to our package GENERIC_COMPLEX_NUMBERS means that its body also needs access to some of the elementary functions applied to the underlying floating type. These can be provided via default parameters in a similar way.

A completely different approach to the whole exercise which applies to both GENERIC_COMPLEX_FUNCTIONS itself as well as to GENERIC_COMPLEX_NUMBERS is to instantiate the elementary functions inside the bodies so that we do not have to pass the functions as parameters. This works but will result in wasteful and unnecessary multiple instantiations, especially since we may well need them at the user level anyway. A possible advantage, however, is that there is then no risk that the wrong function is passed by default which would happen if the user were foolish enough to redeclare perhaps LOG to have a completely different meaning (which might be something to do with logging a result). This would be both unfortunate and unlikely.

It is hoped that the general principles have been understood and that the mathematics has not clouded the issues. The principles are important but not easily illustrated with short examples. It should also be noted that although the package GENERIC_ELEMENTARY_FUNCTIONS described above is exactly as the proposed standard, the complex number packages are just an illustration of how generics can be used.

Note added during reprinting: The proposed standard package MATHEMATICAL_EXCEPTIONS is now named ELEMENTARY_FUNCTIONS_EXCEPTIONS and the package MATHEMATICAL_CONSTANTS is no longer a part of the proposed standard (since it is not required for the specification of GENERIC_ELEMENTARY_FUNCTIONS).

Exercise 13.4

1   Write a body for the package SIMPLE_MATHS of Exercise 2.2(**1**) using an instantiation of GENERIC_ELEMENTARY_FUNCTIONS. Raise NUMERIC_ERROR for all exceptional circumstances.

2   Write a body for the package GENERIC_COMPLEX_FUNCTIONS using the formulae defined above. Ignore exceptions.

3   Write the renaming of CONS required to overcome the parameter mismatch discussed above.

4   Rewrite the package GENERIC_COMPLEX_NUMBERS adding the extra generic parameters to supply the required elementary functions. Implement the type COMPLEX in cartesian form.

Checklist 13

The generic mechanism is not text replacement; non-local name binding would be different.

Object **in out** parameters are bound by renaming.

Object **in** parameters are always copied unlike parameters of subprograms.

Subprogram generic parameters are bound by renaming.

Generic subprograms may not overload – only the instantiations can.

Generic subprograms always have a separate specification and body.

Formal parameters (and defaults) may depend upon preceding parameters.

Generic formal parameters and their attributes are not static.

Chapter 14
Tasking

The final major topic to be introduced is tasking. This has been left to the end, not because it is unimportant or particularly difficult, but because, apart from the interaction with exceptions, it is a fairly self-contained part of the language.

14.1   Parallelism

So far we have only considered sequential programs in which statements are obeyed in order. In many applications it is convenient to write a program as several parallel activities which cooperate as necessary. This is particularly true of programs which interact in real time with physical processes in the real world, simulation programs (which mimic parallel activities in the real world), and programs which wish to exploit multi-processor architectures directly.

In Ada, parallel activities are described by means of tasks. In simple cases a task is lexically described by a form very similar to a package. This consists of a specification describing the interface presented to other tasks and a body describing the dynamic behaviour of the task.

```
task T is              -- specification
   ...
end T;

task body T is         -- body
   ...
end T;
```

In some cases a task presents no interface to other tasks in which case the specification reduces to just

task T;

As a simple example of parallelism, consider a family going shopping to buy ingredients for a meal. Suppose they need meat, salad and wine and that the purchase of these items can be done by calling procedures BUY_MEAT, BUY_SALAD and BUY_WINE respectively. The whole expedition could be represented by

```
procedure SHOPPING is
begin
    BUY_MEAT;
    BUY_SALAD;
    BUY_WINE;
end;
```

However, this solution corresponds to the family buying each item in sequence. It would be far more efficient for them to split up so that, for example, mother buys the meat, the children buy the salad and father buys the wine. They agree to meet again perhaps in the car park. This parallel solution can be represented by

```
procedure SHOPPING is
    task GET_SALAD;

    task body GET_SALAD is
    begin
        BUY_SALAD;
    end GET_SALAD;

    task GET_WINE;

    task body GET_WINE is
    begin
        BUY_WINE;
    end GET_WINE;

begin
    BUY_MEAT;
end SHOPPING;
```

In this formulation, mother is represented as the main processor and calls BUY_MEAT directly from the procedure SHOPPING. The children and father are considered as subservient processors and perform the locally declared tasks GET_SALAD and GET_WINE which respectively call the procedures BUY_SALAD and BUY_WINE.

The example illustrates the declaration, activation and termination of tasks. A task is a program component like a package and is declared in a similar way inside a subprogram, block, package or indeed another task body. A task specification can also be declared in a package specification, in which case the task body must be declared in the corresponding package body. However, a task specification cannot be declared in the specification of another task but only in the body.

The activation of a task is automatic. In the above example the local tasks become active when the parent unit reaches the **begin** following the task declaration.

Such a task will terminate when it reaches its final **end**. Thus the task GET_SALAD calls the procedure BUY_SALAD and then promptly terminates.

A task declared in the declarative part of a subprogram, block or task body is said to depend on that unit. It is an important rule that a unit cannot be left until all dependent tasks have terminated. This termination rule ensures that objects declared in the unit, and therefore potentially visible to local tasks, cannot disappear while there exists a task which could access them. (Note that a task cannot depend on a package – we will return to this later.)

It is important to realize that the main program is itself considered to be called by a hypothetical main task. We can now trace the sequence of actions when this main task calls the procedure SHOPPING. First the tasks GET_SALAD and GET_WINE are declared and then when the main task reaches the **begin** these dependent tasks are set active in parallel with the main task. The dependent tasks call their respective procedures and terminate. Meanwhile the main task calls BUY_MEAT and then reaches the **end** of SHOPPING. The main task then waits until the dependent tasks have terminated if they have not already done so. This corresponds to mother waiting for father and children to return with their purchases.

In the general case termination therefore occurs in two stages. We say that a unit is completed when it reaches its final **end**. It will subsequently become terminated only when all dependent tasks, if any, are also terminated. Of course, if a unit has no dependent tasks then it naturally becomes completed and terminated at the same time.

Exercise 14.1

1   Rewrite procedure SHOPPING to contain three local tasks so that the symmetry of the situation is revealed.

14.2 The rendezvous

In the SHOPPING example the various tasks did not interact with each other once they had been set active except that their parent unit had to wait for them to terminate. Generally, however, tasks will interact with each other during their lifetime. In Ada this is done by a mechanism known as a rendezvous. This is similar to the human situation where two people meet, perform a transaction and then go on independently.

A rendezvous between two tasks occurs as a consequence of one task calling an entry declared in another. An entry is declared in a task specification in a similar way to a procedure in a package specification.

```
task T is
    entry E( ... );
end;
```

An entry can have **in**, **out** and **in out** parameters in the same way as a procedure. It cannot however have a result like a function. An entry is called in a similar way to a procedure

```
T.E( ... );
```

A task name cannot appear in a use clause and so the dotted notation is necessary to call the entry from outside the task. Of course, a local task could call an entry of its parent directly – the usual scope and visibility rules apply.

The statements to be obeyed during a rendezvous are described by corresponding accept statements in the body of the task containing the declaration of the entry. An accept statement usually takes the form

```
accept E( ... ) do
    -- sequence of statements
end E;
```

The formal parameters of the entry E are repeated in the same way that a procedure body repeats the formal parameters of a corresponding procedure declaration. The **end** is optionally followed by the name of the entry. A significant difference is that the body of the accept statement is just a sequence of statements. Any local declarations or exception handlers must be provided by writing a local block.

The most important difference between an entry call and a procedure call is that in the case of a procedure, the task that calls the procedure also immediately executes the procedure body, whereas in the case of an entry, one task calls the entry but the corresponding accept statement is executed by the task owning the entry. Moreover, the accept statement cannot be executed until a task calls the entry and the task owning the entry reaches the accept statement. Naturally one of these will occur first and the task concerned will then be suspended until the other reaches its corresponding statement. When this occurs the sequence of statements of the accept statement is executed by the called task while the calling task remains suspended. This interaction is called a rendezvous. When the end of the accept statement is reached the rendezvous is completed and both tasks then proceed independently. The parameter mechanism is exactly as for a subprogram call; note that expressions in the actual parameter list are evaluated before the call is issued.

We can elaborate our shopping example by giving the task GET_ SALAD two entries, one for mother to hand the children the money for the salad and one to collect the salad from them afterwards. We do the same for GET_WINE (although perhaps father has his own funds in which case he might keep the wine to himself anyway).

We can also replace the procedures BUY_SALAD, BUY_WINE and BUY_MEAT by functions which take money as a parameter and return the appropriate ingredient. Our shopping procedure might now become

```
procedure SHOPPING is
    task GET_SALAD is
        entry PAY(M: in MONEY);
        entry COLLECT(S: out SALAD);
    end GET_SALAD;

    task body GET_SALAD is
        CASH: MONEY;
        FOOD: SALAD;
    begin
        accept PAY(M: in MONEY) do
            CASH:= M;
        end PAY;

        FOOD:= BUY_SALAD(CASH);

        accept COLLECT(S: out SALAD) do
            S:= FOOD;
        end COLLECT;
    end GET_SALAD;

    -- GET_WINE similarly

begin
    GET_SALAD.PAY(50);
    GET_WINE.PAY(100);
    MM:= BUY_MEAT(200);
    GET_SALAD.COLLECT(SS);
    GET_WINE.COLLECT(WW);
end SHOPPING;
```

The final outcome is that the various ingredients end up in the variables MM, SS and WW whose declarations are left to the imagination.

The logical behaviour should be noted. As soon as the tasks GET_SALAD and GET_WINE become active they encounter accept statements and wait until the main task calls the entries PAY in each of them. After calling the function BUY_MEAT, the main task calls the COLLECT entries. Curiously, mother is unable to collect the wine until after she has collected the salad from the children.

As a more abstract example consider the problem of providing a task to act as a single buffer between one or more tasks producing items and one or more tasks consuming them. Our intermediate task can hold just one item.

```
task BUFFERING is
    entry PUT(X: in ITEM);
    entry GET(X: out ITEM);
end;

task body BUFFERING is
    V: ITEM;
begin
    loop
        accept PUT(X: in ITEM) do
            V:= X;
        end PUT;
        accept GET(X: out ITEM) do
            X:= V;
        end GET;
    end loop;
end BUFFERING;
```

Other tasks may then dispose of or acquire items by calling

```
BUFFERING.PUT( ... );
BUFFERING.GET( ... );
```

Intermediate storage for the item is the variable V. The body of the task is an endless loop which contains an accept statement for PUT followed by one for GET. Thus the task alternately accepts calls of PUT and GET which fill and empty the variable V.

Several different tasks may call PUT and GET and consequently may have to be queued. Every entry has a queue of tasks waiting to call the entry – this queue is processed in a first-in-first-out manner and may, of course, be empty at a particular moment. The number of tasks on the queue of entry E is given by E'COUNT but this attribute may only be used inside the body of the task owning the entry.

An entry may have several corresponding accept statements (usually only one). Each execution of an accept statement removes one task from the queue.

Note the asymmetric naming in a rendezvous. The calling task must name the called task but not vice versa. Moreover, several tasks may call an entry and be queued but a task can only be on one queue at a time.

Entries may be overloaded both with each other and with subprograms and obey the same rules. An entry may be renamed as a procedure

procedure WRITE(X: **in** ITEM) **renames** BUFFERING.PUT;

This mechanism may be useful in avoiding excessive use of the dotted notation. An entry, renamed or not, may be an actual or default generic parameter corresponding to a formal subprogram.

An entry may have no parameters, such as

entry SIGNAL;

and it could then be called by

T.SIGNAL;

An accept statement need have no body as in

accept SIGNAL;

In such a case the purpose of the call is merely to effect a synchronization and not to pass information. However, an entry without parameters can have an accept statement with a body and vice versa. There is nothing to prevent us writing

accept SIGNAL **do**
    FIRE;
end;

in which case the task calling SIGNAL is only allowed to continue after the call of FIRE is completed. We could also have

accept PUT(X: ITEM);

although clearly the parameter value is not used.

There are few constraints on the statements in an accept statement. They may include entry calls, subprogram calls, blocks and further accept statements (but not for the same entry or one of the same family – see Section 14.8). On the other hand, an accept statement may not appear in a subprogram body but must be in the sequence of statements of the task, although it could be in a block or other accept statement. The execution of a **return** statement in an accept statement corresponds to reaching the final end and therefore terminates the rendezvous. Similarly to a subprogram body, a **goto** or **exit** statement cannot transfer control out of an accept statement.

A task may call one of its own entries but, of course, will promptly deadlock. This may seem foolish but programming languages allow lots of silly things such as endless loops and so on. We could expect a good compiler to warn us of obvious potential deadlocks.

Exercise 14.2

1   Write the body of a task whose specification is

        task BUILD_COMPLEX **is**
            entry PUT_RL(X: **in** REAL);
            entry PUT_IM(X: **in** REAL);

```
        entry GET_COMP(X: out COMPLEX);
    end;
```

and which alternately puts together a complex number from calls of PUT_RL and PUT_IM and then delivers the result on a call of GET_COMP.

2   Write the body of a task whose specification is

```
    task CHAR_TO_LINE is
        entry PUT(C: in CHARACTER);
        entry GET(L: out LINE);
    end;
```

where

```
    type LINE is array (1 .. 80) of CHARACTER;
```

The task acts as a buffer which alternately builds up a line by accepting successive calls of PUT and then delivers a complete line on a call of GET.

14.3   Timing and scheduling

As we have seen, an Ada program may contain several tasks. Conceptually, it is best to think of these tasks as each having its own personal processor so that, provided a task is not waiting for something to happen, it will actually be executing.

In practice, of course, most implementations will not be able to allocate a unique processor to each task and indeed, in many cases, there will be only one physical processor. It will then be necessary to allocate the processor(s) to the tasks that are logically able to execute by some scheduling algorithm. This can be done in many ways.

One of the simplest mechanisms is to use time slicing. This means giving the processor to each task in turn for some fixed time interval such as 10 milliseconds. Of course, if a task cannot use its turn (perhaps because it is held up awaiting a partner in a rendezvous), then a sensible scheduler would allocate its turn to the next task. Similarly, if a task cannot use all of its turn then the remaining time could be allocated to another task.

Time slicing is somewhat rudimentary since it treats all tasks equally. It is often the case that some tasks are more urgent than others and in the face of a shortage of processing power this equality is a bit wasteful. The idea of a task having a priority is therefore introduced. A simple scheduling system would be one where each task had a distinct priority and the processor would then be given to the highest priority task which could actually run. Combinations of time slicing and priority scheduling are also possible. A system might permit several tasks to have the same priority and time slice between them.

Ada allows various scheduling strategies to be used. If an implementation has the concept of priority, then the priority of a task can be indicated by a pragma appearing somewhere in the task specification as for example

```
task BUFFERING is
    pragma PRIORITY(7);
    entry PUT ...
        ...
end;
```

In the case of the main program, which, as we have seen, is also considered to be a task, the pragma goes in its outermost declarative part.

The priority must be a static expression of the subtype PRIORITY of the type INTEGER but the actual range of the subtype PRIORITY depends upon the implementation. Note that the priority of a task is static and therefore cannot be changed in the course of execution of the program. A larger priority indicates a higher degree of urgency. Several tasks can have the same priority but on the other hand a task need not have an explicit priority at all.

The effect of priorities on the scheduling of Ada tasks is given by the following rule taken from the *LRM*

'If two tasks with different priorities are both eligible for execution and could sensibly be executed using the same physical processors and the same other processing resources, then it cannot be the case that the task with the lower priority is executing while the task with the higher priority is not.'

Basically this says that scheduling must be preemptive – a higher priority task *always* preempts a lower priority task. This rule has been misinterpreted but AI-32 confirms that preemption is mandatory.

However, this rule says nothing about tasks whose priorities are not defined, nor does it say anything about tasks with the same priority. The implementation is therefore free to do whatever seems appropriate in these cases. Moreover, nothing prevents an implementation from having PRIORITY'FIRST = PRIORITY'LAST in which case all tasks could be time sliced equally and the concept of priority disappears. The rule also contains the phrase 'could sensibly be executed using the same ... processing resources'; this is directed towards distributed systems where it may not be at all sensible for a processor in one part of the system to be used to execute a task in a different part of the system.

In the case of a rendezvous (and activation, to be discussed later), a complication arises because two tasks are involved. If both tasks have explicit priorities, the rendezvous is executed with the higher priority. If only one task has an explicit priority, then the rendezvous is executed with at least that priority. If neither task has a defined priority then the priority of the rendezvous is not defined. Of course, if the accept statement contains a further entry call or accept statement, then the rules are applied once more.

The rendezvous rules ensure that a high priority task is not held up just because it is engaged in a rendezvous with a low priority task. On the other hand, the order of accepting the tasks in an entry queue is always first-in-first-out and is not affected by priorities. If a high priority task wishes to guard against being held up because of lower priority tasks in the same entry queue, it can always use timed out or conditional calls as we shall see in the next section.

The use of priorities needs care. They are intended as a means of adjusting relative degrees of urgency and should not be used for synchronization. It should not be assumed that the execution of task A precludes the execution of task B just because task A has a higher priority than task B. There might be several processors or later program maintenance might result in a change of priorities because of different realtime requirements. Synchronization should be done with the rendezvous and priorities should be avoided except for fine tuning of responsiveness.

A task may be held up for various reasons; it might be waiting for a partner in a rendezvous or for a dependent task to terminate. It can also be held up by executing a delay statement such as

delay 3.0;

This suspends the task (or main program) executing the statement for three seconds. The expression after the reserved word **delay** is of a predefined fixed point type DURATION and gives the period in seconds. (The *LRM* says the task is suspended for 'at least' the duration specified. This is solely because, after the expiry of the interval, there might not be a processor immediately available to execute the task since in the meantime a higher priority task might have obtained control. It does not mean that the scheduler can leave the suspended task rotting indefinitely. If it has a higher priority than a task running when the interval expires then it will preempt.)

The type DURATION is a fixed point type so that the addition of durations can be done without systematic loss of accuracy. If we add together two fixed point model numbers, we always get another model number; this does not apply to floating point. On the other hand, we need to express fractions of a second in a convenient way and so the use of a real type rather than an integer type is much more satisfactory.

Delays can be more easily expressed by using suitable constant declarations, thus

SECONDS: **constant** DURATION:= 1.0;
MINUTES: **constant** DURATION:= 60.0;
HOURS: **constant** DURATION:= 3600.0;

We can then write for example

delay 2*HOURS+40*MINUTES;

in which the expression uses the rule that a fixed point value can be multiplied by an integer giving a result of the same fixed point type.

A delay statement with a zero or negative argument has no effect.

Although the type DURATION is implementation defined we are guaranteed that it will allow durations (both positive and negative) of up to at least one day (86 400 seconds). Delays of more than a day (which are unusual) would have to be programmed with a loop. At the other end of the scale, the smallest value of DURATION, that is DURATION'SMALL, is guaranteed to be not greater than 20 milliseconds. This should not be confused with SYSTEM'TICK which gives the basic clock cycle and is, for example, and as confirmed by AI-201, the accuracy with which a delay statement must be executed (as opposed to being requested).

More sophisticated timing operations can be performed by using the predefined package CALENDAR whose specification is

```ada
package CALENDAR is

   type TIME is private;

   subtype YEAR_NUMBER is INTEGER range 1901 .. 2099;
   subtype MONTH_NUMBER is INTEGER range 1 .. 12;
   subtype DAY_NUMBER is INTEGER range 1 .. 31;
   subtype DAY_DURATION is DURATION range 0.0 .. 86_400.0;

   function CLOCK return TIME;

   function YEAR(DATE: TIME) return YEAR_NUMBER;
   function MONTH(DATE: TIME) return MONTH_NUMBER;
   function DAY(DATE: TIME) return DAY_NUMBER;
   function SECONDS(DATE: TIME) return DAY_DURATION;

   procedure SPLIT(DATE: in TIME;
                   YEAR: out YEAR_NUMBER;
                   MONTH: out MONTH_NUMBER;
                   DAY: out DAY_NUMBER;
                   SECONDS: out DAY_DURATION);

   function TIME_OF(YEAR: YEAR_NUMBER;
                    MONTH: MONTH_NUMBER;
                    DAY: DAY_NUMBER;
                    SECONDS: DAY_DURATION:= 0.0)
                                              return TIME;

   function "+" (LEFT: TIME; RIGHT: DURATION) return TIME;
   function "+" (LEFT: DURATION; RIGHT: TIME) return TIME;
   function "-" (LEFT: TIME; RIGHT: DURATION) return TIME;
   function "-" (LEFT: TIME; RIGHT: TIME) return DURATION;
   function "<" (LEFT, RIGHT: TIME) return BOOLEAN;
   function "<=" (LEFT, RIGHT: TIME) return BOOLEAN;
   function ">" (LEFT, RIGHT: TIME) return BOOLEAN;
   function ">=" (LEFT, RIGHT: TIME) return BOOLEAN;
```

```
TIME_ERROR: exception;
                        -- can be raised by TIME_OF, +, and -

private
    -- implementation dependent
end CALENDAR;
```

A value of the private type TIME is a combined time and date; it can be decomposed into the year, month, day and the duration since midnight of the day concerned by the procedure SPLIT. Alternatively the functions YEAR, MONTH, DAY and SECONDS may be used to obtain the individual values. On the other hand, the function TIME_OF can be used to build a value of TIME from the four constituents; the seconds parameter has a default of zero. Note the subtypes YEAR_NUMBER, MONTH_NUMBER and DAY_NUMBER; the range of YEAR_NUMBER is such that the leap year calculation is simplified. The exception TIME_ERROR is raised if the parameters of TIME_OF satisfy the constraints but nevertheless do not form a proper date. A careful distinction must be made between TIME and DURATION. TIME is absolute but DURATION is relative.

The current TIME is returned by a call of the function CLOCK. The result is, of course, returned in an indivisible way and there is no risk of getting the time of day and the date inconsistent around midnight as there would be if there were separate functions delivering the individual components of the current time and date.

The various overloadings of "+", "−" and the relational operators allow us to add, subtract and compare times and durations as appropriate. Attempts to create a time outside the allowed range of years or to create a duration outside the implemented range will result in TIME_ERROR being raised. Note the strange formal parameter names LEFT and RIGHT; these are the normal names for the parameters of the predefined operators in the package STANDARD.

As an example of the use of the package CALENDAR suppose we wish a task to call a procedure ACTION at regular intervals, every five minutes perhaps. Our first attempt might be to write

```
loop
    delay 5*MINUTES;
    ACTION;
end loop;
```

However, this is unsatisfactory for various reasons. First, we have not taken account of the time of execution of the procedure ACTION and the overhead of the loop itself, and secondly, we have seen that a delay statement sets a minimum delay only (since a higher priority task may retain the processor on the expiry of the delay). Furthermore, we might get preempted by a higher priority task at any time anyway. So we will inevitably get a cumulative timing drift. This can be overcome by writing for example

```
declare
   use CALENDAR;
   INTERVAL: constant DURATION:= 5*MINUTES;
   NEXT_TIME: TIME:= FIRST_TIME;
begin
   loop
      delay NEXT_TIME - CLOCK;
      ACTION;
      NEXT_TIME:= NEXT_TIME + INTERVAL;
   end loop;
end;
```

In this formulation NEXT_TIME contains the time when ACTION is next to be called; its initial value is in FIRST_TIME and it is updated exactly on each iteration by adding INTERVAL. The delay statement is then used to delay by the difference between NEXT_TIME and the current time obtained by calling CLOCK. This solution will have no cumulative drift provided the mean duration of ACTION plus the overheads of the loop and updating NEXT_TIME and so on do not exceed INTERVAL. Of course, there may be a local drift if a particular call of ACTION takes a long time or other tasks temporarily use the processors. There is one other condition that must be satisfied for the required timing to be obtained: the interval has to be a safe number.

Exercise 14.3

1   Write a generic procedure to call a procedure regularly. The generic parameters should be the procedure to be called, the time of the first call, the interval and the number of calls. If the time of the first call passed as parameter is in the past use the current time as the first time.

2   What is the least number of bits required to implement the type DURATION?

14.4   Simple select statements

The select statement allows a task to select from one of several possible rendezvous.

Consider the problem of protecting a variable V from uncontrolled access. We might consider using a package and two procedures READ and WRITE.

```
package PROTECTED_VARIABLE is
   procedure READ(X: out ITEM);
   procedure WRITE(X: in ITEM);
end;
```

```
package body PROTECTED_VARIABLE is
    V: ITEM;

    procedure READ(X: out ITEM) is
    begin
        X:= V;
    end;

    procedure WRITE(X: in ITEM) is
    begin
        V:= X;
    end;

begin
    V:= initial value;
end PROTECTED_VARIABLE;
```

However this is generally unsatisfactory. For one thing, the initial value is set in a rather arbitrary way. It would be better if somehow we could ensure that a call of WRITE had to be done first. We could, of course, have an internal state marker and raise an exception if READ is called first but this complicates the interface. The major problem, however, is that nothing prevents different tasks in our system from calling READ and WRITE simultaneously and thereby causing interference. As a more specific example, suppose that the type ITEM is a record giving the coordinates of an aircraft or ship

```
type ITEM is
    record
        X_COORD: REAL;
        Y_COORD: REAL;
    end record;
```

Suppose that a task A acquires pairs of values and uses a call of WRITE to store them into V and that another task B calls READ whenever it needs the latest position. Now assume that A is halfway through executing WRITE when it is interrupted by task B which promptly calls READ. It is clear that B could get a value consisting of the new *x*-coordinate and the old *y*-coordinate which would no doubt represent a location where the vessel had never been. The use of such inconsistent data for calculating the heading of the vessel from regularly read pairs of readings would obviously lead to inaccuracies.

The reader may wonder how the task A could be interrupted by task B anyway. In a single processor system with time slicing it may merely have been that B's turn came at an unfortunate moment. Alternatively B might have a higher priority than A; if B had been waiting for time to elapse before taking the next reading by obeying a delay statement, then A might be allowed to execute and B's delay might expire just at the wrong moment. In practical realtime situations things are always happening at the wrong moment!

The proper solution is to use a task rather than a package, and entry calls rather than procedure calls. Consider now

```
task PROTECTED_VARIABLE is
    entry READ(X: out ITEM);
    entry WRITE(X: in ITEM);
end;

task body PROTECTED_VARIABLE is
    V: ITEM;
begin
    accept WRITE(X: in ITEM) do
        V:= X;
    end;
    loop
        select
            accept READ(X: out ITEM) do
                X:= V;
            end;
        or
            accept WRITE(X: in ITEM) do
                V:= X;
            end;
        end select;
    end loop;
end PROTECTED_VARIABLE;
```

The body of the task starts with an accept statement for the entry WRITE; this ensures that the first call accepted is for WRITE so that there is no risk of the variable being read before it is assigned a value. Of course, a task could call READ before any task had called WRITE but the calls of READ will be queued until a call of WRITE has been accepted.

Having accepted a call of WRITE, the task enters an endless loop containing a single select statement. A select statement starts with the reserved word **select** and finishes with **end select**; it contains two or more alternatives separated by **or**. In this example each alternative consists of an accept statement – one for READ and one for WRITE.

When we encounter the select statement various possibilities have to be considered according to whether calls of READ or WRITE or both or neither have been made. We consider these in turn.

- If neither READ nor WRITE has been called then the task is suspended until one or the other is called and then the corresponding accept statement is obeyed.

- If one or more calls of READ are queued but there are no queued calls of WRITE then the first call of READ is accepted and vice versa with the roles of READ and WRITE reversed.

- If calls of both READ and WRITE are queued then an arbitrary choice is made.

Thus each execution of the select statement results in one of its branches being obeyed and one call of READ or WRITE being dealt with. We can think of the task as corresponding to a person serving two queues of customers waiting for two different services. If only one queue has customers then the server deals with it; if there are no customers then the server waits for the first irrespective of the service required; if both queues exist, the server rather capriciously serves either and makes an arbitrary choice each time.

So each time round the loop the task PROTECTED_VARIABLE will accept a call of READ or WRITE according to the demands upon it. It thus prevents multiple access to the variable V since it can only deal with one call at a time but does not impose any order upon the calls. Compare this with the task BUFFERING in Section 14.2 where an order was imposed upon the calls of PUT and GET.

Another point to notice is that this example illustrates a case where we have two accept statements for the same entry (WRITE). It so happens that the bodies are identical but they need not be.

The reader may wonder what the phrase 'arbitrary choice' means when deciding which alternative to choose. The intent is that there is no rule and the implementor is free to choose some efficient mechanism that nevertheless introduces an adequate degree of nondeterminism so that the various queues are treated fairly and none gets starved. A random choice with equal probability would be acceptable but hard to implement efficiently. The most important point is that a program must not rely on the selection algorithm used; if it does, it is erroneous.

A more complex form of select statement is illustrated by the classic problem of the bounded buffer. This is similar to the problem in Section 14.2 except that up to N items can be buffered. A solution is

```
task BUFFERING is
    entry PUT(X: in ITEM);
    entry GET(X: out ITEM);
end;

task body BUFFERING is
    N: constant:= 8;          -- for instance
    A: array (1 .. N) of ITEM;
    I, J: INTEGER range 1 .. N:= 1;
    COUNT: INTEGER range 0 .. N:= 0;
begin
    loop
        select
            when COUNT < N =>
            accept PUT(X: in ITEM) do
                A(I):= X;
            end;
            I:= I mod N+1; COUNT:= COUNT+1;
        or
            when COUNT > 0 =>
            accept GET(X: out ITEM) do
```

```
            X:= A(J);
        end;
        J:= J mod N+1; COUNT:= COUNT−1;
      end select;
    end loop;
  end BUFFERING;
```

The buffer is the array A of length N which is a number set to 8 in this example. The variables I and J index the next free and last used locations of the buffer respectively and COUNT is the number of locations of the buffer which are full. Not only is it convenient to have COUNT, but it is also necessary in order to distinguish between a completely full and completely empty buffer which both have I = J. The buffer is used cyclically so I need not be greater than J. The situation in Figure 14.1 shows a partly filled buffer with COUNT = 5, I = 3 and J = 6. The portion of the buffer in use is shaded. The variables I and J are both initialized to 1 and COUNT is initialized to 0 so that the buffer is initially empty.

The objective of the task is to allow items to be added to and removed from the buffer in a first-in-first-out manner but to prevent the buffer from being overfilled or under-emptied. This is done with a more general form of select statement which includes the use of guarding conditions.

Each branch of the select statement commences with

when condition =>

and is then followed by an accept statement and then some further statements. Each time the select statement is encountered, all the guarding conditions are evaluated. The behaviour is then as for a select statement without guards but containing only those branches for which the conditions were true. So a branch will be taken and the corresponding rendezvous performed. After the accept statement a branch may contain further statements. These are executed by the server task as part of the select statement but outside the rendezvous.

So the guarding conditions are conditions which have to be true before a service can be offered. The accept statement represents the rendezvous with the customer and the giving of the service. The statements after the accept statement represent bookkeeping actions performed as a consequence of giving the service and which can be done after the customer has left but, of course, need to be done before the next customer is served.

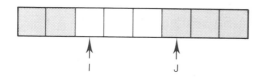

Figure 14.1   The bounded buffer.

In our example the condition for being able to accept a call of PUT is simply that the buffer must not be full; this is the condition COUNT < N. Similarly, we can accept a call of GET provided that the buffer is not empty; this is the condition COUNT > 0. The statements in the bodies of the accept statements copy the item to or from the buffer. After the rendezvous is completed, the index I or J as appropriate and COUNT are updated to reflect the change of state. Note the use of **mod** to update I and J in a cyclic manner.

Thus we see that the first time the select statement is executed, the condition COUNT < N is true but COUNT > 0 is false. Hence, only a call of PUT can be accepted. This puts the first item in the buffer. The next time both conditions will be true so either PUT or GET can be accepted, adding a further item or removing the one item. And so it goes on; allowing items to be added or removed with one of the guarding conditions becoming false in the extreme situations and thereby preventing overfilling or underemptying.

A few points need emphasis. The guards are re-evaluated at the beginning of each execution of the select statement (but their order of evaluation is not defined). An absent guard is taken as true. If all guards turn out to be false then the exception PROGRAM_ERROR is raised. It should be realized that a guard need not still be true when the corresponding rendezvous is performed because it might use global variables and therefore be changed by another task. Later we will discuss an example where guards could change unexpectedly. In the example here, of course, nothing can go wrong. One guard is always true, so PROGRAM_ERROR can never be raised and they both only involve the local variable COUNT and so cannot be changed between their evaluation and the rendezvous.

For our next example consider again the task PROTECTED_VARIABLE. This allowed either read or write access but only one at a time. This is somewhat severe; the usual classical problem is to allow only one writer of course, but to allow several readers together. A simple solution is shown below. It takes the form of a package containing a local task.

```
package READER_WRITER is
   procedure READ(X: out ITEM);
   procedure WRITE(X: in ITEM);
end;

package body READER_WRITER is
   V: ITEM;

   task CONTROL is
      entry START;
      entry STOP:
      entry WRITE(X: in ITEM);
   end;

   task body CONTROL is
      READERS: INTEGER:= 0;
   begin
```

```
      accept WRITE(X: in ITEM) do
         V:= X;
      end;
      loop
         select
            accept START;
            READERS:= READERS+1;
         or
            accept STOP;
            READERS:= READERS-1;
         or
            when READERS = 0 =>
            accept WRITE(X: in ITEM) do
               V:= X;
            end;
         end select;
      end loop;
   end CONTROL;

   procedure READ(X: out ITEM) is
   begin
      CONTROL.START;
      X:= V;
      CONTROL.STOP;
   end READ;

   procedure WRITE(X: in ITEM) is
   begin
      CONTROL.WRITE(X);
   end WRITE;

end READER_WRITER;
```

The task CONTROL has three entries: WRITE to do the writing and START and STOP associated with reading. A call of START indicates a wish to start reading and a call of STOP indicates that reading has finished. The task is wrapped up in a package because we wish to provide multiple reading access. This can be done by providing a procedure READ which can then be called reentrantly; it also enforces the protocol of calling START and then STOP.

So the whole thing is a package containing the variable V, the task CONTROL and the access procedures READ and WRITE. As stated, READ enforces the desired calls of START and STOP around the statement X:= V; the procedure WRITE merely calls the entry WRITE.

The task CONTROL declares a variable READERS which indicates how many readers are present. As before it begins with an accept statement for WRITE to ensure that the variable is initialized and then enters a loop containing a select statement. This has three branches, one for each entry. On a call of START or STOP the count of number of readers is incremented or decremented. A call of WRITE can only be accepted if the condition

READERS = 0 is true. Hence writing when readers are present is forbidden. Of course, since the task CONTROL actually does the writing, multiple writing is prevented and, moreover, it cannot at the same time accept calls of START and so reading is not possible when writing is in progress. However, multiple reading is allowed as we have seen.

Although the above solution does fulfil the general conditions, it is not really satisfactory. A steady stream of readers will completely block out a writer. Since writing is probably rather important, this is not acceptable. An obvious improvement would be to disallow further reading if one or more writers are waiting. We can do this by using the attribute WRITE'COUNT in a guard so that the select statement now becomes

```
select
   when WRITE'COUNT = 0 =>
   accept START;
   READERS:= READERS+1;
or
   accept STOP;
   READERS:= READERS-1;
or
   when READERS = 0 =>
   accept WRITE(X: in ITEM) do
      V:= X;
   end;
end select;
```

The attribute WRITE'COUNT is the number of tasks currently on the queue for the entry WRITE. The use of the count attribute in guards needs care. It gives the value when the guard is evaluated and can well change before a rendezvous is accepted. It could increase because another task joins the queue – that would not matter in this example. But, as we shall see later, it could also decrease unexpectedly and this would indeed give problems. We will return to this example in a moment.

Exercise 14.4

1   Rewrite the body of the task BUILD_COMPLEX of Exercise 14.2(**1**) so that the calls of PUT_RL and PUT_IM are accepted in any order.

14.5   Timed and conditional rendezvous

There are also various other forms of select statement. It is possible for one or more of the branches to start with a delay statement rather than an accept statement. Consider

```
select
   accept READ( ... ) do
      ...
```

```
      end;
   or
      accept WRITE( ... ) do
      ...
      end;
   or
      delay 10*MINUTES;
      -- time out statements
   end select;
```

If neither a call of READ nor WRITE is received within ten minutes, then the third branch is taken and the statements following the delay are executed. The task might decide that since its services are no longer apparently required it can do something else or maybe it can be interpreted as an emergency. In a process control system we might be awaiting an acknowledgement from the operator that some action has been taken and after a suitable interval take our own emergency action

```
OPERATOR.CALL("PUT OUT FIRE");

select
   accept ACKNOWLEDGE;
or
   delay 1*MINUTES;
   FIRE_BRIGADE.CALL;
end select;
```

A delay alternative can be guarded and indeed there could be several in a select statement although clearly only the shortest one with a true guard can be taken. It should be realized that if one of the accept statements is obeyed then any delay is cancelled – we can think of a delay alternative as waiting for a rendezvous with the clock. A delay is, of course, set from the start of the select statement and reset each time the select statement is encountered. Finally, note that it is the start of the rendezvous that matters rather than its completion as far as the time out is concerned.

Another form of select statement is one with an else part. Consider

```
select
   accept READ( ... ) do
   ...
   end;
or
   accept WRITE( ... ) do
   ...
   end;
else
   -- alternative statements
end select;
```

In this case the final branch is preceded by **else** rather than **or** and consists of just a sequence of statements. The else branch is taken at once if none of the other branches can be immediately accepted. A select statement with an else part is rather like one with a branch starting **delay** 0.0; it times out at once if there are no customers to be dealt with. A select statement cannot have both an else part and delay alternatives.

There is a subtle distinction between an accept statement starting a branch of a select and an accept statement anywhere else. In the first case the accept statement is bound up with the workings of the select statement and is to some extent conditional. In the second case, once encountered, it will be obeyed come what may. The same distinction applies to a delay statement starting a branch of a select statement and one elsewhere. Thus if we change the **or** to **else** in our emergency action to give

```
select
    accept ACKNOWLEDGE;
else
    delay 1*MINUTES;
    FIRE_BRIGADE.CALL;
end select;
```

then the status of the delay is quite different. It just happens to be one of a sequence of statements and will be obeyed in the usual way. So if we cannot accept a call of ACKNOWLEDGE at once, we immediately take the else part. The fact that the first statement is a delay is fortuitous – we immediately delay for one minute and then call the fire brigade. There is no time out. We see therefore that the simple change from **or** to **else** causes a dramatic difference in meaning which may not be immediately obvious; so take care!

If a select statement has an else part then PROGRAM_ERROR can never be raised. The else part cannot be guarded and so will always be taken if all branches have guards and they all turn out to be false.

There are two other forms of select statement which are rather different; they concern a single entry call rather than one or more accept statements. The timed out entry call allows a sequence of statements to be taken as an alternative to an entry call if it is not accepted within the specified duration. Thus

```
select
    OPERATOR.CALL("PUT OUT FIRE");
or
    delay 1*MINUTES;
    FIRE_BRIGADE.CALL;
end select;
```

will call the fire brigade if the operator does not accept the call within one minute. Again, it is the start of the rendezvous that matters rather than its completion. Finally there is the conditional entry call. Thus

```
select
    OPERATOR.CALL("PUT OUT FIRE");
else
    FIRE_BRIGADE.CALL;
end select;
```

will call the fire brigade if the operator cannot immediately accept the call.

The timed out and conditional entry calls are quite different to the general select statement. They concern only a single unguarded call and so these select statements always have exactly two branches – one with the entry call and the other with the alternative sequence of statements. Timed out and conditional calls apply only to entries. They do not apply to procedures or even to entries renamed as procedures.

Timed out and conditional calls are useful if a task does not want to be unduly delayed when a server task is busy. They correspond to a customer in a shop giving up and leaving the queue after waiting for a time or, in the conditional case, a highly impatient customer leaving at once if not immediately served.

Timed out calls, however, need some care particularly if the COUNT attribute is used. A decision based on the value of that attribute may be invalidated because of a timed out call unexpectedly removing a task from an entry queue. Consider for example the package READER_WRITER. As it stands the entry calls cannot be timed out because they are encapsulated in the procedures READ and WRITE. However, we might decide to provide further overloadings of these procedures in order to provide timed out facilities. We might add, for example

```
procedure WRITE(X: in ITEM; T: DURATION; OK: out BOOLEAN) is
begin
    select
        CONTROL.WRITE(X);
        OK:= TRUE;
    or
        delay T;
        OK:= FALSE;
    end select;
end WRITE;
```

Unfortunately this is invalid. Suppose that one writer is waiting (so that WRITE'COUNT = 1) but the call is timed out between the evaluation of the guards and the execution of an accept statement. There are two cases to consider according to the value of READERS. If READERS = 0, then no task can call STOP since there are no current readers; a call of START cannot be accepted because its guard was false and the expected call of WRITE will not occur because it has been timed out; the result is that all new readers will be unnecessarily blocked until a new writer arrives. On the other hand, if READERS > 0, then although further calls of WRITE correctly cannot be accepted, nevertheless further calls of START are unnecessarily delayed until an existing reader calls STOP despite there being no waiting writers. We therefore seek an alternative solution.

The original reason for using WRITE'COUNT was to prevent readers from overtaking waiting writers. One possibility in cases of this sort is to make all the customers call a common entry to start with. This ensures that they are dealt with in order. This entry call can be parameterized to indicate the service required and the callers can then be placed on a secondary queue if necessary. This technique is illustrated by the solution which now follows. The package specification is as before.

```
package body READER_WRITER is
    V: ITEM;
    type SERVICE is (READ, WRITE);

    task CONTROL is
        entry START(S: SERVICE);
        entry STOP_READ;
        entry WRITE;
        entry STOP_WRITE;
    end CONTROL;

    task body CONTROL is
        READERS: INTEGER:= 0;
        WRITERS: INTEGER:= 0;
    begin
        loop
            select
                when WRITERS = 0 =>
                accept START(S: SERVICE) do
                    case S is
                        when READ =>
                            READERS:= READERS+1;
                        when WRITE =>
                            WRITERS:= 1;
                    end case;
                end START;
            or
                accept STOP_READ;
                READERS:= READERS-1;
            or
                when READERS = 0 =>
                accept WRITE;
            or
                accept STOP_WRITE;
                WRITERS:= 0;
            end select;
        end loop;
    end CONTROL;
```

```
      procedure READ(X: out ITEM) is
      begin
         CONTROL.START(READ);
         X:= V;
         CONTROL.STOP_READ;
      end READ;

      procedure WRITE(X: in ITEM) is
      begin
         CONTROL.START(WRITE);
         CONTROL.WRITE;
         V:= X;
         CONTROL.STOP_WRITE;
      end WRITE;

   end READER_WRITER;
```

We have introduced a variable WRITERS to indicate how many writers are in the system; it can only take values of 0 and 1. All requests initially call the common entry START but have to wait until there are no writers. The count of readers or writers is then updated as appropriate. In the case of a reader it can then go ahead as before and finishes by calling STOP_READ. A writer, on the other hand, must wait until there are no readers; it does this by calling WRITE and then finally calls STOP_WRITE in order that the control task can set WRITERS back to zero. Separating STOP_WRITE from WRITE enables us to cope with time outs as we shall see; we also take the opportunity to place the actual writing statement in the procedure WRITE so that it is similar to the read case.

In this solution, the variable WRITERS performs the function of WRITE'COUNT in the previous but incorrect solution. By counting for ourselves we can keep the situation under control. The calls of START and WRITE can now be timed out provided that we always call STOP_READ or STOP_WRITE once a call of START has been accepted. The details of suitable overloadings of READ and WRITE to provide timed out calls are left as an exercise.

Note that the above solution has ignored the problem of ensuring that the first call is a write. This can be catered for in various ways, by using a special initial entry, for instance, or by placing the readers on a second auxiliary queue so that they are forced to wait for the first writer.

We finish this section by showing a rather slick alternative to the above

```
   task CONTROL is
      entry START(S: SERVICE);
      entry STOP;
   end CONTROL;

   task body CONTROL is
      READERS: INTEGER:= 0;
   begin
      loop
         select
```

```
                        accept START(S: SERVICE) do
                            case S is
                                when READ =>
                                    READERS:= READERS+1;
                                when WRITE =>
                                    while READERS > 0 loop
                                        accept STOP;        -- from readers
                                        READERS:= READERS-1
                                    end loop;
                            end case;
                        end START;

                        if READERS = 0 then
                            accept STOP;                    -- from the writer
                        end if;
                    or
                        accept STOP;                        -- from a reader
                        READERS:= READERS-1;
                    end select;
                end loop;
            end CONTROL;

            procedure READ(X: out ITEM) is
            begin
                CONTROL.START(READ);
                X:= V;
                CONTROL.STOP;
            end READ;

            procedure WRITE(X: in ITEM) is
            begin
                CONTROL.START(WRITE);
                V:= X;
                CONTROL.STOP;
            end WRITE;
```

The essence of this solution is that the writer waits in the rendezvous for any readers to finish and the whole of the writing process is dealt with in the one branch of the select statement. No guards are required at all and the control task only has two entries. A common STOP entry is possible because the structure is such that each accept statement deals with only one category of caller. A minor disadvantage of the solution is that less flexible timed calls are possible. Once the writer has been accepted by the call of START, he is committed to wait for all the readers to finish.

Exercise 14.5

1   Write additional procedures READ and WRITE for the (penultimate) package READER_WRITER in order to provide

timed out calls. Take care with the procedure WRITE so that the calls of the entries START and WRITE are both timed out appropriately.

14.6   Task types and activation

It is sometimes useful to have several similar but distinct tasks. Moreover, it is often not possible to predict the number of such tasks required. For example, we might wish to create distinct tasks to follow each aircraft within the zone of control of an air traffic control system. Clearly, such tasks need to be created and disposed of in a dynamic way not related to the static structure of the program.

A template for similar tasks is provided by a task type declaration. This is identical to the simple task declarations we have seen so far except that the reserved word **type** follows **task** in the specification. Thus we may write

```
task type T is
    entry E( ... );
end T;

task body T is
    ...
end T;
```

The task body follows the same rules as before.

To create an actual task we use the normal form of object declaration. So we can write

```
X: T;
```

and this declares a task X of type T. In fact the simple form of task declaration we have been using so far such as

```
task SIMPLE is
    ...
end SIMPLE;
```

is exactly equivalent to writing

```
task type anon is
    ...
end anon;
```

followed by

```
SIMPLE: anon;
```

Task objects can be used in structures in the usual way. Thus we can declare arrays of tasks

```
AOT: array (1 .. 10) of T;
```

records containing tasks

```
type REC is
    record
        CT: T;
        ...
    end record;
R: REC;
```

and so on.

The entries of such tasks are called using the task object name; thus we write

```
X.E( ... );
AOT(I).E( ... );
R.CT.E( ... );
```

A most important consideration is that task objects are not variables but behave as constants. A task object declaration creates a task which is permanently bound to the object. Hence assignment is not allowed for task types and nor are the comparisons for equality and inequality. A task type is therefore another form of limited type and so could be used as the actual type corresponding to a formal generic parameter specified as limited private and as the actual type in a private part corresponding to a limited private type. Although task objects behave as constants, they cannot be declared as such since a constant declaration needs an explicit initial value. Subprogram parameters may be of task types; they are always effectively passed by reference and so the formal and actual parameters always refer to the same task. As in the case of other limited types, outside their defining package, parameters of mode **out** are not allowed; of course there is no defining package in the case of task types anyway.

In Section 14.1 we briefly introduced the idea of dependency. Each task is dependent on some unit and there is a general rule that a unit cannot be left until all tasks dependent upon it have terminated.

A task declared as a task object (or using the abbreviated simple form) is dependent upon the enclosing block, subprogram or task body in which it is declared. Inner packages do not count in this rule – this is because a package is merely a passive scope wall and has no dynamic life. If a task is declared in a package (or nested packages) then the task is dependent upon the block, subprogram or task body in which the package or packages are themselves declared. For completeness, a task declared in a library package is said to depend on that package and we refer to it as a library task. After termination of the main program, the main environment task (which calls the main program) must wait for all library tasks to terminate. Only then does the program as a whole terminate (AI-222).

We saw earlier that a task becomes active only when the declaring unit reaches the **begin** following the declaration. The execution of a task can be thought of as a two-stage process. The first stage, known as activation, consists of the elaboration of the declarations of the task body whereas the second stage consists, of course, of the execution of its statements. During the activation stage the parent unit is not allowed to proceed. If several tasks are declared in a unit, then their activations and the subsequent execution of their statements occur independently and in parallel. But it is only when the activation of all the tasks is complete that the parent unit can continue with the execution of the statements following the **begin** in parallel with the new tasks.

Note that the activation of a task (like the rendezvous) involves two tasks: the parent and itself. Similar priority rules apply as for the rendezvous so that the activation occurs at the higher of the priority of the task and that of its parent (if defined) and so on (AI-288).

The activation process is depicted in Figure 14.2 which illustrates the behaviour of a block containing the declarations of two tasks A and B

```
declare
   ...
   A: T;
   B: T;
   ...
begin
   ...
end;
```

Time flows from left to right and a solid line indicates that a unit is actively doing something whereas a dashed line indicates that it exists but is suspended.

For the sake of illustration, we show task A finishing its activation after task B so that the parent resumes execution when task A enters its execution stage. We also show task A finishing its execution and therefore becoming completed and terminated before task B. The parent is shown reaching its **end** and therefore completing execution of the block after task A has terminated but before task B has terminated. The parent is

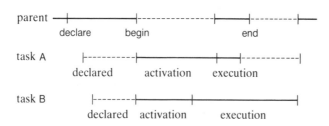

Figure 14.2   Task activation.

therefore suspended until task B is terminated when it can then resume execution with the statements following the block.

The reason for treating task activation in this way concerns exceptions. The reader may recall that an exception raised during the elaboration of declarations is not handled at that level but immediately propagated. So an exception raised in the declarations in a new task could not be handled by that task at all. However, since it is clearly desirable that some means be provided for detecting such an exception, it is obvious that an exception has to be raised in the parent unit. In fact the predefined exception TASKING_ERROR is raised irrespective of the original exception. It would clearly make life rather difficult if this exception were raised in the parent unit after it had moved on in parallel and so it is held up until all the new tasks have been activated. The exception TASKING_ERROR is then raised in the parent unit as soon as it attempts to move on from the **begin**. Note that if several of the new tasks raise exceptions during activation then TASKING_ERROR is only raised once. Such tasks become completed (not terminated) and do not affect sibling tasks being simultaneously activated.

The other thing that can go wrong is that an exception can occur in the declarations of the parent unit itself. In this case any new tasks which have been declared (but of course will not have been activated because the parent unit has not yet reached its **begin**) will automatically become terminated and are never activated at all.

Task objects can be declared in a package and although not dependent on the package are nevertheless set active at the **begin** of the package body. If the package body has no initialization statements and therefore no **begin**, then a null initialization statement is assumed. Worse, if a package has no body, then a body with just a null initialization statement is assumed. So the task CONTROL in the package READER_WRITER of the previous section is set active at the end of the declaration of the package body.

Tasks can also be created through access types. We can write

type REF_T **is access** T;

and then we can create a task using an allocator in the usual way

RX: REF_T:= **new** T;

The type REF_T is a normal access type and so assignment and equality comparisons of objects of the type are allowed. The entry E of the task accessed by RX can be called as expected by

RX.E(...);

Tasks created through access types obey slightly different rules for activation and dependency. They commence activation immediately upon evaluation of the allocator whether it occurs in a sequence of statements or in an initial value – we do not wait until the ensuing **begin**. Furthermore, such tasks are not dependent upon the unit where they are created but are dependent upon the block, subprogram body or task body containing the declaration of the access type itself. The strong analogies between tasks declared as objects and those created through an allocator are revealed when we consider tasks which are components of a composite object.

Suppose we have the following somewhat artificial type

```
type R is
    record
        A: T;
        I: INTEGER:= E;
        B: T;
    end record;
```

where A and B are components of some task type T and E is the default initial expression for the component I.

If we declare an object X of type R thus

```
declare
    X: R;
begin
```

then it is much as if we declared the individual objects

```
declare
    XA: T;
    XI: INTEGER:= E;
    XB: T;
begin
```

using the rules explained above.

Now suppose we have an access type

```
type REF_R is access R;
```

and create an object using an allocator

```
RR: REF_R:= new R;
```

The first thing that happens is that the various components are declared and the initial expression is evaluated and assigned to RR.I. It is only when this has been done that activation of the tasks RR.A and RR.B can commence; in a sense we wait until reaching **end record** by analogy with waiting until we reach **begin** in the case of directly declared objects. The component tasks are then activated in parallel but the parent unit is suspended and the access value is not returned until all the activations are complete just as we could not move past the **begin**. Similarly, if an exception is raised by the activation of one or both component tasks, then, on return from the allocator, TASKING_ERROR is raised just once in the parent unit. Such rogue tasks will then become completed but will not interfere with any other sibling component tasks. Finally, if the evaluation of E raises an exception in the parent unit then the component tasks will automatically become terminated without even being activated.

The reader will probably feel that the activation mechanism is somewhat elaborate. However, in practice, the details will rarely need to be considered. They are mentioned in order to show that the mechanism is well defined rather than because of their everyday importance.

Note that entries in a task can be called as soon as it is declared and even before activation commences – the call will just be queued. However, situations in which this is sensibly possible are rare.

An interesting use of task types is for the creation of agents. An agent is a task that does something on behalf of another task. As an example suppose a task SERVER provides some service that is asked for by calling an entry REQUEST. Suppose also that it may take SERVER some time to provide the service so that it is reasonable for the calling task USER to go away and do something else while waiting for the answer to be prepared. There are various ways in which the USER could expect to collect his answer. He could call another entry ENQUIRE; the SERVER task would need some means of recognizing the caller – he could do this by issuing a key on the call of REQUEST and insisting that it be presented again when calling ENQUIRE. This corresponds to taking something to be repaired, being given a ticket and then having to exchange it when the repaired item is collected later. An alternative approach which avoids the issue of keys, is to create an agent. This corresponds to leaving your address and having the repaired item mailed back to you. We will now illustrate this approach.

First of all we declare a task type as follows

```
task type MAILBOX is
    entry DEPOSIT(X: in ITEM);
    entry COLLECT(X: out ITEM);
end;

task body MAILBOX is
    LOCAL: ITEM;
begin
    accept DEPOSIT(X: in ITEM) do
        LOCAL:= X;
    end;
    accept COLLECT(X: out ITEM) do
        X:= LOCAL;
    end;
end MAILBOX;
```

A task of this type acts as a simple mailbox. An item can be deposited and collected later. What we are going to do is to give the identity of the mailbox to the server so that the server can deposit the item in the mailbox from which the user can collect it later. We need an access type

```
type ADDRESS is access MAILBOX;
```

The tasks SERVER and USER now take the following form

```
task SERVER is
    entry REQUEST(A: ADDRESS; X: ITEM);
end;

task body SERVER is
    REPLY: ADDRESS;
    JOB: ITEM;
begin
    loop
        accept REQUEST(A: ADDRESS; X: ITEM) do
            REPLY:= A;
            JOB:= X;
        end;

        -- work on job

        REPLY.DEPOSIT(JOB);
    end loop;
end SERVER;

task USER;

task body USER is
    MY_BOX: ADDRESS:= new MAILBOX;
    MY_ITEM: ITEM;
begin
    SERVER.REQUEST(MY_BOX, MY_ITEM);

    -- do something while waiting

    MY_BOX.COLLECT(MY_ITEM);
end USER;
```

In practice the user might poll the mailbox from time to time to see if the item is ready. This is easily done using a conditional entry call.

```
select
    MY_BOX.COLLECT(MY_ITEM);
    -- item collected successfully
else
    -- not ready yet
end select;
```

It is important to realize that the agent serves several purposes. It enables the deposit and collect to be decoupled so that the server can get on with the next job. Moreover, and perhaps of more importance, it means that the server need know nothing about the user; to call the user directly would mean that the user would have to be of a particular task type and this would be most unreasonable. The agent enables us to factor off the only property required of the user, namely the existence of the entry DEPOSIT.

If the decoupling property were not required then the body of the agent could be written as

```
task body MAILBOX is
begin
    accept DEPOSIT(X: in ITEM) do
        accept COLLECT(X: out ITEM) do
            COLLECT.X:= DEPOSIT.X;
        end;
    end;
end MAILBOX;
```

The agent does not need a local variable in this case since the agent now only exists in order to aid closely coupled communication. Note also the use of the dotted notation in the nested accept statements in order to distinguish the two uses of X; we could equally have written X:= DEPOSIT.X; but the use of COLLECT is more symmetric.

14.7 Termination and exceptions

A task can become completed and then terminate in various ways as well as running into its final end. It will have been noticed that in many of our earlier examples, the body of a task was an endless loop and clearly never terminated. This means that it would never be possible to leave the unit on which the task was dependent. Suppose, for example, that we needed to have several protected variables in our program. We could declare a task type

```
task type PROTECTED_VARIABLE is
    entry READ(X: out ITEM);
    entry WRITE(X: in ITEM);
end;
```

so that we can just declare variables such as

```
PV: PROTECTED_VARIABLE;
```

and then access them by

```
PV.READ( ... );
PV.WRITE( ... );
```

However, we could not leave the unit on which PV depends without terminating the task in some way. We could, of course, add a special entry

STOP and call it just before leaving the unit, but this would be inconvenient. Instead it is possible to make a task automatically terminate itself when it is of no further use by a special form of select alternative.

The body of the task can be written as

```
task body PROTECTED_VARIABLE is
    V: ITEM;
begin
    accept WRITE(X: in ITEM) do
        V:= X;
    end;
    loop
        select
            accept READ(X: out ITEM) do
                X:= V;
            end;
        or
            accept WRITE(X: in ITEM) do
                V:= X;
            end;
        or
            terminate;
        end select;
    end loop;
end PROTECTED_VARIABLE;
```

The terminate alternative is taken if the unit on which the task depends has reached its end and so is completed and all sibling tasks and dependent tasks are terminated or are similarly able to select a terminate alternative. In such circumstances all the tasks are of no use since they are the only tasks that could call their entries and they are all dormant. Thus the whole set automatically terminates.

In practice, this merely means that all service tasks should have a terminate alternative and will then quietly terminate themselves without more ado.

Strictly speaking, the initial WRITE should also be in a select statement with a terminate alternative otherwise we are still stuck if the task is never called at all.

A terminate alternative may be guarded. However, it cannot appear in a select statement with a delay alternative or an else part.

Selection of a terminate alternative is classified as normal termination – the task is under control of the situation and terminates voluntarily.

At the other extreme the abort statement unconditionally terminates one or more tasks. It consists of the reserved word **abort** followed by a list of task names as for example

```
abort X, AOT(3), RX.all;
```

If a task is aborted then all tasks dependent upon it or a subprogram or block currently called by it are also aborted. If the task is suspended for some reason, then it immediately becomes completed; any delay is cancelled; if the task is on an entry queue, it is removed; other possibilities are that it has not yet even commenced activation or it is at an accept or select statement awaiting a partner. If the task is not suspended, then completion will occur as soon as convenient and certainly no new communication with the task will be possible. The reason for this somewhat vague statement concerns the rendezvous. If the task is engaged in a rendezvous when it is aborted, then we also have to consider the effect on the partner. This depends on the situation. If the called task is aborted, then the calling task receives the exception TASKING_ERROR. On the other hand, if the calling task is aborted, then the called task is not affected; the rendezvous carries on to completion with the caller in a somewhat abnormal state and it is only when the rendezvous is complete that the caller becomes properly completed. The rationale is simple; if a task asks for a service and the server dies so that it cannot be provided, then the customer should be told. On the other hand, if the customer dies, too bad – but we must avoid upsetting the server who might have the database in a critical state.

Note that the above rules are formulated in terms of completing the tasks rather than terminating them. This is because a parent task cannot be terminated until its dependent tasks are terminated and if one of those is the caller in a rendezvous with a third party, then its termination will be delayed. Thus completion of the tasks is the best that can be individually enforced and their termination will then automatically occur in the usual way.

The abort statement is very disruptive and should only be used in extreme situations. It might be appropriate for a command task to abort a complete subsystem in response to an operator command.

Another possible use for the abort statement might be in an exception handler. Remember that we cannot leave a unit until all dependent tasks are terminated. Hence, if an exception is raised in a unit, then we cannot tidy up that unit and propagate the exception on a layered basis while dependent taks are still alive and so one of the actions of tidying up might be to abort all dependent tasks. Thus the procedure CLEAN_UP of Section 10.2 might do just this.

However, it is probably always best to attempt a controlled shutdown and only resort to the abort statement as a desperate measure. Statements in the command task might be as follows

```
select
    T.CLOSEDOWN;
or
    delay 60*SECONDS;
    abort T;
end select;
```

If the slave task does not accept the CLOSEDOWN call within a minute, then it is ruthlessly aborted. We are assuming, of course, that the slave task polls the CLOSEDOWN entry at least every minute using a conditional accept statement such as

```
select
    accept CLOSEDOWN;
```

```
        -- tidy up and die
    else
        -- carry on normally
    end select;
```

If we cannot trust the slave to close down properly even after accepting the entry call, then the command task can always issue an abort after a due interval just in case. Aborting a task which has already terminated has no effect. So the command task might read

```
    select
        T.CLOSEDOWN;
        delay 10*SECONDS;
    or
        delay 60*SECONDS;
    end select;
    abort T;
```

Of course, even this is not foolproof since the malevolent slave might continue for ever in the rendezvous itself

```
    accept CLOSEDOWN do
        loop
            PUT("CAN'T CATCH ME");
        end loop;
    end;
```

Some minimal degree of cooperation is obviously needed!

The status of task T can be ascertained by the use of two attributes. Thus T'TERMINATED is true if a task is terminated. The other attribute, T'CALLABLE, is true unless the task is completed or terminated or in the abnormal state pending final abortion. The use of these attributes needs care. For example, between discovering that a task has not terminated and taking some action based on that information, the task could become terminated. However, the reverse is not possible since a task cannot be restarted and so it is quite safe to take an action based on the information that a task has terminated.

As an illustration of the impact of abnormal termination and how it can be coped with, we will reconsider the task CONTROL in the package READER_WRITER in Section 14.5 in its final form

```
    task body CONTROL is
        READERS: INTEGER:= 0;
    begin
        loop
            select
                accept START(S: SERVICE) do
                    case S is
                        when READ =>
                            READERS:= READERS+1;
```

```
        when WRITE =>
            while READERS > 0 loop
                accept STOP;     -- from readers
                READERS:= READERS-1;
            end loop;
        end case;
    end START;
    if READERS = 0 then
        accept STOP;                -- from the writer
    end if;
or
    accept STOP;                    -- from a reader
    READERS:= READERS-1;
end select;
    end loop;
end CONTROL;
```

Suppose that a reading task has called START and is then aborted before it can call STOP. The variable READERS will then be inconsistent and can never be zero again. The next writer will then be locked out for ever. Similarly, if a writing task has called START and is then aborted before it can call STOP, then all other users will be locked out for ever.

The difficulty we have run into is that our task CONTROL assumes certain behaviour on the part of the calling tasks and this behaviour is not guaranteed. (We had a similar difficulty with our elementary solution to this example in Section 14.5 regarding the COUNT attribute and timed out entry calls.) We can overcome our new difficulty by the use of intermediate agent tasks which we can guarantee cannot be aborted.

The following shows the use of agents for the readers; a similar technique can be applied to the writers. The package body now becomes

```
package body READER_WRITER is
    V: ITEM;
    type SERVICE is (READ, WRITE);

    task type READ_AGENT is
        entry READ(X: out ITEM);
    end;

    type RRA is access READ_AGENT;

    task CONTROL is
        entry START(S: SERVICE);
        entry STOP;
    end;

    task body CONTROL is
        -- as before
    end CONTROL;
```

```
task body READ_AGENT is
begin
   select
      accept READ(X: out ITEM) do
         CONTROL.START(READ);
         X:= V;
         CONTROL.STOP;
      end;
   or
      terminate;
   end select;
end READ_AGENT;

procedure READ(X: out ITEM) is
   TASK_007: RRA:= new READ_AGENT;
begin
   TASK_007.READ(X);
end READ;

procedure WRITE(X: in ITEM) is
begin
   ...
end WRITE;

end READER_WRITER;
```

If we now abort the task calling the procedure READ, then either the
rendezvous with its agent (TASK_007) will be in progress, in which case it
will be completed, or the rendezvous will not be in progress, in which case
there will be no interference. The agent therefore either does its job
completely or not at all. Note that if we made the agent a direct task object
(rather than an access to a task object), then aborting the task calling the
procedure READ would also immediately abort the agent because it would
be a dependent task. Using an access type makes the agent dependent on
the unit in which the READER_WRITER is declared and so it can live on.

The agent task body contains a select statement with a terminate
alternative. This ensures that if the user task is aborted between creating
the agent and calling the agent then nevertheless the agent can quietly die
when the unit on which it depends is left.

It is worth summarizing why the above solution works

- the agent is invisible and so cannot be aborted,
- if the calling task in a rendezvous is abnormally terminated, the
  called task (the agent) is not affected,
- the agent is an access task and is not dependent on the caller.

The moral is not to use abort without due care; or, as in life, if you cannot
trust the calling tasks, use indestructible secret agents.

We finish this section by discussing a few remaining points on exceptions. The exception TASKING_ERROR is concerned with general communication failure. As we have seen, it is raised if a failure occurs during task activation and it is also raised in the caller of a rendezvous if the server is aborted. In addition, no matter how a task is completed, all tasks still queued on its entries receive TASKING_ERROR. Similarly calling an entry of a task that is already completed also raises TASKING_ERROR in the caller.

If an exception is raised during a rendezvous (that is as a consequence of an action by the called task) and is not handled by the accept statement, then it is propagated into both tasks as the same exception on the grounds that both need to know. Of course, if the accept statement handles the exception internally, then that is the end of the matter anyway.

It might be convenient for the called task, the server, to inform the calling task, the user, of some event by the explicit raising of an exception. In such a case it is likely that the server task will not wish to take any action and so a null handler will be required. So in outline we might write

```
begin
   select
      accept E( ... ) do
         ...
         raise ERROR;          -- tell user
         ...
      end E;

   or
      ...
   end select;
exception
   when ERROR =>
      null;                    -- server forgets
end;
```

Finally, if an exception is not handled by a task at all, then, like the main program, the task is abandoned and the exception is lost; it is not propagated to the parent unit because it would be too disruptive to do so. However, we might expect the run time environment to provide a diagnostic message. If it does not, it might be good practice for all significant tasks to have a general handler at the outermost level in order to guard against the loss of exceptions and consequential silent death of the task.

Exercise 14.7

1   Rewrite the task BUFFERING of Section 14.4 so that it has the following specification

```
task BUFFERING is
   entry PUT(X: in ITEM);
```

```
      entry FINISH;
      entry GET(X: out ITEM);
   end;
```

The writing task calls PUT as before and finally calls FINISH. The reading task calls GET as before; a call of GET when there are no further items raises the global exception DONE.

14.8 Resource scheduling

When designing tasks in Ada it is important to remember that the only queues over which we have any control are entry queues and that such queues are handled on a strictly first-in-first-out basis. This might be thought to be a problem in situations where requests are of different priorities or where later requests can be serviced even though earlier ones have to wait. (Note that in this section we will assume that calling tasks are not aborted.)

Requests with priorities can be handled by a family of entries. A family is rather like a one-dimensional array. Suppose we have three levels of priority given by

```
type PRIORITY is (URGENT, NORMAL, LOW);
```

and that we have a task CONTROLLER providing access to some action on a type DATA but with requests for the action on three queues according to their priority. We could do this with three distinct entries but it is neater to use a family of entries. Consider

```
task CONTROLLER is
   entry REQUEST(PRIORITY) (D: DATA);
end;

task body CONTROLLER is
begin
   loop
      select
         accept REQUEST(URGENT) (D: DATA) do
            ACTION(D);
         end;
      or
         when REQUEST(URGENT)'COUNT = 0 =>
         accept REQUEST(NORMAL) (D: DATA) do
            ACTION(D);
         end;
      or
         when REQUEST(URGENT)'COUNT = 0 and
               REQUEST(NORMAL)'COUNT = 0 =>
         accept REQUEST(LOW) (D: DATA) do
```

```
                    ACTION(D);
                end;
            end select;
        end loop;
    end CONTROLLER;
```

REQUEST is a family of entries, indexed by a discrete range which in this case is the type PRIORITY. Clearly this approach is only feasible if the number of priority values is small. If it is large, a more sophisticated technique is necessary. We could try checking each queue in turn thus

```
task body CONTROLLER is
begin
    loop
        for P in PRIORITY loop
            select
                accept REQUEST(P) (D: DATA) do
                    ACTION(D);
                end;
                exit;
            else
                null;
            end select;
        end loop;
    end loop;
end CONTROLLER;
```

Unfortunately this is not satisfactory since it results in the task CONTROLLER continuously polling when all the queues are empty. We need a mechanism whereby the task can wait for the first of any request. This can be done by a two-stage process; the calling task must first sign in by calling a common entry and then call the appropriate entry of the family. The details are left as an exercise for the reader.

We now illustrate a quite general technique which effectively allows the requests in a single entry queue to be handled in an arbitrary order. Consider the problem of allocating a group of resources from a set. We do not wish to hold up a later request that can be satisfied just because an earlier request must wait for the release of some of the resources it wants. We suppose that the resources are represented by a discrete type RESOURCE. We can conveniently use the generic package SET_OF from Section 13.2.

```
package RESOURCE_SETS is new SET_OF(RESOURCE);
use RESOURCE_SETS;
```

and then

```
package RESOURCE_ALLOCATOR is
    procedure REQUEST(S: SET);
    procedure RELEASE(S: SET);
end;
```

```ada
package body RESOURCE_ALLOCATOR is
   task CONTROL is
      entry FIRST(S: SET; OK: out BOOLEAN);
      entry AGAIN(S: SET; OK: out BOOLEAN);
      entry RELEASE(S: SET);
   end;

   task body CONTROL is
      FREE: SET:= FULL;
      WAITERS: INTEGER:= 0;
      procedure TRY(S: SET; OK: out BOOLEAN) is
      begin
         if S <= FREE then
            FREE:= FREE-S;
            OK:= TRUE;          -- allocation successful
         else
            OK:= FALSE;         -- no good, try later
         end if;
      end TRY;

   begin
      loop
         select
            accept FIRST(S: SET; OK: out BOOLEAN) do
               TRY(S, OK);
               if not OK then
                  WAITERS:= WAITERS+1;
               end if;
            end;
         or
            accept RELEASE(S: SET) do
               FREE:= FREE+S;
            end;
            for I in 1 .. WAITERS loop
               accept AGAIN(S: SET; OK: out BOOLEAN) do
                  TRY(S, OK);
                  if OK then
                     WAITERS:= WAITERS-1;
                  end if;
               end;
            end loop;
         end select;
      end loop;
   end CONTROL;

   procedure REQUEST(S: SET) is
      ALLOCATED: BOOLEAN;
   begin
      CONTROL.FIRST(S, ALLOCATED);
```

```
          while not ALLOCATED loop
             CONTROL.AGAIN(S, ALLOCATED);
          end loop;
       end REQUEST;

       procedure RELEASE(S: SET) is
       begin
          CONTROL.RELEASE(S);
       end RELEASE;

    end RESOURCE_ALLOCATOR;
```

This is another example of a package containing a control task; the overall structure is similar to that of the package READER_WRITER introduced in Section 14.4. The package RESOURCE_ALLOCATOR contains two procedures REQUEST and RELEASE which have as parameters the set S of resources to be acquired or returned; the type SET is from the instantiation of SET_OF. These procedures call the entries of the task CONTROL as appropriate.

The task CONTROL has three entries: FIRST, AGAIN and RELEASE. The entries FIRST and AGAIN are similar; as well as the parameter S giving the set of resources required, they also have an out parameter OK which indicates whether the attempt to acquire the resources was successful or not. The accept statements for FIRST and AGAIN are identical and call a common procedure TRY. This checks the set S against the set FREE of available resources using the inclusion operator "<=" from (the instantiation of) SET_OF. If all the resources are available, FREE is altered correspondingly using the symmetric difference operator "−" from SET_OF and OK is set TRUE; if they are not all available, OK is set FALSE. The entry RELEASE returns the resources passed as the parameter S by updating FREE using the union operator "+" from SET_OF. Note that the declaration of FREE gives it the initial value FULL which is also from SET_OF.

The entries FIRST and AGAIN are called by the procedure REQUEST. It makes an immediate attempt to acquire the resources by a call of FIRST; if they are not all available, the Boolean ALLOCATED is set FALSE and the request is queued by calling AGAIN. This call is then repeated until successful. The entry RELEASE is merely called by the procedure RELEASE.

The body of CONTROL is the inevitable select statement in a loop. It has two branches, one for FIRST and one for RELEASE. Thus a call of RELEASE is always acceptable and a call of FIRST is also accepted promptly except when the task is dealing with the consequences of RELEASE. After a call of RELEASE, the requests which could not be satisfied on their call of FIRST and were consequently placed on the AGAIN queue are reconsidered since the resources made available by the call of RELEASE may be able to satisfy one or more requests at arbitrary points in the queue. The queue is scanned by doing a rendezvous with each call; a user which cannot be satisfied places itself back on the queue by a further call of AGAIN in the procedure REQUEST. In order that each user should only have one retry the scan is done by a loop controlled by the variable WAITERS. This indicates how many callers have called FIRST unsuccessfully and so are waiting in the system; it is initially zero and is incremented on an unsuccessful call of FIRST and decremented on a successful call of AGAIN. Note that we cannot use AGAIN'COUNT; deadlock might arise if all the resources were released between a task unsuccessfully calling FIRST and actually calling AGAIN. The moral of the readers and writers example is thus echoed; avoid the COUNT attribute – we must count for ourselves.

The above solution is reasonably satisfactory although there is a risk of unfairness. Tasks could overtake each other in the race from the front of the queue to the back; a newcomer could also miss a turn.

It is interesting to modify the above solution so that the requests are always satisfied in order. That is, a later request is always held up for an earlier one even if the resources they require are quite different. The essence of the solution is to allow only one waiting task in the system at a time. The modification is left as an exercise for the reader.

For this modified problem the following alternative solution is perhaps better. It has the merit of avoiding the task scheduling associated with the waiting task repeatedly calling AGAIN. We show just the task CONTROL and the procedure REQUEST.

```
task CONTROL is
   entry SIGN_IN(S: SET);
   entry REQUEST;
   entry RELEASE(S: SET);
end;

task body CONTROL is
   FREE: SET:= FULL;
   WAITERS: INTEGER range 0 .. 1:= 0;
   WANTED: SET;

begin
   loop
      select
         when WAITERS = 0 =>
         accept SIGN_IN(S: SET) do
            WANTED:= S;
         end;
         WAITERS:= WAITERS+1;
      or
         when WAITERS > 0 and then WANTED <= FREE =>
         accept REQUEST do
            FREE:= FREE-WANTED;
         end;
         WAITERS:= WAITERS-1;
      or
         accept RELEASE(S: SET) do
            FREE:= FREE+S;
         end;
```

```
            end select;
          end loop;
        end CONTROL;

        procedure REQUEST(S: SET) is
        begin
           CONTROL.SIGN_IN(S);
           CONTROL.REQUEST;
        end REQUEST;
```

In this solution we use a guarding condition which is true when the request can be honoured. A sign in call is required in order to hand over the parameter first because of course a guarding condition cannot depend upon the parameters of the actual entry call it is guarding. Note the short circuit condition which prevents the evaluation of WANTED when there is no waiting task. The variable WAITERS should perhaps be a Boolean; it can only be zero or one.

Exercise 14.8

1   Modify the first form of the package RESOURCE_ALLOCATOR so that requests are dealt with strictly in order.

2   Rewrite the task CONTROLLER as a package containing a task in a way which avoids continuous polling. The package specification should be

```
        package CONTROLLER is
           procedure REQUEST(P: PRIORITY; D: DATA);
        end;
```

14.9 Examples of task types

In this final section on tasking we briefly summarize the main differences between packages and tasks and then give a number of examples which illustrate various ways in which task types can be used.

Tasks and packages have a superficial lexical similarity – they both have specifications and bodies. However, there are many differences

- A task is an active construction whereas a package is passive.
- A task can only have entries in its specification. A package can have anything except entries. A task cannot have a private part.
- A package can be generic but a task cannot. The general effect of a parameterless generic task can be obtained by a task type. Alternatively the task can be encapsulated by a generic package.
- A package can appear in a use clause but a task cannot.

- A package can be a library unit but a task cannot. However, a task body can be a subunit.

The overall distinction is that the package should be considered to be the main tool for structuring purposes whereas the task is intended for synchronization. Thus typical subsystems will consist of a (possibly generic) package containing one or more tasks. This general structure has as we have seen the merit of giving complete control over the facilities provided; internal tasks cannot be unwillingly aborted and entry calls cannot be unwillingly timed out if they are not visible.

Our first example illustrates the use of task types as private types by the following generic package which provides a general type BUFFER.

```
generic
    N: POSITIVE;
    type ITEM is private;
package BUFFERS is
    type BUFFER is limited private;
    procedure PUT(B: in out BUFFER; X: in ITEM);
    procedure GET(B: in out BUFFER; X: out ITEM);
private
    task type CONTROL is
        entry PUT(X: in ITEM);
        entry GET(X: out ITEM);
    end;
    type BUFFER is new CONTROL;
end;

package body BUFFERS is

    task body CONTROL is
        A: array (1 .. N) of ITEM;
        I, J: INTEGER range 1 .. N:= 1;
        COUNT: INTEGER range 0 .. N:= 0;
    begin
        loop
            select
                when COUNT < N =>
                accept PUT(X: in ITEM) do
                    A(I):= X;
                end;
                I:= I mod N+1; COUNT:= COUNT+1;
            or
                when COUNT > 0 =>
                accept GET(X: out ITEM) do
                    X:= A(J);
                end;
                J:= J mod N+1; COUNT:= COUNT-1;
            or
                terminate;
```

```
            end select;
          end loop;
      end CONTROL;

      procedure PUT(B: in out BUFFER; X: in ITEM) is
      begin
          B.PUT(X);
      end PUT;

      procedure GET(B: in out BUFFER; X: out ITEM) is
      begin
          B.GET(X);
      end GET;

  end BUFFERS;
```

The buffer is implemented as a task object of a task type derived from CONTROL so that when we declare an object of the type BUFFER a new task is created which in turn declares the storage for the actual buffer. Calls of the procedures PUT and GET access the buffer by calling the corresponding entries of the appropriate task. Note that the select statement contains a terminate alternative so that the task object automatically disappears when we leave the scope of its declaration. Moreover, the system is robust even if the calling task is aborted.

We could have dispensed with the derived type and have written directly

```
  task type BUFFER is
      entry PUT(X: in ITEM);
      entry GET(X: out ITEM);
  end;
```

thus illustrating that a task type declaration can give the full type corresponding to a limited private type – remember that a task type is limited. However, the derived type enables us to use two different names according to whether we are thinking about the buffer or the control aspects of the one concept.

We now come to an interesting demonstration example which illustrates the dynamic creation of task objects. The objective is to find and display the first few prime numbers using the Sieve of Eratosthenes.

This ancient algorithm works using the observation that if we have a list of all the primes below N so far, then N is also prime if none of these divide exactly into it. So we try the existing primes in turn and as soon as one divides N we discard N and try again with N set to $N + 1$. On the other hand, if we get to the end of our list of primes without dividing N, then N must be prime, so we add it to our list and also start again with $N + 1$.

Our implementation (reproduced by permission of Alsys) uses a separate task for each prime P which is linked (via an access value) to the previous prime task and next prime task as shown in Figure 14.3. Its duty is to take a trial number N from the previous task and to check whether it is

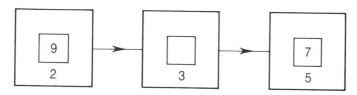

Figure 14.3   The Sieve of Eratosthenes.

divisible by its prime P. If it is, the number is discarded; if it is not, the number is passed to the next prime task. If there is no next prime task then P was the largest prime so far and N is a newly found prime; the P task then creates a new task whose duty is to check for divisibility by N and links itself to it. Each task thus acts as a filter removing multiples of its own prime value.

On the screen each task displays a frame containing its own prime and an inner box which displays the trial value currently being tested, if any. Figure 14.3 shows the situation when the primes 2, 3 and 5 have been found. The 5 task is testing 7 (which will prove to be a new prime), the 3 task is resting and waiting to receive another number from the 2 task, the 2 task (having just discarded 8) is testing 9 (which it will pass to the 3 task in a moment).

The program comprises a package FRAME containing subprograms which manipulate the display (the body of this package is not shown), a task type FILTER which describes the activities of the prime tasks and a main program SIEVE.

```
package FRAME is
    type POSITION is private;
    function MAKE_FRAME(DIVISOR: INTEGER) return POSITION;
    procedure WRITE_TO_FRAME(VALUE: INTEGER;
                                        WHERE: POSITION);
    procedure CLEAR_FRAME(WHERE: POSITION);
private
    ...
end FRAME;

use FRAME;

task type FILTER is
    entry INPUT(NUMBER: INTEGER);
end FILTER;

type A_FILTER is access FILTER;

function MAKE_FILTER return A_FILTER is
begin
    return new FILTER;
end MAKE_FILTER;

task body FILTER is
    P: INTEGER;                    -- prime divisor
```

```
          N: INTEGER;              -- trial number
          HERE: POSITION;
          NEXT: A_FILTER;
        begin
          accept INPUT(NUMBER: INTEGER) do
            P:= NUMBER;
          end;
          HERE:= MAKE_FRAME(P);
          loop
            accept INPUT(NUMBER: INTEGER) do
              N:= NUMBER;
            end;
            WRITE_TO_FRAME(N, HERE);
            if N mod P /= 0 then
              if NEXT = null then
                NEXT:= MAKE_FILTER;
              end if;
              NEXT.INPUT(N);
            end if;
            CLEAR_FRAME(HERE);
          end loop;
        end FILTER;

        procedure SIEVE is
          FIRST: A_FILTER:= new FILTER;
          N: INTEGER:= 2;
        begin
          loop
            FIRST.INPUT(N);
            N:= N+1;
          end loop;
        end SIEVE;
```

The subprograms in the package FRAME behave as follows. The function MAKE_FRAME draws a new frame on the screen and permanently writes the divisor number (that is P for the task calling it) into the frame; the inner box is left empty. The function returns a value of the private type POSITION which identifies the position of the frame; this value is later passed as a parameter to the two other procedures which manipulate the inner box in order to identify the frame concerned. The procedure WRITE_TO_FRAME has a further parameter giving the value to be written in the inner box; the procedure CLEAR_FRAME wipes the inner box clean.

The task type FILTER is fairly straightforward. It has a single entry INPUT which is called by the preceding task to give it the next trial divisor except that the first call passes the value of P which identifies the task. Hence FILTER has two accept statements, the first collects the value of P and the other is within the main loop. After collecting P it creates its frame (noting the position in HERE) and then enters the loop and awaits a number N to test. Having collected N it displays it in the inner box and then tests for divisibility by P. If it is divisible, it clears the inner box and goes to the beginning of the loop for a new value of N. If N is not divisible by P, it makes a successor task if necessary and in any event passes the value of N to it by calling its entry INPUT. Only after the successor task has taken the value does it clear the inner box and go back to the beginning. (The use of the function MAKE_FILTER is necessary to overcome a rule that in the body of a task type its name refers to the current task and not to the type.)

Note that the task FILTER automatically creates its own storage when it is activated (just as the task CONTROL in the previous example). It should also be noticed that the task does not know who it is until told; this is a characteristic of Ada task types since there is no way of parameterizing them.

The driving procedure SIEVE makes the first task, sets N to 2 and then enters an endless loop giving the task successive integer values until the end of time (or some other limitation is reached).

Our final example illustrates in outline a typical application using several processors. In recent years the cost of processors has fallen dramatically and for many applications it is now more sensible to use several individual processors rather than one very high performance processor. Indeed the finite value of the velocity of light coupled with the nonzero value of Planck's constant places physical limits to the performance that one can get from a single processor. We are then faced with the software organizational problem of how to use several processors effectively. For many applications this is hard, but for those where there is a replication of some sort it is often feasible. The processing of algorithms on arrays in graphics, signal processing and so on are good examples.

In Ada the task type gives us a natural means of describing a process which can be run in parallel on several processors simultaneously. For the moment we will suppose that we have a computer comprising several processors with a common address space. Thus when several tasks are active they really will be active and we assume that there are enough processors for all the tasks in the program to truly run in parallel.

Suppose we wish to solve the differential equation

$$\frac{\partial^2 P}{\partial x^2} + \frac{\partial^2 P}{\partial y^2} = F(x, y)$$

over a square region. The value of P is given on the boundary and the value of F is given throughout. The problem is to find the value of P at internal points of the region. This equation arises in many physical situations. One example might concern the flow of heat in a thin sheet of material; $P(x, y)$ would be the temperature of point (x, y) in the sheet and $F(x, y)$ would be the external heat flux applied at that point. However, the physics doesn't really matter.

The standard approach is to consider the region as a grid and to replace the differential equation by a corresponding set of difference equations. For simplicity we consider a square region of side N with unit grid. We end up with something like having to solve

$$4P(i, j) = P(i - 1, j) + P(i + 1, j) + P(i, j - 1)$$
$$+ P(i, j + 1) - F(i, j) \qquad 0 < i, j < N$$

This equation gives a value for each point in terms of its four neighbours. Remember that the values on the boundary are known and fixed. We use an iterative approach (Gauss-Seidel) and allocate a task to each point (i, j). The tasks then repeatedly compute the value of their point from the neighbouring points until the values cease to change. The function F could be of arbitrary complexity. A possible program is as follows

```
procedure GAUSS_SEIDEL is
    N: constant:= 5;
    subtype FULL_GRID is INTEGER range 0 .. N;
    subtype GRID is FULL_GRID range 1 .. N−1;
    type REAL is digits 7;
    type MATRIX is (INTEGER range <>, INTEGER range <>)
                                                    of REAL;

    P: MATRIX(FULL_GRID, FULL_GRID);
    DELTA_P: MATRIX(GRID, GRID);
    TOLERANCE: constant REAL:= 0.0001;
    ERROR_LIMIT: constant REAL:= TOLERANCE * (N−1)**2;
    CONVERGED: BOOLEAN:= FALSE;
    ERROR_SUM: REAL;
    pragma SHARED(CONVERGED);

    function F(I, J: GRID) return REAL is separate;

    task type ITERATOR is
        entry START(I, J: in GRID);
    end;

    PROCESS: array (GRID, GRID) of ITERATOR;

    task body ITERATOR is
        I, J: GRID;
        NEW_P: REAL;
    begin

        accept START(I, J: in GRID) do
            ITERATOR.I:= START.I;
            ITERATOR.J:= START.J;
        end START;

        loop
            NEW_P:= 0.25 * (P(I−1, J) + P(I+1, J) + P(I, J−1)
                                        + P(I, J+1) − F(I, J));
            DELTA_P(I, J):= NEW_P − P(I, J);
            P(I, J):= NEW_P;
            exit when CONVERGED;
        end loop;
```

```
      end ITERATOR;

   begin      -- of main program; the ITERATOR tasks are now active

      ...       -- initialize P and DELTA_P

      for I in GRID loop
         for J in GRID loop
            PROCESS(I, J).START(I, J);      -- tell them who they are
         end loop;
      end loop;

      loop
         ERROR_SUM:= 0.0;
         for I in GRID loop
            for J in GRID loop
               ERROR_SUM:= ERROR_SUM + DELTA_P(I, J)**2;
            end loop;
         end loop;

         CONVERGED:= ERROR_SUM < ERROR_LIMIT;
         exit when CONVERGED;
      end loop;

      ...       -- output results

   end GAUSS_SEIDEL;
```

The main task starts by telling the ITERATOR tasks who they are through the call of the entry START. Thereafter the individual tasks execute independently and communicate through shared variables. The ITERATOR tasks continue until the Boolean CONVERGED is set by the main task; they then exit their loop and terminate. The main task repeatedly computes the sum of squares of the errors from DELTA_P (set by the ITERATOR tasks) and sets CONVERGED accordingly. When stability is reached the main task outputs the results.

The normal way in which tasks communicate is through the rendez-vous but there are occasions as here when this might prove too slow. In this example there are three shared objects: the Boolean CONVERGED and the two arrays P and DELTA_P. Ada discourages the use of shared variables on the grounds that optimization through holding values in registers is impeded. The rules in the *LRM* (to which the reader is referred) guarantee that sharing works only under certain circumstances. One such circumstance is that the pragma SHARED is specified for the variables concerned. We have done this for CONVERGED but the *LRM* appears to forbid this for composite objects. So our program is strictly erroneous but we will assume that our implementation keeps the arrays P and DELTA_P in store so that sharing works.

The program as shown (with $N = 5$) requires 17 tasks and thus 17 processors. This is not unreasonable and of course the program is based on the assumption of one asynchronous processor per task. Nevertheless, the reader will observe a number of flaws. The convergence criterion is a bit suspect. It might be possible for waves of divergence to slurp around the grid in a manner which escapes the attention of the asynchronous main task – but this is unlikely. Another point is that the ITERATOR tasks might still be computing one last iteration while the main task is printing the results. It would be better to add a STOP entry so that the main task can wait until the ITERATOR tasks have finished their loops. Alternatively the array of tasks could be declared in an inner block and the main task could do the printing outside that block where it would know that the other tasks must have terminated. Thus

```
begin      -- main program

   ...      -- initialize arrays

declare
   PROCESS: array (GRID, GRID) of ITERATOR;
begin      -- ITERATOR tasks active
   ...
   ...
end;       -- wait for ITERATOR tasks to terminate

   ...      -- output results

end GAUSS_SEIDEL;
```

Many multiprocessor systems will not have a shared memory in which case a different approach is necessary. A naive first attempt might be to give each ITERATOR an entry which when called delivers the current value of the corresponding point of the grid. Direct *ad hoc* calls from one task to another in a casual design will quickly lead to deadlock. A better approach is to have two tasks per point; one to do the computation and one to provide controlled access to the point (much like the task type PROTECTED_VARIABLE of Section 14.4). We might use one physical processor for each pair of tasks.

It is hoped that our simple example has given the reader some glimpse of how tasking may be distributed over a multiprocessor system. It is a complex subject which is only now being addressed seriously. Of course our example had a ludicrously trivial computation in each task and the system (especially without shared memory) will spend much of its time on communication rather than computation. Nevertheless the principles should be clear. Note that we have not discussed how the different tasks become associated with the different processors; this lies outside the domain of the language itself.

Exercise 14.9

1   A boot repair shop has one man taking orders and three others actually repairing the boots. The shop has storage for 100 boots awaiting repair. The person taking the orders notes the address of the owner and this is attached to the boots; he then puts the boots in the store. Each repairman takes boots from the store when he is free, repairs them and then mails them.

   Write a package COBBLERS whose specification is

```
package COBBLERS is
    procedure MEND(A: ADDRESS; B: BOOTS);
end;
```

   The package body should contain four tasks representing the various men. Use an instantiation of the package BUFFERS to provide a store for the boots and agent tasks as mailboxes to deliver them.

2   Sketch a solution of the differential equations using two tasks for each point and no shared variables. Assume one physical processor per point and set the priorities so that the data manager task is of a higher priority than the iterator task. Evaluate and store DELTA_P in the data task. The main program should use the same convergence rule as before. You will not need arrays (other than for the tasks) since the data will be distributed in the data manager tasks.

Checklist 14

A task is active whereas a package is passive.

A task specification can contain only entries.

A task cannot be generic.

A task name cannot appear in a use clause.

Entries may be overloaded and renamed as procedures.

The COUNT attribute can only be used inside the task owning the entry.

An accept statement must not appear in a subprogram.

Do not attempt to use priorities for synchronization.

Scheduling is preemptive.

The order of evaluation of guards is not defined.

A select statement can have just one of an else part, a single terminate alternative, one or more delay alternatives.

A terminate or delay alternative can be guarded.

Several alternatives can refer to the same entry.

Beware of the COUNT attribute in guards.

Task types are limited.

A task declared as an object is dependent on a block, subprogram or task body but not an inner package.

A task created by an allocator is dependent on the block, subprogram or task body containing the access type definition.

A task declared as an object is made active at the following (possibly notional) **begin**.

A task created by an allocator is made active at once.

Do not use **abort** without good reason.

Chapter 15
External Interfaces

In this chapter we consider various aspects of how an Ada program interfaces to the outside world. This includes obvious areas such as input–output, interrupt handling and so on, but we will also consider the mapping of our abstract Ada program onto an implementation. However, the discussion in this chapter cannot be exhaustive because many details of this area will depend upon the implementation. The intent, therefore, is to give the reader a general overview of the facilities available.

15.1 Input and output

Unlike many other languages, Ada does not have any intrinsic features for input–output. Instead existing general features such as subprogram overloading and generic instantiation are used. This has the merit of enabling different input–output packages to be developed for different application areas without affecting the language itself. On the other hand this approach can lead to a consequential risk of anarchy in this area; the reader may recall that this was one of the reasons for the downfall of Algol 60. In order to prevent such anarchy the *LRM* defines standard packages for input–output. We discuss the general principles of these packages in this and the next section. For further fine detail the reader should consult the *LRM*.

Two categories of input–output are recognized and we can refer to these as binary and text respectively. As an example consider

    I: INTEGER:= 75;

We can output the binary image of I onto file F by

    WRITE(F, I);

and the pattern transmitted might be (on a 16 bit machine)

0000 0000 0100 1011

In fact the file can be thought of as essentially an array of the type INTEGER. On the other hand we can output the text form of I by

PUT(F, I);

and the pattern transmitted might then be

0011 0111 0011 0101

which is the representation of the characters '7' and '5' without parity bits. In this case the file can be thought of as an array of the type CHARACTER.

Input–output of the binary category is in turn subdivided into sequential and direct access and is provided by distinct generic packages with identifiers SEQUENTIAL_IO and DIRECT_IO respectively. Text input–output (which is always sequential) is provided by the special non-generic package TEXT_IO. There is also a package IO_EXCEPTIONS which contains the declarations of the exceptions used by the three other packages. We will deal here first with SEQUENTIAL_IO and then with DIRECT_IO and consider TEXT_IO in the next section.

The specification of the package SEQUENTIAL_IO is as follows

```
with IO_EXCEPTIONS;
generic
    type ELEMENT_TYPE is private;
package SEQUENTIAL_IO is
    type FILE_TYPE is limited private;
    type FILE_MODE is (IN_FILE, OUT_FILE);

    -- File management

    procedure CREATE(FILE: in out FILE_TYPE;
                     MODE: in FILE_MODE:= OUT_FILE;
                     NAME: in STRING:= "";
                     FORM: in STRING:= "");
    procedure OPEN(FILE: in out FILE_TYPE;
                   MODE: in FILE_MODE;
                   NAME: in STRING;
                   FORM: in STRING:= "");
    procedure CLOSE(FILE: in out FILE_TYPE);
    procedure DELETE(FILE: in out FILE_TYPE);
    procedure RESET(FILE: in out FILE_TYPE;
                                          MODE: in FILE_MODE);
    procedure RESET(FILE: in out FILE_TYPE);
    function MODE(FILE: in FILE_TYPE) return FILE_MODE;
    function NAME(FILE: in FILE_TYPE) return STRING;
    function FORM(FILE: in FILE_TYPE) return STRING;
```

```
function IS_OPEN(FILE: in FILE_TYPE) return BOOLEAN;

-- Input and output operations

procedure READ(FILE: in FILE_TYPE;
                                            ITEM: out ELEMENT_TYPE);
procedure WRITE(FILE: in FILE_TYPE; ITEM: in ELEMENT_TYPE);
function END_OF_FILE(FILE: in FILE_TYPE) return BOOLEAN;

-- Exceptions

STATUS_ERROR: exception renames
                              IO_EXCEPTIONS.STATUS_ERROR;
MODE_ERROR: exception renames
                              IO_EXCEPTIONS.MODE_ERROR;
NAME_ERROR: exception renames
                              IO_EXCEPTIONS.NAME_ERROR;
USE_ERROR: exception renames
                              IO_EXCEPTIONS.USE_ERROR;
DEVICE_ERROR: exception renames
                              IO_EXCEPTIONS.DEVICE_ERROR;
END_ERROR: exception renames
                              IO_EXCEPTIONS.END_ERROR;
DATA_ERROR: exception renames
                              IO_EXCEPTIONS.DATA_ERROR;

private
  -- implementation-dependent
end SEQUENTIAL_IO;
```

The package has a single generic parameter giving the type of element to be manipulated. Note that limited types (and that, thankfully, includes task types) cannot be handled since the generic formal parameter is private rather than limited private.

Externally a file has a name which is a string but internally we refer to a file by using objects of type FILE_TYPE. An open file also has an associated value of the enumeration type FILE_MODE; there are two possible values, IN_FILE or OUT_FILE according to whether read-only or write-only access is required. Read–write access is not allowed for sequential files. The mode of a file is originally set when the file is opened or created but can be changed later by a call of the procedure RESET. Manipulation of sequential files is done using various subprograms whose behaviour is generally as expected.

As an example, suppose we have a file containing measurements of various populations and that we wish to compute the sum of these measurements. The populations are recorded as values of type INTEGER and the name of the file is "CENSUS 47". (The actual conventions for the external file name are dependent upon the implementation.) The computed sum is to be written onto a new file to be called "TOTAL 47". This could be done by the following program

```
with SEQUENTIAL_IO;
procedure COMPUTE_TOTAL_POPULATION is
    package INTEGER_IO is new SEQUENTIAL_IO(INTEGER);
    use INTEGER_IO;

    DATA_FILE: FILE_TYPE;
    RESULT_FILE: FILE_TYPE;
    VALUE: INTEGER;
    TOTAL: INTEGER:= 0;
begin
    OPEN(DATA_FILE, IN_FILE, "CENSUS 47");

    while not END_OF_FILE(DATA_FILE) loop
        READ(DATA_FILE, VALUE);
        TOTAL:= TOTAL+VALUE;
    end loop;
    CLOSE(DATA_FILE);

    -- now write the result

    CREATE(RESULT_FILE, NAME => "TOTAL 47");
    WRITE(RESULT_FILE, TOTAL);
    CLOSE(RESULT_FILE);
end COMPUTE_TOTAL_POPULATION;
```

We start by instantiating the generic package SEQUENTIAL_IO with the actual parameter INTEGER. The use clause enables us to refer to the entities in the created package directly.

The file with the data to be read is referred to via the object DATA_FILE and the output file is referred to via the object RESULT_FILE of the type FILE_TYPE. Note that this type is limited private; this enables the implementation to use techniques similar to those described in Section 9.3 where we discussed the example of the key manager.

The call of OPEN establishes the object DATA_FILE as referring to the external file "CENSUS 47" and sets its mode as read-only. The external file is then opened for reading and positioned at the beginning.

We then obey the loop statement until the function END_OF_FILE indicates that the end of the file has been reached. On each iteration the call of READ copies the item into VALUE and positions the file at the next item. TOTAL is then updated. When all the values on the file have been read, it is closed by a call of CLOSE.

The call of CREATE creates a new external file named "TOTAL 47" and establishes RESULT_FILE as referring to it and sets its mode by default to write-only. We then write our total onto the file and then close it.

The procedures CREATE and OPEN have a further parameter FORM; this is provided so that auxiliary implementation dependent information can be specified; the default value is a null string so its use is not mandatory. Note that the NAME parameter of CREATE also has a default null value; such a value corresponds to a temporary file. The procedures CLOSE and DELETE both close the file and thereby sever the connection between the file variable and the external file. The variable can then be reused for another file. DELETE also destroys the external file if the implementation so allows.

The overloaded procedures RESET cause a file to be repositioned at the beginning as for OPEN. RESET can also change the access mode so that, for example, having written a file, we can now read it.

The functions MODE, NAME and FORM return the corresponding properties of the file. The function IS_OPEN indicates whether the file is open; that is, indicates whether the file variable is associated with an external file or not.

The procedures READ and WRITE automatically reposition the file ready for a subsequent call so that the file is processed sequentially. The function END_OF_FILE only applies to an input file and returns true if there are no more elements to be read.

If we do something wrong then one of the exceptions in the package IO_EXCEPTIONS will be raised. This package is as follows

```
package IO_EXCEPTIONS is
    STATUS_ERROR:     exception;
    MODE_ERROR:       exception;
    NAME_ERROR:       exception;
    USE_ERROR:        exception;
    DEVICE_ERROR:     exception;
    END_ERROR:        exception;
    DATA_ERROR:       exception;
    LAYOUT_ERROR:     exception;
end IO_EXCEPTIONS;
```

This is an example of a package that does not need a body. The various exceptions are declared in this package rather than in SEQUENTIAL_IO so that the same exceptions apply to all instantiations of SEQUENTIAL_IO. If they were inside SEQUENTIAL_IO then each instantiation would create different exceptions and this would be rather more inconvenient in the case of a program manipulating files of various types since general purpose exception handlers would need to refer to all the instances. The renaming declarations on the other hand enable the exceptions to be referred to without use of the name IO_EXCEPTIONS. (A similar technique was used with the mathematical library in Section 13.4.)

The following brief summary gives the general flavour of the circumstances giving rise to each exception

STATUS_ERROR	File is open when expected to be closed or vice versa.
MODE_ERROR	File of wrong mode, for example, IN_FILE when should be OUT_FILE.
NAME_ERROR	Something wrong with NAME parameter of CREATE or OPEN.

USE_ERROR	Various such as unacceptable FORM parameter or trying to print on card reader.
DEVICE_ERROR	Physical device broken or not switched on.
END_ERROR	Malicious attempt to read beyond end of file.
DATA_ERROR	READ or GET (see next section) cannot interpret data as value of desired type.
LAYOUT_ERROR	Something wrong with layout in TEXT_IO (see next section) or PUT overfills string parameter.

For fuller details of which exception is actually raised in various circumstances the reader is referred to the *LRM* and to the documentation for the implementation concerned.

We continue by considering the package DIRECT_IO which is very similar to SEQUENTIAL_IO but gives us more flexibility by enabling us to manipulate the file position directly.

As mentioned earlier, a file can be considered as a one-dimensional array. The elements in the file are ordered and each has an associated positive index. This ranges from 1 to an upper value which can change since elements can be added to the end of the file. Not all elements necessarily have a defined value in the case of a direct file as we shall see.

Associated with a direct file is a current index which indicates the position of the next element to be transferred. When a file is opened or created this index is set to 1 so that the program is ready to read or write the first element. The main difference between sequential and direct input–output is that in the sequential case this index is implicit and can only be altered by calls of READ, WRITE and RESET whereas in the direct case, the index is explicit and can be directly manipulated.

The extra facilities of DIRECT_IO are as follows. The enumeration type FILE_MODE has a third value INOUT_FILE so that read-write access is possible; this is also the default mode when a new file is created (thus the MODE parameter of CREATE has a different default for direct and sequential files). The type and subtype

```
type COUNT is range 0 .. implementation_defined;
subtype POSITIVE_COUNT is COUNT range 1 .. COUNT'LAST;
```

are introduced so that the current index can be referred to and finally there are various extra subprograms whose specifications are as follows

```
procedure READ(FILE: in FILE_TYPE; ITEM: out ELEMENT_TYPE;
                      FROM: POSITIVE_COUNT);
procedure WRITE(FILE: in FILE_TYPE; ITEM: in ELEMENT_TYPE;
                      TO: POSITIVE_COUNT);
procedure SET_INDEX(FILE: in FILE_TYPE;
                               TO: in POSITIVE_ COUNT);
function INDEX(FILE: in FILE_TYPE) return POSITIVE_COUNT;
function SIZE(FILE: in FILE_TYPE) return COUNT;
```

The extra overloadings of READ and WRITE first position the current index to the value given by the third parameter and then behave as before. A call of INDEX returns the current index value; SET_INDEX sets the current index to the given value and a call of SIZE returns the number of elements in the file. Note that a file cannot have holes in it; all elements from 1 to SIZE exist although some may not have defined values.

As an illustration of the manipulation of these positions we can alter our example to use DIRECT_IO and we can then write the total population onto the end of an existing file called "TOTALS". The last few statements then become

```
-- now write the result

OPEN(RESULT_FILE, OUT_FILE, "TOTALS");
SET_INDEX(RESULT_FILE, SIZE(RESULT_FILE)+1);
WRITE(RESULT_FILE, TOTAL);
CLOSE(RESULT_FILE);
end COMPUTE_TOTAL_POPULATION;
```

Note that if we set the current index well beyond the end of the file and then write to it, the result will be to add several undefined elements to the file and then finally the newly written element.

Note also that the language does not define whether it is possible to write a file with SEQUENTIAL_IO and then read it with DIRECT_IO or vice versa. This depends upon the implementation.

Exercise 15.1

1   Write a generic library procedure to copy a file onto another file but with the elements in reverse order. Pass the external names as parameters.

15.2   Text input–output

Text input–output, which we first met in Chapter 2, is the more familiar form and provides two overloaded procedures PUT and GET to transmit values as streams of characters as well as various other subprograms such as NEW_LINE for layout control. In addition the concept of current default files is introduced so that every call of the various subprograms need not tiresomely repeat the file name. Thus if F is the current default output file, we can write

```
PUT("MESSAGE");
```

rather than

```
PUT(F, "MESSAGE");
```

There are two current default files, one of mode OUT_FILE for output, and one of mode IN_FILE for input. There is no mode INOUT_FILE in the package TEXT_IO.

When we enter our program these two files are set to standard default files which are automatically open; we can assume that these are attached to convenient external files such as an interactive terminal or (in olden days) a card reader and line printer. If we wish to use other files and want to avoid repeating the file names in the calls of PUT and GET then we can change the default files to refer to our other files. We can also set them back to their original values. This is done with subprograms

```
function STANDARD_OUTPUT return FILE_TYPE;
function CURRENT_OUTPUT return FILE_TYPE;
procedure SET_OUTPUT(FILE: FILE_TYPE);
```

with similar subprograms for input. The function STANDARD_OUTPUT returns the initial default output file, CURRENT_OUTPUT returns the current default output file and the procedure SET_OUTPUT enables us to change the current default output file to the file passed as parameter.

Thus we could bracket a fragment of program with

```
F: FILE_TYPE;
...
OPEN(F, ... );
SET_OUTPUT(F);
-- use PUT
SET_OUTPUT(STANDARD_OUTPUT);
```

so that having used the file F, we can reset the default file to its standard value.

The more general case is where we wish to reset the default file to its previous value which may, of course, not be the standard value. The reader may recall that the type FILE_TYPE is limited private and therefore values cannot be assigned; at first sight, therefore, it might not seem possible to make a copy of the original current value. However, with suitable contortion it can be done by using the parameter mechanism. We could write

```
procedure JOB(OLD_FILE, NEW_FILE: FILE_TYPE) is
begin
    SET_OUTPUT(NEW_FILE);
    ACTION;
    SET_OUTPUT(OLD_FILE);
end;
```

and then

```
JOB(CURRENT_OUTPUT, F);
```

When we call JOB, the present current value is preserved in the parameter OLD_FILE from whence it can be retrieved for the restoring call of

SET_OUTPUT. However, although this works, it does feel a bit like standing on one's head!

The full specification of TEXT_IO is rather long and so only the general form is reproduced here.

```
with IO_EXCEPTIONS;
package TEXT_IO is
    type FILE_TYPE is limited private;
    type FILE_MODE is (IN_FILE, OUT_FILE);


    type COUNT is range 0 .. implementation_defined;
    subtype POSITIVE_COUNT is COUNT range 1 .. COUNT'LAST;
    UNBOUNDED: constant COUNT:= 0;      -- line and page length

    subtype FIELD is INTEGER range 0 .. implementation_defined;
    subtype NUMBER_BASE is INTEGER range 2 .. 16;
    type TYPE_SET is (LOWER_CASE, UPPER_CASE);

    -- File management

    -- CREATE, OPEN, CLOSE, DELETE, RESET, MODE, NAME,
    -- FORM and IS_OPEN as for SEQUENTIAL_IO

    -- Control of default input and output files

    procedure SET_OUTPUT(FILE: in FILE_TYPE);
    function STANDARD_OUTPUT return FILE_TYPE;
    function CURRENT_OUTPUT return FILE_TYPE;

    -- Similarly for input

    -- Specification of line and page lengths

    procedure SET_LINE_LENGTH(TO: in COUNT);
    procedure SET_PAGE_LENGTH(TO: in COUNT);
    function LINE_LENGTH return COUNT;
    function PAGE_LENGTH return COUNT;

    -- also with FILE parameter

    -- Column, line and page control

    procedure NEW_LINE(SPACING: in POSITIVE_COUNT:= 1);
    procedure SKIP_LINE(SPACING: in POSITIVE_COUNT:= 1);
    function END_OF_LINE return BOOLEAN:
    procedure NEW_PAGE;
    procedure SKIP_PAGE;
    function END_OF_PAGE return BOOLEAN;
    function END_OF_FILE return BOOLEAN;
```

```
        procedure SET_COL(TO: in POSITIVE_COUNT);
        procedure SET_LINE(TO: in POSITIVE_COUNT);
        function COL return POSITIVE_COUNT;
        function LINE return POSITIVE_COUNT;
        function PAGE return POSITIVE_COUNT;

        -- also with FILE parameter

        -- Character input-output

        procedure GET(FILE: in FILE_TYPE; ITEM: out CHARACTER);
        procedure GET(ITEM: out CHARACTER);
        procedure PUT(FILE: in FILE_TYPE; ITEM: in CHARACTER);
        procedure PUT(ITEM: in CHARACTER);

        -- String input-output

        procedure GET(ITEM: out STRING);
        procedure PUT(ITEM: in STRING);
        procedure GET_LINE(ITEM: out STRING; LAST: out NATURAL);
        procedure PUT_LINE(ITEM: in STRING);

        -- Generic package for input-output of integer types

    generic
        type NUM is range <>;
    package INTEGER_IO is
        DEFAULT_WIDTH: FIELD:= NUM'WIDTH;
        DEFAULT_BASE: NUMBER_BASE:= 10;

        procedure GET(ITEM: out NUM; WIDTH: in FIELD:= 0);
        procedure PUT(ITEM: in NUM;
                        WIDTH: in FIELD:= DEFAULT_WIDTH;
                        BASE: in NUMBER_BASE:= DEFAULT_BASE);
        procedure GET(FROM: in STRING; ITEM: out NUM;
                        LAST: out POSITIVE);
        procedure PUT(TO: out STRING;
                        ITEM: in NUM;
                        BASE: in NUMBER_BASE:= DEFAULT_BASE);
    end INTEGER_IO;

        -- Generic packages for input-output of real types

    generic
        type NUM is digits <>;
    package FLOAT_IO is
        DEFAULT_FORE: FIELD:= 2;
        DEFAULT_AFT: FIELD:= NUM'DIGITS-1;
        DEFAULT_EXP: FIELD:= 3;
```

```
        procedure GET(ITEM: out NUM; WIDTH: in FIELD:= 0);
        procedure PUT(ITEM: in NUM;
                      FORE: in FIELD:= DEFAULT_FORE;
                      AFT: in FIELD:= DEFAULT_AFT;
                      EXP: in FIELD:= DEFAULT_EXP);
        procedure GET(FROM: in STRING;
                      ITEM: out NUM;
                      LAST: out POSITIVE);
        procedure PUT(TO: out STRING;
                      ITEM: in NUM;
                      AFT: in FIELD:= DEFAULT_AFT;
                      EXP: in FIELD:= DEFAULT_EXP);
    end FLOAT_IO;

generic
    type NUM is delta <>;
package FIXED_IO is
    DEFAULT_FORE: FIELD:= NUM'FORE;
    DEFAULT_AFT: FIELD:= NUM'AFT;
    DEFAULT_EXP: FIELD:= 0;
    -- then as for FLOAT_IO
end FIXED_IO;

-- Generic package for input–output of enumeration types

generic
    type ENUM is (<>);
package ENUMERATION_IO is
    DEFAULT_WIDTH: FIELD:= 0;
    DEFAULT_SETTING: TYPE_SET:= UPPER CASE;

    procedure GET(ITEM: out ENUM);
    procedure PUT(ITEM: in ENUM;
                  WIDTH: in FIELD:= DEFAULT_WIDTH;
                  SET: in TYPE_SET:= DEFAULT_SETTING);
    procedure GET(FROM: in STRING;
                  ITEM: out ENUM;
                  LAST: out POSITIVE);
    procedure PUT(TO: out STRING;
                  ITEM: out ENUM;
                  SET: in TYPE_SET:= DEFAULT_SETTING);
end ENUMERATION_IO;

-- Exceptions

STATUS_ERROR: exception renames
                        IO_EXCEPTIONS.STATUS_ERROR;
...
LAYOUT_ERROR: exception renames
                        IO_EXCEPTIONS.LAYOUT_ERROR;
```

private

    −− implementation-dependent

end TEXT_IO;

The types FILE_TYPE and FILE_MODE and the various file management procedures are similar to those for SEQUENTIAL_IO since text files are of course sequential in nature.

Procedures PUT and GET occur in two forms for characters and strings, one with the file and one without; both are shown only for type CHARACTER.

In the case of type CHARACTER, a call of PUT just outputs that character; for type STRING a call of PUT outputs the characters of the string.

A problem arises in the case of numeric and enumeration types since there is not a fixed number of such types. This is overcome by the use of internal generic packages for each category. Thus for integer input–output we instantiate the package INTEGER_IO with the appropriate type thus

    type MY_INTEGER **is range** −1E6 .. +1E6;
    ...
    package MY_INTEGER_IO **is new** INTEGER_IO(MY_INTEGER);
    use MY_INTEGER_IO;

For integer output, PUT occurs in three forms, one with the file, one without and one with a string as the destination; only the last two are shown.

In the case of PUT to a file, there are two format parameters WIDTH and BASE which have default values provided by the variables DEFAULT_WIDTH and DEFAULT_BASE. The default width is initially NUM' WIDTH which gives the smallest field which is adequate for all values of the type expressed with base 10 (including a leading space or minus). Base 10 also happens to be the initial default base. These default values can be changed by the user by directly assigning new values to the variables DEFAULT_WIDTH and DEFAULT_BASE (they are directly visible); remember that a default parameter is re-evaluated on each call requiring it and so the default obtained is always the current value of these variables. The integer is output as an integer literal without underlines and leading zeros but with a preceding minus sign if negative. It is padded with leading spaces to fill the field width specified; if the field width is too small, it is expanded as necessary. Thus a default width of 0 results in the field being the minimum to contain the literal. If base 10 is specified explicitly or by default, the value is output using the syntax of decimal literal; if the base is not 10, the syntax of based literal is used.

The attribute 'WIDTH deserves attention. It is a property of the subtype of the actual generic type parameter and not that of the base type. Thus the default format is appropriate to the type as the user sees it and not to the predefined type from which it is derived. This is important for portability. So in the case of MY_INTEGER, the attribute has the value 8 (seven digits for one million plus the space or sign).

The general effect is shown by the following sequence of statements where the output is shown in a comment. The quotes delimit the output and s designates a space. We start with the initial default values for the format parameters.

```
X: MY_INTEGER:= 1234;
...
PUT(X);                          -- "ssss1234"
PUT(X, 5);                       -- "s1234"
PUT(X, 0);                       -- "1234"
PUT(X, BASE => 8);               -- "s8#2322#"
PUT(X, 11, 8);                   -- "ssss8#2322#"
DEFAULT_BASE:= 8;
PUT(X);                          -- "s8#2322#"
```

In the case of PUT to a string, the field width is taken as the length of the string. If this is too small, then LAYOUT_ERROR is raised. PUT to strings is useful for building up strings containing various bits and pieces and perhaps editing them before actually sending them to a file. It will be found that slices are useful for this sort of manipulation.

Similar techniques are used for real types. A value is output as a decimal literal without underlines and leading zeros but with a preceding minus sign if negative. If EXP is zero, then there is no exponent and the format consists of FORE characters before the decimal point and AFT after the decimal point. If EXP is nonzero, then a signed exponent in a field of EXP characters is output after a letter E with leading zeros if necessary; the exponent value is such that only one significant digit occurs before the decimal point. If the FORE or EXP parts of the field are inadequate, then they are expanded as necessary. Base 10 is always used and the value is rounded to the size of AFT specified.

The initial default format parameters for floating point types are 2, NUM'DIGITS−1 and 3; this gives an exponent form with a space or minus sign plus single digit before the decimal point, NUM'DIGITS−1 digits after the decimal point and a two-digit exponent. The corresponding parameters for fixed point types are NUM'FORE, NUM'AFT and 0; this gives a form without an exponent and the attributes give the smallest field such that all values of the type can be expressed with appropriate precision.

Enumeration types use a similar technique. A default field of zero is used. If the field has to be padded then the extra spaces go after the value and not before as with the numeric types. Upper case is normally used, but lower case may be specified. A value of a character type which is a character literal is output in single quotes.

Note the subtle distinction between PUT defined directly for the type CHARACTER and for enumeration values.

```
TEXT_IO.PUT('X');
```

outputs the single character X, whereas

```
package CHAR_IO is new TEXT_IO.ENUMERATION_IO(CHARACTER);
...
CHAR_IO.PUT('X');
```

outputs the character X between single quotes.

Input using GET works in an analogous way; a call of GET always skips line and page terminators. In the case of the type CHARACTER the next character is read. In the case of the type STRING, the procedure GET reads the exact number of characters as determined by the actual parameter. In the case of enumeration types, leading blanks (spaces or horizontal tabs) are also skipped; input is terminated by a character which is not part of the value or by a line terminator. Numeric types normally have the same behaviour but they also have an additional and optional WIDTH parameter and if this has a value other than zero, then reading stops after this number of characters including skipped blanks. In the case of GET where the source is a string rather than a file, the value of LAST indexes the last character read; the end of the string behaves as the end of a file.

The allowed form of data for reading an enumeration value is an identifer (case of letters being ignored), or a character literal in single quotes. The allowed form for an integer value is first and optionally a plus or minus sign and then according to the syntax of an integer literal which may be a based literal and possibly have an exponent (see Section 3.4). The allowed form for a real value is similarly an optional sign followed by a real literal (one with a radix point in it). If the data item is not of the correct form or not a value of the subtype NUM then DATA_ERROR is raised. The collector of Ada curiosities will note that PUT cannot output integer based forms where the base is 10 such as

```
10#41#
```

although GET can read them. Similarly PUT cannot output real based forms at all although GET can read them. On the other hand GET can read whatever PUT can write.

A text file is considered as a sequence of lines. The characters in a line have a column position starting at 1. The line length on output can be fixed or variable. A fixed line length is appropriate for the output of tables, a variable line length for dialogue. The line length can be changed within a single file. It is initially not fixed. The lines are similarly grouped into pages starting at page 1.

On output a call of PUT will result in all the characters going on the current line starting at the current position in the line. If, however, the line length is fixed and the characters cannot fit in the remainder of the line, a new line is started and all the characters are placed on that line starting at the beginning. If they still will not fit, LAYOUT_ERROR is raised. If the length is not fixed, the characters always go on the end of the current line.

The layout may be controlled by various subprograms. In some cases they apply to both input and output files; in these cases if the file is omitted then it is taken to apply to the output case and the default output file is assumed. In most cases, a subprogram only applies to one direction and then omitting the file naturally gives the default in that direction.

The function COL returns the current position in the line and the procedure SET_COL sets the position to the given value. A call of SET_COL never goes backwards. On output extra spaces are produced and on input characters are skipped. If the parameter of SET_COL equals the current value of COL then there is no effect; if it is less then a call of NEW_LINE or SKIP_LINE is implied.

The procedure NEW_LINE (output only) outputs the given number of newlines (default 1) and resets the current column to 1. Spare positions at the end of a line are filled with spaces. The procedure SKIP_LINE (input only) similarly moves on the given number of lines (default 1) and resets the current column. The function END_OF_LINE (input only) returns TRUE if we have reached the end of a line.

The function LINE_LENGTH (output only) returns the current line length if it is fixed and zero if it is not. The procedure SET_LINE_LENGTH (output only) sets the line length fixed to the given value; a value of zero indicates that it is not to be fixed.

There are also similar subprograms for the control of lines within pages. These are LINE, SET_LINE, NEW_PAGE, SKIP_PAGE, END_OF_PAGE, PAGE_LENGTH and SET_PAGE_LENGTH. Finally the function PAGE returns the current page number from the start of the file. There is no SET_PAGE.

The procedures PUT_LINE and GET_LINE are particularly appropriate for manipulating whole lines. A call of PUT_LINE outputs the string and then moves to the next line (by calling NEW_LINE). A call of GET_LINE reads successive characters into the string until the end of the string or the end of the line is encountered; in the latter case it then moves to the next line (by calling SKIP_LINE); LAST indexes the last character moved into the string. Successive calls of PUT_LINE and GET_LINE therefore manipulate whole lines. However, AI-50 places a curious interpretation on GET_LINE when the string is exactly the right length to accommodate the remaining characters on the line – it does not move to the next line! So, given a series of lines of length 80, successive calls of GET_LINE with a string of length 80 (bounds 1 .. 80) return alternately lines of 80 characters and null strings (or in other words the value of LAST is alternately 80 and 0). This unhelpful behaviour can be overcome by using a string of length 81 or calling SKIP_LINE ourselves after each call of GET_LINE.

It will be found helpful to use slices with GET_LINE and PUT_LINE; thus to copy a text file (with lines of less than 100 characters) and adding the string "--" to each line we could write

```
S: STRING(1 .. 100);
N: NATURAL;
...
while not END_OF_FILE loop
   GET_LINE(S, N);
```

```
        PUT_LINE("--" & S(1 .. N));
    end loop;
```

where we have assumed default files throughout.

The package TEXT_IO may seem somewhat elaborate but for simple output all we need is PUT and NEW_LINE and these are quite straightforward as we have seen.

Exercise 15.2

1   What do the following calls output? Assume the initial values for the default parameters.

(a)	PUT("FRED");	(f)	PUT(120, 8, 8);
(b)	PUT(120);	(g)	PUT(-38.0);
(c)	PUT(120, 8);	(h)	PUT(0.07, 6, 2, 2);
(d)	PUT(120, 0);	(i)	PUT(3.14159, 1, 4);
(e)	PUT(-120, 0);	(j)	PUT(9_999_999_999.9, 1, 1, 1);

Assume that the real values are of a type with **digits** = 6 and the integer values are of a type with 16 bits.

2   Write a body for the package SIMPLE_IO of Section 2.2. Ignore exceptions.

15.3 Interrupts

An interrupt is another form of input. In Ada this can be achieved through the rendezvous mechanism. From within the program, an interrupt appears as an entry call performed by an external task whose priority is higher than that of any task in the program. The interrupt handler is then naturally represented in the program by a task with accept statements for the corresponding entry. The entry is identified as an interrupt by what is known as a representation clause giving the relevant hardware address.

As an example suppose a program wishes to act upon an interrupt arising from the closing of an electrical contact and the interrupt is associated with the address 8#72#. We could write

```
task CONTACT_HANDLER is
    entry CONTACT;
    for CONTACT use at 8#72#;
end;

task body CONTACT_HANDLER is
begin
    loop
        accept CONTACT do
```

```
            ...
        end;
    end loop;
end CONTACT_HANDLER;
```

The body of the accept statement corresponds to the direct response to the interrupt. The rule that the external mythical task has a priority higher than that of any software task ensures that the response takes precedence over ordinary tasks.

An interrupt entry will usually have no parameters but it can have **in** parameters through which control information is passed. An accept statement for an interrupt entry can also occur in a select statement.

The detailed behaviour of interrupt entry calls is somewhat dependent upon the implementation. They could, for example, appear as conditional entry calls and therefore be lost if the response task is not ready to execute the corresponding accept statement. The exact interpretation of the address in the representation clause is also dependent on the implementation.

15.4 Representation clauses

In the last section we introduced the representation clause as a means of informing the compiler of additional information about the interrupt entry. Representation clauses take various forms and apply to various entities. Their general purpose is to provide the compiler with directions regarding how the entity is to be implemented. A representation clause must occur in the same declaration list as the declaration of the entity it refers to.

An address clause is of the form used for the entry. It can be used to assign an explicit address to an object, to indicate the start address of the code body of a subprogram, package or task, or as we have seen, to specify an interrupt to which an entry is to be linked.

A length clause allows us to specify the amount of storage to be allocated for objects of a type, for the collection of an access type and for the working storage of a task type. This is done by indicating the value of certain attributes. Thus

```
type BYTE is range 0 .. 255;
for BYTE'SIZE use 8;
```

ensures that objects of the type BYTE occupy only 8 bits.

The space for access collections and tasks is indicated using the attribute STORAGE_SIZE. In these cases the unit is not bits but storage units. The number of bits in a storage unit is implementation dependent and is given by the constant STORAGE_UNIT in the package SYSTEM. Thus if we wanted to ensure that the access collection for

```
type LIST is access CELL;
```

will accommodate 500 cells then we write

for LIST'STORAGE_SIZE **use**
    500*(CELL'SIZE / SYSTEM.STORAGE_UNIT);

Similarly the data space for each task of a task type can be indicated by

for MAILBOX'STORAGE_SIZE **use** 128;

The value of *small* for a fixed point type can also be indicated by a length clause as was discussed in Section 12.4.

An enumeration representation clause can be used to specify, as an aggregate, the internal integer codes for the literals of an enumeration type. We might have a status value transmitted into our program as single bit settings, thus

type STATUS **is** (OFF, READY, ON);
for STATUS **use** (OFF => 1, READY => 2, ON => 4);

There is a constraint that the ordering of the values must be the same as the logical ordering of the literals. However, despite the holes, the functions SUCC, PRED, POS and VAL always work in logical terms.

If these single bit values were autonomously loaded into our machine at location octal 100 then we could conveniently access them in our program by declaring a variable of type STATUS and placing it at that location using an address clause

S: STATUS;
for S **use at** 8#100#;

However, if by some hardware mishap a value which is not 1, 2 or 4 turns up then the program will be erroneous and its behaviour quite unpredictable. We will see how to overcome this difficulty in Section 15.6.

The final form of representation clause is used to indicate the layout of a record type. Thus if we have

type REGISTER **is range** 0 .. 15;
type OPCODE **is** (...);

type RR **is**
    record
        CODE: OPCODE;
        R1   : REGISTER;
        R2   : REGISTER;
    end record;

which represents a machine instruction of the RR format in the IBM System 370, then we can specify the exact mapping by

for RR **use**
    record at mod 2;

```
        CODE  at 0 range 0 .. 7;
        R1    at 1 range 0 .. 3;
        R2    at 1 range 4 .. 7;
    end record;
```

The optional alignment clause

```
    at mod 2;
```

indicates that the record is to be aligned on a double byte boundary; the alignment is given in terms of the number of storage units and in the case of the 370 a storage unit would naturally be one 8 bit byte.

The position and size of the individual components are given relative to the start of the record. The value after **at** gives a storage unit and the range is in terms of bits. The bit number can extend outside the storage unit; we could equally have written

```
    R1 at 0 range 8 .. 11;
```

If we do not specify the location of every component, the compiler is free to juggle the rest as best it can. However, we must allow enough space for those we do specify and they must not overlap unless they are in different alternatives of a variant. There may also be hidden components (array dope information for example) and this may interfere with our freedom.

We conclude this section by noting an important rule that only one representation clause is allowed for (a particular aspect of) any type. Moreover, any type derived from a type after the declaration of a representation clause will inherit that representation. Nevertheless, we can have two types, one derived from the other with different representations by placing the representation clauses after the derivation. So, in essence, derived types allow us to have different representations for essentially the same type and conveniently force us to use explicit type conversions to transfer from one representation to another.

15.5 Implementation considerations

It is hard to be specific in this area since so much depends upon the implementation. However, there is a package SYSTEM which includes the values of various machine constants. Its specification is as follows

```
    package SYSTEM is
        type ADDRESS    is implementation_defined;
        type NAME       is implementation_defined_enumeration_type;

        SYSTEM_NAME   : constant NAME:= implementation_defined;

        STORAGE_UNIT  : constant:= implementation_defined;
```

```
MEMORY_SIZE      : constant:= implementation_defined;

-- system-dependent named numbers

MIN_INT          : constant:= implementation_defined;
MAX_INT          : constant:= implementation_defined;
MAX_DIGITS       : constant:= implementation_defined;
MAX_MANTISSA     : constant:= implementation_defined;
FINE_DELTA       : constant:= implementation_defined;
TICK             : constant:= implementation_defined;

-- other system-dependent declarations

subtype PRIORITY is INTEGER range implementation_defined;
...
end SYSTEM;
```

The type ADDRESS is that used in an address clause and given by the corresponding attribute; it might be an integer type or possibly a record type. The numbers STORAGE_UNIT and MEMORY_SIZE give the size of a storage unit in bits and the memory size in storage units; both are of type universal integer. MIN_INT and MAX_INT give the most negative and most positive values of an integer type, MAX_DIGITS is the largest number of decimal digits of a floating type and MAX_MANTISSA is the largest number of binary digits of a fixed type; they are all of type universal integer. FINE_DELTA is a bit redundant since it always has the value $2.0**$ ($-$MAX_MANTISSA) and TICK is the clock period in seconds; they are both of type universal real.

Various pragmas enable us to set certain parameters of the implementation, and attributes enable us to read the value of certain parameters. The predefined pragmas and attributes are listed in Appendix 1 although an implementation is free to add others.

Some pragmas enable us to guide the compiler regarding the balance of the implementation between integrity and efficiency and also between space and time.

The pragma SUPPRESS can be used to indicate that the run-time checks associated with detecting conditions which could give rise to exceptions can be omitted if to do so would lead to a more efficient program. However, it should be remembered that a pragma is merely a recommendation and so there is no guarantee that the exception will not be raised. Indeed it could be propagated from another unit compiled with checks.

The checks corresponding to the exception CONSTRAINT_ERROR are ACCESS_CHECK (checking that an access value is not null when attempting to access a component), DISCRIMINANT_CHECK (checking that a discriminant value is consistent with the component being accessed or a constraint), INDEX_CHECK (checking that an index is in range), LENGTH_CHECK (checking that the number of components of an array match) and RANGE_CHECK (checking that various constraints are satisfied).

The checks corresponding to NUMERIC_ERROR are DIVISION_ CHECK (checking the second operand of /, **rem** and **mod**) and OVERFLOW_ CHECK (checking for numeric overflow).

The check corresponding to STORAGE_ERROR is STORAGE_CHECK (checking that space for an access collection or task has not been exceeded).

The check corresponding to PROGRAM_ERROR is ELABORATION_ CHECK (checking that the body of a unit has been elaborated).

The pragma takes the form

pragma SUPPRESS(RANGE_CHECK);

in which case it applies to all operations in the unit concerned or it can list the types and objects to which it is to be applied. Thus

pragma SUPPRESS(ACCESS_CHECK, LIST);

indicates that no checks are to be applied when accessing objects of the access type LIST.

The other pragmas in this category apply to the balance between speed and time. They are CONTROLLED, INLINE, OPTIMIZE and PACK; they are described in Appendix 1.

Finally, there are various machine dependent attributes defined for real types. For example there is the attribute MACHINE_ROUNDS which indicates whether rounding is performed for the type concerned. Another is the attribute MACHINE_OVERFLOWS which indicates whether NUMERIC_ ERROR is raised for computations which exceed the range of the type. If a program uses these attributes then care is required if portability is to be ensured.

15.6 Unchecked programming

Sometimes the strict integrity of a fully typed language is a nuisance. This particularly applies to system programs where, in different parts of a program, an object is thought of in different terms. This difficulty can be overcome by the use of a generic function called UNCHECKED_CONVERSION. Its specification is

```
generic
    type SOURCE is limited private;
    type TARGET is limited private;
function UNCHECKED_CONVERSION(S: SOURCE) return TARGET;
```

As an example, we can overcome our problem with possible erroneous values of the type STATUS of Section 15.4. We can receive the values into our program as values of type BYTE, check their validity in numeric terms and then convert the values to type STATUS for the remainder of the program. In order to perform the conversion we first instantiate the generic function thus

```
function BYTE_TO_STATUS is
    new UNCHECKED_CONVERSION(BYTE, STATUS);
```

and we can then write

```
B: BYTE;
for B use at 8#100#;
S: STATUS;
...
case B is
    when 1 | 2 | 4 =>
        null;
    when others =>
        raise BAD_DATA;
end case;

S:= BYTE_TO_STATUS(B);
```

The effect of the unchecked conversion is nothing; the bit pattern of the source type is merely passed on unchanged and reinterpreted as the bit pattern of the target type. Clearly, certain conditions must be satisfied for this to be possible; an obvious one which may be imposed by the implementation is that the number of bits in the representations of the two types must be the same. We cannot get a quart into a pint pot.

Another area where the programmer can be given extra freedom is in the deallocation of access types. As mentioned in Section 11.4 there may or may not be a garbage collector. In any event we may prefer to do our own garbage collection perhaps on the grounds that this gives us better timing control in a realtime program. We can do this with a generic procedure called UNCHECKED_DEALLOCATION. Its specification is

```
generic
    type OBJECT is limited private;
    type NAME is access OBJECT;
procedure UNCHECKED_DEALLOCATION(X: in out NAME);
```

If we take our old friend

```
type LIST is access CELL;
```

then we can write

```
procedure FREE is
    new UNCHECKED_DEALLOCATION(CELL, LIST);
```

and then

L: LIST;

...

FREE(L);

After calling FREE, the value of L will be **null** and the cell will have been returned to free storage. Of course, if we mistakenly still had another variable referring to the cell then we would be in a mess; the program would be erroneous. If we use unchecked deallocation then the onus is on us to get it right. We should also insert

pragma CONTROLLED(LIST);

to tell the compiler that we are looking after ourselves and that any garbage collector should not be used for this access type.

The use of both these forms of unchecked programming needs care and it would be sensible to restrict the use of these generic subprograms to privileged parts of the program. Note that since both generic functions are library functions then any compilation unit using them must refer to them in a with clause. This makes it fairly straightforward for a tool to check for their use. And also for our manager to peer over our shoulders to see whether we are writing naughty programs!

15.7   Other languages

Another possible form of communication between an Ada program and the outside world is via other languages. These could be machine languages or other high level languages such as FORTRAN. The *LRM* prescribes general methods but the actual details will obviously depend so much upon the implementation that an outline description seems pointless and the reader is therefore referred to specific documentation for the implementation concerned.

Chapter 16
Finale

This final chapter covers various overall aspects of Ada. The first four sections consider in more detail and consolidate some important topics which have of necessity been introduced in stages throughout the book. There is then a section on the important issue of portability. Finally, we discuss the general topic of program design as it relates to Ada.

16.1 Names and expressions

The idea of a name should be carefully distinguished from that of an identifier. An identifier is a syntactic form such as FRED which is used for various purposes including introducing entities when they are declared. A name, on the other hand, may be more complex and is the form used to denote entities in general. In the *LRM* and in particular in the syntax rules, the term simple name is used to refer to an identifier other than when it is first introduced; we have not used this term since it seems unnecessarily pedantic.

Syntactically, a name starts with an identifier such as FRED or an operator symbol such as "+" and can then be followed by one or more of the following in an arbitrary order

- one or more index expressions in brackets; this denotes a component of an array,
- a discrete range in brackets; this denotes a slice of an array,
- a dot followed by an identifier, operator or **all**; this denotes a record component, an access value or an entity in a package, task, subprogram, block or loop,

- a prime and then an identifier, possibly indexed; this denotes an atrribute,
- an actual parameter list in brackets; this denotes a function call.

A function call in a name must deliver an array, record or access value and must be followed by indexing, slicing, attribution or component selection. This is not to say that a function call must always be followed by one of these things; it could deliver a value as part of an expression, but as part of a name it must be so followed. This point is clarified by considering the assignment statement. The left-hand side must be a name whereas the right-hand side is an expression. Hence, as we saw in Section 11.6, we can write

```
SPOUSE(P).BIRTH:= NEWDATE;
```

but not

```
SPOUSE(P):= Q;
```

although

```
Q:= SPOUSE(P);
```

is of course perfectly legal. (Ada is somewhat less consistent than Algol 68 in this respect.)

Names are just one of the primary components of an expression. The others are literals (numeric literals, enumeration literals, strings and **null**), aggregates, allocators, function calls (not considered as names), type conversions and qualified expressions as well as expressions in brackets. Expressions involving scalar operators were summarized in Section 4.9.

For convenience, all the operators and their predefined uses are shown in Table 16.1. They are grouped according to precedence level. We have also included the short circuit forms **and then** and **or else** and the membership tests **in** and **not in** although these are not technically classed as operators (they cannot be overloaded).

Note the careful distinction between BOOLEAN which means the predefined type and 'Boolean' which means BOOLEAN or any type derived from it. Similarly INTEGER means the predefined type and 'integer' means any integer type (including universal integer). Also 'floating' means any floating type plus universal real.

Observe that the membership tests apply to any type and not just scalar types which were discussed in Section 4.9. Thus we can check whether an array or record has a particular subtype by using a membership test rather than testing the bounds or discriminant. So we can write

```
V in VECTOR_5       -- true, see Section 6.2
JOHN in WOMAN       -- false, see Section 11.3
```

Table 16.1 Predefined operators.

Operator	Operand(s)		Result
and **or** **xor**	Boolean one dim Boolean array		same same
and then **or else**	Boolean		same
= /=	any, not limited		BOOLEAN
< <= > >=	scalar one dim discrete array		BOOLEAN BOOLEAN
in **not in**	scalar any	range type mark	BOOLEAN BOOLEAN
+ − (binary)	numeric		same
&	one dim array | component		same array
+ − (unary)	numeric		same
*	integer fixed INTEGER fixed floating univ real univ integer	integer INTEGER fixed fixed floating univ integer univ real	same same fixed same fixed univ fixed same univ real univ real
/	integer fixed fixed floating univ real	integer INTEGER fixed floating univ integer	same same fixed univ fixed same univ real
mod **rem**	integer	integer	same
**	integer floating	NATURAL INTEGER	same integer same floating
not	Boolean one dim Boolean array		same same
abs	numeric		same

rather than

```
V'FIRST = 1 and V'LAST = 5
JOHN.SEX = FEMALE
```

which are equivalent.

Finally, remember that & can take either an array or a component for both operands so four cases arise.

The observant reader will notice that the syntax in Appendix 4 uses the syntactic form 'simple_expression' in some cases where 'expression' might have been expected. One reason for this is to avoid a potential ambiguity regarding the use of **in** as a membership test with ranges.

From time to time we have referred to the need for certain scalar expressions to be static. As explained in Chapter 2 this means that they can be evaluated at compilation time. An expression is static if all its constituents are one of the following

- a numeric or enumeration literal,
- a named number,
- a constant initialized by a static expression,
- a predefined operator,
- a static attribute or a functional attribute with static parameters,
- a qualified static expression provided that any constraint involved is static.

Note that renaming preserves staticness so a renaming of one of the above (for which renaming is allowed) is also an allowed constituent of a static expression (AI-1 and AI-438). However, membership tests and short circuit forms are not allowed (AI-128). Observe that staticness only applies to scalar expressions and that all intermediate subexpressions must also be scalar (AI-219). This excludes bizarre examples such as 'a'&'b'='c'&'d' where the intermediate expressions are arrays although the result is scalar.

The final point we wish to make about expressions concerns array bounds. If an expression delivers an array value then it will have bounds for each dimension. Such an expression can be used in various contexts which can be divided into categories according to the rules regarding the matching of the bounds.

The first category (sliding semantics) includes assignment and initialization in an object declaration. In these cases the bounds of the expression do not have to match the bounds of the object; all that matters is that the number of components in each dimension is the same. Thus as we saw in Section 6.2 we can write

```
V: VECTOR(1 .. 5);
W: VECTOR(0 .. 4);
...
V:= W;
```

The same sliding rules apply in the case of the predefined equality and relational operators.

The second category (matching semantics) includes using an array as an actual parameter, as a function result, as an initial value in an allocator or in a qualified expression. In all of these cases an array type or subtype is involved but it may or may not be constrained. If it is constrained, then the bounds must exactly match; if it is not constrained, then the 'result' takes the bounds of the expression. Thus if we had a function

```
function F return VECTOR_5 is
    V: VECTOR(1 .. 5);
    W: VECTOR(0 .. 4);
begin
    ...
```

then we could write **return** V but not **return** W. If, however, the specification had been

```
function F return VECTOR
```

then we could write either **return** V or **return** W.

There are complications with array aggregates. In the case of a named aggregate without **others** the bounds are evident; such an aggregate can be used in any of the above contexts. In the case of a positional aggregate without **others** the bounds are not evident although the number of components is; such an aggregate can also be used in any of the above contexts – in all the cases of the first category (sliding) and those of the second category (matching) with a constrained type the bounds are taken to be those required by the constraint – in cases of the second category with an unconstrained type the lower bound is given by S'FIRST where S is the index subtype. Finally, if an aggregate (positional or named) contains **others**, then neither the bounds nor the number of components is evident. Such an aggregate can be used in a situation of the second category with a constrained type; in addition a positional aggregate with **others** (or just **others** on its own) is also allowed in a situation of the first category.

Similar rules apply to nested aggregates; the context of the whole aggregate is applied transitively to its components.

Somewhat surprisingly, array type conversion described in Section 6.2 does not fit neatly into either of the above two categories. If the type is constrained, then the sliding rules of assignment are used; if the type is unconstrained, then the result takes the bounds of the operand as for qualification.

Exercise 16.1

1   Given

```
L: INTEGER:= 6;
M: constant INTEGER:= 7;
N: constant:= 8;
```

then classify the following as static or dynamic expressions and give their type

(a)   L+1
(b)   M+1
(c)   N+1

16.2 Type equivalence

It is perhaps worth emphasizing the rules for type equivalence. The basic rule is that every type definition introduces a new type. Remember the difference between a type definition and a type declaration. A type definition introduces a type whereas a type declaration also introduces an identifier referring to it. Thus

type T **is** (A, B, C);

is a type declaration whereas

(A, B, C)

is a type definition.

Most types have names but in a few cases a type may be anonymous. The obvious cases occur with the declarations of arrays and tasks. Thus

A: **array** (I **range** L .. R) **of** C;

is short for

type anon **is array** (I **range** <>) **of** C;
A: anon(L .. R);

and

task T **is** ...

is short for

task type anon **is** ...
T: anon;

More subtle cases occur where an apparent type declaration is actually only a subtype declaration. This occurs with array types, derived types and numeric types and so

type T **is array** (I **range** L .. R) **of** C;

is short for

> **subtype** index **is** I **range** L .. R;
> **type** anon **is array** (index **range** <>) **of** C;
> **subtype** T **is** anon(L .. R);

and

> **type** S **is new** T constraint;

is short for

> **type** anon **is new** T;
> **subtype** S **is** anon constraint;

and

> **type** T **is range** L .. R;

is short for

> **type** anon **is new** integer_type;
> **subtype** T **is** anon **range** L .. R;

where integer_type is one of the predefined integer types. Similar expansions apply to floating and fixed types.

When interpreting the rule that each type definition introduces a new type, remember that generic instantiation is equivalent to text substitution in this respect. Thus each instantiation of a package with a type definition in its specification introduces a distinct type. It will be remembered that a similar rule applies to the identification of different exceptions. Each textually distinct exception declaration introduces a new exception; an exception in a recursive procedure is the same for each incarnation but generic instantiation introduces different exceptions.

Remember also that multiple declarations are equivalent to several single declarations written out explicitly. Thus if we have

> A, B: **array** (I **range** L .. R) **of** C;

then A and B are of different anonymous types.

In summary then, Ada has named equivalence rather than the weaker structural equivalence of some languages such as Algol 68. As a consequence Ada gives greater security in the sense that more errors can be found during compilation. However, the Ada type model requires more care in program design. Overzealous use of lots of different types can lead to trouble and there are stories of programs that could never be got to compile.

An obvious area of caution is with numeric types (a novice programmer often uses lots of numeric types with great glee). Attempts to use different numeric types to separate different units of measurement (for example the lengths and areas of Exercise 11.7(**1**)) can lead to messy situations where either lots of overloadings of operators have to be introduced or so many type conversions are required that the clarity sought · is lost by the extra clutter. Another problem is that each different numeric type will require a separate instantiation of the relevant package in TEXT_IO if input–output is required. An example of possible overuse of numeric types is in TEXT_IO itself where the distinct integer type COUNT (used for counting characters, lines and pages) is a frequent irritant.

So too many types can be unwise. However, the use of appropriate constraints (as explicit subtypes or directly) always seems to be a good idea. Remember that subtypes are merely shorthands for a base type plus constraint and as a consequence have structural equivalence. Thus, recalling an example in Section 4.4, we can declare

```
subtype DAY_NUMBER is INTEGER range 1 .. 31;
subtype FEB_DAY is DAY_NUMBER range 1 .. 29;
D1: INTEGER range 1 .. 29;
D2: DAY_NUMBER range 1 .. 29;
D3: FEB_DAY;
```

and then D1, D2 and D3 all have exactly the same subtype.

When to use a subtype and when to use a new type is a matter of careful judgement. The guidelines must be the amount of separation between the abstract concepts. If the abstractions are quite distinct then separate types are justified but if there is much overlap and thus much conversion then subtypes are probably appropriate. Thus we could make a case for DAY_NUMBER being a distinct derived type

```
type DAY_NUMBER is range 1 .. 31;
```

but we would find it hard to justify making FEB_DAY not simply a subtype of DAY_NUMBER.

Another important distinction between types and subtypes is in their representation. The basic rule is that a subtype has the same representation as the base type whereas a derived type can have a different representation. Of course, the compiler can still optimize, but that is another matter.

It should also be remembered that checking subtype properties is strictly a run-time matter. Thus

```
S: STRING(1 .. 4):= "abc";
```

raises CONSTRAINT_ERROR although we can expect that any reasonable compiler would pick this up during compilation.

16.3 Structure summary and the main program

Ada has four structural units in which declarations can occur; these are blocks, subprograms, packages and tasks. They can be classified in various ways. First of all, packages and tasks have separate specifications and bodies; for subprograms this separation is optional; for blocks it is not possible or relevant since a block has no specification. We can also consider separate compilation: packages, tasks and subprogram bodies can all be subunits but only packages and subprograms can be library units. Note also that only packages and subprograms can be generic. Finally, tasks, subprograms and blocks can have dependent tasks but packages cannot since they are only passive scope control units. These various properties of units are summarized in Table 16.2.

We can also consider the scope and nesting of these four structural units. (Note that a block is a statement whereas the others are declarations.) Each unit can appear inside any of the other units and this lexical nesting can in principle go on indefinitely, although in practical programs a depth of three will not often be exceeded. The only restrictions to this nesting are that a block, being a statement, cannot appear in a package specification but only in its body (and directly only in the initialization sequence) and of course none of these units can appear in a task specification but again only in its body. In practice, however, some of the combinations will arise rarely. Blocks will usually occur inside subprograms and task bodies and occasionally inside other blocks. Subprograms will occur as library units and inside packages and less frequently inside tasks and other subprograms. Packages will usually be library units or inside other packages. Tasks will probably nearly always be inside packages and occasionally inside other tasks or subprograms.

The *Language Reference Manual* is a little vague about the concept of an Ada program. This is perhaps to be expected since Ada is about software components, and undue concern regarding what constitutes a complete program is probably out of place particularly bearing in mind the growing concern with distributed and parallel systems. However, for simple systems we can regard a program as composed out of the library units in a particular program library. The *LRM* does not prescribe how the program is to be started but as discussed in Sections 2.2 and 8.2 we can imagine that one of the library units which is a subprogram (or an instance of a generic subprogram (AI-513)) is called by some magic outside the language itself. Moreover, we must imagine that this originating flow of control is associated with an anonymous task. The priority of this task can be set by the pragma PRIORITY in the outermost declarative part of this main subprogram.

Table 16.2 Properties of units.

Property	Blocks	Subprograms	Packages	Tasks
Separation	no	optional	yes	yes
Subunits	no	yes	yes	yes
Library units	no	yes	yes	no
Generic units	no	yes	yes	no
Dependent tasks	yes	yes	no	yes

The main program will almost inevitably use dependent library units such as TEXT_IO. These have to be elaborated before the main program is entered and again we can imagine that this is done by our anonymous task. The order of these elaborations is not precisely specified but it must be consistent with the dependencies between the units. In addition, the pragma ELABORATE can be used to ensure that a body is elaborated before a unit that calls it; this may be necessary to prevent PROGRAM_ERROR. Consider the situation mentioned at the end of Section 8.1 thus

```
package P is
    function A return INTEGER;
end P;

package body P is
    function A return INTEGER is
    begin
        return 0;
    end A;
end P;

with P;
package Q is
    I: INTEGER:= P.A;
end Q;
```

The three units can be compiled separately and the requirements are that the body of P and the specification of Q must both be compiled after the specification of P. But there is no need for the body of P to be compiled before the specification of Q. However, when we come to elaborate the three units it is important that the body of P be elaborated before the specification of Q otherwise PROGRAM_ERROR will be raised. The dependency rules are not enough to ensure this and so we have to use the pragma ELABORATE and write

```
with P;
pragma ELABORATE(P);
package Q is
    I: INTEGER:= P.A;
end Q;
```

The pragma immediately follows the context clause and can refer to one or more of the library units mentioned in the context clause.

If the dependencies and any pragmas ELABORATE are such that no consistent order of elaboration exists then the program is illegal; if there are several possible orders and the behaviour of the program depends on the particular order, then it is also illegal (since it then has an incorrect order dependency).

A further point is that whether a main program can have parameters or not or whether there are restrictions on their types and modes or indeed whether the main program can be a function, is dependent on the implementation. Again this is in line with the view that Ada is about the open world of components rather than the closed world of complete programs. It may indeed be very convenient for a main program to have parameters, and for the calling and parameter passing to be performed by the magic associated with the interpretation of a statement in some non-Ada command language.

The above general description is confirmed by AI-222 which also summarizes a number of issues which have been clarified and then illustrates the effect of various rules by the following model

```
task body ... is
begin
   begin
      declare
         package STANDARD is     -- This is Appendix 2
            ...
         end;

         package body STANDARD is
            -- Library units and secondary units needed by
            --      the main program and the main program
            --      (procedure or function), in an order
            --      consistent with the with clauses and any
            --      pragmas ELABORATE.
         begin
            -- Get parameters required by the main program,
            -- if any.
            -- Call the main program.
         exception
            -- Handle any exceptions associated with main
            -- program execution.
         end STANDARD;
      begin
         null;
      end;          -- Wait for library tasks to terminate.
   exception
      -- Handle any exceptions associated with library unit
      -- elaboration.
   end;
   -- Close external files (optional).
   -- Communicate main program function result, if any.
end;
```

This model captures the following

- The environment task is expressed as an anonymous task.
- Library units and the main program are contained in the package STANDARD.
- Library units needed by the main program, corresponding library unit bodies and the main program are elaborated in an implemen-

tation defined order consistent with the with clauses and any ELABORATE pragmas. These elaborations occur before the main program is called.

- Delay statements executed by the environment task during the elaboration of a library package delay the environment task.

- Tasks that depend on a library unit (and that are not designated by an access value) are started at the end of the declarative part of STANDARD and before the main program is called.

- After normal termination of the main program the environment task must wait for all library tasks to terminate. If all library tasks terminate, then the program as a whole terminates.

- If the main program terminates abnormally by the propagation of an exception then the exception is handled by the environment task. The environment task then waits for any library tasks to terminate. The effect of the environment task's exception handler on unterminated tasks is not defined. In particular, unterminated tasks can be aborted.

- If any external files are used by statements executed in library package bodies, then such operations are performed before execution of the main program begins. If external files are used by library tasks, then these files are processed in accordance with normal Ada semantics, whether or not execution of the main program has begun or has finished. After the main program and all library tasks have terminated (or if execution of the main program is abandoned because of an unhandled exception), any further effects on the external files are not defined; in particular, any files that have been left open may (but need not) be closed.

The reader is warned not to read more into the model than the points listed (it does not cover every subtlety). Nevertheless the model does help to dispel a certain mystery about the nature of the main program and its environment.

16.4 Visibility and program composition

The visibility and scope rules have been introduced by stages. The basic rules applicable to the simple block structure were introduced in Section 4.2 and further discussed in Section 7.6 when we considered the use of the dotted notation to provide visibility of an outer identifier which had been hidden by an inner redeclaration. The overloading rules were discussed in Section 7.2 and we recall that the use of identifiers fell into two categories: overloadable (subprograms) and not overloadable (the rest). We then considered the impact of packages in Section 8.4 and the rules regarding the use clause. We also noted in Section 10.3 that exceptions had some special characteristics. We do not intend to repeat all these rules here but rather to illustrate some of their effects particularly with regard to building programs from components.

We begin by recalling from Section 7.5 that enumeration literals behave much like parameterless functions. We could not therefore declare both an enumeration type and a parameterless function returning that type and with the same identifier as one of the literals in the same declarative region thus

```
type COLOUR is (RED, AMBER, GREEN);
function RED return COLOUR;              -- illegal
```

although we could of course declare the function RED in an inner scope where it would hide the literal RED (AI-330). A more subtle illustration is given by

```
package P is
    type LIGHT is new COLOUR;
    function RED return LIGHT;
end;
```

where (assuming COLOUR as above) the function RED replaces the literal RED of the derived type LIGHT. So if we then declared

```
type MORE_LIGHT is new LIGHT;
```

after the package specification then MORE_LIGHT would inherit the function RED rather than the literal RED.

We will now discuss the visibility rules and similar properties of generic packages in more detail. Reconsider the package SET_OF from Section 13.2

```
generic
    type BASE is (<>);
package SET_OF is
    type SET is private;
    type LIST is array (POSITIVE range <>) of BASE;
    ...
end;
```

It is very important to grasp the difference between the rules for the template (the generic text as written) and an instance (the effective text after instantiation).

The first point is that the generic package is not a genuine package and in particular does not export anything. So no meaning can be attached to SET_OF.LIST outside the generic package and nor can SET_OF appear in a use clause. Of course, inside the generic package we can indeed write SET_OF.LIST if we wished to be pedantic or had hidden LIST by an inner redeclaration.

If we now instantiate the generic package thus

```
package CHARACTER_SET is new SET_OF(CHARACTER);
```

then CHARACTER_SET is a genuine package and so we can refer to CHARACTER_SET.LIST outside the package and CHARACTER_SET can appear in a use clause. In this case there is no question of writing CHARACTER_SET.LIST *inside* the package because the inside text is quite ephemeral.

Another very important point concerns the properties of an identifier such as LIST. Inside the generic template we can only use the properties common to all possible actual parameters as expressed by the formal parameter notation. Outside we can additionally use the properties of the particular instantiation. So, inside we cannot write

```
S: LIST(1 .. 6):= "string";
```

because we do not know that the actual type is going to be a character type – it could be an integer type. However, outside we can indeed write

```
S: CHARACTER_SET.LIST(1 .. 6):= "string";
```

because we know full well that the actual type is, in this instance, a character type (AI-398).

Constructing a total program requires putting together various components whose interfaces match much as we can put together hardware components by the use of various plugs and sockets. In order for an entity from one component to be used by another, its name must be exported from the component declaring it and then imported into the component using it. Our normal component is naturally a library package which will often be generic. We will now summarize the various tools at our disposal.

Entities are exported by being in the visible part of a package.

Entities are imported by being generic parameters and also through with clauses. Direct visibility is given by use clauses.

We have also seen that generic actual parameters can be imported into a package and then used to create entities that are exported (the example LIST above); we also noted that specific properties of the actual parameters were reexported but not visible internally (the fact that the actual type was a character type).

The Ada export and import rules work on groups of entities rather than individual entities as in some languages. The Ada technique avoids clutter and is very appropriate when the entities are highly cohesive (that is are strongly related). However, if they are not cohesive then the coarse grouping is a nuisance; there are various (not altogether satisfactory) techniques that can be used to give finer control.

An obvious technique for giving finer control of entities exported from the visible part of a package is simply to declare a hierarchical set of nested packages.

```
package OUTER is
   package INNER1 is
      ...
   end;
```

```
    package INNER2 is
        ...
        end;
    end;
```

We could then write

```
with OUTER;
package USER is
    use OUTER.INNER1;
```

and then INNER2 and its internal entities will not be directly visible. Note that we cannot put the use clause immediately after the with clause because a use clause in such a position can only refer to the packages mentioned in the with clause itself.

There is no directly corresponding technique for grouping imported generic parameters. Sometimes we would like to only partially instantiate a generic package. Consider the more general function INTEGRATE of Section 13.3

```
generic
    type FLOATING is digits <>;
    with function F(X: FLOATING) return FLOATING;
function INTEGRATE(A, B: FLOATING) return FLOATING;
```

If we want to do lots of different integrations but all with the same floating type, then it would be rather nice to fix the type parameter once and then only have to bother with the function parameter thereafter. This could be done if our generic function were rewritten as a nested generic thus

```
generic
    type FLOATING is digits <>;
package GENERIC_INTEGRATE is
    generic
        with function F(X: FLOATING) return FLOATING;
    function INTEGRATE(A, B: FLOATING) return FLOATING;
end GENERIC_INTEGRATE;
```

We can then write

```
package REAL_INTEGRATE is new GENERIC_INTEGRATE(REAL);
use REAL_INTEGRATE;
```

and now we can instantiate the inner generic with our actual function G as in Section 13.3. This technique obviously works but we do have to impose a predetermined order on our partial parameterization.

Renaming is a useful (although somewhat heavy) tool for filtering visibility. We can import some entities into a package and then just rename

those that we wish to reexport. As an example consider again the package
SET_OF. Suppose we wish to instantiate this for type CHARACTER but only
want the user to have access to MAKE_SET on single values, "+", "−" and
SIZE on the grounds that the other operations are superfluous. (This is only
an example!) We write and compile

```
with SET_OF;
package XYZ is new SET_OF(CHARACTER);
```

and then

```
with XYZ;
package CHARACTER_SET is
    subtype SET is XYZ.SET;
    function MAKE_SET(X: CHARACTER) return SET renames
                                                XYZ.MAKE_SET;
    function "+" (X, Y: SET) return SET renames XYZ."+";
    function "−" (X, Y: SET) return SET renames XYZ."−";
    function SIZE(X: SET) return NATURAL renames XYZ.SIZE;
end CHARACTER_SET;
```

The user can now access the reexported facilities from the package
CHARACTER_SET without having visibility of the facilities of XYZ. Of
course the user could still write **with** XYZ; and this would defeat the object
of the exercise. However, it might be that our program library has
additional tools which can hide library units without deleting them. Thus
we see that the flat library structure of Ada without additional tools is not
entirely adequate.
    Note also that we had to use a subtype because we cannot rename a
type. The subtype declaration also makes available the intrinsic ability to
declare objects and perform assignment. However, if we wish to do
equality comparisons then we must explicitly rename "=" as well thus

```
function "=" (LEFT, RIGHT: SET) return BOOLEAN renames
                                                XYZ."=";
```

This also makes "/=" available as one would expect. The general rule
therefore is that predefined operators can be imported by renaming but
intrinsic properties which cannot be dealt with that way are available
automatically. In order to properly comprehend the mechanism it must be
realized that predefined operators such as "=" are implicitly declared
immediately after the declaration of the type to which they refer.
    Another example is provided by enumeration types; if we want to
have visibility of the literals then they have to be renamed. So writing

```
package C is
    type COLOUR is (RED, AMBER, GREEN);
    -- predefined operators such as = and < applying to the
    -- type COLOUR are implicitly declared here
end;
```

```
with C;
package P is
    subtype LIGHT is C.COLOUR;
    function RED return LIGHT renames C.RED;
    function AMBER return LIGHT renames C.AMBER;
    function "<" (LEFT, RIGHT: LIGHT) return BOOLEAN renames
                                                        C."<";
end;
```

will provide visibility (from P) of the literals RED and AMBER but not GREEN and also of "<" but none of the other relational operators. Further details can be found in the *LRM*.

Rather simpler examples of the renaming technique for controlling visibility are given by the renaming of the exceptions declared in IO_EXCEPTIONS at the end of the three input–output packages.

We conclude this section by reconsidering the rules for order of compilation and recompilation of the units in a program library. The various different units are categorized as library units or secondary units as summarized in Table 16.3 which also shows their basic inter-relationships.

The reader will recall from Chapter 8 that the compilation order is determined by the dependency relationships. A unit cannot be compiled unless all the units on which it depends have already been compiled. And contrariwise, if a unit is recompiled then all units depending upon it also have to be recompiled. The basic rules for dependency are

- A body is dependent on its specification.

- A subunit is dependent on its parent.

- A unit is also dependent on the specifications of units mentioned in its with clauses.

Table 16.3   Compilation units.

Unit	Category	Depends on
package spec	library	
package body	secondary	[generic] package spec
subprogram spec	library	
subprogram body	library	
	secondary	[generic] subprogram spec
gen package spec	library	
gen subprogram spec	library	
subunit	secondary	package body | subprogram body | subunit
gen package instance	library	
gen subprogram instance	library	

In addition, for implementation reasons, there are also the following auxiliary rules

- If a subprogram call is inlined using the pragma INLINE (see Appendix 1) then the calling unit will be dependent upon the called subprogram body (as well as the specification).

- If several units are compiled together then the compiler may carry out fancy optimizations not otherwise possible and this may result in dependencies between the units.

- An implementation is also allowed to create other dependencies concerning generics; a unit containing an instantiation may be dependent on the generic body (as well as the specification) and on any subunits of that body (AI-408 and AI-506). An implementation may also require that a generic specification and body be compiled together and that a generic body and its stubs be compiled together.

The last rule says in effect that an implementation may require that the whole of a generic unit be compiled before any instantiation. The philosophy of separation of specification and body (and subunits) is difficult in the case of generics and likely to lead to poor implementations.

The basic rules for recompilation are as follows. A newly compiled library unit will replace an existing library unit (of any sort) with the same name. A secondary unit will be rejected unless there already exists a matching unit on which it can depend – a body is rejected unless its specification exists and a subunit is rejected unless its parent body or subunit exists. A successfully compiled secondary unit naturally replaces an existing one. If a unit is replaced then all units dependent on it are also deleted.

These fairly straightforward rules are complicated by the fact that a subprogram need not have a distinct specification and a package may not need a body.

If we start with an empty library and compile a procedure body P, then it will be accepted as a library unit (and not needing a distinct specification). If we subsequently compile a new version of the body then it will replace the previous library unit. If, however, we subsequently compile just the specification of P, then it will make the old body obsolete and we must then compile a new body which will now be classed as a secondary unit. In other words we cannot add the specification as an afterthought and then provide a new body perhaps in the expectation that units dependent just on the specification could avoid recompilation. Moreover, once we have a distinct specification and body we cannot join them up again – if we provide a new body which matches the existing distinct specification, then it will replace the old body, if it does not match the specification then it will be rejected.

The situation is somewhat reversed in the case of a package. We remember that some packages do not need a body but that a body might be useful for initialization. There is a certain risk here since we will not get an error if we mistakenly forget to compile the missing but apparently not necessary body (a good implementation will give a warning). Note that once we have provided such a body, we can only get rid of it by providing a new specification and that will mean that all dependent units have to be recompiled. Of course, we can always provide an explicit null body.

Generics also have to be considered and we need to take care to distinguish between generic units and their instantiations. A generic subprogram always has a distinct specification but a generic package may not need a body. Note carefully that the body of a generic package or subprogram looks just like the body of a plain package or subprogram. It will be classed as one or the other according to the category of the existing specification (a body is rejected if there is no existing specification except in the case of a subprogram which we discussed above (AI-225)). An instantiation however is all in one lump, it is classed as a library unit in its own right and the separation of specification and body does not occur. The notional body of a generic instance cannot be replaced by a newly compiled plain body. For example, suppose we first compile

```
generic
procedure GP;

procedure GP is
begin ... end GP;
```

and then separately compile

```
with GP;
procedure P is new GP;
```

and then submit

```
procedure P is
begin ... end P;
```

The result is that the new unit P will be accepted. However, it will be classed as a library unit and completely replace the existing instantiation. It cannot be taken as a new secondary unit since the instantiation is treated as one lump (AI-199).

We conclude by observing that we have been discussing the Ada language rules regarding the behaviour of the program library. We can expect an implementation to provide utility programs which manipulate the library in additional ways. Any such facilities are outside the scope of this book and we must hence refer the reader to the documentation for the implementation concerned.

Exercise 16.4

1   Draw a dependency graph for the program PRINT_ROOTS modified to use the package SIMPLE_MATHS as well as SIMPLE_IO as described in Exercise 2.2(**1**). Assume that the bodies of

SIMPLE_MATHS and SIMPLE_IO are as in the answers to Exercises 13.4(**1**) and 15.2(**2**). Assume also that our implementation requires generic units to be compiled as a whole.

16.5 Portability

An Ada program may or may not be portable. In many cases a program will be intimately concerned with the particular hardware on which it is running; this is particularly true of embedded applications. Such a program cannot be transferred to another machine without significant alteration. On the other hand it is highly desirable to write portable program libraries so that they can be reused in different applications. In some cases a library component will be totally portable; more often it will make certain demands on the implementation or be parameterized so that it can be tailored to its environment in a straightforward manner. This section contains general guidelines on the writing of portable Ada programs.

One thing to avoid is erroneous programs and those with incorrect order dependencies. They can be insidious. A program may work quite satisfactorily on one implementation and may seem superficially to be portable. However, if it happens to depend upon some undefined feature then its behaviour on another implementation cannot be guaranteed. A common example in most programming languages occurs with variables which accidentally are not initialized. It is often the case that the intended value is zero and furthermore many operating systems clear the program area before loading the program. Under such circumstances the program will behave correctly but may give surprising results when transferred to a different implementation. So the concept of erroneous programs is not confined to Ada. In the previous chapters we have mentioned various causes of such illegal programs. For convenience we summarize them here.

An important group of situations concerns the order of evaluation of expressions. Since an expression can include a function call and a function call can have side effects, it follows that different orders of evaluation can sometimes produce different results. The order of evaluation of the following is not defined

- the operands of a binary operator,
- the destination and value in an assignment,
- the components in an aggregate,
- the parameters in a subprogram or entry call,
- the index expressions in a multidimensional name,
- the expressions in a range,
- the guards in a select statement.

There is an important situation where a junk value can arise

- reading an uninitialized variable before assigning to it.

There are two situations where the language mechanism is not defined

- the passing of array, record and private parameters,
- the algorithm for choosing a branch of a select statement.

There are also situations where the programmer is given extra freedom to overcome the stringency of the type model; abuse of this freedom can lead to erroneous programs. Examples are

- suppressing exceptions,
- unchecked deallocation,
- unchecked conversion.

Finally, we recall from Section 16.3 that the order of elaboration of library units is not defined.

Numeric types are another important source of portability problems. The reason is, of course, the compromise necessary between achieving absolutely uniform behaviour on all machines and maximizing efficiency. Ada uses the concept of model numbers as the formalization of this compromise. In principle, if we rely only on the properties of the model numbers then our programs will be portable. In practice this is not easy to do; the reader will recall the problems of overflow in intermediate expressions discussed in Section 12.1.

There are various attributes which, if used correctly, can make our programs more portable. Thus we can use BASE to find out what is really going on and MACHINE_OVERFLOWS to see whether NUMERIC_ERROR (CONSTRAINT_ERROR) will occur or not. But the misuse of these attributes can lead to very non-portable programs.

There is, however, one simple rule that can be followed. We should always declare our own real types and not directly use the predefined types such as FLOAT. Ideally, a similar approach should be taken with integer types, but the language does encourage us to assume that the predefined type INTEGER has a sensible range.

Another area to consider is tasking. Any program that uses tasking is likely to suffer from portability problems because instruction execution times vary from machine to machine. This will affect the relative execution times of tasks as well as their individual execution times. In some cases a program may not be capable of running at all on a particular machine because it does not have adequate processing power. Hard guidelines are almost impossible to give but the following points should be kept in mind.

Take care that the type DURATION is accurate enough for the application. Remember that regular loops cannot easily be achieved if the interval required is not a safe number.

Avoid the unsynchronized use of shared variables as far as possible. Sometimes, timing considerations demand quick and dirty techniques; consult your friendly realtime specialist if tempted. In simple cases the pragma SHARED may be able to prevent interference between tasks.

The use of the abort statement will also give portability problems because of its asynchronous nature.

Avoid also the overuse of priorities. If you need to use priorities to obtain adequate responsiveness then the program is probably stretching the resources of the machine.

The finite speed of the machine leads to our final topic in this section – the finite space available. It is clear that different machines have different sizes and so a program that runs satisfactorily on one machine might raise STORAGE_ERROR on another. Moreover, different implementations may use different storage allocation strategies for access types and task data. We have seen how representation clauses can be used to give control of storage allocation and thereby reduce portability problems. However, the unconsidered use of recursion and access types is best avoided.

Exercise 16.5

1   The global variable I is of type INTEGER and the function F is

```
function F return INTEGER is
begin
    I:= I+1;
    return I;
end F;
```

Explain why the following fragments of program are illegal. Assume in each case that I is reset to 1.

(a)   I:= I+F;
(b)   A(I):= F;
(c)   AA(I, F):= 0;

16.6 Program design

This final section considers the question of designing Ada programs. As stated in Section 1.3, this book does not claim to be a treatise on program design. Indeed, program design is still largely an art and the value of different methods of design is often a matter of opinion rather than a matter of fact. We have therefore tried to stick to the facts of Ada and to remain neutral regarding design. Nevertheless much has been learnt about design methods over the last decade and many millions of lines of Ada programs have been designed and written. In particular, Object Oriented Design, which matches Ada well, has gained popularity. So although the general guidelines in this section must be treated with some caution there seems little reason to doubt their general validity. Note also that we are only addressing the question of design issues as they relate to Ada.

There are various low level and stylistic issues which are perhaps obvious. Identifiers should be meaningful. The program should be laid out neatly – the style used in this book is based on that recommended from the syntax in the *LRM*. Useful comments should be added. The block structure should be used to localize declarations to their use. Whenever possible a piece of information should only be written once; thus number and constant declarations should be used rather than explicit literals. And so on.

Programming is really all about abstraction and the mapping of the problem onto constructions in the programming language. We recall from Section 1.2 that the development of programming languages has been concerned with the introduction of various levels of abstraction and that Ada in particular introduces a degree of data abstraction not present in other practically used languages.

An important concept in design and the use of abstractions is information hiding. Information should only be accessible to those parts of a program that need to know. The use of packages and private data types to hide unnecessary detail is the cornerstone of good Ada programming. Indeed as we have stated before Ada is a language which aims to encourage the development of reusable software components; the package is the key component.

Designing an Ada program is therefore largely concerned with designing a group of packages and the interfaces between them. Often we will hope to use one or more existing packages. For this to be possible it is clear that they must have been designed with consistent, clean and sufficiently general interfaces. The difficulties are perhaps in deciding what items are sufficiently related or fundamental to belong together in a package and also how general to make the package. If a package is too general it might be clumsy and inefficient; if not general enough it will not be as useful as it might.

The interface to a package is provided by its specification; at least that provides the syntax of how to use the interface, the semantics must also be defined and that can only be provided by a natural language commentary. Thus consider the package STACK of Section 8.1; its specification (in the Ada sense) guarantees that it will provide subprograms PUSH and POP with certain parameter and result types. However, the specification does not, of itself, guarantee that a call of POP will in fact remove and deliver the top item from the stack. From the point of view of the language it would be quite acceptable for the package body to be

```
package body STACK is
    procedure PUSH(X: INTEGER) is
    begin
        null;
    end;

    function POP return INTEGER is
    begin
        return 0;
    end;
end STACK;
```

However, in our imagined future world of the software components industry, anyone selling such package bodies would soon go out of business.

We will now discuss some categories of related items that might make up useful packages.

A very simple form of package is one which merely consists of a group of related types and constants and has no body. The packages SYSTEM and ASCII are in this category. A further example in Section 8.1 is the package DIURNAL; this does not seem a good example – if it has an array TOMORROW then surely it should also have YESTERDAY. Better examples might be packages of related mathematical constants, conversion constants (metric to imperial say), tables of physical and chemical constants and so on. The last could be

```
package ELEMENTS is
    type ELEMENT is (H, He, Li, ... );
        -- beware of Indium – In is reserved!
    ATOMIC_WEIGHT: array (ELEMENT) of REAL
                := (1.008, 4.003, 6.940, ... );
    ...
end ELEMENTS;
```

Another case is where the package contains functions related by application area. An obvious example is the mathematical library discussed in Section 13.4. The individual functions in such a case are really independent although for efficiency SIN and COS for example are likely to share a common procedure. The package body enables us to hide such a procedure from the user because its existence is merely an implementation detail.

Sometimes a package is needed in order to hide a benevolent side effect – an obvious example is the package RANDOM in Exercise 8.1(**1**).

Packages such as SEQUENTIAL_IO encapsulate a great deal of hidden information and provide a number of related services. A problem here is deciding whether to provide additional subprograms for convenience or to stick to only those absolutely necessary. The package TEXT_IO contains many convenience subprograms.

Many packages can be classified as a means of providing controlled access to some form of database. The database may consist of just one item as in the package RANDOM or it could be the symbol tables of a compiler or a grand commercial style database and so on. The package BANK in Section 9.3 is another example.

An important use of packages is to provide new data types and associated operations. Obvious examples are the packages COMPLEX_NUMBERS (Section 9.1), RATIONAL_NUMBERS (Exercise 9.1(**3**)) and QUEUES (Exercise 11.5(**3**)). In such cases the use of private types enables us to separate the representation of the type from the operations upon it. In a way the new types can be seen as natural extensions to the language.

Packages of this sort raise the question of whether we should use operators rather than functions. Ada is not so flexible as some other languages; new operator forms cannot be introduced and the precedence levels are fixed. This ensures that over-enthusiastic use of operators cannot lead to programs that do not even look like Ada programs as can happen with languages such as POP-2. Even so Ada provides opportunities for surprises. We could write

```
function "–" (X, Y: INTEGER) return INTEGER is
begin
    return STANDARD."+" (X, Y);
end "–";
```

but it would obviously be very foolish to do so. Hence a good general guideline is to minimize surprises.

Operators should be considered for functions with a natural mathematical flavour. As a general rule the normal algebraic properties of the operators should be preserved if this is possible. Thus "+" and "*" should be commutative. Mixed type arithmetic is best avoided but there are situations where it is necessary.

The definitions of the operators in the package COMPLEX_ NUMBERS have the expected properties and do not allow mixed working. It would be nice if type conversion could be done by overloading the type name so that we could write COMPLEX(2.0) rather than CONS(2.0, 0.0). However, Ada does not allow this. Type conversion of this form is restricted to the predefined and derived numeric types.

On the other hand, consider the operators in the predefined package CALENDAR in Section 14.3. Here the very essence of the problem requires mixed type addition but commutivity is preserved by providing two overloadings of "+".

When introducing mathematical types such as COMPLEX and RATIONAL, it is always best to use private types. We will then need to provide constructor and selector functions as well as the natural operations themselves. It will usually be the case that construction and selection are best done with functional notation whereas the natural operations can be done with the operators. However, in the case of rational numbers the division operator "/" provides a natural notation for construction.

There is a general and difficult question of how much to provide in a package for a mathematical type. The bare minimum may be rather spartan and incur all users in unnecessary creation of additional subprograms. To be generous might make the package too cumbersome. For instance should we provide a relational operator and if so should we provide all four? Should input–output be included? Such questions are left for the reader to answer from his or her own experience according to the needs of the application.

Another important issue is storage allocation. This is well illustrated by a type such as POLYNOMIAL introduced in Section 11.1. If this is implemented using a discriminated record thus

```
type POLYNOMIAL(N: INDEX:= 0) is
    record
        A: INTEGER_VECTOR(0 .. N);
    end record;
```

then in the case of unconstrained polynomials the compiler will (unless very clever) allocate the maximum space that could be required. Hence it is important that the range of the discriminant has a sensible upper bound. If we had written

type POLYNOMIAL(N: INTEGER:= 0) **is** ...

then each unconstrained polynomial would have had the space for an array of length INTEGER'LAST and we would presumably soon run out of storage.

If all the polynomials are to be fairly small, then using a discriminated record is probably satisfactory. On the other hand, if they are likely to be of greatly varying size then it is probably better to use access types. Indeed a mixed strategy could be used – a fixed array for the first few terms and then the use of an access type for the remainder. In order that such alternative implementation strategies can be properly organized and hidden from the user it is clear that the polynomial should be a private type. The design of a suitable package is left as an informal exercise for the reader.

In designing packages there is the question of what to do when something goes wrong. This brings us to exceptions. Although not new to programming languages they are nevertheless not widely used except in PL/I and the experience with PL/I has not been satisfactory. However, exceptions in Ada are different to those in PL/I in one most important aspect. In Ada one cannot go back to the point where the exception was raised but is forced to consider a proper alternative to the part of the program that went wrong.

Having said that, exceptions nevertheless need care. In Chapter 10 we warned against the unnecessary use of exceptions and in particular the casual raising of the predefined exceptions since we have no guarantee, when handling such an exception, that it was raised for the reason we had in mind.

The first goal should always be to have clean and complete interfaces. As an example consider again the factorial function and the action to be taken when the parameter is illegal. We could consider

- printing a message,
- returning a default value,
- returning a status via a Boolean parameter,
- calling an error procedure,
- raising an exception.

Printing a message is highly unsatisfactory because it raises a host of detailed problems such as the identity of the file, the format of the message and so on. Moreover, it gives the calling program no control over the action it would like to take and some file is cluttered with messages. Furthermore, there is still the question of what to do after having printed the message.

Another possibility is to return a default value such as −1 as in Exercise 10.1(**2**). This is not satisfactory since there is no guarantee that the user will check for this default value upon return. If we could rely upon the user doing so then we could equally rely upon the user checking the parameter of the function before calling it in the first place.

If we wish to return an auxiliary status value via another parameter then, as we saw when discussing PUSH and POP in Section 10.2, we can no longer use a function anyway and would have to use a procedure instead. We also have to rely upon the caller again as in the case of the default value.

We could call a global procedure to be supplied by the user. This means agreeing on a standard name which is unsatisfactory. We cannot pass the error procedure as a parameter and to resort to the generic mechanism really is using a steam hammer to crack a nut. In any case we still have the problem, as with printing a message, of what to do afterwards and how to return finally from the function. It is highly naive to suppose that the program can just stop. The manager of the steelworks would not wish the control part of the program to stop just because of a minor error in some other part; there must be a way of carrying on.

There are only two ways out of a subprogram in Ada; back to the point of call or by a propagated exception (the global goto and label parameters of other languages are effectively replaced by the exception). We seem to have eliminated the possibility of returning to the point of call as not reliable and so have to come to the conclusion that the raising of an exception is the appropriate solution.

Another criterion we should consider when deciding whether to use exceptions is whether we expect the condition to arise in the normal course of events or not. If we do then an exception is probably wrong. As an example the end of file condition in the package SEQUENTIAL_IO is tested for by a Boolean function and not an exception. We naturally expect to come to the end of the file and so must test for it − see the answer to Exercise 15.1(**1**).

On the other hand, if we are using the package STACK in say an interpreter for mathematical expressions, then, provided that the interpreter is written correctly, we know that the stack cannot underflow. An exception for this unexpected condition is acceptable. Note also that when using SEQUENTIAL_IO, if we accidentally attempt to read after the end of the file then an exception (END_ERROR) is raised.

The raising of exceptions is, however, not a panacea. We cannot sweep the problem under the carpet in this way. The exception must be handled somewhere otherwise the program will terminate. In fact this is one of their advantages − if the user does nothing then the program will terminate safely, whereas if we return status values and the user does nothing then the program will probably ramble on in a fruitless way.

The indiscriminate use of **others** in an exception handler should be avoided. If we write **others** we are really admitting that anything could have gone wrong and we should take appropriate action; we should not use **others** as shorthand for the exceptions we anticipate.

Another major design area concerns the use of tasks. It is usually fairly clear that a problem needs a solution involving tasks but it is not always clear how the various activities should be allocated to individual tasks.

There are perhaps two major problems to be solved regarding the interactions between tasks. One concerns the transmission of messages between tasks, the other the controlling of access to common data by several tasks.

The rendezvous provides a natural mechanism for the closely coupled transmission of a message; examples are provided by the interaction between mother and the other members of her family in the procedure SHOPPING in Section 14.2 and by the interaction between the server and the customer in the package COBBLERS of Exercise 14.9(**1**). If the transmission needs to be decoupled so that the sender can carry on before the message is received then some intermediary task is required. Examples are the task BUFFERING in Section 14.4 and the task type MAILBOX in Section 14.6.

Controlled access to common data is, in Ada, also done by an intermediary task whereas in other languages it may use passive constructions such as monitors or low level primitives such as semaphores. The Ada approach usually provides a clearer and safer solution to the problem. An example is the task PROTECTED_VARIABLE in Section 14.4. Quite often the task is encapsulated in a package in order to enforce the required protocol; examples are the package READER_WRITER of Section 14.4 and the package RESOURCE_ALLOCATOR of Section 14.8.

Sometimes the distinction between message passing and controlling data access is blurred; the task BUFFERING at the macro level is passing messages whereas at the micro level it is controlling access to the buffer.

Another categorization of tasks is between users and servers. A pure server task is one with entries but which calls no other tasks whereas a pure user has no entries but calls other tasks. The distinction is emphasized by the asymmetry of the naming in the rendezvous. The server does not know the names of user tasks whereas the user tasks must know the names of the server tasks in order to call their entries. Sometimes a task is part server and part user; an example is the task type READ_AGENT in Section 14.7.

One problem when designing a set of interacting tasks is deciding which way round the entries are to go. Our intuitive model of servers and users should help. The entries belong in the servers. Another criterion is provided by the consideration of alternatives; if a task is to have a choice of rendezvous via a select statement then it must own the entries and therefore be a server. A select statement can be used to accept one of several entry calls but cannot be used to call one of several entries.

It cannot be emphasized too much that aborting tasks must not be done casually. The abort statement is for extreme situations only. One possible use is in a supervisory task where it may be desirable to close down a complete subsystem in response to a command from a human operator.

The reason for wishing to avoid abort is that it makes it very difficult to provide reliable services as we saw with the package READER_WRITER in Section 14.7. If we know that the users cannot be abnormally terminated then the fancy use of secret agents is not necessary; indeed that example should be considered as illustrating what can be done rather than what should be done.

A multitasking Ada program will often be seen as a set of cooperating tasks designed together. In such circumstances we can rely on the calling tasks to obey the necessary protocols and the design of the servers is then simplified.

The use of timed out entry calls also needs some care but is a very natural and common requirement in real time systems. Services should where possible be able to cope with timed out calls.

Finally, there are generics and the whole question of parameterization. Should we write specific packages or very general ones? This is a familiar problem with subprograms and generics merely add a new dimension. Indeed, in the imagined future market for software components it is likely that packages of all sorts of generalities and performance will be available. We conclude by imagining a future conversation in our local software shop

Customer: Could I have a look at the reader-writer package you have in the window?

Server: Certainly. Would you be interested in this robust version – proof against abort? Or we have this slick version for trusty callers. Just arrived this week.

Customer: Well – it's for a cooperating system so the new one sounds good. How much is it?

Server: It's 250 Eurodollars but as it's new there is a special offer with it – a free copy of this random number generator and 10% off your next certification.

Customer: Great. Is it validated?

Server: All our products conform to the highest standards. The parameter mechanism conforms to ES98263 and it has the usual international multitasking certificate.

Customer: OK, I'll take it.

Server: Will you take it as it is or shall I instantiate it for you?

Customer: As it is please. I prefer to do my own instantiation.
                 . . .

On this fantasy note we come to the end of this book. It is hoped that the reader will have gained some general understanding of the principles of Ada as well as a lot of the detail. Further understanding will come with use and the author hopes that he has in some small way prepared the reader for the future.

Appendix 1
Reserved Words, Attributes and Pragmas

In this edition, this appendix refers to the appropriate sections of the *LRM* for full details. An implementation may define additional attributes and pragmas but not additional reserved words.

A1.1 Reserved words

A list of reserved words will be found in Section 2.9 of the *LRM*. The reserved words **delta**, **digits** and **range** are also used as attributes.

A1.2 Predefined attributes

A list of predefined attributes will be found in Annex A of the *LRM*.

A1.3 Predefined pragmas

A list of predefined pragmas will be found in Annex B of the *LRM*.

Appendix 2
Predefined Language Environment

As mentioned earlier, certain entities are predefined through their declaration in a special package STANDARD. It should not be thought that this package necessarily actually exists; it is just that the compiler behaves as if it does. Indeed, some entities notionally declared in STANDARD cannot be truly declared in Ada at all. The general effect of STANDARD is indicated by the outline specification which will be found in Annex C of the *LRM*.

That specification is, however, not complete. For example, although the type BOOLEAN can be written showing the literals FALSE and TRUE, the short circuit control forms cannot be expressed explicitly. Moreover, each further type definition introduces new overloadings of some operators. All types, except limited types, introduce new overloadings of = and /=. All scalar types and discrete one-dimensional array types introduce new overloadings of & and those with BOOLEAN components also introduce new overloadings of **and**, **or**, **xor** and **not**. Finally, all fixed point types introduce new overloadings of +, −, *, / and **abs**.

Appendix 3
Glossary

A glossary will be found in Appendix D of the *LRM*.

Appendix 4
Syntax

The following syntax rules are taken from Appendix E of the *LRM*. The rules have been rearranged to correspond to the order of introduction of the topics in this book but individual rules have not been changed.

It should be noted that the rules for the construction of lexical elements, which are under the subheading of Chapter 3, have a slightly different status to the other rules since spaces and newlines may be freely inserted between lexical elements but not within lexical elements.

The rules have been sequentially numbered for ease of reference; an index to them will be found in Section A4.2. Note that in rules 65, 81, 124, 131 and 133 the vertical bar stands for itself and is not a metasymbol.

A4.1 Syntax rules

Chapter 2

1   pragma ::= **pragma** identifier [(argument_association
                                  {, argument_association})];

2   argument_association ::= [*argument*_identifier =>] name
                          | [*argument*_identifier =>] expression

Chapter 3

3   graphic_character ::= basic_graphic_character
                       | lower_case_letter
                       | other_special_character

4   basic_graphic_character ::= upper_case_letter | digit
                             | special_character | space_character

5   basic_character ::= basic_graphic_character | format_effector

6   identifier ::= letter {[underline] letter_or_digit}

7   letter_or_digit ::= letter | digit

8   letter ::= upper_case_letter | lower_case_letter

9   numeric_literal ::= decimal_literal | based_literal

10   decimal_literal ::= integer [. integer] [exponent]

11   integer ::= digit {[underline] digit}

12   exponent ::= E [+] integer | E − integer

13   based_literal ::=
             base # based_integer [. based_integer] # [exponent]

14   base ::= integer

15   based_integer ::= extended_digit {[underline] extended_digit}

16   extended_digit ::= digit | letter

17   character_literal ::= 'graphic_character'

18   string_literal ::= "{graphic_character}"

Chapter 4

19   basic_declaration ::=
             object_declaration | number_declaration
             | type_declaration | subtype_declaration
             | subprogram_declaration | package_declaration
             | task_declaration | generic_declaration
             | exception_declaration | generic_instantiation
             | renaming_declaration | deferred_constant_declaration

20   object_declaration ::=
             identifier_list : [**constant**] subtype_indication [:= expression];
             | identifier_list : [**constant**] constrained_array_definition
                                                      [:= expression];

21   number_declaration ::=
             identifier_list : **constant** := *universal_static*_expression;

22   identifier_list ::= identifier {, identifier}

23   assignment_statement ::= *variable*_name:= expression;

24   block_statement ::= [*block*_simple_name :]
                              [**declare**
                                  declarative_part]
                              begin
                                  sequence_of_statements
                              [**exception**
                                  exception_handler
                                  {exception_handler}
                              end [*block*_simple_name];

25   type_declaration ::= full_type_declaration
                              | incomplete_type_declaration
                              | private_type_declaration

26   full_type_declaration ::=
             type identifier [discriminant_part] **is** type_definition;

27   type_definition ::=
              enumeration_type_definition | integer_type_definition
              | real_type_definition | array_type_definition
              | record_type_definition | access_type_definition
              | derived_type_definition

28   subtype_declaration ::= **subtype** identifier **is** subtype_indication;

29   subtype_indication ::= type_mark [constraint]

30   type_mark ::= *type*_name | *subtype*_name

31   constraint ::= range_constraint | floating_point_constraint
                      | fixed_point_constraint | index_constraint
                      | discriminant_constraint

32   range_constraint ::= **range** range

33   range ::= *range*_attribute | simple_expression .. simple_expression

34   enumeration_type_definition ::=
              (enumeration_literal_specification
                                {, enumeration_literal_specification})

35   enumeration_literal_specification ::= enumeration_literal

36   enumeration_literal ::= identifier | character_literal

37   name ::= simple_namc | character_literal | operator_symbol
              | indexed_component | slice | selected_component | attribute

38   simple_name ::= identifier

39   prefix ::= name | function_call

40   attribute ::= prefix ' attribute_designator

41   attribute_designator ::= simple_name
                                    [(*universal_static*_expression)]

42   expression ::= relation {**and** relation}
                      | relation {**and then** relation}
                      | relation {**or** relation}
                      | relation {**or else** relation}
                      | relation {**xor** relation}

43   relation ::=
              simple_expression [relational_operator simple_expression]
              | simple_expression [**not**] **in** range
              | simple_expression [**not**] **in** type_mark

44   simple_expression ::=
              [unary_adding_operator] term {binary_adding_operator term}

45   term ::= factor {multiplying_operator factor}

46   factor ::= primary [** primary] | **abs** primary | **not** primary

47   primary ::= numeric_literal | **null** | aggregate | string_literal | name
                | allocator | function_call | type_conversion
                | qualified_expression | (expression)

48   logical_operator ::= **and** | **or** | **xor**

49   relational_operator ::= = | /= | < | <= | > | >=

50   binary_adding_operator ::= + | − | &

51   unary_adding_operator ::= + | −

52   multiplying_operator ::= * | / | **mod** | **rem**

53   highest_precedence_operator ::= ** | **abs** | **not**

54   type_conversion ::= type_mark (expression)

55   qualified_expression ::= type_mark (expression)
                            | type_mark ' aggregate

Chapter 5

56   sequence_of_statements ::= statement {statement}

57   statement ::= {label} simple_statement
                   | {label} compound_statement

58   simple_statement ::=
                    null_statement | assignment_statement
                  | procedure_call_statement | exit_statement
                  | return_statement | goto_statement
                  | entry_call_statement | delay_statement
                  | abort_statement | raise_statement
                  | code_statement

59   compound_statement ::= if_statement | case_statement
                            | loop_statement | block_statement
                            | accept_statement | select_statement

60   label ::= <<*label*_simple_name>>

61   null_statement ::= **null**;

62   if_statement ::= **if** condition **then**
                        sequence_of_statements
                     {**elsif** condition **then**
                        sequence_of_statements}
                     [**else**
                        sequence_of_statements]
                     end if;

63   condition ::= *boolean*_expression

64   case_statement ::= **case** expression **is**
                        case_statement_alternative
                        {case_statement_alternative}
                     end case;

65   case_statement_alternative ::=
        when choice { | choice} => sequence_of_statements

66   choice ::= simple_expression | discrete_range | **others**
        | *component*_simple_name

67   discrete_range ::= *discrete*_subtype_indication | range

68   loop_statement ::= [*loop*_simple_name :]
                [iteration_scheme] **loop**
                    sequence_of_statements
             end loop [*loop*_simple_name];

69   iteration_scheme ::= **while** condition
                   | **for** loop_parameter_specification

70   loop_parameter_specification ::=
                  identifier **in** [**reverse**] discrete_range

71   exit_statement ::= **exit** [*loop*_name] [**when** condition];

72   goto_statement ::= **goto** *label*_name;

Chapter 6

73   array_type_definition ::=
        unconstrained_array_definition | constrained_array_definition

74   unconstrained_array_definition ::=
        array (index_subtype_dcfinition {, index_subtype_definition}) **of**
                  *component*_subtype_indication

75   constrained_array_definition ::=
        array index_constraint **of** *component*_subtype_indication

76   index_subtype_definition ::= type_mark **range** <>

77   index_constraint ::= (discrete_range {, discrete_range})

78   indexed_component ::= prefix (expression {, expression})

79   slice ::= prefix (discrete_range)

80   aggregate ::= (component_association {, component_association})

81   component_association ::= [choice { | choice} =>] expression

82   record_type_definition ::= **record**
                      component_list
             end record

83   component_list ::=
                component_declaration {component_declaration}
             | {component_declaration} variant_part
             | **null**;

84   component_declaration ::=
        identifier_list : component_subtype_definition [:= expression];

85   component_subtype_definition ::= subtype_indication

86   selected_component ::= prefix . selector

87   selector ::= simple_name | character_literal | operator_symbol | **all**

Chapter 7

88   subprogram_declaration ::= subprogram_specification;

89   subprogram_specification ::=
        procedure identifier [formal_part]
      | **function** designator [formal_part] **return** type_mark

90   designator ::= identifier | operator_symbol

91   operator_symbol ::= string_literal

92   formal_part ::=
                (parameter_specification {; parameter_specification})

93   parameter_specification ::=
        identifier_list : mode type_mark [:= expression]

94   mode ::= [**in**] | **in out** | **out**

95   subprogram_body ::= subprogram_specification **is**
                            [declarative_part]
                        begin
                            sequence_of_statements
                        [**exception**
                            exception_handler
                            {exception_handler}]
                        end [designator];

96   procedure_call_statement ::=
                            *procedure*_name [actual_parameter_part];

97   function_call ::= *function*_name [actual_parameter_part]

98   actual_parameter_part ::=
        (parameter_association {, parameter_association})

99   parameter_association ::=
                            [formal_parameter =>] actual_parameter

100   formal_parameter ::= *parameter*_simple_name

101   actual_parameter ::=
                            expression | *variable*_name | type_mark (*variable*_name)

102   return_statement ::= **return** [expression];

Chapter 8

103   package_declaration ::= package_specification;

104   package_specification ::= **package** identifier **is**
                                {basic_declarative_item}
                                [**private**
                                    {basic_declarative_item}]
                                end [*package*_simple_name]

105   package_body ::= **package body** *package*_simple_name **is**
                       [declarative_part]
                       [**begin**
                          sequence_of_statements
                       [**exception**
                          exception_handler
                          {exception_handler}]]
                       end [*package*_simple_name];

106   declarative_part ::=
      {basic_declarative_item} {later_declarative_item}

107   basic_declarative_item ::= basic_declaration | representation_clause
                                 | use_clause

108   later_declarative_item ::= body
                       | subprogram_declaration
                       | package_declaration
                       | task_declaration
                       | generic_declaration
                       | use_clause
                       | generic_instantiation

109   body ::= proper_body | body_stub

110   proper_body ::= subprogram_body | package_body | task_body

111   use_clause ::= **use** *package*_name {, *package*_name};

112   compilation ::= {compilation_unit}

113   compilation_unit ::= context_clause library_unit
                       | context_clause secondary_unit

114   library_unit ::= subprogram_declaration | package_declaration
                   | generic_declaration | generic_instantiation
                   | subprogram_body

115   secondary_unit ::= library_unit_body | subunit

116   library_unit_body ::= subprogram_body | package_body

117   context_clause ::= {with_clause {use_clause}}

118   with_clause ::= **with** *unit*_simple_name {, *unit*_simple_name};

119   body_stub ::= subprogram_specification **is separate**;
               | **package body** *package*_simple_name **is separate**;
               | **task body** *task*_simple_name **is separate**;

120   subunit ::= **separate** (*parent_unit*_name) proper_body

121   renaming_declaration ::=
      identifier : type_mark **renames** *object*_name;
     | identifier : **exception renames** *exception*_name;
     | **package** identifier **renames** *package*_name;
     | subprogram_specification **renames** *subprogram_or_entry*_name;

Chapter 9

122   private_type_declaration ::=
    type identifier [discriminant_part] **is** [**limited**] **private**;

123   deferred_constant_declaration ::=
    identifier_list: **constant** type_mark;

Chapter 10

124   exception_handler ::=
    when exception_choice { | exception_choice} =>
      sequence_of_statements

125   exception_choice ::= *exception*_name | **others**

126   exception_declaration ::= identifier_list : **exception**;

127   raise_statement ::= **raise** [*exception*_name];

Chapter 11

128   discriminant_part ::=
    (discriminant_specification {; discriminant_specification})

129   discriminant_specification ::=
    identifier_list : type_mark [:= expression]

130   discriminant_constraint ::=
    (discriminant_association {, discriminant_association})

131   discriminant_association ::=
    [*discriminant*_simple_name { | *discriminant*_simple_name} =>]
                           expression

132   variant_part ::= **case** *discriminant*_simple_name **is**
             variant
             {variant}
        end case;

133   variant ::= **when** choice { | choice} => component_list

134   access_type_definition ::= **access** subtype_indication

135   incomplete_type_declaration ::= **type** identifier [discriminant_part];

136   allocator ::= **new** subtype_indication | **new** qualified_expression

137   derived_type_definition ::= **new** subtype_indication

Chapter 12

138   integer_type_definition ::= range_constraint

139   real_type_definition ::=
          floating_point_constraint | fixed_point_constraint

140   floating_point_constraint ::=
          floating_accuracy_definition [range_constraint]

141   floating_accuracy_definition ::= **digits** *static*_simple_expression

142   fixed_point_constraint ::=
                        fixed_accuracy_definition [range_constraint]

143   fixed_accuracy_definition ::= **delta** *static*_simple_expression

Chapter 13

144   generic_declaration ::= generic_specification;

145   generic_specification ::=
                        generic_formal_part subprogram_specification
                        | generic_formal_part package_specification

146   generic_formal_part ::= **generic** {generic_parameter_declaration}

147   generic_parameter_declaration ::=
            identifier_list: [**in** [**out**]] type_mark [:= expression];
          | **type** identifier **is** generic_type_definition;
          | private_type_declaration
          | **with** subprogram_specification [**is** name];
          | **with** subprogram_specification [**is** <>];

148   generic_type_definition ::=
            (<>) | **range** <> | **digits** <> | **delta** <>
          | array_type_definition | access_type_definition

149   generic_instantiation ::=
            package identifier **is**
                new *generic_package*_name [generic_actual_part];
          | **procedure** identifier **is**
                new *generic_procedure*_name [generic_actual_part];
          | **function** designator **Is**
                new *generic_function*_name [generic_actual_part];

150   generic_actual_part ::=
                        (generic_association {, generic_association})

151   generic_association ::=
                [generic_formal_parameter =>] generic_actual_parameter

152   generic_formal_parameter ::=
                        *parameter*_simple_name | operator_symbol

153   generic_actual_parameter ::= expression | *variable*_name
          | *subprogram*_name | *entry*_name | type_mark

Chapter 14

154   task_declaration ::= task_specification;

155   task_specification ::= **task** [**type**] identifier [**is**
                        {entry_declaration}
                        {representation_clause}
                    end [*task*_simple_name]]

156   task_body ::= **task body** *task*_simple_name **is**
                     [declarative_part]
                 begin
                     sequence_of_statements
                 [**exception**
                     exception_handler
                     {exception_handler}]
                 end [*task*_simple_name];

157   entry_declaration ::=
          entry identifier [(discrete_range)] [formal_part];

158   entry_call_statement ::= *entry*_name [actual_parameter_part];

159   accept_statement ::=
          accept *entry*_simple_name [(entry_index)] [formal_part] [**do**
             sequence_of_statements
          end [*entry*_simple_name]];

160   entry_index ::= expression

161   delay_statement ::= **delay** simple_expression;

162   select_statement ::= selective_wait
          | conditional_entry_call | timed_entry_call

163   selective_wait ::= **select**
                          select_alternative
                      {**or**
                          select_alternative}
                      [**else**
                          sequence_of_statements]
                      end select;

164   select_alternative ::=
                          [**when** condition =>] selective_wait_alternative

165   selective_wait_alternative ::= accept_alternative
          | delay_alternative | terminate_alternative

166   accept_alternative ::= accept_statement [sequence_of_statements]

167   delay_alternative ::= delay_statement [sequence_of_statements]

168   terminate_alternative ::= **terminate**;

169   conditional_entry_call ::= **select**
                                  entry_call_statement
                                  [sequence_of_statements]
                              else
                                  sequence_of_statements
                              end_select;

170   timed_entry_call ::= **select**
                            entry_call_statement
                            [sequence_of_statements]
                        or
                            delay_alternative
                        end select;

171   abort_statement ::= **abort** *task*_name {, *task*_name};

Chapter 15

172   representation_clause ::=
                              type_representation_clause | address_clause

173   type_representation_clause ::= length_clause
       | enumeration_representation_clause
       | record_representation_clause

174   length_clause ::= **for** attribute **use** simple_expression;

175   enumeration_representation_clause ::=
       for *type*_simple_name **use** aggregate;

176   record_representation_clause ::= **for** *type*_simple_name **use**
                                     record [alignment_clause]
                                     {component_clause}
                                     end record;

177   alignment_clause ::= **at mod** *static*_simple_expression;

178   component_clause ::=
       *component*_name **at** *static*_simple_expression **range** *static*_range;

179   address_clause ::= **for** simple_name **use at** simple_expression;

180   code_statement ::= type_mark ' *record*_aggregate;

A4.2 Syntax index

This index lists the syntactic categories in alphabetical order and gives the number of their definition in the previous section.

Category	Definition number
based_integer	15
based_literal	13
basic_character	5
basic_declaration	19
basic_declarative_item	107
basic_graphic_character	4
binary_adding_operator	50
block_statement	24
body	109
body_stub	119
case_statement	64
case_statement_alternative	65
character_literal	17
choice	66
code_statement	180
compilation	112
compilation_unit	113
component_association	81
component_clause	178
component_declaration	84
component_list	83
component_subtype_definition	85
compound_statement	59
condition	63
conditional_entry_call	169
constrained_array_definition	75
constraint	31
context_clause	117
decimal_literal	10
declarative_part	106
deferred_constant_declaration	123
delay_alternative	167
delay_statement	161
derived_type_definition	137
designator	90
discrete_range	67
discriminant_association	131
discriminant_constraint	130
discriminant_part	128
discriminant_specification	129
entry_call_statement	158
entry_declaration	157
entry_index	160
enumeration_literal	36
enumeration_literal_specification	35
enumeration_type_definition	34
enumeration_representation_clause	175

Answers to Exercises

Specimen answers are given to all the exercises. In some cases they do not necessarily represent the best technique for solving a problem but merely one which uses the material introduced at that point in the discussion.

Answers 2

Exercise 2.2

1
```
package SIMPLE_MATHS is
    function SQRT(F: FLOAT) return FLOAT;
    function LOG(F: FLOAT) return FLOAT;
    function LN(F: FLOAT) return FLOAT;
    function EXP(F: FLOAT) return FLOAT;
    function SIN(F: FLOAT) return FLOAT;
    function COS(F: FLOAT) return FLOAT;
end SIMPLE_MATHS;
```

The first few lines of our program PRINT_ROOTS could now become

```
with SIMPLE_MATHS, SIMPLE_IO;
procedure PRINT_ROOTS is
    use SIMPLE_MATHS, SIMPLE_IO;
```

Exercise 2.7

1
```
with TEXT_IO, ETC;
use TEXT_IO, ETC;
procedure TEN_TIMES_TABLE is
    use INT_IO;
    ROW, COLUMN: INTEGER;
begin
    ROW:= 1;
    loop
        COLUMN:= 1;
        loop
            PUT(ROW * COLUMN, 5);
            exit when COLUMN = 10;
            COLUMN:= COLUMN+1;
        end loop;
        NEW_LINE;
```

```
            exit when ROW = 10;
            ROW:= ROW+1;
          end loop;
      end TEN_TIMES_TABLE;

2     with TEXT_IO, ETC;
      use TEXT_IO, ETC;
      procedure TABLE_OF_SQUARE_ROOTS is
          use INT_IO, REAL_IO, REAL_MATHS;
          N: INTEGER;
          LAST_N: INTEGER;
          TAB: COUNT;
      begin
          TAB:= 10;
          PUT("What is the largest value please? "); GET(LAST_N);
          NEW_LINE(2);
          PUT("Number"); SET_COL(TAB); PUT("Square root");
          NEW_LINE(2);
          N:= 1;
          loop
              PUT(N, 4); SET_COL(TAB); PUT(SQRT(REAL(N)), 3, 5, 0);
              NEW_LINE;
              exit when N = LAST_N;
              N:= N+1;
          end loop;
      end TABLE_OF_SQUARE_ROOTS;
```

Answers 3

Exercise 3.3

1   The following are not legal identifiers

    (b)   contains &
    (c)   contains hyphens not underlines
    (e)   adjacent underlines
    (f)   does not start with a letter
    (g)   trailing underline
    (h)   this is two legal identifiers
    (i)   this is legal – but it is a reserved word

Exercise 3.4

1   (a)   legal – real
    (b)   illegal – no digit before point
    (c)   legal – integer
    (d)   illegal – integer with negative exponent
    (e)   illegal – closing # missing
    (f)   legal – real
    (g)   illegal – C not a digit of base 12
    (h)   illegal – no number before exponent
    (i)   legal – integer – case of letter immaterial
    (j)   legal – integer
    (k)   illegal – underline at start of exponent
    (l)   illegal – integer with negative exponent

2   (a) $224 = 14 \times 16$
    (b) $6144 = 3 \times 2^{11}$

    (c)   4095.0
    (d)   4095.0

3   (a)   32 ways

               41, 2#101001#, 3#1112#, ...
                       10#41#, ... 16#29#
               41E0, 2#101001#E0, ... 16#29#E0

    (b)   40 ways. As for example (a) plus, since 150 is not prime but $2 \times 3 \times 5^2 = 150$ also

               2#1001011#E1
               3#1212#E1
               5#110#E1
               5#11#E2
               6#41#E1
               10#15#E1
               15#A#E1

           and of course

               15E1

Exercise 3.5

1   (a)   7
    (b)   1
    (c)   1
    (d)   12

2   (a)   This has 3 units
               the identifier   delay
               the literal   2.0
               the single symbol   ;

    (b)   This has 4 units
               the identifier   delay2
               the single symbol   .
               the literal   0
               the single symbol   ;

    Case (a) is a legal delay statement, (b) is just a mess.

Answers 4

Exercise 4.1

1   R: REAL:= 1.0;

2   ZERO: **constant** REAL:= 0.0;
     ONE: **constant** REAL:= 1.0;

     but better to write number declarations

     ZERO: **constant**:= 0.0;
     ONE: **constant**:= 1.0;

3   (a)   **var** is illegal – this is Ada not Pascal
    (b)   terminating semicolon is missing
    (c)   a constant declaration must have an initial value
    (d)   no multiple assignment – this is Ada not Algol
    (e)   nothing – assuming M and N are of integer type
    (f)   2PI is not a legal identifier

Exercise 4.2

1   There are four errors

    (1)   semicolon missing after declaration of J, K
    (2)   K used before a value has been assigned to it
    (3)   = instead of := in declaration of P
    (4)   Q not declared and initialized

Exercise 4.4

1   This analysis assumes that the values of all variables originally satisfy their constraints; this will be the case if the program is not erroneous.

    (a)   the ranges of I and J are identical so no checks are required and consequently CONSTRAINT_ERROR cannot be raised,

    (b)   the range of J is a subset of that of K and again CONSTRAINT_ERROR cannot be raised,

    (c)   in this case a check is required since if K > 10 it cannot be assigned to J in which case CONSTRAINT_ERROR will be raised.

Exercise 4.5

1
(a)	-105	(d)	-3	(g)	-1
(b)	-3	(e)	-3	(h)	2
(c)	0	(f)	illegal		

2   All variables are real

    (a)   M*R**2
    (b)   B**2 − 4.0*A*C
    (c)   (4.0/3.0)*PI*R**3   −− brackets not necessary
    (d)   (P*PI*A**4)/(8.0*L*ETA)   −− brackets are necessary

Exercise 4.6

1   (a)   SAT
    (b)   SAT   note that SUCC applies to the base type
    (c)   2

2   (a)   **type** RAINBOW **is** (RED, ORANGE, YELLOW, GREEN, BLUE, INDIGO, VIOLET);
    (b)   **type** FRUIT **is** (APPLE, BANANA, ORANGE, PEAR);

3   GROOM'VAL ((N−1) **mod** 8)

or perhaps better

GROOM'VAL ((N−1) **mod** (GROOM'POS(GROOM'LAST) + 1))

4   D:= DAY'VAL((DAY'POS(D) + N−1) **mod** 7);

5   If X and Y are both overloaded literals then X < Y will be ambiguous. We would have to use qualification such as T'(X) < T'(Y).

Exercise 4.7

1   T: **constant** BOOLEAN:= TRUE;
    F: **constant** BOOLEAN:= FALSE;

2   The values are TRUE and FALSE, not T or F which are the names of constants.

    (a)   FALSE   (c)   TRUE   (e)   FALSE
    (b)   TRUE   (d)   TRUE

3   The expression is always TRUE. The predefined operators **xor** and /= operating on BOOLEAN values are the same.

Exercise 4.9

1   All variables are real except for N in example (c) which is integer.
     (a)   2.0*PI*SQRT(L/G)
     (b)   M_0/SQRT(1.0 − (V/C)**2)
     (c)   SQRT(2.0*PI*REAL(N))*(REAL(N)/E)**N

2   SQRT(2.0*PI*X)*EXP(X*LN(X)−X)

Answers 5

Exercise 5.1

1
```
declare
    END_OF_MONTH: INTEGER;
begin
    if MONTH = SEP or MONTH = APR or MONTH = JUN or MONTH = NOV then
        END_OF_MONTH:= 30;
    elsif MONTH = FEB then
        if YEAR mod 4 = 0 then
            END_OF_MONTH:= 29;
        else
            END_OF_MONTH:= 28;
        end if;
    else
        END_OF_MONTH:= 31;
    end if;
    if DAY /= END_OF_MONTH then
        DAY:= DAY+1;
    else
        DAY:= 1;
        if MONTH /= DEC then
            MONTH:= MONTH_NAME'SUCC(MONTH);
        else
            MONTH:= JAN;
            YEAR:= YEAR+1;
        end if;
    end if;
end;
```
If today is 31 DEC 2099 then CONSTRAINT_ERROR will be raised on attempting to assign 2100 to YEAR. Note that the range 1901 .. 2099 simplifies the leap year calculation.

2
```
if X < Y then
    declare
        T: REAL:= X;
    begin
        X:= Y;    Y:= T;
    end;
end if;
```

Exercise 5.2

1
```
declare
    END_OF_MONTH: INTEGER;
begin
    case MONTH is
        when SEP | APR | JUN | NOV =>
            END_OF_MONTH:= 30;
```

```
        when FEB =>
            if YEAR mod 4 = 0 then
                END_OF_MONTH:= 29;
            else
                END_OF_MONTH:= 28;
            end if;
        when others =>
            END_OF_MONTH:= 31;
    end case;
    -- then as before
        ...
end;
```

2   ```
    subtype WINTER is MONTH_NAME range JAN .. MAR;
    subtype SPRING is MONTH_NAME range APR .. JUN;
    subtype SUMMER is MONTH_NAME range JUL .. SEP;
    subtype AUTUMN is MONTH_NAME range OCT .. DEC;

        ...
    case M is
        when WINTER => DIG;
        when SPRING => SOW;
        when SUMMER => TEND;
        when AUTUMN => HARVEST;
    end case;
    ```

Note that if we wished to consider winter as December to February then we could not declare a suitable subtype.

3    ```
    case D is
        when 1 .. 10 => GORGE;
        when 11 .. 20 => SUBSIST;
        when others => STARVE;
    end case;
    ```

We cannot write 21 .. END_OF_MONTH because it is not a static range. In fact **others** covers all values of type INTEGER because although D is constrained, nevertheless the constraints are not static.

Exercise 5.3

1   ```
    declare
        SUM: INTEGER:= 0;
        I: INTEGER;
    begin
        loop
            GET(I);
            exit when I < 0;
            SUM:= SUM+I;
        end loop;
    end;
    ```

2    ```
    declare
        COPY: INTEGER:= N;
        COUNT: INTEGER:= 0;
    begin
        while COPY mod 2 = 0 loop
            COPY:= COPY/2;
            COUNT:= COUNT+1;
        end loop;
            ...
    end;
    ```

3   **declare**
            G: REAL:= −LN(REAL(N));
        begin
            for P **in** 1 .. N **loop**
                G:= G+1.0/REAL(P);
            end loop;
            ...
        end;

Exercise 5.4

1   **for** I **in** 1 .. N **loop**
            for J **in** 1 .. M **loop**
                if condition_OK **then**
                    I_VALUE:= I;
                    J_VALUE:= J;
                    goto SEARCH;
                end if;
            end loop;
        end loop;

        <<SEARCH>>

This is not such a good solution because we have no guarantee that there may not be other places in the program from where a goto statement leads to the label. It is also a silly name for the label anyway – it ought to be FOUND!

Answers 6

Exercise 6.1

1   **declare**
            F: **array** (0 .. N) **of** INTEGER;
        begin
            F(0):= 0; F(1):= 1;
            for I **in** 2 .. F'LAST **loop**
                F(I):= F(I−1)+F(I−2);
            end loop;
            ...
        end;

2   **declare**
            MAXI: INTEGER:= A'FIRST(1);
            MAXJ: INTEGER:= A'FIRST(2);
            MAX: REAL:= A(MAXI, MAXJ);
        begin
            for I **in** A'RANGE(1) **loop**
                for J **in** A'RANGE(2) **loop**
                    if A(I, J) > MAX **then**
                        MAX:= A(I, J);
                        MAXI:= I;
                        MAXJ:= J;
                    end if;
                end loop;
            end loop;
            −− MAXI, MAXJ now contain the result
        end;

3   **declare**
　　　　DAYS_IN_MONTH: **array** (MONTH_NAME) **of** INTEGER
　　　　　　:= (31, 28, 31, 30, 31, 30, 31, 31, 30, 31, 30, 31);
　　　　END_OF_MONTH: INTEGER;
　　begin
　　　　if YEAR **mod** 4 = 0 **then**
　　　　　　DAYS_IN_MONTH(FEB):= 29;
　　　　end if;
　　　　END_OF_MONTH:= DAYS_IN_MONTH(MONTH);

　　　　－－ then as Exercise 5.1(1)

　　end;

4   YESTERDAY: **constant array** (DAY) **of** DAY
　　　　:= (SUN, MON, TUE, WED, THU, FRI, SAT);

5   BOR: **constant array** (BOOLEAN, BOOLEAN) **of** BOOLEAN
　　　　:= ((FALSE, TRUE), (TRUE, TRUE));

6   UNIT: **constant array** (1 .. 3, 1 .. 3) **of** REAL
　　　　:= ((1.0, 0.0, 0.0),
　　　　　　(0.0, 1.0, 0.0),
　　　　　　(0.0, 0.0, 1.0));

Exercise 6.2

1   **type** BBB **is array** (BOOLEAN, BOOLEAN) **of** BOOLEAN;

2   **type** RING5_TABLE **is array** (RING5, RING5) **of** RING5;

　　ADD: **constant** RING5_TABLE
　　　　:= ((0, 1, 2, 3, 4),
　　　　　　(1, 2, 3, 4, 0),
　　　　　　(2, 3, 4, 0, 1),
　　　　　　(3, 4, 0, 1, 2),
　　　　　　(4, 0, 1, 2, 3));

　　MULT: **constant** RING5_TABLE
　　　　:= ((0, 0, 0, 0, 0),
　　　　　　(0, 1, 2, 3, 4),
　　　　　　(0, 2, 4, 1, 3),
　　　　　　(0, 3, 1, 4, 2),
　　　　　　(0, 4, 3, 2, 1));

　　A, B, C, D: RING5;
　　...
　　D:= MULT(ADD(A, B), C));

Exercise 6.3

1   DAYS_IN_MONTH: **array** (MONTH_NAME) **of** INTEGER
　　　　:= MONTH_NAME'(SEP | APR | JUN | NOV => 30, FEB => 28, **others** => 31);

2   ZERO: **constant** MATRIX:= (1 .. N => (1 .. N => 0.0));

3   This cannot be done with the material at our disposal at the moment. See Exercise 7.1(**6**).

4   **type** MOLECULE **is** (METHANOL, ETHANOL, PROPANOL, BUTANOL);
　　type ATOM **is** (H, C, O);

```
ALCOHOL: constant array (MOLECULE, ATOM) of INTEGER
     := (METHANOL => (H =>4, C =>1, O =>1),
         ETHANOL   => (    6,     2,     1),
         PROPANOL  => (    8,     3,     1),
         BUTANOL   => (   10,     4,     1));
```

Note the danger in the above. We have used named notation in the first inner aggregate to act as a sort of heading but omitted it in the others to avoid clutter. However, if we had written H, C and O in other than positional order then it would have been very confusing because the positional aggregates would not have had the meaning suggested by the heading.

Exercise 6.4

1
```
ROMAN_TO_INTEGER: constant array (ROMAN_DIGIT) of INTEGER
         := (1, 5, 10, 50, 100, 500, 1000);
```

2
```
declare
    V: INTEGER:= 0;
begin
    for I in R'RANGE loop
        if I /= R'LAST and then
            ROMAN_TO_INTEGER(R(I)) < ROMAN_TO_INTEGER(R(I+1)) then
            V:= V − ROMAN_TO_INTEGER(R(I));
        else
            V:= V + ROMAN_TO_INTEGER(R(I));
        end if;
    end loop;
    ...
end;
```

Note the use of **and then** to avoid attempting to access R(I+1) when I = R'LAST.

Exercise 6.5

1 `AOA(1 .. 2):= (AOA(2), AOA(1));`

2
```
FARMYARD: STRING_3_ARRAY(1 .. 6)
    := ("pig", "oat", "dog", "cow", "rat", "ass");
...
FARMYARD(4)(1):= 's';
```

3
```
if R'LAST >= 2 and then R(R'LAST−1 .. R'LAST) = "IV" then
    R(R'LAST−1 .. R'LAST):= "VI";
end if;
```

Exercise 6.6

1 WHITE, BLUE, YELLOW, GREEN, RED, PURPLE, ORANGE, BLACK

2 (a)   BLACK   (b)   GREEN   (c)   RED

3
```
not (TRUE xor TRUE) = TRUE
not (TRUE xor FALSE) = FALSE
```

the result follows.

4 An aggregate of length one must be named.

5 "123", "ABC", "Abc", "aBc", "abC", "abc"

6 (a)   1   (b)   5

We note therefore that & like **and**, **or** and **xor** is not strictly commutative.

Exercise 6.7

1
```
declare
    DAYS_IN_MONTH: array (MONTH_NAME) of INTEGER
        := MONTH_NAME ' (SEP | APR | JUN | NOV => 30, FEB => 28, others => 31);
    END_OF_MONTH: INTEGER;
begin
    if D.YEAR mod 4 = 0 then
        DAYS_IN_MONTH(FEB):= 29;
    end if;
    END_OF_MONTH:= DAYS_IN_MONTH(D.MONTH);
    if D.DAY /= END_OF_MONTH then
        D.DAY:= D.DAY+1;
    else
        D.DAY:= 1;
        if D.MONTH /= DEC then
            D.MONTH:= MONTH_NAME ' SUCC(D.MONTH);
        else
            D.MONTH:= JAN;
            D.YEAR:= D.YEAR+1;
        end if;
    end if;
end;
```

2
```
C1, C2, C3: COMPLEX;
(a)    C3:= (C1.RL+C2.RL, C1.IM+C2.IM);
(b)    C3:= (C1.RL*C2.RL – C1.IM*C2.IM, C1.RL*C2.IM + C1.IM*C2.RL);
```

3
```
declare
    INDEX: INTEGER;
begin
    for I in PEOPLE ' RANGE loop
        if PEOPLE(I).BIRTH.YEAR >= 1950 then
            INDEX:= I;
            exit;
        end if;
    end loop;
    -- we assume that there is such a person
end;
```

Answers 7

Exercise 7.1

1
```
function EVEN(X: INTEGER) return BOOLEAN is
begin
    return X mod 2 = 0;
end EVEN;
```

2
```
function FACTORIAL(N: NATURAL) return POSITIVE is
begin
    if N = 0 then
        return 1;
    else
        return N*FACTORIAL(N-1);
    end if;
end FACTORIAL;
```

3
```
function OUTER(A, B: VECTOR) return MATRIX is
    C: MATRIX(A ' RANGE, B ' RANGE);
```

```ada
begin
    for I in A'RANGE loop
        for J in B'RANGE loop
            C(I, J):= A(I)*B(J);
        end loop;
    end loop;
    return C;
end OUTER;
```

4
```ada
type PRIMARY_ARRAY is array (INTEGER range <>) of PRIMARY;

function MAKE_COLOUR(P: PRIMARY_ARRAY) return COLOUR is
    C: COLOUR:= (F, F, F);
begin
    for I in P'RANGE loop
        C(P(I)):= T;
    end loop;
    return C;
end MAKE_COLOUR;
```

Note that multiple values are allowed so that

```ada
MAKE_COLOUR((R, R, R)) = RED
```

5
```ada
function VALUE(R: ROMAN_NUMBER) return INTEGER is
    V: INTEGER:= 0;
begin
    for I in R'RANGE loop
        if I /= R'LAST and then
            ROMAN_TO_INTEGER(R(I)) < ROMAN_TO_INTEGER(R(I+1)) then
            V:= V − ROMAN_TO_INTEGER(R(I));
        else
            V:− V + ROMAN_TO_INTEGER(R(I));
        end if;
    end loop;
    return V;
end VALUE;
```

6
```ada
function MAKE_UNIT(N: NATURAL) return MATRIX is
    M: MATRIX(1 .. N, 1 .. N);
begin
    for I in 1 .. N loop
        for J in 1 .. N loop
            if I = J then
                M(I, J):= 1.0;
            else
                M(I, J):= 0.0;
            end if;
        end loop;
    end loop;
    return M;
end MAKE_UNIT;
```

We can then declare

```ada
UNIT: constant MATRIX:= MAKE_UNIT(N);
```

7
```ada
function GCD(X, Y: NATURAL) return NATURAL is
begin
    if Y = 0 then
        return X;
    else
        return GCD(Y, X mod Y);
    end if;
end GCD;
```

or

```
function GCD(X, Y: NATURAL) return NATURAL is
    XX: INTEGER:= X;
    YY: INTEGER:= Y;
    ZZ: INTEGER;
begin
    while YY /= 0 loop
        ZZ:= XX mod YY;
        XX:= YY;
        YY:= ZZ;
    end loop;
    return XX;
end GCD;
```

Note that X and Y have to be copied because formal parameters behave as constants.

8
```
function INNER(A, B: VECTOR) return REAL is
    RESULT: REAL:= 0.0;
begin
    if A'LENGTH /= B'LENGTH then
        raise CONSTRAINT_ERROR;
    end if;
    for I in A'RANGE loop
        RESULT:= RESULT + A(I)*B(I+B'FIRST-A'FIRST);
    end loop;
    return RESULT;
end INNER;
```

Exercise 7.2

1
```
function "<" (X, Y: ROMAN_NUMBER) return BOOLEAN is
begin
    return VALUE(X) < VALUE(Y);
end "<";
```

2
```
function "+" (X, Y: COMPLEX) return COMPLEX is
begin
    return (X.RL + Y.RL, X.IM + Y.IM);
end "+";

function "*" (X, Y: COMPLEX) return COMPLEX is
begin
    return (X.RL*Y.RL - X.IM*Y.IM, X.RL*Y.IM + X.IM*Y.RL);
end "*";
```

3
```
function "<" (P: PRIMARY; C: COLOUR) return BOOLEAN is
begin
    return C(P);
end "<";
```

4
```
function "<=" (X, Y: COLOUR) return BOOLEAN is
begin
    return (X and Y) = X;
end "<=";
```

5
```
function "<" (X, Y: DATE) return BOOLEAN is
begin
    if X.YEAR /= Y.YEAR then
        return X.YEAR < Y.YEAR;
    elsif X.MONTH /= Y.MONTH then
```

```
          return X.MONTH < Y.MONTH;
      else
          return X.DAY < Y.DAY;
      end if;
  end "<";
```

Exercise 7.3

1
```
    procedure SWAP(X, Y: in out REAL) is
        T: REAL;
    begin
        T:= X;  X:= Y;  Y:= T;
    end SWAP;
```

2
```
    procedure REV(X: in out VECTOR) is
        R: VECTOR(X'RANGE);
    begin
        for I in X'RANGE loop
            R(I):= X(X'FIRST + X'LAST – I);
        end loop;
        X:= R;
    end REV;
```

or maybe

```
    procedure REV(X: in out VECTOR) is
    begin
        for I in X'FIRST .. X'FIRST + X'LENGTH/2 – 1 loop
            SWAP(X(I), X(X'FIRST + X'LAST – I));
        end loop;
    end REV;
```

This procedure can be applied to an array R of type ROW by

REV(VECTOR(R));

3   The fragment is erroneous because the outcome depends upon whether the
parameter is passed by copy or by reference. If it is copied then A(1) ends up as
2.0; if it is passed by reference then A(1) ends up as 4.0.

4

		calling mode (actual)		
		in	in out	out
called mode (formal)	in	✓	✓	✗
	in out	✗	✓	✗
	out	✗	✓	✓

Exercise 7.4

1
```
    function ADD(X: INTEGER; Y: INTEGER:= 1) return INTEGER is
    begin
        return X + Y;
    end ADD;
```

The following six calls are equivalent

```
ADD(N)
ADD(N, 1)
ADD(X => N, Y => 1)
```

```
ADD(X => N)
ADD(N, Y => 1)
ADD(Y => 1, X => N)
```

2   **function** FAVOURITE_SPIRIT **return** SPIRIT **is**
begin
    case TODAY **is**
        when MON .. FRI => **return** GIN;
        when SAT | SUN => **return** VODKA;
    end case;
end FAVOURITE_SPIRIT;

    procedure DRY_MARTINI(BASE: SPIRIT:= FAVOURITE_SPIRIT;
                    HOW: STYLE:= ON_THE_ROCKS;
                    PLUS: TRIMMING:= OLIVE);

This example illustrates that defaults are evaluated each time they are required and can therefore be changed from time to time.

Exercise 7.5

1   The named form of call

SELL(C => JERSEY);

is unambiguous since the formal parameter names are different.

Answers 8

Exercise 8.1

1   **package** RANDOM **is**
    MODULUS: **constant**:= 2**13;
    subtype SMALL **is** INTEGER **range** 0 .. MODULUS;
    procedure INIT(SEED: SMALL);
    function NEXT **return** SMALL;
end;

package body RANDOM **is**
    MULTIPLIER: **constant**:= 5**5;
    X: SMALL;

    procedure INIT(SEED: SMALL) **is**
    begin
        X:= SEED;
    end INIT;

    function NEXT **return** SMALL **is**
    begin
        X:= X*MULTIPLIER **mod** MODULUS;
        return X;
    end NEXT;

end RANDOM;

2   **package** COMPLEX_NUMBERS **is**
    type COMPLEX **is**
        record
            RL, IM: REAL:= 0.0;
        end record;

    I: **constant** COMPLEX:= (0.0, 1.0);

    function "+" (X: COMPLEX) **return** COMPLEX; -- unary +

```ada
    function "−" (X: COMPLEX) return COMPLEX;  −− unary −

    function "+" (X, Y: COMPLEX) return COMPLEX;
    function "−" (X, Y: COMPLEX) return COMPLEX;
    function "∗" (X, Y: COMPLEX) return COMPLEX;
    function "/" (X, Y: COMPLEX) return COMPLEX;
end;

package body COMPLEX_NUMBERS is

    function "+" (X: COMPLEX) return COMPLEX is
    begin
        return X;
    end "+";

    function "−" (X: COMPLEX) return COMPLEX is
    begin
        return (−X.RL, −X.IM);
    end "+";

    function "+" (X, Y: COMPLEX) return COMPLEX is
    begin
        return (X.RL + Y.RL, X.IM + Y.IM);
    end "+";

    function "−" (X, Y: COMPLEX) return COMPLEX is
    begin
        return (X.RL − Y.RL, X.IM − Y.IM);
    end "−";

    function "∗" (X, Y: COMPLEX) return COMPLEX is
    begin
        return (X.RL∗Y.RL − X.IM∗Y.IM, X.RL∗Y.IM + X.IM∗Y.RL);
    end "∗";

    funotion "/" (X, Y: COMPLEX) return COMPLEX is
        D: REAL:= Y.RL∗∗2+Y.IM∗∗2;
    begin
        return ((X.RL∗Y.RL + X.IM∗Y.IM)/D,
                (X.IM∗Y.RL − X.RL∗Y.IM)/D);
    end "/";

end COMPLEX_NUMBERS;
```

Exercise 8.2

1

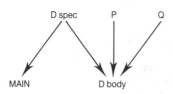

There are 18 different possible orders of compilation.

Exercise 8.3

1

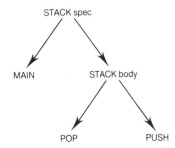

There are 8 different possible orders of compilation.

Exercise 8.5

1   **function** MONDAY **return** DIURNAL.DAY **renames** DIURNAL.MON;

2   This cannot be done because NEXT_WORK_DAY is of an anonymous type.

3   PETS: STRING_3_ARRAY **renames** FARMYARD(2 .. 3);

Note that the bounds of PETS are 2 and 3.

Answers 9

Exercise 9.1

1   Inside the package body we could write

```
function "*" (X: REAL; Y: COMPLEX) return COMPLEX is
begin
    return (X*Y.RL, X*Y.IM);
end "*";
```

but outside we could only write

```
function "*" (X: REAL; Y: COMPLEX) return COMPLEX is
    use COMPLEX_NUMBERS;
begin
    return CONS(X, 0.0)*Y;
end "*";
```

and similarly with the operands interchanged.

2
```
declare
    C, D: COMPLEX_NUMBERS.COMPLEX;
    R, S: REAL;
begin
    C:= COMPLEX_NUMBERS.CONS(1.5, −6.0);
    D:= COMPLEX_NUMBERS."+" (C, COMPLEX_NUMBERS.I);
    R:= COMPLEX_NUMBERS.RL_PART(D) + 6.0;
    ...
end;
```

3
```
package RATIONAL_NUMBERS is
    type RATIONAL is private;
    function "+" (X: RATIONAL) return RATIONAL; −− unary +
    function "−" (X: RATIONAL) return RATIONAL; −− unary −
    function "+" (X, Y: RATIONAL) return RATIONAL;
    function "−" (X, Y: RATIONAL) return RATIONAL;
    function "*" (X, Y: RATIONAL) return RATIONAL;
    function "/" (X, Y: RATIONAL) return RATIONAL;
```

```
    function "/" (X: INTEGER; Y: POSITIVE) return RATIONAL;
    function NUMERATOR(R: RATIONAL) return INTEGER;
    function DENOMINATOR(R: RATIONAL) return POSITIVE;
private
    type RATIONAL is
        record
            NUM: INTEGER:= 0;  -- numerator
            DEN: POSITIVE:= 1;  -- denominator
        end record;
end;

package body RATIONAL_NUMBERS is

    function NORMAL(R: RATIONAL) return RATIONAL is
        -- cancel common factors
        G: POSITIVE:= GCD(abs R.NUM, R.DEN);
    begin
        return (R.NUM/G, R.DEN/G);
    end NORMAL;

    function "+" (X: RATIONAL) return RATIONAL is
    begin
        return X;
    end "+";

    function "-" (X: RATIONAL) return RATIONAL is
    begin
        return (-X.NUM, X.DEN);
    end "-";

    function "+" (X, Y: RATIONAL) return RATIONAL is
    begin
        return NORMAL((X.NUM*Y.DEN + Y.NUM*X.DEN, X.DEN*Y.DEN));
    end "+";

    function "-" (X, Y: RATIONAL) return RATIONAL is
    begin
        return NORMAL((X.NUM*Y.DEN - Y.NUM*X.DEN, X.DEN*Y.DEN));
    end "-";

    function "*" (X, Y: RATIONAL) return RATIONAL is
    begin
        return NORMAL((X.NUM*Y.NUM, X.DEN*Y.DEN));
    end "*";

    function "/" (X, Y: RATIONAL) return RATIONAL is
    begin
        return NORMAL((X.NUM*Y.DEN, X.DEN*Y.NUM));
    end "/";

    function "/" (X: INTEGER; Y: POSITIVE) return RATIONAL is
    begin
        return NORMAL((X, Y));
    end "/";

    function NUMERATOR(R: RATIONAL) return INTEGER is
    begin
        return R.NUM;
    end NUMERATOR;

    function DENOMINATOR(R: RATIONAL) return POSITIVE is
    begin
        return R.DEN;
```

```
  end DENOMINATOR;

end RATIONAL_NUMBERS;
```

4   Although the parameter base types are both INTEGER and therefore the same as for predefined integer division, nevertheless the result types are different. The result types are considered in the hiding rules for functions. See Section 7.5.

Exercise 9.2

1
```
package STACKS is
    type STACK is limited private;
    EMPTY: constant STACK;

    ...
private
    ...
    EMPTY: constant STACK:= ((1 .. MAX => 0), 0);
end;
```

Note that EMPTY has to be initialized because it is a **constant** despite the fact that TOP which is the only component whose value is of interest is automatically initialized anyway.

2
```
function EMPTY(S: STACK) return BOOLEAN is
begin
    return S.TOP = 0;
end EMPTY;

function FULL(S: STACK) return BOOLEAN is
begin
    return S.TOP = MAX;
end FULL;
```

3
```
function "=" (S, T: STACK) return BOOLEAN is
begin
    return S.S(1 .. S.TOP) = T.S(1 .. T.TOP);
end "=";
```

4
```
function "=" (A, B: STACK_ARRAY) return BOOLEAN is
begin
    if A'LENGTH /= B'LENGTH then
        return FALSE;
    end if;
    for I in A'RANGE loop
        if A(I) /= B(I + B'FIRST - A'FIRST) then
            return FALSE;
        end if;
    end loop;
    return TRUE;
end "=";
```

Note that this uses the redefined = (via /=) applying to the type STACK. This pattern of definition of array equality clearly applies to any type. Beware that we cannot use slice comparison (as in the previous answer) because that always uses predefined equality – surprise, surprise!

5
```
procedure ASSIGN(S: in STACK; T: out STACK) is
begin
    T.TOP:= S.TOP;
    for I in 1 .. S.TOP loop
        T.S(I):= S.S(I);
    end loop;
end ASSIGN;
```

The loop could be replaced by the slice assignment

```
T.S(1 .. S.TOP):= S.S(1 .. S.TOP);
```

6
```
package STACKS is
   type STACK is private;
   procedure PUSH(S: in out STACK; X: in INTEGER);
   procedure POP(S: in out STACK; X: out INTEGER);
private
   MAX: constant:= 100;
   DUMMY: constant:= 0;
   type INTEGER_VECTOR is array (INTEGER range <>) of INTEGER;
   type STACK is
      record
         S: INTEGER_VECTOR(1 .. MAX):= (1 .. MAX => DUMMY);
         TOP: INTEGER range 0 .. MAX:= 0;
      end record;
end;

package body STACKS is
   procedure PUSH(S: in out STACK; X: in INTEGER) is
   begin
      S.TOP:= S.TOP+1;
      S.S(S.TOP):= X;
   end;

   procedure POP(S: in out STACK; X: out INTEGER) is
   begin
      X:= S.S(S.TOP);
      S.S(S.TOP):= DUMMY;
      S.TOP:- S.TOP-1;
   end;
end STACKS;
```

Note the use of DUMMY as default value for unused components of the stack.

Exercise 9.3

1
```
private
   MAX: constant:= 1000;  -- no of accounts
   subtype KEY_CODE is INTEGER range 0 .. MAX;
   type KEY is
      record
         CODE: KEY_CODE:= 0;
      end record;
end;

package body BANK is
   BALANCE: array (KEY_CODE range 1 .. KEY_CODE'LAST) of MONEY:=
                                                    (others => 0);
   FREE: array (KEY_CODE range 1 .. KEY_CODE'LAST) of BOOLEAN:=
                                                    (others => TRUE);

   function VALID(K: KEY) return BOOLEAN is
   begin
      return K.CODE /= 0;
   end VALID;

   procedure OPEN_ACCOUNT(K: in out KEY; M: in MONEY) is
   begin
      if K.CODE = 0 then
         for I in FREE'RANGE loop
```

```
                    if FREE(I) then
                        FREE(I):= FALSE;
                        BALANCE(I):= M;
                        K.CODE:= I;
                        return;
                    end if;
                end loop;
            end if;
        end OPEN_ACCOUNT;

        procedure CLOSE_ACCOUNT(K: in out KEY; M: out MONEY) is
        begin
            if VALID(K) then
                M:= BALANCE(K.CODE);
                FREE(K.CODE):= TRUE;
                K.CODE:= 0;
            end if;
        end CLOSE_ACCOUNT;

        procedure DEPOSIT(K: in KEY; M: in MONEY) is
        begin
            if VALID(K) then
                BALANCE(K.CODE):= BALANCE(K.CODE)+M;
            end if;
        end DEPOSIT;

        procedure WITHDRAW(K: in out KEY; M: in out MONEY) is
        begin
            if VALID(K) then
                if M > BALANCE(K.CODE) then
                    CLOSE_ACCOUNT(K, M);
                else
                    BALANCE(K.CODE):= BALANCE(K.CODE)-M;
                end if;
            end if;
        end WITHDRAW;

        function STATEMENT(K: KEY) return MONEY is
        begin
            if VALID(K) then
                return BALANCE(K.CODE);
            end if;
        end STATEMENT;

end BANK;
```

Various alternative formulations are possible. It might be neater to declare a record type representing an account containing the two components FREE and BALANCE.

Note that the function STATEMENT will raise PROGRAM_ERROR if the key is not valid. Alternatively we could return a dummy value of zero but it might be better to raise our own exception as described in the next chapter.

2   An alternative formulation which represents the home savings box could be that where the limited private type is given by

```
type BOX is
    record
        CODE: BOX_CODE:= 0;
        BALANCE: MONEY;
    end record;
```

In this case the money is kept in the variable declared by the user. The bank only knows which boxes have been issued but does not know how much is in a particular box. The details are left to the reader.

3   Since the parameter is of a private type, it is not defined whether the parameter is passed by copy or by reference. If it is passed by copy then the call of ACTION will succeed whereas if it is passed by reference it will not. The program is therefore erroneous. However, this does not seem a very satisfactory answer and might be considered a loophole in the design of Ada.

A slight improvement would be for ACTION to check (via VALID say) whether the passed key is free or not by reference to the array FREE but this would not be any protection once the key were reissued. However, a foolproof solution can be devised using access types which will be described in Chapter 11.

4   He is thwarted because of the rule mentioned in the previous section that, outside the defining package, a procedure cannot be declared having an **out** parameter of a limited type. The purpose of this rule is precisely to prevent just this kind of violation of privacy. (As a minor aside note that in any case the parameter may be passed by reference.)

Answers 10

Exercise 10.1

1
```
procedure QUADRATIC(A, B, C: in REAL;
                    ROOT_1, ROOT_2: out REAL; OK: out BOOLEAN) is
    D: constant REAL:= B**2 − 4.0*A*C;
begin
    ROOT_1:= (−B+SQRT(D))/(2.0*A);
    ROOT_2:= (−B−SQRT(D))/(2.0*A);
    OK:= TRUE;
exception
    when NUMERIC_ERROR =>
        OK:= FALSE;
end QUADRATIC;
```

2
```
function FACTORIAL(N: INTEGER) return INTEGER is

    function SLAVE(N: NATURAL) return POSITIVE is
    begin
        if N = 0 then
            return 1;
        else
            return N*SLAVE(N−1);
        end if;
    end SLAVE;

begin
    return SLAVE(N);
exception
    when CONSTRAINT_ERROR | STORAGE_ERROR | NUMERIC_ERROR =>
        return −1;
end FACTORIAL;
```

Exercise 10.2

1
```
package RANDOM is
    BAD: exception;
    MODULUS: constant:= 2**13;
```

```
        subtype SMALL is INTEGER range 0 .. MODULUS;
        procedure INIT(SEED: SMALL);
        function NEXT return SMALL;
    end;

    package body RANDOM is
        MULTIPLIER: constant:= 5**5;
        X: SMALL;

        procedure INIT(SEED: SMALL) is
        begin
            if SEED mod 2 = 0 then
                raise BAD;
            end if;
            X:= SEED;
        end INIT;

        function NEXT return SMALL is
        begin
            X:= X*MULTIPLIER mod MODULUS;
            return X;
        end NEXT;

    end RANDOM;
```

2
```
    function FACTORIAL(N: INTEGER) return INTEGER is

        function SLAVE(N: NATURAL) return POSITIVE is
        begin
            if N = 0 then
                return 1;
            else
                return N*SLAVE(N-1);
            end if;
        end SLAVE;

    begin
        return SLAVE(N);
    exception
        when NUMERIC_ERROR | STORAGE_ERROR =>
            raise CONSTRAINT_ERROR;
    end FACTORIAL;
```

3
```
    function "+" (X, Y: VECTOR) return VECTOR is
        R: VECTOR(X'RANGE);
    begin
        if X'LENGTH /= Y'LENGTH then
            raise CONSTRAINT_ERROR;
        end if;
        for I in X'RANGE loop
            R(I):= X(I) + Y(I + Y'FIRST - X'FIRST);
        end loop;
        return R;
    end "+";
```

4   No. A malevolent user could write **raise** STACK.ERROR; outside the package. It
     would be nice if the language provided some sort of 'private' exception that
     could be handled but not raised explicitly outside its defining package.

Exercise 10.3

1   Three checks are required. The one inserted by the user plus the two for the
      assignment to S(TOP) which cannot be avoided since we can say little about the
      value of TOP (except that it is not equal to MAX). So this is the worst of all worlds
      thus emphasizing the need to give appropriate constraints.

Exercise 10.4

1
```
package BANK is
    ALARM: exception;
    subtype MONEY is NATURAL;
    type KEY is limited private;
    -- as before
private
    -- as before
end;

package body BANK is
    BALANCE: array (KEY_CODE range 1 .. KEY_CODE'LAST) of MONEY:=
                                                (others => 0);
    FREE: array (KEY_CODE range 1 .. KEY_CODE'LAST) of BOOLEAN:=
                                                (others => TRUE);

    function VALID(K: KEY) return BOOLEAN is
    begin
        return K.CODE /= 0;
    end VALID;

    procedure VALIDATE(K: KEY) is
    begin
        if not VALID(K) then
            raise ALARM;
        end if;
    end VALIDATE;

    procedure OPEN_ACCOUNT(K: in out KEY; M: in MONEY) is
    begin
        if K.CODE = 0 then
            for I in FREE'RANGE loop
                if FREE(I) then
                    FREE(I):= FALSE;
                    BALANCE(I):= M;
                    K.CODE:= I;
                    return;
                end if;
            end loop;
        else
            raise ALARM;
        end if;
    end OPEN_ACCOUNT;

    procedure CLOSE_ACCOUNT(K: in out KEY; M: out MONEY) is
    begin
        VALIDATE(K);
        M:= BALANCE(K.CODE);
        FREE(K.CODE):= TRUE;
        K.CODE:= 0;
    end CLOSE_ACCOUNT;

    procedure DEPOSIT(K: in KEY; M: in MONEY) is
    begin
```

```
        VALIDATE(K);
        BALANCE(K.CODE):= BALANCE(K.CODE)+M;
    end DEPOSIT;

    procedure WITHDRAW(K: in out KEY; M: in out MONEY) is
    begin
        VALIDATE(K);
        if M > BALANCE(K.CODE) then
            raise ALARM;
        else
            BALANCE(K.CODE):= BALANCE(K.CODE)-M;
        end if;
    end WITHDRAW;

    function STATEMENT(K: KEY) return MONEY is
    begin
        VALIDATE(K);
        return BALANCE(K.CODE);
    end STATEMENT;

end BANK;
```

For convenience we have declared a procedure VALIDATE which raises the alarm in most cases. The ALARM is also explicitly raised if we attempt to overdraw but as remarked in the text we cannot also close the account. An attempt to open an account with a key which is in use also causes ALARM to be raised. We do not however raise the ALARM if the bank runs out of accounts but have left it to the user to check with a call of VALID that he was issued a genuine key; the rationale is that it is not the user's fault if the bank runs out of keys.

2   Suppose N is 2. Then on the third call, P is not entered but the exception is raised and handled at the second level. The handler again calls P without success but this time, since an exception raised in a handler is not handled there but propagated up a level, the exception is handled at the first level. The pattern then repeats but the exception is finally propagated out of the first level to the originating call. In all there are three successful calls and four unsuccessful ones. The following diagram may help.

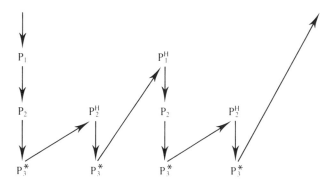

An * indicates an unsuccessful call, H indicates a call from a handler.

More generally suppose C_n is the total number of calls for the case $N = n$. Then by induction

$$C_{n+1} = 2C_n + 1$$

with the initial condition $C_0 = 1$ since in the case $N = 0$ it is obvious that there is only one call which fails. It follows that the total number of calls C_N is $2^{N+1} - 1$. Of these 2^N are unsuccessful and $2^N - 1$ are successful.

I am grateful to Bob Bishop for this example.

Answers 11

Exercise 11.1

1   TRACE((M'LENGTH, M))

If the two dimensions of M were not equal then CONSTRAINT_ERROR would be raised. Note that the lower bounds of M do not have to be 1; all that matters is that the number of components in each dimension is the same.

2   **package** STACKS **is**
  type STACK(MAX: NATURAL) **is limited private**;
  EMPTY: **constant** STACK;

  ...

 private
  type INTEGER_VECTOR **is array** (INTEGER **range** <>) **of** INTEGER;
  type STACK(MAX: NATURAL) **is**
   record
    S: INTEGER_VECTOR(1 .. MAX);
    TOP: INTEGER:= 0;
   end record;
  EMPTY: **constant** STACK(0):= (0, (**others** => 0), 0);
 end;

We have naturally chosen to make EMPTY a stack whose value of MAX is zero. Note that the function "=" only compares the parts of the stacks which are in use. Thus we can write S = EMPTY to test whether a stack S is empty irrespective of its value of MAX.

3   **function** FULL(S: STACK) **return** BOOLEAN **is**
 begin
  return S.TOP = S.MAX;
 end FULL;

4   S: **constant** SQUARE:= (N, MAKE_UNIT(N));

Exercise 11.2

1   Z: POLYNOMIAL:= (0, (0 => 0));

The named notation has to be used because the array has only one component.

2   **function** "*" (P, Q: POLYNOMIAL) **return** POLYNOMIAL **is**
  R: POLYNOMIAL(P.N+Q.N):= (P.N+Q.N, (**others** => 0));
 begin
  for I **in** P.A'RANGE **loop**
   for J **in** Q.A'RANGE **loop**
    R.A(I+J):= R.A(I+J) + P.A(I)*Q.A(J);
   end loop;
  end loop;
  return R;
 end "*";

It is largely a matter of taste whether we write P.A'RANGE rather than 0 .. P.N.

3   **function** "−" (P, Q: POLYNOMIAL) **return** POLYNOMIAL **is**
  SIZE: INTEGER;
 begin
  if P.N > Q.N **then**
   SIZE:= P.N;
  else
   SIZE:= Q.N;
  end if;

```
    declare
        R: POLYNOMIAL(SIZE);
    begin
        for I in 0 .. P.N loop
            R.A(I):= P.A(I);
        end loop;
        for I in P.N+1 .. R.N loop
            R.A(I):= 0;
        end loop;
        for I in 0 .. Q.N loop
            R.A(I):= R.A(I)−Q.A(I);
        end loop;
        return NORMAL(R);
    end;
end "−";
```

There are various alternative ways of writing this function. We could initialize R.A by using slice assignments

```
R.A(0 .. P.N):= P.A;
R.A(P.N+1 .. R.N):= (P.N+1 .. R.N => 0);
```

or even more succinctly by

```
R.A:= P.A & (P.N+1 .. R.N => 0);
```

4
```
procedure TRUNCATE(P: in out POLYNOMIAL) is
begin
    if P'CONSTRAINED then
        raise TRUNCATE_ERROR;
    else
        P:= (P.N−1, P.A(0 .. P.N−1));
    end if;
end TRUNCATE;
```

5   Any unconstrained POLYNOMIAL could then include an array whose range is 0 .. INTEGER'LAST. This will take a lot of space. Since most implementations are likely to adopt the strategy of setting aside the maximum possible space for an unconstrained record it is thus wise to keep the maximum to a practical limit by the use of a suitable subtype such as INDEX.

6
```
function "&" (X, Y: V_STRING) return V_STRING is
begin
    return (X.N + Y.N, X.S & Y.S);
end "&";
```

7
```
function "+" (V: V_STRING) return STRING is
begin
    return V.S;
end "+";
```

and then PUT(+ZOO(3)); will output the string "camel".

Exercise 11.3

1
```
procedure SHAVE(P: in out PERSON) is
begin
    if P.SEX = FEMALE then
        raise SHAVING_ERROR;
    else
        P.BEARDED:= FALSE;
    end if;
end SHAVE;
```

2   **procedure** STERILIZE(M: **in out** MUTANT) **is**
     begin
         if M'CONSTRAINED **and** M.SEX /= NEUTER **then**
             raise STERILIZE_ERROR;
         else
             M:= (NEUTER, M.BIRTH);
         end if;
     end STERILIZE;

3   **type** FIGURE **is** (CIRCLE, SQUARE, RECTANGLE);

     type OBJECT(SHAPE: FIGURE) **is**
         record
             case SHAPE **is**
                 when CIRCLE =>
                     RADIUS: REAL;
                 when SQUARE =>
                     SIDE: REAL;
                 when RECTANGLE =>
                     LENGTH, BREADTH: REAL;
             end case;
         end record;

4   **function** AREA(X: OBJECT) **return** REAL **is**
     begin
         case X.SHAPE **is**
             when CIRCLE =>
                 return PI*X.RADIUS**2;
             when SQUARE =>
                 return X.SIDE**2;
             when RECTANGLE =>
                 return X.LENGTH*X.BREADTH;
         end case;
     end AREA;

Note the similarity between the case statement in the function AREA and the variant part of the type OBJECT.

5   **function** F(N: INTEGER) **return** INTEGER_VECTOR;

     type POLYNOMIAL(N: INDEX:= 0) **is**
         record
             A: INTEGER_VECTOR(0 .. N):= F(N);
         end record;

     function F(N: INTEGER) **return** INTEGER_VECTOR **is**
         R: INTEGER_VECTOR(0 .. N);
     begin
         for I **in** 0 .. N−1 **loop**
             R(I):= 0;
         end loop;
         R(N):= 1;
         return R;
     end;

In order to declare both the function and the type in the same declarative part we have to give the function specification on its own first. This is because a type declaration may not follow a body as explained in Section 7.6. It does not matter that F is referred to before its body is elaborated provided that it is not actually called. Thus if we declared a polynomial (without an initial value) before the body of F then PROGRAM_ERROR would be raised.

6   If the user declared a constrained key with a nonzero discriminant thus

K: KEY(7);

then he will have bypassed GET_KEY and be able to call the procedure ACTION without authority. Note also that if he calls RETURN_KEY then CONSTRAINT_ERROR will be raised on the attempt to set the code to zero because the key is constrained.

Hence forged keys can be recognized since they are constrained and so we could rewrite VALID to check for this

function VALID(K: KEY) **return** BOOLEAN **is**
begin
    return not K'CONSTRAINED **and then** K.CODE /= 0;
end VALID;

We use the short circuit form so that we only test K.CODE when we are sure it exists. We must also insert calls of VALID into GET_KEY and RETURN_KEY.

7   **package** RATIONAL_POLYNOMIALS **is**
    MAX: **constant**:= 10;
    subtype INDEX **is** INTEGER **range** 0 .. MAX;
    type RATIONAL_POLYNOMIAL(N, D: INDEX:= 0) **is private**;

    function "+" (X: RATIONAL_POLYNOMIAL) **return** RATIONAL_POLYNOMIAL;
    function "−" (X: RATIONAL_POLYNOMIAL) **return** RATIONAL_POLYNOMIAL;

    function "+" (X, Y: RATIONAL_POLYNOMIAL) **return** RATIONAL_POLYNOMIAL;
    function "−" (X, Y: RATIONAL_POLYNOMIAL) **return** RATIONAL_POLYNOMIAL;
    function "*" (X, Y: RATIONAL_POLYNOMIAL) **return** RATIONAL_POLYNOMIAL;
    function "/" (X, Y: RATIONAL_POLYNOMIAL) **return** RATIONAL_POLYNOMIAL;

    function "/" (X, Y: POLYNOMIAL) **return** RATIONAL_POLYNOMIAL;
    function NUMERATOR(R: RATIONAL_POLYNOMIAL) **return** POLYNOMIAL;
    function DENOMINATOR(R: RATIONAL_POLYNOMIAL) **return** POLYNOMIAL;

private

    function ZERO(N: INDEX) **return** POLYNOMIAL;
    function ONE(N: INDEX) **return** POLYNOMIAL;

    type RATIONAL_POLYNOMIAL(N, D: INDEX:= 0) **is**
        record
            NUM: POLYNOMIAL(N):= ZERO(N);
            DEN: POLYNOMIAL(D):= ONE(D);
        end record;
end;

The functions ZERO and ONE are required in order to supply appropriate safe initial values. It is not possible to write a suitable aggregate for ONE although it is for ZERO. Nevertheless the function ZERO is written for symmetry

function ZERO(N: INDEX) **return** POLYNOMIAL **is**
begin
    return (N, (0 .. N => 0));   −− all coefficients zero
end;

function ONE(N: INDEX) **return** POLYNOMIAL **is**
    R: POLYNOMIAL(N):= ZERO(N);
begin
    R.A(0):= 1;   −− coefficient of x^0 is one
    return R;
end;

We make no attempt to impose any special language constraint on the denominator as we did in the type RATIONAL where the denominator has subtype POSITIVE.

Exercise 11.4

1
```
procedure APPEND(FIRST: in out LINK; SECOND: in LINK) is
    L: LINK:= FIRST;
begin
    if FIRST = null then
        FIRST:= SECOND;
    else
        while L.NEXT /= null loop
            L:= L.NEXT;
        end loop;
        L.NEXT:= SECOND;
    end if;
end APPEND;
```

2
```
function SIZE(T: TREE) return INTEGER is
begin
    if T = null then
        return 0;
    else
        return SIZE(T.LEFT)+SIZE(T.RIGHT)+1;
    end if;
end SIZE;
```

3
```
function COPY(T: TREE) return TREE is
begin
    if T = null then
        return null;
    else
        return new NODE'(T.VALUE, COPY(T.LEFT), COPY(T.RIGHT));
    end if;
end COPY;
```

Exercise 11.5

1
```
procedure PUSH(S: in out STACK; X: in INTEGER) is
begin
    S:= new CELL'(X, S);
exception
    when STORAGE_ERROR =>
        raise ERROR;
end;

procedure POP(S: in out STACK; X: out INTEGER) is
begin
    if S = null then
        raise ERROR;
    else
        X:= S.VALUE;
        S:= S.NEXT;
    end if;
end;
```

2
```
procedure PUSH(S: in out STACK; X: in INTEGER) is
begin
    S.LIST:= new CELL'(X, S.LIST);
end;

procedure POP(S: in out STACK; X: out INTEGER) is
begin
    X:= S.LIST.VALUE;
```

```
            S.LIST:= S.LIST.NEXT;
      end;

      function "=" (S, T: STACK) return BOOLEAN is
         SL: LINK:= S.LIST;
         TL: LINK:= T.LIST;
      begin
         while SL /= null and TL /= null loop
            SL:= SL.NEXT;
            TL:= TL.NEXT;
            if SL.VALUE /= TL.VALUE then
               return FALSE;
            end if;
         end loop;
         return SL = TL;
      end "=";
```

3
```
   package QUEUES is
      EMPTY: exception;
      type QUEUE is limited private;
      procedure JOIN(Q: in out QUEUE; X: in ITEM);
      procedure REMOVE(Q: in out QUEUE; X: out ITEM);
      function LENGTH(Q: QUEUE) return INTEGER;
   private
      type CELL;
      type LINK is access CELL;
      type CELL is
         record
            DATA: ITEM;
            NEXT: LINK;
         end record;
      type QUEUE is
         record
            COUNT: INTEGER:= 0;
            FIRST, LAST: LINK;
         end record;
   end;

   package body QUEUES is

      procedure JOIN(Q: in out QUEUE; X: in ITEM) is
         L: LINK;
      begin
         L:= new CELL'(DATA => X, NEXT => null);
         Q.LAST.NEXT:= L;
         Q.LAST:= L;
         Q.COUNT:= Q.COUNT+1;
      end JOIN;

      procedure REMOVE(Q: in out QUEUE; X: out ITEM) is
      begin
         if Q.COUNT = 0 then
            raise EMPTY;
         end if;
         X:= Q.FIRST.DATA;
         Q.FIRST:= Q.FIRST.NEXT;
         Q.COUNT:= Q.COUNT-1;
      end REMOVE;

      function LENGTH(Q: QUEUE) return INTEGER is
      begin
```

```
            return Q.COUNT;
        end LENGTH;

    end QUEUES;
```

Exercise 11.6

1
```
    function HEIR(P: PERSON_NAME) return PERSON_NAME is
        MOTHER: WOMANS_NAME;
    begin
        if P.SEX = MALE then
            MOTHER:= P.WIFE;
        else
            MOTHER:= P;
        end if;
        if MOTHER = null or else MOTHER.FIRST_CHILD = null then
            return null;
        end if;
        declare
            CHILD: PERSON_NAME:= MOTHER.FIRST_CHILD;
        begin
            while CHILD.SEX = FEMALE loop
                if CHILD.NEXT_SIBLING = null then
                    return MOTHER.FIRST_CHILD;
                end if;
                CHILD:= CHILD.NEXT_SIBLING;
            end loop;
            return CHILD;
        end;
    end HEIR;
```

2
```
    procedure DIVORCE(W: WOMANS_NAME) is
    begin
        if W.HUSBAND = null or W.FIRST_CHILD /= null then
            return;              -- divorce not possible
        end if;
        W.HUSBAND.WIFE:= null;
        W.HUSBAND:= null;
    end DIVORCE;
```

3
```
    procedure MARRY(BRIDE: WOMANS_NAME; GROOM: MANS_NAME) is
    begin
        if BRIDE.FATHER = GROOM.FATHER then
            raise INCEST;
        end if;
        -- then as before
    end MARRY;
```

Note that there is no need to check for marriage to a parent because the check
for bigamy will detect this anyway. Our model does not allow remarriage.

4
```
    function NO_OF_CHILDREN(P: PERSON_NAME) return INTEGER is
        MOTHER: WOMANS_NAME;
    begin
        if P.SEX = MALE then
            MOTHER:= P.WIFE;
        else
            MOTHER:= P;
        end if;
        if MOTHER = null then
            return 0;
```

```
        end if;
        declare
           CHILD: PERSON_NAME:= MOTHER.FIRST_CHILD;
           COUNT: INTEGER:= 0;
        begin
           while CHILD /= null loop
              COUNT:= COUNT+1;
              CHILD:= CHILD.NEXT_SIBLING;
           end loop;
           return COUNT;
        end;
   end NO_OF_CHILDREN;

   function NO_OF_SIBLINGS(P: PERSON_NAME) return INTEGER is
   begin
        return NO_OF_CHILDREN(P.FATHER)-1;
   end NO_OF_SIBLINGS;

   function NO_OF_GRANDCHILDREN(P: PERSON_NAME) return INTEGER is
        MOTHER: WOMANS_NAME;
   begin
        if P.SEX = MALE then
           MOTHER:= P.WIFE;
        else
           MOTHER:= P;
        end if;
        if MOTHER = null then
           return 0;
        end if;
        declare
           CHILD: PERSON_NAME:= MOTHER.FIRST_CHILD;
           COUNT: INTEGER:= 0;
        begin
           while CHILD /= null loop
              COUNT:= COUNT + NO_OF_CHILDREN(CHILD);
              CHILD:= CHILD.NEXT_SIBLING;
           end loop;
           return COUNT;
        end;
   end NO_OF_GRANDCHILDREN;

   function NO_OF_COUSINS(P: PERSON_NAME) return INTEGER is
   begin
        return NO_OF_GRANDCHILDREN(P.FATHER.FATHER)
              + NO_OF_GRANDCHILDREN(P.FATHER.WIFE.FATHER)
              - 2 * NO_OF_CHILDREN(P.FATHER);
   end NO_OF_COUSINS;
```

We and our siblings get counted twice among the grandchildren and have to be deducted. We have assumed no intermarriage between our maternal and paternal aunts and uncles. If there is then some of our cousins may have been counted twice as well. We leave further contemplation of this complication to the reader.

Exercise 11.7

1
```
   package P is
      type LENGTH is new REAL;
      type AREA is new REAL;
      function "*" (X, Y: LENGTH) return LENGTH;
```

```
        function "*" (X, Y: LENGTH) return AREA;
        function "*" (X, Y: AREA) return AREA;
    end;

    package body P is

        function "*" (X, Y: LENGTH) return LENGTH is
        begin
            raise NUMERIC_ERROR;
        end "*";

        function "*" (X, Y: LENGTH) return AREA is
        begin
            return AREA(REAL(X)*REAL(Y));
        end "*";

        function "*" (X, Y: AREA) return AREA is
        begin
            raise NUMERIC_ERROR;
        end "*";

    end P;
```

Answers 12

Exercise 12.1

1   P: on A: INTEGER, on B: SHORT_INTEGER
     Q: on A: LONG_INTEGER, on B: INTEGER
     R: on A: cannot be implemented, on B: LONG_INTEGER

2   No, the only critical case is type Q on machine A. Changing to one's complement
     changes the range of INTEGER to

     −32767 .. +32767

     and so only INTEGER'FIRST is altered.

3   (a)   INTEGER
     (b)   illegal – type conversion must be explicit
     (c)   MY_INTEGER'BASE
     (d)   INTEGER
     (e)   universal integer
     (f)   MY_INTEGER'BASE

4   type LONGEST_INTEGER is range SYSTEM.MIN_INT .. SYSTEM.MAX_INT;

Exercise 12.2

1   (a)   illegal
     (b)   INTEGER
     (c)   universal real
     (d)   INTEGER
     (e)   universal real
     (f)   universal integer

2   R: constant:= N*1.0;

Exercise 12.3

1    $\frac{1}{16}$

2   REAL has B=18.
         The values of the variables P and Q are model numbers. However, the result

P/Q = ⅔ is not. The nearest model numbers can be determined by considering ⅔ as a binary recurring fraction

0.10101010...

The model number below (L say) is obtained by truncating after 18 digits. The difference between ⅔ and L is clearly ⅔ shifted down by 18 places. So L is ⅔ $(1 - 2^{-18})$. The model number above is obtained by adding 2^{-18} to L. Hence P/Q lies in the model interval

$$⅔(1 - 2^{-18}), ⅔(1 + 2^{-19})$$

The mathematical bounds for (P/Q)⋆Q are obtained by multiplying the bounds of this interval by 3. The lower bound is then $2(1 - 2^{-18})$ and this is a model number. The upper bound is $2(1 + 2^{-19})$ but this is not a model number; the next model number above is $2(1 + 2^{-17})$. So the final model interval in which R must lie is

$$2(1 - 2^{-18}), 2(1 + 2^{-17})$$

3   In this example P and Q are numbers of type universal real and since the operators ⋆ and / apply to the type universal real we might think that the expression (P/Q)⋆Q is always of type universal real and thus evaluated exactly at compilation. However, remember that implicit conversion of the universal types is only performed in the case of single literals, numbers and attributes and that general expressions must be converted explicitly. In the case of the assignment to R the only interpretation is that the individual numbers are implicitly converted to type REAL before the operations ⋆ and / are performed. The result is that R is assigned a value in the same model interval as in the previous exercise. In the case of S, however, an explicit conversion is given and the complete expression is thus of type universal real. The result is that S is assigned the model number 2.0.

4   1313 = 16 (= possible mantissae)
   ×   41 (= possible exponents)
   ×   2 (= possible signs)
   +   1 (= zero)

5   **function** HYPOTENUSE(X, Y: REAL) **return** REAL **is**
      TINY: **constant** REAL:= 2.0⋆⋆(−REAL'EMAX/2);
   begin
      if abs X < TINY **and abs** Y < TINY **then**
         return SQRT((X/TINY)⋆⋆2+(Y/TINY)⋆⋆2)⋆TINY;
      else
         return SQRT(X⋆⋆2+Y⋆⋆2);
      end if;
   end HYPOTENUSE;

Note that REAL'EMAX is always even.

6   In the case of type ROUGH we have requested one decimal digit which implies a maximum relative precision of 1 in 10. If we took $B = 4$ then the relative precision would vary from 1 in 8 to 1 in 16. There would therefore be occasional places where the binary numbers are slightly further apart than the decimal ones. In fact, around 10 000 the decimal model numbers for $D = 1$ are

8000,   9000,   10 000,   20 000

whereas the binary model numbers for $B = 4$ are

7680,   8192,   9216,   10 240

and we see that 8192 and 9216 are more than 1000 apart. Hence we have to take $B = 5$ so that the minimum relative precision is 1 in 16. The general result follows.

7   The ratio is 2^{B-1} or 1/EPSILON. Thus the hole around zero is relatively more dangerous for higher values of B.

8
```
function INNER(A, B: VECTOR) return REAL is
    type LONG_REAL is digits 14;
    RESULT: LONG_REAL:= 0.0;
begin
    for I in A'RANGE loop
        RESULT:= RESULT + LONG_REAL(A(I))*LONG_REAL(B(I));
    end loop;
    return REAL(RESULT);
end INNER;
```

Exercise 12.4

1 $\frac{1}{10}(1 - 2^{-12})$, $\frac{1}{10}(1 + 2^{-14})$

2   The operation $\star$ cannot be universal real because the general expression 2.0$\star$PI cannot be implicitly converted to type ANGLE before the subtraction. Nor can it be the $\star$ applying to two operands of type ANGLE because that delivers a result of the type universal fixed which always has to be explicitly converted and moreover a universal real operand of fixed point multiplication cannot be implicitly converted because of lack of uniqueness. It is fortunate that this is so; otherwise we would have got the wrong answer because 2.0 is not a model number of type ANGLE.

3
```
function "**" (X: COMPLEX; N: INTEGER) return COMPLEX is
    RESULT_THETA: ANGLE:= 0.0;
begin
    for I in 1 .. abs N loop
        RESULT_THETA:= NORMAL(RESULT_THETA+X.THETA);
    end loop;
    if N < 0 then RESULT_THETA:= −RESULT_THETA; end if;
    return (X.R**N, RESULT_THETA);
end "**";
```

We cannot simply write

```
return (X.R**N, NORMAL(X.THETA*N));
```

because if **abs** N is larger than 3 the multiplication is likely to overflow; so we have to repeatedly normalize. A clever solution which is faster for all but the smallest values of **abs** N is

```
function "**" (X: COMPLEX; N: INTEGER) return COMPLEX is
    RESULT_THETA: ANGLE:= 0.0;
    TERM: ANGLE:= X.THETA;
    M: INTEGER:= abs N;
begin
    while M > 0 loop
        if M rem 2 /= 0 then
            RESULT_THETA:= NORMAL(RESULT_THETA + TERM);
        end if;
        M:= M/2;
        TERM:= NORMAL(TERM*2);
    end loop;
    if N < 0 then RESULT_THETA:= −RESULT_THETA; end if;
    return (X.R**N, RESULT_THETA);
end "**";
```

This is a variation of the standard algorithm for computing exponentials by decomposing the exponent into its binary form and doing a minimal number of multiplications. In our case it is the multiplier N which we decompose and then do a minimal number of additions. Note that we cannot write TERM∗2.0 because a universal real operand cannot be implicitly converted in the case of fixed point multiplication. In any event such a product would be of type universal fixed and as mentioned in a previous answer 2.0 is not a model number and so errors would be introduced.

One of the major points about fixed point is the ability to do exact addition; multiplication by integers is treated conceptually as repeated addition which is why it produces a result of the same fixed point type. Multiplication by real values (universal or otherwise) is to be treated with suspicion and hence the concept of universal fixed and compulsory conversion which draws the matter to the programmer's attention. It is hence very appropriate that we are using repeated addition in order to multiply by our integer N. Recognizing that our repeated addition algorithm is essentially the same as for exponentiation, we can in parallel compute X.R∗∗N by the same method. A little manipulation soon makes us realize that we might as well write

```
function "**" (X: COMPLEX; N: INTEGER) return COMPLEX is
    RESULT: COMPLEX= (1.0, 0.0);
    TERM: COMPLEX:= X;
    M: INTEGER:= abs N;
begin
    while M > 0 loop
        if M rem 2 /= 0 then
            RESULT:= RESULT * TERM;      -- COMPLEX *
        end if;
        M:= M/2;
        TERM:= TERM * TERM;              -- COMPLEX *
    end loop;
    if N < 0 then RESULT:= - RESULT; end if;   -- COMPLEX -
    return RESULT;
end "**";
```

This brings us back full circle. This is indeed the standard algorithm for computing exponentials and we are now applying it in the abstract to our type COMPLEX. Note the calls of the functions "∗" and unary "−" applying to the type COMPLEX. This version of "∗∗" can be declared outside the package COMPLEX_NUMBERS and is quite independent of the internal representation (but it will be very inefficient unless the internal representation is polar).

4
```
    private
        type ANGLE is delta 0.05 range -720.0 .. 720.0;
        type COMPLEX is
            record
                R: REAL;
                THETA: ANGLE range 0.0 .. 360.0;
            end record;
        I: constant COMPLEX:= (1.0, 90.0);
    end;
        ...
    function NORMAL(A: ANGLE) return ANGLE is
    begin
        if A >= 360.0 then
            return A - 360.0;
        elsif A < 0.0 then
            return A + 360.0;
        else
            return A;
        end if;
    end NORMAL;
```

The choice of delta is derived as follows. We need 10 bits to cover the range 0 .. 720 plus one bit for the sign thus leaving 5 bits after the binary point. So *small* will be 2^{-5} and thus any value of delta greater than that but less than 2^{-4} will do. We have chosen 0.05.

Answers 13

Exercise 13.1

1
```
generic
    type ITEM is private;
package STACKS is
    type STACK(MAX: NATURAL) is limited private;
    procedure PUSH(S: in out STACK; X: in ITEM);
    procedure POP(S: in out STACK; X: out ITEM);
    function "=" (S, T: STACK) return BOOLEAN;
private
    type ITEM_ARRAY is array (INTEGER range <>) of ITEM;
    type STACK(MAX: NATURAL) is
        record
            S: ITEM_ARRAY(1 .. MAX);
            TOP: INTEGER:= 0;
        end record;
end;
```

The body is much as before. To declare a stack we must first instantiate the package.

```
package BOOLEAN_STACKS is new STACKS(ITEM => BOOLEAN);
use BOOLEAN_STACKS;
S: STACK(MAX => 30);
```

2
```
generic
    type THING is private;
package P is
    procedure SWAP(A, B: in out THING);
    procedure CAB(A, B, C: in out THING);
end P;

package body P is
    procedure SWAP(A, B: in out THING) is
        T: THING;
    begin
        T:= A;  A:= B;  B:= T;
    end;
    procedure CAB(A, B, C: in out THING) is
    begin
        SWAP(A, B);
        SWAP(A, C);
    end;
end P;
```

Exercise 13.2

1
```
function "not" is new NEXT(BOOLEAN);
```

```
2       generic
            type BASE is range <>;
        package RATIONAL_NUMBERS is
            type RATIONAL is private;
            function "+" (X: RATIONAL) return RATIONAL;
            function "-" (X: RATIONAL) return RATIONAL;
            function "+" (X, Y: RATIONAL) return RATIONAL;
            function "-" (X, Y: RATIONAL) return RATIONAL;
            function "*" (X, Y: RATIONAL) return RATIONAL;
            function "/" (X, Y: RATIONAL) return RATIONAL;

            subtype POS_BASE is BASE range 1 .. BASE'LAST;
            function "/" (X: BASE; Y: POS_BASE) return RATIONAL;
            function NUMERATOR(R: RATIONAL) return BASE;
            function DENOMINATOR(R: RATIONAL) return POS_BASE;
        private
            type RATIONAL is
                record
                    NUM: BASE:= 0;
                    DEN: POS_BASE:= 1;
                end record;
        end;

3       generic
            type INDEX is (<>);
            type FLOATING is digits <>;
            type VEC is array (INDEX range <>) of FLOATING;
            type MAT is array (INDEX range <>, INDEX range <>) of FLOATING;
        function OUTER(A, B: VEC) return MAT;

        function OUTER(A, B: VEC) return MAT is
            C: MAT(A'RANGE, B'RANGE);
        begin
            for I in A'RANGE loop
                for J in B'RANGE loop
                    C(I, J):= A(I)*B(J);
                end loop;
            end loop;
            return C;
        end OUTER;

        function OUTER_VECTOR is new OUTER(INTEGER, REAL, VECTOR, MATRIX);

4       package body SET_OF is

            function MAKE_SET(X: LIST) return SET is
                S: SET:= EMPTY;
            begin
                for I in X'RANGE loop
                    S(X(I)):= TRUE;
                end loop;
                return S;
            end MAKE_SET;

            function MAKE_SET(X: BASE) return SET is
                S: SET:= EMPTY;
            begin
                S(X):= TRUE;
                return S;
            end MAKE_SET;
```

```
function DECOMPOSE(X: SET) return LIST is
    L: LIST(1 .. SIZE(X));
    I: POSITIVE:= 1;
begin
    for E in SET'RANGE loop
        if X(E) then
            L(I):= E;
            I:= I+1;
        end if;
    end loop;
    return L;
end DECOMPOSE;

function "+" (X, Y: SET) return SET is
begin
    return X or Y;
end "+";

function "*" (X, Y: SET) return SET is
begin
    return X and Y;
end "*";

function "−" (X, Y: SET) return SET is
begin
    return X xor Y;
end "−";

function "<" (X: BASE; Y: SET) return BOOLEAN is
begin
    return Y(X);
end "<";

function "<=" (X, Y: SET) return BOOLEAN is
begin
    return (X and Y) = X;
end "<=";

function SIZE(X: SET) return NATURAL is
    N: NATURAL:= 0;
begin
    for E in SET'RANGE loop
        if X(E) then
            N:= N+1;
        end if;
    end loop;
    return N;
end SIZE;

end SET_OF;

private
    type BASE_ARRAY is array (BASE) of BOOLEAN;
    type SET is
        record
            VALUE: BASE_ARRAY:= (BASE_ARRAY'RANGE => FALSE);
        end record;

    EMPTY: constant SET:= (VALUE => (BASE_ARRAY'RANGE => FALSE));
    FULL: constant SET:= (VALUE => (BASE_ARRAY'RANGE => TRUE));
end;
```

We have to make the full type into a record containing the array as a single component so that we can give it a default initial expression. Unfortunately, this means that the body needs rewriting and moreover the functions become rather untidy. Sadly we cannot write the default expression as EMPTY.VALUE. This is because we cannot use the component name VALUE in its own declaration. In general, however, we can use a deferred constant as a default value before its full declaration. Note also that we have to use the named notation for the single component record aggregates.

Exercise 13.3

1   First we have to declare our function "<" which we define as follows: if the polynomials have different degrees, the one with the lower degree is smaller; if the same degree, then we compare coefficients starting at the highest power. So

```
function "<" (X, Y: POLYNOMIAL) return BOOLEAN is
begin
    if X.N /= Y.N then
        return X.N < Y.N;
    end if;
    for I in reverse 0 .. X.N loop      -- or X.A'RANGE
        if X.A(I) /= Y.A(I) then
            return X.A(I) < Y.A(I);
        end if;
    end loop;
    return FALSE;          -- they are identical
end "<";

procedure SORT_POLY is new SORT(INTEGER, POLYNOMIAL, POLY_ARRAY);
```

2   ```
type MUTANT_ARRAY is array (INTEGER range <>) of MUTANT;

function "<" (X, Y: MUTANT) return BOOLEAN is
begin
    if X.SEX /= Y.SEX then
        return X.SEX > Y.SEX;
    else
        return Y.BIRTH < X.BIRTH;
    end if;
end "<";

procedure SORT_MUTANT is new SORT(INTEGER, MUTANT, MUTANT_ARRAY);
```

Note that the order of sexes asked for is precisely the reverse order to that in the type GENDER and so we can directly use ">" applied to that type. Similarly younger first means later birth date first and so we use the function "<" we have already defined for the type DATE but with the arguments reversed.

We could not sort an array of type PERSON because we cannot declare such an array anyway. See the end of Section 11.3.

3    We cannot do this because the array is of an anonymous type.

4    We might get CONSTRAINT_ERROR. If C'FIRST = INDEX'FIRST then the attempt to evaluate INDEX'PRED(C'LAST) will raise CONSTRAINT_ERROR. Considerable care can be required to make such extreme cases foolproof. The easy way out in this case is simply to insert

```
if C'LENGTH < 2 then return; end if;
```

5   The generic body corresponds closely to the procedure SORT in Section 11.4. The type VECTOR is replaced by COLLECTION. I is of type INDEX. The types NODE and TREE are declared inside SORT because they depend on the generic type ITEM. The incrementing of I cannot be done with "+" since the index type may not be an integer and so we have to use INDEX'SUCC. Care is needed not to cause CONSTRAINT_ERROR if the array embraces the full range of values of INDEX. However, the important thing is that the generic specification is completely unchanged and so we see how an alternative body can be sensibly supplied.
```

6   Assuming

type BOOL_ARRAY **is array** (INTEGER **range** <>) **of** BOOLEAN;

we have

function AND_ALL **is new** APPLY(INTEGER, BOOLEAN, BOOL_ARRAY, "**and**");

7   A further generic parameter is required to supply a value for zero.

generic
    type INDEX **is** (<>);
    type ITEM **is private**;
    ZERO: **in** ITEM;
    type VEC **is array** (INDEX **range** <>) **of** ITEM;
    with function "+" (X, Y: ITEM) **return** ITEM;
function APPLY(A: VEC) **return** ITEM;

function APPLY(A: VEC) **return** ITEM **is**
    RESULT: ITEM:= ZERO;
begin
    for I **in** A'RANGE **loop**
        RESULT:= RESULT+A(I);
    end loop;
    return RESULT;
end APPLY;

and then

function AND_ALL **is**
                new APPLY(INTEGER, BOOLEAN, TRUE, BOOL_ARRAY, "**and**");

8   **generic**
    type ITEM **is limited private**;
    type VECTOR **is array** (INTEGER **range** <>) **of** ITEM;
    with function "=" (X, Y: ITEM) **return** BOOLEAN **is** <>;
function EQUALS(A, B: VECTOR) **return** BOOLEAN;

function EQUALS(A, B: VECTOR) **return** BOOLEAN **is**
begin
    -- body exactly as for Exercise 9.2(3)
end EQUALS;

We can instantiate by

function "=" **is new** EQUALS(STACK, STACK_ARRAY, "=");

or simply by

function "=" **is new** EQUALS(STACK, STACK_ARRAY);

in which case the default parameter is used.

9   **function** G(X: REAL) **return** REAL **is**
begin
    return EXP(X)+X-7.0;
end;
...
function SOLVE_G **is new** SOLVE(G);
...
ANSWER: REAL:= SOLVE_G;

Exercise 13.4

1   **with** GENERIC_ELEMENTARY_FUNCTIONS;
package body SIMPLE_MATHS **is**

```ada
package FLOAT_FUNCTIONS is
   new GENERIC_ELEMENTARY_FUNCTIONS(FLOAT);

function SQRT(F: FLOAT) return FLOAT is
begin
   return FLOAT_FUNCTIONS.SQRT(F);
exception
   when FLOAT_FUNCTIONS.ARGUMENT_ERROR =>
      raise NUMERIC_ERROR;
end SQRT;

function LOG(F: FLOAT) return FLOAT is
begin
   return FLOAT_FUNCTIONS.LOG(F, 10.0);
exception
   when FLOAT_FUNCTIONS.ARGUMENT_ERROR =>
      raise NUMERIC_ERROR;
end LOG;

function LN(F: FLOAT) return FLOAT is
begin
   return FLOAT_FUNCTIONS.LOG(F);
exception
   when FLOAT_FUNCTIONS.ARGUMENT_ERROR =>
      raise NUMERIC_ERROR;
end LN;

function EXP(F: FLOAT) return FLOAT is
begin
   return FLOAT_FUNCTIONS.EXP(F);
end EXP;

function SIN(F: FLOAT) return FLOAT is
begin
   return FLOAT_FUNCTIONS.SIN(F);
end SIN;

function COS(F: FLOAT) return FLOAT is
begin
   return FLOAT_FUNCTIONS.COS(F);
end COS;

end SIMPLE_MATHS;
```

We did not write a use clause for FLOAT_FUNCTIONS largely because it would not have enabled us to write simply

```ada
return SQRT(F);
```

since this would have resulted in an infinite recursion.

2   ```ada
package body GENERIC_COMPLEX_FUNCTIONS is

   function SQRT(X: COMPLEX_TYPE) return COMPLEX_TYPE is
   begin
      return CONS_POLAR(SQRT(abs X), 0.5*ARG(X)));
   end SQRT;

   function LOG(X: COMPLEX_TYPE) return COMPLEX_TYPE is
   begin
      return CONS(LOG(abs X), ARG(X));
   end LOG;

   function EXP(X: COMPLEX_TYPE) return COMPLEX_TYPE is
   begin
```
```

```
      return CONS_POLAR(EXP(RL_PART(X)), IM_PART(X));
    end EXP;

    function SIN(X: COMPLEX_TYPE) return COMPLEX_TYPE is
      RL: REAL_TYPE:= RL_PART(X);
      IM: REAL_TYPE:= IM_PART(X);
    begin
      return CONS(SIN(RL)*COSH(IM)), COS(RL)*SINH(IM));
    end SIN;

    function COS(X: COMPLEX_TYPE) return COMPLEX_TYPE is
      RL: REAL_TYPE:= RL_PART(X);
      IM: REAL_TYPE:= IM_PART(X);
    begin
      return CONS(COS(RL)*COSH(IM)), −SIN(RL)*SINH(IM));
    end COS;

  end GENERIC_COMPLEX_FUNCTIONS;
```

3
```
    function CONS_CARTESIAN(R, I: MY_REAL) return COMPLEX renames CONS;
```

4
```
    generic
      type REAL is digits <>;
      with function SQRT(X: REAL) return REAL is <>;
      with function SIN(X: REAL) return REAL is <>;
      with function COS(X: REAL) return REAL is <>;
      with function ARCTAN(Y, X: REAL) return REAL is <>;
    package GENERIC_COMPLEX_NUMBERS is
      type COMPLEX is private;

      -- as in Section 9.1 plus

      function CONS_POLAR(R, THETA: REAL) return COMPLEX;
      function "abs" (X: COMPLEX) return REAL;
      function ARG(X: COMPLEX) return REAL;
    private

      -- as before

    end;

    package body GENERIC_COMPLEX_NUMBERS is

      -- as before plus

      function CONS_POLAR(R, THETA: REAL) return COMPLEX is
      begin
        return (R*COS(THETA), R*SIN(THETA));
      end CONS_POLAR;

      function "abs" (X: COMPLEX) return REAL is
      begin
        return SQRT(X.RL**2 + X.IM**2);
      end "abs";

      function ARG(X: COMPLEX) return REAL is
        return ARCTAN(X.IM, X.RL);
      end ARG;

    end GENERIC_COMPLEX_NUMBERS;
```

Numerical analysts will writhe at the poor implementation of **abs** which can
unnecessarily overflow in computing the parameter of SQRT. This can be
avoided by suitable rescaling.

Note also that if the private type COMPLEX is implemented in polar form then the same set of auxiliary functions will suffice. Thus the formal functions provided do not dictate the internal representation and so the abstraction is not compromised.

Answers 14

Exercise 14.1

1
```
procedure SHOPPING is

    task GET_SALAD;

    task body GET_SALAD is
    begin
        BUY_SALAD;
    end GET_SALAD;

    task GET_WINE;

    task body GET_WINE is
    begin
        BUY_WINE;
    end GET_WINE;

    task GET_MEAT;

    task body GET_MEAT is
    begin
        BUY_MEAT;
    end GET_MEAT;

begin
    null;
end SHOPPING;
```

Exercise 14.2

1
```
task body BUILD_COMPLEX is
    C: COMPLEX;
begin
    loop
        accept PUT_RL(X: REAL) do
            C.RL:= X;
        end;
        accept PUT_IM(X: REAL) do
            C.IM:= X;
        end;
        accept GET_COMP(X: out COMPLEX) do
            X:= C;
        end;
    end loop;
end BUILD_COMPLEX;
```

2
```
task body CHAR_TO_LINE is
    BUFFER: LINE;
begin
    loop
        for I in BUFFER'RANGE loop
            accept PUT(C: in CHARACTER) do
                BUFFER(I):= C;
            end;
```

```
          end loop;
          accept GET(L: out LINE) do
             L:= BUFFER;
          end;
       end loop;
    end CHAR_TO_LINE;
```

Exercise 14.3

1
```
generic
   FIRST_TIME: CALENDAR.TIME;
   INTERVAL: DURATION;
   NUMBER: INTEGER;
   with procedure P;
procedure CALL;

procedure CALL is
   use CALENDAR;
   NEXT_TIME: TIME:= FIRST_TIME;
begin
   if NEXT_TIME < CLOCK then
      NEXT_TIME:= CLOCK;
   end if;
   for I in 1 .. NUMBER loop
      delay NEXT_TIME-CLOCK;
      P;
      NEXT_TIME:= NEXT_TIME+INTERVAL;
   end loop;
end CALL;
```

2   The type DURATION requires at least 24 bits.

Exercise 14.4

1
```
task body BUILD_COMPLEX is
   C: COMPLEX;
   GOT_RL, GOT_IM: BOOLEAN:= FALSE;
begin
   loop
      select
         when not GOT_RL =>
         accept PUT_RL(X: REAL) do
            C.RL:= X;
         end;
         GOT_RL:= TRUE;
      or
         when not GOT_IM =>
         accept PUT_IM(X: REAL) do
            C.IM:= X;
         end;
         GOT_IM:= TRUE;
      or
         when GOT_RL and GOT_IM =>
         accept GET_COMP(X: out COMPLEX) do
            X:= C;
         end;
         GOT_RL:= FALSE;
         GOT_IM:= FALSE;
      end select;
```

```
      end loop;
  end BUILD_COMPLEX;
```

An alternative solution is

```
task body BUILD_COMPLEX is
    C: COMPLEX;
begin
    loop
        select
            accept PUT_RL(X: REAL) do
                C.RL:= X;
            end;
            accept PUT_IM(X: REAL) do
                C.IM:= X;
            end;
        or
            accept PUT_IM(X: REAL) do
                C.IM:= X;
            end;
            accept PUT_RL(X: REAL) do
                C.RL:= X;
            end;
        end select;
        accept GET_COMP(X: out COMPLEX) do
            X:= C;
        end;
    end loop;
end BUILD_COMPLEX;
```

At first reading this might seem simpler but the technique does not extrapolate easily when a moderate number of components are involved because of the combinatorial explosion.

Exercise 14.5

1
```
procedure READ(X: out ITEM; T: DURATION; OK: out BOOLEAN) is
begin
    select
        CONTROL.START(READ);
    or
        delay T;
        OK:= FALSE;
        return;
    end select;
    X:= V;
    CONTROL.STOP_READ;
    OK:= TRUE;
end READ;

procedure WRITE(X: in ITEM; T: DURATION; OK: out BOOLEAN) is
    use CALENDAR;
    START_TIME: TIME:= CLOCK;
begin
    select
        CONTROL.START(WRITE);
    or
        delay T;
        OK:= FALSE;
        return;
```

```
      end select;
      select
         CONTROL.WRITE;
      or
         delay T-(CLOCK-START_TIME);
         CONTROL.STOP_WRITE;
         OK:= FALSE;
         return;
      end select;
      V:= X;
      CONTROL.STOP_WRITE;
      OK:= TRUE;
   end WRITE;
```

Note how a shorter time out is imposed on the call of WRITE.

Exercise 14.7

1
```
      task BUFFERING is
         entry PUT(X: in ITEM);
         entry FINISH;
         entry GET(X: out ITEM);
      end;

      task body BUFFERING is
         N: constant:= 8;
         A: array (1 .. N) of ITEM;
         I, J: INTEGER range 1 .. N:= 1;
         COUNT: INTEGER range 0 .. N:= 0;
         FINISHED: BOOLEAN:= FALSE;
      begin
         loop
            select
               when COUNT < N =>
               accept PUT(X: in ITEM) do
                  A(I):= X;
               end;
               I:= I mod N+1; COUNT:= COUNT+1;
            or
               accept FINISH;
               FINISHED:= TRUE;
            or
               when COUNT > 0 =>
               accept GET(X: out ITEM) do
                  X:= A(J);
               end;
               J:= J mod N+1; COUNT:= COUNT-1;
            or
               when COUNT = 0 and FINISHED =>
               accept GET(X: out ITEM) do
                  raise DONE;
               end;
            end select;
         end loop;
      exception
         when DONE =>
            null;
      end BUFFERING;
```

This example illustrates that there may be several accept statements for the same entry in the one select statement. The exception DONE is propagated to the caller and also terminates the loop in BUFFERING before being quietly handled. Of course the exception need not be handled by BUFFERING because exceptions propagated out of tasks are lost, but it is cleaner to do so.

Exercise 14.8

1   The select statement becomes

```
select
    when WAITERS = 0 =>
    accept FIRST(S: SET; OK: out BOOLEAN) do
        TRY(S, OK);
        if not OK then
            WAITERS:= WAITERS+1;
        end if;
    end;
or
    accept RELEASE(S: SET) do
        FREE:= FREE+S;
    end;
    accept AGAIN(S: SET; OK: out BOOLEAN) do
        TRY(S, OK);
        if OK then
            WAITERS:= WAITERS-1;
        end if;
    end;
end select;
```

2
```
package CONTROLLER is
    procedure REQUEST(P: PRIORITY; D: DATA);
end;

package body CONTROLLER is

    task CONTROL is
        entry SIGN_IN(P: PRIORITY);
        entry REQUEST(PRIORITY)(D: DATA);
    end;

    task body CONTROL is
        TOTAL: INTEGER:= 0;
        PENDING: array (PRIORITY) of INTEGER:= (PRIORITY => 0);
    begin
        loop
            if TOTAL = 0 then
                accept SIGN_IN(P: PRIORITY) do
                    PENDING(P):= PENDING(P)+1;
                    TOTAL:= 1;
                end;
            end if;
            loop
                select
                    accept SIGN_IN(P: PRIORITY) do
                        PENDING(P):= PENDING(P)+1;
                        TOTAL:= TOTAL+1;
                    end;
                else
                    exit;
```

```
            end select;
        end loop;

        for P in PRIORITY loop
            if PENDING(P) > 0 then
                accept REQUEST(P)(D: DATA) do
                    ACTION(D);
                end;
                PENDING(P):= PENDING(P)-1;
                TOTAL:= TOTAL-1;
                exit;
            end if;
        end loop;
    end loop;
end CONTROL;

procedure REQUEST(P: PRIORITY; D: DATA) is
begin
    CONTROL.SIGN_IN(P);
    CONTROL.REQUEST(P)(D);
end REQUEST;

end CONTROLLER;
```

The variable TOTAL records the total number of requests outstanding and the array PENDING records the number at each priority. Each time round the outer loop, the task waits for a call of SIGN_IN if no requests are in the system, it then services any outstanding calls of SIGN_IN and finally deals with a request of the highest priority. We could dispense with the array PENDING and scan the queues as before but there is a slight risk of polling if a user has called SIGN_IN but not yet called REQUEST.

Finally, note that the solution will not work if a calling task is aborted; this could be overcome by the use of agents.

Exercise 14.9

1
```
package COBBLERS is
    procedure MEND(A: ADDRESS; B: BOOTS);
end;

package body COBBLERS is
    type JOB is
        record
            REPLY: ADDRESS;
            ITEM: BOOTS;
        end record;

    package P is new BUFFERS(100, JOB);
    use P;
    BOOT_STORE: BUFFER;

    task SERVER is
        entry REQUEST(A: ADDRESS; B: BOOTS);
    end;

    task type REPAIRMAN;
    TOM, DICK, HARRY: REPAIRMAN;

    task body SERVER is
        NEXT_JOB: JOB;
    begin
        loop
            accept REQUEST(A: ADDRESS; B: BOOTS) do
```

```
                        NEXT_JOB:= (A, B);
                    end;
                    PUT(BOOT_STORE, NEXT_JOB);
                end loop;
            end SERVER;

        task body REPAIRMAN is
            MY_JOB: JOB;
        begin
            loop
                GET(BOOT_STORE, MY_JOB);
                REPAIR(MY_JOB.ITEM);
                MY_JOB.REPLY.DEPOSIT(MY_JOB.ITEM);
            end loop;
        end REPAIRMAN;

        procedure MEND(A: ADDRESS; B: BOOTS) is
        begin
            SERVER.REQUEST(A, B);
        end;

    end COBBLERS;
```

We have assumed that the type ADDRESS is an access to a mailbox for handling boots. Note one anomaly; the stupid server accepts boots from the customer before checking the store – if it turns out to be full, he is left holding them. In all, the shop can hold 104 pairs of boots – 100 in store, 1 with the server and 1 with each repairman.

2
```
    procedure GAUSS_SEIDEL is
        N: constant:= 5;
        subtype FULL_GRID is INTEGER range 0 .. N;
        subtype GRID is FULL_GRID range 1 .. N−1;
        type REAL is digits 7;
        DELTA_P: REAL;
        TOLERANCE: constant REAL:= 0.0001;
        ERROR_LIMIT: constant REAL:= TOLERANCE * (N−1)**2;
        CONVERGED: BOOLEAN:= FALSE;
        ERROR_SUM: REAL;

        function F(I, J: GRID) return REAL is separate;

        task type ITERATOR is
            pragma PRIORITY(1);
            entry START(I, J: in GRID);
        end;

        task type POINT is
            pragma PRIORITY(2);
            entry SET_P(X: in REAL);
            entry GET_P(X: out REAL);
            entry GET_DELTA_P(X: out REAL);
            entry SET_CONVERGED(B: in BOOLEAN);
            entry GET_CONVERGED(B: out BOOLEAN);
        end;

        PROCESS: array (GRID, GRID) of ITERATOR;
        DATA: array (GRID, GRID) of POINT;

        task body ITERATOR is
            I, J: GRID;
            P, P1, P2, P3, P4: REAL;
```

```
        CONVERGED: BOOLEAN;
    begin

        accept START(I, J: in GRID) do
            ITERATOR.I:= START.I;
            ITERATOR.J:= START.J;
        end START;

        loop      -- needs modification if adjacent to boundary
            DATA(I-1, J).GET_P(P1);
            DATA(I+1, J).GET_P(P2);
            DATA(I, J-1).GET_P(P3);
            DATA(I, J+1).GET_P(P4);
            P:= 0.25 * (P1+P2+P3+P4-F(I, J));
            DATA(I, J).SET_P(P);
            DATA(I, J).GET_CONVERGED(CONVERGED);
            exit when CONVERGED;
        end loop;

    end ITERATOR;

    task body POINT is
        CONVERGED: BOOLEAN:= FALSE;
        P: REAL;
        DELTA_P: REAL;
    begin

        loop
            select
                accept SET_P(X: in REAL) do
                    DELTA_P:= X-P;
                    P:= X;
                end;
            or
                accept GET_P(X: out REAL) do
                    X:= P;
                end;
            or
                accept GET_DELTA_P(X: out REAL) do
                    X:= DELTA_P;
                end;
            or
                accept SET_CONVERGED(B: in BOOLEAN) do
                    CONVERGED:= B;
                end;
            or
                accept GET_CONVERGED(B: out BOOLEAN) do
                    B:= CONVERGED;
                end;
            or
                terminate;
            end select;
        end loop;

    end POINT;

begin  -- of main program; the tasks are now active

    for I in GRID loop
        for J in GRID loop
            PROCESS(I, J).START(I, J); -- tell them who they are
```

```
            end loop;
        end loop;

        loop
            ERROR_SUM:= 0.0;
            for I in GRID loop
                for J in GRID loop
                    DATA(I, J).GET_DELTA_P(DELTA_P);
                    ERROR_SUM:= ERROR_SUM + DELTA_P**2;
                end loop;
            end loop;

            CONVERGED:= ERROR_SUM < ERROR_LIMIT;
            exit when CONVERGED;
        end loop;

        -- tell the data tasks that it has converged

        for I in GRID loop
            for J in GRID loop
                DATA(I, J).SET_CONVERGED(TRUE);
            end loop;
        end loop;

        -- output results

    end GAUSS_SEIDEL;
```

The main problem with this solution is that we have not taken account of the boundary. Nor have we considered how to initialize the system. However, it must now be clear that using the rendezvous rather than shared variables means that the communication must completely overwhelm the computation unless the function F is extremely complex. Practical applications of distributed tasks of this kind will have much larger computational tasks to perform.

The main loop of the ITERATOR task is a bit painful. It is a pity that we cannot have entry functions. However, it could be made neater by using renaming in order to avoid repeated evaluation of DATA(I, J) and so on; this would also speed things up. Thus we could write

```
procedure GET_P1(X: out REAL) renames DATA(I-1, J).GET_P;
procedure GET_P2(X: out REAL) renames DATA(I+1, J).GET_P;
...
procedure SET_P(X: in REAL) renames DATA(I, J).SET_P;
procedure GET_CONVERGED(B: out BOOLEAN) renames
                                    DATA(I, J).GET_CONVERGED;
```

and then

```
GET_P1(P1); GET_P2(P2); GET_P3(P3); GET_P4(P4);
SET_P(0.25 * (P1+P2+P3+P4-F(I, J)));
GET_CONVERGED(CONVERGED);
exit when CONVERGED;
```

Answers 15

Exercise 15.1

```
1       with DIRECT_IO;
        generic
            type ELEMENT is private;
        procedure REV(FROM, TO: STRING);
```

```
procedure REV(FROM, TO: STRING) is
   package IO is new DIRECT_IO(ELEMENT);
   use IO;
   INPUT: FILE_TYPE;
   OUTPUT: FILE_TYPE;
   X: ELEMENT;
begin
   OPEN(INPUT, IN_FILE, FROM);
   OPEN(OUTPUT, OUT_FILE, TO);
   SET_INDEX(OUTPUT, SIZE(INPUT));
   loop
      READ(INPUT, X);
      WRITE(OUTPUT, X);
      exit when END_OF_FILE(INPUT);
      SET_INDEX(OUTPUT, INDEX(OUTPUT)−2);
   end loop;
   CLOSE(INPUT);
   CLOSE(OUTPUT);
end REV;
```

Remember that **reverse** is a reserved word. Note also that this does not work if the file is empty (the first call of SET_INDEX will raise CONSTRAINT_ERROR). However, this is an improvement on the solution in earlier editions of this book which always raised CONSTRAINT_ERROR. I am very grateful to Vittorio Frigo of CERN for pointing out this blunder.

Exercise 15.2

1   The output is shown in string quotes in order to reveal the layout. Spaces are indicated by s. In reality of course, there are no quotes and spaces are spaces.

    (a)   "FRED"
    (b)   "sss120"
    (c)   "sssss120"
    (d)   "120"
    (e)   "−120"
    (f)   "ss8#170#"
    (g)   "−3.80000E+01"
    (h)   "sssss7.00E−2"
    (i)   "3.1416E+01"
    (j)   "1.0E+10"

2   with TEXT_IO;
     package body SIMPLE_IO is

```
     package FLOAT_IO is new TEXT_IO.FLOAT_IO(FLOAT);

     procedure GET(F: out FLOAT) is
     begin
        FLOAT_IO.GET(F);
     end GET;

     procedure PUT(F: in FLOAT) is
     begin
        FLOAT_IO.PUT(F);
     end PUT;

     procedure PUT(S: in STRING) is
     begin
        TEXT_IO.PUT(S);
     end PUT;
```

```
procedure NEW_LINE(N: in INTEGER:= 1) is
begin
    TEXT_IO.NEW_LINE(TEXT_IO.COUNT(N));
end NEW_LINE;

end SIMPLE_IO;
```

Note that we have chosen to call the instantiated package FLOAT_IO; this causes no confusion (except perhaps for the reader) since the new package merely prevents direct access (via a use clause) to the generic one of the same name. This does not matter since we are using the full dotted notation to access the generic one. In any event we have to use the full notation in the procedures in order to avoid recursion so there is little point in a use clause for TEXT_IO.

The other point of note is the type conversion in NEW_LINE.

Answers 16

Exercise 16.1

1 (a) dynamic – INTEGER
     (b) static – INTEGER
     (c) static – universal integer

Exercise 16.4

1

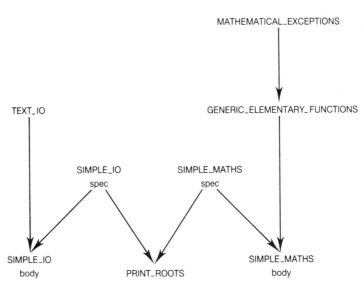

We have assumed that TEXT_IO and GENERIC_ELEMENTARY_FUNCTIONS are self-contained. Note moreover that insisting that generic specifications and bodies are compiled together requires that the specification and body of TEXT_IO are also compiled together; this is because the specifications and bodies of the generic units INTEGER_IO, FLOAT_IO and so on are themselves in the specification and body of TEXT_IO respectively.

Exercise 16.5

1 (a) The order of evaluation of the operands I and F of " + " is not defined. As a result the effect could be

```
        I:= 1+2;                        —— I first
or      I:= 2+2;                        —— F first
```

(b)   The order of evaluation of the destination A(I) and the value F is not defined. The effect could be

```
        A(1):= 2;                       —— I first
or      A(2):= 2;                       —— F first
```

(c)   The order of evaluation of the two indexes is not defined. The effect could be

```
        AA(1, 2):= 0;                   —— I first
or      AA(2, 2):= 0;                   —— F first
```

Bibliography

The following selection for further reading comprises a number of books which the author believes will be found helpful. It is by no means exhaustive and omits many other books which make a valuable contribution to the Ada literature. However, if you are new to Ada and wish to build a library then this list is a good starting point.

Nissen, J. C. and Wallis, P. J. L., eds. (1984). *Portability and Style in Ada*. Cambridge University Press
This covers in much more detail some of the topics addressed in Sections 16.5 and 16.6. The section on portability is comprehensive and accurate; that on style is naturally more a matter of opinion. Anyone writing serious portable Ada programs should read this book.

Burns, A. (1986). *Concurrent Programming in Ada*. Cambridge University Press
This is a very complete account of Ada tasking and contains further examples which complement those in Chapter 14.

Ford, B., Kok, J. and Rogers, M. W., eds. (1986). *Scientific Ada*. Cambridge University Press
Do not be put off by the apparently specialized topic. This book does indeed deal in depth with the use of Ada for numerical calculations. But it also includes much useful discussion about separate compilation and generics which is relevant to all applications.

Cohen, N. H. (1986). *Ada as a Second Language*. McGraw-Hill
This is a rather comprehensive account of the Ada language. It is a large book and contains many examples explored in detail. Its coverage of Ada is not quite complete; it omits a number of minor issues which we have addressed in this book but on the other hand it discusses some topics that we have skimped (especially the pragmas and machine-dependent bits). It also has myriads of exercises but no solutions (just as well because otherwise it would be 2000 pages!).

Booch, G. (1986). *Software Engineering with Ada*, 2nd edn. Benjamin Cummings
This well-known classic was one of the first books to discuss how to design programs in Ada; it is especially famed for Object Oriented Programming.

Sommerville, I. and Morrison, R. (1987). *Software Development with Ada*. Addison-Wesley
This book covers a broad number of topics concerning how to develop well structured reliable Ada programs. A good book to dip into. It contains a large bibliography.

Le Verrand, D. (1985). *Evaluating Ada* (English translation). North Oxford Academic
This is a critical review of Ada and gives the reader further insight into the design of Ada and how to get the most out of it.

Hibbard, P., Hisgen, A., Rosenberg, J., Shaw, M. and Sherman, M. (1983). *Studies in Ada Style*, 2nd edn. Springer-Verlag
This excellent book contains a detailed analysis of a small number of intricate programs which explore important issues of structure. A lot can be learnt from really understanding them.

Ausnit, C. N., Cohen, N. H., Goodenough, J. B. and Eanes, R. S. (1985). *Ada in Practice*. Springer-Verlag
This is another book containing a number of examples explored in depth.

Wallis, P. J. L. and Gautier, R. J., eds. (1990). *Software Reuse with Ada*. Peter Peregrinus
This contains a very good discussion on how to design reusable software components in Ada.

Dawes, J. (1988). *Ada*. Pitman
This useful little book is a handy reference guide to Ada. It covers the whole language in 200 pages.

The following books are of a more general nature.

Langley Moore, D. (1977). *Ada, Countess of Lovelace*. John Murray
This is a classical biography of Lord Byron's daughter after whom the language is named.

Stein, D. (1985). *Ada, A Life and a Legacy*. MIT Press
This biography contains more about Ada's relationship and technical work with Charles Babbage.

Nabokov, V. (1969). *Ada*. Weidenfeld and Nicolson
The title of this book is an illustration of overloading. It has nothing to do with either Ada the language or the Countess of Lovelace. However, if you are fed up with programming languages, this novel brings light relief and will provoke interesting comment if placed in your library.

Index

ANSI/MIL-STD-1815A-1983
February 17, 1983

REFERENCE MANUAL FOR THE

Ada®

PROGRAMMING LANGUAGE

ANSI/MIL-STD-1815A-1983

United States Department of Defense

Approved February 17, 1983
American National Standards Institute, Inc.

Foreword

Ada is the result of a collective effort to design a common language for programming large scale and real-time systems.

The common high order language program began in 1974. The requirements of the United States Department of Defense were formalized in a series of documents which were extensively reviewed by the Services, industrial organizations, universities, and foreign military departments. The Ada language was designed in accordance with the final (1978) form of these requirements, embodied in the Steelman specification.

The Ada design team was led by Jean D. Ichbiah and has included Bernd Krieg-Brueckner, Brian A. Wichmann, Henry F. Ledgard, Jean-Claude Heliard, Jean-Loup Gailly, Jean-Raymond Abrial, John G.P. Barnes, Mike Woodger, Olivier Roubine, Paul N. Hilfinger, and Robert Firth.

At various stages of the project, several people closely associated with the design team made major contributions. They include J.B. Goodenough, R.F. Brender, M.W. Davis, G. Ferran, K. Lester, L. MacLaren, E. Morel, I.R. Nassi, I.C. Pyle, S.A. Schuman, and S.C. Vestal.

Two parallel efforts that were started in the second phase of this design had a deep influence on the language. One was the development of a formal definition using denotational semantics, with the participation of V. Donzeau-Gouge, G. Kahn, and B. Lang. The other was the design of a test translator with the participation of K. Ripken, P. Boullier, P. Cadiou, J. Holden, J.F. Hueras, R.G. Lange, and D.T. Cornhill. The entire effort benefitted from the dedicated assistance of Lyn Churchill and Marion Myers, and the effective technical support of B. Gravem, W.L. Heimerdinger, and P. Cleve. H.G. Schmitz served as program manager.

Over the five years spent on this project, several intense week-long design reviews were conducted, with the participation of P. Belmont, B. Brosgol, P. Cohen, R. Dewar, A. Evans, G. Fisher, H. Harte, A.L. Hisgen, P. Knueven, M. Kronental, N. Lomuto, E. Ploedereder, G. Seegmueller, V. Stenning, D. Taffs, and also F. Belz, R. Converse, K. Correll, A.N. Habermann, J. Sammet, S. Squires, J. Teller, P. Wegner, and P.R. Wetherall.

Several persons had a constructive influence with their comments, criticisms and suggestions. They include P. Brinch Hansen, G. Goos, C.A.R. Hoare, Mark Rain, W.A. Wulf, and also E. Boebert, P. Bonnard, H. Clausen, M. Cox, G. Dismukes, R. Eachus, T. Froggatt, H. Ganzinger, C. Hewitt, S. Kamin, R. Kotler, O. Lecarme, J.A.N. Lee, J.L. Mansion, F. Minel, T. Phinney, J. Roehrich, V. Schneider, A. Singer, D. Slosberg, I.C. Wand, the reviewers of Ada-Europe, AdaTEC, Afcet, those of the LMSC review team, and those of the Ada Tokyo Study Group.

These reviews and comments, the numerous evaluation reports received at the end of the first and second phase, the nine hundred language issue reports and test and evaluation reports received from fifteen different countries during the third phase of the project, the thousands of comments received during the ANSI Canvass, and the on-going work of the IFIP Working Group 2.4 on system implementation languages and that of the Purdue Europe LTPL-E committee, all had a substantial influence on the final definition of Ada.

The Military Departments and Agencies have provided a broad base of support including funding, extensive reviews, and countless individual contributions by the members of the High Order Language Working Group and other interested personnel. In particular, William A. Whitaker provided leadership for the program during the formative stages. David A. Fisher was responsible for the successful development and refinement of the language requirement documents that led to the Steelman specification.

This language definition was developed by Cii Honeywell Bull and later Alsys, and by Honeywell Systems and Research Center, under contract to the United States Department of Defense. William E. Carlson, and later Larry E. Druffel and Robert F. Mathis, served as the technical representatives of the United States Government and effectively coordinated the efforts of all participants in the Ada program.

This reference manual was prepared with a formatter specialized for Ada texts. It was developed by Jon F. Hueras for Multics, using the Cii Honeywell Bull photocomposition system.

Table of Contents

Annexes

Appendices

Index

Postscript: Submission of Comments

1. Introduction

Ada is a programming language designed in accordance with requirements defined by the United States Department of Defense: the so-called Steelman requirements. Overall, these requirements call for a language with considerable expressive power covering a wide application domain. As a result, the language includes facilities offered by classical languages such as Pascal as well as facilities often found only in specialized languages. Thus the language is a modern algorithmic language with the usual control structures, and with the ability to define types and subprograms. It also serves the need for modularity, whereby data, types, and subprograms can be packaged. It treats modularity in the physical sense as well, with a facility to support separate compilation.

In addition to these aspects, the language covers real-time programming, with facilities to model parallel tasks and to handle exceptions. It also covers systems programming; this requires precise control over the representation of data and access to system-dependent properties. Finally, both application-level and machine-level input-output are defined.

1.1 Scope of the Standard

This standard specifies the form and meaning of program units written in Ada. Its purpose is to promote the portability of Ada programs to a variety of data processing systems.

1.1.1 Extent of the Standard

This standard specifies:

(a) The form of a program unit written in Ada.

(b) The effect of translating and executing such a program unit.

(c) The manner in which program units may be combined to form Ada programs.

(d) The predefined program units that a conforming implementation must supply.

(e) The permissible variations within the standard, and the manner in which they must be specified.

(f) Those violations of the standard that a conforming implementation is required to detect, and the effect of attempting to translate or execute a program unit containing such violations.

(g) Those violations of the standard that a conforming implementation is not required to detect.

Extent of the Standard 1.1.1

9   This standard does not specify:

10   (h) The means whereby a program unit written in Ada is transformed into object code executable by a processor.

11   (i) The means whereby translation or execution of program units is invoked and the executing units are controlled.

12   (j) The size or speed of the object code, or the relative execution speed of different language constructs.

13   (k) The form or contents of any listings produced by implementations; in particular, the form or contents of error or warning messages.

14   (l) The effect of executing a program unit that contains any violation that a conforming implementation is not required to detect.

15   (m) The size of a program or program unit that will exceed the capacity of a particular conforming implementation.

16   Where this standard specifies that a program unit written in Ada has an exact effect, this effect is the operational meaning of the program unit and must be produced by all conforming implementations. Where this standard specifies permissible variations in the effects of constituents of a program unit written in Ada, the operational meaning of the program unit as a whole is understood to be the range of possible effects that result from all these variations, and a conforming implementation is allowed to produce any of these possible effects. Examples of permissible variations are:

17   ● The represented values of fixed or floating numeric quantities, and the results of operations upon them.

18   ● The order of execution of statements in different parallel tasks, in the absence of explicit synchronization.

1.1.2 Conformity of an Implementation with the Standard

1   A conforming implementation is one that:

2   (a) Correctly translates and executes legal program units written in Ada, provided that they are not so large as to exceed the capacity of the implementation.

3   (b) Rejects all program units that are so large as to exceed the capacity of the implementation.

4   (c) Rejects all program units that contain errors whose detection is required by the standard.

5   (d) Supplies all predefined program units required by the standard.

6   (e) Contains no variations except where the standard permits.

7   (f) Specifies all such permitted variations in the manner prescribed by the standard.

1.2 Structure of the Standard

This reference manual contains fourteen chapters, three annexes, three appendices, and an index.   1

Each chapter is divided into sections that have a common structure. Each section introduces its   2
subject, gives any necessary syntax rules, and describes the semantics of the corresponding
language constructs. Examples and notes, and then references, may appear at the end of a section.

Examples are meant to illustrate the possible forms of the constructs described. Notes are meant   3
to emphasize consequences of the rules described in the section or elsewhere. References are
meant to attract the attention of readers to a term or phrase having a technical meaning defined in
another section.

The standard definition of the Ada programming language consists of the fourteen chapters and   4
the three annexes, subject to the following restriction: the material in each of the items listed
below is informative, and not part of the standard definition of the Ada programming language:

- Section 1.3 Design goals and sources   5

- Section 1.4 Language summary   6

- The examples, notes, and references given at the end of each section   7

- Each section whose title starts with the word "Example" or "Examples"   8

1.3 Design Goals and Sources

Ada was designed with three overriding concerns: program reliability and maintenance, program-   1
ming as a human activity, and efficiency.

The need for languages that promote reliability and simplify maintenance is well established.   2
Hence emphasis was placed on program readability over ease of writing. For example, the rules of
the language require that program variables be explicitly declared and that their type be specified.
Since the type of a variable is invariant, compilers can ensure that operations on variables are compatible with the properties intended for objects of the type. Furthermore, error-prone notations
have been avoided, and the syntax of the language avoids the use of encoded forms in favor of
more English-like constructs. Finally, the language offers support for separate compilation of
program units in a way that facilitates program development and maintenance, and which
provides the same degree of checking between units as within a unit.

Concern for the human programmer was also stressed during the design. Above all, an attempt   3
was made to keep the language as small as possible, given the ambitious nature of the application
domain. We have attempted to cover this domain with a small number of underlying concepts
integrated in a consistent and systematic way. Nevertheless we have tried to avoid the pitfalls of
excessive involution, and in the constant search for simpler designs we have tried to provide
language constructs that correspond intuitively to what the users will normally expect.

Like many other human activities, the development of programs is becoming ever more   4
decentralized and distributed. Consequently, the ability to assemble a program from independently produced software components has been a central idea in this design. The concepts of
packages, of private types, and of generic units are directly related to this idea, which has ramifica-
tions in many other aspects of the language.

5   No language can avoid the problem of efficiency. Languages that require over-elaborate compilers, or that lead to the inefficient use of storage or execution time, force these inefficiencies on all machines and on all programs. Every construct of the language was examined in the light of present implementation techniques. Any proposed construct whose implementation was unclear or that required excessive machine resources was rejected.

6   None of the above design goals was considered as achievable after the fact. The design goals drove the entire design process from the beginning.

7   A perpetual difficulty in language design is that one must both identify the capabilities required by the application domain and design language features that provide these capabilities. The difficulty existed in this design, although to a lesser degree than usual because of the Steelman requirements. These requirements often simplified the design process by allowing it to concentrate on the design of a given system providing a well defined set of capabilities, rather than on the definition of the capabilities themselves.

8   Another significant simplification of the design work resulted from earlier experience acquired by several successful Pascal derivatives developed with similar goals. These are the languages Euclid, Lis, Mesa, Modula, and Sue. Many of the key ideas and syntactic forms developed in these languages have counterparts in Ada. Several existing languages such as Algol 68 and Simula, and also recent research languages such as Alphard and Clu, influenced this language in several respects, although to a lesser degree than did the Pascal family.

9   Finally, the evaluation reports received on an earlier formulation (the Green language), and on alternative proposals (the Red, Blue, and Yellow languages), the language reviews that took place at different stages of this project, and the thousands of comments received from fifteen different countries during the preliminary stages of the Ada design and during the ANSI canvass, all had a significant impact on the standard definition of the language.

1.4 Language Summary

1   An Ada program is composed of one or more program units. These program units can be compiled separately. Program units may be subprograms (which define executable algorithms), package units (which define collections of entities), task units (which define parallel computations), or generic units (which define parameterized forms of packages and subprograms). Each unit normally consists of two parts: a specification, containing the information that must be visible to other units, and a body, containing the implementation details, which need not be visible to other units.

2   This distinction of the specification and body, and the ability to compile units separately, allows a program to be designed, written, and tested as a set of largely independent software components.

3   An Ada program will normally make use of a library of program units of general utility. The language provides means whereby individual organizations can construct their own libraries. The text of a separately compiled program unit must name the library units it requires.

4   *Program Units*

5   A subprogram is the basic unit for expressing an algorithm. There are two kinds of subprograms: procedures and functions. A procedure is the means of invoking a series of actions. For example, it may read data, update variables, or produce some output. It may have parameters, to provide a controlled means of passing information between the procedure and the point of call.

A function is the means of invoking the computation of a value. It is similar to a procedure, but in addition will return a result.   6

A package is the basic unit for defining a collection of logically related entities. For example, a package can be used to define a common pool of data and types, a collection of related subprograms, or a set of type declarations and associated operations. Portions of a package can be hidden from the user, thus allowing access only to the logical properties expressed by the package specification.   7

A task unit is the basic unit for defining a task whose sequence of actions may be executed in parallel with those of other tasks. Such tasks may be implemented on multicomputers, multiprocessors, or with interleaved execution on a single processor. A task unit may define either a single executing task or a task type permitting the creation of any number of similar tasks.   8

Declarations and Statements   9

The body of a program unit generally contains two parts: a declarative part, which defines the logical entities to be used in the program unit, and a sequence of statements, which defines the execution of the program unit.   10

The declarative part associates names with declared entities. For example, a name may denote a type, a constant, a variable, or an exception. A declarative part also introduces the names and parameters of other nested subprograms, packages, task units, and generic units to be used in the program unit.   11

The sequence of statements describes a sequence of actions that are to be performed. The statements are executed in succession (unless an exit, return, or goto statement, or the raising of an exception, causes execution to continue from another place).   12

An assignment statement changes the value of a variable. A procedure call invokes execution of a procedure after associating any actual parameters provided at the call with the corresponding formal parameters.   13

Case statements and if statements allow the selection of an enclosed sequence of statements based on the value of an expression or on the value of a condition.   14

The loop statement provides the basic iterative mechanism in the language. A loop statement specifies that a sequence of statements is to be executed repeatedly as directed by an iteration scheme, or until an exit statement is encountered.   15

A block statement comprises a sequence of statements preceded by the declaration of local entities used by the statements.   16

Certain statements are only applicable to tasks. A delay statement delays the execution of a task for a specified duration. An entry call statement is written as a procedure call statement; it specifies that the task issuing the call is ready for a rendezvous with another task that has this entry. The called task is ready to accept the entry call when its execution reaches a corresponding accept statement, which specifies the actions then to be performed. After completion of the rendezvous, both the calling task and the task having the entry may continue their execution in parallel. One form of the select statement allows a selective wait for one of several alternative rendezvous. Other forms of the select statement allow conditional or timed entry calls.   17

18   Execution of a program unit may encounter error situations in which normal program execution cannot continue. For example, an arithmetic computation may exceed the maximum allowed value of a number, or an attempt may be made to access an array component by using an incorrect index value. To deal with such error situations, the statements of a program unit can be textually followed by exception handlers that specify the actions to be taken when the error situation arises. Exceptions can be raised explicitly by a raise statement.

19   *Data Types*

20   Every object in the language has a type, which characterizes a set of values and a set of applicable operations. The main classes of types are scalar types (comprising enumeration and numeric types), composite types, access types, and private types.

21   An enumeration type defines an ordered set of distinct enumeration literals, for example a list of states or an alphabet of characters. The enumeration types BOOLEAN and CHARACTER are predefined.

22   Numeric types provide a means of performing exact or approximate numerical computations. Exact computations use integer types, which denote sets of consecutive integers. Approximate computations use either fixed point types, with absolute bounds on the error, or floating point types, with relative bounds on the error. The numeric types INTEGER, FLOAT, and DURATION are predefined.

23   Composite types allow definitions of structured objects with related components. The composite types in the language provide for arrays and records. An array is an object with indexed components of the same type. A record is an object with named components of possibly different types. The array type STRING is predefined.

24   A record may have special components called discriminants. Alternative record structures that depend on the values of discriminants can be defined within a record type.

25   Access types allow the construction of linked data structures created by the evaluation of allocators. They allow several variables of an access type to designate the same object, and components of one object to designate the same or other objects. Both the elements in such a linked data structure and their relation to other elements can be altered during program execution.

26   Private types can be defined in a package that conceals structural details that are externally irrelevant. Only the logically necessary properties (including any discriminants) are made visible to the users of such types.

27   The concept of a type is refined by the concept of a subtype, whereby a user can constrain the set of allowed values of a type. Subtypes can be used to define subranges of scalar types, arrays with a limited set of index values, and records and private types with particular discriminant values.

28   *Other Facilities*

29   Representation clauses can be used to specify the mapping between types and features of an underlying machine. For example, the user can specify that objects of a given type must be represented with a given number of bits, or that the components of a record are to be represented using a given storage layout. Other features allow the controlled use of low level, nonportable, or implementation-dependent aspects, including the direct insertion of machine code.

30   Input-output is defined in the language by means of predefined library packages. Facilities are provided for input-output of values of user-defined as well as of predefined types. Standard means of representing values in display form are also provided.

Finally, the language provides a powerful means of parameterization of program units, called   31
generic program units. The generic parameters can be types and subprograms (as well as objects)
and so allow general algorithms to be applied to all types of a given class.

1.5 Method of Description and Syntax Notation

The form of Ada program units is described by means of a context-free syntax together with   1
context-dependent requirements expressed by narrative rules.

The meaning of Ada program units is described by means of narrative rules defining both the   2
effects of each construct and the composition rules for constructs.   This narrative employs
technical terms whose precise definition is given in the text (references to the section containing
the definition of a technical term appear at the end of each section that uses the term).

All other terms are in the English language and bear their natural meaning, as defined in Webster's   3
Third New International Dictionary of the English Language.

The context-free syntax of the language is described using a simple variant of Backus-Naur-Form.   4
In particular,

(a) Lower case words, some containing embedded underlines, are used to denote syntactic   5
     categories, for example:

     adding_operator

     Whenever the name of a syntactic category is used apart from the syntax rules themselves,   6
     spaces take the place of the underlines (thus: adding operator).

(b) Boldface words are used to denote reserved words, for example: 7

     array

(c) Square brackets enclose optional items. Thus the two following rules are equivalent.   8

          return_statement ::= **return** [expression];
          return_statement ::= **return**; | **return** expression;

(d) Braces enclose a repeated item. The item may appear zero or more times; the repetitions   9
     occur from left to right as with an equivalent left-recursive rule. Thus the two following rules
     are equivalent.

          term ::= factor {multiplying_operator factor}
          term ::= factor | term multiplying_operator factor

10   (e)   A vertical bar separates alternative items unless it occurs immediately after an opening brace, in which case it stands for itself:

```
letter_or_digit ::= letter | digit
component_association ::= [choice {| choice} =>] expression
```

11   (f)   If the name of any syntactic category starts with an italicized part, it is equivalent to the category name without the italicized part. The italicized part is intended to convey some semantic information. For example *type*_name and *task*_name are both equivalent to name alone.

Note:

12   The syntax rules describing structured constructs are presented in a form that corresponds to the recommended paragraphing. For example, an if statement is defined as

```
if_statement ::=
    if condition then
      sequence_of_statements
  { elsif condition then
      sequence_of_statements}
  [ else
      sequence_of_statements]
    end if;
```

13   Different lines are used for parts of a syntax rule if the corresponding parts of the construct described by the rule are intended to be on different lines. Indentation in the rule is a recommendation for indentation of the corresponding part of the construct. It is recommended that all indentations be by multiples of a basic step of indentation (the number of spaces for the basic step is not defined). The preferred places for other line breaks are after semicolons. On the other hand, if a complete construct can fit on one line, this is also allowed in the recommended paragraphing.

1.6 Classification of Errors

1   The language definition classifies errors into several different categories:

2   (a)   Errors that must be detected at compilation time by every Ada compiler.

3   These errors correspond to any violation of a rule given in this reference manual, other than the violations that correspond to (b) or (c) below. In particular, violation of any rule that uses the terms *must*, *allowed*, *legal*, or *illegal* belongs to this category. Any program that contains such an error is not a legal Ada program; on the other hand, the fact that a program is legal does not mean, per se, that the program is free from other forms of error.

4   (b)   Errors that must be detected at run time by the execution of an Ada program.

5   The corresponding error situations are associated with the names of the predefined exceptions. Every Ada compiler is required to generate code that raises the corresponding exception if such an error situation arises during program execution. If an exception is certain to be raised in every execution of a program, then compilers are allowed (although not required) to report this fact at compilation time.

(c) Erroneous execution.

6

The language rules specify certain rules to be obeyed by Ada programs, although there is no requirement on Ada compilers to provide either a compilation-time or a run-time detection of the violation of such rules. The errors of this category are indicated by the use of the word *erroneous* to qualify the execution of the corresponding constructs. The effect of erroneous execution is unpredictable.

7

(d) Incorrect order dependences.

8

Whenever the reference manual specifies that different parts of a given construct are to be executed *in some order that is not defined by the language*, this means that the implementation is allowed to execute these parts in any given order, following the rules that result from that given order, but not in parallel. Furthermore, the construct is incorrect if execution of these parts in a different order would have a different effect. Compilers are not required to provide either compilation-time or run-time detection of incorrect order dependences. The foregoing is expressed in terms of the process that is called execution; it applies equally to the processes that are called evaluation and elaboration.

9

If a compiler is able to recognize at compilation time that a construct is erroneous or contains an incorrect order dependence, then the compiler is allowed to generate, in place of the code otherwise generated for the construct, code that raises the predefined exception PROGRAM_ERROR. Similarly, compilers are allowed to generate code that checks at run time for erroneous constructs, for incorrect order dependences, or for both. The predefined exception PROGRAM_ERROR is raised if such a check fails.

10

2. Lexical Elements

The text of a program consists of the texts of one or more compilations. The text of a compilation   1
is a sequence of lexical elements, each composed of characters; the rules of composition are given
in this chapter. Pragmas, which provide certain information for the compiler, are also described in
this chapter.

References: character 2.1, compilation 10.1, lexical element 2.2, pragma 2.8   2

2.1 Character Set

The only characters allowed in the text of a program are the graphic characters and format effec-   1
tors. Each graphic character corresponds to a unique code of the *ISO* seven-bit coded character
set (*ISO* standard 646), and is represented (visually) by a graphical symbol. Some graphic
characters are represented by different graphical symbols in alternative national representations of
the *ISO* character set. The description of the language definition in this standard reference manual
uses the *ASCII* graphical symbols, the *ANSI* graphical representation of the *ISO* character set.

```
graphic_character ::= basic_graphic_character
   | lower_case_letter | other_special_character
```
2
```
basic_graphic_character ::=
     upper_case_letter | digit
   | special_character | space_character
```
```
basic_character ::=
     basic_graphic_character | format_effector
```

The basic character set is sufficient for writing any program. The characters included in each of the   3
categories of basic graphic characters are defined as follows:

(a) upper case letters   4
 A B C D E F G H I J K L M N O P Q R S T U V W X Y Z

(b) digits   5
  0 1 2 3 4 5 6 7 8 9

(c) special characters   6
  " # & ' ( ) . * + , - . / : ; < = > _ |

(d) the space character   7

Format effectors are the *ISO* (and *ASCII*) characters called horizontal tabulation, vertical tabula-   8
tion, carriage return, line feed, and form feed.

The characters included in each of the remaining categories of graphic characters are defined as follows:

(e)   lower case letters
      a b c d e f g h i j k l m n o p q r s t u v w x y z

(f)   other special characters
      ! $ % ? @ [\ ] ^ ` { } ~

Allowable replacements for the special characters vertical bar (|), sharp (#), and quotation (") are defined in section 2.10.

Notes:

The *ISO* character that corresponds to the sharp graphical symbol in the *ASCII* representation appears as a pound sterling symbol in the French, German, and United Kingdom standard national representations. In any case, the font design of graphical symbols (for example, whether they are in italic or bold typeface) is not part of the *ISO* standard.

The meanings of the acronyms used in this section are as follows: *ANSI* stands for American National Standards Institute, *ASCII* stands for American Standard Code for Information Interchange, and *ISO* stands for International Organization for Standardization.

The following names are used when referring to special characters and other special haracters:

symbol	name	symbol	name
"	quotation	>	greater than
#	sharp	_	underline
&	ampersand	|	vertical bar
'	apostrophe	!	exclamation mark
(	left parenthesis	$	dollar
)	right parenthesis	%	percent
*	star, multiply	?	question mark
+	plus	@	commercial at
,	comma	[	left square bracket
-	hyphen, minus	\	back-slash
.	dot, point, period	]	right square bracket
/	slash, divide	^	circumflex
:	colon	`	grave accent
;	semicolon	{	left brace
<	less than	}	right brace
=	equal	~	tilde

2.2 Lexical Elements, Separators, and Delimiters

The text of a program consists of the texts of one or more compilations. The text of each compilation is a sequence of separate lexical elements. Each lexical element is either a delimiter, an identifier (which may be a reserved word), a numeric literal, a character literal, a string literal, or a comment. The effect of a program depends only on the particular sequences of lexical elements that form its compilations, excluding the comments, if any.

In some cases an explicit *separator* is required to separate adjacent lexical elements (namely,   2
when without separation, interpretation as a single lexical element is possible). A separator is any
of a space character, a format effector, or the end of a line. A space character is a separator except
within a comment, a string literal, or a space character literal. Format effectors other than horizontal tabulation are always separators. Horizontal tabulation is a separator except within a comment.

The end of a line is always a separator. The language does not define what causes the end of a line.   3
However if, for a given implementation, the end of a line is signified by one or more characters,
then these characters must be format effectors other than horizontal tabulation. In any case, a
sequence of one or more format effectors other than horizontal tabulation must cause at least one
end of line.

One or more separators are allowed between any two adjacent lexical elements, before the first of   4
each compilation, or after the last. At least one separator is required between an identifier or a
numeric literal and an adjacent identifier or numeric literal.

A *delimiter* is either one of the following special characters (in the basic character set)   5

    & ' ( ) * + , - . / : ; < = > |

or one of the following *compound delimiters* each composed of two adjacent special characters   6

    =>   ..   **   :=   /=   >=   <=   <<   >>   <>

Each of the special characters listed for single character delimiters is a single delimiter except if   7
this character is used as a character of a compound delimiter, or as a character of a comment, string literal, character literal, or numeric literal.

The remaining forms of lexical element are described in other sections of this chapter.   8

Notes:

Each lexical element must fit on one line, since the end of a line is a separator. The quotation,   9
sharp, and underline characters, likewise two adjacent hyphens, are not delimiters, but may form
part of other lexical elements.

The following names are used when referring to compound delimiters: 10

delimiter	name
=>	arrow
..	double dot
**	double star, exponentiate
:=	assignment (pronounced: "becomes")
/=	inequality (pronounced: "not equal")
>=	greater than or equal
<=	less than or equal
<<	left label bracket
>>	right label bracket
<>	box

References: character literal 2.5, comment 2.7, compilation 10.1, format effector 2.1, identifier 2.3, numeric literal   11
2.4, reserved word 2.9, space character 2.1, special character 2.1, string literal 2.6

2.3 Identifiers

1   Identifiers are used as names and also as reserved words.

2
```
identifier ::=
    letter {[underline] letter_or_digit}

letter_or_digit ::= letter | digit

letter ::= upper_case_letter | lower_case_letter
```

3   All characters of an identifier are significant, including any underline character inserted between a letter or digit and an adjacent letter or digit. Identifiers differing only in the use of corresponding upper and lower case letters are considered as the same.

4   *Examples:*

COUNT	X	get_symbol	Ethelyn	Marion
SNOBOL_4	X1	PageCount	STORE_NEXT_ITEM	

Note:

5   No space is allowed within an identifier since a space is a separator.

6   *References:* digit 2.1, lower case letter 2.1, name 4.1, reserved word 2.9, separator 2.2, space character 2.1, upper case letter 2.1

2.4 Numeric Literals

1   There are two classes of numeric literals: real literals and integer literals. A real literal is a numeric literal that includes a point; an integer literal is a numeric literal without a point. Real literals are the literals of the type *universal_real*. Integer literals are the literals of the type *universal_integer*.

2
```
numeric_literal ::= decimal_literal | based_literal
```

3   *References:* literal 4.2, universal_integer type 3.5.4, universal_real type 3.5.6

2.4.1 Decimal Literals

1   A decimal literal is a numeric literal expressed in the conventional decimal notation (that is, the base is implicitly ten).

2
```
decimal_literal ::= integer [.integer] [exponent]

integer ::= digit {[underline] digit}

exponent ::= E [+] integer | E - integer
```

An underline character inserted between adjacent digits of a decimal literal does not affect the value of this numeric literal. The letter E of the exponent, if any, can be written either in lower case or in upper case, with the same meaning.   3

An exponent indicates the power of ten by which the value of the decimal literal without the exponent is to be multiplied to obtain the value of the decimal literal with the exponent. An exponent for an integer literal must not have a minus sign.   4

Examples: 5

```
12        0        1E6     123_456        --   integer literals

12.0      0.0      0.456   3.14159_26     --   real literals

1.34E-12  1.0E+6   --   real literals with exponent
```

Notes:

Leading zeros are allowed. No space is allowed in a numeric literal, not even between constituents of the exponent, since a space is a separator. A zero exponent is allowed for an integer literal.   6

References: digit 2.1, lower case letter 2.1, numeric literal 2.4, separator 2.2, space character 2.1, upper case letter 2.1   7

2.4.2 Based Literals

A based literal is a numeric literal expressed in a form that specifies the base explicitly. The base must be at least two and at most sixteen.   1

```
based_literal ::=
    base # based_Integer [.based_integer] # [exponent]

base ::= integer

based_integer ::=
    extended_digit {[underline] extended_digit}

extended_digit ::= digit | letter
```

An underline character inserted between adjacent digits of a based literal does not affect the value of this numeric literal. The base and the exponent, if any, are in decimal notation. The only letters allowed as extended digits are the letters A through F for the digits ten through fifteen. A letter in a based literal (either an extended digit or the letter E of an exponent) can be written either in lower case or in upper case, with the same meaning.   3

The conventional meaning of based notation is assumed; in particular the value of each extended digit of a based literal must be less than the base. An exponent indicates the power of the base by which the value of the based literal without the exponent is to be multiplied to obtain the value of the based literal with the exponent.   4

5   *Examples:*

  2#1111_1111#   16#FF#   016#0FF#   -- integer literals of value 255
  16#E#E1   2#1110_0000#   -- integer literals of value 224
  16#F.FF#E+2   2#1.1111_1111_111#E11   -- real literals of value 4095.0

6   *References:* digit 2.1, exponent 2.4.1, letter 2.3, lower case letter 2.1, numeric literal 2.4, upper case letter 2.1

2.5 Character Literals

1   A character literal is formed by enclosing one of the 95 graphic characters (including the space) between two apostrophe characters. A character literal has a value that belongs to a character type.

2   character_literal ::= 'graphic_character'

3   *Examples:*

  'A'   '*'   '''   ' '

4   *References:* character type 3.5.2, graphic character 2.1, literal 4.2, space character 2.1

2.6 String Literals

1   A string literal is formed by a sequence of graphic characters (possibly none) enclosed between two quotation characters used as *string brackets*.

2   string_literal ::= "{graphic_character}"

3   A string literal has a value that is a sequence of character values corresponding to the graphic characters of the string literal apart from the quotation character itself. If a quotation character value is to be represented in the sequence of character values, then a pair of adjacent quotation characters must be written at the corresponding place within the string literal. (This means that a string literal that includes two adjacent quotation characters is never interpreted as two adjacent string literals.)

4   The *length* of a string literal is the number of character values in the sequence represented. (Each doubled quotation character is counted as a single character.)

5   *Examples:*

  "Message of the day:"

  ""   -- an empty string literal
  " "   "A"   """"   -- three string literals of length 1

  "Characters such as $, %, and } are allowed in string literals"

Note:

A string literal must fit on one line since it is a lexical element (see 2.2). Longer sequences of   6
graphic character values can be obtained by catenation of string literals. Similarly catenation of
constants declared in the package ASCII can be used to obtain sequences of character values that
include nongraphic character values (the so-called control characters). Examples of such uses of
catenation are given below:

    "FIRST PART OF A SEQUENCE OF CHARACTERS " &
    "THAT CONTINUES ON THE NEXT LINE"

    "sequence that includes the" & ASCII.ACK & "control character"

References: ascii predefined package C, catenation operation 4.5.3, character value 3.5.2, constant 3.2.1,   7
declaration 3.1, end of a line 2.2, graphic character 2.1, lexical element 2.2

2.7 Comments

A comment starts with two adjacent hyphens and extends up to the end of the line. A comment   1
can appear on any line of a program. The presence or absence of comments has no influence on
whether a program is legal or illegal. Furthermore, comments do not influence the effect of a
program; their sole purpose is the enlightenment of the human reader.

Examples: 2

    —   the last sentence above echoes the Algol 68 report

    end; --   processing of LINE is complete

    --   a long comment may be split onto
    --   two or more consecutive lines

    ----------------   the first two hyphens start the comment

Note:

Horizontal tabulation can be used in comments, after the double hyphen, and is equivalent to one   3
or more spaces (see 2.2).

References: end of a line 2.2, illegal 1.6, legal 1.6, space character 2.1   4

2.8 Pragmas

A pragma is used to convey information to the compiler. A pragma starts with the reserved word   1
pragma followed by an identifier that is the name of the pragma.

    pragma ::=
        pragma identifier [(argument_association {, argument_association})];   2

    argument_association ::=
        [*argument*_identifier =>] name
      | [*argument*_identifier =>] expression

3   Pragmas are only allowed at the following places in a program:

4   • After a semicolon delimiter, but not within a formal part or discriminant part.

5   • At any place where the syntax rules allow a construct defined by a syntactic category whose name ends with "declaration", "statement", "clause", or "alternative", or one of the syntactic categories variant and exception handler; but not in place of such a construct. Also at any place where a compilation unit would be allowed.

6   Additional restrictions exist for the placement of specific pragmas.

7   Some pragmas have arguments. Argument associations can be either positional or named as for parameter associations of subprogram calls (see 6.4). Named associations are, however, only possible if the argument identifiers are defined. A name given in an argument must be either a name visible at the place of the pragma or an identifier specific to the pragma.

8   The pragmas defined by the language are described in Annex B: they must be supported by every implementation. In addition, an implementation may provide implementation-defined pragmas, which must then be described in Appendix F. An implementation is not allowed to define pragmas whose presence or absence influences the legality of the text outside such pragmas. Consequently, the legality of a program does not depend on the presence or absence of implementation-defined pragmas.

9   A pragma that is not language-defined has no effect if its identifier is not recognized by the (current) implementation. Furthermore, a pragma (whether language-defined or implementation-defined) has no effect if its placement or its arguments do not correspond to what is allowed for the pragma. The region of text over which a pragma has an effect depends on the pragma.

10   *Examples:*

```
pragma LIST(OFF);
pragma OPTIMIZE(TIME);
pragma INLINE(SETMASK);
pragma SUPPRESS(RANGE_CHECK, ON => INDEX);
```

Note:

11   It is recommended (but not required) that implementations issue warnings for pragmas that are not recognized and therefore ignored.

12   *References:* compilation unit 10.1, delimiter 2.2, discriminant part 3.7.1, exception handler 11.2, expression 4.4, formal part 6.1, identifier 2.3, implementation-defined pragma F, language-defined pragma B, legal 1.6, name 4.1, reserved word 2.9, statement 5, static expression 4.9, variant 3.7.3, visibility 8.3

13   *Categories ending with "declaration" comprise:* basic declaration 3.1, component declaration 3.7, entry declaration 9.5, generic parameter declaration 12.1

14   *Categories ending with "clause" comprise:* alignment clause 13.4, component clause 13.4, context clause 10.1.1, representation clause 13.1, use clause 8.4, with clause 10.1.1

15   *Categories ending with "alternative" comprise:* accept alternative 9.7.1, case statement alternative 5.4, delay alternative 9.7.1, select alternative 9.7.1, selective wait alternative 9.7.1, terminate alternative 9.7.1

2.9 Reserved Words

The identifiers listed below are called *reserved words* and are reserved for special significance in the language. For readability of this manual, the reserved words appear in lower case boldface. 1

abort	**declare**	**generic**	**of**	**select**	2
abs	**delay**	**goto**	**or**	**separate**	
accept	**delta**		**others**	**subtype**	
access	**digits**	**if**	**out**		
all	**do**	**in**		**task**	
and		**is**	**package**	**terminate**	
array			**pragma**	**then**	
at	**else**		**private**	**type**	
	elsif	**limited**	**procedure**		
	end	**loop**			
begin	**entry**		**raise**	**use**	
body	**exception**		**range**		
	exit	**mod**	**record**	**when**	
			rem	**while**	
		new	**renames**	**with**	
case	**for**	**not**	**return**		
constant	**function**	**null**	**reverse**	**xor**	

A reserved word must not be used as a declared identifier. 3

Notes:

Reserved words differing only in the use of corresponding upper and lower case letters are considered as the same (see 2.3). In some attributes the identifier that appears after the apostrophe is identical to some reserved word. 4

References: attribute 4.1.4, declaration 3.1, identifier 2.3, lower case letter 2.1, upper case letter 2.1 5

2.10 Allowable Replacements of Characters

The following replacements are allowed for the vertical bar, sharp, and quotation basic characters: 1

- A vertical bar character (|) can be replaced by an exclamation mark (!) where used as a delimiter. 2

- The sharp characters (#) of a based literal can be replaced by colons (:) provided that the replacement is done for both occurrences. 3

- The quotation characters (") used as string brackets at both ends of a string literal can be replaced by percent characters (%) provided that the enclosed sequence of characters contains no quotation character, and provided that both string brackets are replaced. Any percent character within the sequence of characters must then be doubled and each such doubled percent character is interpreted as a single percent character value. 4

5   These replacements do not change the meaning of the program.

Notes:

6   It is recommended that use of the replacements for the vertical bar, sharp, and quotation characters be restricted to cases where the corresponding graphical symbols are not available. Note that the vertical bar appears as a broken bar on some equipment; replacement is not recommended in this case.

7   The rules given for identifiers and numeric literals are such that lower case and upper case letters can be used indifferently; these lexical elements can thus be written using only characters of the basic character set. If a string literal of the predefined type STRING contains characters that are not in the basic character set, the same sequence of character values can be obtained by catenating string literals that contain only characters of the basic character set with suitable character constants declared in the predefined package ASCII. Thus the string literal "AB$CD" could be replaced by "AB" & ASCII.DOLLAR & "CD". Similarly, the string literal "ABcd" with lower case letters could be replaced by "AB" & ASCII.LC_C & ASCII.LC_D.

8   *References:* ascii predefined package C, based literal 2.4.2, basic character 2.1, catenation operation 4.5.3, character value 3.5.2, delimiter 2.2, graphic character 2.1, graphical symbol 2.1, identifier 2.3, lexical element 2.2, lower case letter 2.1, numeric literal 2.4, string bracket 2.6, string literal 2.6, upper case letter 2.1

3. Declarations and Types

This chapter describes the types in the language and the rules for declaring constants, variables, and named numbers. [1]

3.1 Declarations

The language defines several kinds of entities that are declared, either explicitly or implicitly, by declarations. Such an entity can be a numeric literal, an object, a discriminant, a record component, a loop parameter, an exception, a type, a subtype, a subprogram, a package, a task unit, a generic unit, a single entry, an entry family, a formal parameter (of a subprogram, entry, or generic subprogram), a generic formal parameter, a named block or loop, a labeled statement, or an operation (in particular, an attribute or an enumeration literal; see 3.3.3). [1]

There are several forms of declaration. A basic declaration is a form of declaration defined as follows. [2]

```
basic_declaration ::=
      object_declaration       | number_declaration
    | type_declaration         | subtype_declaration
    | subprogram_declaration   | package_declaration
    | task_declaration         | generic_declaration
    | exception_declaration    | generic_instantiation
    | renaming_declaration     | deferred_constant_declaration
```
[3]

Certain forms of declaration always occur (explicitly) as part of a basic declaration; these forms are discriminant specifications, component declarations, entry declarations, parameter specifications, generic parameter declarations, and enumeration literal specifications. A loop parameter specification is a form of declaration that occurs only in certain forms of loop statement. [4]

The remaining forms of declaration are implicit: the name of a block, the name of a loop, and a statement label are implicitly declared. Certain operations are implicitly declared (see 3.3.3). [5]

For each form of declaration the language rules define a certain region of text called the *scope* of the declaration (see 8.2). Several forms of declaration associate an identifier with a declared entity. Within its scope, and only there, there are places where it is possible to use the identifier to refer to the associated declared entity; these places are defined by the visibility rules (see 8.3). At such places the identifier is said to be a *name* of the entity (its simple name); the name is said to *denote* the associated entity. [6]

Certain forms of enumeration literal specification associate a character literal with the corresponding declared entity. Certain forms of declaration associate an operator symbol or some other notation with an explicitly or implicitly declared operation. [7]

The process by which a declaration achieves its effect is called the *elaboration* of the declaration; this process happens during program execution. [8]

9   After its elaboration, a declaration is said to be *elaborated*. Prior to the completion of its elaboration (including before the elaboration), the declaration is not yet elaborated. The elaboration of any declaration has always at least the effect of achieving this change of state (from not yet elaborated to elaborated). The phrase *"the elaboration has no other effect"* is used in this manual whenever this change of state is the only effect of elaboration for some form of declaration. An elaboration process is also defined for declarative parts, declarative items, and compilation units (see 3.9 and 10.5).

10   Object, number, type, and subtype declarations are described here. The remaining basic declarations are described in later chapters.

Note:

11   The syntax rules use the term *identifier* for the first occurrence of an identifier in some form of declaration; the term *simple name* is used for any occurrence of an identifier that already denotes some declared entity.

12   *References:* attribute 4.1.4, block name 5.6, block statement 5.6, character literal 2.5, component declaration 3.7, declarative item 3.9, declarative part 3.9, deferred constant declaration 7.4, discriminant specification 3.7.1, elaboration 3.9, entry declaration 9.5, enumeration literal specification 3.5.1, exception declaration 11.1, generic declaration 12.1, generic instantiation 12.3, generic parameter declaration 12.1, identifier 2.3, label 5.1, loop name 5.5, loop parameter specification 5.5, loop statement 5.5, name 4.1, number declaration 3.2.2, numeric literal 2.4, object declaration 3.2.1, operation 3.3, operator symbol 6.1, package declaration 7.1, parameter specification 6.1, record component 3.7, renaming declaration 8.5, representation clause 13.1, scope 8.2, simple name 4.1, subprogram body 6.3, subprogram declaration 6.1, subtype declaration 3.3.2, task declaration 9.1, type declaration 3.3.1, visibility 8.3

3.2 Objects and Named Numbers

1   An *object* is an entity that contains (has) a value of a given type. An object is one of the following:

2   • an object declared by an object declaration or by a single task declaration,

3   • a formal parameter of a subprogram, entry, or generic subprogram,

4   • a generic formal object,

5   • a loop parameter,

6   • an object designated by a value of an access type,

7   • a component or a slice of another object.

8   A number declaration is a special form of object declaration that associates an identifier with a value of type *universal_integer* or *universal_real*.

9
```
object_declaration ::=
      identifier_list : [constant] subtype_indication [:= expression];
    | identifier_list : [constant] constrained_array_definition [:= expression];

number_declaration ::=
      identifier_list : constant := universal_static_expression;

identifier_list ::=   identifier {, identifier}
```

An object declaration is called a *single object declaration* if its identifier list has a single identifier; it   10
is called a *multiple object declaration* if the identifier list has two or more identifiers. A multiple
object declaration is equivalent to a sequence of the corresponding number of single object
declarations. For each identifier of the list, the equivalent sequence has a single object declaration
formed by this identifier, followed by a colon and by whatever appears at the right of the colon in
the multiple object declaration; the equivalent sequence is in the same order as the identifier list.

A similar equivalence applies also for the identifier lists of number declarations, component   11
declarations, discriminant specifications, parameter specifications, generic parameter declarations,
exception declarations, and deferred constant declarations.

In the remainder of this reference manual, explanations are given for declarations with a single   12
identifier; the corresponding explanations for declarations with several identifiers follow from the
equivalence stated above.

Example: 13

```
--  the multiple object declaration

JOHN, PAUL : PERSON_NAME := new PERSON(SEX => M);   --  see 3.8.1

--  is equivalent to the two single object declarations in the order given

JOHN  : PERSON_NAME := new PERSON(SEX => M);
PAUL  : PERSON_NAME := new PERSON(SEX => M);
```

References: access type 3.8, constrained array definition 3.6, component 3.3, declaration 3.1, deferred constant   14
declaration 7.4, designate 3.8, discriminant specification 3.7.1, entry 9.5, exception declaration 11.1, expression 4.4,
formal parameter 6.1, generic formal object 12.1.1, generic parameter declaration 12.1, generic unit 12, generic subprogram 12.1, identifier 2.3, loop parameter 5.5, numeric type 3.5, parameter specification 6.1, scope 8.2, simple
name 4.1, single task declaration 9.1, slice 4.1.2, static expression 4.9, subprogram 6, subtype indication 3.3.2, type
3.3, universal_integer type 3.5.4, universal_real type 3.5.6

3.2.1 Object Declarations

An object declaration declares an object whose type is given either by a subtype indication or by a   1
constrained array definition. If the object declaration includes the assignment compound delimiter
followed by an expression, the expression specifies an initial value for the declared object; the type
of the expression must be that of the object.

The declared object is a *constant* if the reserved word **constant** appears in the object declaration;   2
the declaration must then include an explicit initialization. The value of a constant cannot be
modified after initialization. Formal parameters of mode **in** of subprograms and entries, and generic
formal parameters of mode **in**, are also constants; a loop parameter is a constant within the corresponding loop; a subcomponent or slice of a constant is a constant.

An object that is not a constant is called a *variable* (in particular, the object declared by an object   3
declaration that does not include the reserved word **constant** is a variable). The only ways to
change the value of a variable are either directly by an assignment, or indirectly when the variable
is updated (see 6.2) by a procedure or entry call statement (this action can be performed either on
the variable itself, on a subcomponent of the variable, or on another variable that has the given
variable as subcomponent).

4   The elaboration of an object declaration proceeds as follows:

5   (a) The subtype indication or the constrained array definition is first elaborated. This establishes the subtype of the object.

6   (b) If the object declaration includes an explicit initialization, the initial value is obtained by evaluating the corresponding expression. Otherwise any implicit initial values for the object or for its subcomponents are evaluated.

7   (c) The object is created.

8   (d) Any initial value (whether explicit or implicit) is assigned to the object or to the corresponding subcomponent.

9   Implicit initial values are defined for objects declared by object declarations, and for components of such objects, in the following cases:

10   ● If the type of an object is an access type, the implicit initial value is the null value of the access type.

11   ● If the type of an object is a task type, the implicit initial (and only) value designates a corresponding task.

12   ● If the type of an object is a type with discriminants and the subtype of the object is constrained, the implicit initial (and only) value of each discriminant is defined by the subtype of the object.

13   ● If the type of an object is a composite type, the implicit initial value of each component that has a default expression is obtained by evaluation of this expression, unless the component is a discriminant of a constrained object (the previous case).

14   In the case of a component that is itself a composite object and whose value is defined neither by an explicit initialization nor by a default expression, any implicit initial values for components of the composite object are defined by the same rules as for a declared object.

15   The steps (a) to (d) are performed in the order indicated. For step (b), if the default expression for a discriminant is evaluated, then this evaluation is performed before that of default expressions for subcomponents that depend on discriminants, and also before that of default expressions that include the name of the discriminant. Apart from the previous rule, the evaluation of default expressions is performed in some order that is not defined by the language.

16   The initialization of an object (the declared object or one of its subcomponents) checks that the initial value belongs to the subtype of the object; for an array object declared by an object declaration, an implicit subtype conversion is first applied as for an assignment statement, unless the object is a constant whose subtype is an unconstrained array type. The exception CONSTRAINT_ERROR is raised if this check fails.

17   The value of a scalar variable is undefined after elaboration of the corresponding object declaration unless an initial value is assigned to the variable by an initialization (explicitly or implicitly).

18   If the operand of a type conversion or qualified expression is a variable that has scalar subcomponents with undefined values, then the values of the corresponding subcomponents of the result are undefined. The execution of a program is erroneous if it attempts to evaluate a scalar variable with an undefined value. Similarly, the execution of a program is erroneous if it attempts to apply a predefined operator to a variable that has a scalar subcomponent with an undefined value.

Examples of variable declarations: [19]

```
COUNT, SUM   : INTEGER;
SIZE         : INTEGER range 0 .. 10_000 := 0;
SORTED       : BOOLEAN := FALSE;
COLOR_TABLE  : array(1 .. N) of COLOR;
OPTION       : BIT_VECTOR(1 .. 10) := (others => TRUE);
```

Examples of constant declarations: [20]

```
LIMIT      : constant INTEGER := 10_000;
LOW_LIMIT  : constant INTEGER := LIMIT/10;
TOLERANCE  : constant REAL := DISPERSION(1.15);
```

Note:

The expression initializing a constant object need not be a static expression (see 4.9). In the above [21] examples, LIMIT and LOW_LIMIT are initialized with static expressions, but TOLERANCE is not if DISPERSION is a user-defined function.

References: access type 3.8, assignment 5.2, assignment compound delimiter 5.2, component 3.3, composite type [22] 3.3, constrained array definition 3.6, constrained subtype 3.3, constraint_error exception 11.1, conversion 4.6, declaration 3.1, default expression for a discriminant 3.7, default initial value for an access type 3.8, depend on a discriminant 3.7.1, designate 3.8, discriminant 3.3, elaboration 3.9, entry 9.5, evaluation 4.5, expression 4.4, formal parameter 6.1, generic formal parameter 12.1 12.3, generic unit 12, in some order 1.6, limited type 7.4.4, mode in 6.1, package 7, predefined operator 4.5, primary 4.4, private type 7.4, qualified expression 4.7, reserved word 2.9, scalar type 3.5, slice 4.1.2, subcomponent 3.3, subprogram 6, subtype 3.3, subtype indication 3.3.2, task 9, task type 9.2, type 3.3, visible part 7.2

3.2.2 Number Declarations

A number declaration is a special form of constant declaration. The type of the static expression [1] given for the initialization of a number declaration must be either the type *universal_integer* or the type *universal_real*. The constant declared by a number declaration is called a *named number* and has the type of the static expression.

Note:

The rules concerning expressions of a universal type are explained in section 4.10. It is a conse- [2] quence of these rules that if every primary contained in the expression is of the type *universal_integer*, then the named number is also of this type. Similarly, if every primary is of the type *universal_real*, then the named number is also of this type.

Examples of number declarations: [3]

```
PI            : constant := 3.14159_26536;   -- a real number
TWO_PI        : constant := 2.0*PI;          -- a real number
MAX           : constant := 500;             -- an integer number
POWER_16      : constant := 2**16;           -- the integer 65_536
ONE, UN, EINS : constant := 1;               -- three different names for 1
```

References: identifier 2.3, primary 4.4, static expression 4.9, type 3.3, universal_integer type 3.5.4, universal_real [4] type 3.5.6, universal type 4.10

3.3 Types and Subtypes

1   A type is characterized by a set of values and a set of operations.

2   There exist several *classes* of types. *Scalar* types are integer types, real types, and types defined by enumeration of their values; values of these types have no components. *Array* and *record* types are composite; a value of a composite type consists of *component* values. An *access* type is a type whose values provide access to objects. *Private* types are types for which the set of possible values is well defined, but not directly available to the users of such types. Finally, there are *task* types. (Private types are described in chapter 7, task types are described in chapter 9, the other classes of types are described in this chapter.)

3   Certain record and private types have special components called *discriminants* whose values distinguish alternative forms of values of one of these types. If a private type has discriminants, they are known to users of the type. Hence a private type is only known by its name, its discriminants if any, and by the corresponding set of operations.

4   The set of possible values for an object of a given type can be subjected to a condition that is called a *constraint* (the case where the constraint imposes no restriction is also included); a value is said to *satisfy* a constraint if it satisfies the corresponding condition. A *subtype* is a type together with a constraint; a value is said to *belong to a subtype* of a given type if it belongs to the type and satisfies the constraint; the given type is called the *base type* of the subtype. A type is a subtype of itself; such a subtype is said to be *unconstrained*: it corresponds to a condition that imposes no restriction. The base type of a type is the type itself.

5   The set of operations defined for a subtype of a given type includes the operations that are defined for the type; however the assignment operation to a variable having a given subtype only assigns values that belong to the subtype. Additional operations, such as qualification (in a qualified expression), are implicitly defined by a subtype declaration.

6   Certain types have *default initial values* defined for objects of the type; certain other types have *default expressions* defined for some or all of their components. Certain operations of types and subtypes are called *attributes*; these operations are denoted by the form of name described in section 4.1.4.

7   The term *subcomponent* is used in this manual in place of the term component to indicate either a component, or a component of another component or subcomponent. Where other subcomponents are excluded, the term component is used instead.

8   A given type must not have a subcomponent whose type is the given type itself.

9   The name of a class of types is used in this manual as a qualifier for objects and values that have a type of the class considered. For example, the term "array object" is used for an object whose type is an array type; similarly, the term "access value" is used for a value of an access type.

Note:

10 The set of values of a subtype is a subset of the values of the base type. This subset need not be a proper subset; it can be an empty subset.

11 *References:* access type 3.8, array type 3.6, assignment 5.2, attribute 4.1.4, component of an array 3.6, component of a record 3.7, discriminant constraint 3.7.2, enumeration type 3.5.1, integer type 3.5.4, object 3.2.1, private type 7.4, qualified expression 4.7, real type 3.5.6, record type 3.7, subtype declaration 3.3.2, task type 9.1, type declaration 3.3.1

3.3.1 Type Declarations

A type declaration declares a type.   1

```
type_declaration ::=  full_type_declaration                                                                           2
    |  incomplete_type_declaration | private_type_declaration

full_type_declaration ::=
    type identifier [discriminant_part] is type_definition;

type_definition ::=
      enumeration_type_definition  |  integer_type_definition
    |  real_type_definition        |  array_type_definition
    |  record_type_definition      |  access_type_definition
    |  derived_type_definition
```

The elaboration of a full type declaration consists of the elaboration of the discriminant part, if any   3
(except in the case of the full type declaration for an incomplete or private type declaration), and of
the elaboration of the type definition.

The types created by the elaboration of distinct type definitions are distinct types. Moreover, the   4
elaboration of the type definition for a numeric or derived type creates both a base type and a subtype of the base type; the same holds for a constrained array definition (one of the two forms of
array type definition).

The simple name declared by a full type declaration denotes the declared type, unless the type   5
declaration declares both a base type and a subtype of the base type, in which case the simple
name denotes the subtype, and the base type is anonymous. A type is said to be *anonymous* if it
has no simple name. For explanatory purposes, this reference manual sometimes refers to an
anonymous type by a pseudo-name, written in italics, and uses such pseudo-names at places
where the syntax normally requires an identifier.

Examples of type definitions: 6

```
(WHITE, RED, YELLOW, GREEN, BLUE, BROWN, BLACK)
range 1 .. 72
array(1 .. 10) of INTEGER
```

Examples of type declarations: 7

```
type COLOR    is (WHITE, RED, YELLOW, GREEN, BLUE, BROWN, BLACK);
type COLUMN   is range 1 .. 72;
type TABLE    is array(1 .. 10) of INTEGER;
```

Notes:

Two type definitions always define two distinct types, even if they are textually identical. Thus, the   8
array type definitions given in the declarations of A and B below define distinct types.

```
A  : array(1 .. 10) of BOOLEAN;
B  : array(1 .. 10) of BOOLEAN;
```

If A and B are declared by a multiple object declaration as below, their types are nevertheless dif-   9
ferent, since the multiple object declaration is equivalent to the above two single object declarations.

```
A, B : array(1 .. 10) of BOOLEAN;
```

10   Incomplete type declarations are used for the definition of recursive and mutually dependent types (see 3.8.1). Private type declarations are used in package specifications and in generic parameter declarations (see 7.4 and 12.1).

11   *References:* access type definition 3.8, array type definition 3.6, base type 3.3, constrained array definition 3.6, constrained subtype 3.3, declaration 3.1, derived type 3.4, derived type definition 3.4, discriminant part 3.7.1, elaboration 3.9, enumeration type definition 3.5.1, identifier 2.3, incomplete type declaration 3.8.1, integer type definition 3.5.4, multiple object declaration 3.2, numeric type 3.5, private type declaration 7.4, real type definition 3.5.6, reserved word 2.9, type 3.3

3.3.2 Subtype Declarations

1   A subtype declaration declares a subtype.

2
```
subtype_declaration  ::=
    subtype identifier is subtype_indication;

subtype_indication  ::=   type_mark [constraint]

type_mark  ::=  type_name | subtype_name

constraint  ::=
      range_constraint    | floating_point_constraint | fixed_point_constraint
    | index_constraint    | discriminant_constraint
```

3   A type mark denotes a type or a subtype. If a type mark is the name of a type, the type mark denotes this type and also the corresponding unconstrained subtype. The *base type of a type mark* is, by definition, the base type of the type or subtype denoted by the type mark.

4   A subtype indication defines a subtype of the base type of the type mark.

5   If an index constraint appears after a type mark in a subtype indication, the type mark must not already impose an index constraint. Likewise for a discriminant constraint, the type mark must not already impose a discriminant constraint.

6   The elaboration of a subtype declaration consists of the elaboration of the subtype indication. The elaboration of a subtype indication creates a subtype. If the subtype indication does not include a constraint, the subtype is the same as that denoted by the type mark. The elaboration of a subtype indication that includes a constraint proceeds as follows:

7   (a) The constraint is first elaborated.

8   (b) A check is then made that the constraint is *compatible* with the type or subtype denoted by the type mark.

9   The condition imposed by a constraint is the condition obtained after elaboration of the constraint. (The rules of constraint elaboration are such that the expressions and ranges of constraints are evaluated by the elaboration of these constraints.) The rules defining compatibility are given for each form of constraint in the appropriate section. These rules are such that if a constraint is compatible with a subtype, then the condition imposed by the constraint cannot contradict any condition already imposed by the subtype on its values. The exception CONSTRAINT_ERROR is raised if any check of compatibility fails.

Examples of subtype declarations: 10

```
subtype RAINBOW    is COLOR range RED .. BLUE;           --  see 3.3.1
subtype RED_BLUE   is RAINBOW;
subtype INT        is INTEGER;
subtype SMALL_INT  is INTEGER range -10 .. 10;
subtype UP_TO_K    is COLUMN range 1 .. K;              --  see 3.3.1
subtype SQUARE     is MATRIX(1 .. 10, 1 .. 10);        --  see 3.6
subtype MALE       is PERSON(SEX => M);                --  see 3.8
```

Note:

A subtype declaration does not define a new type.   11

References: base type 3.3, compatibility of discriminant constraints 3.7.2, compatibility of fixed point constraints   12
3.5.9, compatibility of floating point constraints 3.5.7, compatibility of index constraints 3.6.1, compatibility of range
constraints 3.5, constraint_error exception 11.1, declaration 3.1, discriminant 3.3, discriminant constraint 3.7.2,
elaboration 3.9, evaluation 4.5, expression 4.4, floating point constraint 3.5.7, fixed point constraint 3.5.9, index constraint 3.6.1, range constraint 3.5, reserved word 2.9, subtype 3.3, type 3.3, type name 3.3.1, unconstrained subtype
3.3

3.3.3 Classification of Operations

The set of operations of a type includes the explicitly declared subprograms that have a parameter   1
or result of the type; such subprograms are necessarily declared after the type declaration.

The remaining operations are each implicitly declared for a given type declaration, immediately   2
after the type definition. These implicitly declared operations comprise the *basic* operations, the
predefined operators (see 4.5), and enumeration literals. In the case of a derived type declaration,
the implicitly declared operations include any derived subprograms. The operations implicitly
declared for a given type declaration occur after the type declaration and before the next explicit
declaration, if any. The implicit declarations of derived subprograms occur last.

A basic operation is an operation that is inherent in one of the following: 3

- An assignment (in assignment statements and initializations), an allocator, a membership test,   4
  or a short-circuit control form.

- A selected component, an indexed component, or a slice.   5

- A qualification (in qualified expressions), an explicit type conversion, or an implicit type con-   6
  version of a value of type *universal_integer* or *universal_real* to the corresponding value of
  another numeric type.

- A numeric literal (for a universal type), the literal **null** (for an access type), a string literal, an   7
  aggregate, or an attribute.

For every type or subtype T, the following attribute is defined: 8

T'BASE   The base type of T. This attribute is allowed only as the prefix of the name of   9
                another attribute: for example, T'BASE'FIRST.

Note:

10 Each literal is an operation whose evaluation yields the corresponding value (see 4.2). Likewise, an aggregate is an operation whose evaluation yields a value of a composite type (see 4.3). Some operations of a type *operate on* values of the type, for example, predefined operators and certain subprograms and attributes. The evaluation of some operations of a type *returns* a value of the type, for example, literals and certain functions, attributes, and predefined operators. Assignment is an operation that operates on an object and a value. The evaluation of the operation corresponding to a selected component, an indexed component, or a slice, yields the object or value denoted by this form of name.

11 *References:* aggregate 4.3, allocator 4.8, assignment 5.2, attribute 4.1.4, character literal 2.5, composite type 3.3, conversion 4.6, derived subprogram 3.4, enumeration literal 3.5.1, formal parameter 6.1, function 6.5, indexed component 4.1.1, initial value 3.2.1, literal 4.2, membership test 4.5 4.5.2, null literal 3.8, numeric literal 2.4, numeric type 3.5, object 3.2.1, 6.1, predefined operator 4.5, qualified expression 4.7, selected component 4.1.3, short-circuit control form 4.5 4.5.1, slice 4.1.2, string literal 2.6, subprogram 6, subtype 3.3, type 3.3, type declaration 3.3.1, universal_integer type 3.5.4, universal_real type 3.5.6, universal type 4.10

3.4 Derived Types

1 A derived type definition defines a new (base) type whose characteristics are derived from those of a *parent type*; the new type is called a *derived type*. A derived type definition further defines a *derived subtype*, which is a subtype of the derived type.

2   derived_type_definition ::= **new** subtype_indication

3 The subtype indication that occurs after the reserved word **new** defines the *parent subtype*. The parent type is the base type of the parent subtype. If a constraint exists for the parent subtype, a similar constraint exists for the derived subtype; the only difference is that for a range constraint, and likewise for a floating or fixed point constraint that includes a range constraint, the value of each bound is replaced by the corresponding value of the derived type. The characteristics of the derived type are defined as follows:

4 • The derived type belongs to the same class of types as the parent type. The set of possible values for the derived type is a copy of the set of possible values for the parent type. If the parent type is composite, then the same components exist for the derived type, and the subtype of corresponding components is the same.

5 • For each basic operation of the parent type, there is a corresponding basic operation of the derived type. Explicit type conversion of a value of the parent type into the corresponding value of the derived type is allowed and vice versa as explained in section 4.6.

6 • For each enumeration literal or predefined operator of the parent type there is a corresponding operation for the derived type.

7 • If the parent type is a task type, then for each entry of the parent type there is a corresponding entry for the derived type.

8 • If a default expression exists for a component of an object having the parent type, then the same default expression is used for the corresponding component of an object having the derived type.

- If the parent type is an access type, then the parent and the derived type share the same collection; there is a null access value for the derived type and it is the default initial value of that type.

- If an explicit representation clause exists for the parent type and if this clause appears before the derived type definition, then there is a corresponding representation clause (an implicit one) for the derived type.

- Certain subprograms that are operations of the parent type are said to be *derivable*. For each derivable subprogram of the parent type, there is a corresponding derived subprogram for the derived type. Two kinds of derivable subprograms exist. First, if the parent type is declared immediately within the visible part of a package, then a subprogram that is itself explicitly declared immediately within the visible part becomes derivable after the end of the visible part, if it is an operation of the parent type. (The explicit declaration is by a subprogram declaration, a renaming declaration, or a generic instantiation.) Second, if the parent type is itself a derived type, then any subprogram that has been derived by this parent type is further derivable, unless the parent type is declared in the visible part of a package and the derived subprogram is hidden by a derivable subprogram of the first kind.

Each operation of the derived type is implicitly declared at the place of the derived type declaration. The implicit declarations of any derived subprograms occur last.

The specification of a derived subprogram is obtained implicitly by systematic replacement of the parent type by the derived type in the specification of the derivable subprogram. Any subtype of the parent type is likewise replaced by a subtype of the derived type with a similar constraint (as for the transformation of a constraint of the parent subtype into the corresponding constraint of the derived subtype). Finally, any expression of the parent type is made to be the operand of a type conversion that yields a result of the derived type.

Calling a derived subprogram is equivalent to calling the corresponding subprogram of the parent type, in which each actual parameter that is of the derived type is replaced by a type conversion of this actual parameter to the parent type (this means that a conversion to the parent type happens before the call for the modes **in** and **in out**; a reverse conversion to the derived type happens after the call for the modes **in out** and **out**, see 6.4.1). In addition, if the result of a called function is of the parent type, this result is converted to the derived type.

If a derived or private type is declared immediately within the visible part of a package, then, within this visible part, this type must not be used as the parent type of a derived type definition. (For private types, see also section 7.4.1.)

For the elaboration of a derived type definition, the subtype indication is first elaborated, the derived type is then created, and finally, the derived subtype is created.

Examples:

```
type LOCAL_COORDINATE is new COORDINATE;      --  two different types
type MIDWEEK is new DAY range TUE .. THU;      --  see 3.5.1
type COUNTER is new POSITIVE;                  --  same range as POSITIVE

type SPECIAL_KEY is new KEY_MANAGER.KEY;      --  see 7.4.2
-- the derived subprograms have the following specifications:

-- procedure GET_KEY(K : out SPECIAL_KEY);
-- function "<"(X,Y : SPECIAL_KEY) return BOOLEAN;
```

Notes:

18 The rules of derivation of basic operations and enumeration literals imply that the notation for any literal or aggregate of the derived type is the same as for the parent type; such literals and aggregates are said to be *overloaded*. Similarly, it follows that the notation for denoting a component, a discriminant, an entry, a slice, or an attribute is the same for the derived type as for the parent type.

19 Hiding of a derived subprogram is allowed even within the same declarative region (see 8.3). A derived subprogram hides a predefined operator that has the same parameter and result type profile (see 6.6).

20 A generic subprogram declaration is not derivable since it declares a generic unit rather than a subprogram. On the other hand, an instantiation of a generic subprogram is a (nongeneric) subprogram, which is derivable if it satisfies the requirements for derivability of subprograms.

21 If the parent type is a boolean type, the predefined relational operators of the derived type deliver a result of the predefined type BOOLEAN (see 4.5.2).

22 If a representation clause is given for the parent type but appears after the derived type declaration, then no corresponding representation clause applies to the derived type; hence an explicit representation clause for such a derived type is allowed.

23 For a derived subprogram, if a parameter belongs to the derived type, the subtype of this parameter need not have any value in common with the derived subtype.

24 *References:* access value 3.8, actual parameter 6.4.1, aggregate 4.3, attribute 4.1.4, base type 3.3, basic operation 3.3.3, boolean type 3.5.3, bound of a range 3.5, class of type 3.3, collection 3.8, component 3.3, composite type 3.3, constraint 3.3, conversion 4.6, declaration 3.1, declarative region 8.1, default expression 3.2.1, default initial value for an access type 3.8, discriminant 3.3, elaboration 3.9, entry 9.5, enumeration literal 3.5.1, floating point constraint 3.5.7, fixed point constraint 3.5.9, formal parameter 6.1, function call 6.4, generic declaration 12.1, immediately within 8.1, implicit declaration 3.1, literal 4.2, mode 6.1, overloading 6.6 8.7, package 7, package specification 7.1, parameter association 6.4, predefined operator 4.5, private type 7.4, procedure 6, procedure call statement 6.4, range constraint 3.5, representation clause 13.1, reserved word 2.9, slice 4.1.2, subprogram 6, subprogram specification 6.1, subtype indication 3.3.2, subtype 3.3, type 3.3, type definition 3.3.1, visible part 7.2

3.5 Scalar Types

1 Scalar types comprise enumeration types, integer types, and real types. Enumeration types and integer types are called *discrete* types; each value of a discrete type has a position number which is an integer value. Integer types and real types are called *numeric* types. All scalar types are ordered, that is, all relational operators are predefined for their values.

2   range_constraint ::= **range** range

        range ::= *range*_attribute
         | simple_expression .. simple_expression

A range specifies a subset of values of a scalar type. The range L .. R specifies the values from L to   3
R inclusive if the relation L <= R is true. The values L and R are called the *lower bound* and *upper
bound* of the range, respectively. A value V is said to *satisfy* a range constraint if it belongs to the
range; the value V is said to *belong* to the range if the relations L <= V and V <= R are both TRUE.
A *null* range is a range for which the relation R < L is TRUE; no value belongs to a null range. The
operators <= and < in the above definitions are the predefined operators of the scalar type.

If a range constraint is used in a subtype indication, either directly or as part of a floating or fixed   4
point constraint, the type of the simple expressions (likewise, of the bounds of a range attribute)
must be the same as the base type of the type mark of the subtype indication. A range constraint is
compatible with a subtype if each bound of the range belongs to the subtype, or if the range constraint defines a null range; otherwise the range constraint is not compatible with the subtype.

The elaboration of a range constraint consists of the evaluation of the range. The evaluation of a   5
range defines its lower bound and its upper bound. If simple expressions are given to specify the
bounds, the evaluation of the range evaluates these simple expressions in some order that is not
defined by the language.

Attributes   6

For any scalar type T or for any subtype T of a scalar type, the following attributes are defined: 7

T'FIRST   Yields the lower bound of T. The value of this attribute has the same type as T.   8

T'LAST   Yields the upper bound of T. The value of this attribute has the same type as T.   9

Note:

Indexing and iteration rules use values of discrete types.   10

References: attribute 4.1.4, constraint 3.3, enumeration type 3.5.1, erroneous 1.6, evaluation 4.5, fixed point   11
constraint 3.5.9, floating point constraint 3.5.7, index 3.6, integer type 3.5.4, loop statement 5.5, range attribute
3.6.2, real type 3.5.6, relational operator 4.5 4.5.2, satisfy a constraint 3.3, simple expression 4.4, subtype indication
3.3.2, type mark 3.3.2

3.5.1 Enumeration Types

An enumeration type definition defines an enumeration type.   1

```
enumeration_type_definition ::=                                                                          2
    (enumeration_literal_specification {, enumeration_literal_specification})

enumeration_literal_specification ::=  enumeration_literal

enumeration_literal ::=  identifier | character_literal
```

The identifiers and character literals listed by an enumeration type definition must be distinct. Each   3
enumeration literal specification is the declaration of the corresponding enumeration literal: this
declaration is equivalent to the declaration of a parameterless function, the designator being the
enumeration literal, and the result type being the enumeration type. The elaboration of an
enumeration type definition creates an enumeration type; this elaboration includes that of every
enumeration literal specification.

4   Each enumeration literal yields a different enumeration value. The predefined order relations between enumeration values follow the order of corresponding position numbers. The position number of the value of the first listed enumeration literal is zero; the position number for each other enumeration literal is one more than for its predecessor in the list.

5   If the same identifier or character literal is specified in more than one enumeration type definition, the corresponding literals are said to be *overloaded*. At any place where an overloaded enumeration literal occurs in the text of a program, the type of the enumeration literal must be determinable from the context (see 8.7).

6   *Examples:*

```
type DAY     is (MON, TUE, WED, THU, FRI, SAT, SUN);
type SUIT    is (CLUBS, DIAMONDS, HEARTS, SPADES);
type GENDER  is (M, F);
type LEVEL   is (LOW, MEDIUM, URGENT);
type COLOR   is (WHITE, RED, YELLOW, GREEN, BLUE, BROWN, BLACK);
type LIGHT   is (RED, AMBER, GREEN); -- RED and GREEN are overloaded

type HEXA    is ('A', 'B', 'C', 'D', 'E', 'F');
type MIXED   is ('A', 'B', '*', B, NONE, '?', '%');

subtype WEEKDAY is DAY    range MON .. FRI;
subtype MAJOR   is SUIT   range HEARTS .. SPADES;
subtype RAINBOW is COLOR  range RED .. BLUE; --   the color RED, not the light
```

Note:

7   If an enumeration literal occurs in a context that does not otherwise suffice to determine the type of the literal, then qualification by the name of the enumeration type is one way to resolve the ambiguity (see 8.7).

8   *References:* character literal 2.5, declaration 3.1, designator 6.1, elaboration 3.9, 6.1, function 6.5, identifier 2.3, name 4.1, overloading 6.6 8.7, position number 3.5, qualified expression 4.7, relational operator 4.5 4.5.2, type 3.3, type definition 3.3.1

3.5.2 Character Types

1   An enumeration type is said to be a character type if at least one of its enumeration literals is a character literal. The predefined type CHARACTER is a character type whose values are the 128 characters of the *ASCII* character set. Each of the 95 graphic characters of this character set is denoted by the corresponding character literal.

2   *Example:*

```
type ROMAN_DIGIT is ('I', 'V', 'X', 'L', 'C', 'D', 'M');
```

Notes:

3   The predefined package ASCII includes the declaration of constants denoting control characters and of constants denoting graphic characters that are not in the basic character set.

A conventional character set such as *EBCDIC* can be declared as a character type; the internal   4
codes of the characters can be specified by an enumeration representation clause as explained in
section 13.3.

References: ascii predefined package C, basic character 2.1, character literal 2.5, constant 3.2.1, declaration 3.1,   5
enumeration type 3.5.1, graphic character 2.1, identifier 2.3, literal 4.2, predefined type C, type 3.3

3.5.3 Boolean Types

There is a predefined enumeration type named BOOLEAN. It contains the two literals FALSE and   1
TRUE ordered with the relation FALSE < TRUE. A boolean type is either the type BOOLEAN or a
type that is derived, directly or indirectly, from a boolean type.

References: derived type 3.4, enumeration literal 3.5.1, enumeration type 3.5.1, relational operator 4.5 4.5.2, type   2
3.3

3.5.4 Integer Types

An integer type definition defines an integer type whose set of values includes at least those of the   1
specified range.

    integer_type_definition ::= range_constraint   2

If a range constraint is used as an integer type definition, each bound of the range must be defined   3
by a static expression of some integer type, but the two bounds need not have the same integer
type. (Negative bounds are allowed.)

A type declaration of the form: 4

    type T **is range** L .. R;

is, by definition, equivalent to the following declarations: 5

    type *integer_type* **is new** predefined_integer_type;
    subtype T **is** *integer_type* **range** *integer_type*(L) .. *integer_type*(R);

where *integer_type* is an anonymous type, and where the predefined integer type is implicitly   6
selected by the implementation, so as to contain the values L to R inclusive. The integer type
declaration is illegal if none of the predefined integer types satisfies this requirement, excepting
universal_integer. The elaboration of the declaration of an integer type consists of the elaboration
of the equivalent type and subtype declarations.

The predefined integer types include the type INTEGER. An implementation may also have   7
predefined types such as SHORT_INTEGER and LONG_INTEGER, which have (substantially) shorter
and longer ranges, respectively, than INTEGER. The range of each of these types must be
symmetric about zero, excepting an extra negative value which may exist in some implementations. The base type of each of these types is the type itself.

8   Integer literals are the literals of an anonymous predefined integer type that is called *univer-sal_integer* in this reference manual. Other integer types have no literals. However, for each integer type there exists an implicit conversion that converts a *universal_integer* value into the corresponding value (if any) of the integer type. The circumstances under which these implicit conversions are invoked are described in section 4.6.

9   The position number of an integer value is the corresponding value of the type *universal_integer*.

10   The same arithmetic operators are predefined for all integer types (see 4.5). The exception NUMERIC_ERROR is raised by the execution of an operation (in particular an implicit conversion) that cannot deliver the correct result (that is, if the value corresponding to the mathematical result is not a value of the integer type). However, an implementation is not required to raise the exception NUMERIC_ERROR if the operation is part of a larger expression whose result can be computed correctly, as described in section 11.6.

11   *Examples:*

```
type PAGE_NUM   is range 1 .. 2_000;
type LINE_SIZE  is range 1 .. MAX_LINE_SIZE;

subtype SMALL_INT    is INTEGER    range -10 .. 10;
subtype COLUMN_PTR   is LINE_SIZE  range 1 .. 10;
subtype BUFFER_SIZE  is INTEGER    range 0 .. MAX;
```

Notes:

12   The name declared by an integer type declaration is a subtype name. On the other hand, the predefined operators of an integer type deliver results whose range is defined by the parent predefined type; such a result need not belong to the declared subtype, in which case an attempt to assign the result to a variable of the integer subtype raises the exception CONSTRAINT_ERROR.

13   The smallest (most negative) value supported by the predefined integer types of an implementation is the named number SYSTEM.MIN_INT and the largest (most positive) value is SYSTEM.MAX_INT (see 13.7).

14   *References:* anonymous type 3.3.1, belong to a subtype 3.3, bound of a range 3.5, constraint_error exception 11.1, conversion 4.6, identifier 2.3, integer literal 2.4, literal 4.2, numeric_error exception 11.1, parent type 3.4, predefined operator 4.5, range constraint 3.5, static expression 4.9, subtype declaration 3.3.2, system predefined package 13.7, type 3.3, type declaration 3.3.1, type definition 3.3.1, universal type 4.10

3.5.5 Operations of Discrete Types

1   The basic operations of a discrete type include the operations involved in assignment, the membership tests, and qualification; for a boolean type they include the short-circuit control forms; for an integer type they include the explicit conversion of values of other numeric types to the integer type, and the implicit conversion of values of the type *universal_integer* to the type.

2   Finally, for every discrete type or subtype T, the basic operations include the attributes listed below. In this presentation, T is referred to as being a subtype (the subtype T) for any property that depends on constraints imposed by T; other properties are stated in terms of the base type of T.

The first group of attributes yield characteristics of the subtype T. This group includes the attribute   3
BASE (see 3.3.2), the attributes FIRST and LAST (see 3.5), the representation attribute SIZE (see
13.7.2), and the attribute WIDTH defined as follows:

T'WIDTH   Yields the maximum image length over all values of the subtype T (the *image* is the   4
               sequence of characters returned by the attribute IMAGE, see below). Yields zero
               for a null range. The value of this attribute is of the type *universal_integer*.

All attributes of the second group are functions with a single parameter. The corresponding actual   5
parameter is indicated below by X.

T'POS   This attribute is a function. The parameter X must be a value of the base type of T.   6
               The result type is the type *universal_integer*. The result is the position number of
               the value of the parameter.

T'VAL   This attribute is a special function with a single parameter which can be of any   7
               integer type. The result type is the base type of T. The result is the value whose
               position number is the *universal_integer* value corresponding to X. The exception
               CONSTRAINT_ERROR is raised if the *universal_integer* value corresponding to X is
               not in the range T'POS(T'BASE'FIRST) .. T'POS(T'BASE'LAST).

T'SUCC   This attribute is a function. The parameter X must be a value of the base type of T.   8
               The result type is the base type of T. The result is the value whose position number
               is one greater than that of X. The exception CONSTRAINT_ERROR is raised if X
               equals T'BASE'LAST.

T'PRED   This attribute is a function. The parameter X must be a value of the base type of T.   9
               The result type is the base type of T. The result is the value whose position number
               is one less than that of X. The exception CONSTRAINT_ERROR is raised if X equals
               T'BASE'FIRST.

T'IMAGE   This attribute is a function. The parameter X must be a value of the base type of T.   10
               The result type is the predefined type STRING. The result is the *image* of the value
               of X, that is, a sequence of characters representing the value in display form. The
               image of an integer value is the corresponding decimal literal; without underlines,
               leading zeros, exponent, or trailing spaces; but with a single leading character that
               is either a minus sign or a space. The lower bound of the image is one.

               The image of an enumeration value is either the corresponding identifier in upper   11
               case or the corresponding character literal (including the two apostrophes);
               neither leading nor trailing spaces are included. The image of a character C, other
               than a graphic character, is implementation-defined; the only requirement is that
               the image must be such that C equals CHARACTER'VALUE (CHARACTER'IMAGE (C)).

T'VALUE   This attribute is a function. The parameter X must be a value of the predefined type   12
               STRING. The result type is the base type of T. Any leading and any trailing spaces
               of the sequence of characters that corresponds to the parameter are ignored.

               For an enumeration type, if the sequence of characters has the syntax of an   13
               enumeration literal and if this literal exists for the base type of T, the result is the
               corresponding enumeration value. For an integer type, if the sequence of
               characters has the syntax of an integer literal, with an optional single leading
               character that is a plus or minus sign, and if there is a corresponding value in the
               base type of T, the result is this value. In any other case, the exception
               CONSTRAINT_ERROR is raised.

Operations of Discrete Types 3.5.5

14   In addition, the attributes A'SIZE and A'ADDRESS are defined for an object A of a discrete type (see 13.7.2).

15   Besides the basic operations, the operations of a discrete type include the predefined relational operators. For enumeration types, operations include enumeration literals. For boolean types, operations include the predefined unary logical negation operator **not**, and the predefined logical operators. For integer types, operations include the predefined *arithmetic* operators: these are the binary and unary adding operators - and +, all multiplying operators, the unary operator **abs**, and the exponentiating operator.

16   The operations of a subtype are the corresponding operations of its base type except for the following: assignment, membership tests, qualification, explicit type conversions, and the attributes of the first group; the effect of each of these operations depends on the subtype (assignments, membership tests, qualifications, and conversions involve a subtype check; attributes of the first group yield a characteristic of the subtype).

Notes:

17   For a subtype of a discrete type, the results delivered by the attributes SUCC, PRED, VAL, and VALUE need not belong to the subtype; similarly, the actual parameters of the attributes POS, SUCC, PRED, and IMAGE need not belong to the subtype. The following relations are satisfied (in the absence of an exception) by these attributes:

```
T'POS(T'SUCC(X))  = T'POS(X) +  1
T'POS(T'PRED(X))  = T'POS(X) -  1

T'VAL(T'POS(X))   = X
T'POS(T'VAL(N))   = N
```

18   *Examples:*

```
--  For the types and subtypes declared in section 3.5.1 we have:

--  COLOR'FIRST    = WHITE,     COLOR'LAST      = BLACK
--  RAINBOW'FIRST  = RED,       RAINBOW'LAST    = BLUE

--  COLOR'SUCC(BLUE)  = RAINBOW'SUCC(BLUE)  = BROWN
--  COLOR'POS(BLUE)   = RAINBOW'POS(BLUE)   = 4
--  COLOR'VAL(0)      = RAINBOW'VAL(0)      = WHITE
```

19   *References:* abs operator 4.5 4.5.6, assignment 5.2, attribute 4.1.4, base type 3.3, basic operation 3.3.3, binary adding operator 4.5 4.5.3, boolean type 3.5.3, bound of a range 3.5, character literal 2.5, constraint 3.3, constraint_error exception 11.1, conversion 4.6, discrete type 3.5, enumeration literal 3.5.1, exponentiating operator 4.5 4.5.6, function 6.5, graphic character 2.1, identifier 2.3, integer type 3.5.4, logical operator 4.5 4.5.1, membership test 4.5 4.5.2, multiplying operator 4.5 4.5.5, not operator 4.5 4.5.6, numeric literal 2.4, numeric type 3.5, object 3.2, operation 3.3, position number 3.5, predefined operator 4.5, predefined type C, qualified expression 4.7, relational operator 4.5 4.5.2, short-circuit control form 4.5 4.5.1, string type 3.6.3, subtype 3.3, type 3.3, unary adding operator 4.5 4.5.4, universal_integer type 3.5.4, universal type 4.10

3.5.6 Real Types

Real types provide approximations to the real numbers, with relative bounds on errors for floating point types, and with absolute bounds for fixed point types.

    real_type_definition ::=
        floating_point_constraint | fixed_point_constraint

A set of numbers called *model numbers* is associated with each real type. Error bounds on the predefined operations are given in terms of the model numbers. An implementation of the type must include at least these model numbers and represent them exactly.

An implementation-dependent set of numbers, called the *safe numbers*, is also associated with each real type. The set of safe numbers of a real type must include at least the set of model numbers of the type. The range of safe numbers is allowed to be larger than the range of model numbers, but error bounds on the predefined operations for safe numbers are given by the same rules as for model numbers. Safe numbers therefore provide guaranteed error bounds for operations on an implementation-dependent range of numbers; in contrast, the range of model numbers depends only on the real type definition and is therefore independent of the implementation.

Real literals are the literals of an anonymous predefined real type that is called *universal_real* in this reference manual. Other real types have no literals. However, for each real type, there exists an implicit conversion that converts a *universal_real* value into a value of the real type. The conditions under which these implicit conversions are invoked are described in section 4.6. If the *universal_real* value is a safe number, the implicit conversion delivers the corresponding value; if it belongs to the range of safe numbers but is not a safe number, then the converted value can be any value within the range defined by the safe numbers next above and below the *universal_real* value.

The execution of an operation that yields a value of a real type may raise the exception NUMERIC_ERROR, as explained in section 4.5.7, if it cannot deliver a correct result (that is, if the value corresponding to one of the possible mathematical results does not belong to the range of safe numbers); in particular, this exception can be raised by an implicit conversion. However, an implementation is not required to raise the exception NUMERIC_ERROR if the operation is part of a larger expression whose result can be computed correctly (see 11.6).

The elaboration of a real type definition includes the elaboration of the floating or fixed point constraint and creates a real type.

Note:

An algorithm written to rely only upon the minimum numerical properties guaranteed by the type definition for model numbers will be portable without further precautions.

References: conversion 4.6, elaboration 3.9, fixed point constraint 3.5.9, floating point constraint 3.5.7, literal 4.2, numeric_error exception 11.1, predefined operation 3.3.3, real literal 2.4, type 3.3, type definition 3.3.1, universal type 4.10

3.5.7 Floating Point Types

1   For floating point types, the error bound is specified as a relative precision by giving the required minimum number of significant decimal digits.

2   floating_point_constraint ::=
         floating_accuracy_definition [range_constraint]

     floating_accuracy_definition ::= **digits** *static*_simple_expression

3   The minimum number of significant decimal digits is specified by the value of the static simple expression of the floating accuracy definition. This value must belong to some integer type and must be positive (nonzero); it is denoted by D in the remainder of this section. If the floating point constraint is used as a real type definition and includes a range constraint, then each bound of the range must be defined by a static expression of some real type, but the two bounds need not have the same real type.

4   For a given *radix*, the following canonical form is defined for any floating point model number other than zero:

         sign * *mantissa* * (*radix* ** *exponent*)

5   In this form: *sign* is either +1 or -1; *mantissa* is expressed in a number base given by *radix*; and *exponent* is an integer number (possibly negative) such that the integer part of mantissa is zero and the first digit of its fractional part is not a zero.

6   The specified number D is the minimum number of decimal digits required after the point in the decimal mantissa (that is, if *radix* is ten). The value of D in turn determines a corresponding number B that is the minimum number of binary digits required after the point in the binary mantissa (that is, if *radix* is two). The number B associated with D is the smallest value such that the relative precision of the binary form is no less than that specified for the decimal form. (The number B is the integer next above $(D*\log(10)/\log(2)) + 1$.)

7   The model numbers defined by a floating accuracy definition comprise zero and all numbers whose binary canonical form has exactly B digits after the point in the mantissa and an exponent in the range $-4*B$ .. $+4*B$. The guaranteed minimum accuracy of operations of a floating point type is defined in terms of the model numbers of the floating point constraint that forms the corresponding real type definition (see 4.5.7).

8   The predefined floating point types include the type FLOAT. An implementation may also have predefined types such as SHORT_FLOAT and LONG_FLOAT, which have (substantially) less and more accuracy, respectively, than FLOAT. The base type of each predefined floating point type is the type itself. The model numbers of each predefined floating point type are defined in terms of the number D of decimal digits returned by the attribute DIGITS (see 3.5.8).

9   For each predefined floating point type (consequently also for each type derived therefrom), a set of safe numbers is defined as follows. The safe numbers have the same number B of mantissa digits as the model numbers of the type and have an exponent in the range $-E$ .. $+E$ where E is implementation-defined and at least equal to the $4*B$ of model numbers. (Consequently, the safe numbers include the model numbers.) The rules defining the accuracy of operations with model and safe numbers are given in section 4.5.7. The safe numbers of a subtype are those of its base type.

A floating point type declaration of one of the two forms (that is, with or without the optional range   10
constraint indicated by the square brackets):

>   **type** T **is digits** D [**range** L .. R];

is, by definition, equivalent to the following declarations: 11

>   **type** *floating_point_type* **is new** predefined_floating_point_type;
>   **subtype** T **is** *floating_point_type* **digits** D
>   [**range** *floating_point_type*(L) .. *floating_point_type*(R)];

where *floating_point_type* is an anonymous type, and where the predefined floating point type is   12
implicitly selected by the implementation so that its model numbers include the model numbers
defined by D; furthermore, if a range L .. R is supplied, then both L and R must belong to the range
of safe numbers. The floating point declaration is illegal if none of the predefined floating point
types satisfies these requirements, excepting *universal_real*. The maximum number of digits that
can be specified in a floating accuracy definition is given by the system-dependent named number
SYSTEM.MAX_DIGITS (see 13.7.1).

The elaboration of a floating point type declaration consists of the elaboration of the equivalent   13
type and subtype declarations.

If a floating point constraint follows a type mark in a subtype indication, the type mark must   14
denote a floating point type or subtype. The floating point constraint is *compatible* with the type
mark only if the number D specified in the floating accuracy definition is not greater than the corresponding number D for the type or subtype denoted by the type mark. Furthermore, if the
floating point constraint includes a range constraint, the floating point constraint is compatible
with the type mark only if the range constraint is, itself, compatible with the type mark.

The elaboration of such a subtype indication includes the elaboration of the range constraint, if   15
there is one; it creates a floating point subtype whose model numbers are defined by the corresponding floating accuracy definition. A value of a floating point type belongs to a floating point
subtype if and only if it belongs to the range defined by the subtype.

The same arithmetic operators are predefined for all floating point types (see 4.5).   16

Notes:

A range constraint is allowed in a floating point subtype indication, either directly after the type   17
mark, or as part of a floating point constraint. In either case the bounds of the range must belong
to the base type of the type mark (see 3.5). The imposition of a floating point constraint on a type
mark in a subtype indication cannot reduce the allowed range of values unless it includes a range
constraint (the range of model numbers that correspond to the specified number of digits can be
smaller than the range of numbers of the type mark). A value that belongs to a floating point subtype need not be a model number of the subtype.

Examples: 18

>   **type** COEFFICIENT **is digits** 10 **range** -1.0 .. 1.0;
>
>   **type** REAL **is digits** 8;
>   **type** MASS **is digits** 7 **range** 0.0 .. 1.0E35;
>
>   **subtype** SHORT_COEFF **is** COEFFICIENT **digits** 5;   --   a subtype with less accuracy
>   **subtype** PROBABILITY **is** REAL **range** 0.0 .. 1.0;   --   a subtype with a smaller range

Notes on the examples:

19   The implemented accuracy for COEFFICIENT is that of a predefined type having at least 10 digits of precision. Consequently the specification of 5 digits of precision for the subtype SHORT_COEFF is allowed. The largest model number for the type MASS is approximately 1.27E30 and hence less than the specified upper bound (1.0E35). Consequently the declaration of this type is legal only if this upper bound is in the range of the safe numbers of a predefined floating point type having at least 7 digits of precision.

20   *References:* anonymous type 3.3.1, arithmetic operator 3.5.5 4.5, based literal 2.4.2, belong to a subtype 3.3, bound of a range 3.5, compatible 3.3.2, derived type 3.4, digit 2.1, elaboration 3.1 3.9, error bound 3.5.6, exponent 2.4.1 integer type 3.5.4, model number 3.5.6, operation 3.3, predefined operator 4.5, predefined type C, range constraint 3.5, real type 3.5.6, real type definition 3.5.6, safe number 3.5.6, simple expression 4.4, static expression 4.9, subtype declaration 3.3.2, subtype indication 3.3.2, subtype 3.3, type 3.3, type declaration 3.3.1, type mark 3.3.2

3.5.8 Operations of Floating Point Types

1   The basic operations of a floating point type include the operations involved in assignment, membership tests, qualification, the explicit conversion of values of other numeric types to the floating point type, and the implicit conversion of values of the type *universal_real* to the type.

2   In addition, for every floating point type or subtype T, the basic operations include the attributes listed below. In this presentation, T is referred to as being a subtype (the subtype T) for any property that depends on constraints imposed by T; other properties are stated in terms of the base type of T.

3   The first group of attributes yield characteristics of the subtype T. The attributes of this group are the attribute BASE (see 3.3.2), the attributes FIRST and LAST (see 3.5), the representation attribute SIZE (see 13.7.2), and the following attributes:

4   T'DIGITS   Yields the number of decimal digits in the decimal mantissa of model numbers of the subtype T. (This attribute yields the number D of section 3.5.7.) The value of this attribute is of the type *universal_integer*.

5   T'MANTISSA   Yields the number of binary digits in the binary mantissa of model numbers of the subtype T. (This attribute yields the number B of section 3.5.7.) The value of this attribute is of the type *universal_integer*.

6   T'EPSILON   Yields the absolute value of the difference between the model number 1.0 and the next model number above, for the subtype T. The value of this attribute is of the type *universal_real*.

7   T'EMAX   Yields the largest exponent value in the binary canonical form of model numbers of the subtype T. (This attribute yields the product $4*B$ of section 3.5.7.) The value of this attribute is of the type *universal_integer*.

8   T'SMALL   Yields the smallest positive (nonzero) model number of the subtype T. The value of this attribute is of the type *universal_real*.

9   T'LARGE   Yields the largest positive model number of the subtype T. The value of this attribute is of the type *universal_real*.

The attributes of the second group include the following attributes which yield characteristics of the safe numbers: [10]

T'SAFE_EMAX Yields the largest exponent value in the binary canonical form of safe numbers of the base type of T. (This attribute yields the number E of section 3.5.7.) The value of this attribute is of the type *universal_integer*. [11]

T'SAFE_SMALL Yields the smallest positive (nonzero) safe number of the base type of T. The value of this attribute is of the type *universal_real*. [12]

T'SAFE_LARGE Yields the largest positive safe number of the base type of T. The value of this attribute is of the type *universal_real*. [13]

In addition, the attributes A'SIZE and A'ADDRESS are defined for an object A of a floating point type (see 13.7.2). Finally, for each floating point type there are machine-dependent attributes that are not related to model numbers and safe numbers. They correspond to the attribute designators MACHINE_RADIX, MACHINE_MANTISSA, MACHINE_EMAX, MACHINE_EMIN, MACHINE_ROUNDS, and MACHINE_OVERFLOWS (see 13.7.3). [14]

Besides the basic operations, the operations of a floating point type include the relational operators, and the following predefined arithmetic operators: the binary and unary adding operators - and +, the multiplying operators * and /, the unary operator **abs**, and the exponentiating operator. [15]

The operations of a subtype are the corresponding operations of the type except for the following: assignment, membership tests, qualification, explicit conversion, and the attributes of the first group; the effects of these operations are redefined in terms of the subtype. [16]

Notes:

The attributes EMAX, SMALL, LARGE, and EPSILON are provided for convenience. They are all related to MANTISSA by the following formulas: [17]

```
T'EMAX      = 4*T'MANTISSA
T'EPSILON   = 2.0**(1 - T'MANTISSA)
T'SMALL     = 2.0**(-T'EMAX - 1)
T'LARGE     = 2.0**T'EMAX * (1.0 - 2.0**(-T'MANTISSA))
```

The attribute MANTISSA, giving the number of binary digits in the mantissa, is itself related to DIGITS. The following relations hold between the characteristics of the model numbers and those of the safe numbers: [18]

```
T'BASE'EMAX    <= T'SAFE_EMAX
T'BASE'SMALL   >= T'SAFE_SMALL
T'BASE'LARGE   <= T'SAFE_LARGE
```

The attributes T'FIRST and T'LAST need not yield model or safe numbers. If a certain number of digits is specified in the declaration of a type or subtype T, the attribute T'DIGITS yields this number. [19]

References: abs operator 4.5 4.5.6, arithmetic operator 3.5.5 4.5, assignment 5.2, attribute 4.1.4, base type 3.3, basic operation 3.3.3, binary adding operator 4.5 4.5.3, bound of a range 3.5, constraint 3.3, conversion 4.6, digit 2.1, exponentiating operator 4.5 4.5.6, floating point type 3.5.7, membership test 4.5 4.5.2, model number 3.5.6, multiplying operator 4.5 4.5.5, numeric type 3.5, object 3.2, operation 3.3, predefined operator 4.5, qualified expression 4.7, relational operator 4.5 4.5.2, safe number 3.5.6, subtype 3.3, type 3.3, unary adding operator 4.5 4.5.4, universal type 4.10, universal_integer type 3.5.4, universal_real type 3.5.6 [20]

3.5.9 Fixed Point Types

1   For fixed point types, the error bound is specified as an absolute value, called the *delta* of the fixed point type.

2   fixed_point_constraint ::=
          fixed_accuracy_definition [range_constraint]

     fixed_accuracy_definition ::=   **delta** *static*_simple_expression

3   The delta is specified by the value of the static simple expression of the fixed accuracy definition. This value must belong to some real type and must be positive (nonzero). If the fixed point constraint is used as a real type definition, then it must include a range constraint; each bound of the specified range must be defined by a static expression of some real type but the two bounds need not have the same real type. If the fixed point constraint is used in a subtype indication, the range constraint is optional.

4   A canonical form is defined for any fixed point model number other than zero. In this form: *sign* is either +1 or -1; *mantissa* is a positive (nonzero) integer; and any model number is a multiple of a certain positive real number called *small*, as follows:

         sign ∗ *mantissa* ∗ *small*

5   For the model numbers defined by a fixed point constraint, the number *small* is chosen as the largest power of two that is not greater than the delta of the fixed accuracy definition. Alternatively, it is possible to specify the value of *small* by a length clause (see 13.2), in which case model numbers are multiples of the specified value. The guaranteed minimum accuracy of operations of a fixed point type is defined in terms of the model numbers of the fixed point constraint that forms the corresponding real type definition (see 4.5.7).

6   For a fixed point constraint that includes a range constraint, the model numbers comprise zero and all multiples of *small* whose *mantissa* can be expressed using exactly B binary digits, where the value of B is chosen as the smallest integer number for which each bound of the specified range is either a model number or lies at most *small* distant from a model number. For a fixed point constraint that does not include a range constraint (this is only allowed after a type mark, in a subtype indication), the model numbers are defined by the delta of the fixed accuracy definition and by the range of the subtype denoted by the type mark.

7   An implementation must have at least one anonymous predefined fixed point type. The base type of each such fixed point type is the type itself. The model numbers of each predefined fixed point type comprise zero and all numbers for which *mantissa* (in the canonical form) has the number of binary digits returned by the attribute MANTISSA, and for which the number *small* has the value returned by the attribute SMALL.

8   A fixed point type declaration of the form:

         type T **is delta** D **range** L .. R;

9   is, by definition, equivalent to the following declarations:

         type *fixed_point_type* **is new** predefined_fixed_point_type;
         subtype T **is** *fixed_point_type*
            range *fixed_point_type*(L) .. *fixed_point_type*(R);

In these declarations, *fixed_point_type* is an anonymous type, and the predefined fixed point type is implicitly selected by the implementation so that its model numbers include the model numbers defined by the fixed point constraint (that is, by D, L, and R, and possibly by a length clause specifying *small*). 10

The fixed point declaration is illegal if no predefined type satisfies these requirements. The safe numbers of a fixed point type are the model numbers of its base type. 11

The elaboration of a fixed point type declaration consists of the elaboration of the equivalent type and subtype declarations. 12

If the fixed point constraint follows a type mark in a subtype indication, the type mark must denote a fixed point type or subtype. The fixed point constraint is *compatible* with the type mark only if the delta specified by the fixed accuracy definition is not smaller than the delta for the type or subtype denoted by the type mark. Furthermore, if the fixed point constraint includes a range constraint, the fixed point constraint is compatible with the type mark only if the range constraint is, itself, compatible with the type mark. 13

The elaboration of such a subtype indication includes the elaboration of the range constraint, if there is one; it creates a fixed point subtype whose model numbers are defined by the corresponding fixed point constraint and also by the length clause specifying small, if there is one. A value of a fixed point type belongs to a fixed point subtype if and only if it belongs to the range defined by the subtype. 14

The same arithmetic operators are predefined for all fixed point types (see 4.5). Multiplication and division of fixed point values deliver results of an anonymous predefined fixed point type that is called *universal_fixed* in this reference manual; the accuracy of this type is arbitrarily fine. The values of this type must be converted explicitly to some numeric type. 15

Notes:

If S is a subtype of a fixed point type or subtype T, then the set of model numbers of S is a subset of those of T. If a length clause has been given for T, then both S and T have the same value for *small*. Otherwise, since *small* is a power of two, the *small* of S is equal to the *small* of T multiplied by a nonnegative power of two. 16

A range constraint is allowed in a fixed point subtype indication, either directly after the type mark, or as part of a fixed point constraint. In either case the bounds of the range must belong to the base type of the type mark (see 3.5). 17

Examples: 18

```
type VOLT is delta 0.125 range 0.0 .. 255.0;
subtype ROUGH_VOLTAGE is VOLT delta 1.0;   --   same range as VOLT

--   A pure fraction which requires all the available space in a word
--   on a two's complement machine can be declared as the type FRACTION:

DEL : constant := 1.0/2**(WORD_LENGTH - 1);
type FRACTION is delta DEL range -1.0 .. 1.0 - DEL;
```

References: anonymous type 3.3.1, arithmetic operator 3.5.5 4.5, base type 3.3, belong to a subtype 3.3, bound of a range 3.5, compatible 3.3.2, conversion 4.6, elaboration 3.9, error bound 3.5.6, length clause 13.2, model number 3.5.6, numeric type 3.5, operation 3.3, predefined operator 4.5, range constraint 3.5, real type 3.5.6, real type definition 3.5.6, safe number 3.5.6, simple expression 4.4, static expression 4.9, subtype 3.3, subtype declaration 3.3.2, subtype indication 3.3.2, type 3.3, type declaration 3.3.1, type mark 3.3.2 19

3.5.10 Operations of Fixed Point Types

1 The basic operations of a fixed point type include the operations involved in assignment, membership tests, qualification, the explicit conversion of values of other numeric types to the fixed point type, and the implicit conversion of values of the type *universal_real* to the type.

2 In addition, for every fixed point type or subtype T the basic operations include the attributes listed below. In this presentation T is referred to as being a subtype (the subtype T) for any property that depends on constraints imposed by T; other properties are stated in terms of the base type of T.

3 The first group of attributes yield characteristics of the subtype T. The attributes of this group are the attributes BASE (see 3.3.2), the attributes FIRST and LAST (see 3.5), the representation attribute SIZE (see 13.7.2) and the following attributes:

4 T'DELTA   Yields the value of the delta specified in the fixed accuracy definition for the subtype T. The value of this attribute is of the type *universal_real*.

5 T'MANTISSA   Yields the number of binary digits in the mantissa of model numbers of the subtype T. (This attribute yields the number B of section 3.5.9.) The value of this attribute is of the type *universal_integer*.

6 T'SMALL   Yields the smallest positive (nonzero) model number of the subtype T. The value of this attribute is of the type *universal_real*.

7 T'LARGE   Yields the largest positive model number of the subtype T. The value of this attribute is of the type *universal_real*.

8 T'FORE   Yields the minimum number of characters needed for the integer part of the decimal representation of any value of the subtype T, assuming that the representation does not include an exponent, but includes a one-character prefix that is either a minus sign or a space. (This minimum number does not include superfluous zeros or underlines, and is at least two.) The value of this attribute is of the type *universal_integer*.

9 T'AFT   Yields the number of decimal digits needed after the point to accommodate the precision of the subtype T, unless the delta of the subtype T is greater than 0.1, in which case the attribute yields the value one. (T'AFT is the smallest positive integer N for which $(10**N)*$T'DELTA is greater than or equal to one.) The value of this attribute is of the type *universal_integer*.

10 The attributes of the second group include the following attributes which yield characteristics of the safe numbers:

11 T'SAFE_SMALL Yields the smallest positive (nonzero) safe number of the base type of T. The value of this attribute is of the type *universal_real*.

12 T'SAFE_LARGE Yields the largest positive safe number of the base type of T. The value of this attribute is of the type *universal_real*.

13 In addition, the attributes A'SIZE and A'ADDRESS are defined for an object A of a fixed point type (see 13.7.2). Finally, for each fixed point type or subtype T, there are the machine-dependent attributes T'MACHINE_ROUNDS and T'MACHINE_OVERFLOWS (see 13.7.3).

Besides the basic operations, the operations of a fixed point type include the relational operators,   14
and the following predefined arithmetic operators: the binary and unary adding operators - and +,
the multiplying operators ∗ and /, and the operator **abs**.

The operations of a subtype are the corresponding operations of the type except for the following: 15
assignment, membership tests, qualification, explicit conversion, and the attributes of the first
group; the effects of these operations are redefined in terms of the subtype.

Notes:

The value of the attribute T'FORE depends only on the range of the subtype T. The value of the   16
attribute T'AFT depends only on the value of T'DELTA. The following relations exist between
attributes of a fixed point type:

```
T'LARGE          = (2∗∗T'MANTISSA - 1) ∗ T'SMALL
T'SAFE_LARGE     = T'BASE'LARGE
T'SAFE_SMALL     = T'BASE'SMALL
```

References: abs operator 4.5 4.5.6, arithmetic operator 3.5.5 4.5, assignment 5.2, base type 3.3, basic operation   17
3.3.3, binary adding operator 4.5 4.5.3, bound of a range 3.5, conversion 4.6, delta 3.5.9, fixed point type 3.5.9,
membership test 4.5 4.5.2, model number 3.5.6, multiplying operator 4.5 4.5.5, numeric type 3.5, object 3.2, operation 3.3, qualified expression 4.7, relational operator 4.5 4.5.2, safe number 3.5.6, subtype 3.3, unary adding operator
4.5 4.5.4, universal_integer type 3.5.4, universal_real type 3.5.6

3.6 Array Types

An array object is a composite object consisting of components that have the same subtype. The   1
name for a component of an array uses one or more index values belonging to specified discrete
types. The value of an array object is a composite value consisting of the values of its components.

```
array_type_definition ::=
    unconstrained_array_definition | constrained_array_definition
```
2

```
unconstrained_array_definition ::=
    array(index_subtype_definition {, index_subtype_definition}) of
            component_subtype_indication
```

```
constrained_array_definition ::=
    array index_constraint of component_subtype_indication
```

```
index_subtype_definition ::= type_mark range <>
```

```
index_constraint ::=   (discrete_range {, discrete_range})
```

```
discrete_range ::= discrete_subtype_indication | range
```

An array object is characterized by the number of indices (the *dimensionality* of the array), the type   3
and position of each index, the lower and upper bounds for each index, and the type and possible
constraint of the components. The order of the indices is significant.

4   A one-dimensional array has a distinct component for each possible index value. A multidimensional array has a distinct component for each possible sequence of index values that can be formed by selecting one value for each index position (in the given order). The possible values for a given index are all the values between the lower and upper bounds, inclusive; this range of values is called the *index range*.

5   An unconstrained array definition defines an array type. For each object that has the array type, the number of indices, the type and position of each index, and the subtype of the components are as in the type definition; the values of the lower and upper bounds for each index belong to the corresponding index subtype, except for null arrays as explained in section 3.6.1. The *index subtype* for a given index position is, by definition, the subtype denoted by the type mark of the corresponding index subtype definition. The compound delimiter <> (called a *box*) of an index subtype definition stands for an undefined range (different objects of the type need not have the same bounds). The elaboration of an unconstrained array definition creates an array type; this elaboration includes that of the component subtype indication.

6   A constrained array definition defines both an array type and a subtype of this type:

7   • The array type is an implicitly declared anonymous type; this type is defined by an (implicit) unconstrained array definition, in which the component subtype indication is that of the constrained array definition, and in which the type mark of each index subtype definition denotes the subtype defined by the corresponding discrete range.

8   • The array subtype is the subtype obtained by imposition of the index constraint on the array type.

9   If a constrained array definition is given for a type declaration, the simple name declared by this declaration denotes the array subtype.

10   The elaboration of a constrained array definition creates the corresponding array type and array subtype. For this elaboration, the index constraint and the component subtype indication are elaborated. The evaluation of each discrete range of the index constraint and the elaboration of the component subtype indication are performed in some order that is not defined by the language.

11   *Examples of type declarations with unconstrained array definitions:*

```
type VECTOR     is array(INTEGER   range <>) of REAL;
type MATRIX     is array(INTEGER   range <>, INTEGER range <>) of REAL;
type BIT_VECTOR is array(INTEGER   range <>) of BOOLEAN;
type ROMAN      is array(POSITIVE  range <>) of ROMAN_DIGIT;
```

12   *Examples of type declarations with constrained array definitions:*

```
type TABLE    is array(1 .. 10) of INTEGER;
type SCHEDULE is array(DAY) of BOOLEAN;
type LINE     is array(1 .. MAX_LINE_SIZE) of CHARACTER;
```

13   *Examples of object declarations with constrained array definitions:*

```
GRID : array(1 .. 80, 1 .. 100) of BOOLEAN;
MIX  : array(COLOR range RED .. GREEN) of BOOLEAN;
PAGE : array(1 .. 50) of LINE;  -- an array of arrays
```

Note:

For a one-dimensional array, the rule given means that a type declaration with a constrained array definition such as   14

    type T **is array**(POSITIVE **range** MIN .. MAX) **of** COMPONENT;

is equivalent (in the absence of an incorrect order dependence) to the succession of declarations   15

    subtype *index_subtype* **is** POSITIVE **range** MIN .. MAX;
    type *array_type* **is array**(*index_subtype* **range** <>) **of** COMPONENT;
    subtype T **is** *array_type*(*index_subtype*);

where *index_subtype* and *array_type* are both anonymous. Consequently, T is the name of a sub-   16
type and all objects declared with this type mark are arrays that have the same bounds. Similar transformations apply to multidimensional arrays.

A similar transformation applies to an object whose declaration includes a constrained array defini-   17
tion. A consequence of this is that no two such objects have the same type.

References: anonymous type 3.3.1, bound of a range 3.5, component 3.3, constraint 3.3, discrete type 3.5,   18
elaboration 3.1 3.9, in some order 1.6, name 4.1, object 3.2, range 3.5, subtype 3.3, subtype indication 3.3.2, type
3.3, type declaration 3.3.1, type definition 3.3.1, type mark 3.3.2

3.6.1 Index Constraints and Discrete Ranges

An index constraint determines the range of possible values for every index of an array type, and   1
thereby the corresponding array bounds.

For a discrete range used in a constrained array definition and defined by a range, an implicit con-   2
version to the predefined type INTEGER is assumed if each bound is either a numeric literal, a named number, or an attribute, and the type of both bounds (prior to the implicit conversion) is the type *universal_integer*. Otherwise, both bounds must be of the same discrete type, other than *universal_integer*; this type must be determinable independently of the context, but using the fact that the type must be discrete and that both bounds must have the same type. These rules apply also to a discrete range used in an iteration rule (see 5.5) or in the declaration of a family of entries (see 9.5).

If an index constraint follows a type mark in a subtype indication, then the type or subtype denoted   3
by the type mark must not already impose an index constraint. The type mark must denote either an unconstrained array type or an access type whose designated type is such an array type. In either case, the index constraint must provide a discrete range for each index of the array type and the type of each discrete range must be the same as that of the corresponding index.

An index constraint is *compatible* with the type denoted by the type mark if and only if the con-   4
straint defined by each discrete range is compatible with the corresponding index subtype. If any of the discrete ranges defines a null range, any array thus constrained is a *null array*, having no components. An array value *satisfies* an index constraint if at each index position the array value and the index constraint have the same index bounds. (Note, however, that assignment and certain other operations on arrays involve an implicit subtype conversion.)

5   The bounds of each array object are determined as follows:

6   ● For a variable declared by an object declaration, the subtype indication of the corresponding
     object declaration must define a constrained array subtype (and, thereby, the bounds). The
     same requirement exists for the subtype indication of a component declaration, if the type of
     the record component is an array type; and for the component subtype indication of an array
     type definition, if the type of the array components is itself an array type.

7   ● For a constant declared by an object declaration, the bounds of the constant are defined by
     the initial value if the subtype of the constant is unconstrained; they are otherwise defined by
     this subtype (in the latter case, the initial value is the result of an implicit subtype conversion).
     The same rule applies to a generic formal parameter of mode **in**.

8   ● For an array object designated by an access value, the bounds must be defined by the
     allocator that creates the array object. (The allocated object is constrained with the cor-
     responding values of the bounds.)

9   ● For a formal parameter of a subprogram or entry, the bounds are obtained from the cor-
     responding actual parameter. (The formal parameter is constrained with the corresponding
     values of the bounds.)

10   ● For a renaming declaration and for a generic formal parameter of mode **in out**, the bounds are
     those of the renamed object or of the corresponding generic actual parameter.

11   For the elaboration of an index constraint, the discrete ranges are evaluated in some order that is
     not defined by the language.

12   *Examples of array declarations including an index constraint:*

```
BOARD        : MATRIX(1 .. 8,   1 .. 8);   --  see 3.6
RECTANGLE    : MATRIX(1 .. 20,  1 .. 30);
INVERSE      : MATRIX(1 .. N,   1 .. N);   --  N need not be static

FILTER       : BIT_VECTOR(0 .. 31);
```

13   *Example of array declaration with a constrained array subtype:*

```
MY_SCHEDULE : SCHEDULE;   --  all arrays of type SCHEDULE have the same bounds
```

14   *Example of record type with a component that is an array:*

```
type VAR_LINE(LENGTH : INTEGER) is
   record
      IMAGE : STRING(1 .. LENGTH);
   end record;

NULL_LINE : VAR_LINE(0);   --  NULL_LINE.IMAGE is a null array
```

Notes:

15   The elaboration of a subtype indication consisting of a type mark followed by an index constraint
     checks the compatibility of the index constraint with the type mark (see 3.3.2).

16   All components of an array have the same subtype. In particular, for an array of components that
     are one-dimensional arrays, this means that all components have the same bounds and hence the
     same length.

3.6.1 Index Constraints and Discrete Ranges   3-30

References: access type 3.8, access type definition 3.8, access value 3.8, actual parameter 6.4.1, allocator 4.8, array [17] bound 3.6, array component 3.6, array type 3.6, array type definition 3.6, bound of a range 3.5, compatible 3.3.2, component declaration 3.7, constant 3.2.1, constrained array definition 3.6, constrained array subtype 3.6, conversion 4.6, designate 3.8, designated type 3.8, discrete range 3.6, entry 9.5, entry family declaration 9.5, expression 4.4, formal parameter 6.1, function 6.5, generic actual parameter 12.3, generic formal parameter 12.1 12.3, generic parameter 12.1, index 3.6, index constraint 3.6.1, index subtype 3.6, initial value 3.2.1, integer literal 2.4, integer type 3.5.4, iteration rule 5.5, mode 12.1.1, name 4.1, null range 3.5, object 3.2, object declaration 3.2.1, predefined type C, range 3.5, record component 3.7, renaming declaration 8.5, result subtype 6.1, satisfy 3.3, subprogram 6, subtype conversion 4.6, subtype indication 3.3.2, type mark 3.3.2, unconstrained array type 3.6, unconstrained subtype 3.3, universal type 4.10, universal_integer type 3.5.4, variable 3.2.1

3.6.2 Operations of Array Types

The basic operations of an array type include the operations involved in assignment and [1] aggregates (unless the array type is limited), membership tests, indexed components, qualification, and explicit conversion; for one-dimensional arrays the basic operations also include the operations involved in slices, and also string literals if the component type is a character type.

If A is an array object, an array value, or a constrained array subtype, the basic operations also [2] include the attributes listed below. These attributes are not allowed for an unconstrained array type. The argument N used in the attribute designators for the N-th dimension of an array must be a static expression of type *universal_integer*. The value of N must be positive (nonzero) and no greater than the dimensionality of the array.

A'FIRST	Yields the lower bound of the first index range. The value of this attribute has the same type as this lower bound.	[3]
A'FIRST(N)	Yields the lower bound of the N-th index range. The value of this attribute has the same type as this lower bound.	[4]
A'LAST	Yields the upper bound of the first index range. The value of this attribute has the same type as this upper bound.	[5]
A'LAST(N)	Yields the upper bound of the N-th index range. The value of this attribute has the same type as this upper bound.	[6]
A'RANGE	Yields the first index range, that is, the range A'FIRST .. A'LAST .	[7]
A'RANGE(N)	Yields the N-th index range, that is, the range A'FIRST (N) .. A'LAST (N).	[8]
A'LENGTH	Yields the number of values of the first index range (zero for a null range). The value of this attribute is of the type *universal_integer*.	[9]
A'LENGTH(N)	Yields the number of values of the N-th index range (zero for a null range). The value of this attribute is of the type *universal_integer*.	[10]

In addition, the attribute T'BASE is defined for an array type or subtype T (see 3.3.3); the attribute [11] T'SIZE is defined for an array type or subtype T, and the attributes A'SIZE and A'ADDRESS are defined for an array object A (see 13.7.2).

12   Besides the basic operations, the operations of an array type include the predefined comparison for equality and inequality, unless the array type is limited. For one-dimensional arrays, the operations include catenation, unless the array type is limited; if the component type is a discrete type, the operations also include all predefined relational operators; if the component type is a boolean type, then the operations also include the unary logical negation operator **not**, and the logical operators.

13   *Examples (using arrays declared in the examples of section 3.6.1):*

```
--   FILTER'FIRST      =    0    FILTER'LAST      =   31    FILTER'LENGTH  =   32
--   RECTANGLE'LAST(1) =   20    RECTANGLE'LAST(2) =  30
```

Notes:

14   The attributes A'FIRST and A'FIRST (1) yield the same value. A similar relation exists for the attributes A'LAST, A'RANGE, and A'LENGTH. The following relations are satisfied (except for a null array) by the above attributes if the index type is an integer type:

```
A'LENGTH    = A'LAST    - A'FIRST    + 1
A'LENGTH(N) = A'LAST(N) - A'FIRST(N) + 1
```

15   An array type is limited if its component type is limited (see 7.4.4).

16   *References:* aggregate 4.3, array type 3.6, assignment 5.2, attribute 4.1.4, basic operation 3.3.3, bound of a range 3.5, catenation operator 4.5 4.5.3, character type 3.5.2, constrained array subtype 3.6, conversion 4.6, designator 6.1, dimension 3.6, index 3.6, indexed component 4.1.1, limited type 7.4.4, logical operator 4.5 4.5.1, membership test 4.5 4.5.2, not operator 4.5 4.5.6, null range 3.5, object 3.2, operation 3.3, predefined operator 4.5, qualified expression 4.7, relational operator 4.5 4.5.2, slice 4.1.2, static expression 4.9, string literal 2.6, subcomponent 3.3, type 3.3, unconstrained array type 3.6, universal type 4.10, universal_integer type 3.5.4

3.6.3 The Type String

1   The values of the predefined type STRING are one-dimensional arrays of the predefined type CHARACTER, indexed by values of the predefined subtype POSITIVE :

```
subtype POSITIVE is INTEGER range 1 .. INTEGER'LAST;
type STRING is array(POSITIVE range <>) of CHARACTER;
```

2   *Examples:*

```
STARS       : STRING(1 .. 120)  := (1 .. 120 => '*' );
QUESTION    : constant STRING   := "HOW MANY CHARACTERS?";
--   QUESTION'FIRST = 1, QUESTION'LAST = 20 (the number of characters)

ASK_TWICE   : constant STRING   := QUESTION & QUESTION;
NINETY_SIX  : constant ROMAN    := "XCVI";          -- see 3.6
```

Notes:

3   String literals (see 2.6 and 4.2) are basic operations applicable to the type STRING and to any other one-dimensional array type whose component type is a character type. The catenation operator is a predefined operator for the type STRING and for one-dimensional array types; it is represented as &. The relational operators <, <=, >, and >= are defined for values of these types, and correspond to lexicographic order (see 4.5.2).

References: aggregate 4.3, array 3.6, catenation operator 4.5 4.5.3, character type 3.5.2, component type (of an
array) 3.6, dimension 3.6, index 3.6, lexicographic order 4.5.2, positional aggregate 4.3, predefined operator 4.5,
predefined type C, relational operator 4.5 4.5.2, string literal 2.6, subtype 3.3, type 3.3

4

3.7 Record Types

A record object is a composite object consisting of named components. The value of a record   1
object is a composite value consisting of the values of its components.

```
record_type_definition ::=
    record
        component_list
    end record
```

2

```
component_list ::=
        component_declaration {component_declaration}
    |  {component_declaration} variant_part
    |  null;
```

```
component_declaration ::=
    identifier_list : component_subtype_definition [:= expression];
```

```
component_subtype_definition ::=   subtype_indication
```

Each component declaration declares a component of the record type. Besides components   3
declared by component declarations, the components of a record type include any components
declared by discriminant specifications of the record type declaration. The identifiers of all components of a record type must be distinct. The use of a name that denotes a record component other
than a discriminant is not allowed within the record type definition that declares the component.

A component declaration with several identifiers is equivalent to a sequence of single component   4
declarations, as explained in section 3.2. Each single component declaration declares a record
component whose subtype is specified by the component subtype definition.

If a component declaration includes the assignment compound delimiter followed by an expres-   5
sion, the expression is the default expression of the record component; the default expression
must be of the type of the component. Default expressions are not allowed for components that
are of a limited type.

If a record type does not have a discriminant part, the same components are present in all values   6
of the type. if the component list of a record type is defined by the reserved word **null** and there is
no discriminant part, then the record type has no components and all records of the type are *null*
records.

The elaboration of a record type definition creates a record type; it consists of the elaboration of   7
any corresponding (single) component declarations, in the order in which they appear, including
any component declaration in a variant part. The elaboration of a component declaration consists
of the elaboration of the component subtype definition.

For the elaboration of a component subtype definition, if the constraint does not depend on a dis-   8
criminant (see 3.7.1), then the subtype indication is elaborated. If, on the other hand, the constraint depends on a discriminant, then the elaboration consists of the evaluation of any included
expression that is not a discriminant.

9   *Examples of record type declarations:*

```
type DATE is
   record
      DAY     : INTEGER range 1 .. 31;
      MONTH : MONTH_NAME;
      YEAR    : INTEGER range 0 .. 4000;
   end record;

type COMPLEX is
   record
      RE  : REAL := 0.0;
      IM  : REAL := 0.0;
   end record;
```

10 *Examples of record variables:*

```
TOMORROW, YESTERDAY : DATE;
A, B, C : COMPLEX;

-- both components of A, B, and C are implicitly initialized to zero
```

Notes:

11 The default expression of a record component is implicitly evaluated by the elaboration of the declaration of a record object, in the absence of an explicit initialization (see 3.2.1). If a component declaration has several identifiers, the expression is evaluated once for each such component of the object (since the declaration is equivalent to a sequence of single component declarations).

12 Unlike the components of an array, the components of a record need not be of the same type.

13 *References:* assignment compound delimiter 2.2, component 3.3, composite value 3.3, constraint 3.3, declaration 3.1, depend on a discriminant 3.7.1, discriminant 3.3, discriminant part 3.7 3.7.1, elaboration 3.9, expression 4.4, identifier 2.3, identifier list 3.2, limited type 7.4.4, name 4.1, object 3.2, subtype 3.3, type 3.3, type mark 3.3.2, variant part 3.7.3

3.7.1 Discriminants

1   A discriminant part specifies the discriminants of a type. A discriminant of a record is a component of the record. The type of a discriminant must be discrete.

2
```
discriminant_part ::=
    (discriminant_specification {; discriminant_specification})

discriminant_specification ::=
    identifier_list : type_mark [:= expression]
```

3   A discriminant part is only allowed in the type declaration for a record type, in a private type declaration or an incomplete type declaration (the corresponding full declaration must then declare a record type), and in the generic parameter declaration for a formal private type.

A discriminant specification with several identifiers is equivalent to a sequence of single discriminant specifications, as explained in section 3.2. Each single discriminant specification declares a discriminant. If a discriminant specification includes the assignment compound delimiter followed by an expression, the expression is the default expression of the discriminant; the default expression must be of the type of the discriminant. Default expressions must be provided either for all or for none of the discriminants of a discriminant part. **4**

The use of the name of a discriminant is not allowed in default expressions of a discriminant part if the specification of the discriminant is itself given in the discriminant part. **5**

Within a record type definition the only allowed uses of the name of a discriminant of the record type are: in the default expressions for record components; in a variant part as the discriminant name; and in a component subtype definition, either as a bound in an index constraint, or to specify a discriminant value in a discriminant constraint. A discriminant name used in these component subtype definitions must appear by itself, not as part of a larger expression. Such component subtype definitions and such constraints are said to *depend on a discriminant*. **6**

A component is said to *depend on a discriminant* if it is a record component declared in a variant part, or a record component whose component subtype definition depends on a discriminant, or finally, one of the subcomponents of a component that itself depends on a discriminant. **7**

Each record value includes a value for each discriminant specified for the record type; it also includes a value for each record component that does not depend on a discriminant. The values of the discriminants determine which other component values are in the record value. **8**

Direct assignment to a discriminant of an object is not allowed; furthermore a discriminant is not allowed as an actual parameter of mode **in out** or **out**, or as a generic actual parameter of mode **in out**. The only allowed way to change the value of a discriminant of a variable is to assign a (complete) value to the variable itself. Similarly, an assignment to the variable itself is the only allowed way to change the constraint of one of its components, if the component subtype definition depends on a discriminant of the variable. **9**

The elaboration of a discriminant part has no other effect. **10**

Examples: **11**

```
type BUFFER(SIZE : BUFFER_SIZE := 100) is          -- see 3.5.4
   record
      POS     : BUFFER_SIZE := 0;
      VALUE   : STRING(1 .. SIZE);
   end record;

type SQUARE(SIDE : INTEGER) is
   record
      MAT : MATRIX(1 .. SIDE, 1 .. SIDE);          -- see 3.6
   end record;

type DOUBLE_SQUARE(NUMBER : INTEGER) is
   record
      LEFT  : SQUARE (NUMBER);
      RIGHT : SQUARE (NUMBER);
   end record;
```

```
type ITEM(NUMBER : POSITIVE) is
  record
    CONTENT : INTEGER;
    --  no component depends on the discriminant
  end record;
```

12   *References:* assignment 5.2, assignment compound delimiter 2.2, bound of a range 3.5, component 3.3, component declaration 3.7, component of a record 3.7, declaration 3.1, discrete type 3.5, discriminant 3.3, discriminant constraint 3.7.2, elaboration 3.9, expression 4.4, generic formal type 12.1, generic parameter declaration 12.1, identifier 2.3, identifier list 3.2, incomplete type declaration 3.8.1, index constraint 3.6.1, name 4.1, object 3.2, private type 7.4, private type declaration 7.4, record type 3.7, scope 8.2, simple name 4.1, subcomponent 3.3, subtype indication 3.3.2, type declaration 3.3.1, type mark 3.3.2, variant part 3.7.3

3.7.2 Discriminant Constraints

1   A discriminant constraint is only allowed in a subtype indication, after a type mark. This type mark must denote either a type with discriminants, or an access type whose designated type is a type with discriminants. A discriminant constraint specifies the values of these discriminants.

2
```
discriminant_constraint ::=
    (discriminant_association {, discriminant_association})

discriminant_association ::=
    [discriminant_simple_name {| discriminant_simple_name} =>] expression
```

3   Each discriminant association associates an expression with one or more discriminants. A discriminant association is said to be *named* if the discriminants are specified explicitly by their names; it is otherwise said to be *positional*. For a positional association, the (single) discriminant is implicitly specified by position, in textual order. Named associations can be given in any order, but if both positional and named associations are used in the same discriminant constraint, then positional associations must occur first, at their normal position. Hence once a named association is used, the rest of the discriminant constraint must use only named associations.

4   For a named discriminant association, the discriminant names must denote discriminants of the type for which the discriminant constraint is given. A discriminant association with more than one discriminant name is only allowed if the named discriminants are all of the same type. Furthermore, for each discriminant association (whether named or positional), the expression and the associated discriminants must have the same type. A discriminant constraint must provide exactly one value for each discriminant of the type.

5   A discriminant constraint is compatible with the type denoted by a type mark, if and only if each discriminant value belongs to the subtype of the corresponding discriminant. In addition, for each subcomponent whose component subtype specification depends on a discriminant, the discriminant value is substituted for the discriminant in this component subtype specification and the compatibility of the resulting subtype indication is checked.

6   A composite value satisfies a discriminant constraint if and only if each discriminant of the composite value has the value imposed by the discriminant constraint.

The initial values of the discriminants of an object of a type with discriminants are determined as follows: 7

- For a variable declared by an object declaration, the subtype indication of the corresponding object declaration must impose a discriminant constraint unless default expressions exist for the discriminants; the discriminant values are defined either by the constraint or, in its absence, by the default expressions. The same requirement exists for the subtype indication of a component declaration, if the type of the record component has discriminants; and for the component subtype indication of an array type, if the type of the array components is a type with discriminants. 8

- For a constant declared by an object declaration, the values of the discriminants are those of the initial value if the subtype of the constant is unconstrained; they are otherwise defined by this subtype (in the latter case, an exception is raised if the initial value does not belong to this subtype). The same rule applies to a generic parameter of mode **in**. 9

- For an object designated by an access value, the discriminant values must be defined by the allocator that creates the object. (The allocated object is constrained with the corresponding discriminant values.) 10

- For a formal parameter of a subprogram or entry, the discriminants of the formal parameter are initialized with those of the corresponding actual parameter. (The formal parameter is constrained if the corresponding actual parameter is constrained, and in any case if the mode is **in** or if the subtype of the formal parameter is constrained.) 11

- For a renaming declaration and for a generic formal parameter of mode **in out**, the discriminants are those of the renamed object or of the corresponding generic actual parameter. 12

For the elaboration of a discriminant constraint, the expressions given in the discriminant associations are evaluated in some order that is not defined by the language; the expression of a named association is evaluated once for each named discriminant. 13

Examples (using types declared in the previous section): 14

```
LARGE    : BUFFER(200);   -- constrained, always 200 characters (explicit discriminant value)
MESSAGE  : BUFFER;        -- unconstrained, initially 100 characters (default discriminant value)

BASIS    : SQUARE(5);     -- constrained, always 5 by 5
ILLEGAL  : SQUARE;        -- illegal, a SQUARE must be constrained
```

Note:

The above rules and the rules defining the elaboration of an object declaration (see 3.2) ensure that discriminants always have a value. In particular, if a discriminant constraint is imposed on an object declaration, each discriminant is initialized with the value specified by the constraint. Similarly, if the subtype of a component has a discriminant constraint, the discriminants of the component are correspondingly initialized. 15

References: access type 3.8, access type definition 3.8, access value 3.8, actual parameter 6.4.1, allocator 4.8, array type definition 3.6, bound of a range 3.5, compatible 3.3.2, component 3.3, component declaration 3.7, component subtype indication 3.7, composite value 3.3, constant 3.2.1, constrained subtype 3.3, constraint 3.3, declaration 3.1, default expression for a discriminant 3.7, depend on a discriminant 3.7.1, designate 3.8, designated type 3.8, discriminant 3.3, elaboration 3.9, entry 9.5, evaluation 4.5, expression 4.4, formal parameter 6.1, generic actual parameter 12.3, generic formal parameter 12.1 12.3, mode in 6.1, mode in out 6.1, name 4.1, object 3.2, object declaration 3.2.1, renaming declaration 8.5, reserved word 2.9, satisfy 3.3, simple name 4.1, subcomponent 3.3, subprogram 6, subtype 3.3, subtype indication 3.3.2, type 3.3, type mark 3.3.2, variable 3.2.1 16

3.7.3 Variant Parts

1   A record type with a variant part specifies alternative lists of components. Each variant defines the components for the corresponding value or values of the discriminant.

2
```
variant_part ::=
    case discriminant_simple_name is
        variant
        { variant}
    end case;

variant ::=
    when choice {| choice} =>
        component_list

choice ::= simple_expression
    | discrete_range | others | component_simple_name
```

3   Each variant starts with a list of choices which must be of the same type as the discriminant of the variant part. The type of the discriminant of a variant part must not be a generic formal type. If the subtype of the discriminant is static, then each value of this subtype must be represented once and only once in the set of choices of the variant part, and no other value is allowed. Otherwise, each value of the (base) type of the discriminant must be represented once and only once in the set of choices.

4   The simple expressions and discrete ranges given as choices in a variant part must be static. A choice defined by a discrete range stands for all values in the corresponding range (none if a null range). The choice **others** is only allowed for the last variant and as its only choice; it stands for all values (possibly none) not given in the choices of previous variants. A component simple name is not allowed as a choice of a variant (although it is part of the syntax of choice).

5   A record value contains the values of the components of a given variant if and only if the discriminant value is equal to one of the values specified by the choices of the variant. This rule applies in turn to any further variant that is, itself, included in the component list of the given variant. If the component list of a variant is specified by **null**, the variant has no components.

6   *Example of record type with a variant part:*

```
type DEVICE is (PRINTER, DISK, DRUM);
type STATE  is (OPEN, CLOSED);

type PERIPHERAL(UNIT : DEVICE := DISK) is
    record
        STATUS : STATE;
        case UNIT is
            when PRINTER =>
                LINE_COUNT : INTEGER range 1 .. PAGE_SIZE;
            when others =>
                CYLINDER    : CYLINDER_INDEX;
                TRACK       : TRACK_NUMBER;
        end case;
    end record;
```

Examples of record subtypes:

7

```
subtype DRUM_UNIT  is PERIPHERAL(DRUM);
subtype DISK_UNIT  is PERIPHERAL(DISK);
```

Examples of constrained record variables:

8

```
WRITER  : PERIPHERAL(UNIT => PRINTER);
ARCHIVE : DISK_UNIT;
```

Note:

Choices with discrete values are also used in case statements and in array aggregates. Choices with component simple names are used in record aggregates.

9

References: array aggregate 4.3.2, base type 3.3, component 3.3, component list 3.7, discrete range 3.6, discriminant 3.3, generic formal type 12.1.2, null range 3.5, record aggregate 4.3.1, range 3.5, record type 3.7, simple expression 4.4, simple name 4.1, static discrete range 4.9, static expression 4.9, static subtype 4.9, subtype 3.3

10

3.7.4 Operations of Record Types

The basic operations of a record type include the operations involved in assignment and aggregates (unless the type is limited), membership tests, selection of record components, qualification, and type conversion (for derived types).

1

For any object A of a type with discriminants, the basic operations also include the following attribute:

2

A'CONSTRAINED   Yields the value TRUE if a discriminant constraint applies to the object A, or if the object is a constant (including a formal parameter or generic formal parameter of mode **in**); yields the value FALSE otherwise. If A is a generic formal parameter of mode **in out**, or if A is a formal parameter of mode **in out** or **out** and the type mark given in the corresponding parameter specification denotes an unconstrained type with discriminants, then the value of this attribute is obtained from that of the corresponding actual parameter. The value of this attribute is of the predefined type BOOLEAN.

3

In addition, the attributes T'BASE and T'SIZE are defined for a record type or subtype T (see 3.3.3); the attributes A'SIZE and A'ADDRESS are defined for a record object A (see 13.7.2).

4

Besides the basic operations, the operations of a record type include the predefined comparison for equality and inequality, unless the type is limited.

5

Note:

A record type is limited if the type of any of its components is limited (see 7.4.4).

6

References: actual parameter 6.4.1, aggregate 4.3, assignment 5.2, attribute 4.1.4, basic operation 3.3.3, boolean type 3.5.3, constant 3.2.1, conversion 4.6, derived type 3.4, discriminant 3.3, discriminant constraint 3.7.2, formal parameter 6.1, generic actual parameter 12.3, generic formal parameter 12.1 12.3, limited type 7.4.4, membership test 4.5 4.5.2, mode 6.1, object 3.2.1, operation 3.3, predefined operator 4.5, predefined type C, qualified expression 4.7, record type 3.7, relational operator 4.5 4.5.2, selected component 4.1.3, subcomponent 3.3, subtype 3.3, type 3.3

7

3.8 Access Types

1. An object declared by an object declaration is created by the elaboration of the object declaration and is denoted by a simple name or by some other form of name. In contrast, there are objects that are created by the evaluation of *allocators* (see 4.8) and that have no simple name. Access to such an object is achieved by an *access value* returned by an allocator; the access value is said to *designate* the object.

2.
```
access_type_definition  ::=  access subtype_indication
```

3. For each access type, there is a literal **null** which has a null access value designating no object at all. The null value of an access type is the default initial value of the type. Other values of an access type are obtained by evaluation of a special operation of the type, called an allocator. Each such access value designates an object of the subtype defined by the subtype indication of the access type definition; this subtype is called the *designated subtype*; the base type of this subtype is called the *designated type*. The objects designated by the values of an access type form a *collection* implicitly associated with the type.

4. The elaboration of an access type definition consists of the elaboration of the subtype indication and creates an access type.

5. If an access object is constant, the contained access value cannot be changed and always designates the same object. On the other hand, the value of the designated object need not remain the same (assignment to the designated object is allowed unless the designated type is limited).

6. The only forms of constraint that are allowed after the name of an access type in a subtype indication are index constraints and discriminant constraints. (See sections 3.6.1 and 3.7.2 for the rules applicable to these subtype indications.) An access value *belongs* to a corresponding subtype of an access type either if the access value is the null value or if the value of the designated object satisfies the constraint.

7. *Examples:*

```
type FRAME is access MATRIX;            -- see 3.6

type BUFFER_NAME is access BUFFER;      -- see 3.7.1
```

Notes:

8. An access value delivered by an allocator can be assigned to several access objects. Hence it is possible for an object created by an allocator to be designated by more than one variable or constant of the access type. An access value can only designate an object created by an allocator; in particular, it cannot designate an object declared by an object declaration.

9. If the type of the objects designated by the access values is an array type or a type with discriminants, these objects are constrained with either the array bounds or the discriminant values supplied implicitly or explicitly for the corresponding allocators (see 4.8).

10. Access values are called *pointers* or *references* in some other languages.

11. *References:* allocator 4.8, array type 3.6, assignment 5.2, belong to a subtype 3.3, constant 3.2.1, constraint 3.3, discriminant constraint 3.7.2, elaboration 3.9, index constraint 3.6.1, index specification 3.6, limited type 7.4.4, literal 4.2, name 4.1, object 3.2.1, object declaration 3.2.1, reserved word 2.9, satisfy 3.3, simple name 4.1, subcomponent 3.3, subtype 3.3, subtype indication 3.3.2, type 3.3, variable 3.2.1

3.8.1 Incomplete Type Declarations

There are no particular limitations on the designated type of an access type. In particular, the type of a component of the designated type can be another access type, or even the same access type. This permits mutually dependent and recursive access types. Their declarations require a prior incomplete (or private) type declaration for one or more types.

> incomplete_type_declaration ::= **type** identifier [discriminant_part];   2

For each incomplete type declaration, there must be a corresponding declaration of a type with the   3
same identifier. The corresponding declaration must be either a full type declaration or the declaration of a task type. In the rest of this section, explanations are given in terms of full type declarations; the same rules apply also to declarations of task types. If the incomplete type declaration occurs immediately within either a declarative part or the visible part of a package specification, then the full type declaration must occur later and immediately within this declarative part or visible part. If the incomplete type declaration occurs immediately within the private part of a package, then the full type declaration must occur later and immediately within either the private part itself, or the declarative part of the corresponding package body.

A discriminant part must be given in the full type declaration if and only if one is given in the   4
incomplete type declaration; if discriminant parts are given, then they must conform (see 6.3.1 for the conformance rules). Prior to the end of the full type declaration, the only allowed use of a name that denotes a type declared by an incomplete type declaration is as the type mark in the subtype indication of an access type definition; the only form of constraint allowed in this subtype indication is a discriminant constraint.

The elaboration of an incomplete type declaration creates a type. If the incomplete type declara-   5
tion has a discriminant part, this elaboration includes that of the discriminant part: in such a case, the discriminant part of the full type declaration is not elaborated.

Example of a recursive type: 6

```
type CELL;  -- Incomplete type declaration
type LINK is access CELL;

type CELL is
  record
    VALUE  : INTEGER;
    SUCC   : LINK;
    PRED   : LINK;
  end record;

HEAD : LINK := new CELL'(0, null, null);
NEXT : LINK := HEAD.SUCC;
```

Examples of mutually dependent access types:

```
type PERSON(SEX : GENDER);  --  incomplete type declaration
type CAR;                   --  incomplete type declaration

type PERSON_NAME  is access PERSON;
type CAR_NAME     is access CAR;

type CAR is
  record
    NUMBER  : INTEGER;
    OWNER   : PERSON_NAME;
  end record;
```

```
type PERSON(SEX : GENDER) is
  record
     NAME     : STRING(1 .. 20);
     BIRTH    : DATE;
     AGE      : INTEGER range 0 .. 130;
     VEHICLE  : CAR_NAME;
     case SEX is
        when M  => WIFE     : PERSON_NAME(SEX => F);
        when F  => HUSBAND  : PERSON_NAME(SEX => M);
     end case;
  end record;

MY_CAR, YOUR_CAR, NEXT_CAR : CAR_NAME;  --   implicitly initialized with null value
```

8   *References:* access type 3.8, access type definition 3.8, component 3.3, conform 6.3.1, constraint 3.3, declaration 3.1, declarative item 3.9, designate 3.8, discriminant constraint 3.7.2, discriminant part 3.7.1, elaboration 3.9, identifier 2.3, name 4.1, subtype indication 3.3.2, type 3.3, type mark 3.3.2

3.8.2 Operations of Access Types

1   The basic operations of an access type include the operations involved in assignment, allocators for the access type, membership tests, qualification, explicit conversion, and the literal **null**. If the designated type is a type with discriminants, the basic operations include the selection of the corresponding discriminants; if the designated type is a record type, they include the selection of the corresponding components; if the designated type is an array type, they include the formation of indexed components and slices; if the designated type is a task type, they include selection of entries and entry families. Furthermore, the basic operations include the formation of a selected component with the reserved word **all** (see 4.1.3).

2   If the designated type is an array type, the basic operations include the attributes that have the attribute designators FIRST, LAST, RANGE, and LENGTH (likewise, the attribute designators of the N-th dimension). The prefix of each of these attributes must be a value of the access type. These attributes yield the corresponding characteristics of the designated object (see 3.6.2).

3   If the designated type is a task type, the basic operations include the attributes that have the attribute designators TERMINATED and CALLABLE (see 9.9). The prefix of each of these attributes must be a value of the access type. These attributes yield the corresponding characteristics of the designated task objects.

4   In addition, the attribute T'BASE (see 3.3.3) and the representation attributes T'SIZE and T'STORAGE_SIZE (see 13.7.2) are defined for an access type or subtype T; the attributes A'SIZE and A'ADDRESS are defined for an access object A (see 13.7.2).

5   Besides the basic operations, the operations of an access type include the predefined comparison for equality and inequality.

6   *References:* access type 3.8, allocator 4.8, array type 3.6, assignment 5.2, attribute 4.1.4, attribute designator 4.1.4, base type 3.3, basic operation 3.3.3, collection 3.8, constrained array subtype 3.6, conversion 4.6, designate 3.8, designated subtype 3.8, designated type 3.8, discriminant 3.3, indexed component 4.1.1, literal 4.2, membership test 4.5 4.5.2, object 3.2.1, operation 3.3, private type 7.4, qualified expression 4.7, record type 3.7, selected component 4.1.3, slice 4.1.2, subtype 3.3, task type 9.1, type 3.3

3.9 Declarative Parts

A declarative part contains declarative items (possibly none).   1

    declarative_part ::=   2
       {basic_declarative_item} {later_declarative_item}

    basic_declarative_item ::= basic_declaration
       | representation_clause | use_clause

    later_declarative_item ::= body
       | subprogram_declaration | package_declaration
       | task_declaration | generic_declaration
       | use_clause | generic_instantiation

    body ::= proper_body | body_stub

    proper_body ::= subprogram_body | package_body | task_body

The elaboration of a declarative part consists of the elaboration of the declarative items, if any, in   3
the order in which they are given in the declarative part. After its elaboration, a declarative item is
said to be *elaborated*. Prior to the completion of its elaboration (including before the elaboration),
the declarative item is not yet elaborated.

For several forms of declarative item, the language rules (in particular scope and visibility rules) are   4
such that it is either impossible or illegal to use an entity before the elaboration of the declarative
item that declares this entity. For example, it is not possible to use the name of a type for an object
declaration if the corresponding type declaration is not yet elaborated. In the case of bodies, the
following checks are performed:

- For a subprogram call, a check is made that the body of the subprogram is already elaborated.   5

- For the activation of a task, a check is made that the body of the corresponding task unit is   6
  already elaborated.

- For the instantiation of a generic unit that has a body, a check is made that this body is   7
  already elaborated.

The exception PROGRAM_ERROR is raised if any of these checks fails.   8

If a subprogram declaration, a package declaration, a task declaration, or a generic declaration is a   9
declarative item of a given declarative part, then the body (if there is one) of the program unit
declared by the declarative item must itself be a declarative item of this declarative part (and must
appear later). If the body is a body stub, then a separately compiled subunit containing the corresponding proper body is required for the program unit (see 10.2).

References: activation 9.3, instantiation 12.3, program_error exception 11.1, scope 8.2, subprogram call 6.4, type   10
3.3, visibility 8.3

Elaboration of declarations: 3.1, component declaration 3.7, deferred constant declaration 7.4.3, discriminant   11
specification 3.7.1, entry declaration 9.5, enumeration literal specification 3.5.1, generic declaration 12.1, generic
instantiation 12.3, incomplete type declaration 3.8.1, loop parameter specification 5.5, number declaration 3.2.2,
object declaration 3.2.1, package declaration 7.2, parameter specification 6.1, private type declaration 7.4.1, renaming declaration 8.5, subprogram declaration 6.1, subtype declaration 3.3.2, task declaration 9.1, type declaration 3.3.1

12   *Elaboration of type definitions:*   3.3.1, access type definition 3.8, array type definition 3.6, derived type definition 3.4, enumeration type definition 3.5.1, integer type definition 3.5.4, real type definition 3.5.6, record type definition 3.7

13   *Elaboration of other constructs:*   context clause 10.1, body stub 10.2, compilation unit 10.1, discriminant part 3.7.1, generic body 12.2, generic formal parameter 12.1 12.3, library unit 10.5, package body 7.1, representation clause 13.1, subprogram body 6.3, subunit 10.2, task body 9.1, task object 9.2, task specification 9.1, use clause 8.4, with clause 10.1.1

4. Names and Expressions

The rules applicable to the different forms of name and expression, and to their evaluation, are given in this chapter.　　　1

4.1 Names

Names can denote declared entities, whether declared explicitly or implicitly (see 3.1). Names can also denote objects designated by access values; subcomponents and slices of objects and values; single entries, entry families, and entries in families of entries. Finally, names can denote attributes of any of the foregoing.　　　1

```
name ::= simple_name
    | character_literal    | operator_symbol
    | indexed_component    | slice
    | selected_component   | attribute

simple_name ::= identifier

prefix ::= name | function_call
```
2

A simple name for an entity is either the identifier associated with the entity by its declaration, or another identifier associated with the entity by a renaming declaration.　　　3

Certain forms of name (indexed and selected components, slices, and attributes) include a *prefix* that is either a name or a function call. If the type of a prefix is an access type, then the prefix must not be a name that denotes a formal parameter of mode **out** or a subcomponent thereof.　　　4

If the prefix of a name is a function call, then the name denotes a component, a slice, an attribute, an entry, or an entry family, either of the result of the function call, or (if the result is an access value) of the object designated by the result.　　　5

A prefix is said to be *appropriate for a type* in either of the following cases:　　　6

- The type of the prefix is the type considered.　　　7

- The type of the prefix is an access type whose designated type is the type considered.　　　8

The evaluation of a name determines the entity denoted by the name. This evaluation has no other effect for a name that is a simple name, a character literal, or an operator symbol.　　　9

The evaluation of a name that has a prefix includes the evaluation of the prefix, that is, of the corresponding name or function call. If the type of the prefix is an access type, the evaluation of the prefix includes the determination of the object designated by the corresponding access value; the exception CONSTRAINT_ERROR is raised if the value of the prefix is a null access value, except in the case of the prefix of a representation attribute (see 13.7.2).　　　10

11   *Examples of simple names:*

PI	--	the simple name of a number	(see 3.2.2)
LIMIT	--	the simple name of a constant	(see 3.2.1)
COUNT	--	the simple name of a scalar variable	(see 3.2.1)
BOARD	--	the simple name of an array variable	(see 3.6.1)
MATRIX	--	the simple name of a type	(see 3.6)
RANDOM	--	the simple name of a function	(see 6.1)
ERROR	--	the simple name of an exception	(see 11.1)

12   *References:* access type 3.8, access value 3.8, attribute 4.1.4, belong to a type 3.3, character literal 2.5, component 3.3, constraint_error exception 11.1, declaration 3.1, designate 3.8, designated type 3.8, entity 3.1, entry 9.5, entry family 9.5, evaluation 4.5, formal parameter 6.1, function call 6.4, identifier 2.3, indexed component 4.1.1, mode 6.1, null access value 3.8, object 3.2.1, operator symbol 6.1, raising of exceptions 11, renaming declarations 8.5, selected component 4.1.3, slice 4.1.2, subcomponent 3.3, type 3.3

4.1.1 Indexed Components

1   An indexed component denotes either a component of an array or an entry in a family of entries.

2   indexed_component ::= prefix(expression {, expression})

3   In the case of a component of an array, the prefix must be appropriate for an array type. The expressions specify the index values for the component; there must be one such expression for each index position of the array type. In the case of an entry in a family of entries, the prefix must be a name that denotes an entry family of a task object, and the expression (there must be exactly one) specifies the index value for the individual entry.

4   Each expression must be of the type of the corresponding index. For the evaluation of an indexed component, the prefix and the expressions are evaluated in some order that is not defined by the language. The exception CONSTRAINT_ERROR is raised if an index value does not belong to the range of the corresponding index of the prefixing array or entry family.

5   *Examples of indexed components:*

MY_SCHEDULE(SAT)	--	a component of a one-dimensional array	(see 3.6.1)
PAGE(10)	--	a component of a one-dimensional array	(see 3.6)
BOARD(M, J + 1)	--	a component of a two-dimensional array	(see 3.6.1)
PAGE(10)(20)	--	a component of a component	(see 3.6)
REQUEST(MEDIUM)	--	an entry in a family of entries	(see 9.5)
NEXT_FRAME(L)(M, N)	--	a component of a function call	(see 6.1)

Notes on the examples:

6   Distinct notations are used for components of multidimensional arrays (such as BOARD) and arrays of arrays (such as PAGE). The components of an array of arrays are arrays and can therefore be indexed. Thus PAGE (10)(20) denotes the 20th component of PAGE (10). In the last example NEXT_FRAME(L) is a function call returning an access value which designates a two-dimensional array.

7   *References:* appropriate for a type 4.1, array type 3.6, component 3.3, component of an array 3.6, constraint_error exception 11.1, dimension 3.6, entry 9.5, entry family 9.5, evaluation 4.5, expression 4.4, function call 6.4, in some order 1.6, index 3.6, name 4.1, prefix 4.1, raising of exceptions 11, returned value 5.8 6.5, task object 9.2

4.1.2 Slices

A slice denotes a one-dimensional array formed by a sequence of consecutive components of a one-dimensional array. A slice of a variable is a variable; a slice of a constant is a constant; a slice of a value is a value.

    slice ::= prefix(discrete_range)

The prefix of a slice must be appropriate for a one-dimensional array type. The type of the slice is the base type of this array type. The bounds of the discrete range define those of the slice and must be of the type of the index; the slice is a *null slice* denoting a null array if the discrete range is a null range.

For the evaluation of a name that is a slice, the prefix and the discrete range are evaluated in some order that is not defined by the language. The exception CONSTRAINT_ERROR is raised by the evaluation of a slice, other than a null slice, if any of the bounds of the discrete range does not belong to the index range of the prefixing array. (The bounds of a null slice need not belong to the subtype of the index.)

Examples of slices:

```
STARS(1 .. 15)            --  a slice of 15 characters       (see 3.6.3)
PAGE(10 .. 10 + SIZE)     --  a slice of 1 + SIZE components (see 3.6 and 3.2.1)
PAGE(L)(A .. B)           --  a slice of the array PAGE(L)   (see 3.6)
STARS(1 .. 0)             --  a null slice                   (see 3.6.3)
MY_SCHEDULE(WEEKDAY)      --  bounds given by subtype         (see 3.6 and 3.5.1)
STARS(5 .. 15)(K)         --  same as STARS(K)               (see 3.6.3)
                          --  provided that K is in 5 .. 15
```

Notes:

For a one-dimensional array A, the name A(N .. N) is a slice of one component; its type is the base type of A. On the other hand, A(N) is a component of the array A and has the corresponding component type.

References: appropriate for a type 4.1, array 3.6, array type 3.6, array value 3.8, base type 3.3, belong to a subtype 3.3, bound of a discrete range 3.6.1, component 3.3, component type 3.3, constant 3.2.1, constraint 3.3, constraint_error exception 11.1, dimension 3.6, discrete range 3.6, evaluation 4.5, index 3.6, index range 3.6, name 4.1, null array 3.6.1, null range 3.5, prefix 4.1, raising of exceptions 11, type 3.3, variable 3.2.1

4.1.3 Selected Components

Selected components are used to denote record components, entries, entry families, and objects designated by access values; they are also used as *expanded names* as described below.

    selected_component ::= prefix.selector

    selector ::= simple_name
        | character_literal | operator_symbol | **all**

3   The following four forms of selected components are used to denote a discriminant, a record component, an entry, or an object designated by an access value:

4   (a) A discriminant:

5   The selector must be a simple name denoting a discriminant of an object or value. The prefix must be appropriate for the type of this object or value.

6   (b) A component of a record:

7   The selector must be a simple name denoting a component of a record object or value. The prefix must be appropriate for the type of this object or value.

8   For a component of a variant, a check is made that the values of the discriminants are such that the record has this component. The exception CONSTRAINT_ERROR is raised if this check fails.

9   (c) A single entry or an entry family of a task:

10   The selector must be a simple name denoting a single entry or an entry family of a task. The prefix must be appropriate for the type of this task.

11   (d) An object designated by an access value:

12   The selector must be the reserved word **all**. The value of the prefix must belong to an access type.

13   A selected component of one of the remaining two forms is called an *expanded name*. In each case the selector must be either a simple name, a character literal, or an operator symbol. A function call is not allowed as the prefix of an expanded name. An expanded name can denote:

14   (e) An entity declared in the visible part of a package:

15   The prefix must denote the package. The selector must be the simple name, character literal, or operator symbol of the entity.

16   (f) An entity whose declaration occurs immediately within a named construct:

17   The prefix must denote a construct that is either a program unit, a block statement, a loop statement, or an accept statement. In the case of an accept statement, the prefix must be either the simple name of the entry or entry family, or an expanded name ending with such a simple name (that is, no index is allowed). The selector must be the simple name, character literal, or operator symbol of an entity whose declaration occurs immediately within the construct.

18   This form of expanded name is only allowed within the construct itself (including the body and any subunits, in the case of a program unit). A name declared by a renaming declaration is not allowed as the prefix. If the prefix is the name of a subprogram or accept statement and if there is more than one visible enclosing subprogram or accept statement of this name, the expanded name is ambiguous, independently of the selector.

19   If, according to the visibility rules, there is at least one possible interpretation of the prefix of a selected component as the name of an enclosing subprogram or accept statement, then the only interpretations considered are those of rule (f), as expanded names (no interpretations of the prefix as a function call are then considered).

The evaluation of a name that is a selected component includes the evaluation of the prefix.   20

Examples of selected components: 21

```
TOMORROW.MONTH        --  a record component              (see 3.7)
NEXT_CAR.OWNER        --  a record component              (see 3.8.1)
NEXT_CAR.OWNER.AGE    --  a record component              (see 3.8.1)
WRITER.UNIT           --  a record component (a discriminant)  (see 3.7.3)
MIN_CELL(H).VALUE     --  a record component of the result (see 6.1 and 3.8.1)
                      --  of the function call MIN_CELL(H)

CONTROL.SEIZE         --  an entry of the task CONTROL     (see 9.1 and 9.2)
POOL(K).WRITE         --  an entry of the task POOL(K)     (see 9.1 and 9.2)

NEXT_CAR.all          --  the object designated by
                      --  the access variable NEXT_CAR    (see 3.8.1)
```

Examples of expanded names: 22

```
TABLE_MANAGER.INSERT  --  a procedure of the visible part of a package  (see 7.5)
KEY_MANAGER."<"       --  an operator of the visible part of a package   (see 7.4.2)

DOT_PRODUCT.SUM       --  a variable declared in a procedure body   (see 6.5)
BUFFER.POOL           --  a variable declared in a task unit         (see 9.12)
BUFFER.READ           --  an entry of a task unit                    (see 9.12)
SWAP.TEMP             --  a variable declared in a block statement   (see 5.6)
STANDARD.BOOLEAN      --  the name of a predefined type              (see 8.6 and C)
```

Note:

For a record with components that are other records, the above rules imply that the simple name   23
must be given at each level for the name of a subcomponent. For example, the name
NEXT_CAR.OWNER.BIRTH.MONTH cannot be shortened (NEXT_CAR.OWNER.MONTH is not
allowed).

References: accept statement 9.5, access type 3.8, access value 3.8, appropriate for a type 4.1, block statement 5.6,   24
body of a program unit 3.9, character literal 2.5, component of a record 3.7, constraint_error exception 11.1, declaration 3.1, designate 3.8, discriminant 3.3, entity 3.1, entry 9.5, entry family 9.5, function call 6.4, index 3.6, loop statement 5.5, object 3.2.1, occur immediately within 8.1, operator 4.5, operator symbol 6.1, overloading 8.3, package 7,
predefined type C, prefix 4.1, procedure body 6.3, program unit 6, raising of exceptions 11, record 3.7, record component 3.7, renaming declaration 8.5, reserved word 2.9, simple name 4.1, subprogram 6, subunit 10.2, task 9, task
object 9.2, task unit 9, variable 3.7.3, variant 3.7.3, visibility 8.3, visible part 3.7.3

4.1.4 Attributes

An attribute denotes a basic operation of an entity given by a prefix.   1

    attribute ::= prefix'attribute_designator   2

    attribute_designator ::= simple_name [(*universal_static_*expression)]

The applicable attribute designators depend on the prefix. An attribute can be a basic operation   3
delivering a value; alternatively it can be a function, a type, or a range. The meaning of the prefix of
an attribute must be determinable independently of the attribute designator and independently of
the fact that it is the prefix of an attribute.

4   The attributes defined by the language are summarized in Annex A. In addition, an implementation may provide implementation-defined attributes; their description must be given in Appendix F. The attribute designator of any implementation-defined attribute must not be the same as that of any language-defined attribute.

5   The evaluation of a name that is an attribute consists of the evaluation of the prefix.

Notes:

6   The attribute designators DIGITS, DELTA, and RANGE have the same identifier as a reserved word. However, no confusion is possible since an attribute designator is always preceded by an apostrophe. The only predefined attribute designators that have a universal expression are those for certain operations of array types (see 3.6.2).

7   *Examples of attributes:*

```
COLOR'FIRST              -- minimum value of the enumeration type COLOR  (see 3.3.1  3.5)
RAINBOW'BASE'FIRST       -- same as COLOR'FIRST                          (see 3.3.2  3.3.3)
REAL'DIGITS              -- precision of the type REAL                   (see 3.5.7  3.5.8)
BOARD'LAST(2)            -- upper bound of the second dimension of BOARD (see 3.6.1  3.6.2)
BOARD'RANGE(1)           -- index range of the first dimension of BOARD  (see 3.6.1  3.6.2)
POOL(K)'TERMINATED       -- TRUE if task POOL(K) is terminated           (see 9.2   9.9)
DATE'SIZE                -- number of bits for records of type DATE      (see 3.7   13.7.2)
MESSAGE'ADDRESS          -- address of the record variable MESSAGE       (see 3.7.2 13.7.2)
```

8   *References:* appropriate for a type 4.1, basic operation 3.3.3, declared entity 3.1, name 4.1, prefix 4.1, reserved word 2.9, simple name 4.1, static expression 4.9, type 3.3, universal expression 4.10

4.2 Literals

1   A literal is either a numeric literal, an enumeration literal, the literal **null**, or a string literal. The evaluation of a literal yields the corresponding value.

2   Numeric literals are the literals of the types *universal_integer* and *universal_real*. Enumeration literals include character literals and yield values of the corresponding enumeration types. The literal **null** yields a null access value which designates no objects at all.

3   A string literal is a basic operation that combines a sequence of characters into a value of a one-dimensional array of a character type; the bounds of this array are determined according to the rules for positional array aggregates (see 4.3.2). For a null string literal, the upper bound is the predecessor, as given by the PRED attribute, of the lower bound. The evaluation of a null string literal raises the exception CONSTRAINT_ERROR if the lower bound does not have a predecessor (see 3.5.5).

4   The type of a string literal and likewise the type of the literal **null** must be determinable solely from the context in which this literal appears, excluding the literal itself, but using the fact that the literal **null** is a value of an access type, and similarly that a string literal is a value of a one-dimensional array type whose component type is a character type.

5   The character literals corresponding to the graphic characters contained within a string literal must be visible at the place of the string literal (although these characters themselves are not used to determine the type of the string literal).

Examples: 6

```
3.14159_26536    --   a  real  literal
1_345            --   an  integer  literal
CLUBS            --   an  enumeration  literal
'A'              --   a  character  literal
"SOME  TEXT"     --   a  string  literal
```

References: access type 3.8, aggregate 4.3, array 3.6, array bound 3.6, array type 3.6, character literal 2.5, character 7
type 3.5.2, component type 3.3, constraint_error exception 11.1, designate 3.8, dimension 3.6, enumeration literal
3.5.1, graphic character 2.1, integer literal 2.4, nul! access value 3.8, null literal 3.8, numeric literal 2.4, object 3.2.1,
real literal 2.4, string literal 2.6, type 3.3, universal_integer type 3.5.4, universal_real type 3.5.6, visibility 8.3

4.3 Aggregates

An aggregate is a basic operation that combines component values into a composite value of a 1
record or array type.

```
aggregate ::=                                                                                  2
    (component_association  {, component_association})

component_association ::=
    [choice {| choice} => ] expression
```

Each component association associates an expression with components (possibly none). A compo- 3
nent association is said to be *named* if the components are specified explicitly by choices; it is
otherwise said to be *positional*. For a positional association, the (single) component is implicitly
specified by position, in the order of the corresponding component declarations for record components, in index order for array components.

Named associations can be given in any order (except for the choice **others**), but if both positional 4
and named associations are used in the same aggregate, then positional associations must occur
first, at their normal position. Hence once a named association is used, the rest of the aggregate
must use only named associations. Aggregates containing a single component association must
always be given in named notation. Specific rules concerning component associations exist for
record aggregates and array aggregates.

Choices in component associations have the same syntax as in variant parts (see 3.7.3). A choice 5
that is a component simple name is only allowed in a record aggregate. For a component association, a choice that is a simple expression or a discrete range is only allowed in an array aggregate;
a choice that is a simple expression specifies the component at the corresponding index value;
similarly a discrete range specifies the components at the index values in the range. The choice
others is only allowed in a component association if the association appears last and has this
single choice; it specifies all remaining components, if any.

Each component of the value defined by an aggregate must be represented once and only once in 6
the aggregate. Hence each aggregate must be complete and a given component is not allowed to
be specified by more than one choice.

The type of an aggregate must be determinable solely from the context in which the aggregate 7
appears, excluding the aggregate itself, but using the fact that this type must be composite and not
limited. The type of an aggregate in turn determines the required type for each of its components.

Notes:

8   The above rule implies that the determination of the type of an aggregate cannot use any information from within the aggregate. In particular, this determination cannot use the type of the expression of a component association, or the form or the type of a choice. An aggregate can always be distinguished from an expression enclosed by parentheses: this is a consequence of the fact that named notation is required for an aggregate with a single component.

9   *References:* array aggregate 4.3.2, array type 3.6, basic operation 3.3.3, choice 3.7.3, component 3.3, composite type 3.3, composite value 3.3, discrete range 3.6, expression 4.4, index 3.6, limited type 7.4.4, primary 4.4, record aggregate 4.3.1, record type 3.7, simple expression 4.4, simple name 4.1, type 3.3, variant part 3.7.3

4.3.1 Record Aggregates

1   If the type of an aggregate is a record type, the component names given as choices must denote components (including discriminants) of the record type. If the choice **others** is given as a choice of a record aggregate, it must represent at least one component. A component association with the choice **others** or with more than one choice is only allowed if the represented components are all of the same type. The expression of a component association must have the type of the associated record components.

2   The value specified for a discriminant that governs a variant part must be given by a static expression (note that this value determines which dependent components must appear in the record value).

3   For the evaluation of a record aggregate, the expressions given in the component associations are evaluated in some order that is not defined by the language. The expression of a named association is evaluated once for each associated component. A check is made that the value of each subcomponent of the aggregate belongs to the subtype of this subcomponent. The exception CONSTRAINT_ERROR is raised if this check fails.

4   *Example of a record aggregate with positional associations:*

        (4, JULY, 1776)   -- see 3.7

5   *Examples of record aggregates with named associations:*

        (DAY => 4, MONTH => JULY, YEAR => 1776)
        (MONTH => JULY, DAY => 4, YEAR => 1776)

        (DISK, CLOSED, TRACK => 5, CYLINDER => 12)   -- see 3.7.3
        (UNIT => DISK, STATUS => CLOSED, CYLINDER => 9, TRACK => 1)

6   *Example of component association with several choices:*

        (VALUE => 0, SUCC|PRED => **new** CELL'(0, **null**, **null**))   -- see 3.8.1
        -- The allocator is evaluated twice: SUCC and PRED designate different cells

Note:

7   For an aggregate with positional associations, discriminant values appear first since the discriminant part is given first in the record type declaration; they must be in the same order as in the discriminant part.

References: aggregate 4.3, allocator 4.8, choice 3.7.3, component association 4.3, component name 3.7, constraint 3.3, constraint_error exception 11.1, depend on a discriminant 3.7.1, discriminant 3.3, discriminant part 3.7.1, evaluate 4.5, expression 4.4, in some order 1.6, program 10, raising of exceptions 11, record component 3.7, record type 3.7, satisfy 3.3, static expression 4.9, subcomponent 3.3, subtype 3.3.2, type 3.3, variant part 3.7.3

8

4.3.2 Array Aggregates

If the type of an aggregate is a one-dimensional array type, then each choice must specify values of the index type, and the expression of each component association must be of the component type.

1

If the type of an aggregate is a multidimensional array type, an n-dimensional aggregate is written as a one-dimensional aggregate, in which the expression specified for each component association is itself written as an (n-1)-dimensional aggregate which is called a *subaggregate*; the index subtype of the one-dimensional aggregate is given by the first index position of the array type. The same rule is used to write a subaggregate if it is again multidimensional, using successive index positions. A string literal is allowed in a multidimensional aggregate at the place of a one-dimensional array of a character type. In what follows, the rules concerning array aggregates are formulated in terms of one-dimensional aggregates.

2

Apart from a final component association with the single choice **others**, the rest (if any) of the component associations of an array aggregate must be either all positional or all named. A named association of an array aggregate is only allowed to have a choice that is not static, or likewise a choice that is a null range, if the aggregate includes a single component association and this component association has a single choice. An **others** choice is static if the applicable index constraint is static.

3

The bounds of an array aggregate that has an **others** choice are determined by the applicable index constraint. An **others** choice is only allowed if the aggregate appears in one of the following contexts (which defines the applicable index constraint):

4

(a) The aggregate is an actual parameter, a generic actual parameter, the result expression of a function, or the expression that follows an assignment compound delimiter. Moreover, the subtype of the corresponding formal parameter, generic formal parameter, function result, or object is a constrained array subtype.

5

For an aggregate that appears in such a context and contains an association with an **others** choice, named associations are allowed for other associations only in the case of a (nongeneric) actual parameter or function result. If the aggregate is a multidimensional array, this restriction also applies to each of its subaggregates.

6

(b) The aggregate is the operand of a qualified expression whose type mark denotes a constrained array subtype.

7

(c) The aggregate is the expression of the component association of an enclosing (array or record) aggregate. Moreover, if this enclosing aggregate is a multidimensional array aggregate then it is itself in one of these three contexts.

8

The bounds of an array aggregate that does not have an **others** choice are determined as follows. For an aggregate that has named associations, the bounds are determined by the smallest and largest choices given. For a positional aggregate, the lower bound is determined by the applicable index constraint if the aggregate appears in one of the contexts (a) through (c); otherwise, the lower bound is given by S'FIRST where S is the index subtype; in either case, the upper bound is determined by the number of components.

9

10   The evaluation of an array aggregate that is not a subaggregate proceeds in two steps. First, the choices of this aggregate and of its subaggregates, if any, are evaluated in some order that is not defined by the language. Second, the expressions of the component associations of the array aggregate are evaluated in some order that is not defined by the language; the expression of a named association is evaluated once for each associated component. The evaluation of a subaggregate consists of this second step (the first step is omitted since the choices have already been evaluated).

11   For the evaluation of an aggregate that is not a null array, a check is made that the index values defined by choices belong to the corresponding index subtypes, and also that the value of each subcomponent of the aggregate belongs to the subtype of this subcomponent. For an n-dimensional multidimensional aggregate, a check is made that all (n-1)-dimensional subaggregates have the same bounds. The exception CONSTRAINT_ERROR is raised if any of these checks fails.

Note:

12   The allowed contexts for an array aggregate including an **others** choice are such that the bounds of such an aggregate are always known from the context.

13   *Examples of array aggregates with positional associations:*

```
(7, 9, 5, 1, 3, 2, 4, 8, 6, 0)
TABLE'(5, 8, 4, 1, others => 0)   --   see 3.6
```

14   *Examples of array aggregates with named associations:*

```
(1 .. 5 => (1 .. 8 => 0.0))      -- two-dimensional
(1 .. N => new CELL)             --  N new cells, in particular for N = 0

TABLE'(2 | 4 | 10 =>   1, others    => 0)
SCHEDULE'(MON .. FRI  => TRUE,  others => FALSE)   --  see 3.6
SCHEDULE'(WED | SUN  => FALSE, others => TRUE )
```

15   *Examples of two-dimensional array aggregates:*

```
-- Three aggregates for the same value of type MATRIX (see 3.6):

((1.1, 1.2, 1.3), (2.1, 2.2, 2.3))
(1 => (1.1, 1.2, 1.3), 2 => (2.1, 2.2, 2.3))
(1 => (1 => 1.1, 2 => 1.2, 3 => 1.3), 2 => (1 => 2.1, 2 => 2.2, 3 => 2.3))
```

16   *Examples of aggregates as initial values:*

```
A :  TABLE := (7, 9, 5, 1, 3, 2, 4, 8, 6, 0);          -- A(1)=7, A(10)=0
B :  TABLE := TABLE'(2 | 4 | 10 => 1, others => 0); -- B(1)=0, B(10)=1
C :  constant MATRIX := (1 .. 5 => (1 .. 8 => 0.0)); -- C'FIRST(1)=1, C'LAST(2)=8

D :  BIT_VECTOR(M .. N) := (M .. N => TRUE);  -- see 3.6
E :  BIT_VECTOR(M .. N) := (others   => TRUE);
F :  STRING(1 .. 1) := (1 => 'F'); -- a one component aggregate: same as "F"
```

17   *References:* actual parameter 6.4.1, aggregate 4.3, array type 3.6, assignment compound delimiter 5.2, choice 3.7.3, component 3.3, component association 4.3, component type 3.3, constrained array subtype 3.6, constraint 3.3, constraint_error exception 11.1, dimension 3.6, evaluate 4.5, expression 4.4, formal parameter 6.1, function 6.5, in some order 1.6, index constraint 3.6.1, index range 3.6, index subtype 3.6, index type 3.6, named component association 4.3, null array 3.6.1, object 3.2, positional component association 4.3, qualified expression 4.7, raising of exceptions 11, static expression 4.9, subcomponent 3.3, type 3.3

4.4 Expressions

An expression is a formula that defines the computation of a value. 1

```
expression ::=
    relation {and relation} | relation {and then relation}
  | relation {or relation}    | relation {or else relation}
  | relation {xor relation}
```
2

```
relation ::=
    simple_expression [relational_operator simple_expression]
  | simple_expression [not] in range
  | simple_expression [not] in type_mark
```

```
simple_expression ::= [unary_adding_operator] term {binary_adding_operator term}
```

```
term ::= factor {multiplying_operator factor}
```

```
factor ::= primary [** primary] | abs primary | not primary
```

```
primary ::=
    numeric_literal | null | aggregate | string_literal | name | allocator
  | function_call | type_conversion | qualified_expression | (expression)
```

Each primary has a value and a type. The only names allowed as primaries are named numbers; 3
attributes that yield values; and names denoting objects (the value of such a primary is the value of
the object) or denoting values. Names that denote formal parameters of mode **out** are not allowed
as primaries; names of their subcomponents are only allowed in the case of discriminants.

The type of an expression depends only on the type of its constituents and on the operators 4
applied; for an overloaded constituent or operator, the determination of the constituent type, or the
identification of the appropriate operator, depends on the context. For each predefined operator,
the operand and result types are given in section 4.5.

Examples of primaries:
5

```
4.0                   --  real literal
PI                    --  named number
(1 .. 10 => 0)        --  array aggregate
SUM                   --  variable
INTEGER'LAST          --  attribute
SINE(X)               --  function call
COLOR'(BLUE)          --  qualified expression
REAL(M*N)             --  conversion
(LINE_COUNT + 10)     --  parenthesized expression
```

Examples of expressions:
6

```
VOLUME                     --  primary
not DESTROYED              --  factor
2*LINE_COUNT               --  term
-4.0                       --  simple expression
-4.0 + A                   --  simple expression
B**2 - 4.0*A*C             --  simple expression
PASSWORD(1 .. 3) = "BWV"   --  relation
COUNT in SMALL_INT         --  relation
COUNT not in SMALL_INT     --  relation
INDEX = 0 or ITEM_HIT         --  expression
(COLD and SUNNY) or WARM      --  expression (parentheses are required)
A**(B**C)                     --  expression (parentheses are required)
```

7   *References:* aggregate 4.3, allocator 4.8, array aggregate 4.3.2, attribute 4.1.4, binary adding operator 4.5 4.5.3, context of overload resolution 8.7, exponentiating operator 4.5 4.5.6, function call 6.4, multiplying operator 4.5 4.5.5, name 4.1, named number 3.2, null literal 3.8, numeric literal 2.4, object 3.2, operator 4.5, overloading 8.3, overloading an operator 6.7, qualified expression 4.7, range 3.5, real literal 2.4, relation 4.5.1, relational operator 4.5 4.5.2, result type 6.1, string literal 2.6, type 3.3, type conversion 4.6, type mark 3.3.2, unary adding operator 4.5 4.5.4, variable 3.2.1

4.5 Operators and Expression Evaluation

1   The language defines the following six classes of operators. The corresponding operator symbols (except /=), and only those, can be used as designators in declarations of functions for user-defined operators. They are given in the order of increasing precedence.

2
logical_operator	::=	**and** | **or** | **xor**
relational_operator	::=	= | /= | < | <= | > | >=
binary_adding_operator	::=	+ | - | &
unary_adding_operator	::=	+ | -
multiplying_operator	::=	* | / | **mod** | **rem**
highest_precedence_operator	::=	** | **abs** | **not**

3   The short-circuit control forms **and then** and **or else** have the same precedence as logical operators. The membership tests **in** and **not in** have the same precedence as relational operators.

4   For a term, simple expression, relation, or expression, operators of higher precedence are associated with their operands before operators of lower precedence. In this case, for a sequence of operators of the same precedence level, the operators are associated in textual order from left to right; parentheses can be used to impose specific associations.

5   The operands of a factor, of a term, of a simple expression, or of a relation, and the operands of an expression that does not contain a short-circuit control form, are evaluated in some order that is not defined by the language (but before application of the corresponding operator). The right operand of a short-circuit control form is evaluated if and only if the left operand has a certain value (see 4.5.1).

6   For each form of type declaration, certain of the above operators are *predefined*, that is, they are implicitly declared by the type declaration. For each such implicit operator declaration, the names of the parameters are LEFT and RIGHT for binary operators; the single parameter is called RIGHT for unary adding operators and for the unary operators **abs** and **not**. The effect of the predefined operators is explained in subsections 4.5.1 through 4.5.7.

7   The predefined operations on integer types either yield the mathematically correct result or raise the exception NUMERIC_ERROR. A predefined operation that delivers a result of an integer type (other than *universal_integer*) can only raise the exception NUMERIC_ERROR if the mathematical result is not a value of the type. The predefined operations on real types yield results whose accuracy is defined in section 4.5.7. A predefined operation that delivers a result of a real type (other than *universal_real*) can only raise the exception NUMERIC_ERROR if the result is not within the range of the safe numbers of the type, as explained in section 4.5.7.

Examples of precedence:

not SUNNY **or** WARM	-- same as (**not** SUNNY) **or** WARM
X > 4.0 **and** Y > 0.0	-- same as (X > 4.0) **and** (Y > 0.0)
-4.0*A**2	-- same as -(4.0 * (A**2))
abs(1 + A) + B	-- same as (**abs** (1 + A)) + B
Y**(-3)	-- parentheses are necessary
A / B * C	-- same as (A/B)*C
A + (B + C)	-- evaluate B + C before adding it to A

References: designator 6.1, expression 4.4, factor 4.4, implicit declaration 3.1, in some order 1.6, integer type 3.5.4, membership test 4.5.2, name 4.1, numeric_error exception 11.1, overloading 6.6 8.7, raising of an exception 11, range 3.5, real type 3.5.6, relation 4.4, safe number 3.5.6, short-circuit control form 4.5 4.5.1, simple expression 4.4, term 4.4, type 3.3, type declaration 3.3.1, universal_integer type 3.5.4, universal_real type 3.5.6

4.5.1 Logical Operators and Short-circuit Control Forms

The following logical operators are predefined for any boolean type and any one-dimensional array type whose components are of a boolean type; in either case the two operands have the same type.

Operator	Operation	Operand type	Result type
and	conjunction	any boolean type array of boolean components	same boolean type same array type
or	inclusive disjunction	any boolean type array of boolean components	same boolean type same array type
xor	exclusive disjunction	any boolean type array of boolean components	same boolean type same array type

The operations on arrays are performed on a component-by-component basis on matching components, if any (as for equality, see 4.5.2). The bounds of the resulting array are those of the left operand. A check is made that for each component of the left operand there is a matching component of the right operand, and vice versa. The exception CONSTRAINT_ERROR is raised if this check fails.

The short-circuit control forms **and then** and **or else** are defined for two operands of a boolean type and deliver a result of the same type. The left operand of a short-circuit control form is always evaluated first. If the left operand of an expression with the control form **and then** evaluates to FALSE, the right operand is not evaluated and the value of the expression is FALSE. If the left operand of an expression with the control form **or else** evaluates to TRUE, the right operand is not evaluated and the value of the expression is TRUE. If both operands are evaluated, **and then** delivers the same result as **and**, and **or else** delivers the same result as **or**.

Note: The conventional meaning of the logical operators is given by the following truth table:

A	B	A **and** B	A **or** B	A **xor** B
TRUE	TRUE	TRUE	TRUE	FALSE
TRUE	FALSE	FALSE	TRUE	TRUE
FALSE	TRUE	FALSE	TRUE	TRUE
FALSE	FALSE	FALSE	FALSE	FALSE

7   *Examples of logical operators:*

        SUNNY **or** WARM
        FILTER(1 .. 10) **and** FILTER(15 .. 24)   --   see 3.6.1

8   *Examples of short-circuit control forms:*

        NEXT_CAR.OWNER /= **null and then** NEXT_CAR.OWNER.AGE > 25   --   see 3.8.1
        N = 0 **or else** A(N) = HIT_VALUE

9   *References:* array type 3.6, boolean type 3.5.3, bound of an index range 3.6.1, component of an array 3.6, constraint_error exception 11.1, dimension 3.6, false boolean value 3.5.3, index subtype 3.6, matching components of arrays 4.5.2, null array 3.6.1, operation 3.3, operator 4.5, predefined operator 4.5, raising of exceptions 11, true boolean value 3.5.3, type 3.3

4.5.2 Relational Operators and Membership Tests

1   The equality and inequality operators are predefined for any type that is not limited. The other relational operators are the ordering operators < (less than), <= (less than or equal), > (greater than), and >= (greater than or equal). The ordering operators are predefined for any scalar type, and for any discrete array type, that is, a one-dimensional array type whose components are of a discrete type. The operands of each predefined relational operator have the same type. The result type is the predefined type BOOLEAN.

2   The relational operators have their conventional meaning: the result is equal to TRUE if the corresponding relation is satisfied; the result is FALSE otherwise. The inequality operator gives the complementary result to the equality operator: FALSE if equal, TRUE if not equal.

3

Operator	Operation	Operand type	Result type
= /=	equality and inequality	any type	BOOLEAN
< <= > >=	test for ordering	any scalar type discrete array type	BOOLEAN BOOLEAN

4   Equality for the discrete types is equality of the values. For real operands whose values are *nearly* equal, the results of the predefined relational operators are given in section 4.5.7. Two access values are equal either if they designate the same object, or if both are equal to the null value of the access type.

5   For two array values or two record values of the same type, the left operand is equal to the right operand if and only if for each component of the left operand there is a *matching component* of the right operand and vice versa; and the values of matching components are equal, as given by the predefined equality operator for the component type. In particular, two null arrays of the same type are always equal; two null records of the same type are always equal.

6   For comparing two records of the same type, *matching components* are those which have the same component identifier.

7   For comparing two one-dimensional arrays of the same type, *matching components* are those (if any) whose index values match in the following sense: the lower bounds of the index ranges are defined to match, and the successors of matching indices are defined to match. For comparing two multidimensional arrays, matching components are those whose index values match in successive index positions.

If equality is explicitly defined for a limited type, it does not extend to composite types having sub-components of the limited type (explicit definition of equality is allowed for such composite types). **8**

The ordering operators <, <=, >, and >= that are defined for discrete array types correspond to *lexicographic* order using the predefined order relation of the component type. A null array is lexicographically less than any array having at least one component. In the case of nonnull arrays, the left operand is lexicographically less than the right operand if the first component of the left operand is less than that of the right; otherwise the left operand is lexicographically less than the right operand only if their first components are equal and the tail of the left operand is lexicographically less than that of the right (the tail consists of the remaining components beyond the first and can be null). **9**

The membership tests **in** and **not in** are predefined for all types. The result type is the predefined type BOOLEAN. For a membership test with a range, the simple expression and the bounds of the range must be of the same scalar type; for a membership test with a type mark, the type of the simple expression must be the base type of the type mark. The evaluation of the membership test **in** yields the result TRUE if the value of the simple expression is within the given range, or if this value belongs to the subtype denoted by the given type mark; otherwise this evaluation yields the result FALSE (for a value of a real type, see 4.5.7). The membership test **not in** gives the complementary result to the membership test **in**. **10**

Examples: **11**

```
X /= Y

"" < "A" and "A" < "AA"        --   TRUE
"AA" < "B" and "A" < "A "      --   TRUE

MY_CAR = null                  -- true if MY_CAR has been set to null (see 3.8.1)
MY_CAR = YOUR_CAR              -- true if we both share the same car
MY_CAR.all = YOUR_CAR.all      -- true if the two cars are identical

N not in 1 .. 10       -- range membership test
TODAY in MON .. FRI    -- range membership test
TODAY in WEEKDAY       -- subtype membership test (see 3.5.1)
ARCHIVE in DISK_UNIT   -- subtype membership test (see 3.7.3)
```

Notes:

No exception is ever raised by a predefined relational operator or by a membership test, but an exception can be raised by the evaluation of the operands. **12**

If a record type has components that depend on discriminants, two values of this type have matching components if and only if their discriminants are equal. Two nonnull arrays have matching components if and only if the value of the attribute LENGTH(N) for each index position N is the same for both. **13**

References: access value 3.8, array type 3.6, base type 3.3, belong to a subtype 3.3, boolean predefined type 3.5.3, bound of a range 3.5, component 3.3, component identifier 3.7, component type 3.3, composite type 3.3, designate 3.8, dimension 3.6, discrete type 3.5, evaluation 4.5, exception 11, index 3.6, index range 3.6, limited type 7.4.4, null access value 3.8, null array 3.6.1, null record 3.7, object 3.2.1, operation 3.3, operator 4.5, predefined operator 4.5, raising of exceptions 11, range 3.5, record type 3.7, scalar type 3.5, simple expression 4.4, subcomponent 3.3, successor 3.5.5, type 3.3, type mark 3.3.2 **14**

4.5.3 Binary Adding Operators

1. The binary adding operators + and - are predefined for any numeric type and have their conventional meaning. The catenation operators & are predefined for any one-dimensional array type that is not limited.

2.

Operator	Operation	Left operand type	Right operand type	Result type
+	addition	any numeric type	same numeric type	same numeric type
-	subtraction	any numeric type	same numeric type	same numeric type
&	catenation	any array type	same array type	same array type
		any array type	the component type	same array type
		the component type	any array type	same array type
		the component type	the component type	any array type

3. For real types, the accuracy of the result is determined by the operand type (see 4.5.7).

4. If both operands are one-dimensional arrays, the result of the catenation is a one-dimensional array whose length is the sum of the lengths of its operands, and whose components comprise the components of the left operand followed by the components of the right operand. The lower bound of this result is the lower bound of the left operand, unless the left operand is a null array, in which case the result of the catenation is the right operand.

5. If either operand is of the component type of an array type, the result of the catenation is given by the above rules, using in place of this operand an array having this operand as its only component and having the lower bound of the index subtype of the array type as its lower bound.

6. The exception CONSTRAINT_ERROR is raised by catenation if the upper bound of the result exceeds the range of the index subtype, unless the result is a null array. This exception is also raised if any operand is of the component type but has a value that does not belong to the component subtype.

7. *Examples:*

```
Z + 0.1          --  Z must be of a real type

"A" & "BCD"      --  catenation of two string literals
'A' & "BCD"      --  catenation of a character literal and a string literal
'A' & 'A'        --  catenation of two character literals
```

8. *References:* array type 3.6, character literal 2.5, component type 3.3, constraint_error exception 11.1, dimension 3.6, index subtype 3.6, length of an array 3.6.2, limited type 7.4.4, null array 3.6.1, numeric type 3.5, operation 3.3, operator 4.5, predefined operator 4.5, raising of exceptions 11, range of an index subtype 3.6.1, real type 3.5.6, string literal 2.6, type 3.3

4.5.4 Unary Adding Operators

1. The unary adding operators + and - are predefined for any numeric type and have their conventional meaning. For each of these operators, the operand and the result have the same type.

Operator	Operation	Operand type	Result type	
+	identity	any numeric type	same numeric type	2
-	negation	any numeric type	same numeric type	

References: numeric type 3.5, operation 3.3, operator 4.5, predefined operator 4.5, type 3.3   3

4.5.5 Multiplying Operators

The operators $*$ and $/$ are predefined for any integer and any floating point type and have their con-   1
ventional meaning; the operators **mod** and **rem** are predefined for any integer type. For each of
these operators, the operands and the result have the same base type. For floating point types, the
accuracy of the result is determined by the operand type (see 4.5.7).

Operator	Operation	Operand type	Result type	
$*$	multiplication	any integer type	same integer type	2
		any floating point type	same floating point type	
/	integer division	any integer type	same integer type	
	floating division	any floating point type	same floating point type	
mod	modulus	any integer type	same integer type	
rem	remainder	any integer type	same integer type	

Integer division and remainder are defined by the relation   3

$$A = (A/B)*B + (A \textbf{ rem } B)$$

where (A **rem** B) has the sign of A and an absolute value less than the absolute value of B. Integer   4
division satisfies the identity

$$(-A)/B = -(A/B) = A/(-B)$$

The result of the modulus operation is such that (A **mod** B) has the sign of B and an absolute value   5
less than the absolute value of B; in addition, for some integer value N, this result must satisfy the
relation

$$A = B*N + (A \textbf{ mod } B)$$

For each fixed point type, the following multiplication and division operators, with an operand of   6
the predefined type INTEGER , are predefined.

Operator	Operation	Left operand type	Right operand type	Result type	
$*$	multiplication	any fixed point type	INTEGER	same as left	7
		INTEGER	any fixed point type	same as right	
/	division	any fixed point type	INTEGER	same as left	

8   Integer multiplication of fixed point values is equivalent to repeated addition. Division of a fixed point value by an integer does not involve a change in type but is approximate (see 4.5.7).

9   Finally, the following multiplication and division operators are declared in the predefined package STANDARD. These two special operators apply to operands of all fixed point types (it is a consequence of other rules that they cannot be renamed or given as generic actual parameters).

10

Operator	Operation	Left operand type	Right operand type	Result type
*	multiplication	any fixed point type	any fixed point type	universal_fixed
/	division	any fixed point type	any fixed point type	universal_fixed

11 Multiplication of operands of the same or of different fixed point types is exact and delivers a result of the anonymous predefined fixed point type *universal_fixed* whose delta is arbitrarily small. The result of any such multiplication must always be explicitly converted to some numeric type. This ensures explicit control of the accuracy of the computation. The same considerations apply to division of a fixed point value by another fixed point value. No other operators are defined for the type *universal_fixed*.

12 The exception NUMERIC_ERROR is raised by integer division, **rem**, and **mod** if the right operand is zero.

13 *Examples:*

```
I   : INTEGER := 1;
J   : INTEGER := 2;
K   : INTEGER := 3;

X   : REAL digits 6 := 1.0;        --      see 3.5.7
Y   : REAL digits 6 := 2.0;

F   : FRACTION delta 0.0001 := 0.1;    --      see 3.5.9
G   : FRACTION delta 0.0001 := 0.1;
```

Expression	Value	Result Type
I*J	2	same as I and J, that is, INTEGER
K/J	1	same as K and J, that is, INTEGER
K **mod** J	1	same as K and J, that is, INTEGER
X/Y	0.5	same as X and Y, that is, REAL
F/2	0.05	same as F, that is, FRACTION
3*F	0.3	same as F, that is, FRACTION
F*G	0.01	*universal_fixed*, conversion needed
FRACTION(F*G)	0.01	FRACTION, as stated by the conversion
REAL(J)*Y	4.0	REAL, the type of both operands after conversion of J

Notes:

For positive A and B, A/B is the quotient and A **rem** B is the remainder when A is divided by B. The   14
following relations are satisfied by the **rem** operator:

    A   rem (-B) =   A rem B
    (-A) rem   B   =   -(A rem B)

For any integer K, the following identity holds: 15

    A mod B   =   (A + K*B) mod B

The relations between integer division, remainder, and modulus are illustrated by the following   16
table:

A	B	A/B	A rem B	A mod B	A	B	A/B	A rem B	A mod B
10	5	2	0	0	-10	5	-2	0	0
11	5	2	1	1	-11	5	-2	-1	4
12	5	2	2	2	-12	5	-2	-2	3
13	5	2	3	3	-13	5	-2	-3	2
14	5	2	4	4	-14	5	-2	-4	1
10	-5	-2	0	0	-10	-5	2	0	0
11	-5	-2	1	-4	-11	-5	2	-1	-1
12	-5	-2	2	-3	-12	-5	2	-2	-2
13	-5	-2	3	-2	-13	-5	2	-3	-3
14	-5	-2	4	-1	-14	-5	2	-4	-4

References: actual parameter 6.4.1, base type 3.3, declaration 3.1, delta of a fixed point type 3.5.9, fixed point type   17
3.5.9, floating point type 3.5.7, generic formal subprogram 12.1, integer type 3.5.4, numeric type 3.5, numeric_error
exception 11.1, predefined operator 4.5, raising of exceptions 11, renaming declaration 8.5, standard predefined
package 8.6, type conversion 4.6

4.5.6 Highest Precedence Operators

The highest precedence unary operator **abs** is predefined for any numeric type. The highest   1
precedence unary operator **not** is predefined for any boolean type and any one-dimensional array
type whose components have a boolean type.

Operator	*Operation*	*Operand type*	*Result type*
abs	absolute value	any numeric type	same numeric type
not	logical negation	any boolean type	same boolean type
		array of boolean components	same array type

The operator **not** that applies to a one-dimensional array of boolean components yields a one-   3
dimensional boolean array with the same bounds; each component of the result is obtained by
logical negation of the corresponding component of the operand (that is, the component that has
the same index value).

4   The highest precedence *exponentiating* operator ∗∗ is predefined for each integer type and for each floating point type. In either case the right operand, called the exponent, is of the predefined type INTEGER.

5

Operator	Operation	Left operand type	Right operand type	Result type
∗∗	exponentiation	any integer type	INTEGER	same as left
		any floating point type	INTEGER	same as left

6   Exponentiation with a positive exponent is equivalent to repeated multiplication of the left operand by itself, as indicated by the exponent and from left to right. For an operand of a floating point type, the exponent can be negative, in which case the value is the reciprocal of the value with the positive exponent. Exponentiation by a zero exponent delivers the value one. Exponentiation of a value of a floating point type is approximate (see 4.5.7). Exponentiation of an integer raises the exception CONSTRAINT_ERROR for a negative exponent.

7   *References:* array type 3.6, boolean type 3.5.3, bound of an array 3.6.1, component of an array 3.6, constraint_error exception 11.1, dimensionality 3.6, floating point type 3.5.9, index 3.6, integer type 3.5.4, multiplication operation 4.5.5, predefined operator 4.5, raising of exceptions 11

4.5.7 Accuracy of Operations with Real Operands

1   A real subtype specifies a set of model numbers. Both the accuracy required from any basic or predefined operation giving a real result, and the result of any predefined relation between real operands are defined in terms of these model numbers.

2   A *model interval* of a subtype is any interval whose bounds are model numbers of the subtype. The model interval associated with a value that belongs to a real subtype is the smallest model interval (of the subtype) that includes the value. (The model interval associated with a model number of a subtype consists of that number only.)

3   For any basic operation or predefined operator that yields a result of a real subtype, the required bounds on the result are given by a model interval defined as follows:

4   • The result model interval is the smallest model interval (of the result subtype) that includes the minimum and the maximum of all the values obtained by applying the (exact) mathematical operation, when each operand is given any value of the model interval (of the operand subtype) defined for the operand.

5   • The model interval of an operand that is itself the result of an operation, other than an implicit conversion, is the result model interval of this operation.

6   • The model interval of an operand whose value is obtained by implicit conversion of a universal expression is the model interval associated with this value within the operand subtype.

7   The result model interval is undefined if the absolute value of one of the above mathematical results exceeds the largest safe number of the result type. Whenever the result model interval is undefined, it is highly desirable that the exception NUMERIC_ERROR be raised if the implementation cannot produce an actual result that is in the range of safe numbers. This is, however, not required by the language rules, in recognition of the fact that certain target machines do not permit easy detection of overflow situations. The value of the attribute MACHINE_OVERFLOWS indicates whether the target machine raises the exception NUMERIC_ERROR in overflow situations (see 13.7.3).

The safe numbers of a real type are defined (see 3.5.6) as a superset of the model numbers, for **8** which error bounds follow the same rules as for model numbers. Any definition given in this section in terms of model intervals can therefore be extended to safe intervals of safe numbers. A consequence of this extension is that an implementation is not allowed to raise the exception NUMERIC_ERROR when the result interval is a safe interval.

For the result of exponentiation, the model interval defining the bounds on the result is obtained by **9** applying the above rules to the sequence of multiplications defined by the exponent, and to the final division in the case of a negative exponent.

For the result of a relation between two real operands, consider for each operand the model inter- **10** val (of the operand subtype) defined for the operand; the result can be any value obtained by applying the mathematical comparison to values arbitrarily chosen in the corresponding operand model intervals. If either or both of the operand model intervals is undefined (and if neither of the operand evaluations raises an exception) then the result of the comparison is allowed to be any possible value (that is, either TRUE or FALSE).

The result of a membership test is defined in terms of comparisons of the operand value with the **11** lower and upper bounds of the given range or type mark (the usual rules apply to these comparisons).

Note:

For a floating point type the numbers 15.0, 3.0, and 5.0 are always model numbers. Hence X/Y **12** where X equals 15.0 and Y equals 3.0 yields exactly 5.0 according to the above rules. In the general case, division does not yield model numbers and in consequence one cannot assume that $(1.0/X)*X = 1.0$.

References: attribute 4.1.4, basic operation 3.3.3, bound of a range 3.5, error bound 3.5.6, exponentiation operation **13** 4.5.6, false boolean value 3.5.3, floating point type 3.5.9, machine_overflows attribute 13.7.1, membership test 4.5.2, model number 3.5.6, multiplication operation 4.5.5, numeric_error exception 11.1, predefined operation 3.3.3, raising of exceptions 11, range 3.5, real type 3.5.6, relation 4.4, relational operator 4.5.2 4.5, safe number 3.5.6, subtype 3.3, true boolean value 3.5.3, type conversion 4.6, type mark 3.3.2, universal expression 4.10

4.6 Type Conversions

The evaluation of an explicit type conversion evaluates the expression given as the operand, and **1** converts the resulting value to a specified *target* type. Explicit type conversions are allowed between closely related types as defined below.

    type_conversion ::= type_mark(expression)   **2**

The target type of a type conversion is the base type of the type mark. The type of the operand of a **3** type conversion must be determinable independently of the context (in particular, independently of the target type). Furthermore, the operand of a type conversion is not allowed to be a literal **null**, an allocator, an aggregate, or a string literal; an expression enclosed by parentheses is allowed as the operand of a type conversion only if the expression alone is allowed.

A conversion to a subtype consists of a conversion to the target type followed by a check that the **4** result of the conversion belongs to the subtype. A conversion of an operand of a given type to the type itself is allowed.

5   The other allowed explicit type conversions correspond to the following three cases:

6   (a) Numeric types

7   The operand can be of any numeric type; the value of the operand is converted to the target type which must also be a numeric type. For conversions involving real types, the result is within the accuracy of the specified subtype (see 4.5.7). The conversion of a real value to an integer type rounds to the nearest integer; if the operand is halfway between two integers (within the accuracy of the real subtype) rounding may be either up or down.

8   (b) Derived types

9   The conversion is allowed if one of the target type and the operand type is derived from the other, directly or indirectly, or if there exists a third type from which both types are derived, directly or indirectly.

10   (c) Array types

11   The conversion is allowed if the operand type and the target type are array types that satisfy the following conditions: both types must have the same dimensionality; for each index position the index types must either be the same or be convertible to each other; the component types must be the same; finally, if the component type is a type with discriminants or an access type, the component subtypes must be either both constrained or both unconstrained. If the type mark denotes an unconstrained array type, then, for each index position, the bounds of the result are obtained by converting the bounds of the operand to the corresponding index type of the target type. If the type mark denotes a constrained array subtype, then the bounds of the result are those imposed by the type mark. In either case, the value of each component of the result is that of the matching component of the operand (see 4.5.2).

12   In the case of conversions of numeric types and derived types, the exception CONSTRAINT_ERROR is raised by the evaluation of a type conversion if the result of the conversion fails to satisfy a constraint imposed by the type mark.

13   In the case of array types, a check is made that any constraint on the component subtype is the same for the operand array type as for the target array type. If the type mark denotes an unconstrained array type and if the operand is not a null array, then, for each index position, a check is made that the bounds of the result belong to the corresponding index subtype of the target type. If the type mark denotes a constrained array subtype, a check is made that for each component of the operand there is a matching component of the target subtype, and vice versa. The exception CONSTRAINT_ERROR is raised if any of these checks fails.

14   If a conversion is allowed from one type to another, the reverse conversion is also allowed. This reverse conversion is used where an actual parameter of mode **in out** or **out** has the form of a type conversion of a (variable) name as explained in section 6.4.1.

15   Apart from the explicit type conversions, the only allowed form of type conversion is the implicit conversion of a value of the type *universal_integer* or *universal_real* into another numeric type. An implicit conversion of an operand of type *universal_integer* to another integer type, or of an operand of type *universal_real* to another real type, can only be applied if the operand is either a numeric literal, a named number, or an attribute; such an operand is called a *convertible* universal operand in this section. An implicit conversion of a convertible universal operand is applied if and only if the innermost complete context (see 8.7) determines a unique (numeric) target type for the implicit conversion, and there is no legal interpretation of this context without this conversion.

Notes:

The rules for implicit conversions imply that no implicit conversion is ever applied to the operand of   15
an explicit type conversion. Similarly, implicit conversions are not applied if both operands of a
predefined relational operator are convertible universal operands.

The language allows implicit subtype conversions in the case of array types (see 5.2.1). An explicit   16
type conversion can have the effect of a change of representation (in particular see 13.6). Explicit
conversions are also used for actual parameters (see 6.4).

Examples of numeric type conversion: 17

```
REAL(2*J)       --   value is converted to floating point
INTEGER(1.6)    --   value is 2
INTEGER(-0.4)   --   value is 0
```

Example of conversion between derived types: 18

```
type A_FORM is new B_FORM;

X  : A_FORM;
Y  : B_FORM;

X  := A_FORM(Y);
Y  := B_FORM(X);   --   the reverse conversion
```

Examples of conversions between array types: 19

```
type SEQUENCE is array (INTEGER range <>) of INTEGER;
subtype DOZEN is SEQUENCE(1 .. 12);
LEDGER : array(1 .. 100) of INTEGER;

SEQUENCE(LEDGER)            --   bounds are those of LEDGER
SEQUENCE(LEDGER(31 .. 42))  --   bounds are 31 and 42
DOZEN(LEDGER(31 .. 42))     --   bounds are those of DOZEN
```

Examples of implicit conversions: 20

```
X : INTEGER := 2;

X + 1 + 2              --   implicit conversion of each integer literal
1 + 2 + X              --   implicit conversion of each integer literal
X + (1 + 2)            --   implicit conversion of each integer literal

2 = (1 + 1)            --   no implicit conversion:   the type is universal_integer
A'LENGTH = B'LENGTH    --   no implicit conversion:   the type is universal_integer
C : constant := 3 + 2; --   no implicit conversion:   the type is universal_integer

X = 3 and 1 = 2        --   implicit conversion of 3, but not of 1 and 2
```

References: actual parameter 6.4.1, array type 3.6, attribute 4.1.4, base type 3.3, belong to a subtype 3.3,   21
component 3.3, constrained array subtype 3.6, constraint_error exception 11.1, derived type 3.4, dimension 3.6,
expression 4.4, floating point type 3.5.7, index 3.6, index subtype 3.6, index type 3.6, integer type 3.5.4, matching
component 4.5.2, mode 6.1, name 4.1, named number 3.2, null array 3.6.1, numeric literal 2.4, numeric type 3.5, raising of exceptions 11, real type 3.5.6, representation 13.1, statement 5, subtype 3.3, type 3.3, type mark 3.3.2,
unconstrained array type 3.6, universal_integer type 3.5.4, universal_real type 3.5.6, variable 3.2.1

4.7 Qualified Expressions

1   A qualified expression is used to state explicitly the type, and possibly the subtype, of an operand that is the given expression or aggregate.

2   qualified_expression ::=
        type_mark'(expression) | type_mark'aggregate

3   The operand must have the same type as the base type of the type mark. The value of a qualified expression is the value of the operand. The evaluation of a qualified expression evaluates the operand and checks that its value belongs to the subtype denoted by the type mark. The exception CONSTRAINT_ERROR is raised if this check fails.

4   *Examples:*

```
type MASK is (FIX, DEC, EXP, SIGNIF);
type CODE is (FIX, CLA, DEC, TNZ, SUB);

PRINT (MASK'(DEC));    -- DEC is of type MASK
PRINT (CODE'(DEC));    -  DEC is of type CODE

for J in CODE'(FIX) .. CODE'(DEC) loop ...   -- qualification needed for either FIX or DEC
for J in CODE range FIX .. DEC loop ...      -- qualification unnecessary
for J in CODE'(FIX) .. DEC loop ...          -- qualification unnecessary for DEC

DOZEN'(1 | 3 | 5 | 7 => 2, others => 0) -- see 4.6
```

Notes:

5   Whenever the type of an enumeration literal or aggregate is not known from the context, a qualified expression can be used to state the type explicitly. For example, an overloaded enumeration literal must be qualified in the following cases: when given as a parameter in a subprogram call to an overloaded subprogram that cannot otherwise be identified on the basis of remaining parameter or result types, in a relational expression where both operands are overloaded enumeration literals, or in an array or loop parameter range where both bounds are overloaded enumeration literals. Explicit qualification is also used to specify which one of a set of overloaded parameterless functions is meant, or to constrain a value to a given subtype.

6   *References:* aggregate 4.3, array 3.6, base type 3.3, bound of a range 3.5, constraint_error exception 11.1, context of overload resolution 8.7, enumeration literal 3.5.1, expression 4.4, function 6.5, loop parameter 5.5, overloading 8.5, raising of exceptions 11, range 3.3, relation 4.4, subprogram 6, subprogram call 6.4, subtype 3.3, type 3.3, type mark 3.3.2

4.8 Allocators

1   The evaluation of an allocator creates an object and yields an access value that designates the object.

2   allocator ::=
        new subtype_indication | **new** qualified_expression

The type of the object created by an allocator is the base type of the type mark given in either the subtype indication or the qualified expression. For an allocator with a qualified expression, this expression defines the initial value of the created object. The type of the access value returned by an allocator must be determinable solely from the context, but using the fact that the value returned is of an access type having the named designated type. 3

The only allowed forms of constraint in the subtype indication of an allocator are index and discriminant constraints. If an allocator includes a subtype indication and if the type of the object created is an array type or a type with discriminants that do not have default expressions, then the subtype indication must either denote a constrained subtype, or include an explicit index or discriminant constraint. 4

If the type of the created object is an array type or a type with discriminants, then the created object is always constrained. If the allocator includes a subtype indication, the created object is constrained either by the subtype or by the default discriminant values. If the allocator includes a qualified expression, the created object is constrained by the bounds or discriminants of the initial value. For other types, the subtype of the created object is the subtype defined by the subtype indication of the access type definition. 5

For the evaluation of an allocator, the elaboration of the subtype indication or the evaluation of the qualified expression is performed first. The new object is then created. Initializations are then performed as for a declared object (see 3.2.1); the initialization is considered explicit in the case of a qualified expression; any initializations are implicit in the case of a subtype indication. Finally, an access value that designates the created object is returned. 6

An implementation must guarantee that any object created by the evaluation of an allocator remains allocated for as long as this object or one of its subcomponents is accessible directly or indirectly, that is, as long as it can be denoted by some name. Moreover, if an object or one of its subcomponents belongs to a task type, it is considered to be accessible as long as the task is not terminated. An implementation may (but need not) reclaim the storage occupied by an object created by an allocator, once this object has become inaccessible. 7

When an application needs closer control over storage allocation for objects designated by values of an access type, such control may be achieved by one or more of the following means: 8

(a) The total amount of storage available for the collection of objects of an access type can be set by means of a length clause (see 13.2). 9

(b) The pragma CONTROLLED informs the implementation that automatic storage reclamation must not be performed for objects designated by values of the access type, except upon leaving the innermost block statement, subprogram body, or task body that encloses the access type declaration, or after leaving the main program. 10

> **pragma** CONTROLLED (*access_type_*simple_name);

A pragma CONTROLLED for a given access type is allowed at the same places as a representation clause for the type (see 13.1). This pragma is not allowed for a derived type. 11

(c) The explicit deallocation of the object designated by an access value can be achieved by calling a procedure obtained by instantiation of the predefined generic library procedure UNCHECKED_DEALLOCATION (see 13.10.1). 12

The exception STORAGE_ERROR is raised by an allocator if there is not enough storage. Note also that the exception CONSTRAINT_ERROR can be raised by the evaluation of the qualified expression, by the elaboration of the subtype indication, or by the initialization. 13

14   *Examples (for access types declared in section 3.8):*

```
new CELL'(0, null, null)                                   -- initialized explicitly
new CELL'(VALUE => 0, SUCC => null, PRED => null)          -- initialized explicitly
new CELL                                                   -- not initialized

new MATRIX(1 .. 10, 1 .. 20)                               -- the bounds only are given
new MATRIX'(1 .. 10 => (1 .. 20 => 0.0))                   -- initialized explicitly

new BUFFER(100)                                            -- the discriminant only is given

new BUFFER'(SIZE => 80, POS => 0, VALUE => (1 .. 80 => 'A'))  -- initialized explicitly
```

15   *References:* access type 3.8, access type definition 3.8, access value 3.8, array type 3.6, block statement 5.6, bound of an array 3.6.1, collection 3.8, constrained subtype 3.3, constraint 3.3, constraint_error exception 11.1, context of overload resolution 8.7, derived type 3.4, designate 3.8, discriminant 3.3, discriminant constraint 3.7.2, elaboration 3.9, evaluation of a qualified expression 4.7, generic procedure 12.1, index constraint 3.6.1, initial value 3.2.1, initialization 3.2.1, instantiation 12.3, length clause 13.2, library unit 10.1, main program 10.1, name 4.1, object 3.2.1, object declaration 3.2.1, pragma 2.8, procedure 6, qualified expression 4.7, raising of exceptions 11, representation clause 13.1, simple name 4.1, storage_error exception 11.1, subcomponent 3.3, subprogram body 6.3, subtype 3.3, subtype indication 3.3.2, task body 9.1, task type 9.2, terminated task 9.4, type 3.3, type declaration 3.3.1, type mark 3.3.2 type with discriminants 3.3

4.9 Static Expressions and Static Subtypes

1   Certain expressions of a scalar type are said to be *static*. Similarly, certain discrete ranges are said to be static, and the type marks of certain scalar subtypes are said to denote static subtypes.

2   An expression of a scalar type is said to be static if and only if every primary is one of those listed in (a) through (h) below, every operator denotes a predefined operator, and the evaluation of the expression delivers a value (that is, it does not raise an exception):

3   (a)   An enumeration literal (including a character literal).

4   (b)   A numeric literal.

5   (c)   A named number.

6   (d)   A constant explicitly declared by a constant declaration with a static subtype, and initialized with a static expression.

7   (e)   A function call whose function name is an operator symbol that denotes a predefined operator, including a function name that is an expanded name; each actual parameter must also be a static expression.

8   (f)   A language-defined attribute of a static subtype; for an attribute that is a function, the actual parameter must also be a static expression.

(g) A qualified expression whose type mark denotes a static subtype and whose operand is a static expression.

(h) A static expression enclosed in parentheses.

A static range is a range whose bounds are static expressions. A static range constraint is a range constraint whose range is static. A static subtype is either a scalar base type, other than a generic formal type; or a scalar subtype formed by imposing on a static subtype either a static range constraint, or a floating or fixed point constraint whose range constraint, if any, is static. A static discrete range is either a static subtype or a static range. A static index constraint is an index constraint for which each index subtype of the corresponding array type is static, and in which each discrete range is static. A static discriminant constraint is a discriminant constraint for which the subtype of each discriminant is static, and in which each expression is static.

Notes:

The accuracy of the evaluation of a static expression having a real type is defined by the rules given in section 4.5.7. If the result is not a model number (or a safe number) of the type, the value obtained by this evaluation at compilation time need not be the same as the value that would be obtained by an evaluation at run time.

Array attributes are not static: in particular, the RANGE attribute is not static.

References: actual parameter 6.4.1, attribute 4.1.4, base type 3.3, bound of a range 3.5, character literal 2.5, constant 3.2.1, constant declaration 3.2.1, discrete range 3.6, discrete type 3.5, enumeration literal 3.5.1, exception 11, expression 4.4, function 6.5, generic actual parameter 12.3, generic formal type 12.1.2, implicit declaration 3.1, initialize 3.2.1, model number 3.5.6, named number 3.2, numeric literal 2.4, predefined operator 4.5, qualified expression 4.7, raising of exceptions 11, range constraint 3.5, safe number 3.5.6, scalar type 3.5, subtype 3.3, type mark 3.3.2

4.10 Universal Expressions

A *universal_expression* is either an expression that delivers a result of type *universal_integer* or one that delivers a result of type *universal_real*.

The same operations are predefined for the type *universal_integer* as for any integer type. The same operations are predefined for the type *universal_real* as for any floating point type. In addition, these operations include the following multiplication and division operators:

Operator	Operation	Left operand type	Right operand type	Result type
*	multiplication	universal_real	universal_integer	universal_real
		universal_integer	universal_real	universal_real
/	division	universal_real	universal_integer	universal_real

The accuracy of the evaluation of a universal expression of type *universal_real* is at least as good as that of the most accurate predefined floating point type supported by the implementation, apart from *universal_real* itself. Furthermore, if a universal expression is a static expression, then the evaluation must be exact.

5   For the evaluation of an operation of a nonstatic universal expression, an implementation is allowed to raise the exception NUMERIC_ERROR only if the result of the operation is a real value whose absolute value exceeds the largest safe number of the most accurate predefined floating point type (excluding *universal_real*), or an integer value greater than SYSTEM.MAX_INT or less than SYSTEM.MIN_INT.

Note:

6   It is a consequence of the above rules that the type of a universal expression is *universal_integer* if every primary contained in the expression is of this type (excluding actual parameters of attributes that are functions, and excluding right operands of exponentiation operators) and that otherwise the type is *universal_real*.

7   *Examples:*

```
1 + 1        -- 2
abs(-10)*3   -- 30

KILO : constant := 1000;
MEGA : constant := KILO*KILO;    -- 1_000_000
LONG : constant := FLOAT'DIGITS*2;

HALF_PI     : constant := PI/2;              -- see 3.2.2
DEG_TO_RAD  : constant := HALF_PI/90;
RAD_TO_DEG  : constant := 1.0/DEG_TO_RAD; -- equivalent to 1.0/((3.14159_26536/2)/90)
```

8   *References:* actual parameter 6.4.1, attribute 4.1.4, evaluation of an expression 4.5, floating point type 3.5.9, function 6.5, integer type 3.5.4, multiplying operator 4.5 4.5.5, predefined operation 3.3.3, primary 4.4, real type 3.5.6, safe number 3.5.6, system.max_int 13.7, system.min_int 13.7, type 3.3, universal_integer type 3.5.4, universal_real type 3.5.6

5. Statements

A *statement* defines an action to be performed; the process by which a statement achieves its   1
action is called *execution* of the statement.

This chapter describes the general rules applicable to all statements. Some specific statements are   2
discussed in later chapters. Procedure call statements are described in Chapter 6 on subprograms.
Entry call, delay, accept, select, and abort statements are described in Chapter 9 on tasks. Raise
statements are described in Chapter 11 on exceptions, and code statements in Chapter 13. The
remaining forms of statements are presented in this chapter.

References: abort statement 9.10, accept statement 9.5, code statement 13.8, delay statement 9.6, entry call   3
statement 9.5, procedure call statement 6.4, raise statement 11.3, select statement 9.7

5.1 Simple and Compound Statements - Sequences of Statements

A statement is either simple or compound. A simple statement encloses no other statement. A   1
compound statement can enclose simple statements and other compound statements.

    sequence_of_statements ::= statement {statement}   2

    statement ::=
       {label} simple_statement | {label} compound_statement

    simple_statement ::= null_statement
       | assignment_statement | procedure_call_statement
       | exit_statement | return_statement
       | goto_statement | entry_call_statement
       | delay_statement | abort_statement
       | raise_statement | code_statement

    compound_statement ::=
          if_statement | case_statement
       | loop_statement | block_statement
       | accept_statement | select_statement

    label ::= <<*label*_simple_name>>

    null_statement ::= **null**;

A statement is said to be *labeled* by the label name of any label of the statement. A label name,   3
and similarly a loop or block name, is implicitly declared at the end of the declarative part of the
innermost block statement, subprogram body, package body, task body, or generic body that
encloses the labeled statement, the named loop statement, or the named block statement, as the
case may be. For a block statement without a declarative part, an implicit declarative part (and
preceding **declare**) is assumed.

4   The implicit declarations for different label names, loop names, and block names occur in the same
     order as the beginnings of the corresponding labeled statements, loop statements, and block state-
     ments. Distinct identifiers must be used for all label, loop, and block names that are implicitly
     declared within the body of a program unit, including within block statements enclosed by this
     body, but excluding within other enclosed program units (a program unit is either a subprogram, a
     package, a task unit, or a generic unit).

5   Execution of a null statement has no other effect than to pass to the next action.

6   The execution of a sequence of statements consists of the execution of the individual statements
     in succession until the sequence is completed, or a transfer of control takes place. A transfer of
     control is caused either by the execution of an exit, return, or goto statement; by the selection of a
     terminate alternative; by the raising of an exception; or (indirectly) by the execution of an abort
     statement.

7   *Examples of labeled statements:*

         <<HERE>> <<ICI>> <<AQUI>> <<HIER>> **null**;

         <<AFTER>> X := 1;

     Note:

8   The scope of a declaration starts at the place of the declaration itself (see 8.2). In the case of a
     label, loop, or block name, it follows from this rule that the scope of the *implicit* declaration starts
     before the first *explicit* occurrence of the corresponding name, since this occurrence is either in a
     statement label, a loop statement, a block statement, or a goto statement. An implicit declaration
     in a block statement may hide a declaration given in an outer program unit or block statement (ac-
     cording to the usual rules of hiding explained in section 8.3).

9   *References:* abort statement 9.10, accept statement 9.5, assignment statement 5.2, block name 5.6, block
     statement 5.6, case statement 5.4, code statement 13.8, declaration 3.1, declarative part 3.9, delay statement 9.6,
     entry call statement 9.5, exception 11, exit statement 5.7, generic body 12.1, generic unit 12, goto statement 5.9,
     hiding 8.3, identifier 2.3, if statement 5.3, implicit declaration 3.1, loop name 5.5, loop statement 5.5, package 7,
     package body 7.1, procedure call statement 6.4, program unit 6, raise statement 11.3, raising of exceptions 11, return
     statement 5.8, scope 8.2, select statement 9.7, simple name 4.1, subprogram 6, subprogram body 6.3, task 9, task
     body 9.1, task unit 9.1, terminate alternative 9.7.1, terminated task 9.4

5.2 Assignment Statement

1   An assignment statement replaces the current value of a variable with a new value specified by an
     expression. The named variable and the right-hand side expression must be of the same type; this
     type must not be a limited type.

2   assignment_statement ::=
            *variable*_name := expression;

3   For the execution of an assignment statement, the variable name and the expression are first
     evaluated, in some order that is not defined by the language. A check is then made that the value
     of the expression belongs to the subtype of the variable, except in the case of a variable that is an
     array (the assignment then involves a subtype conversion as described in section 5.2.1). Finally,
     the value of the expression becomes the new value of the variable.

The exception CONSTRAINT_ERROR is raised if the above-mentioned subtype check fails; in such a   1
case the current value of the variable is left unchanged. If the variable is a subcomponent that
depends on discriminants of an unconstrained record variable, then the execution of the assignment is erroneous if the value of any of these discriminants is changed by this execution.

Examples: 5

```
VALUE  := MAX_VALUE - 1;
SHADE  := BLUE;

NEXT_FRAME(F)(M, N) := 2.5;        --  see 4.1.1
U := DOT_PRODUCT(V, W);            --  see 6.5

WRITER := (STATUS => OPEN, UNIT => PRINTER, LINE_COUNT => 60);  -- see 3.7.3
NEXT_CAR.all := (72074, null);     --  see 3.8.1
```

Examples of constraint checks: 6

```
I, J : INTEGER range 1 .. 10;
K    : INTEGER range 1 .. 20;
  ...

I  := J;  --  identical ranges
K  := J;  --  compatible ranges
J  := K;  --  will raise the exception CONSTRAINT_ERROR if K > 10
```

Notes:

The values of the discriminants of an object designated by an access value cannot be changed (not   7
even by assigning a complete value to the object itself) since such objects, created by allocators,
are always constrained (see 4.8); however, subcomponents of such objects may be unconstrained.

If the right-hand side expression is either a numeric literal or named number, or an attribute that   8
yields a result of type *universal_integer* or *universal_real*, then an implicit type conversion is performed, as described in section 4.6.

The determination of the type of the variable of an assignment statement may require considera-   9
tion of the expression if the variable name can be interpreted as the name of a variable designated
by the access value returned by a function call, and similarly, as a component or slice of such a
variable (see section 8.7 for the context of overload resolution).

References: access type 3.8, allocator 4.8, array 3.6, array assignment 5.2.1, component 3.6 3.7, constraint_error   10
exception 11.1, designate 3.8, discriminant 3.7.1, erroneous 1.6, evaluation 4.5, expression 4.4, function call 6.4,
implicit type conversion 4.6, name 4.1, numeric literal 2.4, object 3.2, overloading 6.6 8.7, slice 4.1.2, subcomponent
3.3, subtype 3.3, subtype conversion 4.6, type 3.3, universal_integer type 3.5.4, universal_real type 3.5.6, variable
3.2.1

5.2.1 Array Assignments

If the variable of an assignment statement is an array variable (including a slice variable), the value   1
of the expression is implicitly converted to the subtype of the array variable; the result of this subtype conversion becomes the new value of the array variable.

2   This means that the new value of each component of the array variable is specified by the matching component in the array value obtained by evaluation of the expression (see 4.5.2 for the definition of matching components). The subtype conversion checks that for each component of the array variable there is a matching component in the array value, and vice versa. The exception CONSTRAINT_ERROR is raised if this check fails; in such a case the value of each component of the array variable is left unchanged.

3   *Examples:*

```
A  : STRING(1 .. 31);
B  : STRING(3 .. 33);
   ...

A  := B;   --   same number of components

A(1 .. 9)  := "tar sauce";
A(4 .. 12) := A(1 .. 9);  --  A(1 .. 12) = "tartar sauce"
```

Notes:

4   Array assignment is defined even in the case of overlapping slices, because the expression on the right-hand side is evaluated before performing any component assignment. In the above example, an implementation yielding A(1 .. 12) = "tartartartar" would be incorrect.

5   The implicit subtype conversion described above for assignment to an array variable is performed only for the value of the right-hand side expression as a whole; it is not performed for subcomponents that are array values.

6   *References:* array 3.6, assignment 5.2, constraint_error exception 11.1, matching array components 4.5.2, slice 4.1.2, subtype conversion 4.6, type 3.3, variable 3.2.1

5.3 If Statements

1   An if statement selects for execution one or none of the enclosed sequences of statements, depending on the (truth) value of one or more corresponding conditions.

2
```
if_statement ::=
    if condition then
      sequence_of_statements
  { elsif condition then
      sequence_of_statements}
  [ else
      sequence_of_statements]
    end if;

condition ::= boolean_expression
```

3   An expression specifying a condition must be of a boolean type.

4   For the execution of an if statement, the condition specified after **if**, and any conditions specified after **elsif**, are evaluated in succession (treating a final **else** as **elsif** TRUE **then**), until one evaluates to TRUE or all conditions are evaluated and yield FALSE. If one condition evaluates to TRUE, then the corresponding sequence of statements is executed; otherwise none of the sequences of statements is executed.

Examples:

```
if MONTH = DECEMBER and DAY = 31 then
   MONTH := JANUARY;
   DAY   := 1;
   YEAR  := YEAR + 1;
end if;

if LINE_TOO_SHORT then
   raise LAYOUT_ERROR;
elsif LINE_FULL then
   NEW_LINE;
   PUT(ITEM);
else
   PUT(ITEM);
end if;

if MY_CAR.OWNER.VEHICLE /= MY_CAR then          -- see 3.8
   REPORT ("Incorrect data");
end if;
```

References: boolean type 3.5.3, evaluation 4.5, expression 4.4, sequence of statements 5.1

5.4 Case Statements

A case statement selects for execution one of a number of alternative sequences of statements; the chosen alternative is defined by the value of an expression.

```
case_statement ::=
   case expression is
      case_statement_alternative
    { case_statement_alternative}
   end case;

case_statement_alternative ::=
   when choice {| choice } =>
      sequence_of_statements
```

The expression must be of a discrete type which must be determinable independently of the context in which the expression occurs, but using the fact that the expression must be of a discrete type. Moreover, the type of this expression must not be a generic formal type. Each choice in a case statement alternative must be of the same type as the expression; the list of choices specifies for which values of the expression the alternative is chosen.

If the expression is the name of an object whose subtype is static, then each value of this subtype must be represented once and only once in the set of choices of the case statement, and no other value is allowed; this rule is likewise applied if the expression is a qualified expression or type conversion whose type mark denotes a static subtype. Otherwise, for other forms of expression, each value of the (base) type of the expression must be represented once and only once in the set of choices, and no other value is allowed.

5   The simple expressions and discrete ranges given as choices in a case statement must be static. A choice defined by a discrete range stands for all values in the corresponding range (none if a null range). The choice **others** is only allowed for the last alternative and as its only choice; it stands for all values (possibly none) not given in the choices of previous alternatives. A component simple name is not allowed as a choice of a case statement alternative.

6   The execution of a case statement consists of the evaluation of the expression followed by the execution of the chosen sequence of statements.

7   *Examples:*

```
case SENSOR is
   when ELEVATION   => RECORD_ELEVATION (SENSOR_VALUE);
   when AZIMUTH     => RECORD_AZIMUTH   (SENSOR_VALUE);
   when DISTANCE    => RECORD_DISTANCE  (SENSOR_VALUE);
   when others      => null;
end case;

case TODAY is
   when MON         => COMPUTE_INITIAL_BALANCE;
   when FRI         => COMPUTE_CLOSING_BALANCE;
   when TUE .. THU  => GENERATE_REPORT(TODAY);
   when SAT .. SUN  => null;
end case;

case BIN_NUMBER(COUNT) is
   when 1           => UPDATE_BIN(1);
   when 2           => UPDATE_BIN(2);
   when 3 | 4  =>
      EMPTY_BIN(1);
      EMPTY_BIN(2);
   when others  => raise ERROR;
end case;
```

Notes:

8   The execution of a case statement chooses one and only one alternative, since the choices are exhaustive and mutually exclusive. Qualification of the expression of a case statement by a static subtype can often be used to limit the number of choices that need be given explicitly.

9   An **others** choice is required in a case statement if the type of the expression is the type *universal_integer* (for example, if the expression is an integer literal), since this is the only way to cover all values of the type *universal_integer*.

10   *References:* base type 3.3, choice 3.7.3, context of overload resolution 8.7, discrete type 3.5, expression 4.4, function call 6.4, generic formal type 12.1, conversion 4.6, discrete type 3.5, enumeration literal 3.5.1, expression 4.4, name 4.1, object 3.2.1, overloading 6.6 8.7, qualified expression 4.7, sequence of statements 5.1, static discrete range 4.9, static subtype 4.9, subtype 3.3, type 3.3, type conversion 4.6, type mark 3.3.2

5.5 Loop Statements

A loop statement includes a sequence of statements that is to be executed repeatedly, zero or more times.

```
loop_statement ::=
    [loop_simple_name:]
      [ iteration_scheme] loop
          sequence_of_statements
      end loop [loop_simple_name];

iteration_scheme ::= while condition
    |  for loop_parameter_specification

loop_parameter_specification ::=
    identifier in [reverse] discrete_range
```

If a loop statement has a loop simple name, this simple name must be given both at the beginning and at the end.

A loop statement without an iteration scheme specifies repeated execution of the sequence of statements. Execution of the loop statement is complete when the loop is left as a consequence of the execution of an exit statement, or as a consequence of some other transfer of control (see 5.1).

For a loop statement with a **while** iteration scheme, the condition is evaluated before each execution of the sequence of statements; if the value of the condition is TRUE, the sequence of statements is executed, if FALSE the execution of the loop statement is complete.

For a loop statement with a **for** iteration scheme, the loop parameter specification is the declaration of the *loop parameter* with the given identifier. The loop parameter is an object whose type is the base type of the discrete range (see 3.6.1). Within the sequence of statements, the loop parameter is a constant. Hence a loop parameter is not allowed as the (left-hand side) variable of an assignment statement. Similarly the loop parameter must not be given as an **out** or **in out** parameter of a procedure or entry call statement, or as an **in out** parameter of a generic instantiation.

For the execution of a loop statement with a **for** iteration scheme, the loop parameter specification is first elaborated. This elaboration creates the loop parameter and evaluates the discrete range.

If the discrete range is a null range, the execution of the loop statement is complete. Otherwise, the sequence of statements is executed once for each value of the discrete range (subject to the loop not being left as a consequence of the execution of an exit statement or as a consequence of some other transfer of control). Prior to each such iteration, the corresponding value of the discrete range is assigned to the loop parameter. These values are assigned in increasing order unless the reserved word **reverse** is present, in which case the values are assigned in decreasing order.

Example of a loop statement without an iteration scheme:

```
loop
   GET(CURRENT_CHARACTER);
   exit when CURRENT_CHARACTER  =  '*';
end loop;
```

10   *Example of a loop statement with a while iteration scheme:*

```
while BID(N).PRICE < CUT_OFF.PRICE loop
   RECORD_BID(BID(N).PRICE);
   N := N + 1;
end loop;
```

11   *Example of a loop statement with a for iteration scheme:*

```
for J in BUFFER'RANGE loop        -- legal even with a null range
   if BUFFER(J) /= SPACE then
      PUT(BUFFER(J));
   end if;
end loop;
```

12   *Example of a loop statement with a loop simple name:*

```
SUMMATION:
   while NEXT /= HEAD loop        -- see 3.8
      SUM   := SUM + NEXT.VALUE;
      NEXT  := NEXT.SUCC;
   end loop SUMMATION;
```

Notes:

13   The scope of a loop parameter extends from the loop parameter specification to the end of the loop statement, and the visibility rules are such that a loop parameter is only visible within the sequence of statements of the loop.

14   The discrete range of a for loop is evaluated just once. Use of the reserved word **reverse** does not alter the discrete range, so that the following iteration schemes are not equivalent; the first has a null range.

```
for J in reverse 1 .. 0
for J in 0 .. 1
```

15   Loop names are also used in exit statements, and in expanded names (in a prefix of the loop parameter).

16   *References:* actual parameter 6.4.1, assignment statement 5.2, base type 3.3, bound of a range 3.5, condition 5.3, constant 3.2.1, context of overload resolution 8.7, conversion 4.6, declaration 3.1, discrete range 3.6.1, elaboration 3.1, entry call statement 9.5, evaluation 4.5, exit statement 5.7, expanded name 4.1.3, false boolean value 3.5.3, generic actual parameter 12.3, generic instantiation 12.3, goto statement 5.9, identifier 2.3, integer type 3.5.4, null range 3.5, object 3.2.1, prefix 4.1, procedure call 6.4, raising of exceptions 11, reserved word 2.9, return statement 5.8, scope 8.2, sequence of statements 5.1, simple name 4.1, terminate alternative 9.7.1, true boolean value 3.5.3 3.5.4, visibility 8.3

5.6 Block Statements

A block statement encloses a sequence of statements optionally preceded by a declarative part   1
and optionally followed by exception handlers.

```
block_statement ::=                                                          2
    [block_simple_name:]
    [ declare
            declarative_part]
      begin
            sequence_of_statements
    [ exception
            exception_handler
            { exception_handler}]
      end [block_simple_name];
```

If a block statement has a block simple name, this simple name must be given both at the beginn-   3
ing and at the end.

The execution of a block statement consists of the elaboration of its declarative part (if any) fol-   4
lowed by the execution of the sequence of statements. If the block statement has exception
handlers, these service corresponding exceptions that are raised during the execution of the
sequence of statements (see 11.2).

Example: 5

```
SWAP:
   declare
      TEMP : INTEGER;
   begin
      TEMP := V; V := U; U := TEMP;
   end SWAP;
```

Notes:

if task objects are declared within a block statement whose execution is completed, the block   6
statement is not left until all its dependent tasks are terminated (see 9.4). This rule applies also to
a completion caused by an exit, return, or goto statement; or by the raising of an exception.

Within a block statement, the block name can be used in expanded names denoting local entities   7
such as SWAP.TEMP in the above example (see 4.1.3 (f)).

References: declarative part 3.9, dependent task 9.4, exception handler 11.2, exit statement 5.7, expanded name   8
4.1.3, goto statement 5.9, raising of exceptions 11, return statement 5.8, sequence of statements 5.1, simple name
4.1, task object 9.2

5.7 Exit Statements

1 An exit statement is used to complete the execution of an enclosing loop statement (called the loop in what follows); the completion is conditional if the exit statement includes a condition.

2
```
exit_statement ::=
    exit [loop_name] [when condition];
```

3 An exit statement with a loop name is only allowed within the named loop, and applies to that loop; an exit statement without a loop name is only allowed within a loop, and applies to the innermost enclosing loop (whether named or not). Furthermore, an exit statement that applies to a given loop must not appear within a subprogram body, package body, task body, generic body, or accept statement, if this construct is itself enclosed by the given loop.

4 For the execution of an exit statement, the condition, if present, is first evaluated. Exit from the loop then takes place if the value is TRUE or if there is no condition.

5 *Examples:*

```
for N in 1 .. MAX_NUM_ITEMS loop
   GET_NEW_ITEM(NEW_ITEM);
   MERGE_ITEM(NEW_ITEM, STORAGE_FILE);
   exit when NEW_ITEM = TERMINAL_ITEM;
end loop;

MAIN_CYCLE:
   loop
      --   initial statements
      exit MAIN_CYCLE when FOUND;
      --   final statements
   end loop MAIN_CYCLE;
```

Note:

6 Several nested loops can be exited by an exit statement that names the outer loop.

7 *References:* accept statement 9.5, condition 5.3, evaluation 4.5, generic body 12.1, loop name 5.5, loop statement 5.5, package body 7.1, subprogram body 6.3, true boolean value 3.5.3

5.8 Return Statements

1 A return statement is used to complete the execution of the innermost enclosing function, procedure, or accept statement.

2
```
return_statement ::= return [expression];
```

3 A return statement is only allowed within the body of a subprogram or generic subprogram, or within an accept statement, and applies to the innermost (enclosing) such construct; a return statement is not allowed within the body of a task unit, package, or generic package enclosed by this construct (on the other hand, it is allowed within a compound statement enclosed by this construct and, in particular, in a block statement).

A return statement for an accept statement or for the body of a procedure or generic procedure must not include an expression. A return statement for the body of a function or generic function must include an expression. **4**

The value of the expression defines the result returned by the function. The type of this expression must be the base type of the type mark given after the reserved word **return** in the specification of the function or generic function (this type mark defines the result subtype). **5**

For the execution of a return statement, the expression (if any) is first evaluated and a check is made that the value belongs to the result subtype. The execution of the return statement is thereby completed if the check succeeds; so also is the execution of the subprogram or of the accept statement. The exception CONSTRAINT_ERROR is raised at the place of the return statement if the check fails. **6**

Examples: **7**

```
return;                          -- in a procedure
return KEY_VALUE(LAST_INDEX);    -- in a function
```

Note:

If the expression is either a numeric literal or named number, or an attribute that yields a result of type *universal_integer* or *universal_real*, then an implicit conversion of the result is performed as described in section 4.6. **8**

References: accept statement 9.5, attribute A, block statement 5.6, constraint_error exception 11.1, expression 4.4, function body 6.3, function call 6.4, generic body 12.1, implicit type conversion 4.6, named number 3.2, numeric literal 2.4, package body 7.1, procedure body 6.3, reserved word 2.9, result subtype 6.1, subprogram body 6.3, subprogram specification 6.1, subtype 3.3, task body 9.1, type mark 3.3.2, universal_integer type 3.5.4, universal_real type 3.5.6 **9**

5.9 Goto Statements

A goto statement specifies an explicit transfer of control from this statement to a *target* statement named by a label. **1**

```
goto_statement ::= goto label_name;
```
2

The innermost sequence of statements that encloses the target statement must also enclose the goto statement (note that the goto statement can be a statement of an inner sequence). Furthermore, if a goto statement is enclosed by an accept statement or the body of a program unit, then the target statement must not be outside this enclosing construct; conversely, it follows from the previous rule that if the target statement is enclosed by such a construct, then the goto statement cannot be outside. **3**

The execution of a goto statement transfers control to the named target statement. **4**

Note:

5   The above rules allow transfer of control to a statement of an enclosing sequence of statements
     but not the reverse. Similarly, they prohibit transfers of control such as between alternatives of a
     case statement, if statement, or select statement; between exception handlers; or from an excep-
     tion handler of a frame back to the sequence of statements of this frame.

6   *Example:*

```
<<COMPARE>>
  if A(I) < ELEMENT then
    if LEFT(I) /= 0 then
      I := LEFT(I);
      goto COMPARE;
    end if;
    --   some statements
  end if;
```

7   *References:* accept statement 9.5, block statement 5.6, case statement 5.4, compound statement 5.1, exception
     handler 11.2, frame 11.2, generic body 12.1, if statement 5.3, label 5.1, package body 7.1, program unit 6, select
     statement 9.7, sequence of statements 5.1, statement 5.1, subprogram body 6.3, task body 9.1, transfer of control
     5.1

6. Subprograms

Subprograms are one of the four forms of *program unit*, of which programs can be composed. The other forms are packages, task units, and generic units. 1

A subprogram is a program unit whose execution is invoked by a subprogram call. There are two forms of subprogram: procedures and functions. A procedure call is a statement; a function call is an expression and returns a value. The definition of a subprogram can be given in two parts: a subprogram declaration defining its calling conventions, and a subprogram body defining its execution. 2

References: function 6.5, function call 6.4, generic unit 12, package 7, procedure 6.1, procedure call 6.4, subprogram body 6.3, subprogram call 6.4, subprogram declaration 6.1, task unit 9

6.1 Subprogram Declarations

A subprogram declaration declares a procedure or a function, as indicated by the initial reserved word. 1

```
subprogram_declaration ::= subprogram_specification;

subprogram_specification ::=
      procedure identifier [formal_part]
    | function designator [formal_part] return type_mark

designator ::= identifier | operator_symbol

operator_symbol ::= string_literal

formal_part ::=
    (parameter_specification {; parameter_specification})

parameter_specification ::=
    identifier_list : mode type_mark [:= expression]

mode ::= [in] | in out | out
```
2

The specification of a procedure specifies its identifier and its *formal parameters* (if any). The specification of a function specifies its designator, its formal parameters (if any) and the subtype of the returned value (the *result subtype*). A designator that is an operator symbol is used for the overloading of an operator. The sequence of characters represented by an operator symbol must be an operator belonging to one of the six classes of overloadable operators defined in section 4.5 (extra spaces are not allowed and the case of letters is not significant). 3

4   A parameter specification with several identifiers is equivalent to a sequence of single parameter specifications, as explained in section 3.2. Each single parameter specification declares a formal parameter. If no mode is explicitly given, the mode **in** is assumed. If a parameter specification ends with an expression, the expression is the *default expression* of the formal parameter. A default expression is only allowed in a parameter specification if the mode is **in** (whether this mode is indicated explicitly or implicitly). The type of a default expression must be that of the corresponding formal parameter.

5   The use of a name that denotes a formal parameter is not allowed in default expressions of a formal part if the specification of the parameter is itself given in this formal part.

6   The elaboration of a subprogram declaration elaborates the corresponding formal part. The elaboration of a formal part has no other effect.

7   *Examples of subprogram declarations:*

```
procedure TRAVERSE_TREE;
procedure INCREMENT(X : in out INTEGER);
procedure RIGHT_INDENT(MARGIN : out LINE_SIZE);        -- see 3.5.4
procedure SWITCH(FROM, TO : in out LINK);              -- see 3.8.1

function RANDOM return PROBABILITY;                    -- see 3.5.7

function MIN_CELL(X : LINK) return CELL;               -- see 3.8.1
function NEXT_FRAME(K : POSITIVE) return FRAME;        -- see 3.8
function DOT_PRODUCT(LEFT,RIGHT: VECTOR) return REAL;  -- see 3.6

function "*"(LEFT,RIGHT : MATRIX) return MATRIX;       -- see 3.6
```

8   *Examples of in parameters with default expressions:*

```
procedure PRINT_HEADER(PAGES   : in NATURAL;
                       HEADER  : in LINE      :=  (1 .. LINE'LAST => ' ');  -- see 3.6
                       CENTER  : in BOOLEAN   :=  TRUE);
```

Notes:

9   The evaluation of default expressions is caused by certain subprogram calls, as described in section 6.4.2 (default expressions are not evaluated during the elaboration of the subprogram declaration).

10   All subprograms can be called recursively and are reentrant.

11   *References:* declaration 3.1, elaboration 3.9, evaluation 4.5, expression 4.4, formal parameter 6.2, function 6.5, identifier 2.3, identifier list 3.2, mode 6.2, name 4.1, elaboration has no other effect 3.9, operator 4.5, overloading 6.6 8.7, procedure 6, string literal 2.6, subprogram call 6.4, type mark 3.3.2

6.2 Formal Parameter Modes

The value of an object is said to be *read* when this value is evaluated; it is also said to be read when one of its subcomponents is read. The value of a variable is said to be *updated* when an assignment is performed to the variable, and also (indirectly) when the variable is used as actual parameter of a subprogram call or entry call statement that updates its value; it is also said to be updated when one of its subcomponents is updated. · 1

A formal parameter of a subprogram has one of the three following modes: · 2

in   The formal parameter is a constant and permits only reading of the value of the associated actual parameter. · 3

in out   The formal parameter is a variable and permits both reading and updating of the value of the associated actual parameter. · 4

out   The formal parameter is a variable and permits updating of the value of the associated actual parameter. · 5

The value of a scalar parameter that is not updated by the call is undefined upon return; the same holds for the value of a scalar subcomponent, other than a discriminant. Reading the bounds and discriminants of the formal parameter and of its subcomponents is allowed, but no other reading.

For a scalar parameter, the above effects are achieved by copy: at the start of each call, if the mode is **in** or **in out**, the value of the actual parameter is copied into the associated formal parameter; then after normal completion of the subprogram body, if the mode is **in out** or **out**, the value of the formal parameter is copied back into the associated actual parameter. For a parameter whose type is an access type, copy-in is used for all three modes, and copy-back for the modes **in out** and **out**. · 6

For a parameter whose type is an array, record, or task type, an implementation may likewise achieve the above effects by copy, as for scalar types. In addition, if copy is used for a parameter of mode **out**, then copy-in is required at least for the bounds and discriminants of the actual parameter and of its subcomponents, and also for each subcomponent whose type is an access type. Alternatively, an implementation may achieve these effects by reference, that is, by arranging that every use of the formal parameter (to read or to update its value) be treated as a use of the associated actual parameter, throughout the execution of the subprogram call. The language does not define which of these two mechanisms is to be adopted for parameter passing, nor whether different calls to the same subprogram are to use the same mechanism. The execution of a program is erroneous if its effect depends on which mechanism is selected by the implementation. · 7

For a parameter whose type is a private type, the above effects are achieved according to the rule that applies to the corresponding full type declaration. · 8

Within the body of a subprogram, a formal parameter is subject to any constraint resulting from the type mark given in its parameter specification. For a formal parameter of an unconstrained array type, the bounds are obtained from the actual parameter, and the formal parameter is constrained by these bounds (see 3.6.1). For a formal parameter whose declaration specifies an unconstrained (private or record) type with discriminants, the discriminants of the formal parameter are initialized with the values of the corresponding discriminants of the actual parameter; the formal parameter is unconstrained if and only if the mode is **in out** or **out** and the variable name given for the actual parameter denotes an unconstrained variable (see 3.7.1 and 6.4.1). · 9

If the actual parameter of a subprogram call is a subcomponent that depends on discriminants of an unconstrained record variable, then the execution of the call is erroneous if the value of any of the discriminants of the variable is changed by this execution; this rule does not apply if the mode is **in** and the type of the subcomponent is a scalar type or an access type. · 10

Notes:

11   For parameters of array and record types, the parameter passing rules have these consequences:

12   ● If the execution of a subprogram is abandoned as a result of an exception, the final value of an actual parameter of such a type can be either its value before the call or a value assigned to the formal parameter during the execution of the subprogram.

13   ● If no actual parameter of such a type is accessible by more than one path, then the effect of a subprogram call (unless abandoned) is the same whether or not the implementation uses copying for parameter passing. If, however, there are multiple access paths to such a parameter (for example, if a global variable, or another formal parameter, refers to the same actual parameter), then the value of the formal is undefined after updating the actual other than by updating the formal. A program using such an undefined value is erroneous.

14   The same parameter modes are defined for formal parameters of entries (see 9.5) with the same meaning as for subprograms. Different parameter modes are defined for generic formal parameters (see 12.1.1).

15   For all modes, if an actual parameter designates a task, the associated formal parameter designates the same task; the same holds for a subcomponent of an actual parameter and the corresponding subcomponent of the associated formal parameter.

16   *References:* access type 3.8, actual parameter 6.4.1, array type 3.6, assignment 5.2, bound of a array 3.6.1, constraint 3.3, depend on a discriminant 3.7.1, discriminant 3.7.1, entry call statement 9.5, erroneous 1.6, evaluation 4.5, exception 11, expression 4.4, formal parameter 6.1, generic formal parameter 12.1, global 8.1 r ode 6.1, null access value 3.8, object 3.2, parameter specification 6.1, private type 7.4, record type 3.7, scalar type   subcomponent 3.3, subprogram body 6.3, subprogram call statement 6.4, task 9, task type 9.2, type mark 3.3.2, unconstrained array type 3.6, unconstrained type with discriminants 3.7.1, unconstrained variable 3.2.1, variable 3.2.1

6.3 Subprogram Bodies

1   A subprogram body specifies the execution of a subprogram.

2
```
subprogram_body ::=
    subprogram_specification is
        [ declarative_part]
    begin
        sequence_of_statements
    [ exception
        exception_handler
        { exception_handler}]
    end [designator];
```

3   The declaration of a subprogram is optional. In the absence of such a declaration, the subprogram specification of the subprogram body (or body stub) acts as the declaration. For each subprogram declaration, there must be a corresponding body (except for a subprogram written in another language, as explained in section 13.9). If both a declaration and a body are given, the subprogram specification of the body must conform to the subprogram specification of the declaration (see section 6.3.1 for conformance rules).

If a designator appears at the end of a subprogram body, it must repeat the designator of the sub-   4
program specification.

The elaboration of a subprogram body has no other effect than to establish that the body can from   5
then on be used for the execution of calls of the subprogram.

The execution of a subprogram body is invoked by a subprogram call (see 6.4). For this execution,   6
after establishing the association between formal parameters and actual parameters, the
declarative part of the body is elaborated, and the sequence of statements of the body is then
executed. Upon completion of the body, return is made to the caller (and any necessary copying
back of formal to actual parameters occurs (see 6.2)). The optional exception handlers at the end
of a subprogram body handle exceptions raised during the execution of the sequence of statements of the subprogram body (see 11.4).

Note:

It follows from the visibility rules that if a subprogram declared in a package is to be visible outside   7
the package, a subprogram specification must be given in the visible part of the package. The same
rules dictate that a subprogram declaration must be given if a call of the subprogram occurs textually before the subprogram body (the declaration must then occur earlier than the call in the
program text). The rules given in sections 3.9 and 7.1 imply that a subprogram declaration and the
corresponding body must both occur immediately within the same declarative region.

Example of subprogram body: 8

```
procedure PUSH(E : in ELEMENT_TYPE; S : in out STACK) is
begin
  if S.INDEX = S.SIZE then
    raise STACK_OVERFLOW;
  else
    S.INDEX := S.INDEX + 1;
    S.SPACE(S.INDEX) := E;
  end if;
end PUSH;
```

References: actual parameter 6.4.1, body stub 10.2, conform 6.3.1, declaration 3.1, declarative part 3.9, declarative
region 8.1, designator 6.1, elaboration 3.9, elaboration has no other effect 3.1, exception 11, exception handler 11.2,
formal parameter 6.1, occur immediately within 8.1, package 7, sequence of statements 5.1, subprogram 6, sub-   9
program call 6.4, subprogram declaration 6.1, subprogram specification 6.1, visibility 8.3, visible part 7.2

6.3.1 Conformance Rules

Whenever the language rules require or allow the specification of a given subprogram to be   1
provided in more than one place, the following variations are allowed at each place:

- A numeric literal can be replaced by a different numeric literal if and only if both have the   2
  same value.

- A simple name can be replaced by an expanded name in which this simple name is the selec-   3
  tor, if and only if at both places the meaning of the simple name is given by the same declaration.

- A string literal given as an operator symbol can be replaced by a different string literal if and   4
  only if both represent the same operator.

5   Two subprogram specifications are said to *conform* if, apart from comments and the above allowed variations, both specifications are formed by the same sequence of lexical elements, and corresponding lexical elements are given the same meaning by the visibility and overloading rules.

6   Conformance is likewise defined for formal parts, discriminant parts, and type marks (for deferred constants and for actual parameters that have the form of a type conversion (see 6.4.1)).

Notes:

7   A simple name can be replaced by an expanded name even if the simple name is itself the prefix of a selected component. For example, Q.R can be replaced by P.Q.R if Q is declared immediately within P.

8   The following specifications do not conform since they are not formed by the same sequence of lexical elements:

```
procedure  P(X,Y : INTEGER)
procedure  P(X : INTEGER; Y : INTEGER)
procedure  P(X,Y : in INTEGER)
```

9   *References:* actual parameter 6.4 6.4.1, allow 1.6, comment 2.7, declaration 3.1, deferred constant 7.4.3, direct visibility 8.3, discriminant part 3.7.1, expanded name 4.1.3, formal part 6.1, lexical element 2, name 4.1, numeric literal 2.4, operator symbol 6.1, overloading 6.6 8.7, prefix 4.1, selected component 4.1.3, selector 4.1.3, simple name 4.1, subprogram specification 6.1, type conversion 4.6, visibility 8.3

6.3.2 Inline Expansion of Subprograms

1   The pragma INLINE is used to indicate that inline expansion of the subprogram body is desired for every call of each of the named subprograms. The form of this pragma is as follows:

2   **pragma** INLINE (name {, name});

Each name is either the name of a subprogram or the name of a generic subprogram. The pragma INLINE is only allowed at the place of a declarative item in a declarative part or package specification, or after a library unit in a compilation, but before any subsequent compilation unit.

3   If the pragma appears at the place of a declarative item, each name must denote a subprogram or a generic subprogram declared by an earlier declarative item of the same declarative part or package specification. If several (overloaded) subprograms satisfy this requirement, the pragma applies to all of them. If the pragma appears after a given library unit, the only name allowed is the name of this unit. If the name of a generic subprogram is mentioned in the pragma, this indicates that inline expansion is desired for calls of all subprograms obtained by instantiation of the named generic unit.

4   The meaning of a subprogram is not changed by the pragma INLINE. For each call of the named subprograms, an implementation is free to follow or to ignore the recommendation expressed by the pragma. (Note, in particular, that the recommendation cannot generally be followed for a recursive subprogram.)

5   *References:* allow 1.6, compilation 10.1, compilation unit 10.1, declarative item 3.9, declarative part 3.9, generic subprogram 12.1, generic unit 12 12.1, instantiation 12.3, library unit 10.1, name 4.1, overloading 6.6 8.7, package specification 7.1, pragma 2.8, subprogram 6, subprogram body 6.3, subprogram call 6.4

6.4 Subprogram Calls

A subprogram call is either a procedure call statement or a function call; it invokes the execution   1
of the corresponding subprogram body. The call specifies the association of the actual parameters,
if any, with formal parameters of the subprogram.

> procedure_call_statement ::=   2
>   procedure_name [actual_parameter_part];
>
> function_call ::=
>   function_name [actual_parameter_part]
>
> actual_parameter_part ::=
>   (parameter_association {, parameter_association})
>
> parameter_association ::=
>   [formal_parameter =>] actual_parameter
>
> formal_parameter ::= parameter_simple_name
>
> actual_parameter ::=
>   expression | variable_name | type_mark(variable_name)

Each parameter association associates an actual parameter with a corresponding formal   3
parameter. A parameter association is said to be *named* if the formal parameter is named explicitly; it is otherwise said to be *positional*. For a positional association, the actual parameter corresponds to the formal parameter with the same position in the formal part.

Named associations can be given in any order, but if both positional and named associations are   4
used in the same call, positional associations must occur first, at their normal position. Hence
once a named association is used, the rest of the call must use only named associations.

For each formal parameter of a subprogram, a subprogram call must specify exactly one cor-   5
responding actual parameter. This actual parameter is specified either explicitly, by a parameter
association, or, in the absence of such an association, by a default expression (see 6.4.2).

The parameter associations of a subprogram call are evaluated in some order that is not defined by   6
the language. Similarly, the language rules do not define in which order the values of **in out** or **out**
parameters are copied back into the corresponding actual parameters (when this is done).

Examples of procedure calls: 7

```
    TRAVERSE_TREE;                                                   --  see 6.1
    TABLE_MANAGER.INSERT(E);                                         --  see 7.5
    PRINT_HEADER(128, TITLE, TRUE);                                  --  see 6.1

    SWITCH(FROM => X, TO => NEXT);                                   --  see 6.1
    PRINT_HEADER(128, HEADER => TITLE, CENTER => TRUE);              --  see 6.1
    PRINT_HEADER(HEADER => TITLE, CENTER => TRUE, PAGES => 128);     --  see 6.1
```

Examples of function calls: 8

```
    DOT_PRODUCT(U, V)     --  see 6.1 and 6.5
    CLOCK                 --  see 9.6
```

9   *References:* default expression for a formal parameter 6.1, erroneous 1.6, expression 4.4, formal parameter 6.1, formal part 6.1, name 4.1, simple name 4.1, subprogram 6, type mark 3.3.2, variable 3.2.1

6.4.1 Parameter Associations

1   Each actual parameter must have the same type as the corresponding formal parameter.

2   An actual parameter associated with a formal parameter of mode **in** must be an expression; it is evaluated before the call.

3   An actual parameter associated with a formal parameter of mode **in out** or **out** must be either the name of a variable, or of the form of a type conversion whose argument is the name of a variable. In either case, for the mode **in out**, the variable must not be a formal parameter of mode **out** or a subcomponent thereof. For an actual parameter that has the form of a type conversion, the type mark must conform (see 6.3.1) to the type mark of the formal parameter; the allowed operand and target types are the same as for type conversions (see 4.6).

4   The variable name given for an actual parameter of mode **in out** or **out** is evaluated before the call. If the actual parameter has the form of a type conversion, then before the call, for a parameter of mode **in out**, the variable is converted to the specified type; after (normal) completion of the sub-program body, for a parameter of mode **in out** or **out**, the formal parameter is converted back to the type of the variable. (The type specified in the conversion must be that of the formal parameter.)

5   The following constraint checks are performed for parameters of scalar and access types:

6   ● Before the call: for a parameter of mode **in** or **in out**, it is checked that the value of the actual parameter belongs to the subtype of the formal parameter.

7   ● After (normal) completion of the subprogram body: for a parameter of mode **in out** or **out**, it is checked that the value of the formal parameter belongs to the subtype of the actual variable. In the case of a type conversion, the value of the formal parameter is converted back and the check applies to the result of the conversion.

8   In each of the above cases, the execution of the program is erroneous if the checked value is undefined.

9   For other types, for all modes, a check is made before the call as for scalar and access types; no check is made upon return.

10   The exception CONSTRAINT_ERROR is raised at the place of the subprogram call if either of these checks fails.

Note:

11   For array types and for types with discriminants, the check before the call is sufficient (a check upon return would be redundant) if the type mark of the formal parameter denotes a constrained subtype, since neither array bounds nor discriminants can then vary.

If this type mark denotes an unconstrained array type, the formal parameter Is constrained with the bounds of the corresponding actual parameter and no check (neither before the call nor upon return) is needed (see 3.6.1). Similarly, no check is needed if the type mark denotes an unconstrained type with discriminants, since the formal parameter is then constrained exactly as the corresponding actual parameter (see 3.7.1).

12

References: actual parameter 6.4, array bound 3.6, array type 3.6, call of a subprogram 6.4, conform 6.3.1, constrained subtype 3.3, constraint 3.3, constraint_error exception 11.1, discriminant 3.7.1, erroneous 1.6, evaluation 4.5, evaluation of a name 4.1, expression 4.4, formal parameter 6.1, mode 6.1, name 4.1, parameter association 6.4, subtype 3.3, type 3.3, type conversion 4.6, type mark 3.3.2, unconstrained array type 3.6, unconstrained type with discriminants 3.7.1, undefined value 3.2.1, variable 3.2.1

13

6.4.2 Default Parameters

If a parameter specification includes a default expression for a parameter of mode **in**, then corresponding subprogram calls need not Include a parameter association for the parameter. If a parameter association is thus omitted from a call, then the rest of the call, following any initial positional associations, must use only named associations.

1

For any omitted parameter association, the default expression is evaluated before the call and the resulting value is used as an implicit actual parameter.

2

Examples of procedures with default values:

3

```
procedure ACTIVATE( PROCESS   : in PROCESS_NAME;
                    AFTER     : in PROCESS_NAME := NO_PROCESS;
                    WAIT      : in DURATION := 0.0;
                    PRIOR     : In BOOLEAN := FALSE);

procedure PAIR(LEFT, RIGHT : PERSON_NAME := new PERSON);
```

Examples of their calls:

4

```
ACTIVATE(X);
ACTIVATE(X, AFTER => Y);
ACTIVATE(X, WAIT => 60.0, PRIOR => TRUE);
ACTIVATE(X, Y, 10.0, FALSE);

PAIR;
PAIR(LEFT => new PERSON, RIGHT => new PERSON);
```

Note:

If a default expression is used for two or more parameters in a multiple parameter specification, the default expression is evaluated once for each omitted parameter. Hence in the above examples, the two calls of PAIR are equivalent.

5

References: actual parameter 6.4.1, default expression for a formal parameter 6.1, evaluation 4.5, formal parameter 6.1, mode 6.1, named parameter association 6.4, parameter association 6.4, parameter specification 6.1, positional parameter association 6.4, subprogram call 6.4

6

6.5 Function Subprograms

1   A function is a subprogram that returns a value (the result of the function call). The specification of a function starts with the reserved word **function**, and the parameters, if any, must have the mode **in** (whether this mode is specified explicitly or implicitly). The statements of the function body (excluding statements of program units that are inner to the function body) must include one or more return statements specifying the returned value.

2   The exception PROGRAM_ERROR is raised if a function body is left otherwise than by a return statement. This does not apply if the execution of the function is abandoned as a result of an exception.

3   *Example:*

```
function DOT_PRODUCT(LEFT, RIGHT : VECTOR) return REAL is
   SUM : REAL := 0.0;
begin
   CHECK(LEFT'FIRST = RIGHT'FIRST and LEFT'LAST = RIGHT'LAST);
   for J in LEFT'RANGE loop
      SUM := SUM + LEFT(J)*RIGHT(J);
   end loop;
   return SUM;
end DOT_PRODUCT;
```

4   *References:* exception 11, formal parameter 6.1, function 6.1, function body 6.3, function call 6.4, function specification 6.1, mode 6.1, program_error exception 11.1, raising of exceptions 11, return statement 5.8, statement 5

6.6 Parameter and Result Type Profile - Overloading of Subprograms

1   Two formal parts are said to have the same *parameter type profile* if and only if they have the same number of parameters, and at each parameter position corresponding parameters have the same base type. A subprogram or entry has the same *parameter and result type profile* as another subprogram or entry if and only if both have the same parameter type profile, and either both are functions with the same result base type, or neither of the two is a function.

2   The same subprogram identifier or operator symbol can be used in several subprogram specifications. The identifier or operator symbol is then said to be *overloaded*; the subprograms that have this identifier or operator symbol are also said to be overloaded and to overload each other. As explained in section 8.3, if two subprograms overload each other, one of them can hide the other only if both subprograms have the same parameter and result type profile (see section 8.3 for the other requirements that must be met for hiding).

3   A call to an overloaded subprogram is ambiguous (and therefore illegal) if the name of the subprogram, the number of parameter associations, the types and the order of the actual parameters, the names of the formal parameters (if named associations are used), and the result type (for functions) are not sufficient to determine exactly one (overloaded) subprogram specification.

Examples of overloaded subprograms: 4

```
procedure PUT(X : INTEGER);
procedure PUT(X : STRING);
procedure SET(TINT    : COLOR);
procedure SET(SIGNAL  : LIGHT);
```

Examples of calls: 5

```
PUT(28);
PUT("no possible ambiguity here");

SET(TINT    => RED);
SET(SIGNAL  => RED);
SET(COLOR'(RED));

--  SET(RED) would be ambiguous since RED may
--  denote a value either of type COLOR or of type LIGHT
```

Notes:

The notion of parameter and result type profile does not include parameter names, parameter   6
modes, parameter subtypes, default expressions and their presence or absence.

Ambiguities may (but need not) arise when actual parameters of the call of an overloaded sub-   7
program are themselves overloaded function calls, literals, or aggregates. Ambiguities may also
(but need not) arise when several overloaded subprograms belonging to different packages are
visible. These ambiguities can usually be resolved in several ways: qualified expressions can be
used for some or all actual parameters, and for the result, if any; the name of the subprogram can
be expressed more explicitly as an expanded name; finally, the subprogram can be renamed.

References: actual parameter 6.4.1, aggregate 4.3, base type 3.3, default expression for a formal parameter 6.1,   8
entry 9.5, formal parameter 6.1, function 6.5, function call 6.4, hiding 8.3, identifier 2.3, illegal 1.6, literal 4.2, mode
6.1, named parameter association 6.4, operator symbol 6.1, overloading 8.7, package 7, parameter of a subprogram
6.2, qualified expression 4.7, renaming declaration 8.5, result subtype 6.1, subprogram 6, subprogram specification
6.1, subtype 3.3, type 3.3

6.7 Overloading of Operators

The declaration of a function whose designator is an operator symbol is used to overload an   1
operator. The sequence of characters of the operator symbol must be either a logical, a relational, a
binary adding, a unary adding, a multiplying, or a highest precedence operator (see 4.5). Neither
membership tests nor the short-circuit control forms are allowed as function designators.

The subprogram specification of a unary operator must have a single parameter. The subprogram   2
specification of a binary operator must have two parameters; for each use of this operator, the first
parameter takes the left operand as actual parameter, the second parameter takes the right
operand. Similarly, a generic function instantiation whose designator is an operator symbol is only
allowed if the specification of the generic function has the corresponding number of parameters.
Default expressions are not allowed for the parameters of an operator (whether the operator is
declared with an explicit subprogram specification or by a generic instantiation).

3   For each of the operators "+" and "-", overloading is allowed both as a unary and as a binary operator.

4   The explicit declaration of a function that overloads the equality operator "=", other than by a renaming declaration, is only allowed if both parameters are of the same limited type. An overloading of equality must deliver a result of the predefined type BOOLEAN; it also implicitly overloads the inequality operator "/=" so that this still gives the complementary result to the equality operator. Explicit overloading of the inequality operator is not allowed.

5   A renaming declaration whose designator is the equality operator is only allowed to rename another equality operator. (For example, such a renaming declaration can be used when equality is visible by selection but not directly visible.)

Note:

6   Overloading of relational operators does not affect basic comparisons such as testing for membership in a range or the choices in a case statement.

7   *Examples:*

```
function "+" (LEFT, RIGHT : MATRIX)  return MATRIX;
function "+" (LEFT, RIGHT : VECTOR)  return VECTOR;

--   assuming that A, B, and C are of the type VECTOR
--   the three following assignments are equivalent

A := B + C;

A := "+"(B, C);
A := "+"(LEFT => B, RIGHT => C);
```

8   *References:* allow 1.6, actual parameter 6.4.1, binary adding operator 4.5 4.5.3, boolean predefined type 3.5.3, character 2.1, complementary result 4.5.2, declaration 3.1, default expression for a formal parameter 6.1, designator 6.1, directly visible 8.3, equality operator 4.5, formal parameter 6.1, function declaration 6.1, highest precedence operator 4.5 4.5.6, implicit declaration 3.1, inequality operator 4.5.2, limited type 7.4.4, logical operator 4.5 4.5.1, membership test 4.5 4.5.2, multiplying operator 4.5 4.5.5, operator 4.5, operator symbol 6.1, overloading 6.6 8.7, relational operator 4.5 4.5.2 short-circuit control form 4.5 4.5.1, type definition 3.3.1, unary adding operator 4.5 4.5.4, visible by selection 8.3

7. Packages

Packages are one of the four forms of program unit, of which programs can be composed. The other forms are subprograms, task units, and generic units. 1

Packages allow the specification of groups of logically related entities. In their simplest form packages specify pools of common object and type declarations. More generally, packages can be used to specify groups of related entities including also subprograms that can be called from outside the package, while their inner workings remain concealed and protected from outside users. 2

References: generic unit 12, program unit 6, subprogram 6, task unit 9, type declaration 3.3.1 3

7.1 Package Structure

A package is generally provided in two parts: a package specification and a package body. Every package has a package specification, but not all packages have a package body. 1

```
package_declaration ::= package_specification;
```
2
```
package_specification ::=
    package identifier is
        {basic_declarative_item}
    [ private
        {basic_declarative_item}]
    end [package_simple_name]

package_body ::=
    package body package_simple_name is
        [ declarative_part]
    [ begin
            sequence_of_statements
    [ exception
            exception_handler
        { exception_handler}]]
    end [package_simple_name];
```

The simple name at the start of a package body must repeat the package identifier. Similarly if a simple name appears at the end of the package specification or body, it must repeat the package identifier. 3

If a subprogram declaration, a package declaration, a task declaration, or a generic declaration is a declarative item of a given package specification, then the body (if there is one) of the program unit declared by the declarative item must itself be a declarative item of the declarative part of the body of the given package. 4

Notes:

5   A simple form of package, specifying a pool of objects and types, does not require a package body.
One of the possible uses of the sequence of statements of a package body is to initialize such
objects. For each subprogram declaration there must be a corresponding body (except for a subprogram written in another language, as explained in section 13.9). If the body of a program unit
is a body stub, then a separately compiled subunit containing the corresponding proper body is
required for the program unit (see 10.2). A body is not a basic declarative item and so cannot
appear in a package specification.

6   A package declaration is either a library package (see 10.2) or a declarative item declared within
another program unit.

7   *References:* basic declarative item 3.9, body stub 10.2, declarative item 3.9, declarative part 3.9, exception handler
11.2, generic body 12.2, generic declaration 12.1, identifier 2.3, library unit 10.1, object 3.2, package body 7.3, program unit 6, proper body 3.9, sequence of statements 5.1, simple name 4.1, subprogram body 6.3, subprogram declaration 6.1, subunit 10.2, task body 9.1, task declaration 9.1, type 3.3

7.2 Package Specifications and Declarations

1   The first list of declarative items of a package specification is called the *visible part* of the package. The optional list of declarative items after the reserved word **private** is called the *private part* of
the package.

2   An entity declared in the private part of a package is not visible outside the package itself (a name
denoting such an entity is only possible within the package). In contrast, expanded names denoting entities declared in the visible part can be used even outside the package; furthermore, direct
visibility of such entities can be achieved by means of use clauses (see 4.1.3 and 8.4).

3   The elaboration of a package declaration consists of the elaboration of its basic declarative items
in the given order.

Notes:

4   The visible part of a package contains all the information that another program unit is able to know
about the package. A package consisting of only a package specification (that is, without a package body) can be used to represent a group of common constants or variables, or a common pool of
objects and types, as in the examples below.

5   *Example of a package describing a group of common variables:*

```
package PLOTTING_DATA is
   PEN_UP : BOOLEAN;

   CONVERSION_FACTOR,
   X_OFFSET,  Y_OFFSET,
   X_MIN,     Y_MIN,
   X_MAX,     Y_MAX:    REAL;      -- see 3.5.7

   X_VALUE  : array (1 .. 500) of REAL;
   Y_VALUE  : array (1 .. 500) of REAL;
end PLOTTING_DATA;
```

Example of a package describing a common pool of objects and types: 6

```
package WORK_DATA is
   type DAY is (MON, TUE, WED, THU, FRI, SAT, SUN);
   type HOURS_SPENT is delta 0.25 range 0.0 .. 24.0;
   type TIME_TABLE    is array (DAY) of HOURS_SPENT;

   WORK_HOURS     : TIME_TABLE;
   NORMAL_HOURS : constant TIME_TABLE :=
                     (MON .. THU => 8.25, FRI => 7.0, SAT | SUN => 0.0);
end WORK_DATA;
```

References: basic declarative item 3.9, constant 3.2.1, declarative item 3.9, direct visibility 8.3, elaboration 3.9, 7
expanded name 4.1.3, name 4.1, number declaration 3.2.2, object declaration 3.2.1, package 7, package declaration
7.1, package identifier 7.1, package specification 7.1, scope 8.2, simple name 4.1, type declaration 3.3.1, use clause
8.4, variable 3.2.1

7.3 Package Bodies

In contrast to the entities declared in the visible part of a package specification, the entities decla- 1
red in the package body are only visible within the package body itself. As a consequence, a package with a package body can be used for the construction of a group of related subprograms (a *package* in the usual sense), in which the logical operations available to the users are clearly isolated
from the internal entities.

For the elaboration of a package body, its declarative part is first elaborated, and its sequence of 2
statements (if any) is then executed. The optional exception handlers at the end of a package body
service exceptions raised during the execution of the sequence of statements of the package body.

Notes:

A variable declared in the body of a package is only visible within this body and, consequently, its 3
value can only be changed within the package body. In the absence of local tasks, the value of
such a variable remains unchanged between calls issued from outside the package to subprograms
declared in the visible part. The properties of such a variable are similar to those of an "own"
variable of Algol 60.

The elaboration of the body of a subprogram declared in the visible part of a package is caused by 4
the elaboration of the body of the package. Hence a call of such a subprogram by an outside program unit raises the exception PROGRAM_ERROR if the call takes place before the elaboration of
the package body (see 3.9).

5   *Example of a package:*

```
package RATIONAL_NUMBERS is

   type RATIONAL is
      record
         NUMERATOR    : INTEGER;
         DENOMINATOR  : POSITIVE;
      end record;

   function EQUAL (X,Y : RATIONAL) return BOOLEAN;

   function "/"   (X,Y : INTEGER) return RATIONAL;   -- to construct a rational number

   function "+"   (X,Y : RATIONAL) return RATIONAL;
   function "-"   (X,Y : RATIONAL) return RATIONAL;
   function "*"   (X,Y : RATIONAL) return RATIONAL;
   function "/"   (X,Y : RATIONAL) return RATIONAL;
end;

package body RATIONAL_NUMBERS is

   procedure SAME_DENOMINATOR (X,Y : in out RATIONAL) is
   begin
      --   reduces X and Y to the same denominator:
      ...
   end;

   function EQUAL(X,Y : RATIONAL) return BOOLEAN is
      U,V : RATIONAL;
   begin
      U := X;
      V := Y;
      SAME_DENOMINATOR (U,V);
      return U.NUMERATOR = V.NUMERATOR;
   end EQUAL;

   function "/" (X,Y : INTEGER) return RATIONAL is
   begin
      if Y > 0 then
         return (NUMERATOR => X, . DENOMINATOR => Y);
      else
         return (NUMERATOR => -X, DENOMINATOR => -Y);
      end if;
   end "/";

   function "+"   (X,Y : RATIONAL) return RATIONAL is ...  end "+";
   function "-"   (X,Y : RATIONAL) return RATIONAL is ...  end "-";
   function "*"   (X,Y : RATIONAL) return RATIONAL is ...  end "*";
   function "/"   (X,Y : RATIONAL) return RATIONAL is ...  end "/";

end RATIONAL_NUMBERS;
```

6   *References:* declaration 3.1, declarative part 3.9, elaboration 3.1 3.9, exception 11, exception handler 11.2, name 4.1, package specification 7.1, program unit 6, program_error exception 11.1, sequence of statements 5.1, subprogram 6, variable 3.2.1, visible part 7.2

7.4 Private Type and Deferred Constant Declarations

The declaration of a type as a private type in the visible part of a package serves to separate the characteristics that can be used directly by outside program units (that is, the logical properties) from other characteristics whose direct use is confined to the package (the details of the definition of the type itself). Deferred constant declarations declare constants of private types.

        private_type_declaration ::=
            type identifier [discriminant_part] **is** [**limited**] **private**;

        deferred_constant_declaration ::=
            identifier_list : **constant** type_mark;

A private type declaration is only allowed as a declarative item of the visible part of a package, or as the generic parameter declaration for a generic formal type in a generic formal part.

The type mark of a deferred constant declaration must denote a private type or a subtype of a private type; a deferred constant declaration and the declaration of the corresponding private type must both be declarative items of the visible part of the same package. A deferred constant declaration with several identifiers is equivalent to a sequence of single deferred constant declarations as explained in section 3.2.

Examples of private type declarations:

        type KEY **is private**;
        type FILE_NAME **is limited private**;

Example of deferred constant declaration:

        NULL_KEY : **constant** KEY;

References: constant 3.2.1, declaration 3.1, declarative item 3.9, deferred constant 7.4.3, discriminant part 3.7.1, generic formal part 12.1, generic formal type 12.1, generic parameter declaration 12.1, identifier 2.3, identifier list 3.2, limited type 7.4.4, package 7, private type 7.4.1, program unit 6, subtype 3.3, type 3.3, type mark 3.3.2, visible part 7.2

7.4.1 Private Types

If a private type declaration is given in the visible part of a package, then a corresponding declaration of a type with the same identifier must appear as a declarative item of the private part of the package. The corresponding declaration must be either a full type declaration or the declaration of a task type. In the rest of this section explanations are given in terms of full type declarations; the same rules apply also to declarations of task types.

2   A private type declaration and the corresponding full type declaration define a single type. The private type declaration, together with the visible part, define the operations that are available to outside program units (see section 7.4.2 on the operations that are available for private types). On the other hand, the full type declaration defines other operations whose direct use is only possible within the package itself.

3   If the private type declaration includes a discriminant part, the full declaration must include a discriminant part that conforms (see 6.3.1 for the conformance rules) and its type definition must be a record type definition. Conversely, if the private type declaration does not include a discriminant part, the type declared by the full type declaration (the *full type*) must not be an unconstrained type with discriminants. The full type must not be an unconstrained array type. A limited type (in particular a task type) is allowed for the full type only if the reserved word **limited** appears in the private type declaration (see 7.4.4).

4   Within the specification of the package that declares a private type and before the end of the corresponding full type declaration, a restriction applies to the use of a name that denotes the private type or a subtype of the private type and, likewise, to the use of a name that denotes any type or subtype that has a subcomponent of the private type. The only allowed occurrences of such a name are in a deferred constant declaration, a type or subtype declaration, a subprogram specification, or an entry declaration; moreover, occurrences within derived type definitions or within simple expressions are not allowed.

5   The elaboration of a private type declaration creates a private type. If the private type declaration has a discriminant part, this elaboration includes that of the discriminant part. The elaboration of the full type declaration consists of the elaboration of the type definition; the discriminant part, if any, is not elaborated (since the conforming discriminant part of the private type declaration has already been elaborated).

Notes:

6   It follows from the given rules that neither the declaration of a variable of a private type, nor the creation by an allocator of an object of the private type are allowed before the full declaration of the type. Similarly before the full declaration, the name of the private type cannot be used in a generic instantiation or in a representation clause.

7   *References:* allocator 4.8, array type 3.6, conform 6.3.1, declarative item 3.9, deferred constant declaration 7.4.3, derived type 3.4, discriminant part 3.7.1, elaboration 3.9, entry declaration 9.5, expression 4.4, full type declaration 3.3.1, generic instantiation 12.3, identifier 2.3, incomplete type declaration 3.8.1, limited type 7.4.4, name 4.1, operation 3.3, package 7, package specification 7.1, private part 7.2, private type 7.4, private type declaration 7.4, record type definition 3.7, representation clause 13.1, reserved word 2.9, subcomponent 3.3, subprogram specification 6.1, subtype 3.3, subtype declaration 3.3.2, type 3.3, type declaration 3.3.1, type definition 3.3.1, unconstrained array type 3.6, variable 3.2.1, visible part 7.2

7.4.2 Operations of a Private Type

1   The operations that are implicitly declared by a private type declaration include basic operations. These are the operations involved in assignment (unless the reserved word **limited** appears in the declaration), membership tests, selected components for the selection of any discriminant, qualification, and explicit conversions.

For a private type T, the basic operations also include the attributes T'BASE (see 3.3.3) and T'SIZE 2
(see 13.7.2). For an object A of a private type, the basic operations include the attribute
A'CONSTRAINED if the private type has discriminants (see 3.7.4), and in any case, the attributes
A'SIZE and A'ADDRESS (see 13.7.2).

Finally, the operations implicitly declared by a private type declaration include the predefined com- 3
parison for equality and inequality unless the reserved word **limited** appears in the private type
declaration.

The above operations, together with subprograms that have a parameter or result of the private 4
type and that are declared in the visible part of the package, are the only operations from the
package that are available outside the package for the private type.

Within the package that declares the private type, the additional operations implicitly declared by 5
the full type declaration are also available. However, the redefinition of these implicitly declared
operations is allowed within the same declarative region, including between the private type
declaration and the corresponding full declaration. An explicitly declared subprogram hides an
implicitly declared operation that has the same parameter and result type profile (this is only possible if the implicitly declared operation is a derived subprogram or a predefined operator).

If a composite type has subcomponents of a private type and is declared outside the package that 6
declares the private type, then the operations that are implicitly declared by the declaration of the
composite type include all operations that only depend on the characteristics that result from the
private type declaration alone. (For example the operator < is not included for a one-dimensional
array type.)

If the composite type is itself declared within the package that declares the private type (including 7
within an inner package or generic package), then additional operations that depend on the
characteristics of the full type are implicitly declared, as required by the rules applicable to the
composite type (for example the operator < is declared for a one-dimensional array type if the full
type is discrete). These additional operations are implicitly declared at the earliest place within the
immediate scope of the composite type and after the full type declaration.

The same rules apply to the operations that are implicitly declared for an access type whose 8
designated type is a private type or a type declared by an incomplete type declaration.

For every private type or subtype T the following attribute is defined: 9

T'CONSTRAINED Yields the value FALSE if T denotes an unconstrained nonformal private type 10
with discriminants; also yields the value FALSE if T denotes a generic formal
private type, and the associated actual subtype is either an unconstrained type
with discriminants or an unconstrained array type; yields the value TRUE
otherwise. The value of this attribute is of the predefined type BOOLEAN .

Note:

A private type declaration and the corresponding full type declaration define two different views of 11
one and the same type. Outside of the defining package the characteristics of the type are those
defined by the visible part. Within these outside program units the type is just a private type and
any language rule that applies only to another class of types does not apply. The fact that the full
declaration might *implement* the private type with a type of a particular class (for example, as an
array type) is only relevant within the package itself.

12 The consequences of this actual implementation are, however, valid everywhere. For example: any default initialization of components takes place; the attribute SIZE provides the size of the full type; task dependence rules still apply to components that are task objects.

13 *Example:*

```
package KEY_MANAGER is
   type KEY is private;
   NULL_KEY : constant KEY;
   procedure GET_KEY(K : out KEY);
   function "<" (X, Y : KEY) return BOOLEAN;
private
   type KEY is new NATURAL;
   NULL_KEY : constant KEY := 0;
end;

package body KEY_MANAGER is
   LAST_KEY : KEY := 0;
   procedure GET_KEY(K : out KEY) is
   begin
      LAST_KEY := LAST_KEY + 1;
      K := LAST_KEY;
   end GET_KEY;

   function "<" (X, Y : KEY) return BOOLEAN is
   begin
      return INTEGER(X) < INTEGER(Y);
   end "<";
end KEY_MANAGER;
```

Notes on the example:

14 Outside of the package KEY_MANAGER, the operations available for objects of type KEY include assignment, the comparison for equality or inequality, the procedure GET_KEY and the operator "<"; they do not include other relational operators such as ">=", or arithmetic operators.

15 The explicitly declared operator "<" hides the predefined operator "<" implicitly declared by the full type declaration. Within the body of the function, an explicit conversion of X and Y to the type INTEGER is necessary to invoke the "<" operator of this type. Alternatively, the result of the function could be written as **not** (X >= Y), since the operator ">=" is not redefined.

16 The value of the variable LAST_KEY, declared in the package body, remains unchanged between calls of the procedure GET_KEY. (See also the Notes of section 7.3.)

17 *References:* assignment 5.2, attribute 4.1.4, basic operation 3.3.3, component 3.3, composite type 3.3, conversion 4.6, declaration 3.1, declarative region 8.1, derived subprogram 3.4, derived type 3.4, dimension 3.6, discriminant 3.3, equality 4.5.2, full type 7.4.1, full type declaration 3.3.1, hiding 8.3, immediate scope 8.2, implicit declaration 3.1, incomplete type declaration 3.8.1, membership test 4.5, operation 3.3, package 7, parameter of a subprogram 6.2, predefined function 8.6, predefined operator 4.5, private type 7.4, private type declaration 7.4, program unit 6, qualification 4.7, relational operator 4.5, selected component 4.1.3, subprogram 6, task dependence 9.4, visible part 7.2

7.4.3 Deferred Constants

If a deferred constant declaration is given in the visible part of a package then a constant declaration (that is, an object declaration declaring a constant object, with an explicit initialization) with the same identifier must appear as a declarative item of the private part of the package. This object declaration is called the *full* declaration of the deferred constant. The type mark given in the full declaration must conform to that given in the deferred constant declaration (see 6.3.1). Multiple or single declarations are allowed for the deferred and the full declarations, provided that the equivalent single declarations conform.

Within the specification of the package that declares a deferred constant and before the end of the corresponding full declaration, the use of a name that denotes the deferred constant is only allowed in the default expression for a record component or for a formal parameter (not for a generic formal parameter).

The elaboration of a deferred constant declaration has no other effect.

The execution of a program is erroneous if it attempts to use the value of a deferred constant before the elaboration of the corresponding full declaration.

Note:

The full declaration for a deferred constant that has a given private type must not appear before the corresponding full type declaration. This is a consequence of the rules defining the allowed uses of a name that denotes a private type (see 7.4.1).

References: conform 6.3.1, constant declaration 3.2.1, declarative item 3.9, default expression for a discriminant 3.7.1, deferred constant 7.4, deferred constant declaration 7.4, elaboration has no other effect 3.1, formal parameter 6.1, generic formal parameter 12.1 12.3, identifier 2.3, object declaration 3.2.1, package 7, package specification 7.1, private part 7.2, record component 3.7, type mark 3.3.2, visible part 7.2

7.4.4 Limited Types

A limited type is a type for which neither assignment nor the predefined comparison for equality and inequality is *implicitly* declared.

A private type declaration that includes the reserved word **limited** declares a limited type. A task type is a limited type. A type derived from a limited type is itself a limited type. Finally, a composite type is limited if the type of any of its subcomponents is limited.

The operations available for a private type that is limited are as given in section 7.4.2 for private types except for the absence of assignment and of a predefined comparison for equality and inequality.

For a formal parameter whose type is limited and whose declaration occurs in an explicit subprogram declaration, the mode **out** is only allowed if this type is private and the subprogram declaration occurs within the visible part of the package that declares the private type. The same holds for formal parameters of entry declarations and of generic procedure declarations. The corresponding full type must not be limited if the mode **out** is used for any such formal parameter. Otherwise, the corresponding full type is allowed (but not required) to be a limited type (in particular, it is allowed to be a task type). If the full type corresponding to a limited private type is not itself limited, then assignment for the type is available within the package, but not outside.

5   The following are consequences of the rules for limited types:

6   ● An explicit initialization is not allowed in an object declaration if the type of the object is limited.

7   ● A default expression is not allowed in a component declaration if the type of the record component is limited.

8   ● An explicit initial value is not allowed in an allocator if the designated type is limited.

9   ● A generic formal parameter of mode **in** must not be of a limited type.

Notes:

10 The above rules do not exclude a default expression for a formal parameter of a limited type; they do not exclude a deferred constant of a limited type if the full type is not limited. An explicit declaration of an equality operator is allowed for a limited type (see 6.7).

11 Aggregates are not available for a limited composite type (see 3.6.2 and 3.7.4). Catenation is not available for a limited array type (see 3.6.2).

12 *Example:*

```
package I_O_PACKAGE is
  type FILE_NAME is limited private;

  procedure OPEN  (F : in out FILE_NAME);
  procedure CLOSE (F : in out FILE_NAME);
  procedure READ  (F : in FILE_NAME; ITEM : out INTEGER);
  procedure WRITE (F : in FILE_NAME; ITEM : in  INTEGER);
private
  type FILE_NAME is
    record
      INTERNAL_NAME : INTEGER := 0;
    end record;
end I_O_PACKAGE;

package body I_O_PACKAGE is
  LIMIT : constant := 200;
  type FILE_DESCRIPTOR is record   ...   end record;
  DIRECTORY : array (1 .. LIMIT) of FILE_DESCRIPTOR;
  ...
  procedure OPEN  (F : in out FILE_NAME) is   ...   end;
  procedure CLOSE (F : in out FILE_NAME) is   ...   end;
  procedure READ  (F : in FILE_NAME; ITEM : out INTEGER) is ... end;
  procedure WRITE (F : in FILE_NAME; ITEM : in  INTEGER) is ... end;
begin
  ...
end I_O_PACKAGE;
```

Notes on the example:

13 In the example above, an outside subprogram making use of I_O_PACKAGE may obtain a file name by calling OPEN and later use it in calls to READ and WRITE. Thus, outside the package, a file name obtained from OPEN acts as a kind of password; its internal properties (such as containing a numeric value) are not known and no other operations (such as addition or comparison of internal names) can be performed on a file name.

This example is characteristic of any case where complete control over the operations of a type is desired. Such packages serve a dual purpose. They prevent a user from making use of the internal structure of the type. They also implement the notion of an *encapsulated* data type where the only operations on the type are those given in the package specification. 14

References: aggregate 4.3, allocator 4.8, assignment 5.2, catenation operator 4.5, component declaration 3.7, component type 3.3, composite type 3.3, default expression for a discriminant 3.7, deferred constant 7.4.3, derived type 3.4, designate 3.8, discriminant specification 3.7.1, equality 4.5.2, formal parameter 6.1, full type 7.4.1, full type declaration 3.3.1, generic formal parameter 12.1 12.3, implicit declaration 3.1, initial value 3.2.1, mode 12.1.1, object 3.2, operation 3.3, package 7, predefined operator 4.5, private type 7.4, private type declaration 7.4, record component 3.7, record type 3.7, relational operator 4.5, subcomponent 3.3, subprogram 6, task type 9.1 9.2, type 3.3 15

7.5 Example of a Table Management Package

The following example illustrates the use of packages in providing high level procedures with a simple interface to the user. 1

The problem is to define a table management package for inserting and retrieving items. The items are inserted into the table as they are supplied. Each inserted item has an order number. The items are retrieved according to their order number, where the item with the lowest order number is retrieved first. 2

From the user's point of view, the package is quite simple. There is a type called ITEM designating table items, a procedure INSERT for inserting items, and a procedure RETRIEVE for obtaining the item with the lowest order number. There is a special item NULL_ITEM that is returned when the table is empty, and an exception TABLE_FULL which is raised by INSERT if the table is already full. 3

A sketch of such a package is given below. Only the specification of the package is exposed to the user. 4

```
package TABLE_MANAGER is

   type ITEM is
      record
         ORDER_NUM   : INTEGER;
         ITEM_CODE   : INTEGER;
         QUANTITY    : INTEGER;
         ITEM_TYPE   : CHARACTER;
      end record;

   NULL_ITEM : constant ITEM :=
      (ORDER_NUM | ITEM_CODE | QUANTITY => 0, ITEM_TYPE => ' ');

   procedure INSERT   (NEW_ITEM   : in   ITEM);
   procedure RETRIEVE (FIRST_ITEM : out ITEM);

   TABLE_FULL : exception;   --   raised by INSERT when table full
end;
```
5

6   The details of implementing such packages can be quite complex; in this case they involve a two-way linked table of internal items. A local housekeeping procedure EXCHANGE is used to move an internal item between the busy and the free lists. The initial table linkages are established by the initialization part. The package body need not be shown to the users of the package.

7
```
package body TABLE_MANAGER is
   SIZE : constant := 2000;
   subtype INDEX is INTEGER range 0 .. SIZE;

   type INTERNAL_ITEM is
      record
         CONTENT  : ITEM;
         SUCC     : INDEX;
         PRED     : INDEX;
      end record;

   TABLE : array (INDEX) of INTERNAL_ITEM;
   FIRST_BUSY_ITEM  : INDEX := 0;
   FIRST_FREE_ITEM  : INDEX := 1;

   function FREE_LIST_EMPTY  return BOOLEAN is ... end;
   function BUSY_LIST_EMPTY  return BOOLEAN is ... end;
   procedure EXCHANGE (FROM : in INDEX; TO : in INDEX) is ... end;

   procedure INSERT (NEW_ITEM : in ITEM) is
   begin
      if FREE_LIST_EMPTY then
         raise TABLE_FULL;
      end if;
      --   remaining code for INSERT
   end INSERT;

   procedure RETRIEVE (FIRST_ITEM : out ITEM) is ... end;

begin
   --   initialization of the table linkages
end TABLE_MANAGER;
```

7.6 Example of a Text Handling Package

1   This example illustrates a simple text handling package. The users only have access to the visible part; the implementation is hidden from them in the private part and the package body (not shown).

2   From a user's point of view, a TEXT is a variable-length string. Each text object has a maximum length, which must be given when the object is declared, and a current value, which is a string of some length between zero and the maximum. The maximum possible length of a text object is an implementation-defined constant.

3   The package defines first the necessary types, then functions that return some characteristics of objects of the type, then the conversion functions between texts and the predefined CHARACTER and STRING types, and finally some of the standard operations on varying strings. Most operations are overloaded on strings and characters as well as on the type TEXT, in order to minimize the number of explicit conversions the user has to write.

```
package TEXT_HANDLER is
   MAXIMUM : constant := SOME_VALUE;  --  implementation-defined
   subtype INDEX is INTEGER range 0 .. MAXIMUM;

   type TEXT(MAXIMUM_LENGTH : INDEX) is limited private;

   function LENGTH   (T : TEXT)  return INDEX;
   function VALUE    (T : TEXT)  return STRING;
   function EMPTY    (T : TEXT)  return BOOLEAN;

   function TO_TEXT (S : STRING;    MAX : INDEX) return TEXT;   --  maximum length MAX
   function TO_TEXT (C : CHARACTER; MAX : INDEX) return TEXT;
   function TO_TEXT (S : STRING)     return TEXT;   --  maximum length S'LENGTH
   function TO_TEXT (C : CHARACTER)  return TEXT;

   function "&" (LEFT : TEXT;       RIGHT : TEXT)       return TEXT;
   function "&" (LEFT : TEXT;       RIGHT : STRING)     return TEXT;
   function "&" (LEFT : STRING;     RIGHT : TEXT)       return TEXT;
   function "&" (LEFT : TEXT;       RIGHT : CHARACTER)  return TEXT;
   function "&" (LEFT : CHARACTER;  RIGHT : TEXT)       return TEXT;

   function "="  (LEFT : TEXT; RIGHT : TEXT) return BOOLEAN;
   function "<"  (LEFT : TEXT; RIGHT : TEXT) return BOOLEAN;
   function "<=" (LEFT : TEXT; RIGHT : TEXT) return BOOLEAN;
   function ">"  (LEFT : TEXT; RIGHT : TEXT) return BOOLEAN;
   function ">=" (LEFT : TEXT; RIGHT : TEXT) return BOOLEAN;

   procedure SET (OBJECT : in out TEXT; VALUE : in TEXT);
   procedure SET (OBJECT : in out TEXT; VALUE : in STRING);
   procedure SET (OBJECT : in out TEXT; VALUE : in CHARACTER);

   procedure APPEND (TAIL : in TEXT;       TO : in out TEXT);
   procedure APPEND (TAIL : in STRING;     TO : in out TEXT);
   procedure APPEND (TAIL : in CHARACTER;  TO : in out TEXT);

   procedure AMEND (OBJECT : in out TEXT; BY : in TEXT;       POSITION : in INDEX);
   procedure AMEND (OBJECT : in out TEXT; BY : in STRING;     POSITION : in INDEX);
   procedure AMEND (OBJECT : in out TEXT; BY : in CHARACTER;  POSITION : in INDEX);

   --  amend replaces part of the object by the given text, string, or character
   --  starting at the given position in the object

   function LOCATE (FRAGMENT : TEXT;       WITHIN : TEXT) return INDEX;
   function LOCATE (FRAGMENT : STRING;     WITHIN : TEXT) return INDEX;
   function LOCATE (FRAGMENT : CHARACTER;  WITHIN : TEXT) return INDEX;

   --  all return 0 if the fragment is not located

private
   type TEXT(MAXIMUM_LENGTH : INDEX) is
      record
         POS   : INDEX := 0;
         VALUE : STRING(1 .. MAXIMUM_LENGTH);
      end record;
end TEXT_HANDLER;
```

5   *Example of use of the text handling package:*

6   A program opens an output file, whose name is supplied by the string NAME. This string has the
    form

        [DEVICE :] [FILENAME [.EXTENSION]]

7   There are standard defaults for device, filename, and extension. The user-supplied name is passed
    to EXPAND_FILE_NAME as a parameter, and the result is the expanded version, with any necessary
    defaults added.

8
```
function EXPAND_FILE_NAME (NAME : STRING) return STRING is
    use TEXT_HANDLER;

    DEFAULT_DEVICE      : constant STRING := "SY:";
    DEFAULT_FILE_NAME   : constant STRING := "RESULTS";
    DEFAULT_EXTENSION   : constant STRING := ".DAT";

    MAXIMUM_FILE_NAME_LENGTH : constant INDEX := SOME_APPROPRIATE_VALUE;
    FILE_NAME : TEXT(MAXIMUM_FILE_NAME_LENGTH);

begin

    SET(FILE_NAME, NAME);

    if EMPTY(FILE_NAME) then
        SET(FILE_NAME, DEFAULT_FILE_NAME);
    end if;

    if LOCATE(':', FILE_NAME) = 0 then
        SET(FILE_NAME, DEFAULT_DEVICE & FILE_NAME);
    end if;

    if LOCATE('.', FILE_NAME) = 0 then
        APPEND(DEFAULT_EXTENSION, TO => FILE_NAME);
    end if;

    return VALUE(FILE_NAME);

end EXPAND_FILE_NAME;
```

8. Visibility Rules

The rules defining the scope of declarations and the rules defining which identifiers are visible at various points in the text of the program are described in this chapter. The formulation of these rules uses the notion of a declarative region.

References: declaration 3.1, declarative region 8.1, identifier 2.3, scope 8.2, visibility 8.3

8.1 Declarative Region

A declarative region is a portion of the program text. A single declarative region is formed by the text of each of the following:

- A subprogram declaration, a package declaration, a task declaration, or a generic declaration, together with the corresponding body, if any. If the body is a body stub, the declarative region also includes the corresponding subunit. If the program unit has subunits, they are also included.

- An entry declaration together with the corresponding accept statements.

- A record type declaration, together with a corresponding private or incomplete type declaration if any, and together with a corresponding record representation clause if any.

- A renaming declaration that includes a formal part, or a generic parameter declaration that includes either a formal part or a discriminant part.

- A block statement or a loop statement.

In each of the above cases, the declarative region is said to be *associated* with the corresponding declaration or statement. A declaration is said to *occur immediately within* a declarative region if this region is the innermost region that encloses the declaration, not counting the declarative region (if any) associated with the declaration itself.

A declaration that occurs immediately within a declarative region is said to be *local* to the region. Declarations in outer (enclosing) regions are said to be *global* to an inner (enclosed) declarative region. A local entity is one declared by a local declaration; a global entity is one declared by a global declaration.

Some of the above forms of declarative region include several disjoint parts (for example, other declarative items can be between the declaration of a package and its body). Each declarative region is nevertheless considered as a (logically) continuous portion of the program text. Hence if any rule defines a portion of text as the text that *extends* from some specific point of a declarative region to the end of this region, then this portion is the corresponding subset of the declarative region (for example it does not include intermediate declarative items between the two parts of a package).

Notes:

10   As defined in section 3.1, the term declaration includes basic declarations, implicit declarations, and those declarations that are part of basic declarations, for example, discriminant and parameter specifications. It follows from the definition of a declarative region that a discriminant specification occurs immediately within the region associated with the enclosing record type declaration. Similarly, a parameter specification occurs immediately within the region associated with the enclosing subprogram body or accept statement.

11   The package STANDARD forms a declarative region which encloses all library units: the implicit declaration of each library unit is assumed to occur immediately within this package (see sections 8.6 and 10.1.1).

12   Declarative regions can be nested within other declarative regions. For example, subprograms, packages, task units, generic units, and block statements can be nested within each other, and can contain record type declarations, loop statements, and accept statements.

13   *References:* accept statement 9.5, basic declaration 3.1, block statement 5.6, body stub 10.2, declaration 3.1, discriminant part 3.7.1, discriminant specification 3.7.1, entry declaration 9.5, formal part 6.1, generic body 12.2, generic declaration 12.1, generic parameter declaration 12.1, implicit declaration 3.1, incomplete type declaration 3.8.1, library unit 10.1, loop statement 5.5, package 7, package body 7.1, package declaration 7.1, parameter specification 6.1, private type declaration 7.4, record representation clause 13.4, record type 3.7, renaming declaration 8.5, standard package 8.6, subprogram body 6.3, subprogram declaration 6.1, subunit 10.2, task body 9.1, task declaration 9.1, task unit 9

8.2 Scope of Declarations

1   For each form of declaration, the language rules define a certain portion of the program text called the *scope* of the declaration. The scope of a declaration is also called the scope of any entity declared by the declaration. Furthermore, if the declaration associates some notation with a declared entity, this portion of the text is also called the scope of this notation (either an identifier, a character literal, an operator symbol, or the notation for a basic operation). Within the scope of an entity, and only there, there are places where it is legal to use the associated notation in order to refer to the declared entity. These places are defined by the rules of visibility and overloading.

2   The scope of a declaration that occurs immediately within a declarative region extends from the beginning of the declaration to the end of the declarative region; this part of the scope of a declaration is called the *immediate scope*. Furthermore, for any of the declarations listed below, the scope of the declaration extends beyond the immediate scope:

3   (a) A declaration that occurs immediately within the visible part of a package declaration.

4   (b) An entry declaration.

5   (c) A component declaration.

6   (d) A discriminant specification.

7   (e) A parameter specification.

8   (f) A generic parameter declaration.

In each of these cases, the given declaration occurs Immediately within some enclosing declaration, and the scope of the given declaration extends to the end of the scope of the enclosing declaration.

In the absence of a subprogram declaration, the subprogram specification given in the subprogram body or in the body stub acts as the declaration and rule (e) applies also in such a case.

Note:

The above scope rules apply to all forms of declaration defined by section 3.1; in particular, they apply also to implicit declarations. Rule (a) applies to a package declaration and thus not to the package specification of a generic declaration. For nested declarations, the rules (a) through (f) apply at each level. For example, if a task unit is declared in the visible part of a package, the scope of an entry of the task unit extends to the end of the scope of the task unit, that is, to the end of the scope of the enclosing package. The scope of a use clause is defined in section 8.4.

References: basic operation 3.3.3, body stub 10.2, character literal 2.5, component declaration 3.7, declaration 3.1, declarative region 8.1, discriminant specification 3.7.1, entry declaration 9.5, extends 8.1, generic declaration 12.1, generic parameter declaration 12.1, identifier 2.3, implicit declaration 3.1, occur immediately within 8.1, operator symbol 6.1, overloading 6.6 8.7, package declaration 7.1, package specification 7.1, parameter specification 6.1, record type 3.7, renaming declaration 8.5, subprogram body 6.3, subprogram declaration 6.1, task declaration 9.1, task unit 9, type declaration 3.3.1, use clause 8.4, visibility 8.3, visible part 7.2

8.3 Visibility

The meaning of the occurrence of an identifier at a given place in the text is defined by the visibility rules and also, in the case of overloaded declarations, by the overloading rules. The identifiers considered in this chapter include any identifier other than a reserved word, an attribute designator, a pragma identifier, the identifier of a pragma argument, or an identifier given as a pragma argument. The places considered in this chapter are those where a lexical element (such as an identifier) occurs. The overloaded declarations considered in this chapter are those for subprograms, enumeration literals, and single entries.

For each identifier and at each place in the text, the visibility rules determine a set of declarations (with this identifier) that define possible meanings of an occurrence of the identifier. A declaration is said to be *visible* at a given place in the text when, according to the visibility rules, the declaration defines a possible meaning of this occurrence. Two cases arise.

- The visibility rules determine *at most one* possible meaning. In such a case the visibility rules are sufficient to determine the declaration defining the meaning of the occurrence of the identifier, or in the absence of such a declaration, to determine that the occurrence is not legal at the given point.

- The visibility rules determine *more than one* possible meaning. In such a case the occurrence of the identifier is legal at this point if and only if *exactly one* visible declaration is acceptable for the overloading rules in the given context (see section 6.6 for the rules of overloading and section 8.7 for the context used for overload resolution).

5   A declaration is only visible within a certain part of its scope; this part starts at the end of the declaration except in a package specification, in which case it starts at the reserved word is given after the identifier of the package specification. (This rule applies, in particular, for implicit declarations.)

6   Visibility is either by selection or direct. A declaration is visible *by selection* at places that are defined as follows.

7   (a) For a declaration given in the visible part of a package declaration: at the place of the selector after the dot of an expanded name whose prefix denotes the package.

8   (b) For an entry declaration of a given task type: at the place of the selector after the dot of a selected component whose prefix is appropriate for the task type.

9   (c) For a component declaration of a given record type declaration: at the place of the selector after the dot of a selected component whose prefix is appropriate for the type; also at the place of a component simple name (before the compound delimiter =>) in a named component association of an aggregate of the type.

10   (d) For a discriminant specification of a given type declaration: at the same places as for a component declaration; also at the place of a discriminant simple name (before the compound delimiter =>) in a named discriminant association of a discriminant constraint for the type.

11   (e) For a parameter specification of a given subprogram specification or entry declaration: at the place of the formal parameter (before the compound delimiter =>) in a named parameter association of a corresponding subprogram or entry call.

12   (f) For a generic parameter declaration of a given generic unit: at the place of the generic formal parameter (before the compound delimiter =>) in a named generic association of a corresponding generic instantiation.

13   Finally, within the declarative region associated with a construct other than a record type declaration, any declaration that occurs immediately within the region is visible by selection at the place of the selector after the dot of an expanded name whose prefix denotes the construct.

14   Where it is not visible by selection, a visible declaration is said to be *directly visible*. A declaration is directly visible within a certain part of its immediate scope; this part extends to the end of the immediate scope of the declaration, but excludes places where the declaration is hidden as explained below. In addition, a declaration occurring immediately within the visible part of a package can be made directly visible by means of a use clause according to the rules described in section 8.4. (See also section 8.6 for the visibility of library units.)

15   A declaration is said to be *hidden* within (part of) an inner declarative region if the inner region contains a homograph of this declaration; the outer declaration is then hidden within the immediate scope of the inner homograph. Each of two declarations is said to be a *homograph* of the other if both declarations have the same identifier and overloading is allowed for at most one of the two. If overloading is allowed for both declarations, then each of the two is a homograph of the other if they have the same identifier, operator symbol, or character literal, as well as the same parameter and result type profile (see 6.6).

16   Within the specification of a subprogram, every declaration with the same designator as the subprogram is hidden; the same holds within a generic instantiation that declares a subprogram, and within an entry declaration or the formal part of an accept statement; where hidden in this manner, a declaration is visible neither by selection   nor directly.

Two declarations that occur immediately within the same declarative region must not be 17
homographs, unless either or both of the following requirements are met: (a) exactly one of them
is the implicit declaration of a predefined operation; (b) exactly one of them is the implicit declaration of a derived subprogram. In such cases, a predefined operation is always hidden by the other
homograph; a derived subprogram hides a predefined operation, but is hidden by any other
homograph. Where hidden in this manner, an implicit declaration is hidden within the entire scope
of the other declaration (regardless of which declaration occurs first); the implicit declaration is
visible neither by selection nor directly.

Whenever a declaration with a certain identifier is visible from a given point, the identifier and the 18
declared entity (if any) are also said to be visible from that point. Direct visibility and visibility by
selection are likewise defined for character literals and operator symbols. An operator is directly
visible if and only if the corresponding operator declaration is directly visible. Finally, the notation
associated with a basic operation is directly visible within the entire scope of this operation.

Example: 19

```
procedure P is
   A, B : BOOLEAN;

   procedure Q is
      C  : BOOLEAN;
      B  : BOOLEAN;   --   an inner homograph of B
   begin
      ...
      B  := A;    --    means Q.B  := P.A;
      C  := P.B;  --    means Q.C  := P.B;
   end;
begin
   ...
   A := B; --   means P.A := P.B;
end;
```

Note on the visibility of library units:

The visibility of library units is determined by with clauses (see 10.1.1) and by the fact that library 20
units are implicitly declared in the package STANDARD (see 8.6).

Note on homographs:

The same identifier may occur in different declarations and may thus be associated with different 21
entities, even if the scopes of these declarations overlap. Overlap of the scopes of declarations
with the same identifier can result from overloading of subprograms and of enumeration literals.
Such overlaps can also occur for entities declared in package visible parts and for entries, record
components, and parameters, where there is overlap of the scopes of the enclosing package
declarations, task declarations, record type declarations, subprogram declarations, renaming
declarations, or generic declarations. Finally overlapping scopes can result from nesting.

Note on immediate scope, hiding, and visibility:

The rules defining immediate scope, hiding, and visibility imply that a reference to an identifier 22
within its own declaration is illegal (except for packages and generic packages). The identifier
hides outer homographs within its immediate scope, that is, from the start of the declaration; on
the other hand, the identifier is visible only after the end of the declaration. For this reason, all but
the last of the following declarations are illegal:

```
K : INTEGER := K * K;               -- illegal
T : T;                              -- illegal
procedure P(X : P);                 -- illegal
procedure Q(X : REAL := Q);         -- illegal, even if there is a function named Q
procedure R(R : REAL);    --  an inner declaration is legal (although confusing)
```

23   *References:* accept statement 9.5, aggregate 4.3, appropriate for a type 4.1, argument 2.8, basic operation 3.3.3, character literal 2.5, component association 4.3, component declaration 3.7, compound delimiter 2.2, declaration 3.1, declarative region 8.1, designate 3.8, discriminant constraint 3.7.2, discriminant specification 3.7.1, entry call 9.5, entry declaration 9.5, entry family 9.5, enumeration literal specification 3.5.1, expanded name 4.1.3, extends 8.1, formal parameter 6.1, generic association 12.3, generic formal parameter 12.1, generic instantiation 12.3, generic package 12.1, generic parameter declaration 12.1, generic unit 12, identifier 2.3, immediate scope 8.2, implicit declaration 3.1, lexical element 2.2, library unit 10.1, object 3.2, occur immediately within 8.1, operator 4.5, operator symbol 6.1, overloading 6.6 8.7, package 7, parameter 6.2, parameter association 6.4, parameter specification 6.1, pragma 2.8, program unit 6, record type 3.7, reserved word 2.9, scope 8.2, selected component 4.1.3, selector 4.1.3, simple name 4.1, subprogram 6, subprogram call 6.4, subprogram declaration 6.1, subprogram specification 6.1, task type 9.1, task unit 9, type 3.3, type declaration 3.3.1, use clause 8.4, visible part 7.2

8.4 Use Clauses

1   A use clause achieves direct visibility of declarations that appear in the visible parts of named packages.

2   use_clause ::= **use** *package*_name {, *package*_name};

3   For each use clause, there is a certain region of text called the *scope* of the use clause. This region starts immediately after the use clause. If a use clause is a declarative item of some declarative region, the scope of the clause extends to the end of the declarative region. If a use clause occurs within a context clause of a compilation unit, the scope of the use clause extends to the end of the declarative region associated with the compilation unit.

4   In order to define which declarations are made directly visible at a given place by use clauses, consider the set of packages named by all use clauses whose scopes enclose this place, omitting from this set any packages that enclose this place. A declaration that can be made directly visible by a use clause (a potentially visible declaration) is any declaration that occurs immediately within the visible part of a package of the set. A potentially visible declaration is actually made directly visible except in the following two cases:

5   • A potentially visible declaration is not made directly visible if the place considered is within the immediate scope of a homograph of the declaration.

6   • Potentially visible declarations that have the same identifier are not made directly visible unless each of them is either an enumeration literal specification or the declaration of a subprogram (by a subprogram declaration, a renaming declaration, a generic instantiation, or an implicit declaration).

7   The elaboration of a use clause has no other effect.

Note:

8   The above rules guarantee that a declaration that is made directly visible by a use clause cannot hide an otherwise directly visible declaration. The above rules are formulated in terms of the set of packages named by use clauses.

Consequently, the following lines of text all have the same effect (assuming only one package P).   9

```
use P;
use P; use P, P;
```

Example of conflicting names in two packages: 10

```
procedure R is
  package TRAFFIC is
    type COLOR is (RED, AMBER, GREEN);
    ...
  end TRAFFIC;

  package WATER_COLORS is
    type COLOR is (WHITE, RED, YELLOW, GREEN, BLUE, BROWN, BLACK);
    ...
  end WATER_COLORS;

  use TRAFFIC;          --  COLOR, RED, AMBER, and GREEN are directly visible
  use WATER_COLORS;     --  two homographs of GREEN are directly visible
                        --  but COLOR is no longer directly visible

  subtype LIGHT  is TRAFFIC.COLOR;         -- Subtypes are used to resolve
  subtype SHADE  is WATER_COLORS.COLOR;    -- the conflicting type name COLOR

  SIGNAL : LIGHT;
  PAINT  : SHADE;
begin
  SIGNAL := GREEN;     --  that of TRAFFIC
  PAINT  := GREEN;     --  that of WATER_COLORS
end R;
```

Example of name identification with a use clause: 11

```
package D is
  T, U, V : BOOLEAN;
end D;

procedure P is
  package E is
    B, W, V : INTEGER;
  end E;

  procedure Q is
    T, X : REAL;
    use D, E;
  begin
    --    the name T    means Q.T, not D.T
    --    the name U    means D.U
    --    the name B    means E.B
    --    the name W    means E.W
    --    the name X    means Q.X
    --    the name V    is illegal : either D.V or E.V must be used
    ...
  end Q;
begin
  ...
end P;
```

12   *References:* compilation unit 10.1, context clause 10.1, declaration 3.1, declarative item 3.9, declarative region 8.1, direct visibility 8.3, elaboration 3.1 3.9, elaboration has no other effect 3.1, enumeration literal specification 3.5.1, extends 8.1, hiding 8.3, homograph 8.3, identifier 2.3, immediate scope 8.2, name 4.1, occur immediately within 8.1, package 7, scope 8.2, subprogram declaration 6.1, visible part 7.2

8.5 Renaming Declarations

1   A renaming declaration declares another name for an entity.

2
```
renaming_declaration ::=
     identifier : type_mark         renames object_name;
   | identifier : exception         renames exception_name;
   | package identifier             renames package_name;
   | subprogram_specification       renames subprogram_or_entry_name;
```

3   The elaboration of a renaming declaration evaluates the name that follows the reserved word **renames** and thereby determines the entity denoted by this name (the renamed entity). At any point where a renaming declaration is visible, the identifier, or operator symbol of this declaration denotes the renamed entity.

4   The first form of renaming declaration is used for the renaming of objects. The renamed entity must be an object of the base type of the type mark. The properties of the renamed object are not affected by the renaming declaration. In particular, its value and whether or not it is a constant are unaffected; similarly, the constraints that apply to an object are not affected by renaming (any constraint implied by the type mark of the renaming declaration is ignored). The renaming declaration is legal only if exactly one object has this type and can be denoted by the object name.

5   The following restrictions apply to the renaming of a subcomponent that depends on discriminants of a variable. The renaming is not allowed if the subtype of the variable, as defined in a corresponding object declaration, component declaration, or component subtype indication, is an unconstrained type; or if the variable is a generic formal object (of mode **in out**). Similarly if the variable is a formal parameter, the renaming is not allowed if the type mark given in the parameter specification denotes an unconstrained type whose discriminants have default expressions.

6   The second form of renaming declaration is used for the renaming of exceptions; the third form, for the renaming of packages.

7   The last form of renaming declaration is used for the renaming of subprograms and entries. The renamed subprogram or entry and the subprogram specification given in the renaming declaration must have the same parameter and result type profile (see 6.6). The renaming declaration is legal only if exactly one visible subprogram or entry satisfies the above requirements and can be denoted by the given subprogram or entry name. In addition, parameter modes must be identical for formal parameters that are at the same parameter position.

8   The subtypes of the parameters and result (if any) of a renamed subprogram or entry are not affected by renaming. These subtypes are those given in the original subprogram declaration, generic instantiation, or entry declaration (not those of the renaming declaration); even for calls that use the new name. On the other hand, a renaming declaration can introduce parameter names and default expressions that differ from those of the renamed subprogram; named associations of calls with the new subprogram name must use the new parameter name; calls with the old subprogram name must use the old parameter names.

A procedure can only be renamed as a procedure. Either of a function or operator can be renamed   9
as either of a function or operator; for renaming as an operator, the subprogram specification given
in the renaming declaration is subject to the rules given in section 6.7 for operator declarations.
Enumeration literals can be renamed as functions; similarly, attributes defined as functions (such
as SUCC and PRED) can be renamed as functions. An entry can only be renamed as a procedure;
the new name is only allowed to appear in contexts that allow a procedure name. An entry of a
family can be renamed, but an entry family cannot be renamed as a whole.

Examples: 10

```
declare
  L : PERSON renames LEFTMOST_PERSON;  -- see 3.8.1
begin
  L.AGE := L.AGE + 1;
end;

FULL : exception renames TABLE_MANAGER.TABLE_FULL; -- see 7.5

package TM renames TABLE_MANAGER;

function REAL_PLUS(LEFT, RIGHT : REAL    ) return REAL     renames "+";
function INT_PLUS  (LEFT, RIGHT : INTEGER) return INTEGER  renames "+";

function ROUGE  return COLOR renames RED;  --   see 3.5.1
function ROT    return COLOR renames RED;
function ROSSO  return COLOR renames ROUGE;

function NEXT(X : COLOR) return COLOR renames COLOR'SUCC; -- see 3.5.5
```

Example of a renaming declaration with new parameter names: 11

```
function "*" (X,Y : VECTOR) return REAL renames DOT_PRODUCT; -- see 6.1
```

Example of a renaming declaration with a new default expression: 12

```
function MINIMUM(L : LINK := HEAD) return CELL renames MIN_CELL; -- see 6.1
```

Notes:

Renaming may be used to resolve name conflicts and to act as a shorthand. Renaming with a dif-   13
ferent identifier or operator symbol does not hide the old name; the new name and the old name
need not be visible at the same points. The attributes POS and VAL cannot be renamed since the
corresponding specifications cannot be written; the same holds for the predefined multiplying
operators with a *universal_fixed* result.

Calls with the new name of a renamed entry are procedure call statements and are not allowed at   14
places where the syntax requires an entry call statement in conditional and timed entry calls;
similarly, the COUNT attribute is not available for the new name.

A task object that is declared by an object declaration can be renamed as an object. However, a   15
single task cannot be renamed since the corresponding task type is anonymous. For similar
reasons, an object of an anonymous array type cannot be renamed. No syntactic form exists for
renaming a generic unit.

A subtype can be used to achieve the effect of renaming a type (including a task type) as in   16

```
subtype MODE is TEXT_IO.FILE_MODE ;
```

17 *References:* allow 1.6, attribute 4.1.4, base type 3.3, conditional entry call 9.7.2, constant 3.2.1, constrained subtype 3.3, constraint 3.3, declaration 3.1, default expression 6.1, depend on a discriminant 3.7.1, discriminant 3.7.1, elaboration 3.1 3.9, entry 9.5, entry call 9.5, entry call statement 9.5, entry declaration 9.5, entry family 9.5, enumeration literal 3.5.1, evaluation of a name 4.1, exception 11, formal parameter 6.1, function 6.5, identifier 2.3, legal 1.6, mode 6.1, name 4.1, object 3.2, object declaration 3.2, operator 6.7, operator declaration 6.7, operator symbol 6.1, package 7, parameter 6.2, parameter specification 6.1, procedure 6.1, procedure call statement 6.4, reserved word 2.9, subcomponent 3.3, subprogram 6, subprogram call 6.4, subprogram declaration 6.1, subprogram specification 6.1, subtype 3.3.2, task object 9.2, timed entry call 9.7.3, type 3.3, type mark 3.3.2, variable 3.2.1, visibility 8.3

8.6 The Package Standard

1 The predefined types (for example the types BOOLEAN, CHARACTER and INTEGER) are the types that are declared in a predefined package called STANDARD; this package also includes the declarations of their predefined operations. The package STANDARD is described in Annex C. Apart from the predefined numeric types, the specification of the package STANDARD must be the same for all implementations of the language.

2 The package STANDARD forms a declarative region which encloses every library unit and consequently the main program; the declaration of every library unit is assumed to occur immediately within this package. The implicit declarations of library units are assumed to be ordered in such a way that the scope of a given library unit includes any compilation unit that mentions the given library unit in a with clause. However, the only library units that are visible within a given compilation unit are as follows: they include the library units named by all with clauses that apply to the given unit, and moreover, if the given unit is a secondary unit of some library unit, they include this library unit.

Notes:

3 If all block statements of a program are named, then the name of each program unit can always be written as an expanded name starting with STANDARD (unless this package is itself hidden).

4 If a type is declared in the visible part of a library package, then it is a consequence of the visibility rules that a basic operation (such as assignment) for this type is directly visible at places where the type itself is not visible (whether by selection or directly). However this operation can only be applied to operands that are visible and the declaration of these operands requires the visibility of either the type or one of its subtypes.

5 *References:* applicable with clause 10.1.1, block name 5.6, block statement 5.6, declaration 3.1, declarative region 8.1, expanded name 4.1.3, hiding 8.3, identifier 2.3, implicit declaration 3.1, library unit 10.1, loop statement 5.5, main program 10.1, must 1.6, name 4.1, occur immediately within 8.1, operator 6.7, package 7, program unit 6, secondary unit 10.1, subtype 3.3, type 3.3, visibility 8.3, with clause 10.1.1

8.7 The Context of Overload Resolution

1 Overloading is defined for subprograms, enumeration literals, operators, and single entries, and also for the operations that are inherent in several basic operations such as assignment, membership tests, allocators, the literal **null**, aggregates, and string literals.

For overloaded entities, overload resolution determines the actual meaning that an occurrence of   2
an identifier has, whenever the visibility rules have determined that more than one meaning is
acceptable at the place of this occurrence; overload resolution likewise determines the actual
meaning of an occurrence of an operator or some basic operation.

At such a place all visible declarations are considered. The occurrence is only legal if there is   3
exactly one interpretation of each constituent of the innermost complete context; a *complete context* is one of the following:

- A declaration.   4

- A statement.   5

- A representation clause.   6

When considering possible interpretations of a complete context, the only rules considered are the   7
syntax rules, the scope and visibility rules, and the rules of the form described below.

(a) Any rule that requires a name or expression to have a certain type, or to have the same type as   8
     another name or expression.

(b) Any rule that requires the type of a name or expression to be a type of a certain class; similar-   9
     ly, any rule that requires a certain type to be a discrete, integer, real, universal, character,
     boolean, or nonlimited type.

(c) Any rule that requires a prefix to be appropriate for a certain type.   10

(d) Any rule that specifies a certain type as the result type of a basic operation, and any rule that   11
     specifies that this type is of a certain class.

(e) The rules that require the type of an aggregate or string literal to be determinable solely from   12
     the enclosing complete context (see 4.3 and 4.2). Similarly, the rules that require the type of
     the prefix of an attribute, the type of the expression of a case statement, or the type of the
     operand of a type conversion, to be determinable independently of the context (see 4.1.4, 5.4,
     4.6, and 6.4.1).

(f) The rules given in section 6.6, for the resolution of overloaded subprogram calls; in section   13
     4.6, for the implicit conversions of universal expressions; in section 3.6.1, for the interpreta-
     tion of discrete ranges with bounds having a universal type; and in section 4.1.3, for the
     interpretation of an expanded name whose prefix denotes a subprogram or an accept state-
     ment.

Subprogram names used as pragma arguments follow a different rule: the pragma can apply to   14
several overloaded subprograms, as explained in section 6.3.2 for the pragma INLINE, in section
11.7 for the pragma SUPPRESS, and in section 13.9 for the pragma INTERFACE.

Similarly, the simple names given in context clauses (see 10.1.1) and in address clauses (see 13.5)   15
follow different rules.

Notes:

16   If there is only one possible interpretation, the identifier denotes the corresponding entity. However, this does not mean that the occurrence is necessarily legal since other requirements exist which are not considered for overload resolution; for example, the fact that an expression is static, the parameter modes, whether an object is constant, conformance rules, forcing occurrences for a representation clause, order of elaboration, and so on.

17   Similarly, subtypes are not considered for overload resolution (the violation of a constraint does not make a program illegal but raises an exception during program execution).

18   A loop parameter specification is a declaration, and hence a complete context.

19   Rules that require certain constructs to have the same parameter and result type profile fall under the category (a); the same holds for rules that require conformance of two constructs since conformance requires that corresponding names be given the same meaning by the visibility and overloading rules.

20   *References:* aggregate 4.3, allocator 4.8, assignment 5.2, basic operation 3.3.3, case statement 5.4, class of type 3.3, declaration 3.1, entry 9.5, enumeration literal 3.5.1, exception 11, expression 4.4, formal part 6.1, identifier 2.3, legal 1.6, literal 4.2, loop parameter specification 5.5, membership test 4.5.2, name 4.1, null literal 3.8, operation 3.3.3, operator 4.5, overloading 6.6, pragma 2.8, representation clause 13.1, statement 5, static expression 4.9, static subtype 4.9, subprogram 6, subtype 3.3, type conversion 4.6, visibility 8.3

21   *Rules of the form (a):* address clause 13.5, assignment 5.2, choice 3.7.3 4.3.2 5.4, component association 4.3.1 4.3.2, conformance rules 9.5, default expression 3.7 3.7.1 6.1 12.1.1, delay statement 9.6, discrete range 3.6.1 5.5 9.5, discriminant constraint 3.7.2, enumeration representation clause 13.3, generic parameter association 12.3.1, index constraint 3.6.1, index expression 4.1.1 4.1.2 9.5, initial value 3.2.1, membership test 4.5.2, parameter association 6.4.1, parameter and result type profile 8.5 12.3.6, qualified expression 4.7, range constraint 3.5, renaming of an object 8.5, result expression 5.8

22   *Rules of the form (b):* abort statement 9.10, assignment 5.2, case expression 5.4, condition 5.3 5.5 5.7 9.7.1, discrete range 3.6.1 5.5 9.5, fixed point type declaration 3.5.9, floating point type declaration 3.5.7, integer type declaration 3.5.4, length clause 13.2, membership test 4.4, number declaration 3.2.2, record representation clause 13.4, selected component 4.1.3, short-circuit control form 4.4, val attribute 3.5.5

23   *Rules of the form (c):* indexed component 4.1.1, selected component 4.1.3, slice 4.1.2

24   *Rules of the form (d):* aggregate 4.3, allocator 4.8, membership test 4.4, null literal 4.2, numeric literal 2.4, short-circuit control form 4.4, string literal 4.2

9. Tasks

The execution of a program that does not contain a task is defined in terms of a sequential execution of its actions, according to the rules described in other chapters of this manual. These actions can be considered to be executed by a single *logical processor*.

Tasks are entities whose executions proceed *in parallel* in the following sense. Each task can be considered to be executed by a logical processor of its own. Different tasks (different logical processors) proceed independently, except at points where they synchronize.

Some tasks have *entries*. An entry of a task can be *called* by other tasks. A task *accepts* a call of one of its entries by executing an accept statement for the entry. Synchronization is achieved by *rendezvous* between a task issuing an entry call and a task accepting the call. Some entries have parameters; entry calls and accept statements for such entries are the principal means of communicating values between tasks.

The properties of each task are defined by a corresponding *task unit* which consists of a *task specification* and a *task body*. Task units are one of the four forms of program unit of which programs can be composed. The other forms are subprograms, packages and generic units. The properties of task units, tasks, and entries, and the statements that affect the interaction between tasks (that is, entry call statements, accept statements, delay statements, select statements, and abort statements) are described in this chapter.

Note:

Parallel tasks (parallel logical processors) may be implemented on multicomputers, multiprocessors, or with interleaved execution on a single *physical processor*. On the other hand, whenever an implementation can detect that the same effect can be guaranteed if parts of the actions of a given task are executed by different physical processors acting in parallel, it may choose to execute them in this way; in such a case, several physical processors implement a single logical processor.

References: abort statement 9.10, accept statement 9.5, delay statement 9.6, entry 9.5, entry call statement 9.5, generic unit 12, package 7, parameter in an entry call 9.5, program unit 6, rendezvous 9.5, select statement 9.7, subprogram 6, task body 9.1, task specification 9.1

9.1 Task Specifications and Task Bodies

A task unit consists of a task specification and a task body. A task specification that starts with the reserved words **task type** declares a task type. The value of an object of a task type designates a task having the entries, if any, that are declared in the task specification; these entries are also called entries of this object. The execution of the task is defined by the corresponding task body.

2   A task specification without the reserved word **type** defines a *single task*. A task declaration with this form of specification is equivalent to the declaration of an anonymous task type immediately followed by the declaration of an object of the task type, and the task unit identifier names the object. In the remainder of this chapter, explanations are given in terms of task type declarations; the corresponding explanations for single task declarations follow from the stated equivalence.

3   task_declaration ::= task_specification;

        task_specification ::=
            task [**type**] identifier [**is**
                {entry_declaration}
                {representation_clause}
            end [*task*_simple_name]]

        task_body ::=
            task body *task*_simple_name **is**
                [declarative_part]
            begin
                    sequence_of_statements
        [**exception**
                    exception_handler
                { exception_handler}]
            end [*task*_simple_name];

4   The simple name at the start of a task body must repeat the task unit identifier. Similarly if a simple name appears at the end of the task specification or body, it must repeat the task unit identifier. Within a task body, the name of the corresponding task unit can also be used to refer to the task object that designates the task currently executing the body; furthermore, the use of this name as a type mark is not allowed within the task unit itself.

5   For the elaboration of a task specification, entry declarations and representation clauses, if any, are elaborated in the order given. Such representation clauses only apply to the entries declared in the task specification (see 13.5).

6   The elaboration of a task body has no other effect than to establish that the body can from then on be used for the execution of tasks designated by objects of the corresponding task type.

7   The execution of a task body is invoked by the activation of a task object of the corresponding type (see 9.3). The optional exception handlers at the end of a task body handle exceptions raised during the execution of the sequence of statements of the task body (see 11.4).

8   *Examples of specifications of task types:*

        task type RESOURCE **is**
            entry SEIZE;
            entry RELEASE;
        end RESOURCE;

        task type KEYBOARD_DRIVER **is**
            entry READ (C : **out** CHARACTER);
            entry WRITE (C : **in** CHARACTER);
        end KEYBOARD_DRIVER;

9.1 Task Specifications and Task Bodies   9-2

Examples of specifications of single tasks: 9

```
task PRODUCER_CONSUMER is
   entry READ (V : out ITEM);
   entry WRITE(E : in   ITEM);
end;

task CONTROLLER is
   entry REQUEST(LEVEL)(D : ITEM);   --  a family of entries
end CONTROLLER;

task USER;   --  has no entries
```

Example of task specification and corresponding body: 10

```
task PROTECTED_ARRAY is
   --  INDEX and ITEM are global types
   entry READ (N : in INDEX; V : out ITEM);
   entry WRITE (N : in INDEX; E : in   ITEM);
end;

task body PROTECTED_ARRAY is
   TABLE : array(INDEX) of ITEM := (INDEX => NULL_ITEM);
begin
   loop
      select
         accept READ (N : in INDEX; V : out  ITEM) do
            V := TABLE(N);
         end READ;
      or
         accept WRITE(N : In INDEX; E : in    ITEM) do
            TABLE(N) := E;
         end WRITE;
      end select;
   end loop;
end PROTECTED_ARRAY;
```

Note:

A task specification specifies the interface of tasks of the task type with other tasks of the same or   11
of different types, and also with the main program.

References: declaration 3.1, declarative part 3.9, elaboration 3.9, entry 9.5, entry declaration 9.5, exception handler   12
11.2, identifier 2.3, main program 10.1, object 3.2, object declaration 3.2.1, representation clause 13.1, reserved
word 2.9, sequence of statements 5.1, simple name 4.1, type 3.3, type declaration 3.3.1

9.2 Task Types and Task Objects

A task type is a limited type (see 7.4.4). Hence neither assignment nor the predefined comparison   1
for equality and inequality are defined for objects of task types; moreover, the mode **out** is not
allowed for a formal parameter whose type is a task type.

2   A task object is an object whose type is a task type. The value of a task object designates a task that has the entries of the corresponding task type, and whose execution is specified by the corresponding task body. If a task object is the object, or a subcomponent of the object, declared by an object declaration, then the value of the task object is defined by the elaboration of the object declaration. If a task object is the object, or a subcomponent of the object, created by the evaluation of an allocator, then the value of the task object is defined by the evaluation of the allocator. For all parameter modes, if an actual parameter designates a task, the associated formal parameter designates the same task; the same holds for a subcomponent of an actual parameter and the corresponding subcomponent of the associated formal parameter; finally, the same holds for generic parameters.

3   *Examples:*

```
CONTROL  : RESOURCE;
TELETYPE : KEYBOARD_DRIVER;
POOL     : array(1 .. 10) of KEYBOARD_DRIVER;
--  see also examples of declarations of single tasks in 9.1
```

4   *Example of access type designating task objects:*

```
type KEYBOARD is access KEYBOARD_DRIVER;

TERMINAL : KEYBOARD := new KEYBOARD_DRIVER;
```

Notes:

5   Since a task type is a limited type, it can appear as the definition of a limited private type in a private part, and as a generic actual parameter associated with a formal parameter whose type is a limited type. On the other hand, the type of a generic formal parameter of mode **in** must not be a limited type and hence cannot be a task type.

6   Task objects behave as constants (a task object always designates the same task) since their values are implicitly defined either at declaration or allocation, or by a parameter association, and since no assignment is available. However the reserved word **constant** is not allowed in the declaration of a task object since this would require an explicit initialization. A task object that is a formal parameter of mode **in** is a constant (as is any formal parameter of this mode).

7   If an application needs to store and exchange task identities, it can do so by defining an access type designating the corresponding task objects and by using access values for identification purposes (see above example). Assignment is available for such an access type as for any access type.

8   Subtype declarations are allowed for task types as for other types, but there are no constraints applicable to task types.

9   *References:* access type 3.8, actual parameter 6.4.1, allocator 4.8, assignment 5.2, component declaration 3.7, composite type 3.3, constant 3.2.1, constant declaration 3.2.1, constraint 3.3, designate 3.8 9.1, elaboration 3.9, entry 9.5, equality operator 4.5.2, formal parameter 6.2, formal parameter mode 6.2, generic actual parameter 12.3, generic association 12.3, generic formal parameter 12.1, generic formal parameter mode 12.1.1, generic unit 12, inequality operator 4.5.2, initialization 3.2.1, limited type 7.4.4, object 3.2, object declaration 3.2.1, parameter association 6.4, private part 7.2, private type 7.4, reserved word 2.9, subcomponent 3.3, subprogram 6, subtype declaration 3.3.2, task body 9.1, type 3.3

9.3 Task Execution - Task Activation

A task body defines the execution of any task that is designated by a task object of the cor-   1
responding task type. The initial part of this execution is called the *activation* of the task object,
and also that of the designated task; it consists of the elaboration of the declarative part, if any, of
the task body. The execution of different tasks, in particular their activation, proceeds in parallel.

If an object declaration that declares a task object occurs immediately within a declarative part,   2
then the activation of the task object starts after the elaboration of the declarative part (that is,
after passing the reserved word **begin** following the declarative part); similarly if such a declaration occurs immediately within a package specification, the activation starts after the elaboration
of the declarative part of the package body. The same holds for the activation of a task object that
is a subcomponent of an object declared immediately within a declarative part or package
specification. The first statement following the declarative part is executed only after conclusion of
the activation of these task objects.

Should an exception be raised by the activation of one of these tasks, that task becomes a com-   3
pleted task (see 9.4); other tasks are not directly affected. Should one of these tasks thus become
completed during its activation, the exception TASKING_ERROR is raised upon conclusion of the
activation of all of these tasks (whether successfully or not); the exception is raised at a place that
is immediately before the first statement following the declarative part (immediately after the
reserved word **begin**). Should several of these tasks thus become completed during their activation, the exception TASKING_ERROR is raised only once.

Should an exception be raised by the elaboration of a declarative part or package specification,   4
then any task that is created (directly or indirectly) by this elaboration and that is not yet activated
becomes terminated and is therefore never activated (see section 9.4 for the definition of a terminated task).

For the above rules, in any package body without statements, a null statement is assumed. For any   5
package without a package body, an implicit package body containing a single null statement is
assumed. If a package without a package body is declared immediately within some program unit
or block statement, the implicit package body occurs at the end of the declarative part of the
program unit or block statement; if there are several such packages, the order of the implicit
package bodies is undefined.

A task object that is the object, or a subcomponent of the object, created by the evaluation of an   6
allocator is activated by this evaluation. The activation starts after any initialization for the object
created by the allocator; if several subcomponents are task objects, they are activated in parallel.
The access value designating such an object is returned by the allocator only after the conclusion
of these activations.

Should an exception be raised by the activation of one of these tasks, that task becomes a com-   7
pleted task; other tasks are not directly affected. Should one of these tasks thus become completed during its activation, the exception TASKING_ERROR is raised upon conclusion of the
activation of all of these tasks (whether successfully or not); the exception is raised at the place
where the allocator is evaluated. Should several of these tasks thus become completed during
their activation, the exception TASKING_ERROR is raised only once.

Should an exception be raised by the initialization of the object created by an allocator (hence   8
before the start of any activation), any task designated by a subcomponent of this object becomes
terminated and is therefore never activated.

9   *Example:*

```
procedure P is
   A, B : RESOURCE;    --  elaborate the task objects A, B
   C    : RESOURCE;    --  elaborate the task object C
begin
   --  the tasks A, B, C are activated in parallel before the first statement
   ...
end;
```

Notes:

10   An entry of a task can be called before the task has been activated. If several tasks are activated in parallel, the execution of any of these tasks need not await the end of the activation of the other tasks. A task may become completed during its activation either because of an exception or because it is aborted (see 9.10).

11   *References:* allocator 4.8, completed task 9.4, declarative part 3.9, elaboration 3.9, entry 9.5, exception 11, handling an exception 11.4, package body 7.1, parallel execution 9, statement 5, subcomponent 3.3, task body 9.1, task object 9.2, task termination 9.4, task type 9.1, tasking_error exception 11.1

9.4 Task Dependence - Termination of Tasks

1   Each task *depends* on at least one master. A *master* is a construct that is either a task, a currently executing block statement or subprogram, or a library package (a package declared within another program unit is not a master). The dependence on a master is a direct dependence in the following two cases:

2   (a) The task designated by a task object that is the object, or a subcomponent of the object, created by the evaluation of an allocator depends on the master that elaborates the corresponding access type definition.

3   (b) The task designated by any other task object depends on the master whose execution creates the task object.

4   Furthermore, if a task depends on a given master that is a block statement executed by another master, then the task depends also on this other master, in an indirect manner; the same holds if the given master is a subprogram called by another master, and if the given master is a task that depends (directly or indirectly) on another master. Dependences exist for objects of a private type whose full declaration is in terms of a task type.

5   A task is said to have *completed* its execution when it has finished the execution of the sequence of statements that appears after the reserved word **begin** in the corresponding body. Similarly a block or a subprogram is said to have completed its execution when it has finished the execution of the corresponding sequence of statements. For a block statement, the execution is also said to be completed when it reaches an exit, return, or goto statement transferring control out of the block. For a procedure, the execution is also said to be completed when a corresponding return statement is reached. For a function, the execution is also said to be completed after the evaluation of the result expression of a return statement. Finally the execution of a task, block statement, or subprogram is completed if an exception is raised by the execution of its sequence of statements and there is no corresponding handler, or, if there is one, when it has finished the execution of the corresponding handler.

If a task has no dependent task, its *termination* takes place when it has completed its execution.   6
After its termination, a task is said to be *terminated*. If a task has dependent tasks, its termination
takes place when the execution of the task is completed and all dependent tasks are terminated. A
block statement or subprogram body whose execution is completed is not left until all of its dependent tasks are terminated.

Termination of a task otherwise takes place if and only if its execution has reached an open ter-   7
minate alternative in a select statement (see 9.7.1), and the following conditions are satisfied:

- The task depends on some master whose execution is completed (hence not a library   8
  package).

- Each task that depends on the master considered is either already terminated or similarly   9
  waiting on an open terminate alternative of a select statement.

When both conditions are satisfied, the task considered becomes terminated, together with all   10
tasks that depend on the master considered.

Example: 11

```
declare
   type GLOBAL is access RESOURCE;          --  see 9.1
   A, B  : RESOURCE;
   G     : GLOBAL;
begin
   --   activation of A and B
   declare
      type LOCAL is access RESOURCE;
      X  : GLOBAL  := new RESOURCE;   --  activation of X.all
      L  : LOCAL   := new RESOURCE;   --  activation of L.all
      C  : RESOURCE;
   begin
      --   activation of C
      G := X;   --  both G and X designate the same task object
      ...
   end;   --   await termination of C and L.all (but not X.all)
   ...
end;   --   await termination of A, B, and G.all
```

Notes:

The rules given for termination imply that all tasks that depend (directly or indirectly) on a given   12
master and that are not already terminated, can be terminated (collectively) if and only if each of
them is waiting on an open terminate alternative of a select statement and the execution of the
given master is completed.

The usual rules apply to the main program. Consequently, termination of the main program awaits   13
termination of any dependent task even if the corresponding task type is declared in a library
package. On the other hand, termination of the main program does not await termination of tasks
that depend on library packages; the language does not define whether such tasks are required to
terminate.

For an access type derived from another access type, the corresponding access type definition is   14
that of the parent type; the dependence is on the master that elaborates the ultimate parent access
type definition.

15   A renaming declaration defines a new name for an existing entity and hence creates no further dependence.

16   *References:* access type 3.8, allocator 4.8, block statement 5.6, declaration 3.1, designate 3.8 9.1, exception 11, exception handler 11.2, exit statement 5.7, function 6.5, goto statement 5.9, library unit 10.1, main program 10.1, object 3.2, open alternative 9.7.1, package 7, program unit 6, renaming declaration 8.5, return statement 5.8, selective wait 9.7.1, sequence of statements 5.1, statement 5, subcomponent 3.3, subprogram body 6.3, subprogram call 6.4, task body 9.1, task object 9.2, terminate alternative 9.7.1

9.5 Entries, Entry Calls, and Accept Statements

1   Entry calls and accept statements are the primary means of synchronization of tasks, and of communicating values between tasks. An entry declaration is similar to a subprogram declaration and is only allowed in a task specification. The actions to be performed when an entry is called are specified by corresponding accept statements.

2
```
entry_declaration ::=
    entry identifier [(discrete_range)] [formal_part];

entry_call_statement ::= entry_name [actual_parameter_part];

accept_statement ::=
    accept entry_simple_name [(entry_index)] [formal_part] [do
        sequence_of_statements
    end [entry_simple_name]];

entry_index ::= expression
```

3   An entry declaration that includes a discrete range (see 3.6.1) declares a *family* of distinct entries having the same formal part (if any); that is, one such entry for each value of the discrete range. The term *single entry* is used in the definition of any rule that applies to any entry other than one of a family. The task designated by an object of a task type has (or owns) the entries declared in the specification of the task type.

4   Within the body of a task, each of its single entries or entry families can be named by the corresponding simple name. The name of an entry of a family takes the form of an indexed component, the family simple name being followed by the index in parentheses; the type of this index must be the same as that of the discrete range in the corresponding entry family declaration. Outside the body of a task an entry name has the form of a selected component, whose prefix denotes the task object, and whose selector is the simple name of one of its single entries or entry families.

5   A single entry overloads a subprogram, an enumeration literal, or another single entry if they have the same identifier. Overloading is not defined for entry families. A single entry or an entry of an entry family can be renamed as a procedure as explained in section 8.5.

6   The parameter modes defined for parameters of the formal part of an entry declaration are the same as for a subprogram declaration and have the same meaning (see 6.2). The syntax of an entry call statement is similar to that of a procedure call statement, and the rules for parameter associations are the same as for subprogram calls (see 6.4.1 and 6.4.2).

An accept statement specifies the actions to be performed at a call of a named entry (it can be an entry of a family). The formal part of an accept statement must conform to the formal part given in the declaration of the single entry or entry family named by the accept statement (see section 6.3.1 for the conformance rules). If a simple name appears at the end of an accept statement, it must repeat that given at the start.

An accept statement for an entry of a given task is only allowed within the corresponding task body; excluding within the body of any program unit that is, itself, inner to the task body; and excluding within another accept statement for either the same single entry or an entry of the same family. (One consequence of this rule is that a task can execute accept statements only for its own entries.) A task body can contain more than one accept statement for the same entry.

For the elaboration of an entry declaration, the discrete range, if any, is evaluated and the formal part, if any, is then elaborated as for a subprogram declaration.

Execution of an accept statement starts with the evaluation of the entry index (in the case of an entry of a family). Execution of an entry call statement starts with the evaluation of the entry name; this is followed by any evaluations required for actual parameters in the same manner as for a sub-program call (see 6.4). Further execution of an accept statement and of a corresponding entry call statement are synchronized.

If a given entry is called by only one task, there are two possibilities:

- If the calling task issues an entry call statement before a corresponding accept statement is reached by the task owning the entry, the execution of the calling task is *suspended*.

- If a task reaches an accept statement prior to any call of that entry, the execution of the task is suspended until such a call is received.

When an entry has been called and a corresponding accept statement has been reached, the sequence of statements, if any, of the accept statement is executed by the called task (while the calling task remains suspended). This interaction is called a *rendezvous*. Thereafter, the calling task and the task owning the entry continue their execution in parallel.

If several tasks call the same entry before a corresponding accept statement is reached, the calls are queued; there is one queue associated with each entry. Each execution of an accept state-ment removes one call from the queue. The calls are processed in the order of arrival.

An attempt to call an entry of a task that has completed its execution raises the exception TASKING_ERROR at the point of the call, in the calling task; similarly, this exception is raised at the point of the call if the called task completes its execution before accepting the call (see also 9.10 for the case when the called task becomes abnormal). The exception CONSTRAINT_ERROR is raised if the index of an entry of a family is not within the specified discrete range.

Examples of entry declarations:

```
entry READ(V : out ITEM);
entry SEIZE;
entry REQUEST(LEVEL)(D : ITEM);   --  a family of entries
```

Examples of entry calls:

```
CONTROL.RELEASE;                      --  see 9.2 and 9.1
PRODUCER_CONSUMER.WRITE(E);           --  see 9.1
POOL(5).READ(NEXT_CHAR);              --  see 9.2 and 9.1
CONTROLLER.REQUEST(LOW)(SOME_ITEM);   --  see 9.1
```

19   *Examples of accept statements:*

      accept SEIZE;

      accept READ(V : **out** ITEM) **do**
        V := LOCAL_ITEM;
      end READ;

      accept REQUEST(LOW)(D : ITEM) **do**
        ...
      end REQUEST;

Notes:

20   The formal part given in an accept statement is not elaborated; it is only used to identify the corresponding entry.

21   An accept statement can call subprograms that issue entry calls. An accept statement need not have a sequence of statements even if the corresponding entry has parameters. Equally, it can have a sequence of statements even if the corresponding entry has no parameters. The sequence of statements of an accept statement can include return statements. A task can call its own entries but it will, of course, deadlock. The language permits conditional and timed entry calls (see 9.7.2 and 9.7.3). The language rules ensure that a task can only be in one entry queue at a given time.

22   If the bounds of the discrete range of an entry family are integer literals, the index (in an entry name or accept statement) must be of the predefined type INTEGER (see 3.6.1).

23   *References:* abnormal task 9.10, actual parameter part 6.4, completed task 9.4, conditional entry call 9.7.2, conformance rules 6.3.1, constraint_error exception 11.1, designate 9.1, discrete range 3.6.1, elaboration 3.1 3.9, enumeration literal 3.5.1, evaluation 4.5, expression 4.4, formal part 6.1, identifier 2.3, indexed component 4.1.1, integer type 3.5.4, name 4.1, object 3.2, overloading 6.6 8.7, parallel execution 9, prefix 4.1, procedure 6, procedure call 6.4, renaming declaration 8.5, return statement 5.8, scope 8.2, selected component 4.1.3, selector 4.1.3, sequence of statements 5.1, simple expression 4.4, simple name 4.1, subprogram 6, subprogram body 6.3, subprogram declaration 6.1, task 9, task body 9.1, task specification 9.1, tasking_error exception 11.1, timed entry call 9.7.3

9.6 Delay Statements, Duration, and Time

1   The execution of a delay statement evaluates the simple expression, and suspends further execution of the task that executes the delay statement, for at least the duration specified by the resulting value.

2   delay_statement ::= **delay** simple_expression;

3   The simple expression must be of the predefined fixed point type DURATION; its value is expressed in seconds; a delay statement with a negative value is equivalent to a delay statement with a zero value.

4   Any implementation of the type DURATION must allow representation of durations (both positive and negative) up to at least 86400 seconds (one day); the smallest representable duration, DURATION'SMALL must not be greater than twenty milliseconds (whenever possible, a value not greater than fifty microseconds should be chosen). Note that DURATION'SMALL need not correspond to the basic clock cycle, the named number SYSTEM.TICK (see 13.7).

The definition of the type TIME is provided in the predefined library package CALENDAR. The 5
function CLOCK returns the current value of TIME at the time it is called. The functions YEAR,
MONTH, DAY and SECONDS return the corresponding values for a given value of the type TIME;
the procedure SPLIT returns all four corresponding values. Conversely, the function TIME_OF
combines a year number, a month number, a day number, and a duration, into a value of type
TIME. The operators "+" and "-" for addition and subtraction of times and durations, and the
relational operators for times, have the conventional meaning.

The exception TIME_ERROR is raised by the function TIME_OF if the actual parameters do not form 6
a proper date. This exception is also raised by the operators "+" and "-" if, for the given operands,
these operators cannot return a date whose year number is in the range of the corresponding subtype, or if the operator "-" cannot return a result that is in the range of the type DURATION.

```ada
package CALENDAR is                                                         7
   type TIME is private;

   subtype YEAR_NUMBER   is INTEGER   range 1901 .. 2099;
   subtype MONTH_NUMBER  is INTEGER   range 1 .. 12;
   subtype DAY_NUMBER    is INTEGER   range 1 .. 31;
   subtype DAY_DURATION  is DURATION  range 0.0 .. 86_400.0;

   function CLOCK return TIME;

   function YEAR    (DATE : TIME) return YEAR_NUMBER;
   function MONTH   (DATE : TIME) return MONTH_NUMBER;
   function DAY     (DATE : TIME) return DAY_NUMBER;
   function SECONDS (DATE : TIME) return DAY_DURATION;

   procedure SPLIT ( DATE     : in  TIME;
                     YEAR     : out YEAR_NUMBER;
                     MONTH    : out MONTH_NUMBER;
                     DAY      : out DAY_NUMBER;
                     SECONDS  : out DAY_DURATION);

   function TIME_OF( YEAR    : YEAR_NUMBER;
                     MONTH   : MONTH_NUMBER;
                     DAY     : DAY_NUMBER;
                     SECONDS : DAY_DURATION := 0.0) return TIME;

   function "+"  (LEFT : TIME;      RIGHT : DURATION)  return TIME;
   function "+"  (LEFT : DURATION;  RIGHT : TIME)      return TIME;
   function "-"  (LEFT : TIME;      RIGHT : DURATION)  return TIME;
   function "-"  (LEFT : TIME;      RIGHT : TIME)      return DURATION;

   function "<"  (LEFT, RIGHT : TIME) return BOOLEAN;
   function "<=" (LEFT, RIGHT : TIME) return BOOLEAN;
   function ">"  (LEFT, RIGHT : TIME) return BOOLEAN;
   function ">=" (LEFT, RIGHT : TIME) return BOOLEAN;

   TIME_ERROR : exception;   --  can be raised by TIME_OF, "+", and "-"

private
   -- implementation-dependent
end;
```

8   *Examples:*

```
delay 3.0;  --  delay 3.0 seconds

declare
  use CALENDAR;
  -  INTERVAL is a global constant of type DURATION
  NEXT_TIME : TIME := CLOCK + INTERVAL;
begin
  loop
    delay NEXT_TIME - CLOCK;
    --  some actions
    NEXT_TIME := NEXT_TIME + INTERVAL;
  end loop;
end;
```

Notes:

9   The second example causes the loop to be repeated every INTERVAL seconds on average. This interval between two successive iterations is only approximate. However, there will be no cumulative drift as long as the duration of each iteration is (sufficiently) less than INTERVAL.

10   *References:* adding operator 4.5, duration C, fixed point type 3.5.9, function call 6.4, library unit 10.1, operator 4.5, package 7, private type 7.4, relational operator 4.5, simple expression 4.4, statement 5, task 9, type 3.3

9.7 Select Statements

1   There are three forms of select statements. One form provides a selective wait for one or more alternatives. The other two provide conditional and timed entry calls.

2   select_statement ::= selective_wait
              | conditional_entry_call | timed_entry_call

3   *References:* selective wait 9.7.1, conditional entry call 9.7.2, timed entry call 9.7.3

9.7.1 Selective Waits

1   This form of the select statement allows a combination of waiting for, and selecting from, one or more alternatives. The selection can depend on conditions associated with each alternative of the selective wait.

```
selective_wait ::=
   select
      select_alternative
   { or
      select_alternative}
   [ else
      sequence_of_statements]
   end select;

select_alternative ::=
   [ when condition =>]
      selective_wait_alternative

selective_wait_alternative ::= accept_alternative
   | delay_alternative | terminate_alternative

accept_alternative  ::=  accept_statement [sequence_of_statements]

delay_alternative   ::=  delay_statement  [sequence_of_statements]

terminate_alternative ::= terminate;
```

A selective wait must contain at least one accept alternative. In addition a selective wait can con-   3
tain either a terminate alternative (only one), or one or more delay alternatives, or an else part;
these three possibilities are mutually exclusive.

A select alternative is said to be *open* if it does not start with **when** and a condition, or if the condi-   4
tion is TRUE . It is said to be *closed* otherwise.

For the execution of a selective wait, any conditions specified after **when** are evaluated in some   5
order that is not defined by the language; open alternatives are thus determined. For an open
delay alternative, the delay expression is also evaluated. Similarly, for an open accept alternative
for an entry of a family, the entry index is also evaluated. Selection and execution of one open
alternative, or of the else part, then completes the execution of the selective wait; the rules for this
selection are described below.

Open accept alternatives are first considered. Selection of one such alternative takes place   6
immediately if a corresponding rendezvous is possible, that is, if there is a corresponding entry call
issued by another task and waiting to be accepted. If several alternatives can thus be selected,
one of them is selected arbitrarily (that is, the language does not define which one). When such an
alternative is selected, the corresponding accept statement and possible subsequent statements
are executed. If no rendezvous is immediately possible and there is no else part, the task waits
until an open selective wait alternative can be selected.

Selection of the other forms of alternative or of an else part is performed as follows: 7

- An open delay alternative will be selected if no accept alternative can be selected before the   8
  specified delay has elapsed (immediately, for a negative or zero delay in the absence of
  queued entry calls); any subsequent statements of the alternative are then executed. If several
  delay alternatives can thus be selected (that is, if they have the same delay), one of them is
  selected arbitrarily.

- The else part is selected and its statements are executed if no accept alternative can be   9
  immediately selected, in particular, if all alternatives are closed.

- An open terminate alternative is selected if the conditions stated in section 9.4 are satisfied.   10
  It is a consequence of other rules that a terminate alternative cannot be selected while there is
  a queued entry call for any entry of the task.

11   The exception PROGRAM_ERROR is raised if all alternatives are closed and there is no else part.

12   *Examples of a select statement:*

```
select
   accept DRIVER_AWAKE_SIGNAL;
or
   delay 30.0*SECONDS;
   STOP_THE_TRAIN;
end select;
```

13   *Example of a task body with a select statement:*

```
task body RESOURCE is
   BUSY : BOOLEAN := FALSE;
begin
   loop
      select
         when not BUSY =>
            accept SEIZE do
               BUSY := TRUE;
            end;
      or
         accept RELEASE do
            BUSY := FALSE;
         end;
      or
         terminate;
      end select;
   end loop;
end RESOURCE;
```

Notes:

14   A selective wait is allowed to have several open delay alternatives. A selective wait is allowed to
      have several open accept alternatives for the same entry.

15   *References:* accept statement 9.5, condition 5.3, declaration 3.1, delay expression 9.6, delay statement 9.6, duration
      9.6, entry 9.5, entry call 9.5, entry index 9.5, program_error exception 11.1, queued entry call 9.5, rendezvous 9.5,
      select statement 9.7, sequence of statements 5.1, task 9

9.7.2 Conditional Entry Calls

1   A conditional entry call issues an entry call that is then canceled if a rendezvous is not immediately
      possible.

2
```
conditional_entry_call ::=
   select
       entry_call_statement
      [ sequence_of_statements]
   else
       sequence_of_statements
   end select;
```

For the execution of a conditional entry call, the entry name is first evaluated. This is followed by any evaluations required for actual parameters as in the case of a subprogram call (see 6.4).   3

The entry call is canceled if the execution of the called task has not reached a point where it is ready to accept the call (that is, either an accept statement for the corresponding entry, or a select statement with an open accept alternative for the entry), or if there are prior queued entry calls for this entry. If the called task has reached a select statement, the entry call is canceled if an accept alternative for this entry is not selected.   4

If the entry call is canceled, the statements of the else part are executed. Otherwise, the rendez-vous takes place; and the optional sequence of statements after the entry call is then executed.   5

The execution of a conditional entry call raises the exception TASKING_ERROR if the called task has already completed its execution (see also 9.10 for the case when the called task becomes abnormal).   6

Example: 7

```
procedure SPIN(R : RESOURCE) is
begin
  loop
    select
      R.SEIZE;
      return;
    else
      null;   --   busy  waiting
    end select;
  end loop;
end;
```

References: abnormal task 9.10, accept statement 9.5, actual parameter part 6.4, completed task 9.4, entry call   8
statement 9.5, entry family 9.5, entry index 9.5, evaluation 4.5, expression 4.4, open alternative 9.7.1, queued entry call 9.5, rendezvous 9.5, select statement 9.7, sequence of statements 5.1, task 9, tasking_error exception 11.1

9.7.3 Timed Entry Calls

A timed entry call issues an entry call that is canceled if a rendezvous is not started within a given delay.   1

```
timed_entry_call ::=
  select
      entry_call_statement
    [ sequence_of_statements]
  or
      delay_alternative
  end select;
```
  2

3   For the execution of a timed entry call, the entry name is first evaluated. This is followed by any evaluations required for actual parameters as in the case of a subprogram call (see 6.4). The expression stating the delay is then evaluated, and the entry call is finally issued.

4   If a rendezvous can be started within the specified duration (or immediately, as for a conditional entry call, for a negative or zero delay), it is performed and the optional sequence of statements after the entry call is then executed. Otherwise, the entry call is canceled when the specified duration has expired, and the optional sequence of statements of the delay alternative is executed.

5   The execution of a timed entry call raises the exception TASKING_ERROR if the called task completes its execution before accepting the call (see also 9.10 for the case when the called task becomes abnormal).

6   *Example:*

```
select
    CONTROLLER.REQUEST(MEDIUM)(SOME_ITEM);
or
    delay  45.0;
    --   controller  too  busy,  try  something  else
end select;
```

7   *References:* abnormal task 9.10, accept statement 9.5, actual parameter part 6.4, completed task 9.4, conditional entry call 9.7.2, delay expression 9.6, delay statement 9.6, duration 9.6, entry call statement 9.5, entry family 9.5, entry index 9.5, evaluation 4.5, expression 4.4, rendezvous 9.5, sequence of statements 5.1, task 9, tasking_error exception 11.1

9.8 Priorities

1   Each task may (but need not) have a priority, which is a value of the subtype PRIORITY (of the type INTEGER) declared in the predefined library package SYSTEM (see 13.7). A lower value indicates a lower degree of urgency; the range of priorities is implementation-defined. A priority is associated with a task if a pragma

       pragma PRIORITY (*static*_expression);

2   appears in the corresponding task specification; the priority is given by the value of the expression. A priority is associated with the main program if such a pragma appears in its outermost declarative part. At most one such pragma can appear within a given task specification or for a subprogram that is a library unit, and these are the only allowed places for this pragma. A pragma PRIORITY has no effect if it occurs in a subprogram other than the main program.

3   The specification of a priority is an indication given to assist the implementation in the allocation of processing resources to parallel tasks when there are more tasks eligible for execution than can be supported simultaneously by the available processing resources. The effect of priorities on scheduling is defined by the following rule:

4   If two tasks with different priorities are both eligible for execution and could sensibly be executed using the same physical processors and the same other processing resources, then it cannot be the case that the task with the lower priority is executing while the task with the higher priority is not.

For tasks of the same priority, the scheduling order is not defined by the language. For tasks without explicit priority, the scheduling rules are not defined, except when such tasks are engaged in a rendezvous. If the priorities of both tasks engaged in a rendezvous are defined, the rendezvous is executed with the higher of the two priorities. If only one of the two priorities is defined, the rendezvous is executed with at least that priority. If neither is defined, the priority of the rendezvous is undefined.

Notes:

The priority of a task is static and therefore fixed. However, the priority during a rendezvous is not necessarily static since it also depends on the priority of the task calling the entry. Priorities should be used only to indicate relative degrees of urgency; they should not be used for task synchronization.

References: declarative part 3.9, entry call statement 9.5, integer type 3.5.4, main program 10.1, package system 13.7, pragma 2.8, rendezvous 9.5, static expression 4.9, subtype 3.3, task 9, task specification 9.1

9.9 Task and Entry Attributes

For a task object or value T the following attributes are defined:

T'CALLABLE   Yields the value FALSE when the execution of the task designated by T is either completed or terminated, or when the task is abnormal. Yields the value TRUE otherwise. The value of this attribute is of the predefined type BOOLEAN.

T'TERMINATED   Yields the value TRUE if the task designated by T is terminated. Yields the value FALSE otherwise. The value of this attribute is of the predefined type BOOLEAN.

In addition, the representation attributes STORAGE_SIZE, SIZE, and ADDRESS are defined for a task object T or a task type T (see 13.7.2).

The attribute COUNT is defined for an entry E of a task unit T. The entry can be either a single entry or an entry of a family (in either case the name of the single entry or entry family can be either a simple or an expanded name). This attribute is only allowed within the body of T, but excluding within any program unit that is, itself, inner to the body of T.

E'COUNT   Yields the number of entry calls presently queued on the entry E (if the attribute is evaluated by the execution of an accept statement for the entry E, the count does not include the calling task). The value of this attribute is of the type *universal_integer*.

Note:

Algorithms interrogating the attribute E'COUNT should take precautions to allow for the increase of the value of this attribute for incoming entry calls, and its decrease, for example with timed entry calls.

References: abnormal task 9.10, accept statement 9.5, attribute 4.1.4, boolean type 3.5.3, completed task 9.4, designate 9.1, entry 9.5, false boolean value 3.5.3, queue of entry calls 9.5, storage unit 13.7, task 9, task object 9.2, task type 9.1, terminated task 9.4, timed entry call 9.7.3, true boolean value 3.5.3, universal_integer type 3.5.4

9.10 Abort Statements

1   An abort statement causes one or more tasks to become *abnormal*, thus preventing any further rendezvous with such tasks.

2   abort_statement ::= **abort** *task*_name {, *task*_name};

3   The determination of the type of each task name uses the fact that the type of the name is a task type.

4   For the execution of an abort statement, the given task names are evaluated in some order that is not defined by the language. Each named task then becomes abnormal unless it is already terminated; similarly, any task that depends on a named task becomes abnormal unless it is already terminated.

5   Any abnormal task whose execution is suspended at an accept statement, a select statement, or a delay statement becomes completed; any abnormal task whose execution is suspended at an entry call, and that is not yet in a corresponding rendezvous, becomes completed and is removed from the entry queue; any abnormal task that has not yet started its activation becomes completed (and hence also terminated). This completes the execution of the abort statement.

6   The completion of any other abnormal task need not happen before completion of the abort statement. It must happen no later than when the abnormal task reaches a synchronization point that is one of the following: the end of its activation; a point where it causes the activation of another task; an entry call; the start or the end of an accept statement; a select statement; a delay statement; an exception handler; or an abort statement. If a task that calls an entry becomes abnormal while in a rendezvous, its termination does not take place before the completion of the rendezvous (see 11.5).

7   The call of an entry of an abnormal task raises the exception TASKING_ERROR at the place of the call. Similarly, the exception TASKING_ERROR is raised for any task that has called an entry of an abnormal task, if the entry call is still queued or if the rendezvous is not yet finished (whether the entry call is an entry call statement, or a conditional or timed entry call); the exception is raised no later than the completion of the abnormal task. The value of the attribute CALLABLE is FALSE for any task that is abnormal (or completed).

8   If the abnormal completion of a task takes place while the task updates a variable, then the value of this variable is undefined.

9   *Example:*

        abort USER, TERMINAL.**all**, POOL(3);

Notes:

10 An abort statement should be used only in extremely severe situations requiring unconditional termination. A task is allowed to abort any task, including itself.

11 *References:* abnormal in rendezvous 11.5, accept statement 9.5, activation 9.3, attribute 4.1.4, callable (predefined attribute) 9.9, conditional entry call 9.7.2, delay statement 9.6, dependent task 9.4, entry call statement 9.5, evaluation of a name 4.1, exception handler 11.2, false boolean value 3.5.3, name 4.1, queue of entry calls 9.5, rendezvous 9.5, select statement 9.7, statement 5, task 9, tasking_error exception 11.1, terminated task 9.4, timed entry call 9.7.3

9.11 Shared Variables

The normal means of communicating values between tasks is by entry calls and accept state-   1
ments.

If two tasks read or update a *shared* variable (that is, a variable accessible by both), then neither of   2
them may assume anything about the order in which the other performs its operations, except at
the points where they synchronize. Two tasks are synchronized at the start and at the end of their
rendezvous. At the start and at the end of its activation, a task is synchronized with the task that
causes this activation. A task that has completed its execution is synchronized with any other task.

For the actions performed by a program that uses shared variables, the following assumptions can   3
always be made:

• If between two synchronization points of a task, this task reads a shared variable whose type   4
  is a scalar or access type, then the variable is not updated by any other task at any time
  between these two points.

• If between two synchronization points of a task, this task updates a shared variable whose   5
  type is a scalar or access type, then the variable is neither read nor updated by any other task
  at any time between these two points.

The execution of the program is erroneous if any of these assumptions is violated.   6

If a given task reads the value of a shared variable, the above assumptions allow an implementa-   7
tion to maintain local copies of the value (for example, in registers or in some other form of temporary storage); and for as long as the given task neither reaches a synchronization point nor
updates the value of the shared variable, the above assumptions imply that, for the given task,
reading a local copy is equivalent to reading the shared variable itself.

Similarly, if a given task updates the value of a shared variable, the above assumptions allow an   8
implementation to maintain a local copy of the value, and to defer the effective store of the local
copy into the shared variable until a synchronization point, provided that every further read or
update of the variable by the given task is treated as a read or update of the local copy. On the
other hand, an implementation is not allowed to introduce a store, unless this store would also be
executed in the canonical order (see 11.6).

The pragma SHARED can be used to specify that every read or update of a variable is a   9
synchronization point for that variable; that is, the above assumptions always hold for the given
variable (but not necessarily for other variables). The form of this pragma is as follows:

    pragma SHARED(*variable*_simple_name);

This pragma is allowed only for a variable declared by an object declaration and whose type is a   10
scalar or access type; the variable declaration and the pragma must both occur (in this order)
immediately within the same declarative part or package specification; the pragma must appear
before any occurrence of the name of the variable, other than in an address clause.

An implementation must restrict the objects for which the pragma SHARED is allowed to objects   11
for which each of direct reading and direct updating is implemented as an indivisible operation.

References: accept statement 9.5, activation 9.3, assignment 5.2, canonical order 11.6, declarative part 3.9, entry   12
call statement 9.5, erroneous 1.6, global 8.1, package specification 7.1, pragma 2.8, read a value 6.2, rendezvous 9.5,
simple name 3.1 4.1, task 9, type 3.3, update a value 6.2, variable 3.2.1

9.12 Example of Tasking

1   The following example defines a buffering task to smooth variations between the speed of output of a producing task and the speed of input of some consuming task. For instance, the producing task may contain the statements

2
```
loop
    --   produce the next character CHAR
    BUFFER.WRITE(CHAR);
    exit when CHAR = ASCII.EOT;
end loop;
```

3   and the consuming task may contain the statements

4
```
loop
    BUFFER.READ(CHAR);
    --   consume the character CHAR
    exit when CHAR = ASCII.EOT;
end loop;
```

5   The buffering task contains an internal pool of characters processed in a round-robin fashion. The pool has two indices, an IN_INDEX denoting the space for the next input character and an OUT_INDEX denoting the space for the next output character.

6
```
task BUFFER is
    entry READ (C : out  CHARACTER);
    entry WRITE(C : in   CHARACTER);
end;

task body BUFFER is
    POOL_SIZE : constant INTEGER := 100;
    POOL      : array(1 .. POOL_SIZE) of CHARACTER;
    COUNT     : INTEGER range 0 .. POOL_SIZE := 0;
    IN_INDEX, OUT_INDEX : INTEGER range 1 .. POOL_SIZE := 1;
begin
    loop
        select
            when COUNT < POOL_SIZE =>
                accept WRITE(C : in CHARACTER) do
                    POOL(IN_INDEX) := C;
                end;
                IN_INDEX := IN_INDEX mod POOL_SIZE + 1;
                COUNT    := COUNT + 1;
        or when COUNT > 0 =>
                accept READ(C : out CHARACTER) do
                    C := POOL(OUT_INDEX);
                end;
                OUT_INDEX := OUT_INDEX mod POOL_SIZE + 1;
                COUNT     := COUNT - 1;
        or
            terminate;
        end select;
    end loop;
end BUFFER;
```

10. Program Structure and Compilation Issues

The overall structure of programs and the facilities for separate compilation are described in this chapter. A program is a collection of one or more compilation units submitted to a compiler in one or more compilations. Each compilation unit specifies the separate compilation of a construct which can be a subprogram declaration or body, a package declaration or body, a generic declaration or body, or a generic instantiation. Alternatively this construct can be a subunit, in which case it includes the body of a subprogram, package, task unit, or generic unit declared within another compilation unit.

References: compilation 10.1, compilation unit 10.1, generic body 12.2, generic declaration 12.1, generic instantiation 12.3, package body 7.1, package declaration 7.1, subprogram body 6.3, subprogram declaration 6.1, subunit 10.2, task body 9.1, task unit 9

10.1 Compilation Units - Library Units

The text of a program can be submitted to the compiler in one or more compilations. Each compilation is a succession of compilation units.

```
compilation ::= {compilation_unit}

compilation_unit ::=
    context_clause library_unit | context_clause secondary_unit

library_unit ::=
      subprogram_declaration   | package_declaration
    | generic_declaration      | generic_instantiation
    | subprogram_body

secondary_unit ::= library_unit_body | subunit

library_unit_body ::= subprogram_body | package_body
```

The compilation units of a program are said to belong to a *program library*. A compilation unit defines either a library unit or a secondary unit. A secondary unit is either the separately compiled proper body of a library unit, or a subunit of another compilation unit. The designator of a separately compiled subprogram (whether a library unit or a subunit) must be an identifier. Within a program library the simple names of all library units must be distinct identifiers.

The effect of compiling a library unit is to define (or redefine) this unit as one that belongs to the program library. For the visibility rules, each library unit acts as a declaration that occurs immediately within the package STANDARD.

The effect of compiling a secondary unit is to define the body of a library unit, or in the case of a subunit, to define the proper body of a program unit that is declared within another compilation unit.

6   A subprogram body given in a compilation unit is interpreted as a secondary unit if the program library already contains a library unit that is a subprogram with the same name; it is otherwise interpreted both as a library unit and as the corresponding library unit body (that is, as a secondary unit).

7   The compilation units of a compilation are compiled in the given order. A pragma that applies to the whole of a compilation must appear before the first compilation unit of that compilation.

8   A subprogram that is a library unit can be used as a *main program* in the usual sense. Each main program acts as if called by some environment task; the means by which this execution is initiated are not prescribed by the language definition. An implementation may impose certain requirements on the parameters and on the result, if any, of a main program (these requirements must be stated in Appendix F). In any case, every implementation is required to allow, at least, main programs that are parameterless procedures, and every main program must be a subprogram that is a library unit.

Notes:

9   A simple program may consist of a single compilation unit. A compilation need not have any compilation units; for example, its text can consist of pragmas.

10   The designator of a library function cannot be an operator symbol, but a renaming declaration is allowed to rename a library function as an operator. Two library subprograms must have distinct simple names and hence cannot overload each other. However, renaming declarations are allowed to define overloaded names for such subprograms, and a locally declared subprogram is allowed to overload a library subprogram. The expanded name STANDARD.L can be used for a library unit L (unless the name STANDARD is hidden) since library units act as declarations that occur immediately within the package STANDARD.

11   *References:* allow 1.6, context clause 10.1.1, declaration 3.1, designator 6.1, environment 10.4, generic declaration 12.1, generic instantiation 12.3, hiding 8.3, identifier 2.3, library unit 10.5, local declaration 8.1, must 1.6, name 4.1, occur immediately within 8.1, operator 4.5, operator symbol 6.1, overloading 6.6 8.7, package body 7.1, package declaration 7.1, parameter of a subprogram 6.2, pragma 2.8, procedure 6.1, program unit 6, proper body 3.9, renaming declaration 8.5, simple name 4.1, standard package 8.6, subprogram 6, subprogram body 6.3, subprogram declaration 6.1, subunit 10.2, task 9, visibility 8.3

10.1.1 Context Clauses - With Clauses

1   A context clause is used to specify the library units whose names are needed within a compilation unit.

2   context_clause ::= {with_clause {use_clause}}

    with_clause ::= **with** *unit*_simple_name {, *unit*_simple_name};

3   The names that appear in a context clause must be the simple names of library units. The simple name of any library unit is allowed within a with clause. The only names allowed in a use clause of a context clause are the simple names of library packages mentioned by previous with clauses of the context clause. A simple name declared by a renaming declaration is not allowed in a context clause.

4   The with clauses and use clauses of the context clause of a library unit *apply* to this library unit and also to the secondary unit that defines the corresponding body (whether such a clause is repeated or not for this unit). Similarly, the with clauses and use clauses of the context clause of a compilation unit *apply* to this unit and also to its subunits, if any.

If a library unit is named by a with clause that applies to a compilation unit, then this library unit is directly visible within the compilation unit, except where hidden; the library unit is visible as if declared immediately within the package STANDARD (see 8.6).

Dependences among compilation units are defined by with clauses; that is, a compilation unit that mentions other library units in its with clauses *depends* on those library units. These dependences between units are taken into account for the determination of the allowed order of compilation (and recompilation) of compilation units, as explained in section 10.3, and for the determination of the allowed order of elaboration of compilation units, as explained in section 10.5.

Notes:

A library unit named by a with clause of a compilation unit is visible (except where hidden) within the compilation unit and hence can be used as a corresponding program unit. Thus within the compilation unit, the name of a library package can be given in use clauses and can be used to form expanded names; a library subprogram can be called; and instances of a library generic unit can be declared.

The rules given for with clauses are such that the same effect is obtained whether the name of a library unit is mentioned once or more than once by the applicable with clauses, or even within a given with clause.

Example 1 : A main program:

The following is an example of a main program consisting of a single compilation unit: a procedure for printing the real roots of a quadratic equation. The predefined package TEXT_IO and a user-defined package REAL_OPERATIONS (containing the definition of the type REAL and of the packages REAL_IO and REAL_FUNCTIONS) are assumed to be already present in the program library. Such packages may be used by other main programs.

```
with TEXT_IO, REAL_OPERATIONS; use REAL_OPERATIONS;
procedure QUADRATIC_EQUATION is
   A, B, C, D : REAL;
   use  REAL_IO,            -- achieves direct visibility of GET and PUT for REAL
        TEXT_IO,            -- achieves direct visibility of PUT for strings and of NEW_LINE
        REAL_FUNCTIONS;     -- achieves direct visibility of SQRT
begin
   GET(A); GET(B); GET(C);
   D := B**2 - 4.0*A*C;
   if D < 0.0 then
      PUT("Imaginary Roots.");
   else
      PUT("Real Roots : X1 = ");
      PUT((-B - SQRT(D))/(2.0*A)); PUT(" X2 = ");
      PUT((-B + SQRT(D))/(2.0*A));
   end if;
   NEW_LINE;
end QUADRATIC_EQUATION;
```

Notes on the example:

The with clauses of a compilation unit need only mention the names of those library subprograms and packages whose visibility is actually necessary within the unit. They need not (and should not) mention other library units that are used in turn by some of the units named in the with clauses, unless these other library units are also used directly by the current compilation unit. For example, the body of the package REAL_OPERATIONS may need elementary operations provided by other packages. The latter packages should not be named by the with clause of QUADRATIC_EQUATION since these elementary operations are not directly called within its body.

12   *References:* allow 1.6, compilation unit 10.1, direct visibility 8.3, elaboration 3.9, generic body 12.2, generic unit 12.1, hiding 8.3, instance 12.3, library unit 10.1, main program 10.1, must 1.6, name 4.1, package 7, package body 7.1, package declaration 7.1, procedure 6.1, program unit 6, secondary unit 10.1, simple name 4.1, standard predefined package 8.6, subprogram body 6.3, subprogram declaration 6.1, subunit 10.2, type 3.3, use clause 8.4, visibility 8.3

10.1.2 Examples of Compilation Units

1   A compilation unit can be split into a number of compilation units. For example, consider the following program.

2
```
procedure PROCESSOR is

    SMALL : constant    := 20;
    TOTAL  : INTEGER  := 0;

    package STOCK is
        LIMIT  : constant := 1000;
        TABLE : array (1 .. LIMIT) of INTEGER;
        procedure RESTART;
    end STOCK;

    package body STOCK is
        procedure RESTART is
        begin
            for N in 1 .. LIMIT loop
                TABLE(N) := N;
            end loop;
        end;
    begin
        RESTART;
    end STOCK;

    procedure UPDATE(X : INTEGER) is
        use STOCK;
    begin
        ...
        TABLE(X) := TABLE(X) + SMALL;
        ...
    end UPDATE;

begin
    ...
    STOCK.RESTART;   -- reinitializes TABLE
    ...
end PROCESSOR;
```

3   The following three compilation units define a program with an effect equivalent to the above example (the broken lines between compilation units serve to remind the reader that these units need not be contiguous texts).

Example 2 : Several compilation units: 4

```
package STOCK is                                                           5
  LIMIT  : constant := 1000;
  TABLE : array (1 .. LIMIT) of INTEGER;
  procedure RESTART;
end STOCK;
```

```
package body STOCK is
  procedure RESTART is                                                    6
  begin
    for N in 1 .. LIMIT loop
      TABLE(N) := N;
    end loop;
  end;
begin
  RESTART;
end STOCK;
```

```
with STOCK;
procedure PROCESSOR is                                                    7

  SMALL  : constant := 20;
  TOTAL  : INTEGER := 0;

  procedure UPDATE(X : INTEGER) is
    use STOCK;
  begin
    ...
    TABLE(X) := TABLE(X) + SMALL;
    ...
  end UPDATE;
begin
  ...
  STOCK.RESTART;   --   reinitializes TABLE
  ...
end PROCESSOR;
```

Note that in the latter version, the package STOCK has no visibility of outer identifiers other than   8
the predefined identifiers (of the package STANDARD). In particular, STOCK does not use any
identifier declared in PROCESSOR such as SMALL or TOTAL; otherwise STOCK could not have
been extracted from PROCESSOR in the above manner. The procedure PROCESSOR, on the other
hand, depends on STOCK and mentions this package in a with clause. This permits the inner
occurrences of STOCK in the expanded name STOCK.RESTART and in the use clause.

These three compilation units can be submitted in one or more compilations. For example, it is   9
possible to submit the package specification and the package body together and in this order in a
single compilation.

References: compilation unit 10.1, declaration 3.1, identifier 2.3, package 7, package body 7.1, package specification   10
7.1, program 10, standard package 8.6, use clause 8.4, visibility 8.3, with clause 10.1.1

10.2 Subunits of Compilation Units

1   A subunit is used for the separate compilation of the proper body of a program unit declared within another compilation unit. This method of splitting a program permits hierarchical program development.

2
```
body_stub ::=
      subprogram_specification is separate;
    | package body package_simple_name is separate;
    | task body task_simple_name is separate;

subunit ::=
      separate (parent_unit_name) proper_body
```

3   A body stub is only allowed as the body of a program unit (a subprogram, a package, a task unit, or a generic unit) if the body stub occurs immediately within either the specification of a library package or the declarative part of another compilation unit.

4   If the body of a program unit is a body stub, a separately compiled subunit containing the corresponding proper body is required. In the case of a subprogram, the subprogram specifications given in the proper body and in the body stub must conform (see 6.3.1).

5   Each subunit mentions the name of its *parent unit*, that is, the compilation unit where the corresponding body stub is given. If the parent unit is a library unit, it is called the *ancestor* library unit. If the parent unit is itself a subunit, the parent unit name must be given in full as an expanded name, starting with the simple name of the ancestor library unit. The simple names of all subunits that have the same ancestor library unit must be distinct identifiers.

6   Visibility within the proper body of a subunit is the visibility that would be obtained at the place of the corresponding body stub (within the parent unit) if the with clauses and use clauses of the subunit were appended to the context clause of the parent unit. If the parent unit is itself a subunit, then the same rule is used to define the visibility within the proper body of the parent unit.

7   The effect of the elaboration of a body stub is to elaborate the proper body of the subunit.

Notes:

8   Two subunits of different library units in the same program library need not have distinct identifiers. In any case, their full expanded names are distinct, since the simple names of library units are distinct and since the simple names of all subunits that have a given library unit as ancestor unit are also distinct. By means of renaming declarations, overloaded subprogram names that rename (distinct) subunits can be introduced.

9   A library unit that is named by the with clause of a subunit can be hidden by a declaration (with the same identifier) given in the proper body of the subunit. Moreover, such a library unit can even be hidden by a declaration given within a parent unit since a library unit acts as if declared in STANDARD; this however does not affect the interpretation of the with clauses themselves, since only names of library units can appear in with clauses.

References: compilation unit 10.1, conform 6.3.1, context clause 10.1.1, declaration 3.1, declarative part 3.9, direct
visibility 8.3, elaboration 3.9, expanded name 4.1.3, generic body 12.2, generic unit 12, hidden declaration 8.3, identifier 2.3, library unit 10.1, local declaration 8.1, name 4.1, occur immediately within 8.1, overloading 8.3, package 7,
package body 7.1, package specification 7.1, program 10, program unit 6, proper body 3.9, renaming declaration 8.5,
separate compilation 10.1, simple name 4.1, subprogram 6, subprogram body 6.3, subprogram specification 6.1, task
9, task body 9.1, task unit 9.1, use clause 8.4, visibility 8.3, with clause 10.1.1

10.2.1 Examples of Subunits

The procedure TOP is first written as a compilation unit without subunits.

```
with  TEXT_IO;
procedure  TOP  is

    type  REAL  is  digits  10;
    R, S : REAL := 1.0;

    package  FACILITY  is
       PI : constant := 3.14159_26536;
       function    F (X : REAL) return REAL;
       procedure   G (Y, Z : REAL);
    end  FACILITY;

    package body  FACILITY  is
       --   some local declarations followed by

       function F(X : REAL) return REAL is
       begin
          --   sequence of statements of F
          ...
       end  F;

       procedure  G(Y, Z : REAL) is
          --   local procedures using TEXT_IO
          ...
       begin
          --   sequence of statements of G
          ...
       end  G;
    end  FACILITY;

    procedure TRANSFORM(U : in out REAL) is
       use  FACILITY;
    begin
       U := F(U);
       ...
    end  TRANSFORM;
begin  -- TOP
    TRANSFORM(R);
    ...
    FACILITY.G(R, S);
end  TOP;
```

3   The body of the package FACILITY and that of the procedure TRANSFORM can be made into separate subunits of TOP. Similarly, the body of the procedure G can be made into a subunit of FACILITY as follows.

4   *Example 3:*

5
```
procedure TOP is

    type REAL is digits 10;
    R, S : REAL := 1.0;

    package FACILITY is
        PI : constant := 3.14159_26536;
        function    F (X : REAL) return REAL;
        procedure   G (Y, Z : REAL);
    end FACILITY;

    package body FACILITY is separate;                  --  stub of FACILITY
    procedure TRANSFORM(U : in out REAL) is separate;   --  stub of TRANSFORM

begin   --  TOP
    TRANSFORM(R);

    ...
    FACILITY.G(R, S);
end TOP;
```

6
```
separate (TOP)
procedure TRANSFORM(U : in out REAL) is
    use FACILITY;
begin
    U := F(U);

    ...
end TRANSFORM;
```

7
```
separate (TOP)
package body FACILITY is
    --  some local declarations followed by

    function F(X : REAL) return REAL is
    begin
        --  sequence of statements of F
        ...
    end F;

    procedure G(Y, Z : REAL) is separate;               -- stub of G
end FACILITY;
```

```
                  -----------------------------------------------
    with TEXT_IO;
    separate (TOP.FACILITY)                           --  full name of FACILITY        8
    procedure G(Y, Z : REAL) is
       --  local procedures using TEXT_IO
       ...
    begin
       --  sequence of statements of G
       ...
    end G;
```

In the above example TRANSFORM and FACILITY are subunits of TOP, and G is a subunit of   9
FACILITY. The visibility in the split version is the same as in the initial version except for one
change: since TEXT_IO is only used within G, the corresponding with clause is written for G
instead of for TOP. Apart from this change, the same identifiers are visible at corresponding
program points in the two versions. For example, all of the following are (directly) visible within
the proper body of the subunit G: the procedure TOP, the type REAL, the variables R and S, the
package FACILITY and the contained named number PI and subprograms F and G.

References: body stub 10.2, compilation unit 10.1, identifier 2.3, local declaration 8.1, named number 3.2, package   10
7, package body 7.1, procedure 6, procedure body 6.3, proper body 3.9, subprogram 6, type 3.3, variable 3.2.1,
visibility 8.3, with clause 10.1.1

10.3 Order of Compilation

The rules defining the order in which units can be compiled are direct consequences of the visibility   1
rules and, in particular, of the fact that any library unit that is mentioned by the context clause of a
compilation unit is visible in the compilation unit.

A compilation unit must be compiled after all library units named by its context clause. A secon-   2
dary unit that is a subprogram or package body must be compiled after the corresponding library
unit. Any subunit of a parent compilation unit must be compiled after the parent compilation unit.

If any error is detected while attempting to compile a compilation unit, then the attempted com-   3
pilation is rejected and it has no effect whatsoever on the program library; the same holds for
recompilations (no compilation unit can become obsolete because of such a recompilation).

The order in which the compilation units of a program are compiled must be consistent with the   4
partial ordering defined by the above rules.

Similar rules apply for recompilations. A compilation unit is potentially affected by a change in any   5
library unit named by its context clause. A secondary unit is potentially affected by a change in the
corresponding library unit. The subunits of a parent compilation unit are potentially affected by a
change of the parent compilation unit. If a compilation unit is successfully recompiled, the compilation units potentially affected by this change are obsolete and must be recompiled unless they
are no longer needed. An implementation may be able to reduce the compilation costs if it can
deduce that some of the potentially affected units are not actually affected by the change.

6   The subunits of a unit can be recompiled without affecting the unit itself. Similarly, changes in a subprogram or package body do not affect other compilation units (apart from the subunits of the body) since these compilation units only have access to the subprogram or package specification. An implementation is only allowed to deviate from this rule for inline inclusions, for certain compiler optimizations, and for certain implementations of generic program units, as described below.

7   ● If a pragma INLINE is applied to a subprogram declaration given in a package specification, inline inclusion will only be achieved if the package body is compiled before units calling the subprogram. In such a case, inline inclusion creates a *dependence* of the calling unit on the package body, and the compiler must recognize this dependence when deciding on the need for recompilation. If a calling unit is compiled before the package body, the pragma may be ignored by the compiler for such calls (a warning that inline inclusion was not achieved may be issued). Similar considerations apply to a separately compiled subprogram for which an INLINE pragma is specified.

8   ● For optimization purposes, an implementation may compile several units of a given compilation in a way that creates further dependences among these compilation units. The compiler must then take these dependences into account when deciding on the need for recompilations.

9   ● An implementation may require that a generic declaration and the corresponding proper body be part of the same compilation, whether the generic unit is itself separately compiled or is local to another compilation unit. An implementation may also require that subunits of a generic unit be part of the same compilation.

10 *Examples of Compilation Order:*

11 (a) In example 1 (see 10.1.1): The procedure QUADRATIC_EQUATION must be compiled after the library packages TEXT_IO and REAL_OPERATIONS since they appear in its with clause.

12 (b) In example 2 (see 10.1.2): The package body STOCK must be compiled after the corresponding package specification.

13 (c) In example 2 (see 10.1.2): The specification of the package STOCK must be compiled before the procedure PROCESSOR. On the other hand, the procedure PROCESSOR can be compiled either before or after the package body STOCK.

14 (d) In example 3 (see 10.2.1): The procedure G must be compiled after the package TEXT_IO since this package is named by the with clause of G. On the other hand, TEXT_IO can be compiled either before or after TOP.

15 (e) In example 3 (see 10.2.1): The subunits TRANSFORM and FACILITY must be compiled after the main program TOP. Similarly, the subunit G must be compiled after its parent unit FACILITY.

Notes:

16 For library packages, it follows from the recompilation rules that a package body is made obsolete by the recompilation of the corresponding specification. If the new package specification is such that a package body is not required (that is, if the package specification does not contain the declaration of a program unit), then the recompilation of a body for this package is not required. In any case, the obsolete package body must not be used and can therefore be deleted from the program library.

10.4 The Program Library

Compilers are required to enforce the language rules in the same manner for a program consisting   1
of several compilation units (and subunits) as for a program submitted as a single compilation.
Consequently, a library file containing information on the compilation units of the program library
must be maintained by the compiler or compiling environment. This information may include symbol tables and other information pertaining to the order of previous compilations.

A normal submission to the compiler consists of the compilation unit(s) and the library file. The   2
latter is used for checks and is updated for each compilation unit successfully compiled.

Notes:

A single program library is implied for the compilation units of a compilation. The possible   3
existence of different program libraries and the means by which they are named are not concerns
of the language definition; they are concerns of the programming environment.

There should be commands for creating the program library of a given program or of a given family   4
of programs. These commands may permit the reuse of units of other program libraries. Finally,
there should be commands for interrogating the status of the units of a program library. The form
of these commands is not specified by the language definition.

References: compilation unit 10.1, context clause 10.1.1, order of compilation 10.3, program 10.1, program library   5
10.1, subunit 10.2, use clause 8.4, with clause 10.1.1

10.5 Elaboration of Library Units

Before the execution of a main program, all library units needed by the main program are   1
elaborated, as well as the corresponding library unit bodies, if any. The library units needed by the
main program are: those named by with clauses applicable to the main program, to its body, and
to its subunits; those named by with clauses applicable to these library units themselves, to the
corresponding library unit bodies, and to their subunits; and so on, in a transitive manner.

The elaboration of these library units and of the corresponding library unit bodies is performed in   2
an order consistent with the partial ordering defined by the with clauses (see 10.3). In addition, a
library unit mentioned by the context clause of a subunit must be elaborated before the body of the
ancestor library unit of the subunit.

An order of elaboration that is consistent with this partial ordering does not always ensure that   3
each library unit body is elaborated before any other compilation unit whose elaboration neces-
sitates that the library unit body be already elaborated. If the prior elaboration of library unit
bodies is needed, this can be requested by a pragma ELABORATE. The form of this pragma is as
follows:

pragma ELABORATE (*library_unit*_simple_name {, *library_unit*_simple_name});

4   These pragmas are only allowed immediately after the context clause of a compilation unit (before the subsequent library unit or secondary unit). Each argument of such a pragma must be the simple name of a library unit mentioned by the context clause, and this library unit must have a library unit body. Such a pragma specifies that the library unit body must be elaborated before the given compilation unit. If the given compilation unit is a subunit, the library unit body must be elaborated before the body of the ancestor library unit of the subunit.

5   The program is illegal if no consistent order can be found (that is, if a circularity exists). The elaboration of the compilation units of the program is performed in some order that is otherwise not defined by the language.

6   *References:* allow 1.6, argument of a pragma 2.8, compilation unit 10.1, context clause 10.1.1, dependence between compilation units 10.3, elaboration 3.9, illegal 1.6, in some order 1.6, library unit 10.1, name 4.1, main program 10.1, pragma 2.8, secondary unit 10.1, separate compilation 10.1, simple name 4.1, subunit 10.2, with clause 10.1.1

10.6 Program Optimization

1   Optimization of the elaboration of declarations and the execution of statements may be performed by compilers. In particular, a compiler may be able to optimize a program by evaluating certain expressions, in addition to those that are static expressions. Should one of these expressions, whether static or not, be such that an exception would be raised by its evaluation, then the code in that path of the program can be replaced by code to raise the exception; the same holds for exceptions raised by the evaluation of names and simple expressions. (See also section 11.6.)

2   A compiler may find that some statements or subprograms will never be executed, for example, if their execution depends on a condition known to be FALSE. The corresponding object machine code can then be omitted. This rule permits the effect of *conditional compilation* within the language.

Note:

3   An expression whose evaluation is known to raise an exception need not represent an error if it occurs in a statement or subprogram that is never executed. The compiler may warn the programmer of a potential error.

4   *References:* condition 5.3, declaration 3.1, elaboration 3.9, evaluation 4.5, exception 11, expression 4.4, false boolean value 3.5.3, program 10, raising of exceptions 11.3, statement 5, static expression 4.9, subprogram 6

11. Exceptions

This chapter defines the facilities for dealing with errors or other exceptional situations that arise during program execution. Such a situation is called an *exception*. To *raise* an exception is to abandon normal program execution so as to draw attention to the fact that the corresponding situation has arisen. Executing some actions, in response to the arising of an exception, is called *handling* the exception.   1

An exception declaration declares a name for an exception. An exception can be raised by a raise statement, or it can be raised by another statement or operation that *propagates* the exception. When an exception arises, control can be transferred to a user-provided exception handler at the end of a block statement or at the end of the body of a subprogram, package, or task unit.   2

References: block statement 5.6, error situation 1.6, exception handler 11.2, name 4.1, package body 7.1, propagation of an exception 11.4.1 11.4.2, raise statement 11.3, subprogram body 6.3, task body 9.1   3

11.1 Exception Declarations

An exception declaration declares a name for an exception. The name of an exception can only be used in raise statements, exception handlers, and renaming declarations.   1

```
exception_declaration ::= identifier_list : exception;
```
     2

An exception declaration with several identifiers is equivalent to a sequence of single exception declarations, as explained in section 3.2. Each single exception declaration declares a name for a different exception. In particular, if a generic unit includes an exception declaration, the exception declarations implicitly generated by different instantiations of the generic unit refer to distinct exceptions (but all have the same identifier). The particular exception denoted by an exception name is determined at compilation time and is the same regardless of how many times the exception declaration is elaborated. Hence, if an exception declaration occurs in a recursive subprogram, the exception name denotes the same exception for all invocations of the recursive subprogram.   3

The following exceptions are predefined in the language; they are raised when the situations described are detected.   4

CONSTRAINT_ERROR   This exception is raised in any of the following situations: upon an attempt to violate a range constraint, an index constraint, or a discriminant constraint; upon an attempt to use a record component that does not exist for the current discriminant values; and upon an attempt to use a selected component, an indexed component, a slice, or an attribute, of an object designated by an access value, if the object does not exist because the access value is null.   5

Exception Declarations 11.1

6   NUMERIC_ERROR   This exception is raised by the execution of a predefined numeric operation
                          that cannot deliver a correct result (within the declared accuracy for real
                          types); this includes the case where an implementation uses a predefined
                          numeric operation for the execution, evaluation, or elaboration of some
                          construct. The rules given in section 4.5.7 define the cases in which an
                          implementation is not required to raise this exception when such an error
                          situation arises; see also section 11.6.

7   PROGRAM_ERROR   This exception is raised upon an attempt to call a subprogram, to activate a
                          task, or to elaborate a generic instantiation, if the body of the cor-
                          responding unit has not yet been elaborated. This exception is also raised if
                          the end of a function is reached (see 6.5); or during the execution of a
                          selective wait that has no else part, if this execution determines that all
                          alternatives are closed (see 9.7.1). Finally, depending on the implementa-
                          tion, this exception may be raised upon an attempt to execute an action
                          that is erroneous, and for incorrect order dependences (see 1.6).

8   STORAGE_ERROR   This exception is raised in any of the following situations: when the dyna-
                          mic storage allocated to a task is exceeded; during the evaluation of an
                          allocator, if the space available for the collection of allocated objects is
                          exhausted; or during the elaboration of a declarative item, or during the
                          execution of a subprogram call, if storage is not sufficient.

9   TASKING_ERROR   This exception is raised when exceptions arise during intertask communi-
                          cation (see 9 and 11.5).

Note:

10   The situations described above can arise without raising the corresponding exceptions, if the
     pragma SUPPRESS has been used to give permission to omit the corresponding checks (see 11.7).

11   *Examples of user-defined exception declarations:*

         SINGULAR : **exception**;
         ERROR   : **exception**;
         OVERFLOW, UNDERFLOW : **exception**;

12   *References:* access value 3.8, collection 3.8, declaration 3.1, exception 11, exception handler 11.2, generic body
     12.2, generic instantiation 12.3, generic unit 12, identifier 2.3, implicit declaration 12.3, instantiation 12.3, name 4.1,
     object 3.2, raise statement 11.3, real type 3.5.6, record component 3.7, return statement 5.8, subprogram 6, sub-
     program body 6.3, task 9, task body 9.1

13   *Constraint_error exception contexts:* aggregate 4.3.1 4.3.2, allocator 4.8, assignment statement 5.2 5.2.1,
     constraint 3.3.2, discrete type attribute 3.5.5, discriminant constraint 3.7.2, elaboration of a generic formal parameter
     12.3.1 12.3.2 12.3.4 12.3.5, entry index 9.5, exponentiating operator 4.5.6, index constraint 3.6.1, indexed compo-
     nent 4.1.1, logical operator 4.5.1, null access value 3.8, object declaration 3.2.1, parameter association 6.4.1,
     qualified expression 4.7, range constraint 3.5, selected component 4.1.3, slice 4.1.2, subtype indication 3.3.2, type
     conversion 4.6

14   *Numeric_error exception contexts:* discrete type attribute 3.5.5, implicit conversion 3.5.4 3.5.6 4.6, numeric
     operation 3.5.5 3.5.8 3.5.10, operator of a numeric type 4.5 4.5.7

15   *Program_error exception contexts:* collection 3.8, elaboration 3.9, elaboration check 3.9 7.3 9.3 12.2, erroneous
     1.6, incorrect order dependence 1.6, leaving a function 6.5, selective wait 9.7.1

Storage_error exception contexts: allocator 4.8   16

Tasking error exception contexts: abort statement 9.10, entry call 9.5 9.7.2 9.7.3, exceptions during task   17
communication 11.5, task activation 9.3

11.2 Exception Handlers

The response to one or more exceptions is specified by an exception handler.   1

```
exception_handler ::=
    when exception_choice {| exception_choice} =>
        sequence_of_statements

exception_choice ::= exception_name | others
```
                                                                                          2

An exception handler occurs in a construct that is either a block statement or the body of a sub-   3
program, package, task unit, or generic unit. Such a construct will be called a *frame* in this
chapter. In each case the syntax of a frame that has exception handlers includes the following
part:

```
begin
    sequence_of_statements
exception
    exception_handler
    { exception_handler}
end
```
                                                                                          4

The exceptions denoted by the exception names given as exception choices of a frame must all be   5
distinct. The exception choice **others** is only allowed for the last exception handler of a frame and
as its only exception choice; it stands for all exceptions not listed in previous handlers of the frame,
including exceptions whose names are not visible at the place of the exception handler.

The exception handlers of a frame handle exceptions that are raised by the execution of the   6
sequence of statements of the frame. The exceptions handled by a given exception handler are
those named by the corresponding exception choices.

Example: 7

```
begin
    --   sequence of statements
exception
    when SINGULAR | NUMERIC_ERROR =>
        PUT(" MATRIX IS SINGULAR ");
    when others =>
        PUT(" FATAL ERROR ");
        raise ERROR;
end;
```
                                                                                          2

Note:

The same kinds of statement are allowed in the sequence of statements of each exception handler   8
as are allowed in the sequence of statements of the frame. For example, a return statement is
allowed in a handler within a function body.

9   *References:* block statement 5.6, declarative part 3.9, exception 11, exception handling 11.4, function body 6.3, generic body 12.2, generic unit 12.1, name 4.1, package body 7.1, raise statement 11.3, return statement 5.8, sequence of statements 5.1, statement 5, subprogram body 6.3, task body 9.1, task unit 9 9.1, visibility 8.3

11.3 Raise Statements

1   A raise statement raises an exception.

2   raise_statement ::= **raise** [*exception*_name];

3   For the execution of a raise statement with an exception name, the named exception is raised. A raise statement without an exception name is only allowed within an exception handler (but not within the sequence of statements of a subprogram, package, task unit, or generic unit, enclosed by the handler); it raises again the exception that caused transfer to the innermost enclosing handler.

4   *Examples:*

```
raise SINGULAR;
raise NUMERIC_ERROR;      --  explicitly raising a predefined exception

raise;                    --  only within an exception handler
```

5   *References:* exception 11, generic unit 12, name 4.1, package 7, sequence of statements 5.1, subprogram 6, task unit 9

11.4 Exception Handling

1   When an exception is raised, normal program execution is abandoned and control is transferred to an exception handler. The selection of this handler depends on whether the exception is raised during the execution of statements or during the elaboration of declarations.

2   *References:* declaration 3.1, elaboration 3.1 3.9, exception 11, exception handler 11.2, raising of exceptions 11.3, statement 5

11.4.1 Exceptions Raised During the Execution of Statements

1   The handling of an exception raised by the execution of a sequence of statements depends on whether the innermost frame or accept statement that encloses the sequence of statements is a frame or an accept statement. The case where an accept statement is innermost is described in section 11.5. The case where a frame is innermost is presented here.

Different actions take place, depending on whether or not this frame has a handler for the exception, and on whether the exception is raised in the sequence of statements of the frame or in that of an exception handler. **2**

If an exception is raised in the sequence of statements of a frame that has a handler for the exception, execution of the sequence of statements of the frame is abandoned and control is transferred to the exception handler. The execution of the sequence of statements of the handler completes the execution of the frame (or its elaboration if the frame is a package body). **3**

If an exception is raised in the sequence of statements of a frame that does not have a handler for the exception, execution of this sequence of statements is abandoned. The next action depends on the nature of the frame: **4**

(a) For a subprogram body, the same exception is raised again at the point of call of the subprogram, unless the subprogram is the main program itself, in which case execution of the main program is abandoned. **5**

(b) For a block statement, the same exception is raised again immediately after the block statement (that is, within the innermost enclosing frame or accept statement). **6**

(c) For a package body that is a declarative item, the same exception is raised again immediately after this declarative item (within the enclosing declarative part). If the package body is that of a subunit, the exception is raised again at the place of the corresponding body stub. If the package is a library unit, execution of the main program is abandoned. **7**

(d) For a task body, the task becomes completed. **8**

An exception that is raised again (as in the above cases (a), (b), and (c)) is said to be *propagated*, either by the execution of the subprogram, the execution of the block statement, or the elaboration of the package body. No propagation takes place in the case of a task body. If the frame is a subprogram or a block statement and if it has dependent tasks, the propagation of an exception takes place only after termination of the dependent tasks. **9**

Finally, if an exception is raised in the sequence of statements of an exception handler, execution of this sequence of statements is abandoned. Subsequent actions (including propagation, if any) are as in the cases (a) to (d) above, depending on the nature of the frame. **10**

Example: **11**

```
function FACTORIAL (N : POSITIVE) return FLOAT is
begin
  if N = 1 then
    return 1.0;
  else
    return FLOAT(N) * FACTORIAL(N-1);
  end if;
exception
  when NUMERIC_ERROR => return FLOAT'SAFE_LARGE;
end FACTORIAL;
```

If the multiplication raises NUMERIC_ERROR, then FLOAT'SAFE_LARGE is returned by the handler. This value will cause further NUMERIC_ERROR exceptions to be raised by the evaluation of the expression in each of the remaining invocations of the function, so that for large values of N the function will ultimately return the value FLOAT'SAFE_LARGE. **12**

13   *Example:*

```
procedure P is
   ERROR : exception;
   procedure R;

   procedure Q is
   begin
      R;
      ...                     --  error situation (2)
   exception
      ...
      when ERROR =>   --  handler E2
      ...
   end Q;

   procedure R is
   begin
      ...                     --  error situation (3)
   end R;

begin
   ...                        --  error situation (1)
   Q;
   ...
exception
   ...
   when ERROR =>      --  handler E1
   ...
end P;
```

14   The following situations can arise:

15   (1) If the exception ERROR is raised in the sequence of statements of the outer procedure P, the
            handler E1 provided within P is used to complete the execution of P.

16   (2) If the exception ERROR is raised in the sequence of statements of Q, the handler E2 provided
            within Q is used to complete the execution of Q. Control will be returned to the point of call of
            Q upon completion of the handler.

17   (3) If the exception ERROR is raised in the body of R, called by Q, the execution of R is abandoned
            and the same exception is raised in the body of Q. The handler E2 is then used to complete
            the execution of Q, as in situation (2).

18   Note that in the third situation, the exception raised in R results in (indirectly) transferring control
       to a handler that is part of Q and hence not enclosed by R. Note also that if a handler were
       provided within R for the exception choice **others**, situation (3) would cause execution of this
       handler, rather than direct termination of R.

19   Lastly, if ERROR had been declared in R, rather than in P, the handlers E1 and E2 could not provide
       an explicit handler for ERROR since this identifier would not be visible within the bodies of P and
       Q. In situation (3), the exception could however be handled in Q by providing a handler for the
       exception choice **others**.

Notes:

The language does not define what happens when the execution of the main program is abandoned after an unhandled exception. [20]

The predefined exceptions are those that can be propagated by the basic operations and the predefined operators. [21]

The case of a frame that is a generic unit is already covered by the rules for subprogram and package bodies, since the sequence of statements of such a frame is not executed but is the template for the corresponding sequences of statements of the subprograms or packages obtained by generic instantiation. [22]

References: accept statement 9.5, basic operation 3.3.3, block statement 5.6, body stub 10.2, completion 9.4, declarative item 3.9, declarative part 3.9, dependent task 9.4, elaboration 3.1 3.9, exception 11, exception handler 11.2, frame 11.2, generic instantiation 12.3, generic unit 12, library unit 10.1, main program 10.1, numeric_error exception 11.1, package 7, package body 7.1, predefined operator 4.5, procedure 6.1, sequence of statements 5.1, statement 5, subprogram 6, subprogram body 6.3, subprogram call 6.4, subunit 10.2, task 9, task body 9.1 [23]

11.4.2 Exceptions Raised During the Elaboration of Declarations

If an exception is raised during the elaboration of the declarative part of a given frame, this elaboration is abandoned. The next action depends on the nature of the frame: [1]

(a) For a subprogram body, the same exception is raised again at the point of call of the subprogram, unless the subprogram is the main program itself, in which case execution of the main program is abandoned. [2]

(b) For a block statement, the same exception is raised again immediately after the block statement. [3]

(c) For a package body that is a declarative item, the same exception is raised again immediately after this declarative item, in the enclosing declarative part. If the package body is that of a subunit, the exception is raised again at the place of the corresponding body stub. If the package is a library unit, execution of the main program is abandoned. [4]

(d) For a task body, the task becomes completed, and the exception TASKING_ERROR is raised at the point of activation of the task, as explained in section 9.3. [5]

Similarly, if an exception is raised during the elaboration of either a package declaration or a task declaration, this elaboration is abandoned; the next action depends on the nature of the declaration. [6]

(e) For a package declaration or a task declaration, that is a declarative item, the exception is raised again immediately after the declarative item in the enclosing declarative part or package specification. For the declaration of a library package, the execution of the main program is abandoned. [7]

An exception that is raised again (as in the above cases (a), (b), (c) and (e)) is said to be *propagated*, either by the execution of the subprogram or block statement, or by the elaboration of the package declaration, task declaration, or package body. [8]

9   *Example of an exception in the declarative part of a block statement (case (b)):*

```
procedure P is
   ...
begin
   declare
      N : INTEGER := F;      --  the function F may raise ERROR
   begin
      ...
   exception
      when ERROR =>          --  handler E1
   end;
   ...
exception
   when ERROR =>             --  handler E2
end P;
```

      -- if the exception ERROR is raised in the declaration of N, it is handled by E2

10   *References:* activation 9.3, block statement 5.6, body stub 10.2, completed task 9.4, declarative item 3.9, declarative part 3.9, elaboration 3.1 3.9, exception 11, frame 11.2, library unit 10.1, main program 10.1, package body 7.1, package declaration 7.1, package specification 7.1, subprogram 6, subprogram body 6.3, subprogram call 6.4, subunit 10.2, task 9, task body 9.1, task declaration 9.1, tasking_error exception 11.1

11.5 Exceptions Raised During Task Communication

1   An exception can be propagated to a task communicating, or attempting to communicate, with another task. An exception can also be propagated to a calling task if the exception is raised during a rendezvous.

2   When a task calls an entry of another task, the exception TASKING_ERROR is raised in the calling task, at the place of the call, if the called task is completed before accepting the entry call or is already completed at the time of the call.

3   A rendezvous can be completed abnormally in two cases:

4   (a) When an exception is raised within an accept statement, but not handled within an inner frame. In this case, the execution of the accept statement is abandoned and the same exception is raised again immediately after the accept statement within the called task; the exception is also propagated to the calling task at the point of the entry call.

5   (b) When the task containing the accept statement is completed abnormally as the result of an abort statement. In this case, the exception TASKING_ERROR is raised in the calling task at the point of the entry call.

6   On the other hand, if a task issuing an entry call becomes abnormal (as the result of an abort statement) no exception is raised in the called task. If the rendezvous has not yet started, the entry call is cancelled. If the rendezvous is in progress, it completes normally, and the called task is unaffected.

References: abnormal task 9.10, abort statement 9.10, accept statement 9.5, completed task 9.4, entry call 9.5,   7
exception 11, frame 11.2, rendezvous 9.5, task 9, task termination 9.4, tasking_error exception 11.1

11.6 Exceptions and Optimization

The purpose of this section is to specify the conditions under which an implementation is allowed   1
to perform certain actions either earlier or later than specified by other rules of the language.

In general, when the language rules specify an order for certain actions (the *canonical order*), an   2
implementation may only use an alternative order if it can guarantee that the effect of the program
is not changed by the reordering. In particular, no exception should arise for the execution of the
reordered program if none arises for the execution of the program in the canonical order. When,
on the other hand, the order of certain actions is not defined by the language, any order can be
used by the implementation. (For example, the arguments of a predefined operator can be evaluated in any order since the rules given in section 4.5 do not require a specific order of evaluation.)

Additional freedom is left to an implementation for reordering actions involving predefined opera-   3
tions that are either predefined operators or basic operations other than assignments. This
freedom is left, as defined below, even in the case where the execution of these predefined operations may propagate a (predefined) exception:

(a)   For the purpose of establishing whether the same effect is obtained by the execution of cer-   4
      tain actions in the canonical and in an alternative order, it can be assumed that none of the
      predefined operations invoked by these actions propagates a (predefined) exception, provided
      that the two following requirements are met by the alternative order: first, an operation must
      not be invoked in the alternative order if it is not invoked in the canonical order; second, for
      each operation, the innermost enclosing frame or accept statement must be the same in the
      alternative order as in the canonical order, and the same exception handlers must apply.

(b)   Within an expression, the association of operators with operands is specified by the syntax.   5
      However, for a sequence of predefined operators of the same precedence level (and in the
      absence of parentheses imposing a specific association), any association of operators with
      operands is allowed if it satisfies the following requirement: an integer result must be equal to
      . that given by the canonical left-to-right order; a real result must belong to the result model
      interval defined for the canonical left-to-right order (see 4.5.7). Such a reordering is allowed
      even if it may remove an exception, or introduce a further predefined exception.

Similarly, additional freedom is left to an implementation for the evaluation of numeric simple   6
expressions. For the evaluation of a predefined operation, an implementation is allowed to use the
operation of a type that has a range wider than that of the base type of the operands, provided that
this delivers the exact result (or a result within the declared accuracy, in the case of a real type),
even if some intermediate results lie outside the range of the base type. The exception
NUMERIC_ERROR need not be raised in such a case. In particular, if the numeric expression is an
operand of a predefined relational operator, the exception NUMERIC_ERROR need not be raised by
the evaluation of the relation, provided that the correct BOOLEAN result is obtained.

A predefined operation need not be invoked at all, if its only possible effect is to propagate a prede-   7
fined exception. Similarly, a predefined operation need not be invoked if the removal of subsequent
operations by the above rule renders this invocation ineffective.

174-752 0 - 87 - 7

Notes:

8   Rule (b) applies to predefined operators but not to the short-circuit control forms.

9   The expression SPEED < 300_000.0 can be replaced by TRUE if the value 300_000.0 lies outside
     the base type of SPEED, even though the implicit conversion of the numeric literal would raise the
     exception NUMERIC_ERROR.

10   *Example:*

```
declare
  N : INTEGER;
begin
  N := 0;                    -- (1)
  for J in 1 .. 10 loop
    N := N + J**A(K);    -- A and K are global variables
  end loop;
  PUT(N);
exception
  when others => PUT("Some error arose"); PUT(N);
end;
```

11   The evaluation of A(K) may be performed before the loop, and possibly immediately before the
     assignment statement (1) even if this evaluation can raise an exception. Consequently, within the
     exception handler, the value of N is either the undefined initial value or a value later assigned. On
     the other hand, the evaluation of A(K) cannot be moved before **begin** since an exception would
     then be handled by a different handler. For this reason, the initialization of N in the declaration
     itself would exclude the possibility of having an undefined initial value of N in the handler.

12   *References:* accept statement 9.5, accuracy of real operations 4.5.7, assignment 5.2, base type 3.3, basic operation
     3.3.3, conversion 4.6, error situation 11, exception 11, exception handler 11.2, frame 11.2, numeric_error exception
     11.1, predefined operator 4.5, predefined subprogram 8.6, propagation of an exception 11.4, real type 3.5.6,
     undefined value 3.2.1

11.7 Suppressing Checks

1   The presence of a SUPPRESS pragma gives permission to an implementation to omit certain run-
     time checks. The form of this pragma is as follows:

pragma SUPPRESS(identifier [, [ON =>] name]);

2   The identifier is that of the check that can be omitted. The name (if present) must be either a sim-
     ple name or an expanded name and it must denote either an object, a type or subtype, a task unit,
     or a generic unit; alternatively the name can be a subprogram name, in which case it can stand for
     several visible overloaded subprograms.

A pragma SUPPRESS is only allowed immediately within a declarative part or immediately within a package specification. In the latter case, the only allowed form is with a name that denotes an entity (or several overloaded subprograms) declared immediately within the package specification. The permission to omit the given check extends from the place of the pragma to the end of the declarative region associated with the innermost enclosing block statement or program unit. For a pragma given in a package specification, the permission extends to the end of the scope of the named entity.

3

If the pragma includes a name, the permission to omit the given check is further restricted: it is given only for operations on the named object or on all objects of the base type of a named type or subtype; for calls of a named subprogram; for activations of tasks of the named task type; or for instantiations of the given generic unit.

4

The following checks correspond to situations in which the exception CONSTRAINT_ERROR may be raised; for these checks, the name (if present) must denote either an object or a type.

5

ACCESS_CHECK | When accessing a selected component, an indexed component, a slice, or an attribute, of an object designated by an access value, check that the access value is not null.

6

DISCRIMINANT_CHECK | Check that a discriminant of a composite value has the value imposed by a discriminant constraint. Also, when accessing a record component, check that it exists for the current discriminant values.

7

INDEX_CHECK | Check that the bounds of an array value are equal to the corresponding bounds of an index constraint. Also, when accessing a component of an array object, check for each dimension that the given index value belongs to the range defined by the bounds of the array object. Also, when accessing a slice of an array object, check that the given discrete range is compatible with the range defined by the bounds of the array object.

8

LENGTH_CHECK | Check that there is a matching component for each component of an array, in the case of array assignments, type conversions, and logical operators for arrays of boolean components.

9

RANGE_CHECK | Check that a value satisfies a range constraint. Also, for the elaboration of a subtype indication, check that the constraint (if present) is compatible with the type mark. Also, for an aggregate, check that an index or discriminant value belongs to the corresponding subtype. Finally, check for any constraint checks performed by a generic instantiation.

10

The following checks correspond to situations in which the exception NUMERIC_ERROR is raised. The only allowed names in the corresponding pragmas are names of numeric types.

11

DIVISION_CHECK | Check that the second operand is not zero for the operations /, **rem** and **mod**.

12

OVERFLOW_CHECK | Check that the result of a numeric operation does not overflow.

13

The following check corresponds to situations in which the exception PROGRAM_ERROR is raised. The only allowed names in the corresponding pragmas are names denoting task units, generic units, or subprograms.

14

ELABORATION_CHECK | When either a subprogram is called, a task activation is accomplished, or a generic instantiation is elaborated, check that the body of the corresponding unit has already been elaborated.

15

16   The following check corresponds to situations in which the exception STORAGE_ERROR is raised. The only allowed names in the corresponding pragmas are names denoting access types, task units, or subprograms.

17   STORAGE_CHECK   Check that execution of an allocator does not require more space than is available for a collection. Check that the space available for a task or subprogram has not been exceeded.

18   If an error situation arises in the absence of the corresponding run-time checks, the execution of the program is erroneous (the results are not defined by the language).

19   *Examples:*

```
pragma SUPPRESS(RANGE_CHECK);
pragma SUPPRESS(INDEX_CHECK, ON => TABLE);
```

Notes:

20   For certain implementations, it may be impossible or too costly to suppress certain checks. The corresponding SUPPRESS pragma can be ignored. Hence, the occurrence of such a pragma within a given unit does not guarantee that the corresponding exception will not arise; the exceptions may also be propagated by called units.

21   *References:* access type 3.8, access value 3.8, activation 9.3, aggregate 4.3, allocator 4.8, array 3.6, attribute 4.1.4, block statement 5.6, collection 3.8, compatible 3.3.2, component of an array 3.6, component of a record 3.7, composite type 3.3, constraint 3.3, constraint_error exception 11.1, declarative part 3.9, designate 3.8, dimension 3.6, discrete range 3.6, discriminant 3.7.1, discriminant constraint 3.7.2, elaboration 3.1 3.9, erroneous 1.6, error situation 11, expanded name 4.1.3, generic body 11.1, generic instantiation 12.3, generic unit 12, identifier 2.3, index 3.6, index constraint 3.6.1, indexed component 4.1.1, null access value 3.8, numeric operation 3.5.5 3.5.8 3.5.10, numeric type 3.5, numeric_error exception 11.1, object 3.2, operation 3.3.3, package body 7.1, package specification 7.1, pragma 2.8, program_error exception 11.1, program unit 6, propagation of an exception 11.4, range constraint 3.5, record type 3.7, simple name 4.1, slice 4.1.2, subprogram 6, subprogram body 6.3, subprogram call 6.4, subtype 3.3, subunit 10.2, task 9, task body 9.1, task type 9.1, task unit 9, type 3.3, type mark 3.3.2

12. Generic Units

A generic unit is a program unit that is either a generic subprogram or a generic package. A generic unit is a *template*, which is parameterized or not, and from which corresponding (nongeneric) subprograms or packages can be obtained. The resulting program units are said to be *instances* of the original generic unit.

A generic unit is declared by a generic declaration. This form of declaration has a generic formal part declaring any generic formal parameters. An instance of a generic unit is obtained as the result of a generic instantiation with appropriate generic actual parameters for the generic formal parameters. An instance of a generic subprogram is a subprogram. An instance of a generic package is a package.

Generic units are templates. As templates they do not have the properties that are specific to their nongeneric counterparts. For example, a generic subprogram can be instantiated but it cannot be called. In contrast, the instance of a generic subprogram is a nongeneric subprogram; hence, this instance can be called but it cannot be used to produce further instances.

References: declaration 3.1, generic actual parameter 12.3, generic declaration 12.1, generic formal parameter 12.1, generic formal part 12.1, generic instantiation 12.3, generic package 12.1, generic subprogram 12.1, instance 12.3, package 7, program unit 6, subprogram 6

12.1 Generic Declarations

A generic declaration declares a generic unit, which is either a generic subprogram or a generic package. A generic declaration includes a generic formal part declaring any generic formal parameters. A generic formal parameter can be an object; alternatively (unlike a parameter of a subprogram), it can be a type or a subprogram.

```
generic_declaration ::= generic_specification;

generic_specification ::=
      generic_formal_part subprogram_specification
    | generic_formal_part package_specification

generic_formal_part ::= generic {generic_parameter_declaration}

generic_parameter_declaration ::=
      identifier_list : [in [out]] type_mark [:= expression];
    | type identifier is generic_type_definition;
    | private_type_declaration
    | with subprogram_specification [is name];
    | with subprogram_specification [is <>];

generic_type_definition ::=
      (<>) | range <> | digits <> | delta <>
    | array_type_definition | access_type_definition
```

3   The terms generic formal object (or simply, *formal object*), generic formal type (or simply, *formal type*), and generic formal subprogram (or simply, *formal subprogram*) are used to refer to corresponding generic formal parameters.

4   The only form of subtype indication allowed within a generic formal part is a type mark (that is, the subtype indication must not include an explicit constraint). The designator of a generic subprogram must be an identifier.

5   Outside the specification and body of a generic unit, the name of this program unit denotes the generic unit. In contrast, within the declarative region associated with a generic subprogram, the name of this program unit denotes the subprogram obtained by the current instantiation of the generic unit. Similarly, within the declarative region associated with a generic package, the name of this program unit denotes the package obtained by the current instantiation.

6   The elaboration of a generic declaration has no other effect.

7   *Examples of generic formal parts:*

```
generic        --  parameterless

generic
   SIZE : NATURAL;  --  formal object

generic
   LENGTH  : INTEGER := 200;              -- formal object with a default expression
   AREA    : INTEGER := LENGTH*LENGTH; -- formal object with a default expression

generic
   type ITEM  is private;                        -- formal type
   type INDEX is (<>);                            -- formal type
   type ROW   is array(INDEX range <>) of ITEM; -- formal type
   with function "<"(X, Y : ITEM) return BOOLEAN;      -- formal subprogram
```

8   *Examples of generic declarations declaring generic subprograms:*

```
generic
   type ELEM is private;
procedure EXCHANGE(U, V : in out ELEM);

generic
   type ITEM is private;
   with function "*"(U, V : ITEM) return ITEM is <>;
function SQUARING(X : ITEM) return ITEM;
```

9   *Example of a generic declaration declaring a generic package:*

```
generic
   type ITEM     is private;
   type VECTOR is array (POSITIVE range <>) of ITEM;
   with function SUM(X, Y : ITEM) return ITEM;
package ON_VECTORS is
   function SUM   (A, B  : VECTOR) return VECTOR;
   function SIGMA (A     : VECTOR) return ITEM;
   LENGTH_ERROR : exception;
end;
```

12.1 Generic Declarations   **12-2**

Notes:

Within a generic subprogram, the name of this program unit acts as the name of a subprogram. Hence this name can be overloaded, and it can appear in a recursive call of the current instantiation. For the same reason, this name cannot appear after the reserved word **new** in a (recursive) generic instantiation. 10

An expression that occurs in a generic formal part is either the default expression for a generic formal object of mode **in**, or a constituent of an entry name given as default name for a formal subprogram, or the default expression for a parameter of a formal subprogram. Default expressions for generic formal objects and default names for formal subprograms are only evaluated for generic instantiations that use such defaults. Default expressions for parameters of formal subprograms are only evaluated for calls of the formal subprograms that use such defaults. (The usual visibility rules apply to any name used in a default expression: the denoted entity must therefore be visible at the place of the expression.) 11

Neither generic formal parameters nor their attributes are allowed constituents of static expressions (see 4.9). 12

References: access type definition 3.8, array type definition 3.6, attribute 4.1.4, constraint 3.3, declaration 3.1, designator 6.1, elaboration has no other effect 3.1, entity 3.1, expression 4.4, function 6.5, generic instantiation 12.3, identifier 2.3, identifier list 3.2, instance 12.3, name 4.1, object 3.2, overloading 6.6 8.7, package specification 7.1, parameter of a subprogram 6.2, private type definition 7.4, procedure 6.1, reserved word 2.9, static expression 4.9, subprogram 6, subprogram specification 6.1, subtype indication 3.3.2, type 3.3, type mark 3.3.2 13

12.1.1 Generic Formal Objects

The first form of generic parameter declaration declares generic formal objects. The type of a generic formal object is the base type of the type denoted by the type mark given in the generic parameter declaration. A generic parameter declaration with several identifiers is equivalent to a sequence of single generic parameter declarations, as explained in section 3.2. 1

A generic formal object has a mode that is either **in** or **in out**. In the absence of an explicit mode indication in a generic parameter declaration, the mode **in** is assumed; otherwise the mode is the one indicated. If a generic parameter declaration ends with an expression, the expression is the *default expression* of the generic formal parameter. A default expression is only allowed if the mode is **in** (whether this mode is indicated explicitly or implicitly). The type of a default expression must be that of the corresponding generic formal parameter. 2

A generic formal object of mode **in** is a constant whose value is a copy of the value supplied as the matching generic actual parameter in a generic instantiation, as described in section 12.3. The type of a generic formal object of mode **in** must not be a limited type; the subtype of such a generic formal object is the subtype denoted by the type mark given in the generic parameter declaration. 3

A generic formal object of mode **in out** is a variable and denotes the object supplied as the matching generic actual parameter in a generic instantiation, as described in section 12.3. The constraints that apply to the generic formal object are those of the corresponding generic actual parameter. 4

Note:

5   The constraints that apply to a generic formal object of mode **in out** are those of the corresponding generic actual parameter (not those implied by the type mark that appears in the generic parameter declaration). Whenever possible (to avoid confusion) it is recommended that the name of a base type be used for the declaration of such a formal object. If, however, the base type is anonymous, it is recommended that the subtype name defined by the type declaration for the base type be used.

6   *References:* anonymous type 3.3.1, assignment 5.2, base type 3.3, constant declaration 3.2, constraint 3.3, declaration 3.1, generic actual parameter 12.3, generic formal object 12.1, generic formal parameter 12.1, generic instantiation 12.3, generic parameter declaration 12.1, identifier 2.3, limited type 7.4.4, matching generic actual parameter 12.3, mode 6.1, name 4.1, object 3.2, simple name 4.1, subtype 3.3, type declaration 3.3, type mark 3.3.2, variable 3.2.1

12.1.2 Generic Formal Types

1   A generic parameter declaration that includes a generic type definition or a private type declaration declares a generic formal type. A generic formal type denotes the subtype supplied as the corresponding actual parameter in a generic instantiation, as described in 12.3(d). However, within a generic unit, a generic formal type is considered as being distinct from all other (formal or nonformal) types. The form of constraint applicable to a formal type in a subtype indication depends on the class of the type as for a nonformal type.

2   The only form of discrete range that is allowed within the declaration of a generic formal (constrained) array type is a type mark.

3   The discriminant part of a generic formal private type must not include a default expression for a discriminant. (Consequently, a variable that is declared by an object declaration must be constrained if its type is a generic formal type with discriminants.)

4   Within the declaration and body of a generic unit, the operations available for values of a generic formal type (apart from any additional operation specified by a generic formal subprogram) are determined by the generic parameter declaration for the formal type:

5   (a) For a private type declaration, the available operations are those defined in section 7.4.2 (in particular, assignment, equality, and inequality are available for a private type unless it is limited).

6   (b) For an array type definition, the available operations are those defined in section 3.6.2 (for example, they include the formation of indexed components and slices).

7   (c) For an access type definition, the available operations are those defined in section 3.8.2 (for example, allocators can be used).

8   The four forms of generic type definition in which a *box* appears (that is, the compound delimiter <>) correspond to the following major forms of scalar type:

9   (d) Discrete types: (<>)

     The available operations are the operations common to enumeration and integer types; these are defined in section 3.5.5.

(e) Integer types: **range** <>

10

The available operations are the operations of integer types defined in section 3.5.5.

(f) Floating point types: **digits** <>

11

The available operations are those defined in section 3.5.8.

(g) Fixed point types: **delta** <>

12

The available operations are those defined in section 3.5.10.

In all of the above cases (a) through (f), each operation implicitly associated with a formal type   13
(that is, other than an operation specified by a formal subprogram) is implicitly declared at the
place of the declaration of the formal type. The same holds for a formal fixed point type, except for
the multiplying operators that deliver a result of the type *universal_fixed* (see 4.5.5), since these
special operators are declared in the package STANDARD.

For an instantiation of the generic unit, each of these operations is the corresponding basic opera-   14
tion or predefined operator of the matching actual type. For an operator, this rule applies even if
the operator has been redefined for the actual type or for some parent type of the actual type.

Examples of generic formal types:

15

```
type ITEM is private;
type BUFFER(LENGTH : NATURAL) is limited private;

type ENUM   is (<>);
type INT    is range <>;
type ANGLE  is delta <>;
type MASS   is digits <>;

type TABLE is array (ENUM) of ITEM;
```

Example of a generic formal part declaring a formal integer type:

16

```
generic
   type RANK is range <>;
   FIRST   : RANK := RANK'FIRST;
   SECOND  : RANK := FIRST + 1;   --   the operator "+" of the type RANK
```

References: access type definition 3.8, allocator 4.8, array type definition 3.6, assignment 5.2, body of a generic unit   17
12.2, class of type 3.3, constraint 3.3, declaration 3.1, declaration of a generic unit 12.1, discrete range 3.6, discrete
type 3.5, discriminant part 3.7.1, enumeration type 3.5.1, equality 4.5.2, fixed point type 3.5.9, floating point type
3.5.7, generic actual type 12.3, generic formal part 12.1, generic formal subprogram 12.1.3, generic formal type 12.1,
generic parameter declaration 12.1, generic type definition 12.1, indexed component 4.1.1, inequality 4.5.2, instantiation 12.3, integer type 3.5.4, limited private type 7.4.4, matching generic actual type 12.3.2 12.3.3 12.3.4 12.3.5,
multiplying operator 4.5 4.5.5, operation 3.3, operator 4.5, parent type 3.4, private type definition 7.4, scalar type 3.5,
slice 4.1.2, standard package 8.6 C, subtype indication 3.3.2, type mark 3.3.2, universal_fixed 3.5.9

12.1.3 Generic Formal Subprograms

1   A generic parameter declaration that includes a subprogram specification declares a generic formal subprogram.

2   Two alternative forms of defaults can be specified in the declaration of a generic formal subprogram. In these forms, the subprogram specification is followed by the reserved word **is** and either a box or the name of a subprogram or entry. The matching rules for these defaults are explained in section 12.3.6.

3   A generic formal subprogram denotes the subprogram, enumeration literal, or entry supplied as the corresponding generic actual parameter in a generic instantiation, as described in section 12.3(f).

4   *Examples of generic formal subprograms:*

```
with function INCREASE(X : INTEGER) return INTEGER;
with function SUM(X, Y : ITEM) return ITEM;

with function "+"(X, Y : ITEM) return ITEM is <>;
with function IMAGE(X : ENUM) return STRING is ENUM'IMAGE;

with procedure UPDATE is DEFAULT_UPDATE;
```

Notes:

5   The constraints that apply to a parameter of a formal subprogram are those of the corresponding parameter in the specification of the matching actual subprogram (not those implied by the corresponding type mark in the specification of the formal subprogram). A similar remark applies to the result of a function. Whenever possible (to avoid confusion), it is recommended that the name of a base type be used rather than the name of a subtype in any declaration of a formal subprogram. If, however, the base type is anonymous, it is recommended that the subtype name defined by the type declaration be used.

6   The type specified for a formal parameter of a generic formal subprogram can be any visible type, including a generic formal type of the same generic formal part.

7   *References:* anonymous type 3.3.1, base type 3.3, box delimiter 12.1.2, constraint 3.3, designator 6.1, generic actual parameter 12.3, generic formal function 12.1, generic formal subprogram 12.1, generic instantiation 12.3, generic parameter declaration 12.1, identifier 2.3, matching generic actual subprogram 12.3.6, operator symbol 6.1, parameter of a subprogram 6.2, renaming declaration 8.5, reserved word 2.9, scope 8.2, subprogram 6, subprogram specification 6.1, subtype 3.3.2, type 3.3, type mark 3.3.2

12.2 Generic Bodies

1   The body of a generic subprogram or generic package is a template for the bodies of the corresponding subprograms or packages obtained by generic instantiations. The syntax of a generic body is identical to that of a nongeneric body.

2   For each declaration of a generic subprogram, there must be a corresponding body.

The elaboration of a generic body has no other effect than to establish that the body can from then on be used as the template for obtaining the corresponding instances.

₃

Example of a generic procedure body:

₄

```
procedure EXCHANGE(U, V : in out ELEM) is    --  see example in 12.1
  T : ELEM;  --   the generic formal type
begin
  T := U;
  U := V;
  V := T;
end EXCHANGE;
```

Example of a generic function body:

₅

```
function SQUARING(X : ITEM) return ITEM is    --  see example in 12.1
begin
  return X*X;  --   the formal operator "*"
end;
```

Example of a generic package body:

₆

```
package body ON_VECTORS is    --  see example in 12.1

  function SUM(A, B : VECTOR) return VECTOR is
    RESULT  : VECTOR(A'RANGE);      --   the formal type VECTOR
    BIAS    : constant INTEGER := B'FIRST - A'FIRST;
  begin
    if A'LENGTH /= B'LENGTH then
      raise LENGTH_ERROR;
    end if;

    for N in A'RANGE loop
      RESULT(N) := SUM(A(N), B(N + BIAS));      --  the formal function SUM
    end loop;
    return RESULT;
  end;

  function SIGMA(A : VECTOR) return ITEM is
    TOTAL : ITEM := A(A'FIRST);               --  the formal type ITEM
  begin
    for N in A'FIRST + 1 .. A'LAST loop
      TOTAL := SUM(TOTAL, A(N));              --  the formal function SUM
    end loop;
    return TOTAL;
  end;
end;
```

References: body 3.9, elaboration 3.9, generic body 12.1, generic instantiation 12.3, generic package 12.1, generic subprogram 12.1, instance 12.3, package body 7.1, package 7, subprogram 6, subprogram body 6.3

₇

12.3 Generic Instantiation

1 An instance of a generic unit is declared by a generic instantiation.

2
```
generic_instantiation ::=
    package identifier is
        new generic_package_name [generic_actual_part];
    | procedure identifier is
        new generic_procedure_name [generic_actual_part];
    | function designator is
        new generic_function_name [generic_actual_part];

generic_actual_part ::=
    (generic_association {, generic_association})

generic_association ::=
    [generic_formal_parameter =>] generic_actual_parameter

generic_formal_parameter ::= parameter_simple_name | operator_symbol

generic_actual_parameter ::= expression | variable_name
    | subprogram_name | entry_name | type_mark
```

3 An explicit generic actual parameter must be supplied for each generic formal parameter, unless the corresponding generic parameter declaration specifies that a default can be used. Generic associations can be either positional or named, in the same manner as parameter associations of subprogram calls (see 6.4). If two or more formal subprograms have the same designator, then named associations are not allowed for the corresponding generic parameters.

4 Each generic actual parameter must *match* the corresponding generic formal parameter. An expression can match a formal object of mode **in**; a variable name can match a formal object of mode **in out**; a subprogram name or an entry name can match a formal subprogram; a type mark can match a formal type. The detailed rules defining the allowed matches are given in sections 12.3.1 to 12.3.6; these are the only allowed matches.

5 The instance is a copy of the generic unit, apart from the generic formal part; thus the instance of a generic package is a package, that of a generic procedure is a procedure, and that of a generic function is a function. For each occurrence, within the generic unit, of a name that denotes a given entity, the following list defines which entity is denoted by the corresponding occurrence within the instance.

6 (a) For a name that denotes the generic unit: The corresponding occurrence denotes the instance.

7 (b) For a name that denotes a generic formal object of mode **in**:   The corresponding name denotes a constant whose value is a copy of the value of the associated generic actual parameter.

8 (c) For a name that denotes a generic formal object of mode **in out**:   The corresponding name denotes the variable named by the associated generic actual parameter.

9 (d) For a name that denotes a generic formal type: The corresponding name denotes the subtype named by the associated generic actual parameter (the actual subtype).

10 (e) For a name that denotes a discriminant of a generic formal type: The corresponding name denotes the corresponding discriminant (there must be one) of the actual type associated with the generic formal type.

(f)   For a name that denotes a generic formal subprogram: The corresponding name denotes the   11
      subprogram, enumeration literal, or entry named by the associated generic actual parameter
      (the actual subprogram).

(g)   For a name that denotes a formal parameter of a generic formal subprogram: The cor-   12
      responding name denotes the corresponding formal parameter of the actual subprogram
      associated with the formal subprogram.

(h)   For a name that denotes a local entity declared within the generic unit: The corresponding   13
      name denotes the entity declared by the corresponding local declaration within the instance.

(i)   For a name that denotes a global entity declared outside of the generic unit: The cor-   14
      responding name denotes the same global entity.

Similar rules apply to operators and basic operations: in particular, formal operators follow a rule   15
similar to rule (f), local operations follow a rule similar to rule (h), and operations for global types
follow a rule similar to rule (i). In addition, if within the generic unit a predefined operator or basic
operation of a formal type is used, then within the instance the corresponding occurrence refers to
the corresponding predefined operation of the actual type associated with the formal type.

The above rules apply also to any type mark or (default) expression given within the generic formal   16
part of the generic unit.

For the elaboration of a generic instantiation, each expression supplied as an explicit generic actual 17
parameter is first evaluated, as well as each expression that appears as a constituent of a variable
name or entry name supplied as an explicit generic actual parameter; these evaluations proceed in
some order that is not defined by the language. Then, for each omitted generic association (if any),
the corresponding default expression or default name is evaluated; such evaluations are performed in the order of the generic parameter declarations. Finally, the implicitly generated instance
is elaborated. The elaboration of a generic instantiation may also involve certain constraint checks
as described in later subsections.

Recursive generic instantiation is not allowed in the following sense: if a given generic unit   18
includes an instantiation of a second generic unit, then the instance generated by this instantiation
must not include an instance of the first generic unit (whether this instance is generated directly, or
indirectly by intermediate instantiations).

Examples of generic instantiations (see 12.1):   19

```
procedure  SWAP  is new  EXCHANGE(ELEM => INTEGER);
procedure  SWAP  is new  EXCHANGE(CHARACTER);   --  SWAP is overloaded

function  SQUARE  is new  SQUARING (INTEGER);   --  "*" of INTEGER used by default
function  SQUARE  is new  SQUARING (ITEM => MATRIX, "*" => MATRIX_PRODUCT);
function  SQUARE  is new  SQUARING (MATRIX, MATRIX_PRODUCT); -- same as previous

package  INT_VECTORS  is new  ON_VECTORS(INTEGER, TABLE, "+");
```

Examples of uses of instantiated units: 20

```
SWAP(A, B);
A := SQUARE(A);

T  : TABLE(1 .. 5) := (10, 20, 30, 40, 50);
N  : INTEGER := INT_VECTORS.SIGMA(T);  --  150 (see 12.2 for the body of SIGMA)

use INT_VECTORS;
M  : INTEGER := SIGMA(T);  --  150
```

Notes:

21   Omission of a generic actual parameter is only allowed if a corresponding default exists. If default expressions or default names (other than simple names) are used, they are evaluated in the order in which the corresponding generic formal parameters are declared.

22   If two overloaded subprograms declared in a generic package specification differ only by the (formal) type of their parameters and results, then there exist legal instantiations for which all calls of these subprograms from outside the instance are ambiguous. For example:

```
generic
   type A is (<>);
   type B is private;
package G is
   function NEXT(X : A)  return A;
   function NEXT(X : B)  return B;
end;

package P is new G(A => BOOLEAN, B => BOOLEAN);
-- calls of P.NEXT are ambiguous
```

23   *References:* declaration 3.1, designator 6.1, discriminant 3.7.1, elaboration 3.1 3.9, entity 3.1, entry name 9.5, evaluation 4.5, expression 4.4, generic formal object 12.1, generic formal parameter 12.1, generic formal subprogram 12.1, generic formal type 12.1, generic parameter declaration 12.1, global declaration 8.1, identifier 2.3, implicit declaration 3.1, local declaration 8.1, mode in 12.1.1, mode in out 12.1.1, name 4.1, operation 3.3, operator symbol 6.1, overloading 6.6 8.7, package 7, simple name 4.1, subprogram 6, subprogram call 6.4, subprogram name 6.1, subtype declaration 3.3.2, type mark 3.3.2, variable 3.2.1, visibility 8.3

12.3.1 Matching Rules for Formal Objects

1   A generic formal parameter of mode **in** of a given type is matched by an expression of the same type. If a generic unit has a generic formal object of mode **in**, a check is made that the value of the expression belongs to the subtype denoted by the type mark, as for an explicit constant declaration (see 3.2.1). The exception CONSTRAINT_ERROR is raised if this check fails.

2   A generic formal parameter of mode **in out** of a given type is matched by the name of a variable of the same type. The variable must not be a formal parameter of mode **out** or a subcomponent thereof. The name must denote a variable for which renaming is allowed (see 8.5).

Notes:

3   The type of a generic actual parameter of mode **in** must not be a limited type. The constraints that apply to a generic formal parameter of mode **in out** are those of the corresponding generic actual parameter (see 12.1.1).

4   *References:* constraint 3.3, constraint_error exception 11.1, expression 4.4, formal parameter 6.1, generic actual parameter 12.3, generic formal object 12.1.1, generic formal parameter 12.1, generic instantiation 12.3, generic unit 12.1, limited type 7.4.4, matching generic actual parameter 12.3, mode in 12.1.1, mode in out 12.1.1, mode out 6.2, name 4.1, raising of exceptions 11, satisfy 3.3, subcomponent 3.3, type 3.3, type mark 3.3.2, variable 3.2.1

12.3.2 Matching Rules for Formal Private Types

A generic formal private type is matched by any type or subtype (the actual subtype) that satisfies the following conditions:

- If the formal type is not limited, the actual type must not be a limited type. (If, on the other hand, the formal type is limited, no such condition is imposed on the corresponding actual type, which can be limited or not limited.)

- If the formal type has a discriminant part, the actual type must be a type with the same number of discriminants; the type of a discriminant that appears at a given position in the discriminant part of the actual type must be the same as the type of the discriminant that appears at the same position in the discriminant part of the formal type; and the actual subtype must be unconstrained. (If, on the other hand, the formal type has no discriminants, the actual type is allowed to have discriminants.)

Furthermore, consider any occurrence of the name of the formal type at a place where this name is used as an unconstrained subtype indication. The actual subtype must not be an unconstrained array type or an unconstrained type with discriminants, if any of these occurrences is at a place where either a constraint or default discriminants would be required for an array type or for a type with discriminants (see 3.6.1 and 3.7.2). The same restriction applies to occurrences of the name of a subtype of the formal type, and to occurrences of the name of any type or subtype derived, directly or indirectly, from the formal type.

If a generic unit has a formal private type with discriminants, the elaboration of a corresponding generic instantiation checks that the subtype of each discriminant of the actual type is the same as the subtype of the corresponding discriminant of the formal type. The exception CONSTRAINT_ERROR is raised if this check fails.

References: array type 3.6, constraint 3.3, constraint_error exception 11.1, default expression for a discriminant 3.7.1, derived type 3.4, discriminant 3.7.1, discriminant part 3.7.1, elaboration 3.9, generic actual type 12.3, generic body 12.2, generic formal type 12.1.2, generic instantiation 12.3, generic specification 12.1, limited type 7.4.4, matching generic actual parameter 12.3, name 4.1, private type 7.4, raising of exceptions 11, subtype 3.3, subtype indication 3.2.2, type 3.3, type with discriminants 3.3, unconstrained array type 3.6, unconstrained subtype 3.3

12.3.3 Matching Rules for Formal Scalar Types

A generic formal type defined by (<>) is matched by any discrete subtype (that is, any enumeration or integer subtype). A generic formal type defined by **range** <> is matched by any integer subtype. A generic formal type defined by **digits** <> is matched by any floating point subtype. A generic formal type defined by **delta** <> is matched by any fixed point subtype. No other matches are possible for these generic formal types.

References: box delimiter 12.1.2, discrete type 3.5, enumeration type 3.5.1, fixed point type 3.5.9, floating point type 3.5.7, generic actual type 12.3, generic formal type 12.1.2, generic type definition 12.1, integer type 3.5.4, matching generic actual parameter 12.3, scalar type 3.5

12.3.4 Matching Rules for Formal Array Types

1   A formal array type is matched by an actual array subtype that satisfies the following conditions:

2   ● The formal array type and the actual array type must have the same dimensionality; the formal type and the actual subtype must be either both constrained or both unconstrained.

3   ● For each index position, the index type must be the same for the actual array type as for the formal array type.

4   ● The component type must be the same for the actual array type as for the formal array type. If the component type is other than a scalar type, then the component subtypes must be either both constrained or both unconstrained.

5   If a generic unit has a formal array type, the elaboration of a corresponding instantiation checks that the constraints (if any) on the component type are the same for the actual array type as for the formal array type, and likewise that for any given index position the index subtypes or the discrete ranges have the same bounds. The exception CONSTRAINT_ERROR is raised if this check fails.

6   *Example:*

```
--  given the generic package

generic
    type ITEM      is private;
    type INDEX     is (<>);
    type VECTOR    is array (INDEX range <>) of ITEM;
    type TABLE     is array (INDEX) of ITEM;
package P is
    ...
end;

--  and the types

type MIX      is array (COLOR range <>) of BOOLEAN;
type OPTION   is array (COLOR) of BOOLEAN;

--  then  MIX  can match VECTOR and OPTION can match TABLE

package R is new P( ITEM      => BOOLEAN,  INDEX => COLOR,
                    VECTOR    => MIX,      TABLE => OPTION);

--  Note that MIX cannot match TABLE and OPTION cannot match VECTOR
```

Note:

7   For the above rules, if any of the index or component types of the formal array type is itself a formal type, then within the instance its name denotes the corresponding actual subtype (see 12.3(d)).

8   *References:* array type 3.6, array type definition 3.6, component of an array 3.6, constrained array type 3.6, constraint 3.3, constraint_error exception 11.1, elaboration 3.9, formal type 12.1, generic formal type 12.1.2, generic instantiation 12.3, index 3.6, index constraint 3.6.1, matching generic actual parameter 12.3, raise statement 11.3, subtype 3.3, unconstrained array type 3.6

12.3.5 Matching Rules for Formal Access Types

A formal access type is matched by an actual access subtype if the type of the designated objects [1]
is the same for the actual type as for the formal type. If the designated type is other than a scalar
type, then the designated subtypes must be either both constrained or both unconstrained.

If a generic unit has a formal access type, the elaboration of a corresponding instantiation checks [2]
that any constraints on the designated objects are the same for the actual access subtype as for
the formal access type. The exception CONSTRAINT_ERROR is raised if this check fails.

Example: [3]

```
--   the formal types of the generic package

generic
   type NODE  is private;
   type LINK   is access NODE;
package P is
   ...
end;

--   can be matched by the actual types

type CAR;
type CAR_NAME is access CAR;

type CAR is
   record
      PRED, SUCC : CAR_NAME;
      NUMBER      : LICENSE_NUMBER;
      OWNER       : PERSON;
   end record;


—   in the following generic instantiation

package R is new P(NODE => CAR, LINK => CAR_NAME);
```

Note:

For the above rules, if the designated type is itself a formal type, then within the instance its name [4]
denotes the corresponding actual subtype (see 12.3(d)).

References: access type 3.8, access type definition 3.8, constraint 3.3, constraint_error exception 11.1, designate [5]
3.8, elaboration 3.9, generic formal type 12.1.2, generic instantiation 12.3, matching generic actual parameter 12.3,
object 3.2, raise statement 11.3, value of access type 3.8

12.3.6 Matching Rules for Formal Subprograms

1   A formal subprogram is matched by an actual subprogram, enumeration literal, or entry if both have the same parameter and result type profile (see 6.6); in addition, parameter modes must be identical for formal parameters that are at the same parameter position.

2   If a generic unit has a default subprogram specified by a name, this name must denote a subprogram, an enumeration literal, or an entry, that matches the formal subprogram (in the above sense). The evaluation of the default name takes place during the elaboration of each instantiation that uses the default, as defined in section 12.3.

3   If a generic unit has a default subprogram specified by a box, the corresponding actual parameter can be omitted if a subprogram, enumeration literal, or entry matching the formal subprogram, and with the same designator as the formal subprogram, is directly visible at the place of the generic instantiation; this subprogram, enumeration literal, or entry is then used by default (there must be exactly one subprogram, enumeration literal, or entry satisfying the previous conditions).

4   *Example:*

```
--  given the generic function specification

generic
    type ITEM is private;
    with function "*" (U, V : ITEM) return ITEM is <>;
function SQUARING(X : ITEM) return ITEM;

--  and the function

function MATRIX_PRODUCT(A, B : MATRIX) return MATRIX;

--  the following instantiation is possible

function SQUARE is new SQUARING(MATRIX, MATRIX_PRODUCT);

--  the following instantiations are equivalent

function SQUARE is new SQUARING(ITEM => INTEGER, "*" => "*");
function SQUARE is new SQUARING(INTEGER, "*");
function SQUARE is new SQUARING(INTEGER);
```

Notes:

5   The matching rules for formal subprograms state requirements that are similar to those applying to subprogram renaming declarations (see 8.5). In particular, the name of a parameter of the formal subprogram need not be the same as that of the corresponding parameter of the actual subprogram; similarly, for these parameters, default expressions need not correspond.

6   A formal subprogram is matched by an attribute of a type if the attribute is a function with a matching specification. An enumeration literal of a given type matches a parameterless formal function whose result type is the given type.

7   *References:* attribute 4.1.4, box delimiter 12.1.2, designator 6.1, entry 9.5, function 6.5, generic actual type 12.3, generic formal subprogram 12.1.3, generic formal type 12.1.2, generic instantiation 12.3, matching generic actual parameter 12.3, name 4.1, parameter and result type profile 6.3, subprogram 6, subprogram specification 6.1, subtype 3.3, visibility 8.3

12.4 Example of a Generic Package

The following example provides a possible formulation of stacks by means of a generic package. The size of each stack and the type of the stack elements are provided as generic parameters.

1

```
generic
   SIZE : POSITIVE;
   type ITEM is private;
package STACK is
   procedure PUSH (E : in    ITEM);
   procedure POP  (E : out   ITEM);
   OVERFLOW, UNDERFLOW : exception;
end STACK;

package body STACK is

   type TABLE is array (POSITIVE range <>) of ITEM;
   SPACE  : TABLE(1 .. SIZE);
   INDEX  : NATURAL := 0;

   procedure PUSH(E : in ITEM) is
   begin
     if INDEX >= SIZE then
       raise OVERFLOW;
     end if;
     INDEX := INDEX + 1;
     SPACE(INDEX) := E;
   end PUSH;

   procedure POP(E : out ITEM) is
   begin
     if INDEX = 0 then
       raise UNDERFLOW;
     end if;
     E := SPACE(INDEX);
     INDEX := INDEX - 1;
   end POP;

end STACK;
```

2

Instances of this generic package can be obtained as follows:

3

```
package STACK_INT    is new STACK(SIZE => 200, ITEM => INTEGER);
package STACK_BOOL   is new STACK(100, BOOLEAN);
```

Thereafter, the procedures of the instantiated packages can be called as follows:

4

```
STACK_INT.PUSH(N);
STACK_BOOL.PUSH(TRUE);
```

5   Alternatively, a generic formulation of the type STACK can be given as follows (package body omitted):

```
generic
   type ITEM is private;
package ON_STACKS is
   type STACK(SIZE : POSITIVE) is limited private;
   procedure PUSH (S : in out STACK; E : in    ITEM);
   procedure POP  (S : in out STACK; E : out   ITEM);
   OVERFLOW, UNDERFLOW : exception;
private
   type TABLE is array (POSITIVE range <>) of ITEM;
   type STACK(SIZE : POSITIVE) is
      record
         SPACE  : TABLE(1 .. SIZE);
         INDEX  : NATURAL := 0;
      end record;
end;
```

6   In order to use such a package, an instantiation must be created and thereafter stacks of the corresponding type can be declared:

```
declare
   package STACK_REAL is new ON_STACKS(REAL); use STACK_REAL;
   S : STACK(100);
begin
   ...
   PUSH(S, 2.54);
   ...
end;
```

13. Representation Clauses and Implementation-Dependent Features

This chapter describes representation clauses, certain implementation-dependent features, and other features that are used in system programming.

13.1 Representation Clauses

Representation clauses specify how the types of the language are to be mapped onto the underlying machine. They can be provided to give more efficient representation or to interface with features that are outside the domain of the language (for example, peripheral hardware).

```
representation_clause ::=
     type_representation_clause | address_clause

type_representation_clause ::= length_clause
     | enumeration_representation_clause | record_representation_clause
```

A type representation clause applies either to a type or to a *first named subtype* (that is, to a subtype declared by a type declaration, the base type being therefore anonymous). Such a representation clause applies to all objects that have this type or this first named subtype. At most one enumeration or record representation clause is allowed for a given type: an enumeration representation clause is only allowed for an enumeration type; a record representation clause, only for a record type. (On the other hand, more than one length clause can be provided for a given type; moreover, both a length clause and an enumeration or record representation clause can be provided.) A length clause is the only form of representation clause allowed for a type derived from a parent type that has (user-defined) derivable subprograms.

An address clause applies either to an object; to a subprogram, package, or task unit; or to an entry. At most one address clause is allowed for any of these entities.

A representation clause and the declaration of the entity to which the clause applies must both occur immediately within the same declarative part, package specification, or task specification; the declaration must occur before the clause. In the absence of a representation clause for a given declaration, a default representation of this declaration is determined by the implementation. Such a default determination occurs no later than the end of the immediately enclosing declarative part, package specification, or task specification. For a declaration given in a declarative part, this default determination occurs before any enclosed body.

In the case of a type, certain occurrences of its name imply that the representation of the type must already have been determined. Consequently these occurrences force the default determination of any aspect of the representation not already determined by a prior type representation clause. This default determination is also forced by similar occurrences of the name of a subtype of the type, or of the name of any type or subtype that has subcomponents of the type. A forcing occurrence is any occurrence other than in a type or subtype declaration, a subprogram specification, an entry declaration, a deferred constant declaration, a pragma, or a representation clause for the type itself. In any case, an occurrence within an expression is always forcing.

7   A representation clause for a given entity must not appear after an occurrence of the name of the entity if this occurrence forces a default determination of representation for the entity.

8   Similar restrictions exist for address clauses. For an object, any occurrence of its name (after the object declaration) is a forcing occurrence. For a subprogram, package, task unit, or entry, any occurrence of a representation attribute of such an entity is a forcing occurrence.

9   The effect of the elaboration of a representation clause is to define the corresponding aspects of the representation.

10   The interpretation of some of the expressions that appear in representation clauses is implementation-dependent, for example, expressions specifying addresses. An implementation may limit its acceptance of representation clauses to those that can be handled simply by the underlying hardware. If a representation clause is accepted by an implementation, the compiler must guarantee that the net effect of the program is not changed by the presence of the clause, except for address clauses and for parts of the program that interrogate representation attributes. If a program contains a representation clause that is not accepted, the program is illegal. For each implementation, the allowed representation clauses, and the conventions used for implementation-dependent expressions, must be documented in Appendix F of the reference manual.

11   Whereas a representation clause is used to impose certain characteristics of the mapping of an entity onto the underlying machine, pragmas can be used to provide an implementation with criteria for its selection of such a mapping. The pragma PACK specifies that storage minimization should be the main criterion when selecting the representation of a record or array type. Its form is as follows:

    pragma PACK (*type*_simple_name);

12   Packing means that gaps between the storage areas allocated to consecutive components should be minimized. It need not, however, affect the mapping of each component onto storage. This mapping can itself be influenced by a pragma (or controlled by a representation clause) for the component or component type. The position of a PACK pragma, and the restrictions on the named type, are governed by the same rules as for a representation clause; in particular, the pragma must appear before any use of a representation attribute of the packed entity.

13   The pragma PACK is the only language-defined representation pragma. Additional representation pragmas may be provided by an implementation; these must be documented in Appendix F. (In contrast to representation clauses, a pragma that is not accepted by the implementation is ignored.)

Note:

14   No representation clause is allowed for a generic formal type.

15   *References:* address clause 13.5, allow 1.6, body 3.9, component 3.3, declaration 3.1, declarative part 3.9, default expression 3.2.1, deferred constant declaration 7.4, derivable subprogram 3.4, derived type 3.4, entity 3.1, entry 9.5, enumeration representation clause 13.3, expression 4.4, generic formal type 12.1.2, illegal 1.6, length clause 13.2, must 1.6, name 4.1, object 3.2, occur immediately within 8.1, package 7, package specification 7.1, parent type 3.4, pragma 2.8, record representation clause 13.4, representation attribute 13.7.2 13.7.3, subcomponent 3.3, subprogram 6, subtype 3.3, subtype declaration 3.3.2, task specification 9.1, task unit 9, type 3.3, type declaration 3.3.1

13.2 Length Clauses

A length clause specifies an amount of storage associated with a type.   1

    length_clause ::= **for** attribute **use** simple_expression;   2

The expression must be of some numeric type and is evaluated during the elaboration of the length   3
clause (unless it is a static expression). The prefix of the attribute must denote either a type or a
first named subtype. The prefix is called T in what follows. The only allowed attribute designators
in a length clause are SIZE, STORAGE_SIZE, and SMALL. The effect of the length clause depends
on the attribute designator:

(a) Size specification: T'SIZE   4

The expression must be a static expression of some integer type. The value of the expression   5
specifies an upper bound for the number of bits to be allocated to objects of the type or first
named subtype T. The size specification must allow for enough storage space to accommodate every allowable value of these objects. A size specification for a composite type may
affect the size of the gaps between the storage areas allocated to consecutive components.
On the other hand, It need not affect the size of the storage area allocated to each component.

The size specification is only allowed if the constraints on T and on its subcomponents (if any)   6
are static. In the case of an unconstrained array type, the index subtypes must also be static.

(b) Specification of collection size: T'STORAGE_SIZE   7

The prefix T must denote an access type. The expression must be of some integer type (but   8
need not be static); its value specifies the number of storage units to be reserved for the collection, that is, the storage space needed to contain all objects designated by values of the
access type and by values of other types derived from the access type, directly or indirectly.
This form of length clause is not allowed for a type derived from an access type.

(c) Specification of storage for a task activation: T'STORAGE_SIZE   9

The prefix T must denote a task type. The expression must be of some integer type (but need   10
not be static); its value specifies the number of storage units to be reserved for an activation
(not the code) of a task of the type.

(d) Specification of *small* for a fixed point type: T'SMALL   11

The prefix T must denote the first named subtype of a fixed point type. The expression must   12
be a static expression of some real type; its value must not be greater than the delta of the
first named subtype. The effect of the length clause is to use this value of *small* for the
representation of values of the fixed point base type. (The length clause thereby also affects
the amount of storage for objects that have this type.)

Notes:

A size specification is allowed for an access, task, or fixed point type, whether or not another form   13
of length clause is also given for the type.

14   What is considered to be part of the storage reserved for a collection or for an activation of a task is implementation-dependent. The control afforded by length clauses is therefore relative to the implementation conventions. For example, the language does not define whether the storage reserved for an activation of a task includes any storage needed for the collection associated with an access type declared within the task body. Neither does it define the method of allocation for objects denoted by values of an access type. For example, the space allocated could be on a stack; alternatively, a general dynamic allocation scheme or fixed storage could be used.

15   The objects allocated in a collection need not have the same size if the designated type is an unconstrained array type or an unconstrained type with discriminants. Note also that the allocator itself may require some space for internal tables and links. Hence a length clause for the collection of an access type does not always give precise control over the maximum number of allocated objects.

16   *Examples:*

```
--  assumed declarations:

type MEDIUM is range  0 .. 65000;
type SHORT  is delta  0.01  range -100.0  .. 100.0;
type DEGREE is delta  0.1   range -360.0  .. 360.0;

BYTE  : constant := 8;
PAGE  : constant := 2000;

--  length clauses:

for COLOR'SIZE    use 1*BYTE;   --  see 3.5.1
for MEDIUM'SIZE   use 2*BYTE;
for SHORT'SIZE    use 15;

for CAR_NAME'STORAGE_SIZE use  --  approximately 2000 cars
    2000*((CAR'SIZE/SYSTEM.STORAGE_UNIT) + 1);

for KEYBOARD_DRIVER'STORAGE_SIZE use 1*PAGE;

for DEGREE'SMALL use 360.0/2**(SYSTEM.STORAGE_UNIT - 1);
```

17   *Notes on the examples:*

In the length clause for SHORT, fifteen bits is the minimum necessary, since the type definition requires SHORT'SMALL = 2.0**(-7) and SHORT'MANTISSA = 14. The length clause for DEGREE forces the model numbers to exactly span the range of the type.

18   *References:* access type 3.8, allocator 4.8, allow 1.6, array type 3.6, attribute 4.1.4, collection 3.8, composite type 3.3, constraint 3.3, delta of a fixed point type 3.5.9, derived type 3.4, designate 3.8, elaboration 3.9, entity 3.1, evaluation 4.5, expression 4.4, first named subtype 13.1, fixed point type 3.5.9, index subtype 3.6, integer type 3.5.4, must 1.6, numeric type 3.5, object 3.2, real type 3.5.6, record type 3.7, small of a fixed point type 3.5.10, static constraint 4.9, static expression 4.9, static subtype 4.9, storage unit 13.7, subcomponent 3.3, system package 13.7, task 9, task activation 9.3, task specification 9.1, task type 9.2, type 3.3, unconstrained array type 3.6

13.3 Enumeration Representation Clauses

An enumeration representation clause specifies the internal codes for the literals of the enumeration type that is named in the clause.

enumeration_representation_clause ::= **for** *type*_simple_name **use** aggregate;

The aggregate used to specify this mapping is written as a one-dimensional aggregate, for which the index subtype is the enumeration type and the component type is *universal_integer*.

All literals of the enumeration type must be provided with distinct integer codes, and all choices and component values given in the aggregate must be static. The integer codes specified for the enumeration type must satisfy the predefined ordering relation of the type.

Example:

    type MIX_CODE **is** (ADD, SUB, MUL, LDA, STA, STZ);

    for MIX_CODE **use**
        (ADD => 1, SUB => 2, MUL => 3, LDA => 8, STA => 24, STZ => 33);

Notes:

The attributes SUCC, PRED, and POS are defined even for enumeration types with a noncontiguous representation; their definition corresponds to the (logical) type declaration and is not affected by the enumeration representation clause. In the example, because of the need to avoid the omitted values, these functions are likely to be less efficiently implemented than they could be in the absence of a representation clause. Similar considerations apply when such types are used for indexing.

References: aggregate 4.3, array aggregate 4.3.2, array type 3.6, attribute of an enumeration type 3.5.5, choice 3.7.3, component 3.3, enumeration literal 3.5.1, enumeration type 3.5.1, function 6.5, index 3.6, index subtype 3.6, literal 4.2, ordering relation of an enumeration type 3.5.1, representation clause 13.1, simple name 4.1, static expression 4.9, type 3.3, type declaration 3.3.1, universal_integer type 3.5.4

13.4 Record Representation Clauses

A record representation clause specifies the storage representation of records, that is, the order, position, and size of record components (including discriminants, if any).

    record_representation_clause ::=
        for *type*_simple_name **use**
            record [alignment_clause]
                {component_clause}
            end **record**;

    alignment_clause ::= **at** **mod** *static*_simple_expression;

    component_clause ::=
        *component*_name **at** *static*_simple_expression **range** *static*_range;

3   The simple expression given after the reserved words **at mod** in an alignment clause, or after the reserved word **at** in a component clause, must be a static expression of some integer type. If the bounds of the range of a component clause are defined by simple expressions, then each bound of the range must be defined by a static expression of some integer type, but the two bounds need not have the same integer type.

4   An alignment clause forces each record of the given type to be allocated at a starting address that is a multiple of the value of the given expression (that is, the address modulo the expression must be zero). An implementation may place restrictions on the allowable alignments.

5   A component clause specifies the *storage place* of a component, relative to the start of the record. The integer defined by the static expression of a component clause is a relative address expressed in storage units. The range defines the bit positions of the storage place, relative to the storage unit. The first storage unit of a record is numbered zero. The first bit of a storage unit is numbered zero. The ordering of bits in a storage unit is machine-dependent and may extend to adjacent storage units. (For a specific machine, the size in bits of a storage unit is given by the configuration-dependent named number SYSTEM.STORAGE_UNIT.) Whether a component is allowed to overlap a storage boundary, and if so, how, is implementation-defined.

6   At most one component clause is allowed for each component of the record type, including for each discriminant (component clauses may be given for some, all, or none of the components). If no component clause is given for a component, then the choice of the storage place for the component is left to the compiler. If component clauses are given for all components, the record representation clause completely specifies the representation of the record type and must be obeyed exactly by the compiler.

7   Storage places within a record variant must not overlap, but overlap of the storage for distinct variants is allowed. Each component clause must allow for enough storage space to accommodate every allowable value of the component. A component clause is only allowed for a component if any constraint on this component or on any of its subcomponents is static.

8   An implementation may generate names that denote implementation-dependent components (for example, one containing the offset of another component). Such implementation-dependent names can be used in record representation clauses (these names need not be simple names; for example, they could be implementation-dependent attributes).

9   *Example:*

```
        WORD : constant := 4;   --  storage unit is byte, 4 bytes per word

        type STATE        is (A, M, W, P);
        type MODE         is (FIX, DEC, EXP, SIGNIF);

        type BYTE_MASK    is array (0 .. 7) of BOOLEAN;
        type STATE_MASK   is array (STATE) of BOOLEAN;
        type MODE_MASK    is array (MODE) of BOOLEAN;

        type PROGRAM_STATUS_WORD is
          record
            SYSTEM_MASK       : BYTE_MASK;
            PROTECTION_KEY    : INTEGER range 0 .. 3;
            MACHINE_STATE     : STATE_MASK;
            INTERRUPT_CAUSE   : INTERRUPTION_CODE;
            ILC               : INTEGER range 0 .. 3;
            CC                : INTEGER range 0 .. 3;
            PROGRAM_MASK      : MODE_MASK;
            INST_ADDRESS      : ADDRESS;
          end record;
```

13.4 Record Representation Clauses

```
for PROGRAM_STATUS_WORD use
    record at mod 8;
        SYSTEM_MASK          at 0*WORD    range 0    .. 7;
        PROTECTION_KEY       at 0*WORD    range 10   .. 11;   -- bits 8, 9 unused
        MACHINE_STATE        at 0*WORD    range 12   .. 15;
        INTERRUPT_CAUSE      at 0*WORD    range 16   .. 31;
        ILC                  at 1*WORD    range 0    .. 1;    -- second word
        CC                   at 1*WORD    range 2    .. 3;
        PROGRAM_MASK         at 1*WORD    range 4    .. 7;
        INST_ADDRESS         at 1*WORD    range 8    .. 31;
    end record;

for PROGRAM_STATUS_WORD'SIZE use 8*SYSTEM.STORAGE_UNIT;
```

Note on the example:

The record representation clause defines the record layout. The length clause guarantees that   10
exactly eight storage units are used.

References: allow 1.6, attribute 4.1.4, constant 3.2.1, constraint 3.3, discriminant 3.7.1, integer type 3.5.4, must   11
1.6, named number 3.2, range 3.5, record component 3.7, record type 3.7, simple expression 4.4, simple name 4.1,
static constraint 4.9, static expression 4.9, storage unit 13.7, subcomponent 3.3, system package 13.7, variant 3.7.3

13.5 Address Clauses

An address clause specifies a required address in storage for an entity.   1

    address_clause ::= **for** simple_name **use at** simple_expression;   2

The expression given after the reserved word **at** must be of the type ADDRESS defined in the   3
package SYSTEM (see 13.7); this package must be named by a with clause that applies to the
compilation unit in which the address clause occurs. The conventions that define the interpretation
of a value of the type ADDRESS as an address, as an interrupt level, or whatever it may be, are
implementation-dependent. The allowed nature of the simple name and the meaning of the corresponding address are as follows:

(a) Name of an object: the address is that required for the object (variable or constant).   4

(b) Name of a subprogram, package, or task unit: the address is that required for the machine   5
    code associated with the body of the program unit.

(c) Name of a single entry: the address specifies a hardware interrupt to which the single entry is   6
    to be linked.

If the simple name is that of a single task, the address clause is understood to refer to the task unit   7
and not to the task object. In all cases, the address clause is only legal if exactly one declaration
with this identifier occurs earlier, immediately within the same declarative part, package specification, or task specification. A name declared by a renaming declaration is not allowed as the simple
name.

Address clauses should not be used to achieve overlays of objects or overlays of program units.   8
Nor should a given interrupt be linked to more than one entry. Any program using address clauses
to achieve such effects is erroneous.

9   *Example:*

> **for** CONTROL **use at** 16#0020#;   --   assuming that SYSTEM.ADDRESS is an integer type

Notes:

10   The above rules imply that if two subprograms overload each other and are visible at a given point, an address clause for any of them is not legal at this point. Similarly if a task specification declares entries that overload each other, they cannot be interrupt entries. The syntax does not allow an address clause for a library unit. An implementation may provide pragmas for the specification of program overlays.

11   *References:* address predefined type 13.7, apply 10.1.1, compilation unit 10.1, constant 3.2.1, entity 3.1, entry 9.5, erroneous 1.6, expression 4.4, library unit 10.1, name 4.1, object 3.2, package 7, pragma 2.8, program unit 6, reserved word 2.9, simple expression 4.4, simple name 4.1, subprogram 6, subprogram body 6.3, system package 13.7, task body 9.1, task object 9.2, task unit 9, type 3.3, variable 3.2.1, with clause 10.1.1

13.5.1 Interrupts

1   An address clause given for an entry associates the entry with some device that may cause an interrupt; such an entry is referred to in this section as an *interrupt entry*. If control information is supplied upon an interrupt, it is passed to an associated interrupt entry as one or more parameters of mode **in**; only parameters of this mode are allowed.

2   An interrupt acts as an entry call issued by a hardware task whose priority is higher than the priority of the main program, and also higher than the priority of any user-defined task (that is, any task whose type is declared by a task unit in the program). The entry call may be an ordinary entry call, a timed entry call, or a conditional entry call, depending on the kind of interrupt and on the implementation.

3   If a select statement contains both a terminate alternative and an accept alternative for an interrupt entry, then an implementation may impose further requirements for the selection of the terminate alternative in addition to those given in section 9.4.

4   *Example:*

```
task INTERRUPT_HANDLER is
   entry DONE;
   for DONE use at 16#40#;   --   assuming that SYSTEM.ADDRESS is an integer type
end INTERRUPT_HANDLER;
```

Notes:

5   Interrupt entry calls need only have the semantics described above; they may be implemented by having the hardware directly execute the appropriate accept statements.

6   Queued interrupts correspond to ordinary entry calls. Interrupts that are lost if not immediately processed correspond to conditional entry calls. It is a consequence of the priority rules that an accept statement executed in response to an interrupt takes precedence over ordinary, user-defined tasks, and can be executed without first invoking a scheduling action.

One of the possible effects of an address clause for an interrupt entry is to specify the priority of   7
the interrupt (directly or indirectly). Direct calls to an interrupt entry are allowed.

References: accept alternative 9.7.1, accept statement 9.5, address predefined type 13.7, allow 1.6, conditional   8
entry call 9.7.2, entry 9.5, entry call 9.5, mode 6.1, parameter of a subprogram 6.2, priority of a task 9.8, select alternative 9.7.1, select statement 9.7, system package 13.7, task 9, terminate alternative 9.7.1, timed entry call 9.7.3

13.6 Change of Representation

At most one representation clause is allowed for a given type and a given aspect of its representa-   1
tion. Hence, if an alternative representation is needed, it is necessary to declare a second type,
derived from the first, and to specify a different representation for the second type.

Example: 2

```
--   PACKED_DESCRIPTOR and DESCRIPTOR are two different types
--   with identical characteristics, apart from their representation

type DESCRIPTOR is
   record
      --   components of a descriptor
   end record;

type PACKED_DESCRIPTOR is new DESCRIPTOR;

for PACKED_DESCRIPTOR use
   record
      --   component clauses for some or for all components
   end record;
```

Change of representation can now be accomplished by assignment with explicit type conversions: 3

```
D  : DESCRIPTOR;
P  : PACKED_DESCRIPTOR;

P  := PACKED_DESCRIPTOR(D);    --  pack D
D  := DESCRIPTOR(P);           --  unpack P
```

References: assignment 5.2, derived type 3.4, type 3.3, type conversion 4.6, type declaration 3.1, representation   4
clause 13.1

13.7 The Package System

For each implementation there is a predefined library package called SYSTEM which includes the   1
definitions of certain configuration-dependent characteristics. The specification of the package
SYSTEM is implementation-dependent and must be given in Appendix F. The visible part of this
package must contain at least the following declarations.

2
```
package SYSTEM is
   type ADDRESS   is implementation_defined;
   type NAME      is implementation_defined_enumeration_type;

   SYSTEM_NAME    : constant NAME   := implementation_defined;

   STORAGE_UNIT   : constant := implementation_defined;
   MEMORY_SIZE    : constant := implementation_defined;

   -- System-Dependent Named Numbers:

   MIN_INT        : constant := implementation_defined;
   MAX_INT        : constant := implementation_defined;
   MAX_DIGITS     : constant := implementation_defined;
   MAX_MANTISSA   : constant := implementation_defined;
   FINE_DELTA     : constant := implementation_defined;
   TICK           : constant := implementation_defined;

   -- Other System-Dependent Declarations

   subtype PRIORITY is INTEGER range implementation_defined;

   ...
end SYSTEM;
```

3 The type ADDRESS is the type of the addresses provided in address clauses; it is also the type of the result delivered by the attribute ADDRESS. Values of the enumeration type NAME are the names of alternative machine configurations handled by the implementation; one of these is the constant SYSTEM_NAME. The named number STORAGE_UNIT is the number of bits per storage unit; the named number MEMORY_SIZE is the number of available storage units in the configuration; these named numbers are of the type *universal_integer*.

4 An alternative form of the package SYSTEM, with given values for any of SYSTEM_NAME, STORAGE_UNIT, and MEMORY_SIZE, can be obtained by means of the corresponding pragmas. These pragmas are only allowed at the start of a compilation, before the first compilation unit (if any) of the compilation.

5   **pragma** SYSTEM_NAME (enumeration_literal);

6 The effect of the above pragma is to use the enumeration literal with the specified identifier for the definition of the constant SYSTEM_NAME. This pragma is only allowed if the specified identifier corresponds to one of the literals of the type NAME.

7   **pragma** STORAGE_UNIT (numeric_literal);

8 The effect of the above pragma is to use the value of the specified numeric literal for the definition of the named number STORAGE_UNIT.

9   **pragma** MEMORY_SIZE (numeric_literal);

10 The effect of the above pragma is to use the value of the specified numeric literal for the definition of the named number MEMORY_SIZE.

The compilation of any of these pragmas causes an implicit recompilation of the package SYSTEM. Consequently any compilation unit that names SYSTEM in its context clause becomes obsolete after this implicit recompilation. An implementation may impose further limitations on the use of these pragmas. For example, an implementation may allow them only at the start of the first compilation, when creating a new program library.

Note:

It is a consequence of the visibility rules that a declaration given in the package SYSTEM is not visible in a compilation unit unless this package is mentioned by a with clause that applies (directly or indirectly) to the compilation unit.

References: address clause 13.5, apply 10.1.1, attribute 4.1.4, compilation unit 10.1, declaration 3.1, enumeration literal 3.5.1, enumeration type 3.5.1, identifier 2.3, library unit 10.1, must 1.6, named number 3.2, number declaration 3.2.2, numeric literal 2.4, package 7, package specification 7.1, pragma 2.8, program library 10.1, type 3.3, visibility 8.3, visible part 7.2, with clause 10.1.1

13.7.1 System-Dependent Named Numbers

Within the package SYSTEM, the following named numbers are declared. The numbers FINE_DELTA and TICK are of the type *universal_real*; the others are of the type *universal_integer*.

MIN_INT	The smallest (most negative) value of all predefined integer types.
MAX_INT	The largest (most positive) value of all predefined integer types.
MAX_DIGITS	The largest value allowed for the number of significant decimal digits in a floating point constraint.
MAX_MANTISSA	The largest possible number of binary digits in the mantissa of model numbers of a fixed point subtype.
FINE_DELTA	The smallest delta allowed in a fixed point constraint that has the range constraint -1.0 .. 1.0.
TICK	The basic clock period, in seconds.

References: allow 1.6, delta of a fixed point constraint 3.5.9, fixed point constraint 3.5.9, floating point constraint 3.5.7, integer type 3.5.4, model number 3.5.6, named number 3.2, package 7, range constraint 3.5, system package 13.7, type 3.3, universal_integer type 3.5.4, universal_real type 3.5.6

13.7.2 Representation Attributes

1   The values of certain implementation-dependent characteristics can be obtained by interrogating appropriate *representation attributes*. These attributes are described below.

2   For any object, program unit, label, or entry X:

3   X'ADDRESS   Yields the address of the first of the storage units allocated to X. For a sub-program, package, task unit or label, this value refers to the machine code associated with the corresponding body or statement. For an entry for which an address clause has been given, the value refers to the corresponding hardware interrupt. The value of this attribute is of the type ADDRESS defined in the package SYSTEM.

4   For any type or subtype X, or for any object X:

5   X'SIZE   Applied to an object, yields the number of bits allocated to hold the object. Applied to a type or subtype, yields the minimum number of bits that is needed by the implementation to hold any possible object of this type or sub-type. The value of this attribute is of the type *universal_integer*.

6   For the above two representation attributes, if the prefix is the name of a function, the attribute is understood to be an attribute of the function (not of the result of calling the function). Similarly, if the type of the prefix is an access type, the attribute is understood to be an attribute of the prefix (not of the designated object: attributes of the latter can be written with a prefix ending with the reserved word **all**).

7   For any component C of a record object R:

8   R.C'POSITION   Yields the offset, from the start of the first storage unit occupied by the record, of the first of the storage units occupied by C. This offset is measured in storage units. The value of this attribute is of the type *universal_integer*.

9   R.C'FIRST_BIT   Yields the offset, from the start of the first of the storage units occupied by C, of the first bit occupied by C. This offset is measured in bits. The value of this attribute is of the type *universal_integer*.

10 R.C'LAST_BIT   Yields the offset, from the start of the first of the storage units occupied by C, of the last bit occupied by C. This offset is measured in bits. The value of this attribute is of the type *universal_integer*.

11 For any access type or subtype T:

12 T'STORAGE_SIZE   Yields the total number of storage units reserved for the collection associated with the base type of T. The value of this attribute is of the type *universal_integer*.

13 For any task type or task object T:

14 T'STORAGE_SIZE   Yields the number of storage units reserved for each activation of a task of the type T or for the activation of the task object T. The value of this attribute is of the type *universal_integer*.

Notes:

For a task object X, the attribute X'SIZE gives the number of bits used to hold the object X, whereas X'STORAGE_SIZE gives the number of storage units allocated for the activation of the task designated by X. For a formal parameter X, if parameter passing is achieved by copy, then the attribute X'ADDRESS yields the address of the local copy; if parameter passing is by reference, then the address is that of the actual parameter.   15

References: access subtype 3.8, access type 3.8, activation 9.3, actual parameter 6.2, address clause 13.5, address   16
predefined type 13.7, attribute 4.1.4, base type 3.3, collection 3.8, component 3.3, entry 9.5, formal parameter 6.1
6.2, label 5.1, object 3.2, package 7, package body 7.1, parameter passing 6.2, program unit 6, record object 3.7,
statement 5, storage unit 13.7, subprogram 6, subprogram body 6.3, subtype 3.3, system predefined package 13.7,
task 9, task body 9.1, task object 9.2, task type 9.2, task unit 9, type 3.3, universal_integer type 3.5.4

13.7.3 Representation Attributes of Real Types

For every real type or subtype T, the following machine-dependent attributes are defined, which   1
are not related to the model numbers. Programs using these attributes may thereby exploit
properties that go beyond the minimal properties associated with the numeric type (see section
4.5.7 for the rules defining the accuracy of operations with real operands). Precautions must
therefore be taken when using these machine-dependent attributes if portability is to be ensured.

For both floating point and fixed point types: 2

T'MACHINE_ROUNDS	Yields the value TRUE if every predefined arithmetic operation on values of the base type of T either returns an exact result or performs rounding; yields the value FALSE otherwise. The value of this attribute is of the predefined type BOOLEAN.

3

T'MACHINE_OVERFLOWS	Yields the value TRUE if every predefined operation on values of the base type of T either provides a correct result, or raises the exception NUMERIC_ERROR in overflow situations (see 4.5.7); yields the value FALSE otherwise. The value of this attribute is of the predefined type BOOLEAN.

4

For floating point types, the following attributes provide characteristics of the underlying machine   5
representation, in terms of the canonical form defined in section 3.5.7:

T'MACHINE_RADIX	Yields the value of the *radix* used by the machine representation of the base type of T. The value of this attribute is of the type *universal_integer*.

6

T'MACHINE_MANTISSA	Yields the number of digits in the *mantissa* for the machine representation of the base type of T (the digits are extended digits in the range 0 to T'MACHINE_RADIX -1). The value of this attribute is of the type *universal_integer*.

7

T'MACHINE_EMAX	Yields the largest value of *exponent* for the machine representation of the base type of T. The value of this attribute is of the type *universal_integer*.

8

T'MACHINE_EMIN	Yields the smallest (most negative) value of *exponent* for the machine representation of the base type of T. The value of this attribute is of the type *universal_integer*.

9

Representation Attributes of Real Types 13.7.3

Note:

10 For many machines the largest machine representable number of type F is almost

   (F'MACHINE_RADIX)**(F'MACHINE_EMAX),

11 and the smallest positive representable number is

   F'MACHINE_RADIX ** (F'MACHINE_EMIN - 1)

12 *References:* arithmetic operator 4.5, attribute 4.1.4, base type 3.3, boolean predefined type 3.5.3, false boolean value 3.5.3, fixed point type 3.5.9, floating point type 3.5.7, model number 3.5.6, numeric type 3.5, numeric_error exception 11.1, predefined operation 3.3.3, radix 3.5.7, real type 3.5.6, subtype 3.3, true boolean value 3.5.3, type 3.3, universal_integer type 3.5.4

13.8 Machine Code Insertions

1 A machine code insertion can be achieved by a call to a procedure whose sequence of statements contains code statements.

2   code_statement ::= type_mark'*record*_aggregate;

3 A code statement is only allowed in the sequence of statements of a procedure body. If a procedure body contains code statements, then within this procedure body the only allowed form of statement is a code statement (labeled or not), the only allowed declarative items are use clauses, and no exception handler is allowed (comments and pragmas are allowed as usual).

4 Each machine instruction appears as a record aggregate of a record type that defines the corresponding instruction. The base type of the type mark of a code statement must be declared within the predefined library package called MACHINE_CODE; this package must be named by a with clause that applies to the compilation unit in which the code statement occurs. An implementation is not required to provide such a package.

5 An implementation is allowed to impose further restrictions on the record aggregates allowed in code statements. For example, it may require that expressions contained in such aggregates be static expressions.

6 An implementation may provide machine-dependent pragmas specifying register conventions and calling conventions. Such pragmas must be documented in Appendix F.

7 *Example:*

```
M : MASK;
procedure SET_MASK; pragma INLINE(SET_MASK);

procedure SET_MASK is
  use MACHINE_CODE;
begin
  SI_FORMAT'(CODE => SSM, B => M'BASE_REG, D => M'DISP);
  --  M'BASE_REG and M'DISP are implementation-specific predefined attributes
end;
```

References: allow 1.6, apply 10.1.1, comment 2.7, compilation unit 10.1, declarative item 3.9, exception handler 8
11.2, inline pragma 6.3.2, labeled statement 5.1, library unit 10.1, package 7, pragma 2.8, procedure 6 6.1, procedure body 6.3, record aggregate 4.3.1, record type 3.7, sequence of statements 5.1, statement 5, static expression 4.9, use clause 8.4, with clause 10.1.1

13.9 Interface to Other Languages

A subprogram written in another language can be called from an Ada program provided that all 1
communication is achieved via parameters and function results. A pragma of the form

   pragma INTERFACE (*language*_name, *subprogram*_name); 2

must be given for each such subprogram; a subprogram name is allowed to stand for several 3
overloaded subprograms. This pragma is allowed at the place of a declarative item, and must apply
in this case to a subprogram declared by an earlier declarative item of the same declarative part or
package specification. The pragma is also allowed for a library unit; in this case the pragma must
appear after the subprogram declaration, and before any subsequent compilation unit. The
pragma specifies the other language (and thereby the calling conventions) and informs the compiler that an object module will be supplied for the corresponding subprogram. A body is not
allowed for such a subprogram (not even in the form of a body stub) since the instructions of the
subprogram are written in another language.

This capability need not be provided by all Implementations.   An implementation may place 4
restrictions on the allowable forms and places of parameters and calls.

Example: 5

```
package FORT_LIB is
   function SQRT (X : FLOAT) return FLOAT;
   function EXP  (X : FLOAT) return FLOAT;
private
   pragma INTERFACE(FORTRAN, SQRT);
   pragma INTERFACE(FORTRAN, EXP);
end FORT_LIB;
```

Notes:

The conventions used by other language processors that call Ada programs are not part of the Ada 6
language definition. Such conventions must be defined by these other language processors.

The pragma INTERFACE is not defined for generic subprograms. 7

References: allow 1.6, body stub 10.2, compilation unit 10.1, declaration 3.1, declarative item 3.9, declarative part 8
3.9, function result 6.5, library unit 10.1, must 1.6, name 4.1, overloaded subprogram 6.6, package specification 7.1,
parameter of a subprogram 6.2, pragma 2.8, subprogram 6, subprogram body 6.3, subprogram call 6.4, subprogram
declaration 6.1

13.10 Unchecked Programming

1 The predefined generic library subprograms UNCHECKED_DEALLOCATION and UNCHECKED_CONVERSION are used for unchecked storage deallocation and for unchecked type conversions.

2
```
generic
    type OBJECT  is limited private;
    type NAME    is access OBJECT;
procedure UNCHECKED_DEALLOCATION(X : in out NAME);
```

3
```
generic
    type SOURCE is limited private;
    type TARGET is limited private;
function UNCHECKED_CONVERSION(S : SOURCE) return TARGET;
```

4 *References:* generic subprogram 12.1, library unit 10.1, type 3.3

13.10.1 Unchecked Storage Deallocation

1 Unchecked storage deallocation of an object designated by a value of an access type is achieved by a call of a procedure that is obtained by instantiation of the generic procedure UNCHECKED_DEALLOCATION. For example:

```
procedure FREE is new UNCHECKED_DEALLOCATION (object_type_name, access_type_name)
```

2 Such a FREE procedure has the following effect:

3 (a) after executing FREE (X), the value of X is **null**;

4 (b) FREE (X), when X is already equal to **null**, has no effect;

5 (c) FREE (X), when X is not equal to **null**, is an indication that the object designated by X is no longer required, and that the storage it occupies is to be reclaimed.

6 If X and Y designate the same object, then accessing this object through Y is erroneous if this access is performed (or attempted) after the call FREE (X); the effect of each such access is not defined by the language.

7 *Notes:*

7 It is a consequence of the visibility rules that the generic procedure UNCHECKED_DEALLOCATION is not visible in a compilation unit unless this generic procedure is mentioned by a with clause that applies to the compilation unit.

8 If X designates a task object, the call FREE (X) has no effect on the task designated by the value of this task object. The same holds for any subcomponent of the object designated by X, if this sub-component is a task object.

9 *References:* access type 3.8, apply 10.1.1, compilation unit 10.1, designate 3.8 9.1, erroneous 1.6, generic instantiation 12.3, generic procedure 12.1, generic unit 12, library unit 10.1, null access value 3.8, object 3.2, procedure 6, procedure call 6.4, subcomponent 3.3, task 9, task object 9.2, visibility 8.3, with clause 10.1.1

13.10.2 Unchecked Type Conversions

An unchecked type conversion can be achieved by a call of a function that is obtained by instantia- 1
tion of the generic function UNCHECKED_CONVERSION.

The effect of an unchecked conversion is to return the (uninterpreted) parameter value as a value 2
of the target type, that is, the bit pattern defining the source value is returned unchanged as the bit
pattern defining a value of the target type. An implementation may place restrictions on unchecked
conversions, for example, restrictions depending on the respective sizes of objects of the source
and target type. Such restrictions must be documented in appendix F.

Whenever unchecked conversions are used, it is the programmer's responsibility to ensure that 3
these conversions maintain the properties that are guaranteed by the language for objects of the
target type.   Programs that violate these properties by means of unchecked conversions are
erroneous.

Note:

It is a consequence of the visibility rules that the generic function UNCHECKED_CONVERSION is 4
not visible in a compilation unit unless this generic function is mentioned by a with clause that
applies to the compilation unit.

References: apply 10.1.1, compilation unit 10.1, erroneous 1.6, generic function 12.1, instantiation 12.3, parameter 5
of a subprogram 6.2, type 3.3, with clause 10.1.1

14. Input-Output

Input-output is provided in the language by means of predefined packages. The generic packages SEQUENTIAL_IO and DIRECT_IO define input-output operations applicable to files containing elements of a given type. Additional operations for text input-output are supplied in the package TEXT_IO. The package IO_EXCEPTIONS defines the exceptions needed by the above three packages. Finally, a package LOW_LEVEL_IO is provided for direct control of peripheral devices.

References: direct_io package 14.2 14.2.4, io_exceptions package 14.5, low_level_io package 14.6, sequential_io package 14.2 14.2.2, text_io package 14.3

14.1 External Files and File Objects

Values input from the external environment of the program, or output to the environment, are considered to occupy *external files*. An external file can be anything external to the program that can produce a value to be read or receive a value to be written. An external file is identified by a string (the *name*). A second string (the *form*) gives further system-dependent characteristics that may be associated with the file, such as the physical organization or access rights. The conventions governing the interpretation of such strings must be documented in Appendix F.

Input and output operations are expressed as operations on objects of some *file type*, rather than directly in terms of the external files. In the remainder of this chapter, the term *file* is always used to refer to a file object; the term *external file* is used otherwise. The values transferred for a given file must all be of one type.

Input-output for sequential files of values of a single element type is defined by means of the generic package SEQUENTIAL_IO. The skeleton of this package is given below.

```
with IO_EXCEPTIONS;
generic
   type ELEMENT_TYPE is private;
package SEQUENTIAL_IO is
   type FILE_TYPE is limited private;

   type FILE_MODE is (IN_FILE, OUT_FILE);
   ...
   procedure OPEN (FILE : in out FILE_TYPE; ...);
   ...
   procedure READ (FILE : in FILE_TYPE; ITEM : out ELEMENT_TYPE);
   procedure WRITE (FILE : in FILE_TYPE; ITEM : in ELEMENT_TYPE);
   ...
end SEQUENTIAL_IO;
```

In order to define sequential input-output for a given element type, an instantiation of this generic unit, with the given type as actual parameter, must be declared. The resulting package contains the declaration of a file type (called FILE_TYPE) for files of such elements, as well as the operations applicable to these files, such as the OPEN, READ, and WRITE procedures.

5   Input-output for direct access files is likewise defined by a generic package called DIRECT_IO. Input-output in human-readable form is defined by the (nongeneric) package TEXT_IO.

6   Before input or output operations can be performed on a file, the file must first be associated with an external file. While such an association is in effect, the file is said to be *open*, and otherwise the file is said to be *closed*.

7   The language does not define what happens to external files after the completion of the main program (in particular, if corresponding files have not been closed). The effect of input-output for access types is implementation-dependent.

8   An open file has a *current mode*, which is a value of one of the enumeration types

```
type FILE_MODE is (IN_FILE, INOUT_FILE, OUT_FILE);   --  for DIRECT_IO
type FILE_MODE is (IN_FILE, OUT_FILE);               --  for SEQUENTIAL_IO  and  TEXT_IO
```

9   These values correspond respectively to the cases where only reading, both reading and writing, or only writing are to be performed. The mode of a file can be changed.

10   Several file management operations are common to the three input-output packages. These operations are described in section 14.2.1 for sequential and direct files. Any additional effects concerning text input-output are described in section 14.3.1.

11   The exceptions that can be raised by a call of an input-output subprogram are all defined in the package IO_EXCEPTIONS; the situations in which they can be raised are described, either following the description of the subprogram (and in section 14.4), or in Appendix F in the case of error situations that are implementation-dependent.

Notes:

12   Each instantiation of the generic packages SEQUENTIAL_IO and DIRECT_IO declares a different type FILE_TYPE; in the case of TEXT_IO, the type FILE_TYPE is unique.

13   A bidirectional device can often be modeled as two sequential files associated with the device, one of mode IN_FILE, and one of mode OUT_FILE. An implementation may restrict the number of files that may be associated with a given external file. The effect of sharing an external file in this way by several file objects is implementation-dependent.

14   *References:* create procedure 14.2.1, current index 14.2, current size 14.2, delete procedure 14.2.1, direct access 14.2, direct file procedure 14.2, direct_io package 14.1 14.2, enumeration type 3.5.1, exception 11, file mode 14.2.3, generic instantiation 12.3, index 14.2, input file 14.2.2, io_exceptions package 14.5, open file 14.1, open procedure 14.2.1, output file 14.2.2, read procedure 14.2.4, sequential access 14.2, sequential file 14.2, sequential input-output 14.2.2, sequential_io package 14.2 14.2.2, string 3.6.3, text_io package 14.3, write procedure 14.2.4

14.2 Sequential and Direct Files

1   Two kinds of access to external files are defined: *sequential access* and *direct access*. The corresponding file types and the associated operations are provided by the generic packages SEQUENTIAL_IO and DIRECT_IO. A file object to be used for sequential access is called a *sequential file*, and one to be used for direct access is called a *direct file*.

2   For sequential access, the file is viewed as a sequence of values that are transferred in the order of their appearance (as produced by the program or by the environment). When the file is opened, transfer starts from the beginning of the file.

For direct access, the file is viewed as a set of elements occupying consecutive positions in linear order; a value can be transferred to or from an element of the file at any selected position. The position of an element is specified by its *index*, which is a number, greater than zero, of the implementation-defined integer type COUNT. The first element, if any, has index one; the index of the last element, if any, is called the *current size*; the current size is zero if there are no elements. The current size is a property of the external file. 3

An open direct file has a *current index*, which is the index that will be used by the next read or write operation. When a direct file is opened, the current index is set to one. The current index of a direct file is a property of a file object, not of an external file. 4

All three file modes are allowed for direct files. The only allowed modes for sequential files are the modes IN_FILE and OUT_FILE. 5

References: count type 14.3, file mode 14.1, in_file 14.1, out_file 14.1 6

14.2.1 File Management

The procedures and functions described in this section provide for the control of external files; their declarations are repeated in each of the three packages for sequential, direct, and text input-output. For text input-output, the procedures CREATE, OPEN, and RESET have additional effects described in section 14.3.1. 1

    procedure CREATE(FILE : **in out** FILE_TYPE; 2
                        MODE : **in** FILE_MODE := *default_mode*;
                        NAME : **in** STRING := "";
                        FORM : **in** STRING := "");

        Establishes a new external file, with the given name and form, and associates this external file with the given file. The given file is left open. The current mode of the given file is set to the given access mode. The default access mode is the mode OUT_FILE for sequential and text input-output; it is the mode INOUT_FILE for direct input-output. For direct access, the size of the created file is implementation-dependent. A null string for NAME specifies an external file that is not accessible after the completion of the main program (a temporary file). A null string for FORM specifies the use of the default options of the implementation for the external file. 3

        The exception STATUS_ERROR is raised if the given file is already open. The exception NAME_ERROR is raised if the string given as NAME does not allow the identification of an external file. The exception USE_ERROR is raised if, for the specified mode, the environment does not support creation of an external file with the given name (in the absence of NAME_ERROR) and form. 4

    procedure OPEN(FILE : **in out** FILE_TYPE; 5
                   MODE : **in** FILE_MODE;
                   NAME : **in** STRING;
                   FORM : **in** STRING := "");

        Associates the given file with an existing external file having the given name and form, and sets the current mode of the given file to the given mode. The given file is left open. 6

7   The exception STATUS_ERROR is raised if the given file is already open. The exception
     NAME_ERROR is raised if the string given as NAME does not allow the identification of an external
     file; in particular, this exception is raised if no external file with the given name exists. The excep-
     tion USE_ERROR is raised if, for the specified mode, the environment does not support opening for
     an external file with the given name (in the absence of NAME_ERROR) and form.

8   **procedure** CLOSE(FILE : **in out** FILE_TYPE);

9   Severs the association between the given file and its associated external file. The
               given file is left closed.

10   The exception STATUS_ERROR is raised if the given file is not open.

11   **procedure** DELETE(FILE : **in out** FILE_TYPE);

12   Deletes the external file associated with the given file. The given file is closed, and
               the external file ceases to exist.

13   The exception STATUS_ERROR is raised if the given file is not open. The exception
               USE_ERROR is raised if (as fully defined in Appendix F) deletion of the external file
               is not supported by the environment.

14   **procedure** RESET(FILE : **in out** FILE_TYPE; MODE : **in** FILE_MODE);
          procedure RESET(FILE : **in out** FILE_TYPE);

15   Resets the given file so that reading from or writing to its elements can be
               restarted from the beginning of the file; in particular, for direct access this means
               that the current index is set to one. If a MODE parameter is supplied, the current
               mode of the given file is set to the given mode.

16   The exception STATUS_ERROR is raised if the file is not open. The exception
               USE_ERROR is raised if the environment does not support resetting for the external
               file and, also, if the environment does not support resetting to the specified mode
               for the external file.

17   **function** MODE(FILE : **in** FILE_TYPE) **return** FILE_MODE;

18   Returns the current mode of the given file.

19   The exception STATUS_ERROR is raised if the file is not open.

20   **function** NAME(FILE : **in** FILE_TYPE) **return** STRING;

21   Returns a string which uniquely identifies the external file currently associated with
               the given file (and may thus be used in an OPEN operation). If an environment
               allows alternative specifications of the name (for example, abbreviations), the str-
               ing returned by the function should correspond to a full specification of the name.

22   The exception STATUS_ERROR is raised if the given file is not open.

function FORM(FILE : **in** FILE_TYPE) **return** STRING;   23

> Returns the form string for the external file currently associated with the given file.   24
> If an environment allows alternative specifications of the form (for example,
> abbreviations using default options), the string returned by the function should cor-
> respond to a full specification (that is, it should indicate explicitly all options
> selected, including default options).
>
> The exception STATUS_ERROR is raised if the given file is not open.   25

function IS_OPEN(FILE : **in** FILE_TYPE) **return** BOOLEAN;   26

> Returns TRUE if the file is open (that is, if it is associated with an external file),   27
> otherwise returns FALSE.

References: current mode 14.1, current size 14.1, closed file 14.1, direct access 14.2, external file 14.1, file 14.1,   28
file_mode type 14.1, file_type type 14.1, form string 14.1, inout_file 14.2.4, mode 14.1, name string 14.1, name_er-
ror exception 14.4, open file 14.1, out_file 14.1, status_error exception 14.4, use_error exception 14.4

14.2.2 Sequential Input-Output

The operations available for sequential input and output are described in this section. The excep-   1
tion STATUS_ERROR is raised if any of these operations is attempted for a file that is not open.

procedure READ(FILE : **in** FILE_TYPE; ITEM : **out** ELEMENT_TYPE);   2

> Operates on a file of mode IN_FILE. Reads an element from the given file, and   3
> returns the value of this element in the ITEM parameter.
>
> The exception MODE_ERROR is raised if the mode is not IN_FILE. The exception   4
> END_ERROR is raised if no more elements can be read from the given file. The
> exception DATA_ERROR is raised if the element read cannot be interpreted as a
> value of the type ELEMENT_TYPE; however, an implementation is allowed to omit
> this check if performing the check is too complex.

procedure WRITE(FILE : **in** FILE_TYPE; ITEM : **in** ELEMENT_TYPE);   5

> Operates on a file of mode OUT_FILE. Writes the value of ITEM to the given file.   6
>
> The exception MODE_ERROR is raised if the mode is not OUT_FILE. The exception   7
> USE_ERROR is raised if the capacity of the external file is exceeded.

function END_OF_FILE(FILE : **in** FILE_TYPE) **return** BOOLEAN;   8

> Operates on a file of mode IN_FILE. Returns TRUE if no more elements can be read   9
> from the given file; otherwise returns FALSE.
>
> The exception MODE_ERROR is raised if the mode is not IN_FILE.   10

References: data_error exception 14.4, element 14.1, element_type 14.1, end_error exception 14.4, external file   11
14.1, file 14.1, file mode 14.1, file_type 14.1, in_file 14.1, mode_error exception 14.4, out_file 14.1, status_error
exception 14.4, use_error exception 14.4

14.2.3 Specification of the Package Sequential_IO

```
with IO_EXCEPTIONS;
generic
   type ELEMENT_TYPE is private;
package SEQUENTIAL_IO is

   type FILE_TYPE is limited private;

   type FILE_MODE is (IN_FILE, OUT_FILE);


   -- File management

   procedure CREATE (FILE    : in out FILE_TYPE;
                     MODE : in FILE_MODE := OUT_FILE;
                     NAME : in STRING := "";
                     FORM : in STRING := "");

   procedure OPEN    (FILE    : in out FILE_TYPE;
                     MODE : in FILE_MODE;
                     NAME : in STRING;
                     FORM : in STRING := "");

   procedure CLOSE  (FILE : in out FILE_TYPE);
   procedure DELETE (FILE : in out FILE_TYPE);
   procedure RESET  (FILE : in out FILE_TYPE; MODE : in FILE_MODE);
   procedure RESET  (FILE : in out FILE_TYPE);

   function MODE     (FILE : in FILE_TYPE) return FILE_MODE;
   function NAME     (FILE : in FILE_TYPE) return STRING;
   function FORM     (FILE : in FILE_TYPE) return STRING;

   function IS_OPEN  (FILE : in FILE_TYPE) return BOOLEAN;

   -- Input and output operations

   procedure READ    (FILE : in FILE_TYPE; ITEM : out ELEMENT_TYPE);
   procedure WRITE   (FILE : in FILE_TYPE; ITEM : in ELEMENT_TYPE);

   function END_OF_FILE(FILE : in FILE_TYPE) return BOOLEAN;

   -- Exceptions

   STATUS_ERROR : exception renames IO_EXCEPTIONS.STATUS_ERROR;
   MODE_ERROR   : exception renames IO_EXCEPTIONS.MODE_ERROR;
   NAME_ERROR   : exception renames IO_EXCEPTIONS.NAME_ERROR;
   USE_ERROR    : exception renames IO_EXCEPTIONS.USE_ERROR;
   DEVICE_ERROR : exception renames IO_EXCEPTIONS.DEVICE_ERROR;
   END_ERROR    : exception renames IO_EXCEPTIONS.END_ERROR;
   DATA_ERROR   : exception renames IO_EXCEPTIONS.DATA_ERROR;

private
   -- implementation-dependent
end SEQUENTIAL_IO;
```

References: close procedure 14.2.1, create procedure 14.2.1, data_error exception 14.4, delete procedure 14.2.1,   2
device_error exception 14.4, end_error exception 14.4, end_of_file function 14.2.2, file_mode 14.1, file_type 14.1,
form function 14.2.1, in_file 14.1, io_exceptions 14.4, is_open function 14.2.1, mode function 14.2.1, mode_error
exception 14.4, name function 14.2.1, name_error exception 14.4, open procedure 14.2.1, out_file 14.1, read
procedure 14.2.2, reset procedure 14.2.1, sequential_io package 14.2 14.2.2, status_error exception 14.4, use_error
exception 14.4, write procedure 14.2.2,

14.2.4 Direct Input-Output

The operations available for direct input and output are described in this section. The exception   1
STATUS_ERROR is raised if any of these operations is attempted for a file that is not open.

    procedure READ(FILE : **in** FILE_TYPE; ITEM : **out** ELEMENT_TYPE;   2
                                       FROM : **in**   POSITIVE_COUNT);
    procedure READ(FILE : **in** FILE_TYPE; ITEM : **out** ELEMENT_TYPE);

        Operates on a file of mode IN_FILE or INOUT_FILE. In the case of the first form,   3
        sets the current index of the given file to the index value given by the parameter
        FROM. Then (for both forms) returns, in the parameter ITEM, the value of the
        element whose position in the given file is specified by the current index of the file;
        finally, increases the current index by one.

        The exception MODE_ERROR is raised if the mode of the given file is OUT_FILE.   4
        The exception END_ERROR is raised if the index to be used exceeds the size of the
        external file. The exception DATA_ERROR is raised if the element read cannot be
        interpreted as a value of the type ELEMENT_TYPE; however, an implementation is
        allowed to omit this check if performing the check is too complex.

    procedure WRITE(FILE : **in** FILE_TYPE; ITEM : **in** ELEMENT_TYPE;   5
                                         TO   : **in** POSITIVE_COUNT);
    procedure WRITE(FILE : **in** FILE_TYPE; ITEM : **in** ELEMENT_TYPE);

        Operates on a file of mode INOUT_FILE or OUT_FILE. In the case of the first form,   6
        sets the index of the given file to the index value given by the parameter TO. Then
        (for both forms) gives the value of the parameter ITEM to the element whose
        position in the given file is specified by the current index of the file; finally,
        increases the current index by one.

        The exception MODE_ERROR is raised if the mode of the given file is IN_FILE. The   7
        exception USE_ERROR is raised if the capacity of the external file is exceeded.

    procedure SET_INDEX(FILE : **in** FILE_TYPE; TO : **in** POSITIVE_COUNT);   8

        Operates on a file of any mode. Sets the current index of the given file to the given   9
        index value (which may exceed the current size of the file).

    function INDEX(FILE : **in** FILE_TYPE) **return** POSITIVE_COUNT;   10

        Operates on a file of any mode. Returns the current index of the given file.   11

12   **function** SIZE(FILE : **in** FILE_TYPE) **return** COUNT;

13   Operates on a file of any mode. Returns the current size of the external file that is associated with the given file.

14   **function** END_OF_FILE(FILE : **in** FILE_TYPE) **return** BOOLEAN;

15   Operates on a file of mode IN_FILE or INOUT_FILE. Returns TRUE if the current index exceeds the size of the external file; otherwise returns FALSE.

16   The exception MODE_ERROR is raised if the mode of the given file is OUT_FILE.

17   *References:* count type 14.2, current index 14.2, current size 14.2, data_error exception 14.4, element 14.1, element_type 14.1, end_error exception 14.4, external file 14.1, file 14.1, file mode 14.1, file_type 14.1, in_file 14.1, index 14.2, inout_file 14.1, mode_error exception 14.4, open file 14.1, positive_count 14.3, status_error exception 14.4, use_error exception 14.4

14.2.5 Specification of the Package Direct_IO

1
```
with IO_EXCEPTIONS;
generic
   type ELEMENT_TYPE is private;
package DIRECT_IO is

   type FILE_TYPE   is limited private;

   type    FILE_MODE is (IN_FILE, INOUT_FILE, OUT_FILE);
   type    COUNT      is range 0 .. implementation_defined;
   subtype POSITIVE_COUNT is COUNT range 1 .. COUNT'LAST;


   -- File management

   procedure CREATE ( FILE   : in out FILE_TYPE;
                      MODE : in FILE_MODE := INOUT_FILE;
                      NAME : in STRING := "";
                      FORM : in STRING := "");

   procedure OPEN    ( FILE   : in out FILE_TYPE;
                      MODE : in FILE_MODE;
                      NAME : in STRING;
                      FORM : in STRING := "");

   procedure CLOSE  (FILE : in out FILE_TYPE);
   procedure DELETE (FILE : in out FILE_TYPE);
   procedure RESET  (FILE : in out FILE_TYPE; MODE : in FILE_MODE);
   procedure RESET  (FILE : in out FILE_TYPE);

   function MODE    (FILE : in FILE_TYPE) return FILE_MODE;
   function NAME    (FILE : in FILE_TYPE) return STRING;
   function FORM    (FILE : in FILE_TYPE) return STRING;

   function IS_OPEN (FILE : in FILE_TYPE) return BOOLEAN;
```

-- Input and output operations

procedure READ (FILE : **in** FILE_TYPE; ITEM : **out** ELEMENT_TYPE; FROM : POSITIVE_COUNT);
procedure READ (FILE : **in** FILE_TYPE; ITEM : **out** ELEMENT_TYPE);

procedure WRITE (FILE : **in** FILE_TYPE; ITEM : **in** ELEMENT_TYPE; TO : POSITIVE_COUNT);
procedure WRITE (FILE : **in** FILE_TYPE; ITEM : **in** ELEMENT_TYPE);

procedure SET_INDEX(FILE : **in** FILE_TYPE; TO : **in** POSITIVE_COUNT);

function INDEX (FILE : **in** FILE_TYPE) **return** POSITIVE_COUNT;
function SIZE (FILE : **in** FILE_TYPE) **return** COUNT;

function END_OF_FILE (FILE : **in** FILE_TYPE) **return** BOOLEAN;

-- Exceptions

STATUS_ERROR : **exception renames** IO_EXCEPTIONS.STATUS_ERROR;
MODE_ERROR   : **exception renames** IO_EXCEPTIONS.MODE_ERROR;
NAME_ERROR   : **exception renames** IO_EXCEPTIONS.NAME_ERROR;
USE_ERROR   : **exception renames** IO_EXCEPTIONS.USE_ERROR;
DEVICE_ERROR : **exception renames** IO_EXCEPTIONS.DEVICE_ERROR;
END_ERROR   : **exception renames** IO_EXCEPTIONS.END_ERROR;
DATA_ERROR   : **exception renames** IO_EXCEPTIONS.DATA_ERROR;

private
  -- implementation-dependent
end DIRECT_IO;

References close procedure 14.2.1, count type 14.2, create procedure 14.2.1, data_error exception 14.4, default_mode 14.2.5, delete procedure 14.2.1, device_error exception 14.4, element_type 14.2.4, end_error exception 14.4, end_of_file function 14.2.4, file_mode 14.2.5, file_type 14.2.4, form function 14.2.1, in_file 14.2.4, index function 14.2.4, inout_file 14.2.4 14.2.1, io_exceptions package 14.4, is_open function 14.2.1, mode function 14.2.1, mode_error exception 14.4, name function 14.2.1, name_error exception 14.4, open procedure 14.2.1, out_file 14.2.1, read procedure 14.2.4, set_index procedure 14.2.4, size function 14.2.4, status_error exception 14.4, use_error exception 14.4, write procedure 14.2.4 14.2.1

14.3 Text Input-Output

This section describes the package TEXT_IO, which provides facilities for input and output in human-readable form. Each file is read or written sequentially, as a sequence of characters grouped into lines, and as a sequence of lines grouped into pages. The specification of the package is given below in section 14.3.10.

The facilities for file management given above, in sections 14.2.1 and 14.2.2, are available for text input-output. In place of READ and WRITE, however, there are procedures GET and PUT that input values of suitable types from text files, and output values to them. These values are provided to the PUT procedures, and returned by the GET procedures, in a parameter ITEM. Several overloaded procedures of these names exist, for different types of ITEM. These GET procedures analyze the input sequences of characters as lexical elements (see Chapter 2) and return the corresponding values; the PUT procedures output the given values as appropriate lexical elements. Procedures GET and PUT are also available that input and output individual characters treated as character values rather than as lexical elements.

3   In addition to the procedures GET and PUT for numeric and enumeration types of ITEM that operate on text files, analogous procedures are provided that read from and write to a parameter of type STRING. These procedures perform the same analysis and composition of character sequences as their counterparts which have a file parameter.

4   For all GET and PUT procedures that operate on text files, and for many other subprograms, there are forms with and without a file parameter. Each such GET procedure operates on an input file, and each such PUT procedure operates on an output file. If no file is specified, a default input file or a default output file is used.

5   At the beginning of program execution the default input and output files are the so-called standard input file and standard output file. These files are open, have respectively the current modes IN_FILE and OUT_FILE, and are associated with two implementation-defined external files. Procedures are provided to change the current default input file and the current default output file.

6   From a logical point of view, a text file is a sequence of pages, a page is a sequence of lines, and a line is a sequence of characters; the end of a line is marked by a *line terminator*; the end of a page is marked by the combination of a line terminator immediately followed by a *page terminator*; and the end of a file is marked by the combination of a line terminator immediately followed by a page terminator and then a *file terminator*. Terminators are generated during output; either by calls of procedures provided expressly for that purpose; or implicitly as part of other operations, for example, when a bounded line length, a bounded page length, or both, have been specified for a file.

7   The actual nature of terminators is not defined by the language and hence depends on the implementation. Although terminators are recognized or generated by certain of the procedures that follow, they are not necessarily implemented as characters or as sequences of characters. Whether they are characters (and if so which ones) in any particular implementation need not concern a user who neither explicitly outputs nor explicitly inputs control characters. The effect of input or output of control characters (other than horizontal tabulation) is not defined by the language.

8   The characters of a line are numbered, starting from one; the number of a character is called its *column number*. For a line terminator, a column number is also defined: it is one more than the number of characters in the line. The lines of a page, and the pages of a file, are similarly numbered. The *current column number* is the column number of the next character or line terminator to be transferred. The *current line number* is the number of the current line. The *current page number* is the number of the current page. These numbers are values of the subtype POSITIVE_COUNT of the type COUNT (by convention, the value zero of the type COUNT is used to indicate special conditions).

     type COUNT **is range** 0 .. *implementation_defined*;
     subtype POSITIVE_COUNT **is** COUNT **range** 1 .. COUNT'LAST;

9   For an output file, a *maximum line length* can be specified and a *maximum page length* can be specified. If a value to be output cannot fit on the current line, for a specified maximum line length, then a new line is automatically started before the value is output; if, further, this new line cannot fit on the current page, for a specified maximum page length, then a new page is automatically started before the value is output. Functions are provided to determine the maximum line length and the maximum page length. When a file is opened with mode OUT_FILE, both values are zero: by convention, this means that the line lengths and page lengths are unbounded. (Consequently, output consists of a single line if the subprograms for explicit control of line and page structure are not used.) The constant UNBOUNDED is provided for this purpose.

10   *References:* count type 14.3.10, default current input file 14.3.2, default current output file 14.3.2, external file 14.1, file 14.1, get procedure 14.3.5, in_file 14.1, out_file 14.1, put procedure 14.3.5, read 14.2.2, sequential access 14.1, standard input file 14.3.2, standard output file 14.3.2

14.3.1 File Management

The only allowed file modes for text files are the modes IN_FILE and OUT_FILE. The subprograms   1
given in section 14.2.1 for the control of external files, and the function END_OF_FILE given in
section 14.2.2 for sequential input-output, are also available for text files. There is also a version of
END_OF_FILE that refers to the current default input file. For text files, the procedures have the following additional effects:

- For the procedures CREATE and OPEN : After opening a file with mode OUT_FILE, the page   2
  length and line length are unbounded (both have the conventional value zero). After opening a
  file with mode IN_FILE or OUT_FILE, the current column, current line, and current page
  numbers are set to one.

- For the procedure CLOSE : If the file has the current mode OUT_FILE, has the effect of calling   3
  NEW_PAGE, unless the current page is already terminated; then outputs a file terminator.

- For the procedure RESET : If the file has the current mode OUT_FILE, has the effect of calling   4
  NEW_PAGE, unless the current page is already terminated; then outputs a file terminator. If
  the new file mode is OUT_FILE, the page and line lengths are unbounded. For all modes, the
  current column, line, and page numbers are set to one.

The exception MODE_ERROR is raised by the procedure RESET upon an attempt to change the   5
mode of a file that is either the current default input file, or the current default output file.

References: create procedure 14.2.1, current column number 14.3, current default input file 14.3, current line   6
number 14.3, current page number 14.3, end_of_file 14.3, external file 14.1, file 14.1, file mode 14.1, file terminator
14.3, in_file 14.1, line length 14.3, mode_error exception 14.4, open procedure 14.2.1, out_file 14.1, page length
14.3, reset procedure 14.2.1

14.3.2 Default Input and Output Files

The following subprograms provide for the control of the particular default files that are used when   1
a file parameter is omitted from a GET, PUT or other operation of text input-output described
below.

procedure SET_INPUT(FILE : **in** FILE_TYPE);   2

  Operates on a file of mode IN_FILE. Sets the current default input file to FILE.   3

  The exception STATUS_ERROR is raised if the given file is not open. The exception   4
  MODE_ERROR is raised if the mode of the given file is not IN_FILE.

procedure SET_OUTPUT(FILE : **in** FILE_TYPE);   5

  Operates on a file of mode OUT_FILE. Sets the current default output file to FILE.   6

  The exception STATUS_ERROR is raised if the given file is not open. The exception   7
  MODE_ERROR is raised if the mode of the given file is not OUT_FILE.

8   **function** STANDARD_INPUT **return** FILE_TYPE;

9   Returns the standard input file (see 14.3).

10   **function** STANDARD_OUTPUT **return** FILE_TYPE;

11   Returns the standard output file (see 14.3).

12   **function** CURRENT_INPUT **return** FILE_TYPE;

13   Returns the current default input file.

14   **function** CURRENT_OUTPUT **return** FILE_TYPE;

15   Returns the current default output file.

Note:

16   The standard input and the standard output files cannot be opened, closed, reset, or deleted, because the parameter FILE of the corresponding procedures has the mode **in out**.

17   *References:* current default file 14.3, default file 14.3, file_type 14.1, get procedure 14.3.5, mode_error exception 14.4, put procedure 14.3.5, status_error exception 14.4

14.3.3 Specification of Line and Page Lengths

1   The subprograms described in this section are concerned with the line and page structure of a file of mode OUT_FILE. They operate either on the file given as the first parameter, or, in the absence of such a file parameter, on the current default output file. They provide for output of text with a specified maximum line length or page length. In these cases, line and page terminators are output implicitly and automatically when needed. When line and page lengths are unbounded (that is, when they have the conventional value zero), as in the case of a newly opened file, new lines and new pages are only started when explicitly called for.

2   In all cases, the exception STATUS_ERROR is raised if the file to be used is not open; the exception MODE_ERROR is raised if the mode of the file is not OUT_FILE.

3   **procedure** SET_LINE_LENGTH(FILE : **in** FILE_TYPE; TO : **in** COUNT);
        procedure SET_LINE_LENGTH(TO   : **in** COUNT);

4   Sets the maximum line length of the specified output file to the number of characters specified by TO. The value zero for TO specifies an unbounded line length.

5   The exception USE_ERROR is raised if the specified line length is inappropriate for the associated external file.

procedure SET_PAGE_LENGTH (FILE : **in** FILE_TYPE; TO : **in** COUNT);   6
procedure SET_PAGE_LENGTH (TO   : **in** COUNT);

      Sets the maximum page length of the specified output file to the number of lines   7
      specified by TO. The value zero for TO specifies an unbounded page length.

      The exception USE_ERROR is raised if the specified page length is inappropriate for   8
      the associated external file.

function LINE_LENGTH(FILE : **in** FILE_TYPE) **return** COUNT;   9
function LINE_LENGTH **return** COUNT;

      Returns the maximum line length currently set for the specified output file, or zero   10
      if the line length is unbounded.

function PAGE_LENGTH(FILE : **in** FILE_TYPE) **return** COUNT;   11
function PAGE_LENGTH **return** COUNT;

      Returns the maximum page length currently set for the specified output file, or zero   12
      if the page length is unbounded.

References: count type 14.3, current default output file 14.3, external file 14.1, file 14.1, file_type 14.1, line 14.3,   13
line length 14.3, line terminator 14.3, maximum line length 14.3, maximum page length 14.3, mode_error exception
14.4, open file 14.1, out_file 14.1, page 14.3, page length 14.3, page terminator 14.3, status_error exception 14.4,
unbounded page length 14.3, use_error exception 14.4

14.3.4 Operations on Columns, Lines, and Pages

The subprograms described in this section provide for explicit control of line and page structure;   1
they operate either on the file given as the first parameter, or, in the absence of such a file
parameter, on the appropriate (input or output) current default file. The exception STATUS_ERROR
is raised by any of these subprograms if the file to be used is not open.

procedure NEW_LINE(FILE : **in** FILE_TYPE; SPACING : **in** POSITIVE_COUNT := 1);   2
procedure NEW_LINE(SPACING : **in** POSITIVE_COUNT := 1);

      Operates on a file of mode OUT_FILE.

      For a SPACING of one: Outputs a line terminator and sets the current column   3
      number to one. Then increments the current line number by one, except in the case
      that the current line number is already greater than or equal to the maximum page
      length, for a bounded page length; in that case a page terminator is output, the
      current page number is incremented by one, and the current line number is set to
      one.

      For a SPACING greater than one, the above actions are performed SPACING times.   4

      The exception MODE_ERROR is raised if the mode is not OUT_FILE.   5

6   **procedure** SKIP_LINE(FILE   : **in** FILE_TYPE; SPACING : **in** POSITIVE_COUNT := 1);
     procedure SKIP_LINE(SPACING : **in** POSITIVE_COUNT := 1);

7   Operates on a file of mode IN_FILE .

8   For a SPACING of one: Reads and discards all characters until a line terminator
          has been read, and then sets the current column number to one. If the line ter-
          minator is not immediately followed by a page terminator, the current line number
          is incremented by one. Otherwise, if the line terminator is immediately followed by
          a page terminator, then the page terminator is skipped, the current page number is
          incremented by one, and the current line number is set to one.

9   For a SPACING greater than one, the above actions are performed SPACING times.

10   The exception MODE_ERROR is raised if the mode is not IN_FILE . The exception
          END_ERROR is raised if an attempt is made to read a file terminator.

11   **function** END_OF_LINE(FILE : **in** FILE_TYPE) **return** BOOLEAN;
     function END_OF_LINE **return** BOOLEAN;

12   Operates on a file of mode IN_FILE . Returns TRUE if a line terminator or a file
          terminator is next; otherwise returns FALSE .

13   The exception MODE_ERROR is raised if the mode is not IN_FILE .

14   **procedure** NEW_PAGE(FILE : **in** FILE_TYPE);
     procedure NEW_PAGE;

15   Operates on a file of mode OUT_FILE . Outputs a line terminator if the current line is
          not terminated, or if the current page is empty (that is, if the current column and
          line numbers are both equal to one). Then outputs a page terminator, which ter-
          minates the current page. Adds one to the current page number and sets the cur-
          rent column and line numbers to one.

16   The exception MODE_ERROR is raised if the mode is not OUT_FILE .

17   **procedure** SKIP_PAGE(FILE : **in** FILE_TYPE);
     procedure SKIP_PAGE;

18   Operates on a file of mode IN_FILE . Reads and discards all characters and line
          terminators until a page terminator has been read. Then adds one to the current
          page number, and sets the current column and line numbers to one.

19   The exception MODE_ERROR is raised if the mode is not IN_FILE . The exception
          END_ERROR is raised if an attempt is made to read a file terminator.

function END_OF_PAGE(FILE : **in** FILE_TYPE) **return** BOOLEAN;   20
function END_OF_PAGE **return** BOOLEAN;

>   Operates on a file of mode IN_FILE. Returns TRUE if the combination of a line   21
>   terminator and a page terminator is next, or if a file terminator is next; otherwise
>   returns FALSE.
>
>   The exception MODE_ERROR is raised if the mode is not IN_FILE.   22

function END_OF_FILE(FILE : **in** FILE_TYPE) **return** BOOLEAN;   23
function END_OF_FILE **return** BOOLEAN;

>   Operates on a file of mode IN_FILE. Returns TRUE if a file terminator is next, or if   24
>   the combination of a line, a page, and a file terminator is next; otherwise returns
>   FALSE.
>
>   The exception MODE_ERROR is raised if the mode is not IN_FILE.   25

The following subprograms provide for the control of the current position of reading or writing in a   26
file. In all cases, the default file is the current output file.

procedure SET_COL(FILE : **in** FILE_TYPE; TO : **in** POSITIVE_COUNT);   27
procedure SET_COL(TO   : **in** POSITIVE_COUNT);

>   If the file mode is OUT_FILE: 28
>
>>   If the value specified by TO is greater than the current column number,   29
>>   outputs spaces, adding one to the current column number after each
>>   space, until the current column number equals the specified value. If the
>>   value specified by TO is equal to the current column number, there is no
>>   effect. If the value specified by TO is less than the current column number,
>>   has the effect of calling NEW_LINE (with a spacing of one), then outputs
>>   (TO - 1) spaces, and sets the current column number to the specified value.
>>
>>   The exception LAYOUT_ERROR is raised if the value specified by TO   30
>>   exceeds LINE_LENGTH when the line length is bounded (that is, when it
>>   does not have the conventional value zero).
>
>   If the file mode is IN_FILE: 31
>
>>   Reads (and discards) individual characters, line terminators, and page ter-   32
>>   minators, until the next character to be read has a column number that
>>   equals the value specified by TO; there is no effect if the current column
>>   number already equals this value.   Each transfer of a character or ter-
>>   minator maintains the current column, line, and page numbers in the same
>>   way as a GET procedure (see 14.3.5). (Short lines will be skipped until a
>>   line is reached that has a character at the specified column position.)
>>
>>   The exception END_ERROR is raised if an attempt is made to read a file   33
>>   terminator.

34   **procedure** SET_LINE(FILE : **in** FILE_TYPE; TO : **in** POSITIVE_COUNT);
      procedure SET_LINE(TO   : **in** POSITIVE_COUNT);

35   If the file mode is OUT_FILE :

36   If the value specified by TO is greater than the current line number, has the
              effect of repeatedly calling NEW_LINE (with a spacing of one), until the
              current line number equals the specified value. If the value specified by TO
              is equal to the current line number, there is no effect. If the value specified
              by TO is less than the current line number, has the effect of calling
              NEW_PAGE followed by a call of NEW_LINE with a spacing equal to (TO -
              1).

37   The exception LAYOUT_ERROR is raised if the value specified by TO
              exceeds PAGE_LENGTH when the page length is bounded (that is, when it
              does not have the conventional value zero).

38   If the mode is IN_FILE :

39   Has the effect of repeatedly calling SKIP_LINE (with a spacing of one), until
              the current line number equals the value specified by TO ; there is no effect
              if the current line number already equals this value. (Short pages will be
              skipped until a page is reached that has a line at the specified line position.)

40   The exception END_ERROR is raised if an attempt is made to read a file
              terminator.

41   **function** COL(FILE : **in** FILE_TYPE) **return** POSITIVE_COUNT;
      function COL **return** POSITIVE_COUNT;

42   Returns the current column number.

43   The exception LAYOUT_ERROR is raised if this number exceeds COUNT'LAST.

44   **function** LINE(FILE : **in** FILE_TYPE) **return** POSITIVE_COUNT;
      function LINE **return** POSITIVE_COUNT;

45   Returns the current line number.

46   The exception LAYOUT_ERROR is raised if this number exceeds COUNT'LAST.

47   **function** PAGE(FILE : **in** FILE_TYPE) **return** POSITIVE_COUNT;
      function PAGE **return** POSITIVE_COUNT;

48   Returns the current page number.

49   The exception LAYOUT_ERROR is raised if this number exceeds COUNT'LAST.

50   The column number, line number, or page number are allowed to exceed COUNT'LAST (as a
      consequence of the input or output of sufficiently many characters, lines, or pages). These events
      do not cause any exception to be raised. However, a call of COL, LINE, or PAGE raises the
      exception LAYOUT_ERROR if the corresponding number exceeds COUNT'LAST.

14.3.4 Operations on Columns, Lines, and Pages   14-16

Note:

A page terminator is always skipped whenever the preceding line terminator is skipped. An 51
implementation may represent the combination of these terminators by a single character,
provided that it is properly recognized at input.

References: current column number 14.3, current default file 14.3, current line number 14.3, current page number 52
14.3, end_error exception 14.4, file 14.1, file terminator 14.3, get procedure 14.3.5, in_file 14.1, layout_error exception 14.4, line 14.3, line number 14.3, line terminator 14.3, maximum page length 14.3, mode_error exception 14.4,
open file 14.1, page 14.3, page length 14.3, page terminator 14.3, positive count 14.3, status_error exception 14.4

14.3.5 Get and Put Procedures

The procedures GET and PUT for items of the types CHARACTER, STRING, numeric types, and 1
enumeration types are described in subsequent sections. Features of these procedures that are
common to most of these types are described in this section. The GET and PUT procedures for
items of type CHARACTER and STRING deal with individual character values; the GET and PUT
procedures for numeric and enumeration types treat the items as lexical elements.

All procedures GET and PUT have forms with a file parameter, written first. Where this parameter 2
is omitted, the appropriate (input or output) current default file is understood to be specified. Each
procedure GET operates on a file of mode IN_FILE. Each procedure PUT operates on a file of
mode OUT_FILE.

All procedures GET and PUT maintain the current column, line, and page numbers of the specified 3
file: the effect of each of these procedures upon these numbers is the resultant of the effects of
individual transfers of characters and of individual output or skipping of terminators. Each transfer
of a character adds one to the current column number. Each output of a line terminator sets the
current column number to one and adds one to the current line number. Each output of a page
terminator sets the current column and line numbers to one and adds one to the current page
number. For input, each skipping of a line terminator sets the current column number to one and
adds one to the current line number; each skipping of a page terminator sets the current column
and line numbers to one and adds one to the current page number. Similar considerations apply to
the procedures GET_LINE, PUT_LINE, and SET_COL.

Several GET and PUT procedures, for numeric and enumeration types, have *format* parameters 4
which specify field lengths; these parameters are of the nonnegative subtype FIELD of the type
INTEGER.

Input-output of enumeration values uses the syntax of the corresponding lexical elements. Any 5
GET procedure for an enumeration type begins by skipping any leading blanks, or line or page terminators; a *blank* being defined as a space or a horizontal tabulation character. Next, characters
are input only so long as the sequence input is an initial sequence of an identifier or of a character
literal (in particular, input ceases when a line terminator is encountered). The character or line terminator that causes input to cease remains available for subsequent input.

For a numeric type, the GET procedures have a format parameter called WIDTH. If the value given 6
for this parameter is zero, the GET procedure proceeds in the same manner as for enumeration
types, but using the syntax of numeric literals instead of that of enumeration literals. If a nonzero
value is given, then exactly WIDTH characters are input, or the characters up to a line terminator,
whichever comes first; any skipped leading blanks are included in the count. The syntax used for
numeric literals is an extended syntax that allows a leading sign (but no intervening blanks, or line
or page terminators).

7   Any PUT procedure, for an item of a numeric or an enumeration type, outputs the value of the item as a numeric literal, identifier, or character literal, as appropriate. This is preceded by leading spaces if required by the format parameters WIDTH or FORE (as described in later sections), and then a minus sign for a negative value; for an enumeration type, the spaces follow instead of leading. The format given for a PUT procedure is overridden if it is insufficiently wide.

8   Two further cases arise for PUT procedures for numeric and enumeration types, if the line length of the specified output file is bounded (that is, if it does not have the conventional value zero). If the number of characters to be output does not exceed the maximum line length, but is such that they cannot fit on the current line, starting from the current column, then (in effect) NEW_LINE is called (with a spacing of one) before output of the item. Otherwise, if the number of characters exceeds the maximum line length, then the exception LAYOUT_ERROR is raised and no characters are output.

9   The exception STATUS_ERROR is raised by any of the procedures GET, GET_LINE, PUT, and PUT_LINE if the file to be used is not open. The exception MODE_ERROR is raised by the procedures GET and GET_LINE if the mode of the file to be used is not IN_FILE; and by the procedures PUT and PUT_LINE, if the mode is not OUT_FILE.

10 The exception END_ERROR is raised by a GET procedure if an attempt is made to skip a file terminator. The exception DATA_ERROR is raised by a GET procedure if the sequence finally input is not a lexical element corresponding to the type, in particular if no characters were input; for this test, leading blanks are ignored; for an item of a numeric type, when a sign is input, this rule applies to the succeeding numeric literal. The exception LAYOUT_ERROR is raised by a PUT procedure that outputs to a parameter of type STRING, if the length of the actual string is insufficient for the output of the item.

11 *Examples:*

12 In the examples, here and in sections 14.3.7 and 14.3.8, the string quotes and the lower case letter b are not transferred: they are shown only to reveal the layout and spaces.

        N : INTEGER;
          ...
        GET(N);

        -- Characters at input   Sequence input   Value of N

        --   bb-12535b   -12535   -12535
        --   bb12_535E1b   12_535E1   125350
        --   bb12_535E;   12_535E   (none) DATA_ERROR raised

13 *Example of overridden width parameter:*

        PUT(ITEM => -23, WIDTH => 2);   --   "-23"

14 *References:* blank 14.3.9, column number 14.3, current default file 14.3, data_error exception 14.4, end_error exception 14.4, file 14.1, fore 14.3.8, get procedure 14.3.6 14.3.7 14.3.8 14.3.9, in_file 14.1, layout_error exception 14.4, line number 14.1, line terminator 14.1, maximum line length 14.3, mode 14.1, mode_error exception 14.4, new_file procedure 14.3.4, out_file 14.1, page number 14.1, page terminator 14.1, put procedure 14.3.6 14.3.7 14.3.8 14.3.9, skipping 14.3.7 14.3.8 14.3.9, status_error exception 14.4, width 14.3.5 14.3.7 14.3.9

14.3.6 Input-Output of Characters and Strings

For an item of type CHARACTER the following procedures are provided: 1

    procedure GET(FILE : **in** FILE_TYPE; ITEM : **out** CHARACTER);   2
    procedure GET(ITEM : **out** CHARACTER);

        After skipping any line terminators and any page terminators, reads the next 3
        character from the specified input file and returns the value of this character in the
        out parameter ITEM.

        The exception END_ERROR is raised if an attempt is made to skip a file terminator. 4

    procedure PUT(FILE : **in** FILE_TYPE; ITEM : **in** CHARACTER);   5
    procedure PUT(ITEM : **in** CHARACTER);

        If the line length of the specified output file is bounded (that is, does not have the 6
        conventional value zero), and the current column number exceeds it, has the effect
        of calling NEW_LINE with a spacing of one. Then, or otherwise, outputs the given
        character to the file.

For an item of type STRING the following procedures are provided: 7

    procedure GET(FILE : **in** FILE_TYPE; ITEM : **out** STRING);   8
    procedure GET(ITEM : **out** STRING);

        Determines the length of the given string and attempts that number of GET 9
        operations for successive characters of the string (In particular, no operation is per-
        formed if the string is null).

    procedure PUT(FILE : **in** FILE_TYPE; ITEM : **in** STRING);   10
    procedure PUT(ITEM : **in** STRING);

        Determines the length of the given string and attempts that number of PUT 11
        operations for successive characters of the string (in particular, no operation is per-
        formed if the string is null).

    procedure GET_LINE(FILE : **in** FILE_TYPE; ITEM : **out** STRING; LAST : **out** NATURAL);   12
    procedure GET_LINE(ITEM : **out** STRING; LAST : **out** NATURAL);

        Replaces successive characters of the specified string by successive characters 13
        read from the specified input file. Reading stops if the end of the line is met, in
        which case the procedure SKIP_LINE is then called (in effect) with a spacing of
        one; reading also stops if the end of the string is met. Characters not replaced are
        left undefined.

        If characters are read, returns in LAST the index value such that ITEM (LAST) is the 14
        last character replaced (the index of the first character replaced is ITEM'FIRST). If
        no characters are read, returns in LAST an index value that is one less than
        ITEM'FIRST.

        The exception END_ERROR is raised if an attempt is made to skip a file terminator. 15

16 **procedure** PUT_LINE(FILE : **in** FILE_TYPE; ITEM : **in** STRING);
    procedure PUT_LINE(ITEM : **in** STRING);

17   Calls the procedure PUT for the given string, and then the procedure NEW_LINE
                with a spacing of one.

Notes:

18 In a literal string parameter of PUT, the enclosing string bracket characters are not output. Each
    doubled string bracket character in the enclosed string is output as a single string bracket
    character, as a consequence of the rule for string literals (see 2.6).

19 A string read by GET or written by PUT can extend over several lines.

20 *References:* current column number 14.3, end_error exception 14.4, file 14.1, file terminator 14.3, get procedure
    14.3.5, line 14.3, line length 14.3, new_line procedure 14.3.4, page terminator 14.3, put procedure 14.3.4, skipping
    14.3.5

14.3.7 Input-Output for Integer Types

1   The following procedures are defined in the generic package INTEGER_IO. This must be
    instantiated for the appropriate integer type (indicated by NUM in the specification).

2   Values are output as decimal or based literals, without underline characters or exponent, and
    preceded by a minus sign if negative. The format (which includes any leading spaces and minus
    sign) can be specified by an optional field width parameter. Values of widths of fields in output for-
    mats are of the nonnegative integer subtype FIELD. Values of bases are of the integer subtype
    NUMBER_BASE.

        subtype NUMBER_BASE **is** INTEGER **range** 2 .. 16;

3   The default field width and base to be used by output procedures are defined by the following
    variables that are declared in the generic package INTEGER_IO :

        DEFAULT_WIDTH   : FIELD := NUM'WIDTH;
        DEFAULT_BASE   : NUMBER_BASE := 10;

4   The following procedures are provided:

5   **procedure** GET(FILE : **in** FILE_TYPE; ITEM : **out** NUM; WIDTH : **in** FIELD := 0);
    procedure GET(ITEM : **out** NUM; WIDTH : **in** FIELD := 0);

6   If the value of the parameter WIDTH is zero, skips any leading blanks, line
                terminators, or page terminators, then reads a plus or a minus sign if present, then
                reads according to the syntax of an integer literal (which may be a based literal). If
                a nonzero value of WIDTH is supplied, then exactly WIDTH characters are input, or
                the characters (possibly none) up to a line terminator, whichever comes first; any
                skipped leading blanks are included in the count.

7   Returns, in the parameter ITEM, the value of type NUM that corresponds to the
                sequence input.

8   The exception DATA_ERROR is raised if the sequence input does not have the
                required syntax or if the value obtained is not of the subtype NUM.

14.3.7 Input-Output for Integer Types   14-20

```
procedure PUT(FILE  : in FILE_TYPE;
              ITEM  : in NUM;
              WIDTH : in FIELD := DEFAULT_WIDTH;
              BASE  : in NUMBER_BASE := DEFAULT_BASE);
```
9

```
procedure PUT(ITEM  : in NUM;
              WIDTH : in FIELD := DEFAULT_WIDTH;
              BASE  : in NUMBER_BASE := DEFAULT_BASE);
```

Outputs the value of the parameter ITEM as an integer literal, with no underlines, no exponent, and no leading zeros (but a single zero for the value zero), and a preceding minus sign for a negative value.
10

If the resulting sequence of characters to be output has fewer than WIDTH characters, then leading spaces are first output to make up the difference.
11

Uses the syntax for decimal literal if the parameter BASE has the value ten (either explicitly or through DEFAULT_BASE); otherwise, uses the syntax for based literal, with any letters in upper case.
12

```
procedure GET(FROM : in STRING; ITEM : out NUM; LAST : out POSITIVE);
```
13

Reads an integer value from the beginning of the given string, following the same rules as the GET procedure that reads an integer value from a file, but treating the end of the string as a file terminator. Returns, in the parameter ITEM, the value of type NUM that corresponds to the sequence input. Returns in LAST the index value such that FROM (LAST) is the last character read.
14

The exception DATA_ERROR is raised if the sequence input does not have the required syntax or if the value obtained is not of the subtype NUM.
15

```
procedure PUT(TO   : out STRING;
              ITEM : in NUM;
              BASE : in NUMBER_BASE := DEFAULT_BASE);
```
16

Outputs the value of the parameter ITEM to the given string, following the same rule as for output to a file, using the length of the given string as the value for WIDTH.
17

Examples:
18

```
package INT_IO is new INTEGER_IO(SMALL_INT); use INT_IO;
-- default format used at instantiation, DEFAULT_WIDTH = 4, DEFAULT_BASE = 10
```

```
PUT(126);                              -- "b126"
PUT(-126, 7);                          -- "bbb-126"
PUT(126, WIDTH => 13, BASE => 2);      -- "bbb2#1111110#"
```

References: based literal 2.4.2, blank 14.3.5, data_error exception 14.4, decimal literal 2.4.1, field subtype 14.3.5, file_type 14.1, get procedure 14.3.5, integer_io package 14.3.10, integer literal 2.4, layout_error exception 14.4, line terminator 14.3, put procedure 14.3.5, skipping 14.3.5, width 14.3.5
19

14.3.8 Input-Output for Real Types

1   The following procedures are defined in the generic packages FLOAT_IO and FIXED_IO, which must be instantiated for the appropriate floating point or fixed point type respectively (indicated by NUM in the specifications).

2   Values are output as decimal literals without underline characters. The format of each value output consists of a FORE field, a decimal point, an AFT field, and (if a nonzero EXP parameter is supplied) the letter E and an EXP field. The two possible formats thus correspond to:

        FORE . AFT

3   and to:

        FORE . AFT E EXP

4   without any spaces between these fields. The FORE field may include leading spaces, and a minus sign for negative values. The AFT field includes only decimal digits (possibly with trailing zeros). The EXP field includes the sign (plus or minus) and the exponent (possibly with leading zeros).

5   For floating point types, the default lengths of these fields are defined by the following variables that are declared in the generic package FLOAT_IO :

        DEFAULT_FORE   : FIELD := 2;
        DEFAULT_AFT   : FIELD := NUM'DIGITS-1;
        DEFAULT_EXP   : FIELD := 3;

6   For fixed point types, the default lengths of these fields are defined by the following variables that are declared in the generic package FIXED_IO :

        DEFAULT_FORE   : FIELD := NUM'FORE;
        DEFAULT_AFT   : FIELD := NUM'AFT;
        DEFAULT_EXP   : FIELD := 0;

7   The following procedures are provided:

8   **procedure** GET(FILE : **in** FILE_TYPE; ITEM : **out** NUM; WIDTH : **in** FIELD := 0);
        procedure GET(ITEM : **out** NUM; WIDTH   : **in** FIELD := 0);

9   If the value of the parameter WIDTH is zero, skips any leading blanks, line terminators, or page terminators, then reads a plus or a minus sign if present, then reads according to the syntax of a real literal (which may be a based literal). If a nonzero value of WIDTH is supplied, then exactly WIDTH characters are input, or the characters (possibly none) up to a line terminator, whichever comes first; any skipped leading blanks are included in the count.

10   Returns, in the parameter ITEM, the value of type NUM that corresponds to the sequence input.

11   The exception DATA_ERROR is raised if the sequence input does not have the required syntax or if the value obtained is not of the subtype NUM.

```
procedure PUT(FILE   : in FILE_TYPE;                                    12
              ITEM   : in NUM;
              FORE   : in FIELD := DEFAULT_FORE;
              AFT    : in FIELD := DEFAULT_AFT;
              EXP    : in FIELD := DEFAULT_EXP);

procedure PUT(ITEM   : in NUM;
              FORE   : in FIELD := DEFAULT_FORE;
              AFT    : in FIELD := DEFAULT_AFT;
              EXP    : in FIELD := DEFAULT_EXP);
```

Outputs the value of the parameter ITEM as a decimal literal with the format   13
defined by FORE, AFT and EXP. If the value is negative, a minus sign is included in
the integer part. If EXP has the value zero, then the integer part to be output has as
many digits as are needed to represent the integer part of the value of ITEM,
overriding FORE if necessary, or consists of the digit zero if the value of ITEM has
no integer part.

If EXP has a value greater than zero, then the integer part to be output has a single   14
digit, which is nonzero except for the value 0.0 of ITEM.

In both cases, however, if the integer part to be output has fewer than FORE   15
characters, including any minus sign, then leading spaces are first output to make
up the difference. The number of digits of the fractional part is given by AFT, or is
one if AFT equals zero. The value is rounded; a value of exactly one half in the last
place may be rounded either up or down.

If EXP has the value zero, there is no exponent part. If EXP has a value greater than   16
zero, then the exponent part to be output has as many digits as are needed to
represent the exponent part of the value of ITEM (for which a single digit integer
part is used), and includes an initial sign (plus or minus). If the exponent part to be
output has fewer than EXP characters, including the sign, then leading zeros
precede the digits, to make up the difference. For the value 0.0 of ITEM, the
exponent has the value zero.

```
procedure GET(FROM : in STRING; ITEM : out NUM; LAST : out POSITIVE);   17
```

Reads a real value from the beginning of the given string, following the same rule   18
as the GET procedure that reads a real value from a file, but treating the end of the
string as a file terminator. Returns, in the parameter ITEM, the value of type NUM
that corresponds to the sequence input. Returns in LAST the index value such that
FROM(LAST) is the last character read.

The exception DATA_ERROR is raised if the sequence input does not have the   19
required syntax, or if the value obtained is not of the subtype NUM.

```
procedure PUT(TO   : out STRING;                                        20
              ITEM : in NUM;
              AFT  : in FIELD   := DEFAULT_AFT;
              EXP  : in INTEGER := DEFAULT_EXP);
```

Outputs the value of the parameter ITEM to the given string, following the same   21
rule as for output to a file, using a value for FORE such that the sequence of
characters output exactly fills the string, including any leading spaces.

22   *Examples:*

```
package REAL_IO is new FLOAT_IO(REAL); use REAL_IO;
-- default format used at instantiation, DEFAULT_EXP = 3

X : REAL := -123.4567;   --   digits 8        (see 3.5.7)

PUT(X); -- default format                         "-1.2345670E+02"
PUT(X, FORE => 5, AFT => 3, EXP => 2);   --  "bbb-1.235E+2"
PUT(X, 5, 3, 0);                          --  "b-123.457"
```

Note:

23   For an item with a positive value, if output to a string exactly fills the string without leading spaces, then output of the corresponding negative value will raise LAYOUT_ERROR.

24   *References:* aft attribute 3.5.10, based literal 2.4.2, blank 14.3.5, data_error exception 14.3.5, decimal literal 2.4.1, field subtype 14.3.5, file_type 14.1, fixed_io package 14.3.10, floating_io package 14.3.10, fore attribute 3.5.10, get procedure 14.3.5, layout_error 14.3.5, line terminator 14.3.5, put procedure 14.3.5, real literal 2.4, skipping 14.3.5, width 14.3.5

14.3.9 Input-Output for Enumeration Types

1   The following procedures are defined in the generic package ENUMERATION_IO, which must be instantiated for the appropriate enumeration type (indicated by ENUM in the specification).

2   Values are output using either upper or lower case letters for identifiers. This is specified by the parameter SET, which is of the enumeration type TYPE_SET.

```
type TYPE_SET is (LOWER_CASE, UPPER_CASE);
```

3   The format (which includes any trailing spaces) can be specified by an optional field width parameter. The default field width and letter case are defined by the following variables that are declared in the generic package ENUMERATION_IO:

```
DEFAULT_WIDTH    : FIELD := 0;
DEFAULT_SETTING  : TYPE_SET := UPPER_CASE;
```

4   The following procedures are provided:

5
```
procedure GET(FILE   : in FILE_TYPE; ITEM : out ENUM);
procedure GET(ITEM   : out ENUM);
```

6   After skipping any leading blanks, line terminators, or page terminators, reads an identifier according to the syntax of this lexical element (lower and upper case being considered equivalent), or a character literal according to the syntax of this lexical element (including the apostrophes). Returns, in the parameter ITEM, the value of type ENUM that corresponds to the sequence input.

7   The exception DATA_ERROR is raised if the sequence input does not have the required syntax, or if the identifier or character literal does not correspond to a value of the subtype ENUM.

```
procedure PUT(FILE   : in FILE_TYPE;                                    8
             ITEM   : in ENUM;
             WIDTH  : in FIELD := DEFAULT_WIDTH;
             SET    : in TYPE_SET := DEFAULT_SETTING);

procedure PUT(ITEM   : in ENUM;
             WIDTH  : in FIELD := DEFAULT_WIDTH;
             SET    : in TYPE_SET := DEFAULT_SETTING);
```

Outputs the value of the parameter ITEM as an enumeration literal (either an   9
identifier or a character literal). The optional parameter SET indicates whether
lower case or upper case is used for identifiers; it has no effect for character
literals. If the sequence of characters produced has fewer than WIDTH characters,
then trailing spaces are finally output to make up the difference.

```
procedure GET(FROM : in STRING; ITEM : out ENUM; LAST : out POSITIVE);    10
```

Reads an enumeration value from the beginning of the given string, following the   11
same rule as the GET procedure that reads an enumeration value from a file, but
treating the end of the string as a file terminator. Returns, in the parameter ITEM,
the value of type ENUM that corresponds to the sequence input. Returns in LAST
the index value such that FROM (LAST) is the last character read.

The exception DATA_ERROR is raised if the sequence input does not have the   12
required syntax, or if the identifier or character literal does not correspond to a
value of the subtype ENUM.

```
procedure PUT(TO   : out STRING;                                         13
             ITEM : in ENUM;
             SET  : in TYPE_SET := DEFAULT_SETTING);
```

Outputs the value of the parameter ITEM to the given string, following the same   14
rule as for output to a file, using the length of the given string as the value for
WIDTH.

Although the specification of the package ENUMERATION_IO would allow instantiation for an   15
integer type, this is not the intended purpose of this generic package, and the effect of such instantiations is not defined by the language.

Notes:

There is a difference between PUT defined for characters, and for enumeration values. Thus   16

```
TEXT_IO.PUT('A');   --  outputs the character A

package CHAR_IO is new TEXT_IO.ENUMERATION_IO(CHARACTER);
CHAR_IO.PUT('A');   --  outputs the character 'A', between single quotes
```

The type BOOLEAN is an enumeration type, hence ENUMERATION_IO can be instantiated for this   17
type.

References: blank 14.3.5, data_error 14.3.5, enumeration_io package 14.3.10, field subtype 14.3.5, file_type 14.1,   18
get procedure 14.3.5, line terminator 14.3.5, put procedure 14.3.5, skipping 14.3.5, width 14.3.5

14.3.10 Specification of the Package Text_IO

1

```
with IO_EXCEPTIONS;
package TEXT_IO is

   type FILE_TYPE   is limited private;

   type FILE_MODE is (IN_FILE, OUT_FILE);

   type COUNT is range 0 .. implementation_defined;
   subtype POSITIVE_COUNT is COUNT range 1 .. COUNT'LAST;
   UNBOUNDED : constant COUNT := 0; -- line and page length

   subtype FIELD         is INTEGER range 0 .. implementation_defined;
   subtype NUMBER_BASE is INTEGER range 2 .. 16;

   type TYPE_SET is (LOWER_CASE, UPPER_CASE);

   -- File Management

   procedure CREATE ( FILE   : in out FILE_TYPE;
                      MODE : in FILE_MODE := OUT_FILE;
                      NAME : in STRING      := "";
                      FORM : in STRING      := "");

   procedure OPEN   ( FILE   : in out FILE_TYPE;
                      MODE : in FILE_MODE;
                      NAME : in STRING;
                      FORM : in STRING := "");

   procedure  CLOSE  (FILE : in out FILE_TYPE);
   procedure  DELETE (FILE : in out FILE_TYPE);
   procedure  RESET  (FILE : in out FILE_TYPE; MODE : in FILE_MODE);
   procedure  RESET  (FILE : in out FILE_TYPE);

   function   MODE   (FILE : in FILE_TYPE) return FILE_MODE ;
   function   NAME   (FILE : in FILE_TYPE) return STRING;
   function   FORM   (FILE : in FILE_TYPE) return STRING;

   function   IS_OPEN(FILE : in FILE_TYPE) return BOOLEAN;

   -- Control of default input and output files

   procedure  SET_INPUT  (FILE : in FILE_TYPE);
   procedure  SET_OUTPUT (FILE : in FILE_TYPE);


   function   STANDARD_INPUT    return FILE_TYPE;
   function   STANDARD_OUTPUT   return FILE_TYPE;

   function   CURRENT_INPUT     return FILE_TYPE;
   function   CURRENT_OUTPUT    return FILE_TYPE;
```

-- Specification of line and page lengths

```
procedure  SET_LINE_LENGTH    (FILE : in FILE_TYPE; TO : in COUNT);
procedure  SET_LINE_LENGTH    (TO : in COUNT);

procedure  SET_PAGE_LENGTH    (FILE : in FILE_TYPE; TO : in COUNT);
procedure  SET_PAGE_LENGTH    (TO : in COUNT);

function   LINE_LENGTH  (FILE : in FILE_TYPE) return COUNT;
function   LINE_LENGTH    return COUNT;

function   PAGE_LENGTH (FILE : in FILE_TYPE) return COUNT;
function   PAGE_LENGTH  return COUNT;
```

— Column, Line, and Page Control

```
procedure  NEW_LINE    (FILE : in FILE_TYPE; SPACING : in POSITIVE_COUNT := 1);
procedure  NEW_LINE    (SPACING : in POSITIVE_COUNT := 1);

procedure  SKIP_LINE    (FILE : in FILE_TYPE; SPACING : in POSITIVE_COUNT := 1);
procedure  SKIP_LINE    (SPACING : in POSITIVE_COUNT := 1);

function   END_OF_LINE  (FILE : in FILE_TYPE) return BOOLEAN;
function   END_OF_LINE    return BOOLEAN;

procedure  NEW_PAGE    (FILE : in FILE_TYPE);
procedure  NEW_PAGE;

procedure  SKIP_PAGE    (FILE : in FILE_TYPE);
procedure  SKIP_PAGE;

function   END_OF_PAGE (FILE : in FILE_TYPE) return BOOLEAN;
function   END_OF_PAGE return BOOLEAN;

function   END_OF_FILE  (FILE : in FILE_TYPE) return BOOLEAN;
function   END_OF_FILE    return BOOLEAN;


procedure  SET_COL (FILE  : in FILE_TYPE; TO : in POSITIVE_COUNT);
procedure  SET_COL (TO    : in POSITIVE_COUNT);

procedure  SET_LINE (FILE  : in FILE_TYPE; TO : in POSITIVE_COUNT);
procedure  SET_LINE (TO    : in POSITIVE_COUNT);


function COL   (FILE : in FILE_TYPE) return POSITIVE_COUNT;
function COL     return POSITIVE_COUNT;

function LINE  (FILE : in FILE_TYPE) return POSITIVE_COUNT;
function LINE return POSITIVE_COUNT;

function PAGE (FILE : in FILE_TYPE) return POSITIVE_COUNT;
function PAGE   return POSITIVE_COUNT;
```

```
-- Character Input-Output

procedure  GET(FILE  : in   FILE_TYPE; ITEM : out CHARACTER);
procedure  GET(ITEM  : out  CHARACTER);
procedure  PUT(FILE  : in   FILE_TYPE; ITEM : in CHARACTER);
procedure  PUT(ITEM  : in   CHARACTER);

-- String Input-Output

procedure  GET(FILE  : in   FILE_TYPE; ITEM : out STRING);
procedure  GET(ITEM  : out  STRING);
procedure  PUT(FILE  : in   FILE_TYPE; ITEM : in STRING);
procedure  PUT(ITEM  : in   STRING);

procedure  GET_LINE(FILE : in   FILE_TYPE;  ITEM : out STRING; LAST : out NATURAL);
procedure  GET_LINE(ITEM : out  STRING; LAST : out NATURAL);
procedure  PUT_LINE(FILE : in   FILE_TYPE; ITEM : in STRING);
procedure  PUT_LINE(ITEM : in   STRING);

-- Generic package for Input-Output of Integer Types

generic
   type NUM is range <>;
package INTEGER_IO is

   DEFAULT_WIDTH  : FIELD := NUM'WIDTH;
   DEFAULT_BASE   : NUMBER_BASE := 10;

   procedure GET(FILE : in   FILE_TYPE; ITEM : out NUM; WIDTH : in FIELD := 0);
   procedure GET(ITEM : out NUM; WIDTH : in FIELD := 0);

   procedure PUT(FILE     : in FILE_TYPE;
                 ITEM     : in NUM;
                 WIDTH    : in FIELD := DEFAULT_WIDTH;
                 BASE     : in NUMBER_BASE := DEFAULT_BASE);
   procedure PUT(ITEM     : in NUM;
                 WIDTH    : in FIELD := DEFAULT_WIDTH;
                 BASE     : in NUMBER_BASE := DEFAULT_BASE);

   procedure GET(FROM : in  STRING; ITEM : out NUM; LAST : out POSITIVE);
   procedure PUT(TO       : out STRING;
                 ITEM     : in NUM;
                 BASE     : in NUMBER_BASE := DEFAULT_BASE);

end INTEGER_IO;
```

-- Generic packages for Input-Output of Real Types

```
generic
  type NUM is digits <>;
package FLOAT_IO is

  DEFAULT_FORE  : FIELD := 2;
  DEFAULT_AFT   : FIELD := NUM'DIGITS-1;
  DEFAULT_EXP   : FIELD := 3;

  procedure  GET(FILE : in FILE_TYPE; ITEM : out NUM; WIDTH : in FIELD := 0);
  procedure  GET(ITEM : out NUM; WIDTH : in FIELD := 0);

  procedure PUT(FILE    : in FILE_TYPE;
                ITEM    : in NUM;
                FORE    : in FIELD := DEFAULT_FORE;
                AFT     : in FIELD := DEFAULT_AFT;
                EXP     : in FIELD := DEFAULT_EXP);
  procedure PUT(ITEM    : in NUM;
                FORE    : in FIELD := DEFAULT_FORE;
                AFT     : in FIELD := DEFAULT_AFT;
                EXP     : in FIELD := DEFAULT_EXP);

  procedure GET(FROM : in STRING; ITEM : out NUM; LAST : out POSITIVE);
  procedure PUT(TO      : out STRING;
                ITEM    : in NUM;
                AFT     : in FIELD := DEFAULT_AFT;
                EXP     : in FIELD := DEFAULT_EXP);
end FLOAT_IO;

generic
  type NUM is delta <>;
package FIXED_IO is

  DEFAULT_FORE  : FIELD := NUM'FORE;
  DEFAULT_AFT   : FIELD := NUM'AFT;
  DEFAULT_EXP   : FIELD := 0;

  procedure GET(FILE : in FILE_TYPE; ITEM : out NUM; WIDTH : in FIELD := 0);
  procedure GET(ITEM : out NUM; WIDTH : in FIELD := 0);

  procedure PUT(FILE    : in FILE_TYPE;
                ITEM    : in NUM;
                FORE    : in FIELD := DEFAULT_FORE;
                AFT     : in FIELD := DEFAULT_AFT;
                EXP     : in FIELD := DEFAULT_EXP);
  procedure PUT(ITEM    : in NUM;
                FORE    : in FIELD := DEFAULT_FORE;
                AFT     : in FIELD := DEFAULT_AFT;
                EXP     : in FIELD := DEFAULT_EXP);

  procedure GET(FROM : in  STRING; ITEM : out NUM; LAST : out POSITIVE);
  procedure PUT(TO      : out STRING;
                ITEM    : in NUM;
                AFT     : in FIELD := DEFAULT_AFT;
                EXP     : in FIELD := DEFAULT_EXP);

end FIXED_IO;
```

-- Generic package for Input-Output of Enumeration Types

```
generic
    type ENUM is (<>);
package ENUMERATION_IO is

    DEFAULT_WIDTH   : FIELD := 0;
    DEFAULT_SETTING : TYPE_SET := UPPER_CASE;

    procedure GET(FILE    : in FILE_TYPE; ITEM : out ENUM);
    procedure GET(ITEM    : out ENUM);

    procedure PUT(FILE    : in FILE_TYPE;
                  ITEM    : in ENUM;
                  WIDTH   : in FIELD      := DEFAULT_WIDTH;
                  SET     : in TYPE_SET   := DEFAULT_SETTING);
    procedure PUT(ITEM    : in ENUM;
                  WIDTH   : in FIELD      := DEFAULT_WIDTH;
                  SET     : in TYPE_SET   := DEFAULT_SETTING);

    procedure GET(FROM    : in  STRING; ITEM : out ENUM; LAST : out POSITIVE);
    procedure PUT(TO      : out STRING;
                  ITEM    : in  ENUM;
                  SET     : in  TYPE_SET := DEFAULT_SETTING);
end ENUMERATION_IO;

-- Exceptions

STATUS_ERROR  : exception renames IO_EXCEPTIONS.STATUS_ERROR;
MODE_ERROR    : exception renames IO_EXCEPTIONS.MODE_ERROR;
NAME_ERROR    : exception renames IO_EXCEPTIONS.NAME_ERROR;
USE_ERROR     : exception renames IO_EXCEPTIONS.USE_ERROR;
DEVICE_ERROR  : exception renames IO_EXCEPTIONS.DEVICE_ERROR;
END_ERROR     : exception renames IO_EXCEPTIONS.END_ERROR;
DATA_ERROR    : exception renames IO_EXCEPTIONS.DATA_ERROR;
LAYOUT_ERROR  : exception renames IO_EXCEPTIONS.LAYOUT_ERROR;

private
    -- implementation-dependent
end TEXT_IO;
```

14.4 Exceptions in Input-Output

1   The following exceptions can be raised by input-output operations. They are declared in the package IO_EXCEPTIONS, defined in section 14.5; this package is named in the context clause for each of the three input-output packages. Only outline descriptions are given of the conditions under which NAME_ERROR, USE_ERROR, and DEVICE_ERROR are raised; for full details see Appendix F. If more than one error condition exists, the corresponding exception that appears earliest in the following list is the one that is raised.

2   The exception STATUS_ERROR is raised by an attempt to operate upon a file that is not open, and by an attempt to open a file that is already open.

The exception MODE_ERROR is raised by an attempt to read from, or test for the end of, a file whose current mode is OUT_FILE, and also by an attempt to write to a file whose current mode is IN_FILE. In the case of TEXT_IO, the exception MODE_ERROR is also raised by specifying a file whose current mode is OUT_FILE in a call of SET_INPUT, SKIP_LINE, END_OF_LINE, SKIP_PAGE, or END_OF_PAGE; and by specifying a file whose current mode is IN_FILE in a call of SET_OUTPUT, SET_LINE_LENGTH, SET_PAGE_LENGTH, LINE_LENGTH, PAGE_LENGTH, NEW_LINE, or NEW_PAGE. 3

The exception NAME_ERROR is raised by a call of CREATE or OPEN if the string given for the parameter NAME does not allow the identification of an external file. For example, this exception is raised if the string is improper, or, alternatively, if either none or more than one external file corresponds to the string. 4

The exception USE_ERROR is raised if an operation is attempted that is not possible for reasons that depend on characteristics of the external file. For example, this exception is raised by the procedure CREATE, among other circumstances, if the given mode is OUT_FILE but the form specifies an input only device, if the parameter FORM specifies invalid access rights, or if an external file with the given name already exists and overwriting is not allowed. 5

The exception DEVICE_ERROR is raised if an input-output operation cannot be completed because of a malfunction of the underlying system. 6

The exception END_ERROR is raised by an attempt to skip (read past) the end of a file. 7

The exception DATA_ERROR may be raised by the procedure READ if the element read cannot be interpreted as a value of the required type. This exception is also raised by a procedure GET (defined in the package TEXT_IO) if the input character sequence fails to satisfy the required syntax, or if the value input does not belong to the range of the required type or subtype. 8

The exception LAYOUT_ERROR is raised (in text input-output) by COL, LINE, or PAGE if the value returned exceeds COUNT'LAST. The exception LAYOUT_ERROR is also raised on output by an attempt to set column or line numbers in excess of specified maximum line or page lengths, respectively (excluding the unbounded cases). It is also raised by an attempt to PUT too many characters to a string. 9

References: col function 14.3.4, create procedure 14.2.1, end_of_line function 14.3.4, end_of_page function 14.3.4, external file 14.1, file 14.1, form string 14.1, get procedure 14.3.5, in_file 14.1, io_exceptions package 14.5, line function 14.3.4, line_length function 14.3.4, name string 14.1, new_line procedure 14.3.4, new_page procedure 14.3.4, open procedure 14.2.1, out_file 14.1, page function 14.3.4, page_length function 14.3.4, put procedure 14.3.5, read procedure 14.2.2 14.2.3, set_input procedure 14.3.2, set_line_length 14.3.3, set_page_length 14.3.3, set_output 14.3.2, skip_line procedure 14.3.4, skip_page procedure 14.3.4, text_io package 14.3 10

14.5 Specification of the Package IO_Exceptions

1   This package defines the exceptions needed by the packages SEQUENTIAL_IO, DIRECT_IO, and TEXT_IO.

2
```
package IO_EXCEPTIONS is

    STATUS_ERROR   : exception;
    MODE_ERROR     : exception;
    NAME_ERROR     : exception;
    USE_ERROR      : exception;
    DEVICE_ERROR   : exception;
    END_ERROR      : exception;
    DATA_ERROR     : exception;
    LAYOUT_ERROR   : exception;

end IO_EXCEPTIONS;
```

14.6 Low Level Input-Output

1   A low level input-output operation is an operation acting on a physical device. Such an operation is handled by using one of the (overloaded) predefined procedures SEND_CONTROL and RECEIVE_CONTROL.

2   A procedure SEND_CONTROL may be used to send control information to a physical device. A procedure RECEIVE_CONTROL may be used to monitor the execution of an input-output operation by requesting information from the physical device.

3   Such procedures are declared in the standard package LOW_LEVEL_IO and have two parameters identifying the device and the data. However, the kinds and formats of the control information will depend on the physical characteristics of the machine and the device. Hence, the types of the parameters are implementation-defined. Overloaded definitions of these procedures should be provided for the supported devices.

4   The visible part of the package defining these procedures is outlined as follows:

5
```
package LOW_LEVEL_IO is
    -- declarations of the possible types for DEVICE and DATA;
    -- declarations of overloaded procedures for these types:
    procedure SEND_CONTROL      (DEVICE : device_type; DATA : in out data_type);
    procedure RECEIVE_CONTROL   (DEVICE : device_type; DATA : in out data_type);
end;
```

6   The bodies of the procedures SEND_CONTROL and RECEIVE_CONTROL for various devices can be supplied in the body of the package LOW_LEVEL_IO. These procedure bodies may be written with code statements.

14.7 Example of Input-Output

The following example shows the use of some of the text input-output facilities in a dialogue with a user at a terminal. The user is prompted to type a color, and the program responds by giving the number of items of that color available in stock, according to an inventory. The default input and output files are used. For simplicity, all the requisite instantiations are given within one sub-program; in practice, a package, separate from the procedure, would be used.

```ada
with TEXT_IO; use TEXT_IO;
procedure DIALOGUE is
    type COLOR is (WHITE, RED, ORANGE, YELLOW, GREEN, BLUE, BROWN);
    package COLOR_IO is new ENUMERATION_IO(ENUM => COLOR);
    package NUMBER_IO is new INTEGER_IO(INTEGER);
    use COLOR_IO, NUMBER_IO;

    INVENTORY : array (COLOR) of INTEGER := (20, 17, 43, 10, 28, 173, 87);
    CHOICE : COLOR;

    procedure ENTER_COLOR (SELECTION : out COLOR) is
    begin
      loop
        begin
          PUT ("Color selected: ");    --  prompts user
          GET (SELECTION);             --  accepts color typed, or raises exception
          return;
        exception
          when DATA_ERROR =>
            PUT("Invalid color, try again.  ");  --  user has typed new line
            NEW_LINE(2);
            --  completes execution of the block statement
        end;
      end loop;  --  repeats the block statement until color accepted
    end;
begin --  statements of DIALOGUE;

    NUMBER_IO.DEFAULT_WIDTH := 5;

    loop

      ENTER_COLOR(CHOICE);  --   user types color and new line

      SET_COL(5);    PUT(CHOICE); PUT(" items available:");
      SET_COL(40);   PUT(INVENTORY(CHOICE));   --   default width is 5
      NEW_LINE;
    end loop;
end DIALOGUE;
```

Example of an interaction (characters typed by the user are italicized):

```
Color selected:  Black
Invalid color, try again.

Color selected:  Blue
   BLUE items available:          173
Color selected:  Yellow
   YELLOW items available:         10
```

A. Predefined Language Attributes

This annex summarizes the definitions given elsewhere of the predefined language attributes.　　1

P'ADDRESS　　For a prefix P that denotes an object, a program unit, a label, or an entry:　　2

Yields the address of the first of the storage units allocated to P. For a subprogram, package, task unit, or label, this value refers to the machine code associated with the corresponding body or statement. For an entry for which an address clause has been given, the value refers to the corresponding hardware interrupt. The value of this attribute is of the type ADDRESS defined in the package SYSTEM. (See 13.7.2.)

P'AFT　　For a prefix P that denotes a fixed point subtype:　　3

Yields the number of decimal digits needed after the point to accommodate the precision of the subtype P, unless the delta of the subtype P is greater than 0.1, in which case the attribute yields the value one. (P'AFT is the smallest positive integer N for which $(10**N)*P'DELTA$ is greater than or equal to one.) The value of this attribute is of the type *universal_integer*. (See 3.5.10.)

P'BASE　　For a prefix P that denotes a type or subtype:　　4

This attribute denotes the base type of P. It is only allowed as the prefix of the name of another attribute: for example, P'BASE'FIRST. (See 3.3.3.)

P'CALLABLE　　For a prefix P that is appropriate for a task type:　　5

Yields the value FALSE when the execution of the task P is either completed or terminated, or when the task is abnormal; yields the value TRUE otherwise. The value of this attribute is of the predefined type BOOLEAN. (See 9.9.)

P'CONSTRAINED　　For a prefix P that denotes an object of a type with discriminants:　　6

Yields the value TRUE if a discriminant constraint applies to the object P, or if the object is a constant (including a formal parameter or generic formal parameter of mode **in**); yields the value FALSE otherwise. If P is a generic formal parameter of mode **in out**, or if P is a formal parameter of mode **in out** or **out** and the type mark given in the corresponding parameter specification denotes an unconstrained type with discriminants, then the value of this attribute is obtained from that of the corresponding actual parameter. The value of this attribute is of the predefined type BOOLEAN. (See 3.7.4.)

7 **P'CONSTRAINED**   For a prefix P that denotes a private type or subtype:

Yields the value FALSE if P denotes an unconstrained nonformal private type with discriminants; also yields the value FALSE if P denotes a generic formal private type and the associated actual subtype is either an unconstrained type with discriminants or an unconstrained array type; yields the value TRUE otherwise. The value of this attribute is of the predefined type BOOLEAN. (See 7.4.2.)

8 **P'COUNT**   For a prefix P that denotes an entry of a task unit:

Yields the number of entry calls presently queued on the entry (if the attribute is evaluated within an accept statement for the entry P, the count does not include the calling task). The value of this attribute is of the type *universal_integer*. (See 9.9.)

9 **P'DELTA**   For a prefix P that denotes a fixed point subtype:

Yields the value of the delta specified in the fixed accuracy definition for the subtype P. The value of this attribute is of the type *universal_real*. (See 3.5.10.)

10 **P'DIGITS**   For a prefix P that denotes a floating point subtype:

Yields the number of decimal digits in the decimal mantissa of model numbers of the subtype P. (This attribute yields the number D of section 3.5.7.) The value of this attribute is of the type *universal_integer*. (See 3.5.8.)

11 **P'EMAX**   For a prefix P that denotes a floating point subtype:

Yields the largest exponent value in the binary canonical form of model numbers of the subtype P. (This attribute yields the product $4*B$ of section 3.5.7.) The value of this attribute is of the type *universal_integer*. (See 3.5.8.)

12 **P'EPSILON**   For a prefix P that denotes a floating point subtype:

Yields the absolute value of the difference between the model number 1.0 and the next model number above, for the subtype P. The value of this attribute is of the type *universal_real*. (See 3.5.8.)

13 **P'FIRST**   For a prefix P that denotes a scalar type, or a subtype of a scalar type:

Yields the lower bound of P. The value of this attribute has the same type as P. (See 3.5.)

14 **P'FIRST**   For a prefix P that is appropriate for an array type, or that denotes a con-strained array subtype:

Yields the lower bound of the first index range. The value of this attribute has the same type as this lower bound. (See 3.6.2 and 3.8.2.)

P'FIRST(N)   For a prefix P that is appropriate for an array type, or that denotes a con-   15
strained array subtype:

Yields the lower bound of the N-th index range. The value of this attribute
has the same type as this lower bound. The argument N must be a static
expression of type *universal_integer*. The value of N must be positive
(nonzero) and no greater than the dimensionality of the array. (See 3.6.2 and
3.8.2.)

P'FIRST_BIT   For a prefix P that denotes a component of a record object: 16

Yields the offset, from the start of the first of the storage units occupied by
the component, of the first bit occupied by the component. This offset is
measured in bits. The value of this attribute is of the type *universal_integer*.
(See 13.7.2.)

P'FORE   For a prefix P that denotes a fixed point subtype: 17

Yields the minimum number of characters needed for the integer part of the
decimal representation of any value of the subtype P, assuming that the
representation does not include an exponent, but includes a one-character
prefix that is either a minus sign or a space. (This minimum number does not
include superfluous zeros or underlines, and is at least two.) The value of
this attribute is of the type *universal_integer*. (See 3.5.10.)

P'IMAGE   For a prefix P that denotes a discrete type or subtype: 18

This attribute is a function with a single parameter. The actual parameter X
must be a value of the base type of P. The result type is the predefined type
STRING. The result is the *image* of the value of X, that is, a sequence of
characters representing the value in display form. The image of an integer
value is the corresponding decimal literal; without underlines, leading
zeros, exponent, or trailing spaces; but with a one character prefix that is
either a minus sign or a space.

The image of an enumeration value is either the corresponding identifier in
upper case or the corresponding character literal (including the two
apostrophes); neither leading nor trailing spaces are included. The image of
a character other than a graphic character is implementation-defined. (See
3.5.5.)

P'LARGE   For a prefix P that denotes a real subtype: 19

The attribute yields the largest positive model number of the subtype P. The
value of this attribute is of the type *universal_real*. (See 3.5.8 and 3.5.10.)

P'LAST   For a prefix P that denotes a scalar type, or a subtype of a scalar type: 20

Yields the upper bound of P. The value of this attribute has the same type as
P. (See 3.5.)

P'LAST   For a prefix P that is appropriate for an array type, or that denotes a con-   21
strained array subtype:

Yields the upper bound of the first index range. The value of this attribute
has the same type as this upper bound. (See 3.6.2 and 3.8.2.)

<table>
<tr><td>22</td><td>P'LAST(N)</td><td>For a prefix P that is appropriate for an array type, or that denotes a constrained array subtype:</td></tr>
</table>

22   P'LAST(N)   For a prefix P that is appropriate for an array type, or that denotes a constrained array subtype:

Yields the upper bound of the N-th index range. The value of this attribute has the same type as this upper bound. The argument N must be a static expression of type *universal_integer*. The value of N must be positive (nonzero) and no greater than the dimensionality of the array. (See 3.6.2 and 3.8.2.)

23   P'LAST_BIT   For a prefix P that denotes a component of a record object:

Yields the offset, from the start of the first of the storage units occupied by the component, of the last bit occupied by the component. This offset is measured in bits. The value of this attribute is of the type *universal_integer*. (See 13.7.2.)

24   P'LENGTH   For a prefix P that is appropriate for an array type, or that denotes a constrained array subtype:

Yields the number of values of the first index range (zero for a null range). The value of this attribute is of the type *universal_integer*. (See 3.6.2.)

25   P'LENGTH(N)   For a prefix P that is appropriate for an array type, or that denotes a constrained array subtype:

Yields the number of values of the N-th index range (zero for a null range). The value of this attribute is of the type *universal_integer*. The argument N must be a static expression of type *universal_integer*. The value of N must be positive (nonzero) and no greater than the dimensionality of the array. (See 3.6.2 and 3.8.2.)

26   P'MACHINE_EMAX   For a prefix P that denotes a floating point type or subtype:

Yields the largest value of *exponent* for the machine representation of the base type of P. The value of this attribute is of the type *universal_integer*. (See 13.7.3.)

27   P'MACHINE_EMIN   For a prefix P that denotes a floating point type or subtype:

Yields the smallest (most negative) value of *exponent* for the machine representation of the base type of P. The value of this attribute is of the type *universal_integer*. (See 13.7.3.)

28   P'MACHINE_MANTISSA   For a prefix P that denotes a floating point type or subtype:

Yields the number of digits in the *mantissa* for the machine representation of the base type of P (the digits are extended digits in the range 0 to P'MACHINE_RADIX - 1). The value of this attribute is of the type *universal_integer*. (See 13.7.3.)

P'MACHINE_OVERFLOWS For a prefix P that denotes a real type or subtype: 29

Yields the value TRUE if every predefined operation on values of the base type of P either provides a correct result, or raises the exception NUMERIC_ERROR in overflow situations; yields the value FALSE otherwise. The value of this attribute is of the predefined type BOOLEAN. (See 13.7.3.)

P'MACHINE_RADIX For a prefix P that denotes a floating point type or subtype: 30

Yields the value of the *radix* used by the machine representation of the base type of P. The value of this attribute is of the type *universal_integer*. (See 13.7.3.)

P'MACHINE_ROUNDS For a prefix P that denotes a real type or subtype: 31

Yields the value TRUE if every predefined arithmetic operation on values of the base type of P either returns an exact result or performs rounding; yields the value FALSE otherwise. The value of this attribute is of the predefined type BOOLEAN. (See 13.7.3.)

P'MANTISSA For a prefix P that denotes a real subtype: 32

Yields the number of binary digits in the binary mantissa of model numbers of the subtype P. (This attribute yields the number B of section 3.5.7 for a floating point type, or of section 3.5.9 for a fixed point type.) The value of this attribute is of the type *universal_integer*. (See 3.5.8 and 3.5.10.)

P'POS For a prefix P that denotes a discrete type or subtype: 33

This attribute is a function with a single parameter. The actual parameter X must be a value of the base type of P. The result type is the type *universal_integer*. The result is the position number of the value of the actual parameter. (See 3.5.5.)

P'POSITION For a prefix P that denotes a component of a record object: 34

Yields the offset, from the start of the first storage unit occupied by the record, of the first of the storage units occupied by the component. This offset is measured in storage units. The value of this attribute is of the type *universal_integer*. (See 13.7.2.)

P'PRED For a prefix P that denotes a discrete type or subtype: 35

This attribute is a function with a single parameter. The actual parameter X must be a value of the base type of P. The result type is the base type of P. The result is the value whose position number is one less than that of X. The exception CONSTRAINT_ERROR is raised if X equals P'BASE'FIRST. (See 3.5.5.)

P'RANGE For a prefix P that is appropriate for an array type, or that denotes a   36
constrained array subtype:

Yields the first index range of P, that is, the range P'FIRST .. P'LAST. (See 3.6.2.)

37	P'RANGE(N)	For a prefix P that is appropriate for an array type, or that denotes a constrained array subtype:
		Yields the N-th index range of P, that is, the range P'FIRST(N) .. P'LAST(N). (See 3.6.2.)
38	P'SAFE_EMAX	For a prefix P that denotes a floating point type or subtype:
		Yields the largest exponent value in the binary canonical form of safe numbers of the base type of P. (This attribute yields the number E of section 3.5.7.) The value of this attribute is of the type *universal_integer*. (See 3.5.8.)
39	P'SAFE_LARGE	For a prefix P that denotes a real type or subtype:
		Yields the largest positive safe number of the base type of P. The value of this attribute is of the type *universal_real*. (See 3.5.8 and 3.5.10.)
40	P'SAFE_SMALL	For a prefix P that denotes a real type or subtype:
		Yields the smallest positive (nonzero) safe number of the base type of P. The value of this attribute is of the type *universal_real*. (See 3.5.8 and 3.5.10.)
41	P'SIZE	For a prefix P that denotes an object:
		Yields the number of bits allocated to hold the object. The value of this attribute is of the type *universal_integer*. (See 13.7.2.)
42	P'SIZE	For a prefix P that denotes any type or subtype:
		Yields the minimum number of bits that is needed by the implementation to hold any possible object of the type or subtype P. The value of this attribute is of the type *universal_integer*. (See 13.7.2.)
43	P'SMALL	For a prefix P that denotes a real subtype:
		Yields the smallest positive (nonzero) model number of the subtype P. The value of this attribute is of the type *universal_real*. (See 3.5.8 and 3.5.10.)
44	P'STORAGE_SIZE	For a prefix P that denotes an access type or subtype:
		Yields the total number of storage units reserved for the collection associated with the base type of P. The value of this attribute is of the type *universal_integer*. (See 13.7.2.)
45	P'STORAGE_SIZE	For a prefix P that denotes a task type or a task object:
		Yields the number of storage units reserved for each activation of a task of the type P or for the activation of the task object P. The value of this attribute is of the type *universal_integer*. (See 13.7.2.)

P'SUCC   For a prefix P that denotes a discrete type or subtype: 46

This attribute is a function with a single parameter. The actual parameter X must be a value of the base type of P. The result type is the base type of P. The result is the value whose position number is one greater than that of X. The exception CONSTRAINT_ERROR is raised if X equals P'BASE'LAST. (See 3.5.5.)

P'TERMINATED   For a prefix P that is appropriate for a task type: 47

Yields the value TRUE if the task P is terminated; yields the value FALSE otherwise. The value of this attribute is of the predefined type BOOLEAN. (See 9.9.)

P'VAL   For a prefix P that denotes a discrete type or subtype: 48

This attribute is a special function with a single parameter X which can be of any integer type. The result type is the base type of P. The result is the value whose position number is the *universal_integer* value corresponding to X. The exception CONSTRAINT_ERROR is raised if the *universal_integer* value corresponding to X is not in the range P'POS (P'BASE'FIRST) .. P'POS (P'BASE'LAST). (See 3.5.5.)

P'VALUE   For a prefix P that denotes a discrete type or subtype: 49

This attribute is a function with a single parameter. The actual parameter X must be a value of the predefined type STRING. The result type is the base type of P. Any leading and any trailing spaces of the sequence of characters that corresponds to X are ignored.

For an enumeration type, if the sequence of characters has the syntax of an enumeration literal and if this literal exists for the base type of P, the result is the corresponding enumeration value. For an integer type, if the sequence of characters has the syntax of an integer literal, with an optional single leading character that is a plus or minus sign, and if there is a corresponding value in the base type of P, the result is this value. In any other case, the exception CONSTRAINT_ERROR is raised. (See 3.5.5.)

P'WIDTH   For a prefix P that denotes a discrete subtype: 50

Yields the maximum image length over all values of the subtype P (the *image* is the sequence of characters returned by the attribute IMAGE). The value of this attribute is of the type *universal_integer*. (See 3.5.5.)

B. Predefined Language Pragmas

This annex defines the pragmas LIST, PAGE, and OPTIMIZE, and summarizes the definitions given elsewhere of the remaining language-defined pragmas.

Pragma   *Meaning*

CONTROLLED   Takes the simple name of an access type as the single argument. This pragma is only allowed immediately within the declarative part or package specification that contains the declaration of the access type; the declaration must occur before the pragma. This pragma is not allowed for a derived type. This pragma specifies that automatic storage reclamation must not be performed for objects designated by values of the access type, except upon leaving the innermost block statement, subprogram body, or task body that encloses the access type declaration, or after leaving the main program (see 4.8).

ELABORATE   Takes one or more simple names denoting library units as arguments. This pragma is only allowed immediately after the context clause of a compilation unit (before the subsequent library unit or secondary unit). Each argument must be the simple name of a library unit mentioned by the context clause. This pragma specifies that the corresponding library unit body must be elaborated before the given compilation unit. If the given compilation unit is a subunit, the library unit body must be elaborated before the body of the ancestor library unit of the subunit (see 10.5).

INLINE   Takes one or more names as arguments; each name is either the name of a subprogram or the name of a generic subprogram. This pragma is only allowed at the place of a declarative item in a declarative part or package specification, or after a library unit in a compilation, but before any subsequent compilation unit. This pragma specifies that the subprogram bodies should be expanded inline at each call whenever possible; in the case of a generic subprogram, the pragma applies to calls of its instantiations (see 6.3.2).

INTERFACE   Takes a language name and a subprogram name as arguments. This pragma is allowed at the place of a declarative item, and must apply in this case to a subprogram declared by an earlier declarative item of the same declarative part or package specification. This pragma is also allowed for a library unit; in this case the pragma must appear after the subprogram declaration, and before any subsequent compilation unit. This pragma specifies the other language (and thereby the calling conventions) and informs the compiler that an object module will be supplied for the corresponding subprogram (see 13.9).

LIST   Takes one of the identifiers ON or OFF as the single argument. This pragma is allowed anywhere a pragma is allowed. It specifies that listing of the compilation is to be continued or suspended until a LIST pragma with the opposite argument is given within the same compilation. The pragma itself is always listed if the compiler is producing a listing.

MEMORY_SIZE   Takes a numeric literal as the single argument. This pragma is only allowed at the start of a compilation, before the first compilation unit (if any) of the compilation. The effect of this pragma is to use the value of the specified numeric literal for the definition of the named number MEMORY_SIZE (see 13.7).

8   OPTIMIZE   Takes one of the identifiers TIME or SPACE as the single argument. This
                          pragma is only allowed within a declarative part and it applies to the block or
                          body enclosing the declarative part. It specifies whether time or space is the
                          primary optimization criterion.

9   PACK   Takes the simple name of a record or array type as the single argument. The
                          allowed positions for this pragma, and the restrictions on the named type, are
                          governed by the same rules as for a representation clause. The pragma
                          specifies that storage minimization should be the main criterion when selecting
                          the representation of the given type (see 13.1).

10   PAGE   This pragma has no argument, and is allowed anywhere a pragma is allowed. It
                          specifies that the program text which follows the pragma should start on a new
                          page (if the compiler is currently producing a listing).

11   PRIORITY   Takes a static expression of the predefined integer subtype PRIORITY as the
                          single argument. This pragma is only allowed within the specification of a task
                          unit or immediately within the outermost declarative part of a main program. It
                          specifies the priority of the task (or tasks of the task type) or the priority of the
                          main program (see 9.8).

12   SHARED   Takes the simple name of a variable as the single argument. This pragma is
                          allowed only for a variable declared by an object declaration and whose type is
                          a scalar or access type; the variable declaration and the pragma must both
                          occur (in this order) immediately within the same declarative part or package
                          specification. This pragma specifies that every read or update of the variable is
                          a synchronization point for that variable. An implementation must restrict the
                          objects for which this pragma is allowed to objects for which each of direct
                          reading and direct updating is implemented as an indivisible operation (see
                          9.11).

13   STORAGE_UNIT   Takes a numeric literal as the single argument. This pragma is only allowed at
                          the start of a compilation, before the first compilation unit (if any) of the com-
                          pilation. The effect of this pragma is to use the value of the specified numeric
                          literal for the definition of the named number STORAGE_UNIT (see 13.7).

14   SUPPRESS   Takes as arguments the identifier of a check and optionally also the name of
                          either an object, a type or subtype, a subprogram, a task unit, or a generic unit.
                          This pragma is only allowed either immediately within a declarative part or
                          immediately within a package specification. In the latter case, the only allowed
                          form is with a name that denotes an entity (or several overloaded subprograms)
                          declared immediately within the package specification. The permission to omit
                          the given check extends from the place of the pragma to the end of the
                          declarative region associated with the innermost enclosing block statement or
                          program unit. For a pragma given in a package specification, the permission
                          extends to the end of the scope of the named entity.

                          If the pragma includes a name, the permission to omit the given check is further
                          restricted: it is given only for operations on the named object or on all objects
                          of the base type of a named type or subtype; for calls of a named subprogram;
                          for activations of tasks of the named task type; or for instantiations of the given
                          generic unit (see 11.7).

15   SYSTEM_NAME   Takes an enumeration literal as the single argument. This pragma is only
                          allowed at the start of a compilation, before the first compilation unit (if any) of
                          the compilation. The effect of this pragma is to use the enumeration literal with
                          the specified identifier for the definition of the constant SYSTEM_NAME. This
                          pragma is only allowed if the specified identifier corresponds to one of the
                          literals of the type NAME declared in the package SYSTEM (see 13.7).

C. Predefined Language Environment

This annex outlines the specification of the package STANDARD containing all predefined [1] identifiers in the language. The corresponding package body is implementation-defined and is not shown.

The operators that are predefined for the types declared in the package STANDARD are given in [2] comments since they are implicitly declared. Italics are used for pseudo-names of anonymous types (such as *universal_real*) and for undefined information (such as *implementation_defined* and *any_fixed_point_type*).

package STANDARD **is** [3]

  type BOOLEAN **is** (FALSE, TRUE); [4]

  -- The predefined relational operators for this type are as follows:

  -- **function** "="   (LEFT, RIGHT : BOOLEAN) **return** BOOLEAN;
  -- **function** "/="   (LEFT, RIGHT : BOOLEAN) **return** BOOLEAN;
  -- **function** "<"   (LEFT, RIGHT : BOOLEAN) **return** BOOLEAN;
  -- **function** "<="   (LEFT, RIGHT : BOOLEAN) **return** BOOLEAN;
  -- **function** ">"   (LEFT, RIGHT : BOOLEAN) **return** BOOLEAN;
  -- **function** ">="   (LEFT, RIGHT : BOOLEAN) **return** BOOLEAN;

  -- The predefined logical operators and the predefined logical negation operator are as follows:

  -- **function** "and" (LEFT, RIGHT : BOOLEAN) **return** BOOLEAN;
  -- **function** "or" (LEFT, RIGHT : BOOLEAN) **return** BOOLEAN;
  -- **function** "xor" (LEFT, RIGHT : BOOLEAN) **return** BOOLEAN;

  -- **function** "not" (RIGHT : BOOLEAN) **return** BOOLEAN;

  -- The universal type *universal_integer* is predefined. [5]

  type INTEGER **is** *implementation_defined*; [6]

  -- The predefined operators for this type are as follows:

  -- **function** "="   (LEFT, RIGHT : INTEGER) **return** BOOLEAN;
  -- **function** "/="   (LEFT, RIGHT : INTEGER) **return** BOOLEAN;
  -- **function** "<"   (LEFT, RIGHT : INTEGER) **return** BOOLEAN;
  -- **function** "<="   (LEFT, RIGHT : INTEGER) **return** BOOLEAN;
  -- **function** ">"   (LEFT, RIGHT : INTEGER) **return** BOOLEAN;
  -- **function** ">="   (LEFT, RIGHT : INTEGER) **return** BOOLEAN;

```
-- function "+"    (RIGHT : INTEGER) return INTEGER;
-- function "-"    (RIGHT : INTEGER) return INTEGER;
-- function "abs"  (RIGHT : INTEGER) return INTEGER;

-- function "+"    (LEFT, RIGHT : INTEGER) return INTEGER;
-- function "-"    (LEFT, RIGHT : INTEGER) return INTEGER;
-- function "*"    (LEFT, RIGHT : INTEGER) return INTEGER;
-- function "/"    (LEFT, RIGHT : INTEGER) return INTEGER;
-- function "rem"  (LEFT, RIGHT : INTEGER) return INTEGER;
-- function "mod"  (LEFT, RIGHT : INTEGER) return INTEGER;

-- function "**"   (LEFT : INTEGER; RIGHT : INTEGER) return INTEGER;
```

7   -- An implementation may provide additional predefined integer types. It is recommended that the
      -- names of such additional types end with INTEGER as in SHORT_INTEGER or LONG_INTEGER.
      -- The specification of each operator for the type *universal_integer*, or for any additional
      -- predefined integer type, is obtained by replacing INTEGER by the name of the type in the
      -- specification of the corresponding operator of the type INTEGER, except for the right operand
      -- of the exponentiating operator.

8   -- The universal type *universal_real* is predefined.

9   type FLOAT is *implementation_defined*;

      -- The predefined operators for this type are as follows:

```
-- function "="    (LEFT, RIGHT : FLOAT) return BOOLEAN;
-- function "/="   (LEFT, RIGHT : FLOAT) return BOOLEAN;
-- function "<"    (LEFT, RIGHT : FLOAT) return BOOLEAN;
-- function "<="   (LEFT, RIGHT : FLOAT) return BOOLEAN;
-- function ">"    (LEFT, RIGHT : FLOAT) return BOOLEAN;
-- function ">="   (LEFT, RIGHT : FLOAT) return BOOLEAN;

-- function "+"    (RIGHT : FLOAT) return FLOAT;
-- function "-"    (RIGHT : FLOAT) return FLOAT;
-- function "abs"  (RIGHT : FLOAT) return FLOAT;

-- function "+"    (LEFT, RIGHT : FLOAT) return FLOAT;
-- function "-"    (LEFT, RIGHT : FLOAT) return FLOAT;
-- function "*"    (LEFT, RIGHT : FLOAT) return FLOAT;
-- function "/"    (LEFT, RIGHT : FLOAT) return FLOAT;

-- function "**"   (LEFT : FLOAT; RIGHT : INTEGER) return FLOAT;
```

10   -- An implementation may provide additional predefined floating point types. It is recom-
      -- mended that the names of such additional types end with FLOAT as in SHORT_FLOAT or
      -- LONG_FLOAT. The specification of each operator for the type *universal_real*, or for any
      -- additional predefined floating point type, is obtained by replacing FLOAT by the name of the
      -- type in the specification of the corresponding operator of the type FLOAT.

-- In addition, the following operators are predefined for universal types: **11**

```
-- function "*"   (LEFT : universal_integer;   RIGHT : universal_real)   return universal_real;
-- function "*"   (LEFT : universal_real;      RIGHT : universal_integer) return universal_real;
-- function "/"   (LEFT : universal_real;      RIGHT : universal_integer) return universal_real;
```

-- The type *universal_fixed* is predefined. The only operators declared for this type are

```
-- function "*"   (LEFT : any_fixed_point_type; RIGHT : any_fixed_point_type) return universal_fixed;
-- function "/"   (LEFT : any_fixed_point_type; RIGHT : any_fixed_point_type) return universal_fixed;
```

-- The following characters form the standard ASCII character set. Character literals cor- **12**
-- responding to control characters are not identifiers; they are indicated in italics in this definition.

type CHARACTER **is** **13**

```
( nul,   soh,   stx,   etx,      eot,   enq,   ack,   bel,
  bs,    ht,    lf,    vt,       ff,    cr,    so,    si,
  dle,   dc1,   dc2,   dc3,      dc4,   nak,   syn,   etb,
  can,   em,    sub,   esc,      fs,    gs,    rs,    us,

  ' ',   '!',   '"',   '#',      '$',   '%',   '&',   ''',
  '(',   ')',   '*',   '+',      ',',   '-',   '.',   '/',
  '0',   '1',   '2',   '3',      '4',   '5',   '6',   '7',
  '8',   '9',   ':',   ';',      '<',   '=',   '>',   '?',

  '@',   'A',   'B',   'C',      'D',   'E',   'F',   'G',
  'H',   'I',   'J',   'K',      'L',   'M',   'N',   'O',
  'P',   'Q',   'R',   'S',      'T',   'U',   'V',   'W',
  'X',   'Y',   'Z',   '[',      '\',   ']',   '^',   '_',

  '`',   'a',   'b',   'c',      'd',   'e',   'f',   'g',
  'h',   'i',   'j',   'k',      'l',   'm',   'n',   'o',
  'p',   'q',   'r',   's',      't',   'u',   'v',   'w',
  'x',   'y',   'z',   '{',      '|',   '}',   '~',   del );
```

for CHARACTER **use**   --   128 ASCII character set without holes
      (0, 1, 2, 3, 4, 5, ..., 125, 126, 127);

-- The predefined operators for the type CHARACTER are the same as for any enumeration type. **14**

15   **package** ASCII **is**

    -- Control characters:

NUL	: **constant** CHARACTER := *nul*;	SOH	: **constant** CHARACTER := *soh*;
STX	: **constant** CHARACTER := *stx*;	ETX	: **constant** CHARACTER := *etx*;
EOT	: **constant** CHARACTER := *eot*;	ENQ	: **constant** CHARACTER := *enq*;
ACK	: **constant** CHARACTER := *ack*;	BEL	: **constant** CHARACTER := *bel*;
BS	: **constant** CHARACTER := *bs*;	HT	: **constant** CHARACTER := *ht*;
LF	: **constant** CHARACTER := *lf*;	VT	: **constant** CHARACTER := *vt*;
FF	: **constant** CHARACTER := *ff*;	CR	: **constant** CHARACTER := *cr*;
SO	: **constant** CHARACTER := *so*;	SI	: **constant** CHARACTER := *si*;
DLE	: **constant** CHARACTER := *dle*;	DC1	: **constant** CHARACTER := *dc1*;
DC2	: **constant** CHARACTER := *dc2*;	DC3	: **constant** CHARACTER := *dc3*;
DC4	: **constant** CHARACTER := *dc4*;	NAK	: **constant** CHARACTER := *nak*;
SYN	: **constant** CHARACTER := *syn*;	ETB	: **constant** CHARACTER := *etb*;
CAN	: **constant** CHARACTER := *can*;	EM	: **constant** CHARACTER := *em*;
SUB	: **constant** CHARACTER := *sub*;	ESC	: **constant** CHARACTER := *esc*;
FS	: **constant** CHARACTER := *fs*;	GS	: **constant** CHARACTER := *gs*;
RS	: **constant** CHARACTER := *rs*;	US	: **constant** CHARACTER := *us*;
DEL	: **constant** CHARACTER := *del*;		

    -- Other characters:

EXCLAM	: **constant** CHARACTER := '!';	QUOTATION	: **constant** CHARACTER := '"';
SHARP	: **constant** CHARACTER := '#';	DOLLAR	: **constant** CHARACTER := '$';
PERCENT	: **constant** CHARACTER := '%';	AMPERSAND	: **constant** CHARACTER := '&';
COLON	: **constant** CHARACTER := ':';	SEMICOLON	: **constant** CHARACTER := ';';
QUERY	: **constant** CHARACTER := '?';	AT_SIGN	: **constant** CHARACTER := '@';
L_BRACKET	: **constant** CHARACTER := '[';	BACK_SLASH	: **constant** CHARACTER := '\';
R_BRACKET	: **constant** CHARACTER := ']';	CIRCUMFLEX	: **constant** CHARACTER := '~';
UNDERLINE	: **constant** CHARACTER := '_';	GRAVE	: **constant** CHARACTER := '`';
L_BRACE	: **constant** CHARACTER := '{';	BAR	: **constant** CHARACTER := '	';
R_BRACE	: **constant** CHARACTER := '}';	TILDE	: **constant** CHARACTER := '~';

    -- Lower case letters:

    LC_A : **constant** CHARACTER := 'a';
    ...
    LC_Z : **constant** CHARACTER := 'z';

end ASCII;

16   -- Predefined subtypes:

    subtype NATURAL **is** INTEGER **range** 0 .. INTEGER'LAST;
    subtype POSITIVE **is** INTEGER **range** 1 .. INTEGER'LAST;

-- Predefined string type:

17

type STRING **is array**(POSITIVE **range** <>) **of** CHARACTER;

pragma PACK(STRING);

-- The predefined operators for this type are as follows:

18

```
-- function "="  (LEFT, RIGHT : STRING) return BOOLEAN;
-- function "/=" (LEFT, RIGHT : STRING) return BOOLEAN;
-- function "<"  (LEFT, RIGHT : STRING) return BOOLEAN;
-- function "<=" (LEFT, RIGHT : STRING) return BOOLEAN;
-- function ">"  (LEFT, RIGHT : STRING) return BOOLEAN;
-- function ">=" (LEFT, RIGHT : STRING) return BOOLEAN;

-- function "&" (LEFT : STRING;    RIGHT : STRING)    return STRING;
-- function "&" (LEFT : CHARACTER; RIGHT : STRING)    return STRING;
-- function "&" (LEFT : STRING;    RIGHT : CHARACTER) return STRING;
-- function "&" (LEFT : CHARACTER; RIGHT : CHARACTER) return STRING;
```

type DURATION **is delta** *implementation_defined* **range** *implementation_defined*;

19

-- The predefined operators for the type DURATION are the same as for any fixed point type.

-- The predefined exceptions:

20

```
CONSTRAINT_ERROR : exception;
NUMERIC_ERROR    : exception;
PROGRAM_ERROR    : exception;
STORAGE_ERROR    : exception;
TASKING_ERROR    : exception;
```

end STANDARD;

Certain aspects of the predefined entities cannot be completely described in the language itself. For example, although the enumeration type BOOLEAN can be written showing the two enumeration literals FALSE and TRUE, the short-circuit control forms cannot be expressed in the language.

21

Note:

The language definition predefines the following library units:

22

- The package CALENDAR   (see 9.6)

- The package SYSTEM   (see 13.7)
- The package MACHINE_CODE (if provided)   (see 13.8)
- The generic procedure UNCHECKED_DEALLOCATION   (see 13.10.1)
- The generic function UNCHECKED_CONVERSION   (see 13.10.2)

- The generic package SEQUENTIAL_IO   (see 14.2.3)
- The generic package DIRECT_IO   (see 14.2.5)
- The package TEXT_IO   (see 14.3.10)
- The package IO_EXCEPTIONS   (see 14.5)
- The package LOW_LEVEL_IO   (see 14.6)

[This glossary is not part of the standard definition of the Ada programming language.]

753

D. Glossary

This appendix is informative and is not part of the standard definition of the Ada programming language. Italicized terms in the abbreviated descriptions below either have glossary entries themselves or are described in entries for related terms.

Accept statement. See *entry*.

Access type. A value of an access type (an *access value*) is either a null value, or a value that *designates* an *object* created by an *allocator*. The designated object can be read and updated via the access value. The definition of an access type specifies the type of the objects designated by values of the access type. See also *collection*.

Actual parameter. See *parameter*.

Aggregate. The evaluation of an aggregate yields a value of a *composite type*. The value is specified by giving the value of each of the *components*. Either *positional association* or *named association* may be used to indicate which value is associated with which component.

Allocator. The evaluation of an allocator creates an *object* and returns a new *access value* which *designates* the object.

Array type. A value of an array type consists of *components* which are all of the same *sub-type* (and hence, of the same type). Each component is uniquely distinguished by an *index* (for a one-dimensional array) or by a sequence of indices (for a multidimensional array). Each index must be a value of a *discrete type* and must lie in the correct index *range*.

Assignment. Assignment is the *operation* that replaces the current value of a *variable* by a new value. An *assignment statement* specifies a variable on the left, and on the right, an *expression* whose value is to be the new value of the variable.

Attribute. The evaluation of an attribute yields a predefined characteristic of a named entity; some attributes are *functions*.

Block statement. A block statement is a single statement that may contain a sequence of statements. It may also include a *declarative part*, and *exception handlers*; their effects are local to the block statement.

Body. A body defines the execution of a *subprogram*, *package*, or *task*. A *body stub* is a form of body that indicates that this execution is defined in a separately compiled *sub-unit*.

Collection. A collection is the entire set of *objects* created by evaluation of *allocators* for an *access type*.

Compilation unit. A compilation unit is the *declaration* or the *body* of a *program unit*, presented for compilation as an independent text. It is optionally preceded by a *context clause*, naming other compilation units upon which it depends by means of one more *with clauses*.

Component. A component is a value that is a part of a larger value, or an *object* that is part of a larger object.

Composite type. A composite type is one whose values have *components*. There are two kinds of composite type: *array types* and *record types*.

Constant. See *object*.

Constraint. A constraint determines a subset of the values of a *type*. A value in that subset *satisfies* the constraint.

Context clause. See *compilation unit*.

Declaration. A declaration associates an identifier (or some other notation) with an entity. This association is in effect within a region of text called the *scope* of the declaration. Within the scope of a declaration, there are places where it is possible to use the identifier to refer to the associated declared entity. At such places the identifier is said to be a *simple name* of the entity; the *name* is said to *denote* the associated entity.

Declarative Part. A declarative part is a sequence of *declarations*. It may also contain related information such as *subprogram bodies* and *representation clauses*.

Denote. See *declaration*.

Derived Type. A derived type is a *type* whose operations and values are replicas of those of an existing type. The existing type is called the *parent type* of the derived type.

Designate. See *access type*, *task*.

Direct visibility. See *visibility*.

Discrete Type. A discrete type is a *type* which has an ordered set of distinct values. The discrete types are the *enumeration* and *integer types*. Discrete types are used for indexing and iteration, and for choices in case statements and record *variants*.

Discriminant. A discriminant is a distinguished *component* of an *object* or value of a *record type*. The *subtypes* of other components, or even their presence or absence, may depend on the value of the discriminant.

Discriminant constraint. A discriminant constraint on a *record type* or *private type* specifies a value for each *discriminant* of the *type*.

Elaboration. The elaboration of a *declaration* is the process by which the declaration achieves its effect (such as creating an *object*); this process occurs during program execution.

Entry. An entry is used for communication between *tasks*. Externally, an entry is called just as a *subprogram* is called; its internal behavior is specified by one or more *accept statements* specifying the actions to be performed when the entry is called.

Enumeration type. An enumeration type is a *discrete type* whose values are represented by enumeration literals which are given explicitly in the *type declaration*. These enumeration literals are either *identifiers* or *character literals*.

Evaluation. The evaluation of an *expression* is the process by which the value of the expression is computed. This process occurs during program execution.

Exception. An exception is an error situation which may arise during program execution. To *raise* an exception is to abandon normal program execution so as to signal that the error has taken place. An *exception handler* is a portion of program text specifying a response to the exception. Execution of such a program text is called *handling* the exception.

Expanded name. An expanded name *denotes* an entity which is *declared* immediately within some construct. An expanded name has the form of a *selected component*: the *prefix* denotes the construct (a *program unit*; or a *block*, loop, or *accept statement*); the *selector* is the *simple name* of the entity.

Expression. An expression defines the computation of a value.

Fixed point type. See *real type*.

Floating point type. See *real type*.

Formal parameter. See *parameter*.

Function. See *subprogram*.

Generic unit. A generic unit is a template either for a set of *subprograms* or for a set of *packages*. A subprogram or package created using the template is called an *instance* of the generic unit. A *generic instantiation* is the kind of *declaration* that creates an instance.

A generic unit is written as a subprogram or package but with the specification prefixed by a *generic formal part* which may declare *generic formal parameters*. A generic formal parameter is either a *type*, a *subprogram*, or an *object*. A generic unit is one of the kinds of *program unit*.

Handler. See *exception*.

Index. See *array type*.

Index constraint. An index constraint for an *array type* specifies the lower and upper bounds for each index *range* of the array type.

Indexed component. An indexed component *denotes* a *component* in an *array*. It is a form of *name* containing *expressions* which specify the values of the *indices* of the array component. An indexed component may also denote an *entry* in a family of entries.

Instance. See *generic unit*.

Integer type. An integer type is a *discrete type* whose values represent all integer numbers within a specific *range*.

Lexical element. A lexical element is an identifier, a *literal*, a delimiter, or a comment.

Limited type. A limited type is a *type* for which neither assignment nor the predefined comparison for equality is implicitly declared. All *task* types are limited. A *private type* can be defined to be limited. An equality operator can be explicitly declared for a limited type.

Literal. A literal represents a value literally, that is, by means of letters and other characters. A literal is either a numeric literal, an enumeration literal, a character literal, or a string literal.

Mode. See *parameter*.

Model number. A model number is an exactly representable value of a *real type*. *Operations* of a real type are defined in terms of operations on the model numbers of the type. The properties of the model numbers and of their operations are the minimal properties preserved by all implementations of the real type.

Name. A name is a construct that stands for an entity: it is said that the name *denotes* the entity, and that the entity is the meaning of the name. See also *declaration*, *prefix*.

Named association. A named association specifies the association of an item with one or more positions in a list, by naming the positions.

Object. An object contains a value. A program creates an object either by *elaborating* an *object declaration* or by *evaluating* an *allocator*. The declaration or allocator specifies a *type* for the object: the object can only contain values of that type.

Operation. An operation is an elementary action associated with one or more *types*. It is either implicitly declared by the *declaration* of the type, or it is a *subprogram* that has a *parameter* or *result* of the type.

Operator. An operator is an operation which has one or two operands. A unary operator is written before an operand; a binary operator is written between two operands. This notation is a special kind of *function call*. An operator can be declared as a function. Many operators are implicitly declared by the *declaration* of a *type* (for example, most type declarations imply the declaration of the equality operator for values of the type).

Overloading. An identifier can have several alternative meanings at a given point in the program text: this property is called *overloading*. For example, an overloaded enumeration literal can be an identifier that appears in the definitions of two or more *enumeration types*. The effective meaning of an overloaded identifier is determined by the context. *Subprograms*, *aggregates*, *allocators*, and string *literals* can also be overloaded.

Package. A package specifies a group of logically related entities, such as *types*, *objects* of those types, and *subprograms* with *parameters* of those types. It is written as a *package declaration* and a *package body*. The package declaration has a *visible part*, containing the *declarations* of all entities that can be explicitly used outside the package. It may also have a *private part* containing structural details that complete the specification of the visible entities, but which are irrelevant to the user of the package. The *package body* contains implementations of *subprograms* (and possibly *tasks* as other *packages*) that have been specified in the package declaration. A package is one of the kinds of *program unit*.

Parameter. A parameter is one of the named entities associated with a *subprogram*, *entry*, or *generic unit*, and used to communicate with the corresponding subprogram body, *accept statement* or generic body. A *formal parameter* is an identifier used to denote the named entity within the body. An *actual parameter* is the particular entity associated with the corresponding formal parameter by a *subprogram call*, *entry call*, or *generic instantiation*. The *mode* of a formal parameter specifies whether the associated actual parameter supplies a value for the formal parameter, or the formal supplies a value for the actual parameter, or both. The association of actual parameters with formal parameters can be specified by *named associations*, by *positional associations*, or by a combination of these.

Parent type. See *derived type*.

Positional association. A positional association specifies the association of an item with a position in a list, by using the same position in the text to specify the item.

Pragma. A pragma conveys information to the compiler.

Prefix. A prefix is used as the first part of certain kinds of name. A prefix is either a *function call* or a *name*.

Private part. See *package*.

Private type. A private type is a *type* whose structure and set of values are clearly defined, but not directly available to the user of the type. A private type is known only by its *discriminants* (if any) and by the set of *operations* defined for it. A private type and its applicable operations are defined in the *visible part* of a *package*, or in a *generic formal part*. *Assignment*, equality, and inequality are also defined for private types, unless the private type is *limited*.

Procedure. See *subprogram*.

Program. A program is composed of a number of *compilation units*, one of which is a *subprogram* called the *main program*. Execution of the program consists of execution of the main program, which may invoke subprograms declared in the other compilation units of the program.

Program unit. A program unit is any one of a *generic unit*, *package*, *subprogram*, or *task unit*.

Qualified expression. A qualified expression is an *expression* preceded by an indication of its *type* or *subtype*. Such qualification is used when, in its absence, the expression might be ambiguous (for example as a consequence of *overloading*).

Raising an exception. See *exception*.

Range. A range is a contiguous set of values of a *scalar type*. A range is specified by giving the lower and upper bounds for the values. A value in the range is said to *belong* to the range.

Range constraint. A range constraint of a *type* specifies a *range*, and thereby determines the subset of the values of the type that *belong* to the range.

Real type. A real type is a *type* whose values represent approximations to the real numbers. There are two kinds of real type: *fixed point types* are specified by absolute error bound; *floating point types* are specified by a relative error bound expressed as a number of significant decimal digits.

Record type. A value of a record type consists of *components* which are usually of different *types* or *subtypes*. For each component of a record value or record *object*, the definition of the record type specifies an identifier that uniquely determines the component within the record.

Renaming declaration. A renaming declaration declares another *name* for an entity.

Rendezvous. A rendezvous is the interaction that occurs between two parallel *tasks* when one task has called an *entry* of the other task, and a corresponding *accept statement* is being executed by the other task on behalf of the calling task.

Representation clause. A representation clause directs the compiler in the selection of the mapping of a *type*, an *object*, or a *task* onto features of the underlying machine that executes a program. In some cases, representation clauses completely specify the mapping; in other cases, they provide criteria for choosing a mapping.

Satisfy. See *constraint*, *subtype*.

Scalar type. An *object* or value of a scalar *type* does not have *components*. A scalar type is either a *discrete type* or a *real type*. The values of a scalar type are ordered.

Scope. See *declaration*.

Selected component. A selected component is a *name* consisting of a *prefix* and of an identifier called the *selector*. Selected components are used to denote record components, *entries*, and *objects* designated by access values; they are also used as *expanded names*.

Selector. See *selected component*.

Simple name. See *declaration*, *name*.

Statement. A statement specifies one or more actions to be performed during the execution of a *program*.

Subcomponent. A subcomponent is either a *component*, or a component of another subcomponent.

Subprogram. A subprogram is either a *procedure* or a *function*. A procedure specifies a sequence of actions and is invoked by a *procedure call* statement. A function specifies a sequence of actions and also returns a value called the *result*, and so a *function call* is an *expression*. A subprogram is written as a *subprogram declaration*, which specifies its *name*, *formal parameters*, and (for a function) its result; and a *subprogram body* which specifies the sequence of actions. The subprogram call specifies the *actual parameters* that are to be associated with the formal parameters. A subprogram is one of the kinds of *program unit*.

Subtype. A subtype of a *type* characterizes a subset of the values of the type. The subset is determined by a *constraint* on the type. Each value in the set of values of a subtype *belongs* to the subtype and *satisfies* the constraint determining the subtype.

Subunit. See *body*.

Task. A task operates in parallel with other parts of the program. It is written as a *task specification* (which specifies the *name* of the task and the names and *formal parameters* of its entries), and a *task body* which defines its execution. A *task unit* is one of the kinds of *program unit*. A *task type* is a *type* that permits the subsequent *declaration* of any number of similar tasks of the type. A value of a task type is said to *designate* a task.

Type.   A type characterizes both a set of values, and a set of *operations* applicable to those values. A *type definition* is a language construct that defines a type. A particular type is either an *access type*, an *array type*, a *private type*, a *record type*, a *scalar type*, or a *task type*.

Use clause. A use clause achieves *direct visibility* of *declarations* that appear in the *visible parts* of named *packages*.

Variable. See *object*.

Variant part.   A variant part of a *record* specifies alternative record *components*, depending on a *discriminant* of the record. Each value of the discriminant establishes a particular alternative of the variant part.

Visibility. At a given point in a program text, the *declaration* of an entity with a certain identifier is said to be *visible* if the entity is an acceptable meaning for an occurrence at that point of the identifier. The declaration is *visible* by *selection* at the place of the *selector* in a *selected component* or at the place of the name in a *named association*. Otherwise, the declaration is *directly visible*, that is, if the identifier alone has that meaning.

Visible part. See *package*.

With clause. See *compilation unit*.

[This syntax summary is not part of the standard definition of the Ada programming language.]

759

E. Syntax Summary

2.1

graphic_character ::= basic_graphic_character
| lower_case_letter | other_special_character

basic_graphic_character ::=
upper_case_letter | digit
| special_character | space_character

basic_character ::=
basic_graphic_character | format_effector

2.3

identifier ::=
letter {[underline] letter_or_digit}

letter_or_digit ::= letter | digit

letter ::= upper_case_letter | lower_case_letter

2.4

numeric_literal ::= decimal_literal | based_literal

2.4.1

decimal_literal ::= integer [.integer] [exponent]

integer ::= digit {[underline] digit}

exponent ::= E [+] integer | E - integer

2.4.2

based_literal ::=
base # based_integer [.based_integer] # [exponent]

base ::= integer

based_integer ::=
extended_digit {[underline] extended_digit}

extended_digit ::= digit | letter

2.5

character_literal ::= 'graphic_character'

2.6

string_literal ::= "{graphic_character}"

2.8

pragma ::=
pragma identifier [(argument_association
{, argument_association})];

argument_association ::=
[argument_identifier =>] name
| [argument_identifier =>] expression

3.1

basic_declaration ::=
object_declaration | number_declaration
| type_declaration | subtype_declaration
| subprogram_declaration | package_declaration
| task_declaration | generic_declaration
| exception_declaration | generic_instantiation
| renaming_declaration | deferred_constant_declaration

3.2

object_declaration ::=
identifier_list : [**constant**] subtype_indication [:= expression];
| identifier_list : [**constant**] constrained_array_definition
[:= expression];

number_declaration ::=
identifier_list : **constant** := universal_static_expression;

identifier_list ::= identifier {, identifier}

3.3.1

type_declaration ::= full_type_declaration
| incomplete_type_declaration | private_type_declaration

full_type_declaration ::=
type identifier [discriminant_part] **is** type_definition;

type_definition ::=
enumeration_type_definition | integer_type_definition
| real_type_definition | array_type_definition
| record_type_definition | access_type_definition
| derived_type_definition

3.3.2

subtype_declaration ::=
subtype identifier **is** subtype_indication;

subtype_indication ::= type_mark [constraint]

type_mark ::= type_name | subtype_name

constraint ::=
range_constraint | floating_point_constraint
| fixed_point_constraint | index_constraint
| discriminant_constraint

3.4

derived_type_definition ::= **new** subtype_indication

3.5

range_constraint ::= **range** range

range ::= range_attribute
| simple_expression .. simple_expression

3.5.1

```
enumeration_type_definition  ::=
    (enumeration_literal_specification
     |, enumeration_literal_specification})

enumeration_literal_specification  ::=   enumeration_literal

enumeration_literal  ::=   identifier | character_literal
```

3.5.4

```
integer_type_definition  ::=   range_constraint
```

3.5.6

```
real_type_definition  ::=
    floating_point_constraint | fixed_point_constraint
```

3.5.7

```
floating_point_constraint  ::=
    floating_accuracy_definition [range_constraint]

floating_accuracy_definition  ::=
    digits static_simple_expression
```

3.5.9

```
fixed_point_constraint  ::=
    fixed_accuracy_definition [range_constraint]

fixed_accuracy_definition  ::=
    delta static_simple_expression
```

3.6

```
array_type_definition  ::=
    unconstrained_array_definition | constrained_array_definition

unconstrained_array_definition  ::=
    array(index_subtype_definition {, index_subtype_definition}) of
         component_subtype_indication

constrained_array_definition  ::=
    array index_constraint of component_subtype_indication

index_subtype_definition  ::=  type_mark range <>

index_constraint  ::=   (discrete_range {, discrete_range})

discrete_range  ::=  discrete_subtype_indication | range
```

3.7

```
record_type_definition  ::=
    record
        component_list
    end record

component_list  ::=
        component_declaration {component_declaration}
    | {component_declaration} variant_part
    | null;

component_declaration  ::=
        identifier_list : component_subtype_definition [:= expression];

component_subtype_definition  ::=   subtype_indication
```

3.7.1

```
discriminant_part  ::=
    (discriminant_specification {; discriminant_specification})

discriminant_specification  ::=
    identifier_list : type_mark [:= expression]
```

3.7.2

```
discriminant_constraint  ::=
    (discriminant_association {, discriminant_association})

discriminant_association  ::=
    [discriminant_simple_name {| discriminant_simple_name} =>]
        expression
```

3.7.3

```
variant_part  ::=
    case discriminant_simple_name is
        variant
      {variant}
    end case;

variant  ::=
    when choice {| choice} =>
        component_list

choice  ::=  simple_expression
    | discrete_range | others | component_simple_name
```

3.8

```
access_type_definition  ::=  access subtype_indication
```

3.8.1

```
incomplete_type_declaration  ::=
    type identifier [discriminant_part];
```

3.9

```
declarative_part  ::=
    {basic_declarative_item} {later_declarative_item}

basic_declarative_item  ::=  basic_declaration
    | representation_clause | use_clause

later_declarative_item  ::=  body
    | subprogram_declaration  | package_declaration
    | task_declaration        | generic_declaration
    | use_clause              | generic_instantiation

body  ::=  proper_body | body_stub

proper_body  ::=
    subprogram_body | package_body | task_body
```

4.1

name ::= simple_name
| character_literal | operator_symbol
| indexed_component | slice
| selected_component | attribute

simple_name ::= identifier

prefix ::= name | function_call

4.1.1

indexed_component ::= prefix(expression {, expression})

4.1.2

slice ::= prefix(discrete_range)

4.1.3

selected_component ::= prefix.selector

selector ::= simple_name
| character_literal | operator_symbol | **all**

4.1.4

attribute ::= prefix'attribute_designator

attribute_designator ::=
   simple_name [(*universal_static*_expression)]

4.3

aggregate ::=
   (component_association {, component_association})

component_association ::=
   [choice {| choice} =>] expression

4.4

expression ::=
   relation {**and** relation} | relation {**and then** relation}
| relation {**or** relation} | relation {**or else** relation}
| relation {**xor** relation}

relation ::=
   simple_expression [relational_operator simple_expression]
| simple_expression [**not**] **in** range
| simple_expression [**not**] **in** type_mark

simple_expression ::=
   [unary_adding_operator] term {binary_adding_operator term}

term ::= factor {multiplying_operator factor}

factor ::= primary [** primary] | **abs** primary | **not** primary

primary ::=
   numeric_literal | **null** | aggregate | string_literal
| name | allocator | function_call | type_conversion
| qualified_expression | (expression)

4.5

logical_operator ::= **and** | **or** | **xor**

relational_operator ::= = | /= | < | <= | > | >=

binary_adding_operator ::= + | - | &

unary_adding_operator ::= + | -

multiplying_operator ::= * | / | **mod** | **rem**

highest_precedence_operator ::= ** | **abs** | **not**

4.6

type_conversion ::= type_mark(expression)

4.7

qualified_expression ::=
   type_mark'(expression) | type_mark'aggregate

4.8

allocator ::=
   new subtype_indication | **new** qualified_expression

5.1

sequence_of_statements ::= statement {statement}

statement ::=
   {label} simple_statement | {label} compound_statement

simple_statement ::= null_statement
| assignment_statement | procedure_call_statement
| exit_statement | return_statement
| goto_statement | entry_call_statement
| delay_statement | abort_statement
| raise_statement | code_statement

compound_statement ::=
   if_statement | case_statement
| loop_statement | block_statement
| accept_statement | select_statement

label ::= <<*label*_simple_name>>

null_statement ::= **null**;

5.2

assignment_statement ::=
   *variable*_name := expression;

5.3

if_statement ::=
   if condition **then**
     sequence_of_statements
   {**elsif** condition **then**
     sequence_of_statements}
   [**else**
     sequence_of_statements]
   end if;

condition ::= *boolean*_expression

5.4

```
case_statement ::=
    case expression is
        case_statement_alternative
      { case_statement_alternative}
    end case;
```

```
case_statement_alternative ::=
    when choice {| choice } =>
        sequence_of_statements
```

5.5

```
loop_statement ::=
    [loop_simple_name:]
      [ iteration_scheme] loop
          sequence_of_statements
      end loop [loop_simple_name];
```

```
iteration_scheme ::= while condition
  | for loop_parameter_specification
```

```
loop_parameter_specification ::=
    identifier in [reverse] discrete_range
```

5.6

```
block_statement ::=
    [block_simple_name:]
      [ declare
            declarative_part]
      begin
            sequence_of_statements
      [ exception
            exception_handler
          { exception_handler}]
      end [block_simple_name];
```

5.7

```
exit_statement ::=
    exit [loop_name] [when condition];
```

5.8

```
return_statement ::= return [expression];
```

5.9

```
goto_statement ::= goto label_name;
```

6.1

```
subprogram_declaration ::= subprogram_specification;
```

```
subprogram_specification ::=
      procedure identifier [formal_part]
    | function designator [formal_part] return type_mark
```

```
designator ::= identifier | operator_symbol
```

```
operator_symbol ::= string_literal
```

```
formal_part ::=
    (parameter_specification {; parameter_specification})
```

```
parameter_specification ::=
    identifier_list : mode type_mark [:= expression]
```

```
mode ::= [in] | in out | out
```

6.3

```
subprogram_body ::=
      subprogram_specification is
        [ declarative_part]
      begin
            sequence_of_statements
    [ exception
          exception_handler
        { exception_handler}]
      end [designator];
```

6.4

```
procedure_call_statement ::=
    procedure_name [actual_parameter_part];
```

```
function_call ::=
    function_name [actual_parameter_part]
```

```
actual_parameter_part ::=
    (parameter_association {, parameter_association})
```

```
parameter_association ::=
    [ formal_parameter =>] actual_parameter
```

```
formal_parameter ::= parameter_simple_name
```

```
actual_parameter ::=
    expression | variable_name | type_mark(variable_name)
```

7.1

```
package_declaration ::= package_specification;
```

```
package_specification ::=
      package identifier is
        {basic_declarative_item}
    [ private
        {basic_declarative_item}]
      end [package_simple_name]
```

```
package_body ::=
      package body package_simple_name is
        [ declarative_part]
    [ begin
            sequence_of_statements
    [ exception
          exception_handler
        { exception_handler}]
      end [package_simple_name];
```

7.4

```
private_type_declaration ::=
      type identifier [discriminant_part] is [limited] private;
```

```
deferred_constant_declaration ::=
    identifier_list : constant type_mark;
```

8.4

```
use_clause ::= use package_name {, package_name};
```

8.5

```
renaming_declaration ::=
      identifier : type_mark            renames object_name;
    | identifier : exception            renames exception_name;
    | package identifier                renames package_name;
    | subprogram_specification   renames
                                          subprogram_or_entry_name;
```

9.1

task_declaration ::= task_specification;

task_specification ::=
   task [type] identifier [is
     {entry_declaration}
     {representation_clause}
   end [task_simple_name]]

task_body ::=
   task body task_simple_name is
     [declarative_part]
   begin
       sequence_of_statements
  [exception
       exception_handler
     | exception_handler}]
   end [task_simple_name];

9.5

entry_declaration ::=
   entry identifier [(discrete_range)] [formal_part];

entry_call_statement ::=
   entry_name [actual_parameter_part];

accept_statement ::=
   accept entry_simple_name [(entry_index)] [formal_part] [do
     sequence_of_statements
   end [entry_simple_name]];

entry_index ::= expression

9.6

delay_statement ::= delay simple_expression;

9.7

select_statement ::= selective_wait
  | conditional_entry_call | timed_entry_call

9.7.1

selective_wait ::=
   select
     select_alternative
  { or
     select_alternative}
  [else
     sequence_of_statements]
   end select;

select_alternative ::=
  [when condition =>]
    selective_wait_alternative

selective_wait_alternative ::= accept_alternative
  | delay_alternative | terminate_alternative

accept_alternative ::=
  accept_statement [sequence_of_statements]

delay_alternative ::=
  delay_statement [sequence_of_statements]

terminate_alternative ::= terminate;

9.7.2

conditional_entry_call ::=
  select
     entry_call_statement
    [sequence_of_statements]
  else
     sequence_of_statements
  end select;

9.7.3

timed_entry_call ::=
  select
     entry_call_statement
    [sequence_of_statements]
  or
     delay_alternative
  end select;

9.10

abort_statement ::= abort task_name {, task_name};

10.1

compilation ::= {compilation_unit}

compilation_unit ::=
    context_clause library_unit
  | context_clause secondary_unit

library_unit ::=
    subprogram_declaration | package_declaration
  | generic_declaration | generic_instantiation
  | subprogram_body

secondary_unit ::= library_unit_body | subunit

library_unit_body ::= subprogram_body | package_body

10.1.1

context_clause ::= {with_clause {use_clause}}

with_clause ::=
  with unit_simple_name {, unit_simple_name};

10.2

body_stub ::=
    subprogram_specification is separate;
  | package body package_simple_name is separate;
  | task body task_simple_name is separate;

subunit ::= separate (parent_unit_name) proper_body

11.1

exception_declaration ::= identifier_list : exception;

11.2

exception_handler ::=
  when exception_choice {| exception_choice} =>
    sequence_of_statements

exception_choice ::= exception_name | others

11.3

raise_statement ::= raise [exception_name];

12.1

generic_declaration ::= generic_specification;

generic_specification ::=
      generic_formal_part subprogram_specification
   | generic_formal_part package_specification

generic_formal_part ::= **generic** {generic_parameter_declaration}

generic_parameter_declaration ::=
      identifier_list : [**in** [**out**]] type_mark [:= expression];
   | **type** identifier **is** generic_type_definition;
   | private_type_declaration
   | **with** subprogram_specification [**is** name];
   | **with** subprogram_specification [**is** <>];

generic_type_definition ::=
      (<>) | **range** <> | **digits** <> | **delta** <>
   | array_type_definition | access_type_definition

12.3

generic_instantiation ::=
      package identifier **is**
         new *generic_package*_name [generic_actual_part];
   | **procedure** identifier **is**
         new *generic_procedure*_name [generic_actual_part];
   | **function** designator **is**
         new *generic_function*_name [generic_actual_part];

generic_actual_part ::=
    (generic_association {, generic_association})

generic_association ::=
    [generic_formal_parameter =>] generic_actual_parameter

generic_formal_parameter ::=
    *parameter*_simple_name | operator_symbol

generic_actual_parameter ::= expression | *variable*_name
   | *subprogram*_name | *entry*_name | type_mark

13.1

representation_clause ::=
      type_representation_clause | address_clause

type_representation_clause ::= length_clause
   | enumeration_representation_clause
   | record_representation_clause

13.2

length_clause ::= **for** attribute **use** simple_expression;

13.3

enumeration_representation_clause ::=
    for *type*_simple_name **use** aggregate;

13.4

record_representation_clause ::=
    for *type*_simple_name **use**
      record [alignment_clause]
        {component_clause}
      end record;

alignment_clause ::= **at mod** *static*_simple_expression;

component_clause ::=
    *component*_name **at** *static*_simple_expression
               range *static*_range;

13.5

address_clause ::=
    for simple_name **use at** simple_expression;

13.8

code_statement ::= type_mark'*record*_aggregate;

Syntax Cross Reference

In the list given below each syntactic category is followed by the section number where it is defined. For example:

adding_operator   4.5

In addition, each syntactic category is followed by the names of other categories in whose definition it appears. For example, adding_operator appears in the definition of simple_expression:

    adding_operator   4.5
        simple_expression   4.4

An ellipsis (...) is used when the syntactic category is not defined by a syntax rule. For example:

    lower_case_letter   ...

All uses of parentheses are combined in the term "()". The italicized prefixes used with some terms have been deleted here.

---

abort   ...
    abort_statement   9.10

abort_statement   9.10
    simple_statement   5.1

abs   ...
    factor   4.4
    highest_precedence_operator   4.5

accept   ...
    accept_statement   9.5

accept_alternative   9.7.1
    selective_wait_alternative   9.7.1

accept_statement   9.5
    accept_alternative   9.7.1
    compound_statement   5.1

access   ...
    access_type_definition   3.8

access_type_definition   3.8
    generic_type_definition   12.1
    type_definition   3.3.1

actual_parameter   6.4
    parameter_association   6.4

actual_parameter_part   6.4
    entry_call_statement   9.5
    function_call   6.4
    procedure_call_statement   6.4

address_clause   13.5
    representation_clause   13.1

aggregate   4.3
    code_statement   13.8
    enumeration_representation_clause   13.3
    primary   4.4
    qualified_expression   4.7

alignment_clause   13.4
    record_representation_clause   13.4

all   ...
    selector   4.1.3

allocator   4.8
    primary   4.4

[This appendix is not part of the standard definition of the Ada programming language.]

775

F. Implementation-Dependent Characteristics

The Ada language definition allows for certain machine-dependences in a controlled manner. No machine-dependent syntax or semantic extensions or restrictions are allowed. The only allowed implementation-dependences correspond to implementation-dependent pragmas and attributes, certain machine-dependent conventions as mentioned in chapter 13, and certain allowed restrictions on representation clauses.

The reference manual of each Ada implementation must include an appendix (called Appendix F) that describes all implementation-dependent characteristics. The appendix F for a given implementation must list in particular:

(1) The form, allowed places, and effect of every implementation-dependent pragma.

(2) The name and the type of every implementation-dependent attribute.

(3) The specification of the package SYSTEM (see 13.7).

(4) The list of all restrictions on representation clauses (see 13.1)

(5) The conventions used for any implementation-generated name denoting implementation-dependent components (see 13.4).

(6) The interpretation of expressions that appear in address clauses, including those for interrupts (see 13.5).

(7) Any restriction on unchecked conversions (see 13.10.2).

(8) Any implementation-dependent characteristics of the input-output packages (see 14).

[This index is not part of the standard definition of the Ada programming language.]

777

Index

An entry exists in this index for each technical term or phrase that is defined in the reference manual. The term or phrase is in boldface and is followed by the section number where it is defined, also in boldface, for example:

Record aggregate 4.3.1

References to other sections that provide additional information are shown after a semicolon, for example:

Record aggregate 4.3.1; **4.3**

References to other related entries in the index follow in brackets, and a line that is indented below a boldface entry gives the section numbers where particular uses of the term or phrase can be found; for example:

Record aggregate 4.3.1; **4.3**
[see also: aggregate]
as a basic operation 3.3.3; **3.7.4**
in a code statement 13.8

The index also contains entries for different parts of a phrase, entries that correct alternative terminology, and entries directing the reader to information otherwise hard to find, for example:

Check
[see: suppress pragma]

Abandon elaboration or evaluation (of declarations or statements)
[see: exception, raise statement]

Abnormal task 9.10; 9.9
[see also: abort statement]
as recipient of an entry call 9.7.2, 9.7.3, 11.5; 9.5
raising tasking_error in a calling task 11.5; 9.5

Abort statement 9.10
[see also: abnormal task, statement, task]
as a simple statement 5.1

Abs unary operator 4.5.6; 4.5
[see also: highest precedence operator]
as an operation of a fixed point type 3.5.10
as an operation of a floating point type 3.5.8
as an operation of an integer type 3.5.5
in a factor 4.4

Absolute value operation 4.5.6

Accept alternative (of a selective wait) **9.7.1**
for an interrupt entry 13.5.1

Accept statement 9.5; 9, D
[see also: entry call statement, simple name in..., statement, task]
accepting a conditional entry call 9.7.2
accepting a timed entry call 9.7.3
and optimization with exceptions 11.6
as a compound statement 5.1
as part of a declarative region 8.1
entity denoted by an expanded name 4.1.3

in an abnormal task 9.10
in a select alternative 9.7.1
including an exit statement 5.7
including a goto statement 5.9
including a return statement 5.8
raising an exception 11.5
to communicate values 9.11

Access to external files 14.2

Access type 3.8; 3.3, D
[see also: allocator, appropriate for a type, class of type, collection, derived type of an access type, null access value, object designated by...]
as a derived type 3.4
as a generic formal type 12.1.2, 12.3.5
deallocation [see: unchecked_deallocation]
designating a limited type 7.4.4
designating a task type determining task dependence 9.4
formal parameter 6.2
name in a controlled pragma 4.8
object initialization 3.2.1
operation 3.8.2
prefix 4.1
value designating an object 3.2, 4.8
value designating an object with discriminants 5.2
with a discriminant constraint 3.7.2
with an index constraint 3.6.1

Access type definition 3.8; 3.3.1, 12.1.2
as a generic type definition 12.1

Access_check
[see: constraint_error, suppress]

Accuracy
of a numeric operation 4.5.7
of a numeric operation of a universal type 4.10

Activation
[see: task activation]

Actual object
[see: generic actual object]

Actual parameter 6.4.1; D; (of an operator) 6.7; (of a sub-program) 6.4; 6.2, 6.3
[see also: entry call, formal parameter, function call, procedure call statement, subprogram call]
characteristics and overload resolution 6.6
in a generic instantiation [see: generic actual parameter]
of an array type 3.6.1
of a record type 3.7.2
of a task type 9.2
that is an array aggregate 4.3.2
that is a loop parameter 5.5

Actual parameter part 6.4
in a conditional entry call 9.7.2
in an entry call statement 9.5
in a function call 6.4
in a procedure call statement 6.4
in a timed entry call 9.7.3

Actual part
[see: actual parameter part, generic actual part]

Actual subprogram
[see: generic actual subprogram]

Actual type
[see: generic actual type]

Adding operator
[see: binary adding operator, unary adding operator]

Addition operation 4.5.3
accuracy for a real type 4.5.7

ADDRESS (predefined attribute) **13.7.2**; 3.5.5, 3.5.8, 3.5.10, 3.6.2, 3.7.4, 3.8.2, 7.4.2, 9.9, 13.7, A
[see also: address clause, system.address]

ADDRESS (predefined type)
[see: system.address]

Address clause 13.5; 13.1, 13.7
[see also: storage address, system.address]
as a representation clause 13.1
for an entry 13.5.1

AFT (predefined attribute) for a fixed point type **3.5.10**; A

Aft field of text_io output **14.3.8**, **14.3.10**

Aggregate 4.3, D
[see also: array aggregate, overloading of..., record aggregate]
as a basic operation 3.3.3; 3.6.2, 3.7.4
as a primary 4.4
in an allocator 4.8
in a code statement 13.8
in an enumeration representation clause 13.3
in a qualified expression 4.7
must not be the argument of a conversion 4.6
of a derived type 3.4

Alignment clause (in a record representation clause) **13.4**

All in a selected component **4.1.3**

Allocation of processing resources **9.8**

Allocator 4.8; 3.8, D
[see also: access type, collection, exception raised during..., initial value, object, overloading of...]
as a basic operation 3.3.3; 3.8.2
as a primary 4.4
creating an object with a discriminant 4.8; 5.2
for an array type 3.6.1
for a generic formal access type 12.1.2
for a private type 7.4.1
for a record type 3.7.2
for a task type 9.2; 9.3
must not be the argument of a conversion 4.6
raising storage_error due to the size of the collection being exceeded 11.1
setting a task value 9.2
without storage check 11.7

Allowed 1.6

Alternative
[see: accept alternative, case statement alternative, closed alternative, delay alternative, open alternative, select alternative, selective wait, terminate alternative]

Ambiguity
[see: overloading]

Ampersand
[see: catenation]
character 2.1
delimiter 2.2

Ancestor library unit 10.2

And operator
[see: logical operator]

And then control form
[see: short circuit control form]

Anonymous type 3.3.1; 3.5.4, 3.5.7, 3.5.9, 3.6, 9.1
anonymous base type [see: first named subtype]

ANSI (american national standards institute) **2.1**

Apostrophe character 2.1
in a character literal 2.5

Apostrophe delimiter 2.2
in an attribute 4.1.4
of a qualified expression 4.7

Apply 10.1.1

Appropriate for a type **4.1**
for an array type 4.1.1, 4.1.2
for a record type 4.1.3
for a task type 4.1.3

Arbitrary selection of select alternatives **9.7.1**

Argument association in a pragma **2.8**

Argument identifier in a pragma **2.8**

Arithmetic operator 4.5
[see also: binary adding operator, exponentiating operator, multiplying operator, predefined operator, unary adding operator]
as an operation of a fixed point type 3.5.10

Basic character 2.1
[see also: basic graphic character, character]

Basic character set 2.1
is sufficient for a program text 2.10

Basic declaration 3.1
as a basic declarative item 3.9

Basic declarative item 3.9
in a package specification 7.1; 7.2

Basic graphic character 2.1
[see also: basic character, digit, graphic character, space character, special character, upper case letter]

Basic operation 3.3.3
[see also: operation, scope of..., visibility...]
accuracy for a real type 4.5.7
implicitly declared 3.1, 3.3.3
of an access type 3.8.2
of an array type 3.6.2
of a derived type 3.4
of a discrete type 3.5.5
of a fixed point type 3.5.10
of a floating point type 3.5.8
of a limited type 7.4.4
of a private type 7.4.2
of a record type 3.7.4
of a task type 9.9
propagating an exception 11.6
raising an exception 11.4.1
that is an attribute 4.1.4

Belong
to a range 3.5
to a subtype 3.3
to a subtype of an access type 3.8

Binary adding operator 4.5; 4.5.3, C
[see also: arithmetic operator, overloading of an operator]
for time predefined type 9.6
in a simple expression 4.4
overloaded 6.7

Binary operation 4.5

Bit
[see: storage bits]

Blank skipped by a text_io procedure **14.3.5**

Block name 5.6
declaration 5.1
implicitly declared 3.1

Block statement 5.6; D
[see also: completed block statement, statement]
as a compound statement 5.1
as a declarative region 8.1
entity denoted by an expanded name 4.1.3
having dependent tasks 9.4
including an exception handler 11.2; 11
including an implicit declaration 5.1
including a suppress pragma 11.7
raising an exception 11.4.1, 11.4.2

Body 3.9; D
[see also: declaration, generic body, generic package body, generic subprogram body, library unit, package body, proper body, subprogram body, task body]
as a later declarative item 3.9

Body stub 10.2; D
acting as a subprogram declaration 6.3
as a body 3.9
as a portion of a declarative region 8.1
must be in the same declarative region as the declaration 3.9, 7.1

BOOLEAN (predefined type) **3.5.3**; C
derived 3.4; 3.5.3
result of a condition 5.3
result of an explicitly declared equality operator 6.7

Boolean expression
[see: condition, expression]

Boolean operator
[see: logical operator]

Boolean type 3.5.3
[see also: derived type of a boolean type, predefined type]
operation 3.5.5; 4.5.1, 4.5.2, 4.5.6
operation comparing real operands 4.5.7

Bound
[see: error bound, first attribute, last attribute]

Bound of an array **3.6, 3.6.1**
[see also: index range, slice]
aggregate 4.3.2
ignored due to index_check suppression 11.7
initialization in an allocator constrains the allocated object 4.8
that is a formal parameter 6.2
that is the result of an operation 4.5.1, 4.5.3, 4.5.6

Bound of a range **3.5**; 3.5.4
of a discrete range in a slice 4.1.2
of a discrete range is of universal_integer type 3.6.1
of a static discrete range 4.9

Bound of a scalar type **3.5**

Bound of a slice **4.1.2**

Box compound delimiter 2.2
in a generic parameter declaration 12.1, 12.1.2, 12.1.3; 12.3.3
in an index subtype definition 3.6

Bracket
[see: label bracket, left parenthesis, parenthesized expression, right parenthesis, string bracket]

CALENDAR (predefined library package) **9.6**; C

Call
[see: conditional entry call, entry call statement, function call, procedure call statement, subprogram call, timed entry call]

CALLABLE (predefined attribute)
for an abnormal task 9.10
for a task object 9.9; A

Calling conventions
[see: subprogram declaration]
of a subprogram written in another language 13.9

Cancelation of an entry call statement **9.7.2, 9.7.3**

Deallocation
[see: access type, unchecked_deallocation]

Decimal literal 2.4.1; 14.3.7, 14.3.8
as a numeric literal 2.4

Decimal number (in text_io) **14.3.7**

Decimal point
[see: fixed point, floating point, point character]

Declaration 3.1; D
[see also: basic declaration, block name declaration, body, component declaration, constant declaration, deferred constant declaration, denote, discriminant specification, entry declaration, enumeration literal specification, exception declaration, exception raised during..., generic declaration, generic formal part, generic instantiation, generic parameter declaration, generic specification, hiding, implicit declaration, incomplete type declaration, label declaration, local declaration, loop name declaration, loop parameter specification, number declaration, object declaration, package declaration, package specification, parameter specification, private type declaration, renaming declaration, representation clause, scope of..., specification, subprogram declaration, subprogram specification, subtype declaration, task declaration, task specification, type declaration, visibility]
as an overload resolution context 8.7
determined by visibility from an identifier 8.3
made directly visible by a use clause 8.4
of an enumeration literal 3.5.1
of a formal parameter 6.1
of a loop parameter 5.5
overloaded 6.6
raising an exception 11.4.2; 11.4
to which a representation clause applies 13.1

Declarative item 3.9
[see also: basic declarative item, later declarative item]
in a code procedure body 13.8
in a declarative part 3.9; 6.3.2
in a package specification 6.3.2
in a visible part 7.4
that is a use clause 8.4

Declarative part 3.9; D
[see also: elaboration of...]
in a block statement 5.6
in a package body 7.1; 7.3
in a subprogram body 6.3
in a task body 9.1; 9.3
including a generic declaration 12.2
including an inline pragma 6.3.2
including an interface pragma 13.9
including a representation clause 13.1
including a suppress pragma 11.7
including a task declaration 9.3
with implicit declarations 5.1

Declarative region 8.1; 8.2, 8.4
[see also: scope of...]
determining the visibility of a declaration 8.3
formed by the predefined package standard 8.6
in which a declaration is hidden 8.3
including a full type definition 7.4.2
including a subprogram declaration 6.3

Declared immediately within
[see: occur immediately within]

Default determination of a representation for an entity **13.1**

Default expression
[see: default initial value, default initialization, discriminant specification, formal parameter, generic formal object, initial value]
cannot include a forcing occurrence 13.1
for a component 3.3; 7.4.3, 7.4.4
for a component of a derived type object 3.4
for a discriminant 3.7.1; 3.2.1, 3.7.2, 12.3.2
for a formal parameter 6.1, 6.4.2; 6.4, 6.7, 7.4.3
for a formal parameter of a generic formal subprogram 12.1; 7.4.3
for a formal parameter of a renamed subprogram or entry 8.5
for a generic formal object 12.1, 12.1.1; 12.3
for the discriminants of an allocated object 4.8
in a component declaration 3.7
in a discriminant specification 3.7.1
including the name of a private type 7.4.1

Default file 14.3.2; 14.3

Default generic formal subprogram **12.1**; 12.1.3, 12.3.6

Default initial value (of a type) **3.3**
[see also: default expression, initial value]
for an access type object 3.8; 3.2.1 [see also: null access value]
for a record type object 3.7; 3.2.1

Default initialization (for an object) **3.2.1, 3.3**
[see also: default expression, default initial value, initial value]

Default mode (of a file) **14.2.1**; 14.2.3, 14.2.5, 14.3.10

Default_aft (field length)
of fixed_io or float_io 14.3.8; 14.3.10

Default_base
of integer_io 14.3.7; 14.3.10

Default_exp (field length)
of fixed_io or float_io 14.3.8; 14.3.10

Default_fore (field length)
of fixed_io or float_io 14.3.8; 14.3.10

Default_setting (letter case)
of enumeration_io 14.3.9; 14.3.10

Default_width (field length)
of enumeration_io 14.3.9; 14.3.10
of integer_io 14.3.7; 14.3.10

Deferred constant 7.4.3
of a limited type 7.4.4

Deferred constant declaration 7.4; 7.4.3
[see also: private part (of a package), visible part (of a package)]
as a basic declaration 3.1
is not a forcing occurrence 13.1

Definition
[see: access type definition, array type definition, component subtype definition, constrained array definition, derived type definition, enumeration type definition, generic type definition, index subtype definition, integer type definition, real type definition, record type definition, type definition, unconstrained array definition]

Delay alternative (of a selective wait) **9.7.1**

Expanded name ● *Fixed point type*

Generic actual part • Generic specification

Predefined operator 4.5, 8.6; C
[see also: abs, arithmetic operator, binary adding operator,
catenation, equality, exponentiating operator, highest
precedence operator, inequality, limited type, logical
operator, multiplying operator, operator, predefined operation, relational operator, unary adding operator]
> applied to an undefined value 3.2.1
> as an operation 3.3.3
> for an access type 3.8.2
> for an array type 3.6.2
> for a record type 3.7.4
> implicitly declared 3.3.3
> in a static expression 4.9
> of a derived type 3.4
> of a fixed point type 3.5.9
> of a floating point type 3.5.7
> of an integer type 3.5.4
> raising an exception 11.4.1

Predefined package 8.6; C
[see also: ascii, library unit, predefined library package,
standard]
> for input-output 14

Predefined pragma
[see: controlled, elaborate, inline, interface, list,
memory_size, optimize, pack, page, priority, shared,
storage_unit, suppress, system_name]

Predefined subprogram 8.6; C
[see also: input-output subprogram, library unit,
predefined generic library subprogram]

Predefined subtype 8.6; C
[see also: field, natural, number_base, positive, priority]

Predefined type 8.6; C
[see also: boolean, character, count, duration, float,
integer, long_float, long_integer, priority, short_float, short_
integer, string, system.address, system .name, time,
universal_integer, universal_real]

Prefix 4.1; D
[see also: appropriate for a type, function call, name,
selected component, selector]
> in an attribute 4.1.4
> in an indexed component 4.1.1
> in a selected component 4.1.3
> in a slice 4.1.2
> that is a function call 4.1
> that is a name 4.1

Primary 4.4
> in a factor 4.4
> in a static expression 4.9

PRIORITY (predefined integer subtype) **9.8**; 13.7, C
[see also: Task priority]

PRIORITY (predefined pragma) **9.8**; 13.7, B
[see also: Task priority]

Private part (of a package) **7.2**; 7.4.1, 7.4.3, D
[see also: deferred constant declaration, private type
declaration]

Private type 3.3, 7.4, 7.4.1; D
[see also: class of type, derived type of a private type,
limited private type, type with discriminants]
> as a generic actual type 12.3.2
> as a generic formal type 12.1.2
> as a parent type 3.4
> corresponding full type declaration 3.3.1
> formal parameter 6.2

> of a deferred constant 7.4; 3.2.1
> operation 7.4.2

Private type declaration 7.4; 7.4.1, 7.4.2
[see also: private part (of a package), visible part (of a
package)]
> as a generic type declaration 12.1
> as a portion of a declarative region 8.1
> including the word 'limited' 7.4.4

Procedure 6.1; 6, D
[see also: parameter and result type profile, parameter,
subprogram]
> as a main program 10.1
> as a renaming of an entry 9.5
> renamed 8.5

Procedure body
[see: subprogram body]
> including code statements 13.8

Procedure call 6.4; 6, D
[see also: subprogram call]

Procedure call statement 6.4
[see also: actual parameter, statement]
> as a simple statement 5.1
> with a parameter of a derived type 3.4

Procedure specification
[see: subprogram specification]

Processor 9

Profile
[see: parameter and result type profile, parameter type
profile]

Program 10; D
[see also: main program]

Program legality 1.6

Program library 10.1, 10.4; 10.5
> creation 10.4; 13.7
> manipulation and status 10.4

Program optimization 11.6; 10.6

Program text 2.2, 10.1; 2.10

Program unit 6, 7, 9, 12; D
[see also: address attribute, generic unit, library unit,
package, subprogram, task unit]
> body separately compiled [see: subunit]
> including a declaration denoted by an expanded
> name 4.1.3
> including a suppress pragma 11.7
> subject to an address clause 13.5
> with a separately compiled body 10.2

PROGRAM_ERROR (predefined exception) **11.1**
[see also: erroneous execution, suppress pragma]
> raised by an erroneous program or incorrect order
> dependence 1.6; 11.1
> raised by a generic instantiation before elaboration
> of the body 3.9; 12.1, 12.2
> raised by a selective wait 9.7.1
> raised by a subprogram call before elaboration of
> the body 3.9; 7.3
> raised by a task activation before elaboration of the
> body 3.9
> raised by reaching the end of a function body 6.5

Recursive
> call of a subprogram 6.1, 12.1; 6.3.2
> generic instantiation 12.1, 12.3
> types 3.8.1; 3.3.1

Reentrant subprogram 6.1

Reference (parameter passing) **6.2**

Relation (in an expression) **4.4**

Relational expression
[see: relation, relational operator]

Relational operation 4.5.2
> of a boolean type 3.5.3
> of a discrete type 3.5.5
> of a fixed point type 3.5.10
> of a floating point type 3.5.8
> of a scalar type 3.5
> result for real operands 4.5.7

Relational operator 4.5; 4.5.2, C
[see also: equality operator, inequality operator, ordering relation, overloading of an operator, predefined operator]
> for an access type 3.8.2
> for an array type 3.6.2
> for a private type 7.4.2
> for a record type 3.7.4
> for time predefined type 9.6
> in a relation 4.4
> overloaded 6.7

Relative address of a component within a record
[see: record representation clause]

Rem operator 4.5.5
[see also: multiplying operator]

Remainder operation 4.5.5

Renaming declaration 8.5; 4.1, 12.1.3, D
[see also: name]
> as a basic declaration 3.1
> as a declarative region 8.1
> cannot rename a universal_fixed operation 4.5.5
> for an array object 3.6.1
> for an entry 9.5
> for a record object 3.7.2
> name declared is not allowed as a prefix of certain expanded names 4.1.3
> to overload a library unit 10.1
> to overload a subunit 10.2
> to resolve an overloading ambiguity 6.6

Rendezvous (of tasks) **9.5**; 9, 9.7.1, 9.7.2, 9.7.3, D
> during which an exception is raised 11.5
> priority 9.8
> prohibited for an abnormal task 9.10

Replacement of characters in program text **2.10**

Representation (of a type and its objects) **13.1**
> recommendation by a pragma 13.1

Representation attribute 13.7.2, 13.7.3
> as a forcing occurrence 13.1
> with a prefix that has a null value 4.1

Representation clause 13.1; 13.6, D
[see also: address clause, elaboration of..., enumeration representation clause, first named subtype, length clause, record representation clause, type]
> as a basic declarative item 3.9

> as a portion of a declarative region 8.1
> cannot include a forcing occurrence 13.1
> for a derived type 3.4
> for a private type 7.4.1
> implied for a derived type 3.4
> in an overload resolution context 8.7
> in a task specification 9.1

Reserved word 2.9; 2.2, 2.3

RESET (input-output procedure)
> in an instance of direct_io 14.2.1; 14.2.5
> in an instance of sequential_io 14.2.1; 14.2.3
> in text_io 14.2.1; 14.3.1, 14.3.10

Resolution of overloading
[see: overloading]

Result subtype (of a function) **6.1**
> of a return expression 5.8

Result type profile
[see: parameter and...]

Result type and overload resolution 6.6

Result of a function
[see: returned value]

Return
[see: carriage return]

Return statement 5.8
[see also: function, statement]
> as a simple statement 5.1
> causing a loop to be exited 5.5
> causing a transfer of control 5.1
> completing block statement execution 9.4
> completing subprogram execution 9.4
> expression that is an array aggregate 4.3.2
> in a function body 6.5

Returned value
[see: function call]
> of a function call 5.8, 6.5; 8.5
> of an instance of a generic formal function 12.1.3
> of a main program 10.1
> of an operation 3.3.3
> of a predefined operator of an integer type 3.5.4
> of a predefined operator of a real type 3.5.6, 4.5.7

Right label bracket compound delimiter **2.2**

Right parenthesis
> character 2.1
> delimiter 2.2

Rounding
> in a real-to-integer conversion 4.6
> of results of real operations 4.5.7; 13.7.3

Run time check 11.7; 11.1

Safe interval 4.5.7

Safe number (of a real type) **3.5.6**; 4.5.7
[see also: model number, real type representation attribute, real type]
> limit to the result of a real operation 4.5.7
> of a fixed point type 3.5.9; 3.5.10
> of a floating point type 3.5.7; 3.5.8
> result of universal expression too large 4.10

SAFE_EMAX (predefined attribute) **3.5.8**; A

SAFE_LARGE (predefined attribute) **3.5.8, 3.5.10**; A

SAFE_SMALL (predefined attribute) **3.5.8, 3.5.10**; A

Satisfy (a constraint) **3.3**; D
[see also: constraint, subtype]
    a discriminant constraint 3.7.2
    an index constraint 3.6.1
    a range constraint 3.5

Scalar type 3.3, 3.5; D
[see also: class of type, discrete type, enumeration type, fixed point type, floating point type, integer type, numeric type, real type, static expression]
    as a generic parameter 12.1.2, 12.3.3
    formal parameter 6.2
    of a range in a membership test 4.5.2
    operation 3.5.5; 4.5.2

Scheduling 9.8; 13.5.1

Scheme
[see: iteration scheme]

Scope 8.2; 8.3, D
[see also: basic operation, character literal, declaration, declarative region, generic instance, identifier, immediate scope, implicit declaration, operator symbol, overloading, visibility]
    of a use clause 8.4

Secondary unit 10.1
[see also: compilation unit, library unit]
    compiled after the corresponding library unit or parent unit 10.3
    subject to pragma elaborate 10.5

SECONDS (predefined function) **9.6**

Select alternative (of a selective wait) **9.7.1**

Select statement 9.7; 9.7.1, 9.7.2, 9.7.3
[see also: statement, task, terminate alternative]
    as a compound statement 5.1
    in an abnormal task 9.10

Selected component 4.1.3; 8.3, D
[see also: direct visibility, prefix, selector, visibility by selection, visibility]
    as a basic operation 3.3.3; 3.3, 3.7.4, 3.8.2, 7.4.2
    as a name 4.1
    as the name of an entry or entry family 9.5
    for selective visibility 8.3
    in a conforming construct 6.3.1
    starting with standard 8.6
    using a block name 5.6
    using a loop name 5.5
    whose prefix denotes a package 8.3
    whose prefix denotes a record object 8.3
    whose prefix denotes a task object 8.3

Selection of an exception handler **11.4, 11.4.1, 11.4.2**; 11.6

Selective visibility
[see: visibility by selection]

Selective wait 9.7.1; 9.7
[see also: terminate alternative]
    accepting a conditional entry call 9.7.2
    accepting a timed entry call 9.7.3
    raising program_error 11.1

Selector 4.1.3; D
[see also: prefix, selected component]

Semicolon character 2.1

Semicolon delimiter 2.2
    followed by a pragma 2.8

SEND_CONTROL (low_level_io procedure) **14.6**

Separate compilation 10, 10.1; 10.5
    of a proper body 3.9
    cf a proper body declared in another compilation unit 10.2

Separator 2.2

Sequence of statements 5.1
    in an accept statement 9.5
    in a basic loop 5.5
    in a block statement 5.6; 9.4
    in a case statement alternative 5.4
    in a conditional entry call 9.7.2
    in an exception handler 11.2
    in an if statement 5.3
    in a package body 7.1; 7.3
    in a selective wait statement 9.7.1
    in a subprogram body 6.3; 9.4, 13.8
    in a task body 9.1; 9.4
    in a timed entry call 9.7.3
    including a raise statement 11.3
    of code statements 13.8
    raising an exception 11.4.1

Sequential access file 14.2; 14.1, 14.2.1

Sequential execution
[see: sequence of statements, statement]

Sequential input-output 14.2.2; 14.2.1

SEQUENTIAL_IO (predefined input-output generic package) **14.2, 14.2.2**; 14, 14.1, 14.2.3, C
    exceptions 14.4; 14.5
    specification 14.2.3

SET_COL (text_io procedure) **14.3.4**; 14.3.10

SET_INDEX (input-output procedure)
    in an instance of direct_io 14.2.4; 14.2.5

SET_INPUT (text_io procedure) **14.3.2**; 14.3.10
    raising an exception 14.4

SET_LINE (text_io procedure) **14.3.4**; 14.3.10

SET_LINE_LENGTH (text_io procedure) **14.3.3**; 14.3.10
    raising an exception 14.4

SET_OUTPUT (text_io procedure) **14.3.2**; 14.3.10
    raising an exception 14.4

SET_PAGE_LENGTH (text_io procedure) **14.3.3**; 14.3.10
    raising an exception 14.4

SHARED (predefined pragma) **9.11**; B

Shared variable (of two tasks) **9.11**
[see also: task]

Sharp character 2.1
[see also: based literal]
    replacement by colon character 2.10

Short circuit control form 4.5, 4.5.1; 4.4
    as a basic operation 3.3.3; 3.5.5
    in an expression 4.4

SHORT_FLOAT (predefined type) **3.5.7**; C

SHORT_INTEGER (predefined type) **3.5.4**; C

Sign of a fixed point number **3.5.9**

Sign of a floating point number **3.5.7**

Significant decimal digits 3.5.7

Simple expression 4.4
    as a choice 3.7.3
    as a choice in an aggregate 4.3
    as a range bound 3.5
    for an entry index in an accept statement 9.5
    in an address clause 13.5
    in a delay statement 9.6
    in a fixed accuracy definition 3.5.9
    in a floating accuracy definition 3.5.7
    in a record representation clause 13.4
    in a relation 4.4

Simple name 4.1; 2.3, D
    [see also: block name, identifier, label, loop name, loop
    simple name, name, overloading, visibility]
        as a choice 3.7.3
        as a formal parameter 6.4
        as a label 5.1
        as a name 4.1
        before arrow compound delimiter 8.3
        in an accept statement 9.5
        in an address clause 13.5
        in an attribute designator 4.1.4
        in a conforming construct 6.3.1
        in a discriminant association 3.7.2
        in an enumeration representation clause 13.3
        in a package body 7.1
        in a package specification 7.1
        in a record representation clause 13.4
        in a selector 4.1.3
        in a suppress pragma 11.7
        in a task body 9.1
        in a variant part 3.7.3
        in a with clause 10.1.1
        versus identifier 3.1

Simple statement 5.1
    [see also: statement]

Single task 9.1

SIZE (input-output function)
    in an instance of direct_io 14.2.4; 14.2.5

SIZE (predefined attribute) **13.7.2**; A
    [see also: storage bits]
    specified by a length clause 13.2

SKIP_LINE (text_io procedure) **14.3.4**; 14.3.10
    raising an exception 14.4

SKIP_PAGE (text_io procedure) **14.3.4**; 14.3.10
    raising an exception 14.4

Slice 4.1.2
    [see also: array type]
        as a basic operation 3.3.3; 3.6.2, 3.8.2
        as a name 4.1
        as destination of an assignment 5.2.1
        of a constant 3.2.1

    of a derived type 3.4
    of an object as an object 3.2
    of a value of a generic formal array type 12.1.2
    of a variable 3.2.1
    starting with a prefix 4.1, 4.1.2

SMALL (predefined attribute) **3.5.8, 3.5.10**; A
    [see also: fixed point type]
    specified by a length clause 13.2

Small of a fixed point model number **3.5.9**

Some order not defined by the language
    [see: incorrect order dependence]

Space character 2.1
    [see also: basic graphic character]
        as a separator 2.2
        in a comment 2.7
        not allowed in an identifier 2.3
        not allowed in a numeric literal 2.4.1

Space character literal 2.5; 2.2

Special character 2.1
    [see also: basic graphic character, other special character]
    in a delimiter 2.2

Specification
    [see: declaration, discriminant specification, enumeration
    literal specification, generic specification, loop parameter
    specification, package specification, parameter specifica-
    tion, subprogram specification, task specification]

STANDARD (predefined package) **8.6**; C
    [see also: library unit]
        as a declarative region 8.1
        enclosing the library units of a program 10.1.1;
        10.1, 10.2
        including implicit declarations of fixed point cross-
        multiplication and cross-division 4.5.5

STANDARD_INPUT (text_io function) **14.3.2**; 14.3.10

STANDARD_OUTPUT (text_io function) **14.3.2**; 14.3.10

Star
    [see: double star]
        character 2.1
        delimiter 2.2

Statement 5.1; 5, D
    [see also: abort statement, accept statement, address
    attribute, assignment statement, block statement, case
    statement, code statement, compound statement, delay
    statement, entry call statement, exit statement, goto state-
    ment, if statement, label, loop statement, null statement,
    procedure call statement, raise statement, return state-
    ment, select statement, sequence of statements, target
    statement]
        allowed in an exception handler 11.2
        as an overload resolution context 8.7
        optimized 10.6
        raising an exception 11.4.1; 11.4
        that cannot be reached 10.6

Statement alternative
    [see: case statement alternative]

Static constraint 4.9
    on a subcomponent subject to a component clause
    13.4
    on a type 3.5.4, 3.5.7, 3.5.9, 13.2

Static discrete range ● *Subprogram body*

having dependent tasks 9.4
in a package body 7.1
including an exception handler 11.2; 11
including an exit statement 5.7
including a goto statement 5.9
including an implicit declaration 5.1
including a return statement 5.8
including code statements must be a procedure
body 13.8
inlined in place of each call 6.3.2
must be in the same declarative region as the
declaration 3.9, 7.1
not allowed for a subprogram subject to an interface
pragma 13.9
not yet elaborated at a call 3.9
raising an exception 11.4.1, 11.4.2
recompiled 10.3

Subprogram call 6.4; 6, 6.3, 12.3
[see also: actual parameter, entry call statement, entry call, function call, procedure call statement, procedure call]
    before elaboration of the body 3.9 , 11.1
    statement replaced by an inlining of the body 6.3.2
    statement with a default actual parameter 6.4.2
    to a derived subprogram 3.4
    to a generic instance 12

Subprogram declaration 6.1; 6, D
    and body as a declarative region 8.1
    as a basic declaration 3.1
    as a later declarative item 3.9
    as a library unit 10.1
    as an overloaded declaration 8.3
    implied by the body 6.3, 10.1
    in a package specification 7.1
    made directly visible by a use clause 8.4
    of an operator 6.7
    recompiled 10.3

Subprogram specification 6.1
    and forcing occurrences 13.1
    conforming to another 6.3.1
    for a function 6.5
    in a body stub 10.2
    in a generic declaration 12.1; 12.1.3
    in a renaming declaration 8.5
    in a subprogram body 6.3
    including the name of a private type 7.4.1
    of a derived subprogram 3.4

Subtraction operation 4.5.3
    for a real type 4.5.7

Subtype 3.3, 3.3.2; D
[see also: attribute of..., base attribute, constrained subtype, constraint, first named subtype, operation of..., result subtype, satisfy, size attribute, static subtype, type, unconstrained subtype]
    declared by a numeric type declaration 3.5.4, 3.5.7, 3.5.9
    in a membership test 4.5.2
    name [see: name of a subtype, type_mark of a subtype]
    not considered in overload resolution 8.7
    of an access type 3.8
    of an actual parameter 6.4.1
    of an array type [see: constrained array type, index constraint]
    of a component of an array 3.6
    of a component of a record 3.7
    of a constant in a static expression 4.9
    of a discriminant of a generic formal type 12.3.2
    of a formal parameter 6.4.1

of a formal parameter or result of a renamed subprogram or entry 8.5
of a generic formal type 12.1.2
of an index of a generic formal array type 12.3.4
of an object [see: elaboration of...]
of a private type 7.4, 7.4.1
of a real type 3.5.7, 3.5.9; 3.5.6, 4.5.7
of a record type [see: constrained record type, discriminant constraint]
of a scalar type 3.5
of a task type 9.2
of a variable 5.2
subject to a representation clause 13.1

Subtype conversion 4.6
[see also: conversion operation, explicit conversion, implicit conversion, type conversion]
    in an array assignment 5.2.1; 5.2
    to a real type 4.5.7

Subtype declaration 3.3.2; 3.1
    and forcing occurrences 13.1
    as a basic declaration 3.1
    including the name of a private type 7.4.1

Subtype definition
[see: component subtype definition, dependence on a discriminant, index subtype definition]

Subtype indication 3.3.2
[see also: elaboration of...]
    as a component subtype indication 3.7
    as a discrete range 3.6
    for a subtype of a generic formal type 12.1.2
    in an access type definition 3.8
    in an allocator 4.8
    in an array type definition 3.6
    in a component declaration 3.7
    in a constrained array definition 3.6
    in a derived type definition 3.4
    in a generic formal part 12.1
    in an object declaration 3.2, 3.2.1
    in an unconstrained array definition 3.6
    including a fixed point constraint 3.5.9
    including a floating point constraint 3.5.7
    with a range constraint 3.5

Subunit 10.2; D
[see also: library unit]
    as a compilation unit 10.4
    as a library unit 10.4
    as a secondary unit 10.1
    compiled after the corresponding parent unit 10.3
    not allowed for a subprogram subject to an interface pragma 13.9
    of a compilation unit subject to a context clause 10.1.1
    raising an exception 11.4.1, 11.4.2
    recompiled (does not affect other compilation units) 10.3

SUCC (predefined attribute) **3.5.5**; 13.3, A

Successor
[see: succ attribute]

SUPPRESS (predefined pragma) **11.7**; 11.1, B

Symbol
[see: graphical symbol, operator symbol]

Synchronization of tasks
[see: task synchronization]

Task unit 9.1; 9
[see also: program unit]
    declaration determining the visibility of another declaration 8.3
    including a raise statement 11.3
    subject to an address clause 13.5
    subject to a representation clause 13.1
    subject to a suppress pragma 11.7
    with a separately compiled body 10.2

TASKING_ERROR (predefined exception) 11.1
[see also: suppress pragma]
    raised by an entry call to an abnormal task 9.10, 11.5
    raised by an entry call to a completed task 9.5, 9.7.2, 9.7.3, 11.5
    raised by an exception in the task body 11.4.2
    raised by failure of an activation 9.3; 11.4.2

Template
[see: generic unit]

Term 4.4
    in a simple expression 4.4

Terminate alternative (of a selective wait) 9.7.1
[see also: select statement]
    causing a transfer of control 5.1
    in a select statement causing a loop to be exited 5.5
    selection 9.4
    selection in the presence of an accept alternative for an interrupt entry 13.5.1

TERMINATED (predefined attribute) for a task object 9.9; A

Terminated task 9.4; 9.3, 9.9
[see also: completed task]
    not becoming abnormal 9.10
    object or subcomponent of an object designated by an access value 4.8
    termination of a task during its activation 9.3

Terminator
[see: file terminator, line terminator, page terminator]

Text input-output **14.3;** 14.2.1

Text of a program **2.2, 10.1**

TEXT_IO (predefined input-output package) 14.3; 14, 14.1, 14.3.9, 14.3.10, C
    exceptions 14.4; 14.5
    specification 14.3.10

TICK
[see: system.tick]

TIME (predefined type) 9.6
[see also: clock, date, day, make_time, month, system.tick, year]

TIME_ERROR (predefined exception) 9.6

TIME_OF (predefined function) 9.6

Timed entry call 9.7.3; 9.7
    and renamed entries 8.5
    subject to an address clause 13.5.1

Times operator
[see: multiplying operator]

Transfer of control 5.1
[see also: exception, exit statement, goto statement, return statement, terminate alternative]

TRUE boolean enumeration literal **3.5.3;** C

Type 3.3; D
[see also: access type, appropriate for a type, array type, attribute of..., base attribute, base type, boolean type, character type, class of type, composite type, constrained type, derived type, discrete types, discriminant of..., enumeration type, fixed point type, floating point type, forcing occurrence, generic actual type, generic formal type, integer type, limited private type, limited type, numeric type, operation of..., parent type, predefined type, private type, real type, record type, representation clause, scalar type, size attribute, storage allocated, subtype, unconstrained subtype, unconstrained type, universal type]
    name 3.3.1
    of an actual parameter 6.4.1
    of an aggregate 4.3.1, 4.3.2
    of an array component of a generic formal array type 12.3.4
    of an array index of a generic formal array type 12.3.4
    of a case statement expression 5.4
    of a condition 5.3
    of a declared object 3.2, 3.2.1
    of a discriminant of a generic formal private type 12.3.2
    of an expression 4.4
    of a file 14.1
    of a formal parameter of a generic formal subprogram 12.1.3
    of a generic actual object 12.3.1
    of a generic formal object 12.1.1; 12.3.1
    of an index 4.1.1
    of a loop parameter 5.5
    of a named number 3.2, 3.2.2
    of an object designated by a generic formal access type 12.3.5
    of a primary in an expression 4.4
    of a shared variable 9.11
    of a slice 4.1.2
    of a string literal 4.2
    of a task object 9.2
    of a universal expression 4.10
    of a value 3.3; 3.2
    of discriminants of a generic formal object and the matching actual object 12.3.2
    of of the literal null 4.2
    of the result of a generic formal function 12.1.3
    renamed 8.5
    subject to a representation clause 13.1; 13.6
    subject to a suppress pragma 11.7
    yielded by an attribute 4.1.4

Type conversion 4.6
[see also: conversion operation, conversion, explicit conversion, subtype conversion, unchecked_conversion]
    as an actual parameter 6.4, 6.4.1
    as a primary 4.4
    in a static expression 4.9
    to a real type 4.5.7

Type declaration 3.3.1
[see also: elaboration of..., incomplete type declaration, private type declaration]
    as a basic declaration 3.1
    as a full declaration 7.4.1
    implicitly declaring operations 3.3.3
    in a package specification 7.1
    including the name of a private type 7.4.1

as a basic declarative item 3.9
as a later declarative item 3.9
in a code procedure body 13.8
in a context clause of a compilation unit 10.1.1
in a context clause of a subunit 10.2
inserted by the environment 10.4

USE_ERROR (input-output exception) **14.4**; 14.2.1, 14.2.3,
14.2.5, 14.3.3, 14.3.10, 14.5

VAL (predefined attribute) **3.5.5**; A

Value
[see: assignment, evaluation, expression, initial value,
returned value, subtype, task designated..., type]
in a constant 3.2.1; 3.2
in a task object 9.2
in a variable 3.2.1, 5.2; 3.2
of an access type [see: object designated, task
object designated]
of an array type 3.6; 3.6.1 [see also: array, slice]
of a based literal 2.4.2
of a boolean type 3.5.3
of a character literal 2.5
of a character type 3.5.2; 2.5, 2.6
of a decimal literal 2.4.1
of a fixed point type 3.5.9, 4.5.7
of a floating point type 3.5.7, 4.5.7
of a record type 3.7
of a record type with discriminants 3.7.1
of a string literal 2.6; 2.10
of a task type [see: task designated]
returned by a function call [see: returned value]

VALUE (predefined attribute) **3.5.5**; A

Variable 3.2.1; D
[see also: object, shared variable]
as an actual parameter 6.2
declared in a package body 7.3
formal parameter 6.2
in an assignment statement 5.2
of an array type as destination of an assignment
5.2.1
of a private type 7.4.1
renamed 8.5
that is a slice 4.1.2

Variable declaration 3.2.1

Variant 3.7.3; 4.1.3
[see also: component clause, record type]
in a variant part 3.7.3

Variant part 3.7.3; D
[see also: dependence on a discriminant]
in a component list 3.7
in a record aggregate 4.3.1

Vertical bar character 2.1
replacement by exclamation character 2.10

Vertical bar delimiter 2.2

Vertical tabulation format effector 2.1

Violation of a constraint
[see: constraint_error exception]

Visibility 8.3; 8.2, D
[see also: direct visibility, hiding, identifier, name, operation, overloading]
and renaming 8.5
determining multiple meanings of an identifier 8.4,
8.7; 8.5
determining order of compilation 10.3
due to a use clause 8.4
of a basic operation 8.3
of a character literal 8.3
of a default for a generic formal subprogram 12.3.6
of a generic formal parameter 12.3
of a library unit due to a with clause 8.6, 10.1.1
of a name of an exception 11.2
of an operation declared in a package 7.4.2
of an operator symbol 8.3
of a renaming declaration 8.5
of a subprogram declared in a package 6.3
of declarations in a package body 7.3
of declarations in a package specification 7.2
of declarations in the package system 13.7
within a subunit 10.2

Visibility by selection 8.3
[see also: basic operation, character literal, operation,
operator symbol, selected component]

Visible part (of a package) **7.2**; 3.2.1, 7.4, 7.4.1, 7.4.3, D
[see also: deferred constant declaration, private type
declaration]
expanded name denoting a declaration in a visible
part 8.2
scope of a declaration in a visible part 4.1.3
use clause naming the package 8.4
visibility of a declaration in a visible part 8.3

Wait
[see: selective wait, task suspension]

While loop
[see: loop statement]

WIDTH (predefined attribute) **3.5.5**; A

With clause 10.1.1; D
[see also: context clause]
determining order of compilation 10.3
determining the implicit order of library units 8.6
in a context clause of a compilation unit 10.1.1
in a context clause of a subunit 10.2
inserted by the environment 10.4
leading to direct visibility 8.3

WRITE (input-output procedure)
in an instance of direct_io 14.2.4; 14.1, 14.2, 14.2.5
in an instance of sequential_io 14.2.2; 14.1, 14.2,
14.2.3

Writing to an output file 14.1, 14.2.2, 14.2.4

Xor operator
[see: logical operator]

YEAR (predefined function) **9.6**

Postscript : Submission of Comments

For submission of comments on this standard Ada reference manual, we would appreciate them being sent by Arpanet to the address

Ada-Comment at ECLB

If you do not have Arpanet access, please send the comments by mail

Ada Joint Program Office
Office of the Under Secretary of Defense Research and Engineering
Washington, DC 20301
United States of America.

For mail comments, it will assist us if you are able to send them on 8-inch single-sided single-density IBM format diskette - but even if you can manage this, please also send us a paper copy, in case of problems with reading the diskette.

All comments are sorted and processed mechanically in order to simplify their analysis and to facilitate giving them proper consideration. To aid this process you are kindly requested to precede each comment with a three line header

!section ...
!version 1983
!topic ...

The section line includes the section number, the paragraph number enclosed in parentheses, your name or affiliation (or both), and the date in ISO standard form (year-month-day). The paragraph number is the one given in the margin of the paper form of this document (it is not contained in the ECLB files); paragraph numbers are optional, but very helpful. As an example, here is the section line of comment #1194 on a previous version:

!section 03.02.01(12) D . Taffs 82-04-26

The version line, for comments on the current standard, should only contain "!version 1983". Its purpose is to distinguish comments that refer to different versions.

The topic line should contain a one line summary of the comment. This line is essential, and you are kindly asked to avoid topics such as "Typo" or "Editorial comment" which will not convey any information when printed in a table of contents. As an example of an informative topic line consider:

!topic Subcomponents of constants are constants

Note also that nothing prevents the topic line from including all the information of a comment, as in the following topic line:

!topic Insert: "... are {implicitly} defined by a subtype declaration"

As a final example here is a complete comment received on a prior version of this manual:

!section 03.02.01(12) D . Taffs 82-04-26
!version 10
!topic Subcomponents of constants are constants

Change "component" to "subcomponent" in the last sentence.

Otherwise the statement is inconsistent with the defined use of subcomponent in 3.3, which says that subcomponents are excluded when the term component is used instead of subcomponent.